PUBLICATIONS

OF THE

NAVY RECORDS SOCIETY

VOL. 125

THE NAVAL MISCELLANY

VOLUME V

THE
NAVAL
MISCELLANY

Volume V

Edited by
N. A. M. RODGER

PUBLISHED BY GEORGE ALLEN & UNWIN
FOR THE NAVY RECORDS SOCIETY
1984

George Allen & Unwin (Publishers) Ltd,
40 Museum Street, London WC1A 1LU, UK

George Allen & Unwin (Publishers) Ltd,
Park Lane, Hemel Hempstead, Herts HP2 4TE, UK

Allen & Unwin, Inc.,
Fifty Cross Street, Winchester, Mass. 01890, USA

George Allen & Unwin Australia Pty Ltd,
8 Napier Street, North Sydney, NSW 2060, Australia

First published in 1984.

British Library Cataloguing in Publication Data

The Naval Miscellany.—Vol. 5—(Publications
of the Navy Records Society; v. 125)
1. Great Britain. *Royal Navy*—History
I. Title
359′.00941   VA454

ISBN 0-04-942184-0

Set in 10 on 12 point Times by Grove Graphics, Tring, Hertfordshire
and printed in Great Britain
by William Clowes Limited, Beccles and London

To the memory of R. C. Anderson
Historian and Benefactor

CONTENTS

THE CONTRIBUTORS

Dr A. P. McGowan is head of the Department of Ships of the National Maritime Museum, and edited the Society's Volume 116, *The Jacobean Commissions of Enquiry, 1608 and 1618.*

Professor Nelson P. Bard is head of the History Department of Davis and Elkins College, West Virginia. He is writing a biography of the second Earl of Warwick.

Dr R. V. Saville is a lecturer in Economic and Social History in the University of St Andrews. He has worked extensively in the records of the Navy Board for the seventeenth century.

Professor John B. Hattendorf was formerly an officer in the United States Navy. He was awarded a D.Phil. by Oxford University, has been visiting Professor in the National University of Singapore, and is now Professor of Naval History at the United States Naval War College.

A. W. H. Pearsall is the Historian of the National Maritime Museum.

Dr N. A. M. Rodger is an Assistant Keeper in the Public Record Office and Honorary Secretary of the Society.

Miss P. K. Crimmin is a lecturer in History at Royal Holloway and Bedford Colleges, University of London.

A. N. Ryan is Reader in History at Liverpool University and Honorary General Editor of the Society. His publications include writings on British maritime policy in the Baltic.

Dr Eric Poole has been senior lecturer in Law at the University of Kent, and a visiting Professor at the University of Texas. He is a palaeographer, has written on documents relating to Shakespeare's family and on computer techniques for ascertaining relationships between manuscripts, and he is also a solicitor.

Dr A. D. Lambert has recently been awarded his Ph.D. at King's College, London, for work on the Russian War of 1854–6, and is now a lecturer at Bristol Polytechnic.

Dr C. I. Hamilton is a lecturer in European History at the University of the Witwatersrand.

Professor Paul G. Halpern is Professor of History at the Florida State University, and edited the Keyes Papers for the Society. He is finishing a book on the naval war in the Mediterranean, 1914–18.

Lieutenant J. V. P. Goldrick is a serving seaman officer in the Royal Australian Navy. His book, *The King's Ships were at Sea*, has been recently published.

PREFACE

This is the fifth volume of the Society's series *The Naval Miscellany*, and although it is the first for more than thirty years, it requires little introduction, for the plan is simple and self-evident. This is a collection of pieces worthy, it is hoped, of publication, but individually too short to form a volume. The sections have been selected to provide a wide coverage both of date and subject, representing in miniature the editorial policy of the Society. Naval operations of various sorts and periods include Warwick's privateering voyage of 1627, Benbow's last fight, amphibious landings in 1758, the capture of Copenhagen in 1807, the bombardment of Bomarsund in 1854, and the Dardanelles expedition of 1915. The letters of Sir James Douglas, Captain Mundy and Midshipman Noel describe naval life from a variety of points of view. The memoirs of Captain Foley not only provide a fascinating view of life in the gunrooms of the Grand Fleet, but are the Society's first publication relating to the Royal Australian Navy. The administration of the dockyards is dealt with by Dr Saville, and of the Admiralty by Dr Hamilton.

As always, the Society is indebted to the owners and custodians of manuscripts without whose kindness nothing could be published. This volume draws on the resources of the National Maritime Museum, the Public Record Office, the Bodleian Library, the British Library, the Somerset and Derbyshire Record Offices, the Naval Historical Library and Churchill College, Cambridge. The Society thanks the authorities of all these, and especially the Trustees of the National Maritime Museum, for permission to print papers in their care. Transcripts of documents in Crown Copyright appear by permission of the Controller of Her Majesty's Stationery Office.

Particular thanks are due to Mrs Gwenllian Day for the Noel letters, to Mrs J. B. Foley, Mrs A. F. Sallman and Commander A. F. Sallman, MVO, RAN, for the Foley memoirs, to the executors of the late Major P. M. Mundy, and to Baron de Robeck and Mrs Jocelyn Proby for permission to use the de Robeck Papers. Other acknowledgements have been made by the several editors of the individual sections, and it is to them that the editor of the volume tenders his own thanks, for they have done all the work for him.

N. A. M. RODGER

1

Further Papers from the Commission of Enquiry, 1608

Edited by

A. P. McGOWAN

Prefatory Note

These documents from the Commission of Enquiry into Abuses in the Navy 1608 were bought by the National Maritime Museum in 1979.[1] They are an addendum to those already printed by the Navy Records Society in 1971.[2] They consist of some 149 folios, bound with one or two others which have nothing to do with the 1608 Enquiry. The papers themselves were in a fairly poor state, without a cover − if indeed they ever had one − and the binding was in a very poor condition. Miss Sally Unwin of the National Maritime Museum's paper conservation staff, released the binding, treated and mounted the folios and rebound them in vellum. At the same time the oversize folios that had been folded in the original binding were rebound between suitable covers and a substantial and handsome case made to contain and protect both bindings.

There is no provenance for the documents. Almost all are in a clerk's hand although one or two appear to have been written by the Earl of Northampton, as are certain of the maginalia.

All dates are shown modern style. The absence of a folio number indicates a blank folio or one containing only a superscription.

I wish to thank the Trustees of the National Maritime Museum for permission to publish this material and I would like to acknowledge the assistance of the staff in the Department of Printed Books and Manuscripts. I am also indebted to the General Editor of this volume, Dr N. A. M. Rodger, for his patience and forbearance.

Introduction

It seems unlikely that we yet have all the documents relating to the Commission of 1608, but it is equally unlikely that anything else that may be found will add significantly to our already considerable knowledge of how the investigation was carried out. At the end of the papers there is a table of contents which,, although accurate as far as it goes, lists nothing beyond p. 183 [fol. **109**] in the original pagination. This was probably the core of this particular collection of documents referring to the Commission of Enquiry of 1608, others being added later. The highest page number in the bound volume is p. 221 [fol. **145**] and one sheet in the oversize binding is marked p. 321 [no folio number], so these papers are clearly only part of a body of material that appears to have become separated from the Cotton manuscripts later deposited in the British Museum. Most of the documents in the oversize binding have neither page nor folio number.

The documents in this collection are more varied perhaps than those from the 1608 Enquiry in the Cotton MSS but they are all the sort of documents that anyone reasonably familiar with the Society's Volume 116 might expect. For that reason, and to avoid rather tedious repetition, for the papers in question contain nearly 40,000 words, I have reduced this edition to a minimum: a full transcription of a number of entries which have a particular interest, with an annotated calendar of the remainder.

Four of the full transcriptions concern an important figure in seventeenth-century shipbuilding: Phineas Pett. Because of his prominence and because his outlook typified that of the senior officers most at fault in the naval administration at the time, a brief sketch of his career until 1608 is appropriate. The view, widely accepted by twentieth-century historians, of Pett's pre-eminence in shipbuilding in the early seventeenth century stems largely from the fact that he had the wit to write an autobiography – and Phineas Pett was never a man to hide his light under a bushel. Published by the Navy Records Society in 1918, *Phineas Pett*[3] was for so long the only account of a seventeenth-century shipbuilder that it established him in a position that is by no means justified. That Pett was capable of building well may be true, but that he was quite content not to do so if thereby he could gain some personal advantage – usually financial – is all too obvious.

Pett had served only two years of his apprenticeship when his master died in 1592. He seems not to have continued his training formally, but found employment sporadically at sea or as an ordinary workman, occasionally with his brother Joseph with whom he fell out in 1595 because Joseph would not accept him as his deputy. He worked twice with Matthew

Baker who attempted to teach him more of his craft, and after a period as a storeman was finally appointed Assistant Master Shipwright at Chatham at 32 years of age in 1602. The commissioners had much to enquire about Phineas Pett in 1608, for apart from their main investigation they held a separate enquiry into the work on the *Prince Royal* then building under Pett's supervision at Woolwich. Matthew Baker, 78 years old and noted associate of Sir John Hawkins in the years before the defeat of the Armada, had no illusions about Pett's ability. When asked if Pett was 'a workman sufficient to be given . . . so great a charge' he answered that 'he never saw any work of his doing whereby he should so think him'.[4] The *Prince Royal* cost £20,000; twelve years later, and having made only two voyages, she required repairs costing £6,000 because she had been built with green unseasoned timber, the very charge levelled by the 1608 Commission.

The masterpiece of peculation, however, occurred in 1605. Pett built the *Resistance* with a third share belonging each to Sir Robert Mansell and Sir John Trevor using the king's materials. The ship was then hired to the crown as a transport in Nottingham's embassy to Spain in 1605 but was, in fact, employed on both the outward and the return voyage in a commercial venture for her owners. It is to this ship that the items demanded in the letter on fol. 77r were to be sent. The cable which is the subject of three other entries fully transcribed was almost certainly for the *Resistance*, built under Pett's control at David Duck's yard at Gillingham and which, after Pett's return home, had been chartered by merchants for a voyage into the Mediterranean.[5] These documents clearly point to collusion between Pett and the Surveyor, Sir John Trevor, even if they do not evince actual proof. One contemporary, presumably a Commissioner and probably either Northampton or his agent, Sir Robert Cotton, had no doubts, as the pencilled annotation makes clear.

A number of the documents in this collection concern misappropriation and the fraudulent obtaining of timber even while it was standing. In this regard the names of Pembury (also written Pamborough) in Kent and Aliceholt (Alesholt) and Dunwood in Hampshire occur frequently, as they do in the Cotton MSS. Dunwood is the subject of most of the questions asked of Esaie Whittiffe and Daniel Lyell (Lisle) [fol. **12**], and also of Lisle, Whittiffe, John Hodsall, John Wells and Sir Peter Buck (Vol. 116, pp. 7–10). This being a typical case of the kind, I have transcribed the indenture between Whittiffe and Lisle and Sir John Trevor. This document, to be found in the oversize binding, may be the original although there is no evidence of either seals or signatures. If it is merely a copy, it is surprising to find the use of properly cut vellum (i.e. making it a fascimile) rather than paper.

The letter to the Principal Officers from the Justices of the Peace of the County of Southampton (copy) [fol. **108bv**] puts into perspective the practical difficulties arising from an apparently straightforward order for the carriage of 500 trees. Such an order required the use of 600 teams of horses, with probably six horses to a team. While it is obvious that this does not mean 600 different teams, the provision of horses for 600 team journeys threw an immense burden upon the resources of the county, and this letter gives some insight into the problems of local administration.

CALENDAR OF DOCUMENTS

> John Apslyn of Chatham, one of the assistants of his Majesty's
> master carpenter there saith that since he was last examined upon
> his oath he hath called to mind many things which then came not
> to his memory both in respect to the shortness of the time and of
> the honourable personages before whom he spake and therefore
> doth now voluntarily in tenderness of conscience present these things
> ensuing which have come to his mind since.

56–58v   Deposition signed by Thomas Venables, boatswain of the *Rainbow* and William Ward, boatswain of the *Answer*.

59   A note of the remainder of boatswain's stores aboard the *Quittance* signed by Thomas Burston, master, and William Ward.

60   A note of remainder of stores signed by Ambrose Dixon and William Ward.

61–63r   Copy of a deposition by Richard Middleton, boatswain of the *Triumph*, and others.

67–68r   Statement by Hildebrand Pruson, purveyor, countersigned by Sir Robert Cotton, Northampton and John Griffiths Esq.

69   An account of prices paid by the Crown for masts 'in the past 4 years'.

70–71   An abstract of the amounts of masts, deals, tar, etc., bought 1600–1607.

72   A request by Phineas Pett for two anchors and cables from the *Elizabeth* and the *Bonadventure* with, immediately following, a warrant for the same signed by Sir Henry Palmer, Sir John Trevor and Sir Peter Buck,[7] dated 17 November 1604.
         Pett's receipt follows, dated 18 November 1604.

73   A warrant to deliver 120 bolts of canvas to Phineas Pett, signed by Sir Robert Mansell and Sir John Trevor.

74   A list of munitions for the *Resistance* in accordance with the Lord Admiral's warrant of 13 March 1605.

75v   An order to Austin Morland signed by Sir John Trevor:

> Austin Morland, I pray you with the privity of Sir Peter Buck (whose favour I pray in this business) to let Phineas Pett have a good new cable of 10 inches out of some of the late returned ships putting bond to redeliver another new one of like size to his Majesty's use as soon as the Russian fleet is returned with cordage or within some convenient time after. Dated the 6 August 1605
> J. Trevor

In a different seventeenth-century hand:

> Note that Sir Peter Buck set not his hand to this warrant though Ph. Pett on the next page at this mark ⊖→ says he had his consent.

Note in pencil:

> Note Sir Peter Buck set not his hand to the warrant yet Pett confesseth he acquainted him on page 137. ⊖→

76r   Letter to Austin Morland from Phineas Pett dated 11 August
        1605:

> Mr Austin Morland I commend unto you and have sent you herein
> enclosed a note from Sir John Trevor concerning a new cable I
> am to have from some of the ships or storehouse. I have acquainted
> Sir Peter Buck with it already and he is very willing to it and
> therefore I earnestly entreat you to be here betimes in the morning
> to give me order for it for I am to ride the tide and thus I bid you
> hearty farewell. Chatham 11 August 1605. Your very loving friend,
> Phineas Pett.

Below, on the same folio:

> Mr Morland I am sorry I could not speak with you myself but I
> have left David Duck to receive the cable for me, to whom I pray
> you deliver it for there is one of eleven inches in the house will
> fit my turn very well, which Nicholas showed me. When I come
> down again I will give you my bond as the warrant importeth and
> so I bid you farewell.
>
>   P. Pett

Pencil hand:

> No bond delivered.

77r   Letter to Austin Morland from Phineas Pett dated 28 March
        1605:

> Mr Morland, I did forget an especial warrant to you from Sir John
> Trevor, which was this that you should deliver me 2 compasses
> and 2 running glasses, a deepsea lead and line, and a sounding lead
> and line the which I pray you to deliver to David Duck to bring
> down to me. I pray give him also one barrel of pitch and one of
> tar and I will undertake you shall have sufficient discharge from
> Sir John Trevor for it. Same I pray also to appoint to him a quarter
> weight [28 lb] of small spikes, with 300 of a sort of 2s nails and
> 20d nails and 540 of a sort of 1s 6d nails and 4d nails and a basket
> to put them in, also I pray send me a warrant to the *Primrose* hoy
> for 12 oars to be delivered to me from her. All these things I will
> undertake you shall have sufficient warrant for at Sir John Trevor's
> return and therefore I pray strain not courtesy to cause them to
> be performed. And this with hearty commendations I commit you
> to get. From aboard the *Beare* this 28 March 1605.
>
>   Your very loving friend
>   Phineas Pett

> Our humble duties to your Lordships. Whereas it hath pleased you by your letters of this 12 April to require 500 trees to be carried out of the forest of Aliceholt unto the nearest places of Thames from thence to be transported to his Majesty's timber yards at Deptford and Woolwich. We find by the deputy of his Majesty's Master Shipwright that the said 500 trees will amount to the rate of 1,500 loads. Before the receipt of your Lordships' letters we proportioned 400 carriages for the reparation of his Majesty's fort at Portsmouth by order of his Majesty's Commission and now 600 teams for the carriage of timber unto the Thames side, whereof two hundred loads presently to be carried; we find the same a very great trouble unto the county, and ourselves enforced to draw many teams thirty miles remote from Aliceholt and thence unto the nearest place of their discharge fifteen miles and unto the other eighteen. We humbly beseech your lordships so much to favour this poor county that Surrey and Sussex confirming [adjoining] unto Aliceholt may carry the rest of the trees already felled and appointed to be cut down. And so humbly referring ourselves unto your favourable considerations of our readiness to perform our best means in furtherance of any his Majesty's Service do most humbly rest your Lordships humbly to be commanded . . . Winchester 15 May 1605.

Whereas it pleases your honourable Lordship to require me to certify under my hand whether there were not in anno 1606 a greater quantity of cordage delivered into his Majesty's store by the Muscovy Company than was contained in my Lord Admiral's warrant, I have informed myself from our agent and books of accounts touching that matter but do not find any express warrant from his Lordship that year. And therefore do think that the order given to the Company by the officers of his Majesty's Navy for the taking in of that year's cordage proceeded from a warrant sent to the Company under my Lord Admiral's sign dated the 10 November 1604, a copy of which warrant I send here enclosed to your Lordship together with the several scantlings and sizes delivered the years 1605 and 1606 towards the performance of the said warrant whereby your Lordship may be pleased to cause a further examination thereof as in your wisdom shall be thought fit.

And whereas your Lordship required me to certify whether the labourers be not paid upon the King's price for handing in the cordage at Deptford I have examined that likewise and do find that we allowed two shillings upon every ton which the Company do pay them. And the same is allowed to the Company again in their debenture, when they receive their money from his Majesty. Thus being desirous to satisfy your Lordship in this or any other thing that may tend to his Majesty's better service which I know your Lordship doth chiefly respect. I humbly rest at your Lordship's service.

Thomas Smythe

135	Copy of the details of the Lord Admiral's warrant for cordage from the Muscovy Company dated 10 November 1604 and referred to in Sir Thomas Smythe's letter to Northampton.
137–138	A note of the quantities of plank bought by Thomas Dymoke 1606–8, signed by Edward Stevens, Nicholas Clay and others.
140v	An estimate of the loss to the Crown by paying squared plank prices for shells [see fol. 131v].
141–142	A list of questions to be asked of those examined in the course of the Commission of Enquiry – directed to Sir Edward Hoby, Sir John Leveson, Sir Alexander Temple and Mr Robert Masters, LL.D.
142v	An account of the employment of the collier *Ellen* of London to carry plank out of Lord Worcester's forests from Portsmouth to the Thames in 1606–7.
143v	An account of the timber actually carried by the *Ellen*.
143b v	A note from William Rowland, master of the *Ellen* to Mr [John] Wells requesting payment to the bearer.
146	Notes on shipbuilding practice by Phineas Pett, headed 'concerning the ship at Woolwich'.
147v	A certified copy of a warrant from Lord Admiral Nottingham requiring assistance for his Majesty's Sergeant Painter in his work on the king's ships.
148–149	Table of contents.

Documents in the oversize binding

Copy of indenture between Esaie Whittiffe and Daniel Lyell and Sir John Trevor:

This Indenture made the 20th day of May in the year of the reign of our Sovereign Lord James by the Grace of God of England, Scotland, France and Ireland, King Defender of the Faith, and that is to say of England, France and Ireland the fourth and of Scotland the nine and thirtieth between Esaie Whittiffe of the town and county of Southampton, Shipwright and Daniel Lyell of the same town and county, Cutter of the one part and Sir John Trevor of Westminster in the county of Middlesex, Knight of the other part witnesseth that the said Esaie Whittiffe and Daniel Lyell for and in consideration of the sum of lawful money of England already in hand paid before their sealing and delivery of these presents by the said Sir John Trevor unto the said Esaie Whittiffe and Daniel Lyell as also for divers and sundry other good causes and considerations therein hereunto sufficiently moving have bargained, sold, conveyed, assigned and set over and by these presents do bargain, sell, convey, assign and set over unto the said Sir John Trevor, his executors, administrators and assignees, all trees of oak, beech, ash and aspe standing, growing, lying, remaining and being and whichever standing, growing, lying, remaining and being on the first day of October last past or at any time sithence within the circuit, precinct, compass and liberty of a certain wood commonly called or known by the name of Downe Wood, also Dunne Wood situated, lying and being within the foresaid county of Southampton or in any part or parcel thereof in as large ample and beneficial manner and form as the aforesaid bargained premission that the appurtenances were bargained, sold, conveyed and confirmed by one William Chamberlayne of Whitley Park within the parish of Titchfield in the aforesaid county of Southampton Esq. to the aforesaid Esaie Whittiffe and Daniel Lyell by one pair of Indentures made between William Chamberlayne of the one part and the said Esaie Whittiffe and Daniel Lyell of the other part bearing date of the first day of October last past, together with the said Indenture of bargain and sale subject to all and all manner of covenants, exceptions, conditions and agreements as are mentioned expressed and declared in the foresaid receipted Indenture, as in and by the said Indenture due reference thereunto being had, more at large appeareth. Provided always and it is covenanted, concluded and agreed by and between the parties to these presents that if the said Esaie Whittiffe and Daniel Lyell or either of them, their or either of their executors or administrators do and shall well and truly deliver or cause to be well and truly delivered before the last day of the month of November next ensuing the date of these present unto the said Sir John Trevor his executors or administrators to his and their own proper use and behoof thereby and freely exonerated of all charges whatsoever unto such of the King's Majesty's yards of Deptford Strand, Woolwich or Chatham within the county of Kent or elsewhere upon any such wharf or quay below London Bridge upon the River of Thames as the said Sir John Trevor shall limit or appoint, so much of good and sound 4 inch plank at the rate of one and twenty shillings for every 100 foot of the same 4 inch plank, so much of good and sound 3 inch plank at the rate of fifteen shillings for every 100 foot of the same 3 inch plank, so much of good and sound 2 inch plank at the rate of ten shillings and six pence for every 100 foot of the same 2 inch plank, so much of good and sound knee and crooked timber fit for building of great ships at the rate of twenty two shillings a load every such load to contain fifty foot, as shall amount in the whole to the value of £700 lawful money of England according to the rates aforesaid. And also if the said Esaie Whittiffe and Daniel Lyell or either of them, their or either of their executors or administrators do and shall well and truly deliver or cause to be well and truly delivered before the Feast of Pentecost, commonly called Whitsuntide which will be in the year of our Lord God according to the computation of the Church of England one thousand six hundred and seven to the said Sir John Trevor his executors or administrators to his and their own proper use and behoof, clearly and freely exonerated of all charges whatsoever unto such of the said places aforesaid as the said Sir John Trevor shall limit or appoint, so much of good and sound 4 inch plank at the rate of one and twenty shillings for every 100 foot of the said 4 inch plank, so much of good and sound 3 inch plank at the rate of fifteen shillings for every 100 foot of the said 3 inch plank, so much of good and sound 2 inch plank at the rate of ten shillings and six pence for every 100 foot of the said 2 inch plank, so much of good and sound knee and crooked timber fit for the building of great ships at the rate of twenty two shillings the load every such load to contain 50 foot as shall amount in the whole to the sum of £300 of lawful money of England according to the rates aforesaid, that then and from thenceforth this present Indenture of bargain and sale to be void and of none effect, anything in these Indentures contained to the contrary notwithstanding. In witness whereof the parties above mentioned to these present Indentures interchangeably have put their hands and seals the day and years first above written.

A note about the deposition of Mr [Hugh] Legat, Clerk of the Cheque at Chatham, and Mr [John] Duffield marked p. 321.

The state of the intended choice of timber in the king's woods. The statement contains numeral references to names and/or depositions in the right-hand margin frequently with page numbers. Marginal notes in a different hand are in the left-hand margin.

Letter from Peter Pett to Robert Lane, carpenter of the *Lion*, dated 24 September 1607, reproaching him for his testimony. Letter from Edward Dalton to Roger Langford at Deptford dated 17 February 1596.

Notes

1 National Maritime Museum MSS. CAD/A13.
2 A. P. McGowan (ed.), *The Jacobean Commissions of Enquiry, 1608 and 1618*, N[avy] R[ecord] S[ociety], Vol. 116 (1971). The original manuscripts for the Commission of Enquiry in 1608 are in the British Library, Cotton MSS. Julius F iii.
3 W. G. Perrin (ed.), *Autobiography of Phineas Pett*, N.R.S. Vol. 51 (1918).
4 Deposition of Matthew Baker, 15 December 1608, in N.R.S. Vol. 116, p. 231.
5 Perrin (ed.), *Autobiography*, pp. 24–6.
6 The first paragraph of this deposition has been transcribed as it throws an interesting light on the deponent's attitude to the Enquiry. One wonders whether Apslyn was nervous, as he may well have been, or whether he had heard of other depositions which might have compromised him. With such powerful and unpleasant figures as Sir Robert Mansell and Sir John Trevor as the object of the investigations, the lesser officers must have been in a considerable dilemma as to the wisdom of their answers. The temptation

to say only so much as would satisfy the Commissioners without unduly incriminating the Principal Officers was no doubt considerable.

7 Respectively, Comptroller, Surveyor and Clerk of the Navy.
8 Almost certainly the Thomas Norreys who appears in other documents and who became a Commissioner in the Enquiry of 1618.
9 Three Master Shipwrights.
10 A City merchant and a governor of the Muscovy and East India Companies. An active member of the Commission of Enquiry in 1618.

2

The Earl of Warwick's Voyage of 1627

Edited by

NELSON P. BARD

Introduction

The Elizabethans, in their feud with Spain, established privateering as an especially glorious and profitable English tradition. Later, between 1625 and 1630 when England was at war with France and Spain, English privateers launched many expeditions, from the very large and disastrous Cadiz expedition sponsored by the government in 1625 to the tiny, extremely lucrative enterprise of Sir Kenelm Digby in 1628.[1] Robert Rich, second Earl of Warwick and perhaps England's greatest privateer since the Elizabethans, set out four fleets in these years, ranging from five ships to ten.

His expedition in 1627 was his largest and by far the best advertised. The earl himself went as admiral, and he carried a special commission from the king to make war on the enemies of England and religion. Such a commission had not been granted since Queen Elizabeth had endowed the Earl of Cumberland in such a manner.

This enterprise has special significance for historians because it has been described in two independent sources. Warwick himself, immediately upon returning to England, wrote a short description of a sea battle between a fragment of his fleet and a large Spanish armada. The master of the *Hector*, the vice-admiral of Warwick's fleet, wrote a more complete account of the voyage, covering the entire time the fleet was at sea. Both accounts are straightforward and reliable, endowing our knowledge of this voyage with a wealth of detail. Besides these, many English and foreign observers took note of the voyage; and Sir James Bagg, the vice-admiral of Devonshire and a devoted follower of the Duke of Buckingham, maintained a running hostile account of the fleet's proceedings in letters to the duke and to the duke's secretary, Edward Nicholas.

William Ball, master of the *Hector* and a mariner who had been at sea for thirty years, composed the detailed narrative of the voyage, nearly day by day, in a candid and vivid style, replete with sea battles, mutinies, treacheries, personal enemies, and divine providence. In 1597 Ball had been apprenticed to Richard Harris – later one of the four Masters of England and the original captain of the *Hector* – and had served under Harris for eight years. Since 1608, Ball had served as master of numerous ships.

Ball was of the artisan class, then, and had done quite well at sea. From his narrative, and there is nothing else on which to rely, he appears to have been a reasonably honest, competent man, deeply religious, perhaps puritanically inclined as was the Earl of Warwick. He wrote with skill, telling an occasionally complex tale with clarity. He had a surprisingly sophisticated vocabulary and used it effectively in conjunction with his wry and often ferocious wit.

Also he wrote for a purpose. When the *Hector* returned to Plymouth, brought there from the voyage by a mutinous crew after an utterly unprofitable voyage, Sir Francis Stewart, the captain of the ship, apparently used Ball as a scapegoat for the failure of the trip. Although Ball never actually listed the charges made against him, and it may be that most charges were just aspersions made in public and never formally placed, it is possible to sort them out from his narrative. He was accused of making the ship's hold available to all seamen, of mishandling the ship, of selling the ship's victuals after they had docked at Plymouth in order to get pocket money – thus starving the sailors – and apparently, of stirring up mutiny. Finally, he was accused of allowing the sailors to run away to other ships in harbour before they had been discharged. These were serious charges, and he was removed from the *Hector* by the ship's owners on the strength of them.

Ball wrote, then, 'clearing himself of an aspersion falsely imputed upon him on the voyage'. He must have written his account very shortly after his removal from the *Hector*, though the document is not dated and is incorrectly catalogued among the state papers. It has been placed among documents dated 1 October 1627, and someone has written that date in pencil on the manuscript; but since the account continues to the end of October and at one point he mentions the 'great storm that blew so forceably in November 1627', it must have been written later [see below page 75]. In any case, Ball wrote *Might and Would Not* shortly after the voyage when the details of the trip, and of his injuries, were still clear. Considering the precision of his dates and weather data, it seems likely that he had kept a personal log of the voyage or had access to the ship's log as he wrote his account.

Fortunately, Ball did not dwell exclusively, or even primarily, upon his injuries. Most of the manuscript he kept shorn of personal complaint, and he was even capable of surprising fairness to his most desperate enemies. In the sea battle between the *Hector* and the vice-admiral of the Spanish fleet, he described Sir Francis Stewart as 'a most valorous, warlike gentleman and soldier in the face of his enemy, not to be persuaded by any means once to descend or go below from the deck' [p. **46**]. In an era that traded heavily in the extremes of diatribe, he dealt rather gently with his enemies, freeing his work from the worst distortions of venomous exaggeration.

On the other hand, he spoke with candour about the misdeeds of his superiors. He described their errors in convincing detail, from mere human errors of judgement to rank folly, vanity, weakness, treachery, cowardice, and gross corruption. In fact, Ball courted the wrath of several great persons with his candour. A first reading of the manuscript sometimes stirs speculation whether he wrote it in prison awaiting judgement for his outspokenness.

Not only did he attack specific enemies who were gentlemen, a dangerous practice for any artisan, but Ball attacked gentlemen as a class, betraying considerable class hostility. He spoke harshly of 'any decayed, forlorn gentleman appointed captain of a ship' [p. **65**] who knew little of the sea and cared less for the well-being of his seamen: 'the poor sailor being made a vassal and a slave to every supposed gentleman that goeth in a gay coat and taketh the name upon him' [p. **79**]. Although he hedged a little, he clearly believed gentlemen incapable of being concerned for seamen 'when their turn is served' [p. **79**]. Part of the overthrow of the voyage at least, according to Ball, was occasioned by the presence of such an over-abundance of idle gentlemen on all of the ships. His attitude, however, towards his superiors did not extend to the Earl of Warwick: 'Many such Warwicks, having the like pity and compassion, [may] God almighty send to increase and prosper in England' [pp. **79–80**].

Ball's chronicle, then, has value from several different perspectives. His lengthy descriptions of the nautical aspects of the voyage are accurate and revealing, based on thirty years' seamanship. His account sheds much light on the reasons for the failure of this expedition and the difficulties that even such a capable and prestigious man as Warwick faced in launching a small fleet. Also his social perspective is of considerable value. There are few enough articulate and coherent responses from the artisan class. Ball wrote with the skill and power of a shrewd, self-educated man who understood the structure of his society.

The manuscript itself survives in one copy among the domestic state papers at the Public Record Office in London (SP 16/80 No. 7). It consists of sixty-one folio pages written in a clear, precise hand. Though he appeals specifically at one point to the leading men at Trinity House, he apparently intended it for publication and for a general audience, 'committing these observations to the press . . . which I hope giveth the world judicially understood satisfaction' [p. **68**]. But the document was not printed and came into the hands of the government. Just why his manuscript should have fallen into government hands so soon is not known. Very shortly after the voyage the government had copied extracts from *Might and Would Not*, of two incidents relating to England's sovereignty of the seas.[2] He nowhere appeals to the government, only to the world and to the masters of Trinity House. But his account obviously was of interest to someone in government circles.

The document includes an account of the voyage of the *Hector* from March, when Ball agreed to sail, to the end of October, when he was relieved as master of the ship at Plymouth. Ball appended to his narrative a hostile description of new punishments for offending sailors devised by the captain of the *Hector*, Sir Francis Stewart; a list of grievances allegedly presented to the captain and signed by thirty officers of the *Hector*; and a list of the orders from the Earl of Warwick for his fleet, composed on 13 April 1627. These appendices add considerable substance to Ball's narrative of the voyage and have been included here.

Warwick's orders for the fleet are similar to those agreed upon by Sir Kenelm Digby and his associates in 1628, except that Warwick's are much more detailed. They reveal much about his intentions and his puritanism.

The list of grievances by the officers, however, is rather suspect. It consists very largely of Ball's personal grievances, written very much in Ball's colourful style. Some of the wording even gives the appearance of having been borrowed from the narrative. This could very well indicate that Ball, attempting to strengthen his case, simply made them up after the voyage was over. It may, alternatively, indicate that he had sufficient sway over his officers to convince them to sign a petition which he had written. Whether the officers of the *Hector* joined Ball in this petition or not, it adds much useful detail to his account of the government of the ship.

Interestingly enough, Ball made fairly extensive use of a code in all parts of the manuscript, except the petition of grievances. The code was a combination of letters and numbers similar to those used by English diplomats, only rather crude and easily deciphered.

His purpose is not clear. If the code was meant for secrecy, then his manuscript was scarcely suitable for publication. Some of the passages in code are merely innocuous proverbs, but most of the passages are rather dangerous. Many of them are bitter accusations and invective directed against those who had wronged Ball, especially Sir Francis Stewart. Others reveal useful information about the voyage which might have been dangerous to publish. Sir Francis Stewart was a man of eminence and some, at least, of what Ball put in code might have been actionable in court. But much of what Ball wrote without benefit of code was just as provocative. Perhaps the code was no more than a toy which Ball employed rather indiscriminately. The coded sections of the manuscript are indicated here by italics.

The Earl of Warwick's account is much shorter, consisting of only two folio pages. Warwick, in the *Great Neptune*, his fleet admiral, met a fleet of thirty galleons on 2 July in the fog. When the fog lifted a little, he found himself separated from the rest of his fleet and surrounded by his enemies. He then proceeded to fight his way out, engaging fourteen different ships and damaging four of them severely, by his own account. After he had fought clear of them, his rear-admiral the *Jonathan* rejoined him, and the two ships eventually returned to England. Warwick rushed off to kiss the king's hands and produced an account of his battle, perhaps written while still out to sea. Bagg included a copy of it in a letter to Nicholas on 26 July, the same day Warwick arrived in port.[3] In the account, Warwick mentioned that he still knew nothing of the fate of Sir Francis Stewart and rest of his fleet.

Warwick had good reason to write his account. He had returned home prizeless with a battered ship full of sick men, after more than two months at sea. He was not popular at court, especially with the duke, and he needed to protect himself with at least a tale of heroism. His enemies must have taken great glee in his failure; and Bagg, at least, did not scruple to belittle the earl's feats in battle:

> the mariners in praise of his Lordship, and their own valours, blow up the business as much as they can. It was fit for him to come away, for there were so great an odds against him as I hardly believe his Lordship made three of the galleons lie by the lee, neither do I think that this Spanish fleet is other than that of Naples, that this season annually keeps the coast.[4]

Two copies of the earl's account exist. One is among the state papers in the Public Record Office (SP 16/72 No. 9.1) and is the version sent by Bagg to Nicholas. The other, here printed, is among the Phelips manuscripts at the Somerset Record Office (Phelips MS. 211/43). On the whole, they are identical with only insignificant variations between them. They are both in a fair hand, though neither is the Earl of Warwick's, and they are written in the first person. There is little reason to suppose the earl did not write the account. Ball was aware that such an account existed:

> As for his honour's valour, noble courage, and bold attempt he passed this day in a dangerous fight with the armada of Spain, I cease to write, being no spectator thereof, knowing there were worthy gentlemen and seamen present of great account which have writ thereof and divulged unto the world the true manner, form, and order, with what courageous valour, manly courage, and resolution it was performed. [p. **40**]

This account was previously published in 1837 by the Abbotsford Club.[5] As their publication, though accurate, is not generally available, it seems worthwhile to reprint Warwick's account here in conjunction with Ball's.

MIGHT AND WOULD NOT

or

The observation of the Right Honourable the Earl of Warwick's voyage made upon the coast of Portingale in the year of our Lord Anno Domini 1627:

With the passages which principally happened; and the proceeding thereof, but especially of the rule and government in the good ship called the Hector, *under the command of Sir Francis Stewart, knight, captain of the said ship.*

And a true relation of the manner of his fight with the Vice-Admiral of Spain the twelfth day of July 1627, three more of the Spanish Armada giving her chase in sight, very near at hand:

Written by William Ball, mariner, clearing himself of an aspersion falsely imputed upon him on the voyage.

The true noble, renowned, most worthy of right, the right honourable the Earl of Warwick of his heroic spirit and love unto martial discipline, for the glory of God, honour of his king and country, and for the suppressing of the enemies of Christ and the haters of England, prepared a fleet of ships at the beginning of the year of our Lord God *Anno Domini* 1627, whose names, with their burdens, number of men and ordnance are hereunder set down:

	tons	*men*	*ordnance*
The *Great Neptune,* admiral	500	160	48
The *Hector,* vice-admiral	400	138	32
The *Jonathan,* rear-admiral	350	125	28
The *Golden Cat,* a Hollander	2—	—	—
The *Flight,* a pinnace	060	040	06
The *Little Neptune*	120	070	14
The *Treasure*	160	084	14
The *Bark Warwick,* a pinnace	060	042	05
The *Robert,* a pinnace	060	050	06
The . . . [*sic*], a pinnace	—	—	—

These ships according to his honour's directions were made ready and furnished with provisions, some of them from London and the rest in the west part of England. The ship *Hector*, being a very proper warlike ship and well appointed, was prepared and victualled in the River of Thames, of which ship the worshipful Richard Harris, one of the four Masters of England, being part owner *with whom I had served apprenticeship seven years* was appointed to be captain, but upon some dislike afterward conceived was dispossessed.

MARCH 1626–7

The 14th day of March 1626 being Wednesday in the morning, Captain Harris sent for me at my house to come to him, I being then in bed and in health, but since heartily wished I had been at the same time sick, for which desire [reason] hereafter shall be declared.

Having had formerly the summer past diverse times conference together concerning the right honourable the Earl of Warwick his voyage, intended to go along with him in the *Hector*, and [I] was now to give an absolute answer, whether to proceed or not.

I having well considered with myself it was a very hopeful voyage, with an honourable earl, and Captain Harris a worthy seaman *and my master unto whom I was bound apprentice in the year of our Lord God anno domini 1597 and served him complete eight years* made me the willinger, and [I] resolve[d] to undertake the voyage. And the 15th day in the afternoon I went to him at his lodging at Tower Wharf and certified him I would proceed along with him on the voyage. Then he confirmed unto me I should be master of the *Hector* under him and willed me to repair aboard to make ready the ship with all expedition (as the Earl of Warwick desired) and to manage all such business with speed as should be for the preferment and good of the voyage. So having received order, taking my leave of him, [I] departed.

The sixteenth day being Friday, according to his appointment, the ship riding at Blackwall, I went aboard and took possession of her, as master under God and him, for the present voyage intended, beginning to prepare and fit all such business as was necessary to be done and afterward was well rewarded for my pains and travail as shall be likewise at large declared.

And by the 31st day and last of this month of March 1627 we had received most of our victuals and provisions aboard, determining the beginning of the next week following to break ground. But only happened a great disaster unto us, which was the cause of our longer stay in the River of Thames, viz. we found so great an imperfection in our ship's mainmast, being rotten above the middle partners, as could by no means possible be made serviceable for the voyage, but forced [us] to have a new mast prepared with all expedition.

APRIL 1627

The fourth day of April being Wednesday, in regard of the *Hector*'s grounding at Blackwall every low water, about two o'clock in the afternoon

[we] weighed with a fresh gale of wind at north-west and went down to Woolwich. The right honourable the Earl of Warwick, being himself in person aboard beginning our hopeful voyage, which God almighty send prosperous.

And the seventh day being Saturday, in the forenoon we hove out our old mainmast and set a new — which was, by great negligence of them in whom the charge lay and were put in trust, made some four foot shorter than the other old mast was, which proved more stubborn and not so pliant as it should, which impediment, with other defects which I omit to speak of, hath wronged much the reputation of the ship.

Three or four days after, the *Hector*, being ready victualled and provisions aboard, [was] ready to depart from Woolwich and to proceed on the voyage.

The twelfth day the wind came up easterly and so continued betwixt the north-east and the south-east quarters nine days following, which with the former disaster in her mainmast, was great hindrance unto us. Myself, having had little time limited for performing of any business of mine own, the managing of the ship being of such great importance which ought not to have been neglected, seeing the wind come easterly, and being bound forth of such a voyage, this day I went to London and stayed there some three days to settle mine affairs in the best manner I could, in order howsoever it should please God to deal with me on the voyage. Which when I came and returned aboard the *Hector* at Woolwich, the seventeenth day being Tuesday, Captain Harris seemed to be much discontented and angry with me for my staying and being so long absent at London. But [after] showing unto him good caution for the same, [he] was afterward pacified and his wrath appeased, although he had a further retch [*sic*] and malicious intention (failing of his enterprise he expected).

The twenty-second day being Sunday, in the morning the wind came up at south-west, and the same day about three o'clock in the afternoon, having half tide under foot, we weighed at Woolwich in the *Hector* and the same evening came to an anchor at Gravesend, where for two days following we were stayed by a general stay by the Duke of Buckingham his Grace's order.

And the twenty-fifth day in the morning, we anchored at Leigh in the road or swatch in six fathom and a half water of the sand, where rode the *Assurance* and *Adventure* of his majesty's, with other ships, bound for the river of Hamburg. And when Captain Harris came aboard the *Hector*, he was very angry, *calling me fool and ass*, asking if any man in England would come to an anchor in that place so near the sand and upon a lee shore, the wind being at south-west, when we rode in the wake of the *Assurance*, or rather to the southward, and other ships betwixt the shore and the *Hector*.

The time of our staying at Leigh proved very foul weather, and the winds westerly. But the twenty-seventh day it blew more amenable and about ten o'clock in the morning this day, we weighed in Leigh road and went over the flats, which are sands lying at the Thames mouth. And the thirtieth and laf April 1627, being Monday, we arrived at the Isle of Wight and went in at St Helen's Point. Captain Harris, in the skiff, departed from the ship and went ashore to Portsmouth, leaving order with me to go with the *Hector* into Stokes Bay. Which about seven o'clock at night, [we] came there to an anchor in eleven fathom water against the west end of the high trees, according to his own direction. But when Captain Harris was returned aboard [and] asked me where the ship was, I answered him with these words: 'Sir, in Stokes Bay.' 'In Stokes Bay,' quoth he, '*thou art an ass and a fool indeed; what a coxcomb art thou*. Thou dost not know Stokes Bay.' − with other opprobrious, reviling speeches most shamefully to my disgrace. But at that time the sign predominant was elevated.

And under correction be it spoken, I know the road as well as he or any man whatsoever.

These vagaries and usage of him to me struck me very much out of heart and weakened my command and authority very much amongst the company, grieving me and making myself not myself, as though I had been a *fool indeed* and knew nothing.

For there is no inferior officer in a ship of whatsoever degree or calling he is of, from the highest to the lowest, if he be not protected and borne out in his command by the superior and chief commander in the ship which they are present in, I say that officer will be daunted and can never bear a good command amongst men, but everyone will seek to suppress his authority and make him a right novice. [Witness] the occasion of Captain Harris, his malice and spleen so taken against me: to my best remembrance since I was his servant, I never gave him distaste but ever acknowledged and honoured him as a master in, and before, all companies whatsoever. Neither can I to this present instant time study, imagine, or conceive whereupon his envy, hatred, and malice should proceed unless because *my wife would not yield to his lascivious lust* at Woolwich.

MAY 1627

The first day being Tuesday, May day, about noon came in at St Helen's Point a Flushing man-of-war, one Captain Adrianyanson, and with him his prize, a Spanish ship of Seville come from the West Indies, about the burden of 180 tons or thereabouts, laden with hides, ginger, certain wood, and indigo. These two ships came sailing along by us near the island side, not showing of any colours of whence they were, upon which I caused two or three piece of ordnance to be shot at them and brought them under command and to an anchor close by us, to examine from whence they came and what they were. Who fearing much the States of Holland men-of-war was the cause, as they said, that they showed no colours, which made me conceive their letter of marque was not authentical and the more to be inquisitive of their proceedings; which the captain, diving into our imagination what we intended, proffered any reasonable composition to be freely cleared, that he might pass away. Which being denied him, [he] desired to go ashore unto Captain Harris, who was then at Portsmouth. And being met together, [they] grew into such a propinquity of loving society that the man-of-war was secretly cleared.

But the two signs Aries and Pisces, being this day in conjunction, was the hindrance that every one fared the worse and that we carried not the man-of-war and her prize unto our admiral, the right honourable the Earl of Warwick. The next morning, Captain Adrianyanson with his prize departed out of Stokes Bay and went to the Cowes, where as afterward we understood [he] was stayed, until such time as he cleared himself of the Admiralty Court of England.

The third day being Thursday, Captain Pennington in the ship *Lion* of the King's Majesty, with a great fleet of ships and French prizes which were taken in the trade at Ushant upon the coast of France, came into the road and anchored as near as convenient they could, every ship taking a fair berth round about us. And then Captain Harris could see the *Hector* ride in Stokes Bay.

The fourth day the *Lion*, with all her whole fleet, weighed in Stokes Bay and went afore the opening of Portsmouth harbour, and there anchored. And likewise we in the *Hector* according to directions went also and anchored among the fleet.

And having very fair calm weather, one Mr John Cheeklie, and certain of our principal men whom Captain Harris much respected, went aboard other ships to take leave of their acquaintance and friends. And before they came aboard themselves again, in the interim, Captain Harris returned from Portsmouth *being half signed* [*sic*] and inquiring for the long boat and such men as he missed that were not present in his sight. Answer was made him, where they were. So with that, he fell into an impassionate humour, railing at me, (by reason they were from the ship, and at his coming aboard absent) *and swore he, 'God's blood, I was a base slave, a rascal, and a very fool'*; I could not keep our men aboard, and not worthy to be master of such a ship as the *Hector*, and disgraced me what he could in the wildest manner before the company, conceiting to himself a vainglory and great applause. Which I think would have disheartened any man in his command amongst and before so many men, [and] for answering which point, I refer to the judicial censure and opinion of his own fraternity.

This reproach and shame without cause, not knowing from whence it should spring or proceed, with the former abuses grieved me to the very heart, in so much I took no joy in anything, resolving with myself, God sending us to the right honourable the Earl of Warwick, to inform his honour of the same and to have a hearing betwixt Captain Harris and myself, and to have redress either one way or other. Upon which being so full of grief, I absented myself from his table, determining not to eat with him until atonement was made betwixt us.

The fifth day we weighed and came out from the Isle of Wight to sea. And the seventh day being Monday, in the afternoon we safely arrived and came to an anchor in Plymouth Sound where rode our admiral, the *Great Neptune*; our rear-admiral, the *Jonathan*; and the *Golden Cat* of Amsterdam in Holland, with the *Flight*; and were all ready to depart and go to sea, staying only for the rest of the fleet. We being come to an anchor and after we had saluted the right honourable the Earl of Warwick and the rest of the ships in the fleet, Captain Harris in the pinnace went aboard the *Great Neptune*, our admiral, unto the earl, and within an hour after returned back aboard the *Hector* with the right honourable the Earl of Warwick, the right worshipful Sir Francis Stewart, knight, the worshipful Sir Michael Geare, knight, Captain James Mountague, Captain Gyles, and Captain Richard Hooper, with diverse other gentlemen attendant. And after salutation to the company, the earl caused his commission under the Broad Seal of England to be throughout read publicly unto all the company, wherein was ratified and confirmed unto his honour for the execution of martial law. This being done, the Earl of Warwick certified our company he had received a special warrant or countermand, from the Duke of Buckingham his Grace, to call back and command Captain Richard Harris to return again for London and not to go out of the land but as he, being one of the four Masters of England, so to attend his majesty's special service and could by no means be permitted to proceed any farther. At which hearing, all the company were much discontented and answered with a general voice, if Captain Harris went not on the voyage, there was but few or none desired likewise to go any farther. The Earl of Warwick protested he was heartily sorry for the losing of his company and for his return back to London. Yet most of the company conceited it was only a plot laid to work Captain Harris out of the *Hector*, and that he was but only made an instrument to fit and victual the ship and to bring her to Plymouth for another man, by reason of the rumour and report at London and in the West Country, Sir Michael Geare should proceed captain of the *Hector*.

The Earl of Warwick gave me straight command and charged me, as I would answer the contrary upon my peril, not to permit and suffer any man to go ashore or out of the ship until I heard further order from his honour. And so [he], with the rest of the knights, captains, and other gentlemen, departed and went ashore to Plymouth.

This sudden unexpected welcome unto the company was not well liked of. First hearing of martial law (which might have been better concealed and published after our coming to sea) and then to hear again of the displacing of Captain Harris out of the ship, bred in them such an inveterate hate and dislike of the voyage, which caused them to be in an uproar, swearing if they could by any means convey away their clothes and get themselves ashore, they would leave the ship and give over the voyage. And much care and watch with all respect I could use, with my best endeavour, to keep many of them aboard that night, which otherwise would have stolen ashore and gone away.

The next morning being the eighth day, the right honourable the Earl of Warwick, with Captain Harris and all the other forenamed gentlemen (only Sir Michael Geare excepted) came aboard the *Hector*, his honour understanding the great discontentment of the company and their resolution [of] going away by reason of Captain Harris his departure from the ship. Wherefore, to accommodate all quietness and peace with them, the company being all called upon the upper deck, [he] spoke as followeth: 'Gentlemen,' quoth the Earl of Warwick, 'I am as truly sorry and grieved for Dick Harris his going away as any of you all, and as loath I am, believe it, to lose his company. But since it is our King's Majesty's pleasure by order from my Lord Duke of Buckingham his Grace to call him back and take him from us, we must all have patience and of force be contented. But,' said the earl, 'here is Sir Francis Stewart whom, if you please to accept of, shall be your captain and my vice-admiral.' Then Sir Francis Stewart made a pleasing apology to the company, leaving it unto their choice what to do. Which being ended, the company, of their own voluntary love and disposition, embraced Sir Francis Stewart and chose him to be our captain of the *Hector* over us. But afterward, most of them wished they had made choice of him whom they refused, which was reported should be captain.

This business being thus established and set in order, and the current now running another way, the Earl of Warwick and all the gentlemen departed ashore to Plymouth, leaving our new chosen captain aboard the *Hector*.

The ninth day, Captain Harris in the forenoon came aboard and fetched away his chests and clothes, and departed from the *Hector* very much discontented. And surely if I had understood of his good offices he wrought for me (as afterward I did) as hereafter shall be spoken of, upon no conditions in the world would I have proceeded in that ship on the voyage.

The tenth day being Thursday in the morning about six o'clock, the right honourable the Earl of Warwick, admiral in the *Great Neptune*; Sir Francis Stewart, vice-admiral in the *Hector*; Mr James Mountague, rear-admiral in the *Jonathan*; Captain Mean the Hollander in the *Golden Cat*; and Captain Pellam, in a Spanish patache named the *Flight*, weighed anchor and set sail in Plymouth Sound with the wind at north north-west and came out to sea, bound for the coast of Portingale, God almighty be our good speed. Leaving in England the *Little Neptune*, Captain Sussex Cammocke; the *Treasure*, Captain John Jones; the *Bark Warwick*, Captain Richard Beaumont; the *Robert*, and the *Scralle*, the earl expecting they would have presently followed out to sea according to directions left for them at Plymouth to the place of rendezvous appointed. But, following their own designs, [they] made the Earl of Warwick, and all the rest that looked daily for their coming to the southward, frustrate of their expectation.

Sailing out of Plymouth Sound, our ship the *Hector*, being the headmost of the fleet, in Cawsand Bay rode the *Patience*, a ship of London with the King's Majesty's colours displayed at the main top-gallant mast head, at whom Sir Francis Stewart commanded the gunner to shoot a saker shot, contemptuously, at his flag and so compelled him to take it in.

Being a seaboard of the Rame Head without the Eddystone, we met with Captain Powell and his pinnace, which were bound for the West Indies, who consorted to keep company with the Earl of Warwick his fleet for three months following, in regard of half our fleet left in England behind us. But [he] performed not according to promise.

And in the afternoon, being athwart the Lizard, we met a small Frenchman, a ship of Dieppe in France, standing into the shore [and] plying to the eastward. To whom the *Flight* [and] Captain Powell and his pinnace gave chase and brought her off to the Earl of Warwick, being as they said (as is rehearsed) of Dieppe. Who, having my Lord the Duke of Buckingham his Grace's pass, without further search or examination was cleared and so departed. But the next day after, as I am credably informed, one Captain H. West, a man-of-war of London, athwart or near about the Start, met with the same Frenchman and surprised her of all that ever they had, and went clear and sheer away with the same.

At eight o'clock this night we set off from the Land's End of England, directing and shaping our course for the coast of Portingale.

And the eleventh day, after we had shifted our company according to directions and order from our admiral, the Earl of Warwick, our men were appointed to sit five and five all the voyage, without altering, to four men's allowance of victuals, which if it might have so continued constantly as it was promised, it had been well comported. But this moved some discontent amongst our company, in regard they being put to that allowance so soon and suddenly after our coming to sea.

Thus having a prosperous gale and a fair wind, the fifteenth day being Tuesday, in the morning we made the land, being Cape Coruna [MS: Corians] and Cape Finisterre and the land thereabouts upon the coast of Galicia.

Our admiral in the *Great Neptune*, the Earl of Warwick, caused a flag of council to be put abroad in the mizzen shrouds, upon which all the captains and masters in the fleet repaired aboard, and it was ordered by council of war that we should sail along the coast of Portingale to the Berlings, spreading ourselves east and west, abreast of one another three or four miles distance.

The sixteenth day in the forenoon, sailing along the coast, our ships which were nearest the shore descried three sail of ships, unto whom all our fleet gave chase; and they next unto them exchanged certain piece of ordnance. But the three ships, being between the shore and our fleet, recovered the harbour of Caminha to friend, and sailed in there, and so got away and cleared themselves of us. We took two or three fishermen, who certified the Earl of Warwick [that] those three ships chased into Caminha were three Portingale men-of-war and also informed his honour the Brazil fleet were not yet arrived home.

The seventeenth day in the afternoon, we saw a sail to the southward of us which all our fleet chased while about six o'clock at night; and then the Earl of Warwick and our fleet, seeing we could not fetch of her, gave over. Only Captain Powell and his pinnace continued his chase, shot off a farewell piece of ordnance, and so with his pinnace departed out of our company but spoke not with our admiral, the Earl of Warwick, completing [MS: compleering] not what he had promised.

The nineteenth day in the morning, we saw the Berlings. And then again council was held, at which time it was ordered that Captain Mean, the Dutchman in the *Golden Cat*, and Captain Pellam in the *Flight* should be the next morning by break of day betwixt the shore and the Berlings, to see what they could descry; who returned back the next day and brought word to the Earl of Warwick they saw certain ships riding in Peniche road. From this time to the end of the month, we saw divers sail of ships, and chased, but none [were] worthy of entertainment, to be spoken of.

JUNE 1627

The first day of June being Friday, one Thomas Ware, the steward, altered the company's ordinary allowance of victuals, which they had wont to have, and at noon gave them cheese in lieu of butter with their fish, which formerly on every fish day they had butter at noon and cheese at night allowed them. So that there was a great error in the steward committed which was never examined nor called in question, which in all reason should have been done, and contrariwise which the steward he ought not to have done, in presuming without order from the captain to alter any property of their allowance or diminish any part thereof.

Whereupon rose an insolent mutiny amongst our vulgar sort of common sailors, and they had chosen one James Addams and one Daniel Fleshman, two deboshed [MS: deboiste] fellows to be their spokesmen, who with some dozen or fourteen together with their platters of fish in their hands — the captain sitting at dinner upon the upper deck — came very rude and peremptorily unto him, and made their complaint for their butter as aforesaid. He entreated them of all love to have patience and be silent until such time he himself had dined, and in the afternoon he would go aboard the admiral to the Earl of Warwick and look what allowance in all victual and other provisions their company had; they [the *Hector*'s crew] should have the like and the same allowed them. So in a muttering sort, they all went forward afore the mast to the cook-room door and set their platters of fish down upon the deck. Quoth this Addams, ' 'Sblood, let's take it, and heave it overboard'. Whereupon Sir Francis Stewart hearing him speak in this reproachful manner, and being of a sudden very much moved in passion, rose very earnestly and hastily from the table and with an East India cane or rattan struck him, and commanded the boatswain to seize a block at the yard's arm and to have Addams dunked. Then said Fleshman and with him all his confederates together, 'Duck one and duck all'. Then seeing that they were gathered to a head and so many parts taking compacted all together, our captain appointed myself and one Mr Mungo Murray, a very honest gentleman and well demeanoured, to carry him aboard the admiral to the Earl of Warwick, and to certify his honour of this mutiny arising in the ship as is aforesaid related. Addams denied to go and swore he would not go to the earl. But by force and compulsion, our chiefest officers by command from our captain put him into the pinnace. When he saw he should of force go indeed, [he] said to his consorts, 'A plague upon you all. Will you forsake me now and not stick to me?' Whereupon many entered the pinnace and said they would go all to the admiral. But Sir Francis Stewart, advising them what an enterprise they undertook, persuaded them, and so they came again into the ship, the gang appointed only excepted, with the rest of us that went with Addams, so being come to the admiral, certified the Earl of Warwick what had passed. Upon which understanding the truth, he commanded the said Addams to be put into the bilboes, who remained not there above the space of two hours, but upon earnest entreaty and his submission to his honour, was released, cleared, and discharged. So we, taking our leave, departed from thence and went aboard our own ship, the *Hector*.

And by the way advised Addams very earnestly when he came aboard [he] should present himself to Sir Francis Stewart, and in submission ask him forgiveness for his fact committed. But he being of a stubborn, perverse nature, and a scornful fellow, refused and disdained our counsel, which turned afterward to his further disgrace and punishment.

The second day in the afternoon, Sir Francis Stewart caused the pinnace to be hoisted out, determining to go aboard the admiral and pretending, or at least making a bravado, to leave our ship and proceed no longer for captain in the *Hector* by reason of the former disgust passed. Which our company was very loath to let him go out of the ship, until such time he had promised to return again aboard the *Hector*. In his cabin, the captain said privately unto me, that if the said Addams had but come and presented himself unto him after the Earl of Warwick had cleared him, and asked pardon and forgiveness in any reasonable fashion, it should have given him satisfaction and have been called no further in question, nor examined any more.

Our captain, myself, and one of my mates went aboard the admiral, where being come, he related anew unto the Earl of Warwick the whole circumstance of the former mutiny, giving him also to understand of the stubborn perverseness of the said Addams. Whereupon the earl commanded me to fetch the two mutineers aboard, Addams and one Fleshman his confederate, brothers in villainy, and bring them unto his honour aboard the *Great Neptune*, who after examination upon certain interrogatories, the earl committed them both into the bilboes, where they remained for a further trial of a martial court to be called, and for a while leave them.

It was ordered by council of war the same time that all our fleet present should sail towards the Cape Roca [MS: Rocksentt] going into the river of Lisbon, and there to remain off and on upon that coast until the latter end of this month of June, expecting daily the residue of our fleet left in England to come to us — which by the northerly winds as we had blew continually since we arrived on the coast, [they] might very well have done. But we looked, as the Jews look for their messiah, for they never intended no such matter for to come unto the Earl of Warwick upon the coast of Portingale, as the event of their proceedings declareth.

The third day being Sunday, in the morning about five o'clock one William Ledbetter, a young man, departed and changed this life for immortality, he having lain sick and diseased the most time of our being out of England. And about noon after sermon was ended, [we] buried the corpse of him in the large sepulchre of the ocean sea.

The fourth day being Monday, about one of the clock in the afternoon, we descried three sail of ships, which bore of us east south-east and, with the wind at south-west, stood upon a tack to the westward. We stood directly with them, which after some small time they perceiving, and coming somewhat near us, began to alter their course and bear room quarter winds to the eastward from us, and with all our admiral, the Earl of Warwick, and all our fleet chasing them. About seven o'clock at night we, in the *Hector*, near fetched them up within the length of two saker shot and might have spoken with them, but night coming on in hand, determined to keep near unto them in sight all the night following. Our admiral caused a piece of ordnance to be shot off and so, with the rest of our fleet, tacked off to the westward, only but ourselves who still held on our course towards them, with a firm resolution not to depart before we knew certain what ships they were. This piece of ordnance being shot off, and they cast about to the westward, caused Sir Francis Stewart our captain to be very much discontented, and likewise all our company, admiring what they intended to do — we still standing after them resolving to have spoken with them before our departure to have known what ships they were. But after some certain time passed, the night growing dark and the rest of our fleet near out of sight of us, our captain, being mutable [and] like other men changing his opinion, fell into consideration what was best to be done, being loath to incur the displeasure of the Earl of Warwick. [He] commanded me to tack and cast about our ship after them, himself and all our company being very much unwilling and discontented as he said unto them, but only forced to follow order and commission.

And so we gave over our chase, not any one ship in our fleet not knowing what they were, from whence they came, nor whither they were bound. Which in my judgement was a great absurdity, but by whom this gross error was committed or who was the cause thereof I certainly know not.

We had diverse opinions held amongst our company, every one expending their judgements what ships they were. Viz. some made them to be three Portingale Admarantazgo [*sic*] men-of-war, some three Turks men-of-war of Algiers or Sallee, others to be three Hamburgers, either bound in or come out of Lisbon, but myself and certain others judged them to be three Lubeckers, being deep laden, which so appeared by their colours displayed. But none of us knew certainly to this present day what nation ships they were. I conceive if they had been any men-of-war whatsoever, Spaniards excepted, they would questionless have spoken with us, although we not with them. And it is naturally used in English men-of-war, if they be of force and upon any reasonable terms, to see and speak with the proudest he that cross the seas whatsoever.

This fourth day of June was the first day and time we had sight of the Rock going into the river of Lisbon in all our traverse since we came to the southward, which is not ordinary; neither, I think, was ever known before that men-of-war lie so long about the Berlings as we did, but at some time or other should have seen and have been near the said land of the Rock, to have seen and known what had passed in and out of the river of Lisbon, being the metropolitan city of trade in all the kingdom of Portingale.

From the nineteenth day of May, which was our first arrival at the Berlings, to this present day, the fourth of June, we met and spoke with divers sail of ships, but most of them English men-of-war and not any ships wherewith to do us any good, profit or benefit, and now having hope and possibility of purchase, [we] let this opportunity overslip. All this night following, we stood off to the westward and bore a press sail, the wind being at south-west, close, misting, sleety weather. And the next morning about four o'clock, we saw the three sail of ships east north-east of us, as far as we could well discern and descry them half shrouds high. Then our admiral and all our fleet gave chase after them again some four hours, and raised them very much so that we saw them upon the deck and questionless might have fetched them up. But they edging to the northward, and the wind veering southerly, our admiral clapt his tacks aboard, gave over the chase, and so departed.

This seemed a bravado and a mere folly to be admired and wondered at, that all our fleet might have kept company with them all the night afore within some two saker shot length which they could not possibly have shunned, and that night to sail away, and the next morning give chase to them again. This working discomforted our company and put them out of heart and any hope for the making of a saving voyage, as it did manifestly appear also by the discontentment of Captain Mean, the Dutchman, and all his company in the *Golden Cat*, who the sixth day of June in the afternoon, being some four miles to leeward of all the fleet, brought his ship by the lee and shot off a piece of ordnance, upon which the Earl of Warwick in his ship the *Great Neptune*, admiral, and all the rest of the fleet bore room withal, who certified his honour that his ship, the *Golden Cat*, was very leaky and his beer most part spent, so being desirous to be freed of our company from the fleet. The earl gave his leave to depart, and about seven o'clock at night he bore up the helm, pretending as he said for England. But our captain and most of our company imagined and conceived this to be only a device and stratagem of the Fleming to be cleared to follow his own designs in regard he did not like our proceedings.

The seventh day being Thursday, our captain went aboard the admiral, and about eight o'clock at night he returned aboard and gave me order presently to cast about, and tack the ship, and stand to the eastward. 'For,' saith he, 'it is appointed by the Earl of Warwick [that] our ship, the *Hector*, and the patache called the *Flight* to be the next morning very early near unto the Cape Roca going into Lisbon to see what we could descry, leaving our admiral the *Great Neptune* and rear-admiral the *Jonathan* in the offing.'

This order having received from our captain, I gave unto the boatswain and fore and aft in the ship amongst the company, to be ready for to go about. In the interim, one Mr John Cheeklie (whom I made account had been shipped by Captain Harris as a mate until this time) – having been with associates and colleagues where their place of rendezvous for good fellowship, eating and drinking was kept all the voyage – came up upon the deck and in the presence of Sir Francis Stewart demanded wherefore we should go about, and by whose and what order. The captain himself answered and told him by order from the Earl of Warwick *for as he was aft that time I would not, neither desired, to speak with or to him.* Then he broke out in a most violent and impassionate humour, saying he was not worthy to be made acquainted therewith, and that Sir Francis should take notice, he had as much command and charge of the ship committed unto him as Ball had, and that he should know. At which being urged to speak, I answered, 'Mr Cheeklie, if it were so, as that you have such authority, it was well. But,' said I, 'I do think to the contrary.' Then swearing this oath, ' 'sblood,' quoth he, 'We are all led up and down, like a crew of fools by Balaam and his ass' (but whom this ass was, or is, I leave it to censure) with other opprobrious speeches which I omit. Our captain and other gentlemen entreated him to be patient and quiet, and if he had any thing to say wherewith he was discontented, [he] should speak and reveal the same to him the next morning. But then nothing at all was said touching this business.

Here now began Mr Cheeklie's emulation to break out and to show his authority, which should seem secretly, as afterward I understood, he had received. As also most of our resident officers were all linked together in the same nature and condition, having all, before our departure and coming from Plymouth, learned their leirypoope [*sic*] of Captain Harris.

This business was never after by our captain called in question to be examined whether unto whom the charge of the *Hector* was committed, so that I well perceived he gave way unto what was spoken overnight and was the protector of this difference and discord. But a long time after, as every true seaman may conceive, there could be no great love nor familiarity betwixt us, but outwardly in show, in regard of such aspiring secret emulation in an inferior.

The eighth day in the morning, before any light appeared, we were both our ships fair by the land. And the *Flight*, being betwixt the shore and us, chased a Portingale caravel which sailed along the coast ashore upon the rocks near unto Cascais Point, [so] that she was bilged and cast away. This caravel arrived some three or four days before, out of Guinea to Peniche, laden with gum and other goods, and was bound in for Lisbon. Also they had taken in at Peniche certain passengers whereof there was six men and two women drowned as they sought to save themselves going ashore in their gondola [MS: Gundell]. Our pinnace brought aboard the *Hector* two Dutchmen whereof one of them was the gunner of the castle at Peniche, the other his son-in-law, and a young Portingale which had been on the voyage in the caravel to Guinea, who related unto our captain [that] they feared we had been Turks men-of-war, and that they also feared, being taken, should have been made slaves all days of their lives. Otherwise, they would not have run ashore and cast away the caravel, neither to endanger themselves. Also, they informed us that the Brazil fleet was not as yet arrived at Lisbon.

After this, we stood off to sea with little wind northerly. And in the offing a-seaboard of us, we descried a sail coming in with the land, which they could not so well perceive us, being under the high land of the Rock. Our admiral and the *Jonathan* giving her chase, but when she perceived us and the *Flight* to stand off and chase her likewise, then the ship altered her course and bore room afore the wind, and quartering for Cape Espichel [MS: Pitcher]. And being too light of foot for us, [she] recovered and got into Sezimbra Road under the command and protection of a castle and there anchored. Where of force, for want of anima, discretion, and understanding, we left her. But certainly if we had presently followed her into the road, as myself, Mr Cheeklie, and most of our men propounded it unto the captain, and were resolutely willing to do, in regard the wind being northerly, that we might leave and take off the shore at our pleasure, there had been no such great danger but that we might have brought her from thence.

In Sezimbra Bay, we took two small Portingale caravels which we had chased into a cove. All the men, forsaking them [and] taking the shore for their best friends, had taken from them their rudders. But with great danger of our men, by reason of the inhabitants which were there present withstanding them, with four of our pinnaces being manned with murderers and small shot, [we] brought two of them by force both off from the enemy. These caravels were laden with pilchards and salt, bound for Lisbon, and might have done us very good service, had not one of them, which was lost carelessly and negligently, been cast away. The biggest was appointed to be attendant upon the admiral, the Earl of Warwick, and the other unto the *Hector*, Sir Francis Stewart, which our captain named the *Snapper*, and caused her to be fitted with men and munition serviceable for war, and appointed one George Larremar to be captain of her, who went ascouting [MS: a scoaking] as he was ordered by the Earl of Warwick's directions. This night and the ninth day following, we stood off to the westward with very much wind at north north-west, intending to ply for the Rock, in so much that we were forced to take all our men that were in the *Snapper* into the *Hector*, and for the night following to tow her at our ship's stern.

The tenth day, being Sunday, proved a storm of wind northerly. In which storm bearing a press sail the night following, we sprang a great leak that forced us to pump upward of five hundred strokes a glass. But the next morning at daylight, we laid our ship by the lee and found the leak on the larboard bow, under the manger scupper, which our carpenter, with sheet lead, tar, and hair, thanks be to God, stopped the same to a very small matter, which afterward we pumped. This afternoon, the wind dulled and blew more amenable.

The twelfth day in the morning, our admiral caused his flag of council to be put abroad in the mizzen shrouds and every captain and master repaired aboard according unto the Earl of Warwick his order so to do, whensoever it was displayed abroad in that place, and it was set down and agreed upon by council of war, that in regard the winds hanging northerly, and the fleet a whole degree and better to leeward of the latitude of our rendezvous, and well considered we should be a long time a-beating back unto that latitude. All thought it fit and convenient [that] we should stand still to the westward for the western islands of Terceira [MS: Traceras], if the wind should so continue. And if it should happen in the interim [for] the wind to come westerly, then to return back for the Cape Roca again, having a great sea, with the wind that formerly blew, though a fair gale of wind present.

The caravel attendant on the admiral, the Earl of Warwick, the commander which was appointed of her, trying his valour and conclusions, by negligence came athwart the *Hector*'s hawse, lying with our foresail aback stays; and, before they could make means to clear themselves of the ship, [he] made means to break her down to the water and was utterly lost and cast away.

This twelfth day of June, there was also a martial court called and appointed, and a jury empanelled upon James Addams, concerning the mutiny by him committed the first day of this month, as also for a shirt he stole aboard our admiral, the *Great Neptune*, the time he was a prisoner, being let loose only to come to prayer and then played the knave. Of which jury there was six of the admiral's men appointed, four of the *Hector*'s, two of the *Jonathan*'s, and one of the *Flight*'s, all chosen officers. And by his indictment whereof he was accused, they found him to be guilty of a mutiny, and so delivered up their verdicts under their handwriting, and left him to the mercy of the right honourable the Earl of Warwick, judge in that place. And the court assembled to be censured [*sic*], who condemned him to be hanged, pronouncing that fearful sentence of death, Lord have mercy upon his soul.

The fourteenth day being Thursday, having fair weather and little wind northerly, in the morning our admiral took in their topsails and brailed up both their two great sails, every one of the fleet doing the like. And the Earl of Warwick by a chief servant of his sent aboard our ship, the *Hector*, James Addams the prisoner, who was condemned to die for the said mutiny, and with a special warrant in the King's Majesty's name to Sir Francis Stewart our captain that he should receive and take, and cause to execute the said Addams, hanging him by the neck while he was dead, according to the law of England.

Having received this strict order and command from the Earl of Warwick, our captain first caused the minister to take the fellow privately unto confession to almighty God, and to prepare himself to die. Which being resolved, he was brought forth to the place of execution, where the halter was put about his neck. So then we went to prayer, which being ended, we sung the first part of the one and fiftieth psalm. And after all ceremonies being done and everything ready, our captain caused a musket to be shot off. And the Earl of Warwick out his ship, the *Neptune*, caused another to be answered as soon as the first immediately was discharged, which was a token betwixt them to save the man's life. And so he was taken down, with much rejoicing of all the company.

Yet nevertheless in the afternoon, the Earl of Warwick sent express order and command aboard the *Hector* that the said James Addams for his punishment should be in the midships of the ship, be hauled under the keel of the *Hector*, and his confederate, Daniel Fleshman, to be ducked three times at the yard's arm, according to the orders of the sea. But he would needs of his own free will be ducked once more, for Sir Francis Stewart's sake. [All] which was executed according unto the earl's and our captain's commandment, and so freed, acquitted, and set at liberty for their defaults.

This business as I conceived was so ordered for example to other men, and very judicially and discreetly carried betwixt the Earl of Warwick and Sir Francis Stewart, which kept our men a long time after in better awe and subjection, *until they broke out in open rebellion*.

Towards evening there came up little wind at north-west, so it was ordered by the earl to return back for the coast of Portingale again and give over our course for the western islands, we being seventy-six leagues or thereabouts off from the land.

The eighteenth day in the morning at the four o'clock watch being out, one of our boatswain's mates calling up the forenamed Daniel Fleshman and commanding him to rise to watch, [he] denied he would not; whereupon the boatswain's mate called him lazy lubber, and such like names passed betwixt them. With that, Fleshman rose hastily out of his cabin, took the boatswain's mate by the ears, and buffetted together. Which our captain understanding the truth thereof, committed him into the bilboes, and about midnight following commanded he should be stripped naked from the middle upward, and fast bound to the capstan with his arms spreading, and there well whipped by one disguised, according as he well deserved.

This morning about six o'clock, we descried two sail of ships which bore of us south south-west some four leagues off, they standing to the eastward and with the wind northerly. These ships came very near unto us, and the biggest of them brailed up her mainsail, purposing to speak with us. But one of our fleet putting abroad her colours (an error committed), which as soon as they perceived and descried what we were, presently [they] let fall her mainsail again and, with all the sail they could make, began to sail and make way from us, as they had most reason. The biggest of them shaped her course south-west and southerly to her best advantage off into sea. And our admiral, our ship the vice-admiral, and the rear-admiral, (being most erroneous) giving her chase, which we all continued after while about twelve o'clock at noon, and finding her too light afoot [so] that she outsailed us, gave over chasing and stood into the eastward, with a very fresh gale of wind at north.

The smallest ship steered away south-east and south-east and by east among [sic], towards Cape Espichel – the *Flight*, Captain Pellam, and the *Snapper*, our caravel, Captain Larremar, giving her chase – and so departed out of our company to leeward. The *Snapper* returned unto us the next day, who related unto the Earl of Warwick and our captain, as far as they could perceive, they were Brazil men. And so [it] was conceived by an old Portingale pilot which was aboard the admiral, prisoner, that by their working they should be so, which as he said is a usual course they take amongst them, that being chased by any men-of-war, every ship, excepting they be a strong fleet, to steer a contrary course in like manner as these did.

The *Flight* never returned unto us, nor [we] never saw her afterward all the voyage, until such time as we arrived in Plymouth Cattewater, where she was sunk and cast away, not for want of negligence.

The twentieth day being Wednesday, in the morning about six o'clock we were all the fleet left of us within some two leagues of the nose of the Cape Roca going into Lisbon, having very close weather. And being new come upon the coast again and loath to be too much discovered, [we] would not stand no nearer towards the Rock or Cascais Point but cast about and stood to the westward, the wind being at north. Our captain commanded and sent the *Snapper* — manned and very well furnished — to keep near the shore to see what they could descry and surprise.

The twenty-first day in the forenoon, the Earl of Warwick gave order unto us to bear room to leeward towards the Rock and to look for the *Flight*, Captain Pellam. But by no means we could neither descry nor see the *Flight*, nor meet with the *Snapper*. This evening Sir Francis Stewart grew to be much discontented and angry with me, by reason our men that were the common sort of sailors were not kept upon the upper deck in time of their watch. And [he] commanded me to go down below and to seize them up aloft upon the deck. Which I denied in this manner: 'Sir,' quoth I, 'I have many times and often complained unto the boatswain concerning the same in your presence, as you very well know, and have given him order and command from your worship, [that] being an article which concerns him, he should look unto it and not suffer them to be under the deck so near him continually as they are, which is a very shame it should be suffered. And likewise, Sir, it is an office that pertaineth not unto me (without great extremity of need), but only unto the boatswain, pertaining to his charge and command. And in these nineteen years that I have taken charge of a ship, I have not been brought up nor used unto it, and I was too old to begin now, but upon necessity.' Then he demanded of me what was the orders we used in merchant ships; and of those affairs, I answered him, that if we had a boatswain or any other officer insufficient, and not capable for to discharge his office and place he undertook, excepting for love or favour, as ours was, we always took another more sufficient. So then he surceased and there was an end and period of this discourse. And this was the first difference and disgust that grew betwixt our captain and myself, and for a business which pertained not unto me, but only to command the inferior officers whom it did concern to see it executed and performed.

The twenty-third day it proved stark calm all the whole day, we being some five leagues west and by south from Cape Roca, in which time this day I went down with our quarter masters and others, and we rummaged our ship so effectually below in hold, insomuch that at an hour's warning or less, we could trim our ship either ahead or stern, port or starboard upon any occasion whatsoever, according as we found it necessary and commodious for the benefit of the ship's going.

The twenty-fourth day being Sunday, and midsummer's day, in the morning we stood in so far into the river of Lisbon that we brought the town of Cascais north of us, near two mile off, and were very near the north Catchup, which are sands going into the river so called. And there was riding in Cascais road under the castle's command three small ships. Also, above St Julian's Castle, certain of our men saw and told twenty-three ships roaders, which were riding within the river, but could not discern what nation ships they were. So we tacked off, having then fair weather, and stood all night following to the westward with a storm of wind which increased at north, under two courses, but the next day after it blew more amenable.

The twenty-sixth day our caravel, the *Snapper*, came to us and brought great store of lobsters and fresh fish, as formerly they did unto the admiral and our captain, which they had taken upon the coast, relating the passage of their business, what they had done the time of their absence from us, but nothing to any purpose to be spoken of.

This day we found a great imperfection in our maintopmast, which was cracked and rent up and down betwixt the heel and the main cap at the head of the mainmast, [so] that we were forced four days after to set a new one which was made of the old mainmast. Otherwise, we had been destitute at present of a maintopmast.

The twenty-ninth day we met with the *Jonathan*, our rear-admiral, Captain James Mountague, whom our captain invited aboard the *Hector* with other gentlemen to dinner, and were very merry and at night departed aboard their own ship.

The thirtieth day and last of June, being Saturday, in the morning before day we met with our admiral, the Earl of Warwick, and in his company two Turks men-of-war of Sallee, a ship and a frigate or Turks' brigantine, and also our caravel, the *Snapper*. Which at first sight [we] took them to be enemies and provided ourselves purposing to fight with them. And they determined the like by us, but our *Snapper* coming within call of us, [we] hailed her, who presently repaired to the Earl of Warwick and certified his honour what we were and so our fight was ended; otherwise, unhappily we had done great spoil one to another. The Turks' men-of-war were both in great want and in distress of victuals, which the earl of his royal disposition supplied and spared unto them for their relief and necessity, [they] promising his honour to consort and keep company with us for some certain time as he pleased. So all this day we stood in to the shore to the eastward and at night tacked off to the westward, having little wind, a smooth sea, and very fair weather.

These Turks related unto us of the truce and league concluded betwixt England and Turkey and had a certificate thereof under the Audience's hand their resident. Also [they related] that all the Englishmen that were their slaves were sent home for England out of Barbary.

JULY 1627

The first day of July, *Anno Domini* 1627, being Sunday, we lay becalmed most part all the day, the Cape Roca going into the river of Lisbon east north-east of us about some seven leagues off.

In the evening about five o'clock, having little wind westerly and standing to the southward, we descried a great fleet of ships some two and twenty sail one or other, which stood to the northwards and bore of us at first sight southeast and by east some five leagues or five leagues and a half off. So our admiral, the Earl of Warwick, bore room with them, and likewise ourselves and all our fleet, making what sail we could towards them. The two Turks' men-of-war, the ship and the brigantine, also giving them chase, being at least a league ahead of us, to see if they could descry and bring word to the Earl of Warwick what fleet of ships they were. But night coming on, growing dark and proving thick, misting, sleety weather, [we] lost sight of them and also of all our own fleet. This night following proved foul weather, but a reasonable pretty fresh gale of wind northerly being extreme marvellous thick, and hazy.

The second day being Monday, in the morning about four o'clock we were fair by Cascais Point, where sometimes the weather being thick and sometimes clear, we came in sight of our admiral and rear-admiral and of all our own fleet but could see none of them we chased, but were certainly satisfied they were not gone into the river of Lisbon.

Our admiral, the renowned noble Earl of Warwick in the *Great Neptune*, being to the southward and to leeward of us as the wind was, hauled up their mainsail in the brails, which I took to be a sign we should come to leeward and speak with his honour. And so I certified our captain, as it had been most necessary and convenient at that time, in regard of such a fleet descried upon the coast, we should have all conferred and have taken counsel one of another, *but as all other business was carried, so was this*. The Turks' ship went room unto the admiral and spoke with him; and I went unto our captain (having a great desire to speak with his honour), he being in his cabin laid down to sleep, and said unto him, 'Sir, it were very fitting we should go to leeward and speak with our admiral for to know his pleasure in regard of the knowledge of this great fleet upon the coast what were best to be done.' His answer was, in the hearing of our minister and a gentleman with his servants, 'Master,' quoth he, 'keep near unto him until anon [MS: a none], and then I will speak with the Earl of Warwick.' I, having my answer, departed out of the cabin. We standing off to the westward close upon a tack with a fresh gale of wind all northerly, where the farther off we came to sea, in the offing at sundry times began to be thick weather. And conferring with my mates, everyone having a desire and saying it were very necessary to speak with our admiral, I went unto our captain the second time into his cabin and certified him how the weather was like to prove and to be very thick and, as before, held it very convenient we should go and speak with the Earl of Warwick. As our captain his answer was at first, so answered he me again, 'Keep as near unto him as you can, and we will speak with him anon towards noon' – as though we had the wind and weather at command to speak with the earl when he listed. But as I say, the farther we ran off, the thicker the weather grew and proved so marvellous extreme thick, misting, sleety weather, the mist continuing and [we] not knowing what sail one another bore. In this extremity of weather, [we] lost company of the Earl of Warwick and also of all our own fleet and of the Turks' men-of-war, the ship and brigantine. This was a great error committed, but as the old sea phrase is, *not done in my watch*. After this present business passed, we never saw nor could hear of our admiral the Earl of Warwick, where his honour was, until such time as we met with the *Great Neptune* outward bound again from England to the southward some seventy odd leagues off from the Land's End of England, who certified us of the earl being in safety.

As for his honour's valour, noble courage, and bold attempt he passed this day in a dangerous fight with the armada of Spain, I cease to write, being no spectator thereof, knowing there were worthy gentlemen and seamen present of great account which have writ thereof and divulged unto the world the true manner, form, and order with what courageous valour, manly courage, and resolution it was performed.

We had not stood off to sea about some four hours, but in the extremity of this thick mist, we heard betwixt ten and eleven o'clock the report of many piece of ordnance shot off, apace and very thick, which sound came from the eastward. So we cast about and stood that ways according as the sound of the ordnance directing us, steering in east south-east and sometimes south-east among, judging it to be our admiral and rear-admiral in fight, as by consequence it could be no otherwise. Our captain and all our company being then heartily sorry we had lost our fleet, having a great desire if it were possible to find them out and come to them again, and went only to assist them. But all the means and endeavour we could make prevailed not to find them. Which if it had pleased almighty God we had met together, all our fleet, it would have been a very bloody day. But, as is aforesaid, being so extreme thick and the report of ordnance ceasing, [we] could not see nor find where any of them were. But as we stood into the eastward, being at prayer, [we] had a glimpse of five sail of ships which passed by to leeward of us, standing to the westward, whom presently our minister ending prayer abruptly, we tacked after. But before we could tack our ship and fully trim our sails, determining to give chase, [we] lost sight of them again. But nevertheless, we still kept on that course standing off to the westward.

Betwixt two and three o'clock in the afternoon, it somewhat cleared up at times. And the first ships we saw was two under our lee bow, standing as we did, unto whom we were bearing up. And presently [we] saw some nine or ten ships more, right astern. Upon which sight, we sprang our luff again and made the best benefit we could to keep the wind of them until such time [as] we could make what fleet they were. And afterward we descried in all fifteen sail very near unto us and seven sail bearing quartering to the southwards. Most of them [were] very great ships which, all our men that had used Spain and formerly seen any built of them being galleons, we made them to be the Spanish armada. And I myself, very well knowing and perceiving them certainly to be so, advised our captain thereof, and kept the wind, and stood our course according as they did as though we had been one of their fleet. And about four o'clock in the afternoon, when they tacked to the northward, we then also tacked the same way and were the same time about some two mile to windward of the windermost of their fleet. And night coming on, and [they] being all bound in for the river of Lisbon, they all bore room in for Cascais road, which we perceiving after some small time passed they had borne up, we cast about and stood to the westward, with the wind at northwest a very fresh gale of wind, the Rock east north-east of us some five leagues off. And thanks be to God [we] cleared ourselves by this means of the Spanish armada for that time. So all this night following, we stood off to the westward.

The third day in the morning we cast about to look for our admiral and consorts. And standing in to the eastward towards the shore, [we] met with our caravel, the *Snapper*, whose captain, George Larremar, the master, and company related unto Sir Francis Stewart they had not seen nor spoken with the Earl of Warwick since Sunday last – upon which report we were all very sorrowful – and that his last order was, his honour gave unto them, directed and appointed us [that] we should meet him at the Berlings, there to make clean, wash and trim our ships, and then to direct our course for the islands of Terceira, according as it was concluded and set down by our admiral. This message being delivered, order was given upon their relation unto me by our captain to ply forthwith with all expedition unto the Berlings, which order I presently followed, but to little purpose. For our admiral, the Earl of Warwick, had shaped his course – upon separation and loss one of another, and after his fight with the Spanish armada – for the western islands and, having a fair wind, arrived there in a very short time. In all which, we were boilting [*sic*] it up for the islands of the Berlings.

The seventh day being Saturday, in the morning as we were plying to windward, we met with a small Breton [MS: brittaine] hull, one Captain Shaplie of Bristowe, an English man-of-war, who had not been out of England above four or five days, for whom our captain sent for to come aboard the *Hector*. Which presently fulfilled his request, who related unto him the unfortunate tidings of six sail of Turks' men-of-war that had taken from the *Little Neptune, Bark Warwick*, and the Captain Scrale, a Dutchman, three of the Earl of Warwick's fleet, three Hamburgers, prizes, come out of Spain, richly laden, which they had formerly surprised. And that the Turks had carried them away for Algiers or Barbary. Our fleet making account the Turks' men-of-war had been Spaniards, without certain knowledge thereof, the *Little Neptune* and *Bark Warwick* ran away and left Scrale with the prizes to certify what they were. Which the Turks, not believing him that he pertained to England and that he served the Earl of Warwick, carried both certain men and prizes clean away alongst with them as is before related, *which three prizes they might very well have kept and would not.*

About two o'clock in the afternoon, Captain Shaplie went aboard his own ship, and he departed out of our company, being bound as he said for the Madeira Island. In the evening we saw the islands of the Berlings east of us some six leagues off.

The eighth day in the evening, contrary to my opinion and certain others, our captain caused the *Snapper* to be new victualled and, with sixteen men and a boy, sent her into the cove at the Berlings, giving them directions to wash and make her clean under water. And the next day we were appointed and purposed ourselves to go in with the *Hector* and to do the like, according as order was given from the Earl of Warwick, hoping we should have met with his honour there. But this sending away the *Snapper* afterwards was repented of, when it was too late, and turned to our great hindrance and disadvantage.

The ninth day being Monday, in the morning determining to go in and anchor between the mainland and the Berlings, about five o'clock very early we descried three sail of ships come room, right afore the wind, [it] being at north-west and we standing to the northwards, very bold and peremptorily unto us. The admiral or biggest of them steering directly with our forefoot, one with our midships, and the other with our larboard transom, as though they would have clapped us aboard presently and that there had been no other way but one with us. [We were] expecting them to be men-of-war, which showed none other by their working but that they were, being two French hulls and a flyboat, all deep laden. We brailed up our mainsail and stayed for them, and likewise they furled their mainsails. But when they came within saker shot of us and well viewed our ship, seeing our ordnance, *as the proverb is, they began to take eggs for their money*, altering their course, and clapped close upon a tack as we stood to the northward, letting fall their mainsails again, putting abroad their topgallant sails, and making all the sail possible they could to sail and be gone from us. And we also spreading all the sail we could chasing after them. One being very near us, we discharged and shot some dozen or fourteen piece of ordnance at her, which shot went half as far beyond the ship as the way she was distant from us, but could not force nor compel any of them to come to leeward, so standing some two hours or thereabouts to the northward, they reaching of us, until they had gotten the advantage. Then they all tacked to the southwards and, being better of sail than we were, got away and so cleared themselves of us. But certainly if the *Snapper* had not been sent away to the Berlings and had been remaining in our company, then she might have gone and entangled any one of them, but especially the nearest; I persuade myself and so did all our company, we had carried one if not two of them along with us. And this was our unfortunate mishap that followed us. In the afternoon our caravel, the *Snapper*, came off to us when we had little occasion to employ her in any service present, not having performed that business which they went about for the making clean the caravel, but [having] followed their own designs upon the Main about the road of Peniche and coasting thereabouts.

In the evening we saw fifteen sail of ships which bore of us west southwest and west and by south some five leagues off, and they standing to the northward with whom we stood towards all night following, having fair weather and plying unto them according as the wind would give leave and permit us.

The tenth day being Tuesday, in the morning standing to the eastward, we descried four sail of these great ships standing off to the westward and striving to weather us. Certain of our men persuading our captain and myself the fleet we saw overnight were Hamburgers and would not be brought out of that conceit nor persuaded otherwise, and [that] these four sail were part of them. So we kept on our course still towards that way, and about noon we were so near unto them, I descried them to be four galleons of the Spanish armada, [which] we formerly met with all the second day of this month, being well acquainted and knowing their build. Which well perceiving, [we] kept to windward of them what possible we could, keeping on our course, making the best means God would direct us to clear ourselves of their company. Having no reason to entangle ourselves with such a force as they were, their consorts not being far off and we not able to encounter with them, [we] could not otherwise well shunn [*sic*] to better ourselves to get away clear of our enemies. They, having come near into our wake, cast about and chased us all this whole day to the northwards, having very little wind westerly and a head sea, with the westerly winds that formerly blew and the *Hector* sailing upon a head sea, being no great glutton. The vice-admiral of Spain towards evening near fetched us up, within some four mile, gaining still upon us and the rest coming after, that they kept in sight of us all the time the moon shined. And after midnight, the moon being down and the night growing somewhat dark, I sent the *Snapper* to stand to the southward some two or three glass, and as they passed by to windward of the ship, to show a light glimmering now and then, as though it had been at a ship's port, that they should conceive and imagine we ourselves had been cast about. Which the armada, perceiving the light and thinking so indeed, cast about to the southward; and so by that stratagem the next morning they were two leagues farther astern than in the evening before.

This tenth day about nine o'clock at night one Henry Mannester, an armourer, died suddenly, he having lain long sick and diseased in a consumption and other diseases, and − being a troublesome, combustious time − [we] buried him as suddenly in the ocean sea as the other that formerly died, *without any ceremonies*.

The eleventh day in the morning at four o'clock, we saw the Berlings east south-east of us some eight leagues off, and then we set off from the coast of Portingale, bound from thence for the islands Flores and Corvo, expecting to meet with our admiral, the right honourable the Earl of Warwick, and the rest of our fleet, [that] being the place appointed for our rendezvous.

This morning at daylight we saw the vice-admiral of Spain some three leagues astern of us and the other three a league farther off, which advantage we gained of them in using that policy sending away the *Snapper* with a light. Also we descried eleven sail of ships more, north north-east of us as far as we could well discern and see them in the maintop, which were very great ships, being also of the Spanish armada. This day having very little wind westerly, we towed our ship, keeping her head upon the sea with our caravel, long boat, and pinnace. But all little prevailed, for they all sailed marvellously well without any towing. About eight o'clock at night, the vice-admiral of Spain fetched us up within saker shot and we, only to shun the danger and force of the rest of the ships being to the northward and which were in sight of us, cast about and stood to the southward, with the wind at north north-east, being for our best advantage. And [we] went ranging along his weather side, little above musket shot off. And so without any hailing one of another, as the ancient sea custom is, exchanged with each other a whole broadside of our ordnance, which they did not very well comport as afterwards appeared, and so passing by, left us for that night. After he was out astern and came into our wake, [he] cast about after us and so kept astern, in sight all night following, expecting the next day to have been resolutely set upon and performed a very hot fight if the rest of the ships should likewise happen to fetch us up. Every man in the *Hector*, from the highest to the lowest according to their degree, vowing and protesting to each other with a firm resolution to fight it out manfully to the death and resolved every man to die [and] the ship sink or burn, rather than to be surprised or taken by the Spaniards. Which resolution gave great encouragement unto our captain and gentlemen − seeing our men so willing − and unto all our company each unto another in general.

Whereupon Sir Francis Stewart, seeing the valorous disposition and resolute courage of our men, of his own free will and voluntary mind, promised unto our company, God sending us clear of this Spanish armada, [that] whatsoever happened unto us for want of purchase to make a saving voyage, every man in the ship according to his degree and office should have the king's wages or pay ordinary allowed unto seamen for the time of their service unto the right honourable the Earl of Warwick. *But now being delivered and arrived at home in safety, that promise is forgotten and drowned in oblivion as all the rest are.* And the better to provide and prepare ourselves for such a desperate and resolute fight, first in humble prayer unto almighty God we commended ourselves, desiring him, as he was the protector, keeper, and defender of all his faithful children and elect chosen, so likewise to defend and save us out of the hands of these our bloody and merciless enemies, and to fight in our behalf and quarrel against them. Which being done, I ordered and appointed our men in such good, ample sort and manner, directing so many men to every piece of ordnance, according as the quality of the piece would deserve to employ, to ply and discharge upon the enemy upon his next coming up and as occasion should require. And also express charge [was] given them by our captain no man to go nor absent himself away from the piece of ordnance where he was quartered, but to be found there either alive or dead. This being likewise done and effected in order our company liked very well, and [it] gave much cheerfulness, courage and alacrity unto all our men, and cried with a general voice and manly courage, 'Saint George for England!'

And being so many of the armada near unto us, our men being somewhat timorous and fearful – which was in the *Snapper* – to remain and keep in her for fear of being surprised, we were forced to take them out into our ship with as much of her provisions as we could preserve conveniently and turned her off from us adrift and wrack in the sea.

Also to full humour and give content unto a self conceit, our long boat was caused this night to be hoisted overboard and utterly thrown away.

The twelfth day of July being Thursday, in the morning at daylight, we displayed on our ship's maintopgallant masthead a bloody ancient, on our foretopgallant masthead St George, and on the poop the right honourable the Earl of Warwick his colours, with a bloody pendant at our mizzen yardarm; resolving and arming ourselves, by God's assistance and protection, under these colours which were shown abroad, to live and die; and that the Spaniards, being well acquainted with the conditions of Englishmen, knew full well. And betwixt five and six of the clock in the morning this vice-admiral of Spain came up with us, our captain waving them with a bright sword upon our poop in defiance to leeward. She being a very proper great ship of some eight hundred tons or thereabouts at the least and as well a moulded-built ship – after our English fashion set out with carved work and gilded very sumptuously both the trail and side boards of her head and galleries – as eye could see and behold or man's heart could desire, full of men and very well appointed with store of brass ordnance and munition answerable. I say about that time in the morning aforenamed, they came up with us on our weather quarter and transom, we standing close upon a wind to the southward, in regard of the fleet being to leeward with the wind at west north-west. And then began [the] fight with us, we welcoming and saluting him again with as many piece of ordnance as could be at present levelled and presented towards them to any good purpose. Upon which, conceiving they should have what they expected and their bellies full to their own content, they fell astern and so continued fight with us more sparingly all the whole day after, placing right astern and sometimes on each transom, never daring once to come up along our ship's broadside, which we all expected and heartily wished that they would have vouchsafed and presumed to have done. And in this manner was our fight performed, plying continually four piece of ordnance right astern at them, and they four out of their prow, a chase continually unto us, never ceasing but as fast as we could charge and discharge one at another, taking the best advantage for the spoil. And about six o'clock at night, he perceiving the other three galleons his consorts which were astern fetched nothing of us, having as I say his bellyful of what they looked for, [he] cast about and stood to the northward towards his consorts and so departed out of our company, being both agreed and well contented.

Surely at our first salutation, we did them great spoil, which we conceived by their fearfulness that would not presume nor dare to adventure to come and look upon our broadside once after our first meeting; or otherwise they were absolute arch cowards that, having so many seconds in sight coming up to assist and aid them, would nor durst not give a better onset and assault upon us.

Which had it not been for to endanger and entangle ourselves with them, while the other armadas should have come up unto us, by God's blessing, we should have given them such a breakfast they would not have very well digested and a little better sport than we did; and happy man [had] been his dole that should have returned to relate it.

In all this fight, Sir Francis Stewart, our captain, showed himself a most valorous, warlike gentleman and soldier in the face of his enemy, not to be persuaded by any means once to descend or go below from the deck, but fore and aft, cheering up our company in these and the like words, 'Courageous my English hearts, we fight for the glory of God, honour of our king and country, and for our own liberties. Therefore, let us not be daunted, although there be so many of the Spanish armada in sight of us and present. And let it be never said nor reported nor never shall, as long as I have any breath in my body, that the proudest Spaniard that ever Spain yielded shall ever surprise or take Frank Stewart or any one of us prisoners.'

We received from them diverse shot, as they from us, amongst which one of them is worthy the noting. Upon our starboard quarter, half way betwixt the mizzen mast and the poop, level with the roundhouse deck, came in a saker shot which hit right against a timber and dulled the force of the shot. It ran through two boarded cabins upon the poop, split a great water jar all in pieces, struck a gentleman's pistol lying upon the poop out of his hand, and another gentleman named Mr James Quarles of very fair condition and quality, sitting by the mizzen mast on the starboard side. The shot fell into his codpiece, bruised his thighs, and what harm else I know not, leaving it to your charitable imagination, but thanks be to God did him not very much harm, only astonished him in a very great maze for a certain time. Sir Francis Stewart, being near him, and every one of the beholders present absolute thinking he had been slain, said 'Lord, have mercy upon him'. One very speedily stepping unto him and taking him in his arms, said 'Courageous man, what cheer? Pluck up a good heart'. And so after a little pause, coming unto himself again, [he] was carried down to the surgeon who very carefully and respectively looked unto him and dressed him as occasion served, and blessed be God, in a short time [he] safely recovered. And this was the most harm any of our company sustained, but only certain shot we received in our masts and sails, which did us some spoil.

After all this passed, first in all humble duty of prayer, as we were bound, giving God thanks and lauding his glorious name for our safe deliverance and keeping us clear from the hands of our cruel enemies, we shaped our course for the islands of Terceira, according to the right honourable the Earl of Warwick his instructions delivered unto our captain, and [which] were now at this time opened and the contents published unto our company.

And having a very constant contrary wind for a long season, [we] happened upon a very long and tedious passage, by which means we lost the meeting of the Earl of Warwick at the islands.

The nineteenth day being Thursday, in the morning about five o'clock we descried a sail to the northward which came with the wind northerly right afore the wind to us, and about ten o'clock this forenoon we spoke with him, being a man-of-war of Flushing, who certified our captain some ten days past he spoke with Captain Pellam in the *Flight*, the Earl of Warwick's patache, which was at the Berlings making clean their ship [and] who determined to stay some eight or ten days thereabouts upon the coast, according to their relation. Expecting the earl's and our coming and not meeting with us, [they] resolved to go for England. All our company were very joyful and glad to hear of their being in health and safety, which before this news, we doubted of her very much. Also Captain Crupp, for so he was called, confirmed the disastrous news to be true of the *Little Neptune, Bark Warwick*, and Captain Scrale's losing of their three Hamburger prizes with the Turks' men-of-war. About two o'clock in the afternoon he departed out of our company, bound as he said for the island of St Mary's.

The twenty-second day being Sunday, about half an hour past ten o'clock in the morning one Ralph Venables departed and changed this life, having lain long sick and diseased, and after evening prayer [we] buried him.

The twenty-sixth day being Monday, about ten o'clock at night one – [*sic*] also departed and changed this life, having lain long sick of an ague and a calenture, and so died, and the next morning [we] buried him according as the other in the ocean sea.

The twenty-ninth day being Sunday, about ten o'clock in the forenoon we spoke with one Captain Baker of Bristowe come from the Madeiras, bound home for England, who had taken a small Portingale prize laden with iron and other commodities, by whom we sent letters for London by the way of Bristowe. And in the afternoon, [he] departed out of our company.

AUGUST 1627

The first day of August being Wednesday, we had very much wind at north-west and a very great grown sea. About eleven o'clock at noon, we spoke with Captain Squib in the *St Claude* of London, come out of Guinea and bound for England, and having as I say so much wind and a great sea, [we] durst not hoist out our skiff to go aboard of them, not so much as to convey a letter home for England. But they certified our captain of the *Little Neptune*'s and *Bark Warwick*'s being at the islands of Flores and Corvo, expecting the Earl of Warwick and our fleet's coming thither according to appointment.

The second day in the morning about a quarter of an hour past seven o'clock, one Nicholas Southcote, our cooper's mate and his own brother by the mother's side, departed and changed this life for immortality, having been sick of a fainting and a sweating sickness – being first bred in the ship's hold – which afterwards turned to another scurvy disease and so [he] died. And about some two hours after, [he] was buried in the sea, contrary to my mind and without my consent, and in my judgement against the nature of a brother so suddenly to permit and suffer the same, being so lately dead.

This day about one o'clock in the afternoon we saw and made the high land at the north-east end of the island of St Michael's, which bore of us west and by south some ten leagues off. It fell calm and so continued all the whole night following.

The third day being Friday, I mustered all our company, and I found by register of all their names we had eight and forty men sick and diseased in our ship not able to perform any business, besides certain others which were somewhat infected, crazy, and not in perfect health. Our captain, being certified thereof, seemed to be sorrowful and made a great show and promise that God sending us to arrive at the islands of Flores and Corvo, if possible it could be had upon any conditions whatsoever, [he] would provide and buy some relief and succour for them, and should not want any fresh victuals or provisions any sick man desired. And not without great need of Christian charity so to do, for there was not so much as a pound of sugar, ounce of spice, or any fruit laid into the ship to minister any comfort, succour, or relief to any sick man whatsoever, but only such salt provisions (oatmeal excepted) as the ship's allowance of victuals yielded. But after our arrival at the island of Flores, this promise was forgotten and neglected, and who durst claim it for fear of displeasure, and nothing at all [was] performed as hereafter shall be declared.

The fifth day we passed along by the south side of the island of Terceira by Angra Road, and the night following we sailed betwixt the islands of St George's and Graciosa with a fresh gale of wind at north-east.

The sixth day being Monday, about half an hour past nine o'clock at night, one George Levoricke departed and changed this life, having lain a long time sick and diseased, and on the morning after prayer [we] buried him in the sea.

The eighth day being Wednesday, in the morning we met with the wind all westerly which continued while about noon, and then veered up to the north north-east a very fresh gale of wind; and in the evening we disembogued betwixt the island of Flores and the island of Corvo, having the wind dullard but continuing at north north-east, and fair weather. Giving God thanks for our safe arrival at the islands appointed by the Earl of Warwick, the place of our rendezvous and meeting of all our fleet together, and the next day in the morning our captain read the earl's letter of direction openly unto all the company.

The tenth day being Friday, being off our distance appointed from the islands some twenty leagues west and by south, and standing in to the eastward, about noon we met and spoke with the *Little Neptune*, Captain Sussex Cammocke, and the *Bark Warwick*, Captain Richard Beaumont, who were appointed and directed to attend the Earl of Warwick's coming thither, according unto our direction. So after salutation one to another they came aboard the *Hector*, and it was concluded we should all go for the island of Flores to get some refreshing and relief for our sick men, as also to take in fresh water and wood for our provision and necessity.

The twelfth day being Sunday, in the morning about nine o'clock one Mr John Eybrooke, an ancient man and one of the mates, departed and changed this life for immortality, he having lain long sick of a black jaundice, which afterward turned and bred to other gross humours and diseases and so [he] died, having also taken an inward grief being appointed to be one of the jury against James Addams when he was condemned to be hanged and speaking at the same present when the execution should be that, for his part, he never gave consent thereunto. Whereupon the Earl of Warwick sent order to our captain to dismiss him of his place and office and to turn him aboard the rear-admiral as an ordinary common man. Which grief and conceit so taken and struck to his heart was partly cause of those inbred diseases growing upon him, and end of his days. And after sermon being done and ended, [we] buried his corpse as the other formerly in the large sepulchre of the ocean sea.

This day, Sir Francis Stewart feasted aboard the *Hector* the captains and masters of the other ships with certain other gentlemen, and [they] were very merry.

The fourteenth day being Tuesday, in the morning standing in to the eastward for the island of Flores, and having a fresh gale of wind northerly half way betwixt the two islands, we descried a sail which, perceiving us, steered away to the eastward betwixt the two islands, unto whom we gave chase. And in some four hours, the *Bark Warwick* fetched her up, being the ship *Treasure* of London, Captain John Davis, one of the Earl of Warwick's fleet, who consorted with our captain to keep company such time as we remained about the islands.

This day one Mr Walter Stewart and three other gentlemen came out of the *Little Neptune* to remain aboard the *Hector*, their company having had enough and weary of him, and [he was] as welcome unto our company as saltwater coming into any ship. For when the said gentleman came aboard the *Hector, then had we the counsel of Achitophel* and never afterward all the voyage had good correspondence, merry countenance, nor familiar discourse with our captain as formerly of the voyage we had been accustomed to have, which in short time bred much discontent and unquietness in the ship amongst our company.

The fifteenth day being Wednesday, in the afternoon, we came to an anchor in a bay at the north-east end of the island of Flores called Saint Pedro's Road, where we rode in fifty-two fathom water, clean ground, but a reasonable fair berth off from the shore. Where after consultation held, our captain sent ashore to treat with the inhabitants for pratique. And a present [went] to the governor of the island which seemed was by him well accepted, who sent order to his inferior officers and gave us free liberty and licence to take in such water as we wanted for our necessities and also to buy for money or truck and barter for such fresh provisions in victuals and fruits of the country for our sick men to relieve them as the island yielded. And so for three days following we watered to our own contents, and our men [had] free truck and trade with the people and inhabitants of the island for such provisions as their necessities required, for clothes, any kind of apparel, linen cloth, soap, shirts, shoes, stockings, knives, or anything else whatsoever they could spare, nothing of any value coming amiss to the inhabitants. As sick men being in such great need, perplexity, and misery of want, [they] spared all that ever they could make, for otherwise if they had not provided such commodities of their own, to have trucked and bartered, they must of force have gone without any relief or succour which was provided for them and have done as the rest formerly did.

For, being now arrived at our desired place of rendezvous, and business sorting to our wished content, and in the very height where we might have had all provisions and necessary fruits such as the country yielded for the preservation of men's healths — which was as much as could be desired or expected being in an enemy's country — our captain, as great men used to do, having enough himself, forgetting what was promised and requisite to be done for poor sick men, solicited the purser of the ship and would have him to disburse money and to buy such provisions as our sick men and company wanted. And if the money he had would not pass on the island, then he might take in lieu thereof certain French canvas which was aboard the *Little Neptune* which they had taken out of a French ship they had surprised, being a very good commodity in that place. Conditionally the purser would indent and pass bills under his hand for it upon the owners' accounts and, at their charges, buy such provisions. The purser, considering with himself, the ship being in the right honourable the Earl of Warwick his service, denied to do the same and would not follow no such order nor direction. Then our captain, seeing that he could not prevail nor persuade with the purser and that his command would not stretch so far to compel and force him, fell to be both agreed; and he would do nothing neither, not so much as buy the value of two pence of any provisions whatsoever to bestow upon a sick man. And so betwixt them both, nothing according to our captain's vain promise was performed. But only as formerly I have said by the company themselves forced to buy their own provisions, which gave them great nourishment, comfort, and relief. For in short time after, most of them that were sick was recovered of their sickness and that filthy disease which most reigned and was predominant in the ship.

The eighteenth day being Saturday, in the morning our captain commanded me to go and take a strict survey of all our victuals and provisions whatsoever in the ship, the which I performed and certified him thereof according to a note taken and delivered him.

And having a remnant of butter remaining in a firkin which was the last to be spent amongst the company — only some reserved for our sick men — our captain commanded me twice to go down into the steward room and to weigh out men's allowance of butter. [This] being a business that was never motioned unto me by him afore, [and] admiring who should be his counsel now to make me a demi-purser or a steward, which command I peremptorily denied and told him it pertained not unto my place, others being appointed for the same office who had executed it all the voyage. Upon which he seemed to be much angry and discontented with me, concealing what he thought. And this was the second distaste by him taken against me, *being very poor conceits to be used in such a commander*.

Thus [we] having provided ourselves with good store of fresh water but little anything else to purpose of the general charge, but only what everyone could do and buy for his relief of his own charge. And as for mine own part, I was forced to do as the rest did. The greatest help under God and preservation of my health I do really persuade myself was garlic. For the prodigious scents, smells, and savours a man should smell and have next his heart in a morning betwixt the decks where our men lodged was able to infect any sound man − [when] coming out of the fresh air − that lay and had his cabin above upon the deck, to cast him down with sickness. Wherefore to prevent infection the best I could, at our first coming out of England from Plymouth every morning before I came out of my cabin, I ate next my heart three or four cloves of garlic with bread and butter, and after it drank a dram of hot water, and so come forward amongst our company; and I should very little or nothing participate of any ill savour that annoyed me. But constantly every day of the voyage, I ate not less than three heads, and sometimes four or five, of garlic. And questionless garlic is the greatest and most forceable antidote against any infection whatsoever. And therefore I could wish and advise all seamen that loveth and respecteth their health, proceeding of such a voyage where there is many men that are given to filthiness and nastiness, to frequent and love the eating of garlic.

The nineteenth day being Sunday, having watered sufficiently, our pinnace with the rest of the other ships' were manned with muskets and pikes, which were secretly hidden in the boats' holds, and under pretence of bartering certain canvas with them for fresh provisions, [they] pretended only to betray, take, and bring aboard our ship either the governor of the islands or the chief father, or both, prisoners. And then before they should have been set at liberty or released again, we purposed to have anything from the shore that it yielded and we desired. But our men being descried and this plot discovered, it took no effect and so [we] was forced to return aboard frustrate of the treachery intended. Upon which the governor peremptorily denied us any more courtesy, as he had just cause and reason so to do, [and] bid us be gone, for we should not have anything else from the island more than formerly we had. And thus was their love and favour showed unto us requited.

The twentieth day being Monday, the wind came up at north-east and a very great sea, that we could not very well ride any longer in St Pedro's Road in safety, but with great danger of our ships. Whereupon we weighed anchor to go to sea out to the southward of the island. Captain Sussex Cammocke and Captain John Davis dined with Sir Francis Stewart aboard the *Hector*, and after dinner being ended, the two captains took their leave and departed in the *Treasure*'s pinnace. The ships all under sail going alongst the coast and they seeing a fisher boat near the shore, made towards her purposing to buy or truck one thing or other for some fresh fish with the Portingales. But the fishermen, perceiving the pinnace coming towards them, being fearful, made also with all expedition towards the shore and, recovering the shore first, went all a-land and began to keep the pinnace off with stones, in so much that they hurt Captain Davis sitting in his own boat. Which he perceiving and feeling himself hurt, being of a valiant courage and bold spirit, [he] would resolutely presume to go ashore, with his sword drawn in his hand, amongst a crew of heathen banditto'd runagates; and having neither musket, half pike, nor any other munition but only a sword in the pinnace to defend themselves, [this] was very ill advised, indiscreetly and desperately performed. The Portingales – with other mountaineers which suddenly came down upon them – being too strong for our Englishmen, slew Captain Davis outright, wounding him in very many places, where they were forced to leave his body slain upon the shore. Also, [they] hurt and wounded Captain Cammocke very dangerously, and all the men there present [were] in great danger to be slain, having much to do to recover themselves. Which by God's great providence, [they] hardly escaped off from the shore with their pinnace, being all the men in the fleet in general heartily sorry for the untimely and unfortunate death of Captain John Davis.

This being a judgement of God that whereas we pretended and plotted mischief against them, [we] was repaid with the same measure that we thought to mete – he [Davis] being the chief instrument and deviser of the project intended. But sithence it was so and having no remedy, consultation being held, it was agreed we should sail west twenty leagues off from the island of Flores, the place of our rendezvous, to look for the right honourable the Earl of Warwick and the rest of our fleet, where we ranged two or three days – in which time Bartholomew Churchman was chosen and made captain, by a general consent of his company of the ship, *Treasure*.

The three and twentieth day being Thursday, in the morning we brailed up our sails, and our captain caused a flag of counsel to be put abroad in the mizzen shrouds, upon which Captain Richard Beaumont and Captain Bartholomew Churchman came aboard the *Hector* and, by reason Captain Sussex Cammocke lay grievously wounded, Mr Charles Kilburne, master of the *Little Neptune*, served in his stead. And, with the other masters and certain principal officers of their ships whom they appointed, [they] repaired also aboard our ship the *Hector*. And it was ordered by council of war and general consent of all that were present that we should stay and remain about these islands of Flores and Corvo until Monday the twenty-seventh present and then to range to the northward in the latitude of forty-two and forty-three degrees, and so to go for Cape

Finisterre in Galicia and there to spend some certain time according as the length of victuals would produce and permit us, to see what we could take and surprise, and afterwards to sail for England. Which had been good if that course and agreement had been put in present execution, for the next day the wind came up westerly and so continued all the time we remained about the islands, which would have carried us upward of a hundred and forty leagues on our way; and afterwards when we came to bear up the helm to shape our course for the place appointed, the wind came contrary, which detained us ten days longer amongst the islands than was determined, which was a great hindrance to our proceedings. This day, having certain friends come aboard the *Hector* − as many times formerly I had − and sending down to the cooper for a quarter can of beer, the boy returned with the can empty and said the cooper would send none, I had my allowance; as indeed divers times he had used me formerly in the like manner; upon which both myself and mates many times complained unto our captain and made him acquainted of the base usage of the cooper but never having no redress nor amendment thereof. And in fine, [I] could have no beer, which strangers perceiving, said it was very strict and hard that either I or my mates could not command a can of beer to make a friend drink. So as the ancient proverb is, taking heart of grace, [I] called a quarter-master with me and went down into the ship's hold, and fetched up beer myself, and told the cooper this: 'It was as well put into the ship for me and company as for the captain and gentlemen and, being so frequent as it was in his cabin − never wanting no supply of can and bottle − I might command a can of beer in the like nature, and would do it upon such and the like occasion.' This message was not long before it was delivered unto the higher power, good notice taken thereof and well recorded; and this is the ground our captain has taken to divulge unto the world I made the hold common to every rascal in the ship. But by his private order and strict command given the cooper, it was kept severe enough from every one, the gentlemen excepted.

The five and twentieth day being Saturday, it blew a fresh gale of wind at west south-west, and all the companies of each ship very willing and desirous to bear room for the Cape Finisterre, according as it was formerly agreed upon, in regard of the fair wind that blew. And [with] no hope nor expectation of meeting the Earl of Warwick, myself and company earnestly solicited our captain that we might bear up the helm and take the benefit of the fair wind now present blowing; but no persuasion would prevail with him, until such time as the day came that was appointed. This day at noon the island of Flores bore east and by north of us, some eighteen leagues off, we standing close upon a wind to the southward, spending time to no purpose, which every man in the fleet (but one) thought it long and tedious, for it was impossible for the Earl of Warwick with the wind that now blew to come where we were. And one day more being expired, the next was the day appointed to go room, so that we spent all this time upon a vainglorious humour and lost that opportunity that would have done us good.

The seven and twentieth day being Monday, which was long wished for, our captain sent aboard their ships for all the captains and masters and the rest that were formerly to come aboard the *Hector*, where being assembled together, it was propounded to sail for Fayal and for the island of St Michael's, and afterward to shape our course according as it was agreed upon and set down. Which proposition, being well considered, was very well liked of, and everyone condescended thereunto, confirming it to be material and holding it very fitting to see and look in every road among the islands in our course for Cape Finisterre. Upon which agreement and opinion so held for our departure from the islands of Flores and Corvo, our captain caused a writing to be drawn and the chiefest in every ship in the fleet to set their hands and affirm thereunto that, having enjoined themselves by the said writing, they should stand unto and follow that course and direction which was by us held most meet and convenient for the benefit of the voyage and adventurers, confirming their own opinions of the course taken, and our captain to certify the Earl of Warwick at his arrival in England, keeping the writing so drawn for his own discharge. Which business being done and ended according to our captain's desire, about eleven o'clock in the forenoon his worship gave order and we bore up the helm with willing minds and joyful hearts for the other islands, with the wind at west south-west, God almighty be our good speed and prosper our proceedings, amen. At the same time that we bore up the helm, the island of Flores bore east of us some three or four and twenty leagues off. And so we steered all night following in for the land, keeping that course with little wind as is aforesaid.

The eight and twentieth day being Tuesday, having very fair weather, Captain Bartholomew Churchman and Mr John Wyles invited Sir Francis Stewart, with the gentlemen and all the captains and masters, with their principal mates, aboard the *Treasure* to dinner, where was provided a great feast for that present and were very merry. And after dinner being ended, Sir Francis Stewart with all the gentlemen departed from thence aboard our ship the *Hector* and, in regard Captain Beaumont and the masters of other ships stayed there, they also entreated myself and Mr John Cheeklie, with two of my mates, not to go away from thence until we had supped. Likewise there was divers other of our principal officers unknown to me which were the same time present aboard the *Treasure*, solemnly invited by their friends and acquaintance, for whom the pinnace was sent for but neglected and went not. Upon which neglect, in the afternoon our captain sailed away with the *Hector* and caused the pinnace, in his spleen *which was the disease he was troubled with*, to be hoisted into the ship, pretending a chase which was the rock that lieth off the north-west end of the island of Flores, not respecting or regarding any one of us that were absent from the ship. So that we were forced to go aboard the *Bark Warwick* with Captain Richard Beaumont and follow him in chase some two or three leagues; and having fetched the *Hector* up, [we] caused the pinnace to be hoisted out again and so went aboard. But we all took this usage from our captain very harshly and received it most discourteously, not knowing how to remedy ourselves. And howsoever he conceited, it was not sea-like carried, being not wont to be curbed by any in such like nature, knowing what pertained to it better than *our shallow commander*. And afterward, being come aboard our ship, the *Hector*, the captain being upon the deck, I said we were returned in spite of fortune and whosoever was against it. He demanded in spite of whom. I answered that might be conceived, but growing into an angry method of discourse, being uncovered and bare headed, I spoke to him as followeth: 'Sir,' quoth I, 'for your birth and nobility I honour you. For your knighthood and gentility, I worship you. And for that you are now captain of the *Hector*, I speak to you as captain of the *Hector* and no otherwise.' And with that I covered my head and put my cap on. Then I told him how grossly I was abused and how slightly myself and others were by him regarded. Not in nineteen year going under the command of any man but himself − only some four months of a voyage to Lisbon, and now to be under command of so worthy a gentleman as he was reputed − I conceived his government to be rather of spleen than of judicial understanding. He excused it and said they took the aforesaid rock for a sail and so gave chase after that. 'Well,' said I, 'another time we shall take and observe better order to repair aboard in time, seeing how slightly we are respected, which if such deserving were equally balanced should cause the like remuneration.'

Mr John Cheeklie, being also very much in passion, amongst divers other speeches passed said unto our captain with a great oath, 'We have not as yet made no voyage nor done any good for ourselves but only followed order and commission like a crew of fools. But before we go home, if the company will be ruled by me, we will make a voyage and carry you where you shall have all your hands full.' And this was the worst that I heard him speak and say unto the captain, which was in the presence of many of the company being then present upon the deck. He being afterward called further in question for contempt of his majesty's commission granted the Earl of Warwick and for a combination plotted to carry away the ship, and witnesses [were] produced against him, on Sir Francis Stewart's side.

The twenty-ninth day after evening prayer, our captain made an apology unto all the company concerning his great love and kind usage of them, which of very few, except some followers of his own, was so conceited − as hereafter shall be shown. Pretending that he had not done the least wrong or any abuse to any of the company, and if any man could tax him with any such indirect wrong or unkindness that was spoken of, [he] desired them to show the same unto him in what he had offended, speaking also of the abuse done to him the night before by Mr Cheeklie, which in conclusion seemed not to comport.

The one and thirtieth day and last of August, we sailed along the south side of the island of Fayal, where we saw riding in Porto Pim [MS: Porta Pinne] Road, two or three caravels and other vessels. And having the wind northerly right off the shore, we plied all the day and this night following to get up into the road.

This day Sir Francis Stewart, according to the tenor of his exordium to the company, sent for all the captains and masters in the fleet to come aboard the *Hector* and summoned a martial court against Mr John Cheeklie, pretending that he should and did hold in contempt the King's Majesty's commission granted unto the right honourable the Earl of Warwick and that it was plotted by him to carry the ship away without our captain's order or direction. This being his accusation, two witnesses were brought in against him to approve the same. But Mr Cheeklie, maintaining himself clear of such a heinous crime (being in nature and quality, petty treason), would confess no such matter, which they would have persuaded him to have done; but confidently standing in the same, [he] denied and would acknowledge as I said no such matter in words that ever he had spoken or plot intended. Yet nevertheless by the instigation of Sir Francis Stewart and vehement pressing of the same, certain of them among themselves brought it to this period that he should confess what they objected against him, and say he had spoken such and the like words, and so to ask the captain forgiveness; and then all matters should be remitted. Or otherwise it was determined that he should be turned out of the *Hector* and be carried home in another ship as a malefactor, and to answer what should be objected against him when God should send us safely to arrive in England, where the accused was content to appeal and there to answer all objections whatsoever that might or could be alleged against him. The captain likewise was so contented and agreed, but would not permit him to remain to go home for England in the ship where he himself went in person. Thus they broke off, and after supper all the captains and masters repaired aboard their own ships.

This evening Mr John Cheeklie, being in much grief and heaviness and very pensive, seeing how vehemently the captain was bent against him — [and] sitting together, being in the cuddy in talk and discoursing of the passages of business — of his own free voluntary will [he] related unto me how that Captain Harris had shipped him to be master of the *Hector*, and that at Plymouth, after he knew he was to depart and leave the ship, [Captain Harris] disgraced me and commended him [John Cheeklie] unto the Earl of Warwick and Sir Francis Stewart, which I make no question but was on both sides in the highest degree by him acted, and that after our coming to sea, he should be fully established master. Which was plotted and contrived in this manner: the first prize that should have been taken by the Earl of Warwick's fleet, 'Peell Garlic' should have been placed master of her, and so sent home for England, and should never have known who had hurt him, but by the falling at discord and variance of our captain and Mr Cheeklie. But God almighty made them frustrate of their expectations and sent us never a prize. After I had heard this treacherous discourse, it grieved me very much *that the master whom I had served seven years by covenant and one year upon liking* should abuse me in such a sort, and [I] never knowing for what defect or any cause I had given him, excepting for that whereof I have given you a touch. I presently private in my cabin made Mr Jonas Styles our minister acquainted what I understood from Mr Cheeklie, relating unto him every word as is of this discourse formerly written, entreating to know of him if he knew of any such matter. Quoth Master Styles in these very words, 'Master, it is very true what he hath spoken and related unto you, upon my knowledge, and he that hath done and did devise you this wrong and disgrace is Captain Harris, and you may give him thanks for it'. And so [he] confirmed the same for certain truth, which from others I should scarce have given any credit, which maketh me the more audacious to show unto the world what a kind office he did and great preferment he had prepared for me, which is my reward for the care and trouble I have taken and my service done in the *Hector*.

But I conceive it to be a part acted out of Machiavell and so I leave it. According to our English proverb, *a man with a red head and a red beard, take him with a good trick, and cut off his head*.

Three days after, Sir Francis Stewart, purposing to have his will and command obeyed and to show his power and magnificence, in the evening would have turned Mr John Cheeklie out of the *Hector* aboard the *Little Neptune* and sent Captain Cammocke for the same purpose to command him to go alongst aboard his ship. Whereupon all the vulgar sort of common sailors rose in an uproar and a very great mutiny, taking Mr Cheeklie's part, and stood very strongly in his behalf, and very boldly and peremptorily told the captain flatly he should not be turned out of the ship but they would keep him perforce, do and say what he could; and this in general was their resolution. Which provoked Sir Francis Stewart into very much passion and choler against them all that took his part, but [he] prevailed to very small purpose. And howsoever, Master Cheeklie he remained still in the ship. But never before was our captain in England brought up to such a bitter [*sic*] by the vulgar sort of ordinary common sailors. He, perceiving how the current ran and but in vain to strive against the stream in regard the company were so strongly bent against his command touching the dismissing of Mr Cheeklie out of the ship replied little, only threatening them they should answer this contempt in England.

SEPTEMBER 1627

The first day of September 1627 being Saturday, we plied into Porto Pim Road, which is at the south-east end of the island of Fayal, where we came to an anchor in fifty fathom water, not far off the shore. In this road were three small vessels, one being a pretty great caravel, which if our small ships had suddenly gone upon them, happily we might have surprised them; but suspecting us to be no friends, although we had all French colours displayed abroad, yet they were very fearful and carried them all close to the shore under a small fort or castle. Yet nevertheless, when it was too late, it was determined by council that the *Bark Warwick* should be double manned out of the other ships and should go into the port and see if they could fetch and bring any of them from thence. But then considering that we knew not the strength of the fort as they were under and the inhabitants very strong to come down upon our men with muskets and small shot, which might annoy us, night being in hand, and we [in] haste to ply our voyage by reason we began all to be short of provisions – these motives alleged – the enterprise was given over. And about eight o'clock at night we weighed anchor with little wind westerly, sleety, misting weather, and came out of Porto Pim Road. And the next day on the south side of the island of Pico, within some two leagues of the shore, we lay becalmed all the whole day, where we washed and tallowed our ship very effectually *contrary to reason on that day, because another time might have served as well.*

The third day being Monday, having little wind easterly, consultation was held aboard our ship the *Hector* by the masters in the fleet to bear room to leeward about Fayal and the other islands and so to stand to the northwards, giving over going to the island of St Michael's. But our opinions in the *Hector* held it more fitting to keep it up and not to lose so much way in sailing as we had gained, so we kept plying to the eastward all the night following. And the next day we had likewise little wind easterly and, being at the east end of the island Pico, stood near unto the shore; and there we set our two Dutchmen and Portingale ashore, which were taken at the Cape Roca going into Lisbon the eighth day of June last, with certain other Portingales out of the other ships. Which being done, the wind freshing in at east south-east, the *Little Neptune* bore room afore the wind and, after her, the *Bark Warwick* to fetch a circuit about to the eastward of all the other islands; and then were we and the *Treasure* forced to bear room after them or otherwise of force to leave their company. And at the west end of the island Pico, it fell calm and so continued most part all the night following.

The fifth day being Wednesday, we sailed about the island of Fayal, our two consorts the *Neptune* and *Bark Warwick* pretending to shape their course directly for England, not regarding the covenant and agreement which they had made with Sir Francis Stewart and unto which they had set to their hands and affirmed the seven and twentieth day of the last month, alleging these reasons following: our long stay about the islands unexpected, since our coming from Flores and Corvo, and falling short of victual and provisions so that they determined not to go for Cape Finisterre but to sail directly for England. This was contrary to Sir Francis Stewart's mind and all our company's, who were all very willing to proceed to the cape, conditionally they were to go alongst with us in company as it was agreed upon and by special order set down. But they shaping their course according as themselves thought good, we were forced to sail after their compass, neither respecting nor regarding Sir Francis Stewart's order, authority, power, and command that he had from the right honourable the Earl of Warwick under the Broad Seal of England, even as much as I respected my old [*sic*]. But these men being lawless, pass currant [*sic*] and nothing spoken nor brought in question against them.

Yet Sir Francis Stewart, to make his power and authority known aboard the *Hector*, tentered it to the uttermost. His malicious envious hatred being set on fire could not so soon be quenched. For this day, not being satisfied concerning Master John Cheeklie, having still an inveterate aiming to turn him out of the ship, [he] devised another course to have his command fulfilled and obeyed, which was this. He sent for all the captains and masters of the fleet to come aboard the *Hector*, and summoned again a martial court against Mr John Cheeklie, and then caused to be called all my mates, the purser, the boatswain, quarter-masters, gunner, and the carpenter, and all our chief officers' mates before him. And them being assembled in his cabin, and caused to be read afore the said officers publicly the right honourable the Earl of Warwick his commission granted him by the King's Majesty, under the Broad Seal of England. Which being done, he charged them by virtue of that commission, in his majesty's name, and of their allegiance to the king as they would answer to the contrary at our coming in to England, they should take Mr John Cheeklie and put him out of the *Hector* aboard of another ship. His speech being ended, [he] broke off abruptly and so departed out of the cabin, leaving all the officers to put the same in present execution. And [they were] communing with themselves what was best to be done and what course were best to be taken, being now put to a strait of extremity. Then they consented to frame a petition in the behalf of Mr Cheeklie, binding themselves to the obedience of Sir Francis Stewart, unto which they all affirmed; and [it] being presented unto our captain, he accepting thereof *and glad such means was made unto him*, atonement was made betwixt them and so, for present, his turning away was remitted and never after any more called in question.

The sixth day in the forenoon we were at the northernmost end of the island of Graciosa, and there Captain Bartholomew Churchman in the *Treasure* came up with the *Hector*, and saluted Sir Francis Stewart, bade him farewell, and departed out of our company bound for the island of St Michael's, having a very fresh gale of wind at south-west. And at six o'clock at night, the body of Graciosa Island bore south-west and by south of us, some nine leagues off. And then we set off from the land into sea, steering our course after our consorts as they directed us. This night following fell great abundance of rain pouring down with great extremity, the most we had seen this voyage, which dullered the wind and, after midnight, proved all weatherly and the next night following after, the wind came up at east north-east and began to blow very hard.

The eighth day being Saturday, in the grey of the morning we descried six sail of ships east of us, which stood to the southward, unto whom we gave chase with as much wind easterly as we could well bear or carry our topsails half mast high, hoisting and striking for every gust of wind that suddenly came; and about one o'clock in the afternoon the *Bark Warwick* and the *Little Neptune* fetched them up and spoke with the admiral and vice-admiral, being as they said Hollanders laden with dry fish out of Newfoundland bound for Marseilles [MS: Mercelia], which came from thence ten days past. And this answer they returned to our captain, as they must say something for themselves who, believing the Flemings' report, gave over our chase and so departed; but most of our men rather conceived them to be Hamburgers bound for Spain. And whether they were or not, we put it not into practice to make no further examination.

The tenth day being Monday, Sir Francis Stewart sent for Captain Sussex Cammocke and Captain Richard Beaumont to come aboard the *Hector*, seeing their unwillingness to keep us company, and demanded of them their resolutions what they intended to do and whether they would steer for Cape Finisterre according as it was agreed upon the twenty-third and twenty-seventh days of the last month or not, claiming their own covenant set down. Captain Cammocke answered that in regard of his shortness of victuals and provisions, he and his company were fully resolved and determined to go directly for England. Captain Beaumont himself was willing to sail alongst with us to Cape Finisterre, conditionally he might have a supply of beer, water, and other necessaries from us that he wanted. Which was by our captain and purser granted, and all the company willingly condescended thereunto that – look what allowance of victuals and provisions our men had – the very same allowance his men should have the like and be supplied out of the *Hector*. And to confirm the same for truth to make it plainly appear it should be so, there should be a master's mate and certain quarter-masters of ours appointed to go and take survey of their hold what victuals and provisions they had in their ship; and contrariwise, there should be the like of his men chosen and appointed to come and take the like survey and view of our hold, what victuals and provisions we had in our ship, which condition was agreed upon. So now there wanted but only his company's good wills and consent, which should seem was the chiefest. For which, one of my mates Sir Francis Stewart appointed to go aboard the *Bark Warwick* with their master (leaving the captain aboard our ship) and to know the resolution of the *Warwick*'s company, how they stood affected unto that which was formerly agreed upon and whether they intended to go with us towards Cape Finisterre or not. Answer was returned from one and all of the *Warwick*'s company to our captain that they would do as the *Neptune*'s company did and no otherwise, and for Captain Beaumont's willingness they cared not, neither respected any command Sir Francis Stewart could impose upon them, as by a warrant under his hand, by virtue of the Broad Seal of England, charged them withal. For that they knew they should answer it in England as well as others, meaning the *Neptune*'s company. Therefore, they were resolved to go directly for England and would steer no other course. So, taking their leave, they departed aboard their own ships and sailed out of our company. Here both his ships failed the right honourable the Earl of Warwick and showed their insolence, forgetting what they had indented with Sir Francis Stewart. So that if any error were committed for not going to the cape for the earl and adventurers' benefits (as it is conceived to be so), surely they are more culpable than any and ought most justly to be blamed. For the *Bark Warwick*, Captain Richard Beaumont, was joined in a French commission to be attendant pinnace on the *Hector* wheresoever our captain pleased to proceed. For which neglect and contempt against his majesty's Broad Seal of England and the right honourable the Earl of Warwick, if it were justly scanned, could not well be answered. But 'tis an old saying and a true, some were better steal a horse, than other some look on. Thus being left unto ourselves, the pinnace which was joined in commission having forsaken us, I said unto our captain as ever formerly I did − as I can justly maintain and approve − I held it not fitting or to small purpose for the *Hector* to go alone towards the Cape Finisterre without a pinnace that sailed well, of which want we had sufficient experience. And to the same purpose, I did in the watch divers and sundry times speak unto my mates and afore our men, never altering my opinion, which all the company being possessed in the like nature thereof held the same resolution.

My allegations shall be hereafter showed, which were delivered in writing to our captain.

The *Neptune* and *Bark Warwick*, being departed out of our company shaping their course for England, we keeping our course for Cape Finisterre, and a great tumult amongst our men what course should be taken in regard of steering more easterly, our captain in this combustious and troublesome time called all my mates and commanded them to go and consult together, and to deliver up their opinions presently in writing under their hands in that case what was best to be done, by reason it did require a sudden and speedy resolution.

Myself and Mr John Cheeklie having formerly given our approbation for denial to sail to the cape, excepting the *Bark Warwick* went and proceeded along with us in company, my mates [were] willing to give our captain content [and] said if the master and we all pleased, it were not much out of our way to go towards Cape Finisterre. I answered their opinions were only desired and it was referred unto them. And for my part, I should be conformable to any reason. Whereupon all of them being suddenly agreed, without any mature consideration, a writing was drawn in these words and to this effect following: 'Our opinions are that we may sail from hence for Cape Finisterre and according as wind and weather shall permit us to range through the trade and so for England, so that your honour can command the company.' This, being written and affirmed, was delivered him.

Now I, being always constant in that resolution which was concluded and agreed upon by general consent the twenty-third and twenty-seventh of the last month, hoping that everyone would have done the like and stood unto that which they had underwritten until such time as at this present, I saw the uttermost and to the contrary and hearing of my mates all to agree in one opinion that we might sail for Cape Finisterre without the company of the *Bark Warwick*, digressing from our former covenant and design which was concluded upon, as though there had been nothing at all done in this business.

Lest I should be accounted obstinate, perverse, and self-conceited above other men and thought to be so strongly wedded to mine own opinion that no persuasion or reason could alter or remove the same, although I knew it to be most absurd and ridiculous, to small purpose, and against wisdom to proceed alone, yet I − willing to fulfil our captain's humour and hoping to give content amongst the rest − condescended thereunto, which if I should not have done, then might our captain have justly condemned me of obstinacy *and disgraced me as he hath done*. But as I say, thinking to give content as the rest did, both myself and Mr Cheeklie underwrote the aforesaid note, as we did the former; but had we known it should have taken no better effect and success than it did, *our captain should first have been at the Mallorie* and I would [have] better advised myself and never astrived to give content where it was undeserved. And being presented unto the captain, *being glad he had had something to work upon*, [he] brought it forth and read the same amongst the company.

Then presently was there a hubbub and an uproar amongst them, making a great tumult. And some four or five base, idle fellows among the rest − viz., Addams, who should have been executed, Fleshman, Ford and Paine, his confederates, with one Martin, whom our captain gave audience − spoke unto him, saying, 'The master hath possessed us all this time hitherto that it is not fitting to go for Cape Finisterre without the company of the *Bark Warwick*, and now there is delivered unto your worship a writing that we may go, if you please and if that the company will be commanded. So that he says one thing unto you and another unto us. Therefore, we perceive and see to be double dealing with him and therefore will not go the cape but do as the other ships do and go along with them.' I desired them to have patience and to hear the reason wherefore I yielded and altered mine opinion, but the more they were entreated, the more obstinate and worse they were; and upon no terms would they be persuaded, pacified, or their yelling appeased, but everyone cried 'for England, for England'. The current now running all one way and our captain following the stream, [he] gave order to bear up the helm and steer after the other ships for England. So then was their envious and malicious wrath appeased, and everyone went willingly to trim the sails according as they were directed.

And this was the great distaste and overthrow of the voyage which our captain excepteth against me and hath divulged unto the world, which for want of better success of the voyage would be sure to bring home something to be famously talked of.

Sir Francis Stewart, our captain – against these ordinary common fellows, which were not above some four or five of them as held together as mutineers, and were speakers for all the rest – used no resistance by force and violence to withstand their purpose, which he ought to have done (being so eminent a commander as he hath been reputed) but did even sympathise with their insurrection and willingly give way to their furious enterprise, as I myself hath done and executed punishment upon the offenders, when any mutiny hath been under my command. And so might he, having the assistance – as he knew he had upon their allegiance unto our sovereign lord the king durst not deny his lawful commands – for myself, five mates, purser, boatswain, quarter-masters, gunners, carpenters, and generally every officer in the ship being bound to follow his direction, as he had it subscribed under every one of these men's hands so to do, and [we] did offer for to do, in no contemptuous manner nor otherwise. It is a very probable and likely matter for any judicial-understanding man to think that all the prime men and officers in the ship would rise in rebellion against the King's Majesty's commission or be led by the nose by a few rascally, idle fellows' pleasure. But I rather conceive and so did most in the ship, and may be by this as is afore written conceived, that he himself was as willing as any man to come for England but concealed to make any show, similitude, or sign thereof to be seen, only to appropriate applause unto himself.

Contrariwise if it were not so, committing such a heinous crime as he conceited and as to the world he hath divulged, why did he not use and execute his authority, having the King's Majesty's commission under the Broad Seal of England, calling me in question for the same as he did Mr John Cheeklie for such or the very like default? Which as they say − his associates and followers − if it were true, as it is not, were a plain contempt against his Royal Majesty's commission granted the right honourable the Earl of Warwick. But I have performed and done the earl as faithful, true, and loyal service as any knight, captain, gentleman, or any tobacco drinker of them all, or any he whatsoever that was of the voyage, according to my degree and quality, having had my bellyful of such or the like service, without better content.

And for my part, except I be commanded by his majesty, I will never desire to go to sea in any ship where there is any more gentlemen than mainmasts, besides the captain. My reasons I will conceal, for not giving distaste to any, yet one particular I will touch without offence.

I speak not to the true noble and gentry inclined to sea (and therefore I would not be mistaken). Neither by [sic] four or five gentlemen that were alongst with us on the voyage, which were as fair conditioned and well demeanoured as men might be. Yet had we two or three rude, rustical, deboshed and ill-conditioned by the name and habit of gentlemen which were in favour and as intimate with our captain as the rest. For now, if there be any decayed, forlorn gentleman appointed captain of a ship, at his first coming aboard, or using the phrase as they term it a-shipboard, his first title that he layeth claim to is: 'This is my ship, my boat, my men'. And so likewise 'mine' of everything pertaineth to the ship, when God knoweth he, nor none of his friends, never owneth part thereof. And he of himself [is] not able to value the beakhead; and when God sendeth her safe return home back, the captain goeth and departeth away, leaveth 'his' ship, 'his' boat, 'his' men, and everything that never was his, behind him. And [he] never returneth to claim any part or parcel thereof, as it is just reason he should so do. (Yet there is likewise certain fantastical green-headed seamen, and gentlemen pursers, that seek for predomination and to oversway the master that taketh charge − framed out of the prodigality of nature, like ours − [who] will use the same phrase *'my'* for *'our'*, which is improper and vainglorious to an understanding seaman, to appropriate that applause particular to himself; when the ship is not all his own, nor peradventure part, neither is able of himself to manage a ship to sea without the help, aid, and assistance of other men.)

Wherefore, it is fitting all creatures should live in their own element, and every man in his own profession and calling God hath called him unto and hath been trained up or served. And if young gentlemen and others will be trained up to sea, they should serve seven year, and in that time they will learn the true sea phrases and gain good experience. *But it is an ancient proverb and true, the sea and the gallows refuseth nobody.*

For there is three principal points [that] pertaineth to a right seaman that taketh charge of a ship and goods, and men's lives that are precious, which gentlemen are not capable of, neither respect. And therefore [they are] unfit to take charge and be commanders at sea. Which are these, viz., to be *careful, fearful, and watchful*; and that master or pilot of a ship in whom the charge apperttaineth that useth these three points in their due order respectively, is a true, proper, wise understanding seaman and worthy of charge committed into his custody and command.

To define the true nature and property of these points aright shall not [have] much need, for there is no man whatsoever he be that taketh so great a charge upon him under his hand as is here expressed – being capable to be master of a ship to sea – but doth know, or a leastwise ought to know, what pertaineth unto it; otherwise, if he do not, [he] is a novice.

But to say the truth, the poor, vulgar seamen are counted the very scum and off-scouring in England of most men (more than in all other nations), and therefore so little respected, being suborned, subpesed [*sic*], and trodden down of every man that his purse can master them for every slight occasion *as I myself have found by woeful experience*. It is certain true there are of sailors, as there are of all other professions. Therefore, I will insist no further to speak of them, for every man knoweth my meaning. And as the saying is, it is an ill bird that will defile his own nest.

Now will I set down my allegations [why] I held it not fitting to go for Cape Finisterre without a pinnace, unto whom I appeal to be censured by the worshipful, judicial, and understanding seamen, the master, wardens, assistants, and elder brethren of the Trinity House of Deptford Strond.

My first and main reason is this: in regard of our ship's going so extraordinary heavily, being foul under water, over that which she formerly had gone and sailed and [having] no hope of fetching up any sail we shall see in the sea, as by good proof and trial we have had sufficient and lamentable experience. For from the time of our departure out of Plymouth to this present day, we had been in chase after sixty-five sail of ships, when we have had some under our lee within shot of us, others again so near us that we have shot over and over them, yet never could fetch any of these up but only them three formerly spoken of, near the Cape Roca going into Lisbon – that might and would not.

Secondly, we had never a sufficient strong foresail in the ship to command her, if need should so require and extremity of weather should have happened, but looked every storm or gust to split or fly away, and generally [had] never a good sail in the ship (neither having canvas sufficient wherewithal to supply the mending of them if occasion should serve) but only a new main course never at yard nor used. And wintertime [was] drawing on, and our Channel very dangerous as all seamen that taketh charge knoweth at that time of the year as we were likely to come home in and subject to foul weather. As the state stood with us, being so badly provided, wanting good sails, I held it not fitting nor no great wisdom without very good caution to keep the ship any longer out at sea and without better hope of success than we have had, or like to have.

Thirdly, for that our men began to mutiny, and every day [they were] agrumbling (but durst not break out) for want of victuals, being a long time abridged of their ordinary allowance, which was the chief cause of their desire to come for England.

Their allowance of victuals was as followeth: viz., two days, or four meals a week, beef and peas; five days a week, Poor John or bacalow fish without either butter, oil, cheese, or mustard to eat with it; and so they had continued a long time, being cold comfort and small sustenance for the nourishment of men's bodies. Bread, four small pounds a day to five men; beer, three quarter cans a day to five men; at this allowance, they were not willing to continue any longer and often times entreated me to speak to our captain to have it amended, which I did but could have no redress. [The men] being scarce able to keep life and soul together but by the provisions and refreshings which they had of their own, although there was reasonably sufficient in the ship – butter, cheese, oil and suchlike excepted. And therefore [they] desired with the rest of the fleet to come along with them for England.

Fourthly, that the *Bark Warwick* being absolute appointed, and joined in commission by letter of marque from the Admiralty Court against the French, to attend and wait upon the *Hector* for pinnace wheresoever it pleased Sir Francis Stewart would proceed with her. And they presuming so contemptuously to leave, depart, and to go away from us in such a sort and manner as they did, we should as well and better answer our coming for England to the right honourable the Earl of Warwick, if it were called in question, than their company could.

Fifthly, for that we had made, in all our time being out and absent from England, not any profit or benefit for the adventurers *the worshipful owners of the* Hector, and [had] no hope taking that course to the Cape Finisterre like for to make [any], the time of year being principally for the ship's employment for the Straits, which if the owners pleased to have sent her, I conceived would have turned more advantage to their benefits than such a desperate voyage.

And sixthly, having such a contentious, turbulent, troublesome, unruly, inhuman company, for a matter of half a score persons one or other, Newgate not yielding worse, nor Tyburn enjoying the like, I heartily desired to come for England as one motive producing me thereunto, only to be rid and clear of such rascally consorts and wicked company, never having sailed with such nor the like.

All the reason that ever I could hear or understand from our captain that he alleged and objected against me many times before this garboil, in a familiar sort, both private and public to the company for our going to Cape Finisterre, was this:

'It were a shame and disgrace for us to go home for England as long as we have any victuals in the ship, and if it be but bread and drink, and to spend all our provisions, until we should make a voyage.' Although there was little possibility thereof, so that, if we had stayed out at sea until we had spent all our victuals and provisions and have come home in to England as we did, and could have lived by the way like chameleons by the air, we had given our captain content — although better content that pleased him — and then happily, never a word hereof spoken.

The clearing of this aspersion laid upon me, to my great defamation, was only the chief cause and ground of committing these observations to the press. Being prolixious, hath held you in long discourse, which I hope giveth the world judicially understood satisfaction. But hath incurred the inveterate heavy wrath and displeasure of our captain, Sir Francis Stewart, for whose favour I crave not, nor hatred I care not.

But, all this while we are sailing our course for England with a merry wind and a prosperous gale, God almighty continue the same, (the *Little Neptune* and *Bark Warwick* in our company) [so] that our ships run after fifty-four or fifty-five leagues in four and twenty hours.

The eleventh day being Tuesday, about two o'clock in the afternoon happened unto us an unkind loss and disaster. I not having the afternoon watch, being new gone into my cabin — viz., on the larboard quarter — one John Scrutton, a marvellous, very fair, honest conditioned man, having formerly hung a shirt about that place overboard awashing, was gone to take it in, and standing carelessly (as by some of the company he was seen) upon a port, let [it] fall upon a piece of ordnance. The ship going within two points right afore the wind, having a very great grown sea, she fetched a great weather seell [*sic*] so forceably to windward that the man fell overboard into the sea and was about half a cable's length astern in the wake of the ship before anybody saw him, or knew of it. All men — in regard of the sudden outcry of the company that was upon the upper deck and likewise [among] them below in the ship — being in amaze or astonished, presently we brought the ship, all her sails in the wind, but before we could make means to hoist the pinnace overboard, the man was out of sight very far astern and was drowned, every man being very sorrowful for the untimely and disastrous death of so honest and well-behavioured fellow.

And the truth is [that] the ship having so much way, sailing after eleven leagues a watch, was very long before she came in the wind to have her way wholly stemmed that, if there might have been given a king's ransom to have saved his life, it had been impossible.

This evening our captain out of his love sent a message unto me by our purser and sequestered, absented me from his table *by reason he had caused a hog to be killed and had fresh victuals provided.*

The fourteenth day being Friday, our captain called a council together with myself and mates to have our opinions what course was best to be taken for the performance of a voyage, now being come somewhat near England, and to use the best endeavour and all diligence that possibly could be conceived. And [he] thought most expedient, whom all of us held it very fitting and convenient, we might steer for the coast of France and so range betwixt the Seams [Isle de Sein?], Ushant, and the Main, and so through the trade and then for England. Whereupon about noon, by order from our captain, we altered our course, according as it was concluded and agreed upon, and steered east for the coast of France, the *Little Neptune* and *Bark Warwick* keeping on their course directly for the coast of England, leaving our company. But our men rose up in a very great mutiny, produced by the old crew Addams, Fleshman, Ford, Paine, and two or three more, which was their spokesmen. Most of them all now (being suffered) joined and ran upon one strain and swore many great, deep, and bitter oaths, telling the captain flat and plain to his face they would neither go that ways nor lay hand to trim a sail nor touch a rope for boatswain or any other officer's command whatsoever, do what they could, all the sails lying loose, fluttering in the wind. Here the insolency of this rascal crew was shown in open rebellion this second time, which if their proceedings, by wisdom, had been cropped in the bud at first, it had never blossomed forth. That for all our being so near unto the coast of England as we were, and [had] but to spend a two or three days upon the coast of France, according as wind and weather gave us leave, to see what good we might or could have done; yet these fellows would yield to nothing, neither by fair nor foul means, but would bear and carry all the sway themselves, which way their idle humours listed.

Being in this combustion and mutiny with our company, in the very interim one descried a sail which bore of us east and by north. So with her they all concluded to steer and then trimmed the sails accordingly. And about four o'clock in the afternoon we spoke with her, being the *Great Neptune*, our admiral that was the right honourable the Earl of Warwick his ship, in whom was principal commander Captain – Gyles, come from Plymouth bound out of a new voyage to the southward, who related unto us of the earl's being in health and safety in England, which we were glad to hear, with the discourse of their fight with the Spanish armada, and the passages of their proceedings since our losing one another off the Rock in the thick mist the second day of July last.

The *Little Neptune* and *Bark Warwick*, being near out of sight and hearing the report of our ordnance when we saluted each other, and seeing us together, came into our company again. And so we all three continued in the *Great Neptune*'s company all the night following, standing to the westward with the wind southerly, attending our captain's pleasure (as it was meet) when we should depart.

All their discourse being ended, the next day being the fifteenth, about twelve o'clock at noon we took our leave of Captain Gyles [and] the *Great Neptune*, saluting one another according to the custom and manner of the sea. And so [we] departed, she being bound for Cape Finisterre and Cape St Vincent, and we three bound in for the Sleeve [the Channel], steering for the coast of England. This afternoon, Sir Francis Stewart gave order to myself and mates that this night following to shape our course and steer over for Ushant upon the coast of France, leaving the other ships, and to never make any of our company acquainted therewith. But some of them amongst the rest (having gained a little experience) perceiving what course was intended to take, began to fall amuttering.

The sixteenth day being Sunday, in the morning the foresaid ragged regiment, in the like manner as they did, began to make a great mutiny again and break out this third time in rebellion and to oppose themselves against our captain's command and authority, and swore plainly to him [that] they would not go towards the coast of France upon no conditions whatsoever, but they would go directly for Plymouth and so willed him to resolve himself. With that, Sir Francis Stewart, he being moved in a very great passion and ecstacy with wrath and anger, immediately ran amongst them with his poniard drawn in his hand and swore he that spoke the next word of denial, [he] would stab him to the heart. But all this prevailed not. Upon this rash and outrageous threatening, they were all silent and none of them would speak a word of discontent, neither touch a rope to trim a sail upon any persuasion. So he, seeing the perverseness and headstrongness of these audacious fellows, and that they were now gathered to a head, (and as the saying is) hung all in a string being so long suffered, could not tell what to say or reply unto them. Sir Francis Stewart called myself and mates together in my cabin and concluded: [he] give me order to shape our course for England and to steer after the *Little Neptune* and the *Bark Warwick*, and then they were all appeased and quiet.

Also he gave me great charge and express command to take special good notice of those fellows' names that were the ringleaders and mutineers, that had animated and produced the rest to this rebellion and great disorder, and when God should send us to arrive in England, he would do to them. Aye, marry, would he.

About noon we descried two sail of ships to the northward of us standing to the westward with the wind at south-east, unto whom we all three gave chase after while towards evening; but, having a long chase and night approaching towards, our captain gave me order to give over chasing, which was obeyed, and so we stood our course to the eastward.

The seventeenth day being Monday, about eight o'clock in the morning we sounded and had some seventy-five fathom water, fair Channel ground, and at twelve o'clock at noon observed the sun and found ourselves to be in the latitude of forty-nine degrees, fifty minutes. And having the wind at south, I directed our course east up the Channel, which I knew was the best course we could steer, having that wind and like to veer easterly. Mr John Cheeklie objected and opposed himself against me and would maintain before our captain that east and by north was a better course. Whereupon the company, taking his part and holding his opinion to be best, conceited Sir Francis Stewart had given me private order to steer up alongst the Channel for Portsmouth, for that was the port which I desired, and many men more in the ship who had their residency and dwelling at London. The crew of rebellious, rascally Newgate birds consulted amongst themselves, vowing and swearing one to another whatsoever order and direction Sir Francis Stewart gave should stand for nothing, neither would they respect his command, and that if the master did not carry them into the harbour of Plymouth, they would heave him overboard. So great was their contempt and disobedience *for want of judicial government* grown unto, that they cared not neither what they said nor what they did. 'Well, my masters,' quoth I, 'by the help of almighty God, I will bring you within the sight of the Rame Head going in to Plymouth, and then I will leave it to our captain's discretion what course he pleaseth to direct; and that, I purpose, God willing, to follow.'

The eighteenth day being Tuesday, in the morning about five o'clock, standing into the eastward with the wind at south-east and fair weather, expecting at daylight to make the land (as about eight o'clock we did, being the Land's End of England and the Mount), we descried three sail of ships close to leeward of us standing off to the southward, unto whom we cast about and gave chase after them. Being a French man-of-war of Brest in France, who had surprised some two days before a ship called the *Elinore* of Salcombe in Devonshire, part of her pertaining to one Mr Hugh Randall of the same place, which was come out of Newfoundland, laden with dry fish called bacalow or Poor John, of whom was master one John Coos. And the other [was] a ship of the island of Jersey called the *Spring*, one Mr Balhash sole owner, being in her ballast bound for Wales to lade coals, part of whose company the Frenchmen had set ashore near about Saint Ives. And with both these ships this French man-of-war, whose captain was called Monsieur Michel Levery, were intended directly and bound over for the coast of France with the residue of the English men they had kept. But it pleased God our fleet, steering in for the land – having a scant wind – came athwart his way unexpected. And coming up with them, discharging some three or four piece of ordnance, we commanded immediately the two English ships and the *Bark Warwick* the French man-of-war to strike (for which there was a distaste taken by the *Little Neptune*'s company by reason they gave not Captain Cammocke the grace and reputation to come first up with the Frenchman). And so in fine [we] took them all three, redeeming the Englishmen out of the hands and possession of the merciless Frenchmen, who intended and were resolved the company for their parts, if their captain would have given his free consent, to have heaved every Englishman of them overboard. But God dealt more merciful unto them in delivering the poor captives from so untimely a death.

The *Bark Warwick*, Captain Richard Beaumont, having entered certain men aboard the French ship, commanded the man-of-war to come to leeward near unto our ship, the *Hector*, being admiral, where she lay by the lee a fair berth off, Sir Francis Stewart sending our pinnace aboard for the captain of the French man-of-war. But in the interim before our pinnace could arrive or get aboard of her for the captain, the *Little Neptune*, Captain Sussex Cammocke, with her two topsails and foresail, with a fresh gale of wind [so] that a ship would have ran near after six leagues a watch – they right afore the wind – willingly, shamefully, and most idly, ran sternlings aboard the man-of-war right in the midships with the *Neptune*'s boltsprit betwixt her masts, tore her down to the water, and forced to cut overboard the prize foremast before they could clear each ship the one of another. And in the meantime, [they] had the first rifling and pillaging of her and of the French company. And so by that fantastical, idle, gentleman-like humorous means, the man-of-war was utterly lost, cast away, and sunk in the sea. Which by all men's judgements and understanding might better have been saved for any great benefit we have gained on our voyage, and would have given a thirty or forty good fellows satisfaction for their service to the right honourable the Earl of Warwick.

This simple, foolish business of the commander of the *Little Neptune* being so carried, Sir Francis Stewart much distasted and seemed to be very angry and discontented. And as I have heard it credibly reported, answer was made [that], if he was angry, he might mend himself; for he was angry with him that cared not for his anger a rush. Howsoever, all business was hushed up in silence *as birds of a feather will hold together*.

But the malicious enmity and cause of this disaster was because Captain Beaumont, as has been afore spoken, would not give way and suffer the *Little Neptune* to come first up with the French man-of-war and surprise her. Which was a poor conceit amongst men of understanding as should be, to commit such an error, for what matter had it been who had taken her as long as she was ours and in possession. And again, in any man's judgement, it had been more grace and fame unto our noble general, the right honourable the Earl of Warwick, to have brought her in to England home in triumph, than that she should have perished and been lost in such vile, a base, and spiteful manner.

Yet these men, for all their abuses to the Earl of Warwick, are winked at, dance in a net, and think themselves unseen.

We having fitted and manned our two prizes, the wind blowing very fresh at east south-east, in the afternoon we put in to St Mary's Sound at Scilly, where we arrived, praised be God, in safety.

In the evening Captain Bassett, of the castle at St Mary's, very courteously presented Sir Francis Stewart and sent aboard a live sheep, a turkey, and certain hens to bid him welcome into England and Scilly, which he most courteously and kindly accepted. And to remunerate his loving kindness, two days after, Sir Francis Stewart invited the captain of the castle, with other gentlemen, aboard the *Hector* to a feast and were very merry.

The one and twentieth day being Friday, about four o'clock in the afternoon, having the wind at north north-west a fresh gale, we weighed with our fleet and divers other ships in St Mary's Sound at Scilly, and came out to sea, and while twelve o'clock at midnight following steered east and by south, and then all night after east up the Channel.

The two and twentieth day being Saturday, in the morning we were within some three leagues of the cape of Cornwall called the Lizard, having the wind westerly, with misting sleety weather, and keeping our course sailing along the coast, we saw divers sail of ships standing several courses, and chased, but could fetch up none. And athwart of the opening off Falmouth, four sail of ships stood with our forefoot, which very earnestly strived to weather us, amongst whom was one Captain Ferran, a French man-of-war of Rochelle and in a Breton French hull built, who came close out to windward of us within hailing. And we not knowing no otherwise but that he was an enemy, as we expected, and by his working appeared, we shot four or five piece of ordnance at him and did his ship some spoil about his boltsprit and bits. And howsoever, it was not repented of by any of us, but only of one or two in the ship, if we had done him five times more harm than we did.

For had he been the proudest French man-of-war in the kingdom of France, friend or foe, to offer and presume to come to windward of the *Hector* in such a nature and a braving, presumptuous manner, having a gentleman aboard of worth, I would have done the best that lay in my power as I did to this Captain Ferran, to sink her or perforce compel him to come to leeward, or otherwise would lie by the lee and sink by her side.

Yet one wise gentleman amongst the rest aboard the *Hector*, out of the quintessence of his wit, said to our captain [that] he deserved to have a poniard clapped in his breast that caused to shoot at her coming so near us and within call, conceiving it was all one and no difference whether she came to windward or to leeward. 'Sir,' quoth I, 'you speak very wisely, or else according to your sea understanding. It had been very good reputation and honour for Sir Francis Stewart and the commanders of the *Hector* under him to have suffered and permit any proud French man-of-war whatsoever, seeing colours abroad displayed, to come close out to windward, braving us, and never have given him a piece of ordnance through his sides to compel him for to come to leeward, that he might report and brag, wheresoever he came, that he presumed and went to windward of such a ship and they durst not shoot at him a piece of ordnance.' Our captain being in presence said it was well enough. So then little was replied by the gentleman again and then ceased.

But the truth is, nothing was executed without the consent and order from our captain unto me, which I − being amongst our ordnance − saw performed and discharged the first piece was fired, being a demi-culverin.

So after he was come out astern of our ship and brought himself to leeward, Captain Ferran came aboard the *Hector*, [where] Sir Francis Stewart kindly embraced and saluted him and, having acquaintance, bade him welcome. Captain Ferran he complained what harm we had done him, being sorry as he said that he presumed so boldly to come to windward of us, pleading he did not know what ship it was − as I verily believed him, yet might he see our colours that we were of England. He certified our captain that all the other ships in sight were friends.

And so after many French compliments used and a running banquet presented him, [he] took his leave and departed as he said for Falmouth to repair his harms which he had sustained.

At eight o'clock at night the Dodman bore north north-west of us some four leagues off. And having a tide of flood and much wind at south-west, [we] clapped close upon a tack to the southward to spend the night, purposing the next day, God willing, to harbour in Plymouth, according to direction received from our captain.

This night following proved a storm of wind at south-west so forceably that about twelve o'clock at midnight we flatted our ship's head about to the westward and was constrained to take in our forecourse and laid it a-try with our maincourse, while towards morning then the wind dulled and the storm broke up and blew more amenable.

Also this night was there a muttering amongst the rabble crew of rebellious rascals, that before morning we should be droven with the storm of wind that blew to the eastward and put to leeward of Plymouth. Which if our captain had pleased so to have done or given his consent, there blew a fair wind and as good an opportunity as men could wish or have in seven years, nothing regarding what any of the rest of the compact company said.

About midnight, I solicited our captain to go for Portsmouth with our ship, which for divers respects had been the more fitter place for all our designs. But by no means possible could I persuade or grant him to yield thereunto, his own conceit and reason − which he concealed − being best known to himself.

The three and twentieth day of September being Sunday, in the morning at daylight we saw the Rame Head north north-west of us and the opening of Plymouth Sound north. So then, having a fresh gale of wind at south-west about ten o'clock in the forenoon, we put into the harbour of Plymouth, into Cattewater, and there anchored, all our fleet and prizes being in company with us, giving God almighty most humble praise and thanks for our safe and good arrival into our native country of England, back of our troublesome, discontented, and unfortunate voyage.

In the afternoon Sir Ferdinando Gorges, with certain other gentlemen, came aboard the *Hector* to the ship's side and fetched Sir Francis Stewart ashore, and other gentlemen that were on the voyage; and, for his welcome into Plymouth, discharged and gave him five piece of ordnance at his departure, *contrary to his own mind, for he gave order not to have any, which showed little generosity but a niggardly penuriousness, howsoever the voyage unexpectedly proved.*

The twenty-fourth day being Monday, we dispatched letters for London to advise our friends and owners of our safe arrival in Plymouth.

The five and twentieth day our captain returned aboard the *Hector* where, by his directions, a feast was prepared, inviting most of the principal officers in the ship with him to dinner, which was to welcome us into England, which every one willingly accepted and took it very kindly at his hands, conceiving we had been all friends; but the violence and enmity of nature of two contrary climates would not permit that affinity of friendship. All this day our captain stayed and night following lay aboard. And the next morning [he] took his leave of the *Hector* and farewell of the company and so departed ashore to Plymouth and no more returned aboard this voyage, few or none being sorry he was no sooner gone and departed from the ship. This day having fair weather and little wind northerly, we warped the *Hector* up to the head of Cattewater, which is esteemed and counted the safest berth in the harbour for a ship to ride and is called the Lion's Hole. And there we new moored our ship in that berth with good anchors and cables according as I would have her to mine own content. Where, blessed be God, she continued and rode in safety the great storm that blew so forceably in November 1627 when two of his majesty's ships miscarried and divers other merchant ships cast away within the harbour of Plymouth. For which great care and diligence I am well rewarded with just nothing.

The twenty-seventh day being Thursday, Sir Francis Stewart sent aboard the *Hector* for his clothes and all his provisions which were delivered out of the ship and carried ashore according to his directions to Plymouth. And whereas he had certain provisions remaining of his store which was left of the voyage, as half a barrel of flour, scotch meal, fresh beef which was bought at Scilly, spice, fruit, sweetmeats, and certain other nourishing things, and knowing that there were many sick men aboard the *Hector* and no order taken for their preservation, it had been a pious deed of charity and a matter of small moment or import unto him if part thereof had been left aboard the ship for the relief and use of poor distressed sick men. But there was not left in the ship to my knowledge not the worth of a penny pertaining unto his worship, or what was his, for the nourishment of any man, but all carried away according to his desire, so free was our worthy captain of his benevolence unto our sick men.

The eight and twentieth day in the morning he sent aboard the *Hector* the master gunner of the ship for four brass guns which were taken in the French man-of-war the eighteenth day of September, which at his first coming for them was denied. But [he] afterwards returning with a warrant under our captain's hand, I caused the boatswain's mate to deliver them unto the gunner, and so they were carried him ashore to Plymouth. Of these brass guns there was six of them in all aboard the French man-of-war, which were first taken out and carried aboard the *Little Neptune* Captain Cammocke, (and two iron piece of ordnance which we received aboard the *Hector*), all which our captain – coming to understand thereof – shared betwixt them and owners, being all agreed. Although others deserving share and part, both of them and what is surprised, [and] must of force be content with a small pittance allotted by them that never adventured for any thing was taken.

In the afternoon Sir Francis Stewart, Sir Ferdinando Gorges, and the commissioners appointed for the right honourable the Earl of Warwick his business sent for me aboard the *Hector* to come ashore to appear before their worships at the castle to be examined upon interrogatories concerning the proceedings of the voyage and objections alleged against me by our captain. Where, when I came to the fort, as my duty was, [I] presented myself unto them and, having stayed and attended their pleasures a long time – longer than I knew wherefore, they having nothing to say nor could not I tell what business they sent for me – I was dismissed. And so [I] returned aboard like a fool as I went ashore, *not like them that sent for me*, and so remain.

OCTOBER 1627

The first day being Monday, most of our chiefest men belonging to the *Hector* went ashore [not] only to take their leave of Sir Francis Stewart, but principally to see how liberal he would be unto them. Whom this day with our minister, Mr Jonas Styles, and certain other gentlemen that did accompany him departed out of Plymouth, beginning to take his journey for London – where God send him safely to arrive – taking no order for any fresh provisions or victuals for the company, nor order for the bringing ashore of the sick men, which every man expected and thought he would have done, as had been most meet and convenient, he being chief commander of the ship. And under his charge [he] ought to have seen it in all reason and conscience performed before his departure or taken strict order and course with the commissioners who were appointed by the Earl of Warwick to have had it executed in his absence.

Thus having passed many dangers, God almighty granting our desires in sending us safely to arrive at Plymouth, having spent and passed one whole week and better since our arrival, and having brought home divers sick men and many weak and feeble, touched with the scurvy, not able to help themselves, and very few of the company belonging to the ship lusty and strong as they were at our departure and going out of England, every man looked and expected − as well the sound and them in health as the sick and feeble − that order should have been taken [that] men should have had fresh victuals and provisions from the shore to nourish and relieve them in regard of the hardness of their fare and eating so long of salt victuals at sea (being the most part of our food for relief, poor dry fish without any other provision to drive it down but only mere hunger, so that, if it had been possible, men might have been metamorphised into fish).

Especially them that were sick, weak, and not healthy, that they should have been respected and carried ashore into houses, and have had that provided for them which was fitting for men to have in that sick and weak estate as they were in, to restore them, if [it] pleased God to see good, unto their former healths and prosperity again. But there was no order nor course in the world at all taken for neither sick nor sound. Only if there were any sick man who had anything of his own to make money of, to relieve his wants, or any friend to assist him, to pass his word for what provisions he should take and receive, or had so much credit of his own in Plymouth, it was some comfort unto them and would pass for current. Otherwise, they might stay aboard, starve, and die. And God knoweth there was but cold comfort and no other allowance nor other victuals provided and allowed them than that the ship brought out of the sea, only bread and beer excepted.

Wherefore, as I say, all the poor men that could make any shift for relief and succour to recover their healths any manner of way, these men went ashore, and the rest that could make no means were forced to stay aboard sick.

For even as it was at the island of Flores, even so it was here in Plymouth; our captain, he referred it and left the same to the purser to supply such wants, by reason the ship was arrived in England and was now to be resigned over to the owners. The purser, on the other side again as formerly he did, in regard the ship being in the Earl of Warwick's service and not discharged thereof, would neither meddle nor make to buy any provisions until such time he had order from the owners, as he thought in his discretion most expedient he should so do. But being a long time before any such order came from London, resting as 'twere betwixt *hawk and buzzard*, between them both no order at all was taken at Plymouth and, by that means, all they that remained and kept belonging unto the ship, in hope of satisfaction for their time, fared all the harder − excepting those that had wherewithal to replenish their own necessity.

And this was the cause and main ground that divers of the company forsook and departed from the *Hector*, took their own courses, and went aroving into other ships, contrary to their friends' minds here at London, to their great discontent and imputation of him that never deserved it, as is well approved.

They, having neither means nor victuals fitting for men according to the custom of England in harbour allowed them, neither could they be cleared nor discharged from the ship by any order as they desired, and so [were] forced to follow their own ways and inventions, which since hath turned to many of them their utter ruin and destruction

For my part, I was one amongst the rest and had as much allowed me as any (the purser excepted, whose expenses in diet for himself had no limitation), only such provisions as I bought for mine own use and succour for myself. And what relief and comfort I did unto others that remained aboard and tasted thereof, I leave it for them to relate.

Yet was there, before the ship's arrival in the river of Thames, a scandal and an exclamation about the town and at my house, railing at my door, [that] I had sold the victuals from aboard the *Hector* to make spending money and starved all the men. But God and the world knoweth otherwise, for our purser, only for the benefit and credit of the owners, kept me short enough for any provisions being chargeable unto them. And for mine own charge and expenses laid out the time I remained to the ship, I must of force have patience and be content to bear it myself.

But for the starving of any man, I leave it to their consciences, and God pardon them that were the cause of it, being a shame to have it spoken and to the world related. But 'tis the truth, and therefore no shame to reveal it, [but] more shame for them that should have redressed it and would not seek to perform it; and to their considerations it must remain.

Amongst the rest, there was four sick men remained aboard the *Hector*, having not wherewithal to supply and relieve their wants, especially two that was very sick, one David Rankin and Antipas Medcalfe. Rankin remained and lay extreme sick, lingering and pining until the five and twentieth day of this month of October, being Thursday, and then about two o'clock in the morning, for want of good sustenance, good kitchen physic, and good looking unto, [he] departed and changed this life for immortality aboard the ship *Hector* in Cattewater, having lain a long time sick, weak, and diseased. And in the afternoon [we] buried him over against Catte Down, no order taken by the commissioners nor purser to allow him Christian burial. Antipas Medcalfe being very weak, sick and feeble — wanting indeed that which the other did to make him strong and lusty — being like a starveling, lived while the *Hector* came about to London, where being arrived with his mother and friends, after he was come to fresh nourishment and good keeping, shortly after died, to the great grief and lamentation of his poor distressed mother. The other two, praised be God, reasonably well recovered of their sickness and gathered their accustomed health and strength.

And this is the care, charity, and respect that gentlemen taketh over poor seafaring men, when their turn is served, which maketh them so unwilling to go under their command and causeth such great love and familiarity betwixt them, that one careth not for another's company at sea and will hardly be truly reconciled – the poor sailor being made a vassal and a slave to every supposed gentleman that goeth in a gay coat and taketh the name upon him, usurping the true title of gentility.

But I speak not this of our captain, he well known to be of the blood royal. Neither dare I say, being of so high a degree and calling made him forget himself and [be] so careless.

To return to the right honourable and noble Earl of Warwick, worthy of all praise and commendation *who was this voyage, as I am credibly informed by certain that were of the ship with his honour, that there was such enmity one against another amongst the chiefest commanders under him that led his honour by their ill counsel which way they listed and brought such confusion as it happened unto the voyage, and therefore no default at all in our worthy general for such ill success.* [He had] little understanding of the passage and carriage of the business before spoken of at Plymouth being full sore against his mind, which if he had known should have been better ordered; but I presume until by this relation [he] never did come to the hearing and knowledge thereof. But let it rest.

Upon suit made unto his honour by the owners of the two prizes taken by the *Hector* on the eighteenth day of September, the *Elinore* of Salcombe laden with one hundred and five thousand of dry fish called bacalow or Poor John and fourteen hundred of corfish with certain train oil from Newfoundland, and the *Spring* of Jersey with her stock of ready money bound for Wales to load coals (which money the French captain had taken and surprised from the master of the said *Spring* but after they were retaken again, and the French man-of-war and were all in our possessions, the *Little Neptune* running aboard her and having the first sacking of the Frenchman, that money never appeared nor was never brought to light, being by the captains concealed), these two ships being in value worth upward of seven hundred and odd pounds. Which the honourable earl, if he would have used the extremity of the law, might have converted them two ships and goods to his own and the adventurers' use, and made them prize and lawful purchase. But he, understanding the poor and weak estate of the said owners and that it would be an impoverishing and undoing of divers poor men, of his great clemency, heroical love, and Christian charity unto his countrymen, sent down order to Plymouth unto his commissioners that the charges his honour had been at in rescuing and redeeming these two ships out of the Frenchmen's possession being paid, they should have them restored and surrendered unto the true owners again; and so [they] were delivered up accordingly to their great comforts and consolation. Many such Warwicks, having the like pity and

compassion, [may] God almighty send to increase and prosper in England
to their ever-flourishing posterity in after ages, amen.

Now our captain of the *Hector*, Sir Francis Stewart, being well arrived
at Westminster and in health, to his haven of happiness and greatest
devotion, the greatest kindness that he could and hath afforded me for
all my care, trouble, turmoil, vexation, and hard fare of the voyage, out
of his malicious, malignant, and envious spirit, hath laid a false aspersion
upon me to the right honourable the Earl of Warwick, disgraced me to
the owners of the *Hector*, and wrongfully scandalised me to the world;
whereupon, without examination of the truth, crediting the discourse
present, who daring or will conceit otherwise than that which is divulged
by reason of a great relater and eminent person spoken it? But all is not
gold that glisters, nor all truth that is carried to and fro; and therefore
the discourse [was] absent — which ought to have been heard as well
as the other, before a rigorous sentence and order passed — never called
nor permitted to appear and answer for itself. But [he] caused the owners
of the ship to send down to Plymouth a new master to take charge and
bring the *Hector* up to London. I remained unto her until his coming
thither who was appointed master, which was the thirtieth day of October
1627, and then resigned her over into the charge and custody of Mr William
Wylds, desiring God almighty to send him much joy, prosperous voyages,
and good success with her as I wish myself. And this is the secret spite
and public mischief that our captain has conspired and done to me, in
disgrace for my true and faithful service to the right honourable the Earl
of Warwick on his voyage made upon the coast of Portingale. Which,
if I were able to parallel or remunerate any manner of way, should want
for no performance. *But God the revenger of all wrong, unto whom
vengeance doth belong and unto whom I leave the disgrace to punish, deal
with his honour as he hath done by my reputation.*

And thus have I finished and made a period of discoursing of our
troublesome and discontented voyage, that only might and would not.

*Only to relate, we had pretty conceited and new devised punishments
for malefactors and offenders never before invented for the sea, viz.*

If our captain sent any cheese to toast — as many times he did, *loving
it as well as a Welshman* — if by accident, or if one man playing or jesting
with another in the cookroom, it happened to fall in the ashes and be all
dirty, the causer thereof being called in question should be compelled by
our captain to stand right afore, close to the mainmast, all the whole time
our company was at supper, with a piece of toasted cheese in his mouth
all besmeared and greased in the ashes, and one tinkling with a frying pan
and a pair of tongs making tinker's music all the time he was appointed
so shamefully to stand.

Likewise, if there were any man that was a talecarrier and transported tales to and again in the ship one from another whereby it should produce any debate and strife betwixt man and man, the same being known and approved, the offender should in the same manner as the former stand right afore the mainmast some certain time limited by our captain with his tongue lil'd [sic] all the length out of his mouth and one anointing it with tar, so that if at any time he were forced to take his tongue into his mouth – as I imagine it is impossible for any man to perform and contain himself any long time in such a nature, but he shall of force do it – he was sure to have his mouth well tarred for sunburning. And this was their punishment.

Also if any ordinary common man, that were not an officer and a commander, struck one another for any slight occasion a box on the ear or anywhere else, the other that was strucken not resisting but as it were taking the advantage of the law – as indeed there ought not a blow to be given in a ship by any of the vulgar – he, I say, complaining to our captain of his grievance, the offender should be adjudged to have both his hands seized across at the wrists and so hoisted up by one of the fore braces, and there [he] should hang by the arms to his great pain and dolour [a] certain long time according to our captain's humour. And when it pleased him he thought the man had suffered punishment and torture enough for his default, he would give order for his taking down. But this punishment and tyranny used unto men for any offence, I hold it not fitting to be executed in a ship, excepting those that are commanders' purpose to break men's arms, laming them, and have no benefit nor use of their labour for which men go to sea and venture their lives. Neither would I wish nor counsel any true bred seaman that hath the charge of a ship and sole commander of men to execute and use this unlawful punishment although it was (the first time as ever I knew since my going to sea) put in execution aboard the *Hector* and by such an eminent gentleman as our captain, Sir Francis Stewart, the devisor thereof.

The grievances of the company of the Hector *in this present, discontented voyage in the service of the right honourable the Earl of Warwick, under the command of the right worshipful Sir Francis Stewart, knight, captain of the said ship*:

Whereas, at the setting forth the good ship called the *Hector* from London, it was agreed and concluded betwixt the right honourable the Earl of Warwick and the worshipful alderman with the rest of the owners of the said ship that she should be fully and complete victualled for six months, having one hundred and twenty men, which was her full proportion set down, [yet] she brought from London to Plymouth one hundred forty and eight men and hath continued all the voyage one hundred and thirty-six men, having so many idlers overplus that doth neither watch nor ward, nor do nothing but only devour the provisions not provided for them. And this being above the true proportion hath bred much discontent and confusion in the ship and is partly an overthrow of the voyage, by reason men are so hardly pinched of victuals and no profit.

At the pretended setting forth of the *Hector* this present voyage, the worshipful Richard Harris, part owner and captain of the said ship, for whose employment she was purposely built and for whose sake and by whose instigation the chiefest officers and best seamen in the ship voluntarily, of their love unto Captain Harris and hopes of the voyage pretended, undertook the prosecution thereof; or otherwise had not, neither would have proceeded. He taking great trouble, care, and pains for the providing and victualling forth the ship to sea, yet nevertheless, at our arrival at Plymouth found [*sic*] it was plotted and contrived that he should be returned back to London and but only made an instrument to procure, provide, and fit the ship for another. As it was pretended, whereof he had true notice at London but [was] not able to withstand it; for otherwise without the consent and assistance of Captain Harris, the ship had not nor could not have proceeded of this voyage.

But being arrived at Plymouth and all men perceiving how the business was carried against him of whom they had agreed to perform the voyage and received money, expecting no other captain, [they] would have all forsaken and left the ship if possible by any means the company could have gotten ashore. But having no remedy, of force [they] must have a new captain appointed of the *Hector* over them, denying utterly the former mentioned; the company, of their own voluntary free will and disposition before the Earl of Warwick, made choice of you, right worshipful Sir Francis Stewart, to be their captain, hoping according to promise they should have been lovingly and kindly respected. But contrary to expectation [they] have received these grievances.

Whereas, in the right honourable the Earl of Warwick his instructions, under his hand, he desireth for the preferment and lengthening of the voyage that men should mess themselves five to the true proportion and order of victuals according to four men's allowance and not to be altered without a general consent. Which at our coming to sea, at the first motion of you, Sir Francis Stewart, and reading of the said instructions, all the company willingly condescended thereunto. Yet falling short a great matter of that allowance in all provisions, not having the full allowance but one day in the week (namely on Sundays) which hath been a great means to plunge and draw the voyage to a larger length yet nothing thereof considered.

For that which is a common courtesy of all seamen and allowed aboard all private men-of-war (excepting lords and gentlemen that do not know the issue and content, neither will understand their own tranquillity and love amongst their company which they gain in such small matters – and no hindrance unto the voyage) that when any friend doth come aboard to visit the master or any principal officer, [he] desireth a can of beer to bid him drink. Which hath been here strictly denied, in such sort men a-dying could not get no beer at the first sending for and before the second return with beer hath been dead. And the sick entreating for beer aboard other ships, in [the] regard they [had] been denied it here, when can or bottle is supplied in the cabin without any allowance as though there were a spring or brewhouse in the ship's hold of new beer every day.

For the dispossessing of seamen which lay upon the upper deck out of their cabins for gentlemen to lie in, which is a thing most ridiculous and not fitting, in regard the sailors are the safeguard of the ship's managing and by all reason ought to lie ready at hand for the handling of the sails and to manage her in the sea.

Upon every least offence of any sailor that hath been committed, he hath been and is sure for to receive severe punishment, according to his desert; yet there is in the habit of gentlemen which hath presumed to quarrel and strike in the ship and to draw swords to maintain private quarrels, for which there hath been no redress nor order taken for any punishment for the offenders.

Whereas it was rumoured voluntarily by the company of the *Little Neptune* and *Warwick* unto our company of the *Hector* that they had taken certain canvas and was part thereof divided amongst their men seven yards apiece, and [they] saying that every one of our company might have as much if they would call for it and knew no reason to the contrary − being that we were all of the earl's fleet and our shares did lie therein − every one desiring the like proportion and none dared to speak unto your worship. [They] entreated the master to move it unto you. Which motion and information you hearkened unto and openly spoke it to all the company, if it were so and that there was canvas sufficient aboard the *Neptune*, they all should have the like. Whereupon the master was sent aboard to know the truth thereof and returned answer, there was canvas three or four bales; but of this nothing performed according to promise.

And whereas at our coming to the island of Flores we had divers sick men and diseased, whereof some of the scurvy, it was spoken by your worship we should have plentiful relief and fresh provisions for them from the shore as indeed of all Christianity there ought to have been done for the preservation of men's lives into whose hands they committed themselves. We lay buzzing about the island six or seven days and nothing to be done nor no order taken, while it was too late, and then a flashing bravado seeming wise to have it by the way of policy and treachery. But in fine, nothing at all [was] performed, without the purser would indent for it; and so, in conclusion, nothing was done neither by you nor him, but only the company themselves were forced to truck and barter away such apparel and commodities as they had for their own relief. Otherwise, they should have had no refreshing, by which means, God be praised, they are reasonably well recovered.

At the island of Flores where we watered, and having received aboard sufficient for our provisions as much as was needful and desired, yet nevertheless you gave great charge and straight command that no man whatsoever should presume to take any fresh water so much as to wash a shirt, upon pain of severe punishment, when poor men had laboured and taken great pains for the same and approved by the surgeon to be a great preservation of men's healths, to have their linen washed in fresh water to keep themselves sweet and clean against infection of sickness. For what both breedeth sickness, diseases, and the scurvy amongst men but only nastiness and filthiness in wearing and lying in their clothes, as we have seen and find by daily experience?

We humbly entreat your worship that you would be pleased to answer these our grievances and then to set down your own, whereby we may clear ourselves of the railing imputation and public disgrace laid upon us by your parson before the whole fleet by way of a sermon in our presence, and not to let us be accounted in your eyes as rascals and base fellows, nor in the eyes of the rest of the fleet as infidels, not knowing any reason to bind us to endure these grievances under you but our own voluntary dispositions, bent rather to obey than displease. So for brevity's sake, we omit many till another time, and so for the present take our leave, desiring God to send your worship health and quietness, with our own, to the end of the voyage and ever after.

These grievances, according as any was touched, presented them in writing and were copied out to be presented unto Sir Francis Stewart, our captain, as appeareth affirmed under thirty of the principal chief officers' and men's hands that served on the voyage in the *Hector*.

Here followeth the orders to be observed:

Laws and orders set down and established by me, Robert Earl of Warwick, by virtue of his majesty's commission under the Broad Seal of England made admiral of this fleet, by God's grace bound to the southward, to be daily observed of every captain, master, chief officer, and others in the said fleet, as they will answer the contrary at their perils, this thirteenth of April, Anno Domini *1627*:

1 First, because no action or enterprise can prosper, be it by land or sea, without the favour or assistance of almighty God, you shall not fail to cause divine service to be read in your ship morning and evening, praising God every night with the singing of a psalm [and] a prayer at the setting of the watch;

2   Secondly, you shall take special care that God be not blasphemed in your ship, but that after admonition given, if the offenders do not reform themselves, you shall cause them all to be punished with such punishments as you, in your judgements, shall think meet and convenient;

3   Thirdly, no man shall refuse to obey his officer in all that he is commanded for the benefit of the journey; no man, being in health, refuse to watch his turn, as he shall be directed by the captain, master, and other officers;

4   You shall take care that the quarter-masters every night do search between the decks that no fire or candle light be carried about the ship after the watch be set, nor that any candle be burning in any cabin, and that no man shall take tobacco between the decks, and therefore forbidden to all men but aloft upon the upper deck, where tubs shall be set with water to receive the ashes, where all men shall empty their pipes, as they will answer the contrary;

5   You shall cause all your landmen to learn all the names and places of the ropes, that they may assist the sailors in all their labour upon the decks, though they cannot go up to top and yard;

6   You shall train and instruct your sailors to handle their arms, so many as shall be found fit, as you do your landmen, making no difference of professions, but that all be esteemed sailors and all soldiers;

7   If you fetch up any ship belonging to any prince or state in league or amity with his majesty, you shall not take anything from them by perforce, upon pain to be punished as pirates, although in manifest extremity or want, you may agree for the price and relieve yourselves with things necessary, giving bond for the same, provided that it be not to the disfurnishing of any ship, whereby the owners or merchants be endangered for the ship and goods;

8   You shall every night fall astern your admiral and follow his light, receiving instructions in the evening what course to hold, and if you shall at any time be separated by foul weather, you shall receive certain billets sealed up to be opened in the height of the North Cape;

9   If you happen to lose our company and find us again, your token shall be to hoist and strike your main topsail twice; if it be foul weather, then to hoist and strike your mizzen twice; our answer shall be to strike and hoist ours once; and so to come in company again;

10   If we happen to meet any fleet of ships likely to be the King of Spain's army, every one of you shall forthwith repair unto me your admiral, to take my directions upon pain of death;

(*This article was broken in the highest degree aboard the* Hector, *wilfully and presumptuously*.)

11   If the admiral at any time by chase or otherwise do lose company, then all the fleet to follow the vice-admiral; if the vice-admiral be absent, then to follow the rear-admiral, until my return, except special order to the contrary;

12   No person whatsoever shall depart out of any ship where he is first placed without special order, and that no captain or master receive any such person without the consent of me, the admiral;

13   Every of you shall, with all diligent care and possible means, follow me, your admiral, as well by night as by day, and that no ship or pinnace, either by wilfullness or negligence, presume to lose my company except it be proved they were severed by extremity or otherwise receiving order by me, upon pain of death. And if it shall happen any of our said ships in such sort to be severed unwillingly, that then you shape your course presently according to such private instructions as you shall receive sealed up;

14   If you discover a fleet of ships, you shall not only strike your maintopsail often, but put out your ensign in the main top; and if such fleet go large before the wind, you shall also, after you have given notice, go large and stand as they do, I mean no longer than that you may judge the admiral and the rest have seen your signs and your so standing − and if you went large at the time of the discovery, you shall hale aft your sheets for a little time and then to go large again − that the rest may know that you go large to show us that the fleet discovered keep that course. So shall you do if the fleet discovered have their tacks aboard at the time of the discovery, you shall bear up for a little time, and afterward hale your sheets again to show us what course a fleet holds;

15   If you discover any fleet or ship by night, if the fleet or ship be to windward of you and you to windward of the admiral, you shall presently bear up to give us knowledge. And if you think that did you not bear up, you might speak with her, then you shall keep your luff and shoot off a piece of ordnance to give us knowledge thereof;

16   For a general rule, let no man presume to shoot off any piece of ordnance but in discovering of a ship or fleet by night, or being in danger

of the enemy, or in danger of fire, or in danger of sinking, that it may be unto us all a most certain intelligence of some matter of importance, and that you shall make us know by this the difference. If you give chase and, being near a ship, you shoot to make her strike, we shall all see and know that you shoot to that end if it be day. If by night, we shall then know that you have seen a ship or fleet, none of our own. And if you suspect that we do not hear the first piece, then you may shoot a second, but not otherwise; and you must take almost a quarter of an hour between your two pieces. If you be in present danger of a leak, you shall shoot off two pieces, one after the other; and if in danger of fire, three pieces presently one after another. But if there be time between, we will know by your second that you doubt we did not hear your first and therefore you shoot a second, to wit by night and to give time between;

17   There is no man shall dare to strike an officer be he captain, lieutenant, master, sergeant, corporal, master's mate, boatswain, quartermaster, or any other officer. I say no man shall strike or offer any violence to any of these, but the supreme officer to the inferior in time of service, upon pain of death;

18   No private man shall strike one another upon pain of receiving such punishment as a martial court shall think him worthy of;

19   If any man steal any victuals, either by breaking into the hold or otherwise, he shall receive the punishment of a thief, and the murderer of his fellows;

20   No man shall keep any feasting or drinking between meals, or drink any health upon the ship's provisions;

21   Every captain, by his purser, steward, and other officer, shall take a weekly account how the victuals waste;

22   The steward shall not deliver any candle to any private man, nor for any private use;

23   Whosoever shall steal from his fellows either apparel or any thing else, he shall be punished as a thief;

24   In foul weather, every man shall fit his sails to keep company with the rest of the fleet, and not to run so far ahead by the day but that he may fall astern the admiral before night. And further you shall give special charge and be careful that your topmasts be favoured and the head of your masts by a wind or in a head sea, which otherwise might endanger the service;

25   If in case we shall be set upon at sea, the captain shall appoint sufficient company to assist the gunners, after which, if the fight require it, the cabins between the decks shall be taken down, all beds and sacks employed for bulwarks. The musketeers of every ship shall be divided under captains to other officers, some for the forecastle, others for the waist, and others for the poop where they shall abide, if they be not otherwise provided;

26   The gunners shall not shoot any great ordnance at other distance than point blank;

27   An officer or two shall be appointed to take care that no loose powder be carried between the decks, nor near any linstock or match in hand. You shall saw divers hogsheads in two parts and filling them with water and set them aloft upon the deck; the carpenters [shall set] some of them in hold, and the rest between decks, if any shot should happen to come in either of these places;

28   The master and boatswain shall appoint a certain number of sailors to every sail, and to every such company a master's mate or a quarter-master. So, as when every man knoweth his charge and his place, things may be done without noise or confusion, and no man to speak but the officers. As for example, if the master bid heave out the maintopsail, the master's mate, boatswain's mate, or quarter-master which hath charge of that sail shall with his company perform it without calling to others and without rumour. And so for the rest. The boatswain himself taking no particular charge of any sail but seeing every man to do his duty;

29   Every ship, if he be under the lee of an enemy, shall labour to recover the wind if the admiral endeavour it, using their best means according unto this article, more at large expressed;

30   The musketeers divided into the quarters of the ship shall not deliver their shot but at such distance as their commander shall direct them for to do;

31   If the admiral give chase and be the headmost ship, the next ship shall take up his boat, if other order be not given, or if any other ship be appointed to give chase, the next ship — if a chasing ship have a boat at the stern — shall take her up;

32   You shall take especial care for the keeping of your ship clean between the decks, to have your ordnance in order, and not cloyed with trunks and chests to hinder any service;

33   Let those that have provision of victuals, deliver it to the steward;

34   Everyone that doth use any weapon of fire, be it musket or other piece, shall keep it clean. And if he be not able to mend it, he shall presently acquaint his officer therewith, who shall command the armourer to amend the same;

35   No man shall play at cards or dice, either for his apparel or arms, upon pain of being disarmed and made a swabber;

36   Whosoever shall show himself a coward in service, he shall be disarmed and made a shifter of victuals for the rest;

37   No man shall land any men in any foreign parts without order from the general or principal officer upon pain of death;

38   And wheresoever we shall find to land, no man shall force any woman, be she Christian or heathen, upon pain of death;

39   You shall take especial care when you land anywhere, not to eat of any fruit unknown, which fruit you do not find eaten with birds on the tree or beasts under the tree;

40   You shall avoid sleeping on the ground and eating of new fish till it be salted two or three hours, which otherwise will breed a most dangerous flux;

41   When I the admiral shall happen or do intend to cast about in the night, you shall see two lights standing one over the other a man's height aboard my ship. Then every [one] of you shall prepare yourselves to make after me, with all diligent speed as you will answer to the contrary;

42   If I chance to take in all my sails and lay it a-hull, I will show three lights, which every ship shall answer to the like;

43   And for the lengthening of our voyage, it is required, according to ancient custom of men-of-war, to sit five men to four men's allowance of victuals and not to alter the same without a general consent;

44   That in thick weather, all ships do keep about me the admiral as near as conveniently they may, as they will answer to the contrary. (*But of this article was breach made in the highest degree by wilfull stubbornness.*)

To destroy and burn all these orders if occasion require, if we be set upon by the Spanish armada.

For other orders, we will establish them as occasion shall arise, by general consent. In the meanwhile, I shall value every man according to his deserts, and so God send us a prosperous voyage, amen.

Finis.

A TRUE RELATION OF MY LORD OF WARWICK'S PASSAGE
THROUGH THE SPANISH ARMADA,
single in his own Ship near the Rock, the 2nd July, 1627

Upon Sunday, being the first of July, towards night there came a Sallee captain (renegade Portingale) that had been in my company some three days before, from whom I redeemed two English captives [and] who told me he had descried the Brazil fleet to the southward and that they could hardly weather Cape Espichel [MS: Pitcher], the wind being northerly. Whereupon I gave order to set sail, having been all that day becalmed, being west south-west of the Rock about seven leagues. And in the morning I got the entrance of the river of Lisbon by the dawning of the day; and at sun rising, perceiving they were not come into Cascais, we cast about and stood off right to sea (in the way which they should come in). And having stood so three hours, I willed the Turk [a companion ship of Warwick's fleet] to run ahead, having an excellent sailing ship, to see if he could descry them, it being very foggy. Only sometimes it did clear, and sometimes a fog again. After some three glasses, the Turk returned and told me they were hard by, standing in to the shore, some thirty sail of them. So I cast about after them, my vice-admiral and rear-admiral keeping the wind of me some two or three leagues, [and] I supposing that when they heard my ordnance, they would have come room unto me.

For in less time than half an hour I fell near the admiral of the galleons and four other great galleons of his fleet, who, I suppose, took me for one of his fleet in the mist. I bore up within half musket shot of them, the admiral having his mainsail brailed up. Which as soon as I had made him, I cast about again from them, to keep our wind. Presently two of them tacked about after us. We were no sooner about, but we espied one of their pinnaces right ahead of us, so we bore up upon him and did all that ever we could to have overrun him, but he escaped us very narrowly, close under our lee, where we paid him soundly with our great ordnance and small shot, which did so amaze him [that] he knew not which way to go. At this instant also three other galleons were close on the weather of me, which I likewise saluted with my whole broadside and small shot as they passed by me, who presently cast about after me.

The vice-admiral, with his squadron being six ships, whereof one was the *George* (an English ship which was one Mallby's), of six hundred tons, gave me chase also. So I commanded all things to be readily prepared for their entertainment. And the first that came up close to me I saluted with a whole broadside, and [we] so plied him that it pleased God we shot down his maintop sail and did so tear him that he durst stay no longer by us, but bore up under our stern and lay by the lee, and we saw him no more. A second came [MS: came came] up close with us and, after an exchange of two or three broadsides, he tacked about, with an intent (as we suppose) to have given us his other broadside. But it pleased God we lighted so right on him with our double and crossbar shot out of our great ordnance, which did so tear him that he also left us and was glad to be gone.

When I did see myself so far engaged, and that some of them had gotten the wind of me, I resolved that we must [sail] through them, and it pleased God so to order it for us [that] the mist sometimes thickened that all the fleet could not see us that were to leeward of us but followed by the sound of ordnance.

A third man came up to us, the bravest and valiantest captain of the whole fleet, and never discharged a piece until he came within less than pistol shot, with an intent to board us, whom we likewise welcomed with the best we had, which we were not sparing of but we sent it him freely. Our case shot took such effect, that at our discharge of a great brass port piece that lay upon our half deck, there was a grievous cry amongst them, '*O vale me Deus*'. Whereat they fell off and lay by the lee, some of our shot having lighted upon him between wind and water, for some of my men said that they discerned she was sunk a yard deeper.

The vice-admiral came up in the weather of us, the mist being now cleared, and five galleons more with him. We stood on still with a boat to our stern, our flag and bloody colours flying. But he was not so good a soldier as he had a ship, which had forty good piece of brass, which our Portingale prisoners told us. For when he came right in the wind of us, he luffed [MS: loft] up in the wind to make shot at us afar off, which we answered again, and so was still now and then in the wind, by which occasion he fell astern when he might have borne up on us, by which means we got ahead and so went through the fleet. Still, he with five more gave me chase, but after some three hours two of them cast about (as we conceive) spying Sir Francis Stewart who was all this time to windward of us. How they [in the *Hector*] speed I do not yet know, but hope well, he being so far to windward and the mist so great as we could not see him. Still the vice-admiral and two others continued following us. Two of them kept somewhat near us on our weather quarter, beating upon us with their great ordnance and we at them, but durst not come within musket shot of us, it growing late and the *Jonathan* being come into our company. So at night when it grew dark, their vice-admiral shot off a piece and drew them off, which we answered with another, and I think they were not sorry, for they durst not come near us although they went far better than we.

All our men behaved themselves passing well, and showed themselves to be right Englishmen. In this fight we lost but three men killed with great shot outright and some twenty more hurt, whereof half of them were hurt by a horn of powder and three or four cartridges that took fire in our own ship by negligence of a match. We received shot from them sans number, but − God be thanked − none low under water or otherwise dangerous saving one through our boltsprit.

Then we shaped our course for the western islands and after six days had sight of St Michael's and St Mary's. We lay long becalmed under the east end of St Michael's, being a continual fog, where our men fell down very fast of the scurvy and calenture, so that Captain Mountague, my rear-admiral (who was only with me now), came aboard my ship with a great complaint that of six score and five men, he had one hundred of them fallen down and in great extremity, besides those that he had heaved dead overboard, so as that he had but nine men on a watch.

Whereupon we considered, to send her away were to hazard her and so many men's lives, and having many sick in my ship also, and the wind contrary, water failing us, and we not knowing how long we might be a-getting the Flores and Corvo whither we intended to go and had none of my small ships and pinnaces with me, being half my fleet or number, whose stays was the overthrow of my best designs both by sea and land. Upon these considerations, it was thought fit by a general consent of both our ships' companies to bear up for our own coast to refresh our men and repair our defects, which accordingly we did, with resolution to hasten away again.

Notes

1   Both of these expeditions have been chronicled and published by the Camden Society: John Bruce (ed.), *Journal of a Voyage into the Mediterranean, by Sir Kenelm Digby, AD 1628,* Camden Society, Vol. 96 (1868), and Alexander B. Grosart (ed.), *The Voyage to Cadiz in 1625: being a Journal Written by John Glanville*, Camden Society, New Series, Vol. 32 (1883).

2   P.R.O. SP 16/79 No. 17. Although this document is not dated, it has been bound with documents dated 22 September 1627 and is calendared under that date. Since Ball could not have written *Might and Would Not* before November at the earliest, this document is plainly misdated. Still, it is reasonable to assume that it was written shortly after Ball's manuscript, indicating clearly that the government had early access to his work.

3   26? July, 1627, Sir James Bagg to Edward Nicholas; P.R.O. SP 16/72 No. 9.

4   ibid.

5   *Miscellany of the Abbotsford Club*, Vol. I (Edinburgh, 1837), pp. 189–94.

3

The Management of the Royal Dockyards, 1672–1678

Edited by
R. V. SAVILLE

Introduction

During the seven years from 1672 to 1678 the English Navy saw action in the third Dutch war from March 1672 to February 1673/4,[1] in the shortlived conflict with the French from December 1677 to July 1678, and in the Mediterranean, notably against Algiers and Tripoli.[2] Naval units were also involved in a variety of actions including operations against pirates in the Caribbean, support for land forces involved in the suppression of Bacon's rebellion in Virginia, attempts to curtail the illegal export of raw wool from England, support for fishermen at Newfoundland against French harassment and the general enforcement of the Navigation system. The formal naval strength from first to sixth rates at the end of 1672 consisted of 95 ships of 55,711 tons; these included six first rates, nine second rates and nineteen third rates.[3] The two first rates, four third rates and nine ships of the smaller rates that were added to the fleet between 1673 and 1676 were barely enough to keep pace with losses; though the huge building programme that was commenced after the passing of the Thirty Ships Act of 1677 (29 Car. II c. 1) added over 34,000 tons, mainly in the form of second and third rate vessels. Repairs and maintenance to the ships, and most of the new building work, were carried out at Chatham, Portsmouth, Woolwich, Deptford and Sheerness. Stores were kept at several ports including Yarmouth (Norfolk), Harwich and Plymouth, and at Kinsale and Dublin in Ireland.[4] We are fortunate in that a considerable volume of the correspondence which related to the

dockyard and supply work has survived and this covers the entire range
of the organisation. After 1672 it gives us information on a day-to-day
basis.[5]

By the 1670s the naval bureaucracy was a well oiled organisation by
the standards of the time and, though there remained considerable scope
for improvement, a major part of the work of the Board and the dockyard
managements could be described as routine [Documents 4, 5]. Therefore
it has been decided to focus here on those aspects of their work which
they and the Admiralty perceived to be in need of attention. Among such
issues were problems of labour relations, attempts to improve productivity,
conflict with the accumulated customs of the yard workmen and officials,
and the difficulties with local credit and supply of stores and finance to
the yards.

These questions loomed large in the correspondence that was exchanged
in the years covered here, and the officials were only too conscious of
the limits of their effectiveness in enforcing improvements. Their work
was seriously hindered by the difficulty of obtaining adequate funding
for dockyard work, a problem that became aggravated during the second
Dutch war by the periodic upturn in work associated with building ships.
This was especially evident during the wartime peaks of activity in 1672–4
and 1677–8, and it was complicated by the general problems of credit
resulting from the Stop of the Exchequer of January 1671/2.[6] The
relative ineffectiveness of officials in improving the work of the dockyards
in the years covered here stems in part from these financial problems. We
should be aware, however, of the tenacity of attitudes to work practices
on the part of the various yard trades, and the widespread support for
such long-established yard customs as the receipt of timber chips. For both
these general areas, finance and customs, the correspondence provides
abundant material.

The periodic ebb and flow in dockyard activity may be measured from
the lists of employment and from the payments made to the workforce
and suppliers of materials.[7] In the last three months of 1671 the main
Thames and Medway yards, Chatham, Woolwich and Deptford, employed
1,613 workmen and owed £8,931; a year later the pressure of wartime had
seen the number employed rise to 2,293, whilst debts rose to £12,172 for
that quarter. Numbers and expenditure rose again in 1673. From the spring
of 1674 the policy of retrenchment more than halved the workforce in
these yards, such that by the Michaelmas quarter only 903 workmen
remained on the books and employment remained below a thousand for
the subsequent three years. The pattern of expansion in 1672 and 1673,
followed by decline in 1674, was paralleled at Portsmouth and Sheerness,
though the latter was only a minor employer. The upturn in work in the
summer of 1677, due to preparations for war and to the Act authorising
thirty new ships to be completed within two years of 24 June 1678, saw

a further expansion of dockyard work at the close of the period covered here.

Payments to workmen were drawn up on the basis of regular musters taken by the Clerks of the Cheque or their servants, and the basic daily pay was enhanced by overtime and additional payments.[8] At the end of each quarter the books were forwarded to London, and at least three months would elapse before payment was made. This meant that workmen were expected to rely on their own savings or the credit of family and landladies to support them when they started work at the yards, though pressed workmen and other special categories received board wages and lodging money at various times. In practice the pay that was due usually accumulated until several quarters were owing, and the situation of these arrears deteriorated rapidly after the start of 1666. From the last two quarters of that year, for example, the sums due to the workmen at Chatham yard were not paid until the end of 1671, and in point of fact all the yards had to wait four years for some quarterly payments owing from the second Dutch war. It is apparent that the pattern of payments was inconsistent both between quarters and between yards. Deptford and Woolwich received prompt payment for the last quarter of 1666 in June 1667, but they had to wait until October 1671 for the previous quarter due whilst Portsmouth had both these quarters cleared by December 1669. By 1673 payments were running roughly one year in arrears, and there was only slight improvement in the peace years down to 1676.

As has been noted above, the dockyard arrears which remained from the second Dutch war were only a part of a wider, chronic, government credit and payments situation that was to affect Navy Board dealings with both workmen and suppliers throughout the subsequent decade, which were worsened by the Stop of the Exchequer which took place immediately before the letters here to be examined commence. The local management of the yards had great difficulty in obtaining supplies on credit and had particular problems in persuading merchants and landowners to part with timber [20, 33]. A standard promise of a part cash payment with the rest to follow 'in course' proved insufficient on several occasions.[9] The artisans who worked in the dockyards were in a similarly difficult situation, and so too were the private shipbuilders who built ships on contract [10, 15, 19].[10]

The credit limits that were applied to workmen forced many of them to sell their old quarters' claims for ready cash in the early 1670s. This particularly applied to credits due from work done during the second Dutch war. A number of employees, including the pressed men, found local credit expensive or non-existent, and left the yards to return home when their lodging money and board wages were not forthcoming [24, 59]. The pressures that were caused by the shortage of ready money help to explain the reluctance of men to enter yards away from their home areas [16,

59, 67]. There was a varied response from the workmen, which included petitions, threats of violence, and occasional strikes [20, 29, 70].

At times the workmen were so severely affected by shortages of pay and credit [1, 25] that many had little choice but to work part of the week elsewhere, and on occasion they reported for duty to the yard musters and then departed [12, 60]. For those like 'one of the best workmen of the joiners' at Chatham, 'grown stark mad to see the necessity himself and family were necessitated to', it must have been a grim life, which was made worse by the spread of diarrhoea and malaria from 1676 to 1680 [61].[11] One response was to grant liberal allowances in the form of 'nights' and 'tides' for difficult work, as this would have increased the credit of the men involved.

The management problem at Portsmouth and Chatham was aggravated by their distance from London, and at the latter yard by the unique strength of the Pett shipbuilding family.[12] Phineas Pett, the Master Shipwright, enjoyed widespread support from the workforce and regarded himself as the foremost official at the yard. He clashed with John Cox, appointed Commissioner in March 1669 (who was killed at Sole Bay on 28 May 1672) and also with his successor Colonel Thomas Middleton, who died in December 1672. Rear-Admiral Richard Beach, a royalist and tough disciplinarian, then took over. Within a few weeks he had taken up the cudgels in a seven-year struggle with Pett [3, 8, 9, 13] and the letters which this conflict generated are a remarkable record of the problems and customs of the Chatham yard. Except in emergencies, such as that of the time of the Popish Plot [72, 73], Beach lacked sufficient authority over the work of the yard; in all routine matters other yard officers could appeal to the Navy Board to arbitrate on decisions. Moreover, both Phineas Pett and Edward Gregory, Clerk of the Cheque, were held in respect by the Board and the Admiralty, and many of the arguments dragged on for several years. Pett and Gregory took a more sympathetic view of yard customs and payments for overtime and difficult work than did Beach who, although concerned over the effect of arrears on workmen, took a decidedly less lenient view on other managerial issues.

It is difficult at a distance of three centuries to appreciate the depth of feeling on many dockyard customs, whether it was opposition to the marriage of apprentices, the insistence on keeping one's own tools, or the right of shipwrights to keep discarded wood chips from timber which they had worked on. Managerial attempts to regulate and restrain existing customs generated the most serious disputes in the four years of peacetime after the end of the second Dutch war. After considerable discussion [13, 17] the Admiralty issued an order on 9 November 1674 banning the custom of taking home wood chips. There was an immediate slowdown in work in all yards; within a few weeks most yard officers expressed the opinion that the move had been a serious error, and further representations followed. The attempt to raise cash by official sales of the chips was a failure, possibly because of resentment against such sales by the workmen, and a modification of the original order was made in February 1674/5 [**43, 44, 45**]. The refusal of the workmen to comply with the spirit of the order led to its withdrawal in the summer of 1677 [**58**], along with an order which had attempted, and failed, to increase the time allotted to tide work, from 1½ hours to 2 hours. Attempts to force men to work during their traditional holidays in peacetime were usually unsuccessful [**21, 22, 35**].

The Navy Board had some success, albeit a modest one, with minor reforms of the work of the three ropeworks, initially in 1672, when the ropespinners were put on a specified productivity of 17 ordinary ropes per day [**2**]. In 1673 the Board carried out a time and motion study for the spinning of cables and other ropeyard work;[13] there was indeed little doubt that more work could be performed in the ropeworks by the workmen, and Commissioner Anthony Deane suggested in 1674 that a day's work (i.e. 17 threads) could be done in five hours [**38**]. In May 1675 the Board, as part of their general policy of retrenchment, ordered that a day's work for spinners was henceforth to be 18 threads [**47, 49**]. The result was the sharpest industrial conflict in the yards in this period, during which the management threatened apprentices with the House of Correction, and all the ropeyard workmen with the loss of their back pay.

The Navy Board and local management had a complex legal framework to support them,[14] in particular the Act of 14 Car. II c. 20 (1662), by which the Navy could requisition carts and horses for transport of timber at rates fixed in the Act, and could require aid from Justices of the Peace and local Corporations [**6, 14, 63**]. This legislation was frequently invoked to speed up the passage of timber to the yards, though these requisitions were not always adequately supported at a local level [**64**].

There were several attempts made in these years to improve the quality of ships and materials. An effort was made with English sailcloth [**50, 51**], though the real breakthrough in quality came after 1690.[15] There was only an imperfect answer to the seaworm *Teredo navalis*. Ships were lined below water with boards nailed over a mixture of tar and hair, and covered on the outside by a mixture of brimstone, tar and oil. This had to be replaced frequently. In 1670 a group of projectors headed by Sir Philip Howard and Francis Watson, with Sir Robert Viner the banker as treasurer, obtained an Act of Parliament incorporating themselves as a company to manufacture sheet lead, with a twenty-five-year monopoly. Charles II ordered the Navy to place a ship at their disposal and the *Phoenix* was lead sheathed and sailed well for three years; by 1673 other ships were protected in like manner. From 1674, however, complaints were made about the effect of the lead on the rudder irons and nails [**48, 55, 65, 66**]; lead sheathing was carried out only intermittently thereafter and the experiment finally ended in 1682. These years witnessed unsuccessful attempts to install a dock-cleansing or dredging machine at Chatham to a design prepared by Sir Samuel Moreland, the failure of which may have been due to opposition from the workmen [42].

Most of the letters that appear below were written by the resident Commissioners and officials at the dockyards to the Navy Board in London, from where, if necessary, copies were forwarded to the Admiralty. In addition certain official orders and letters from other sources have been added where appropriate. As a general rule, spelling and punctuation have been modernised and some material in square brackets has been added for clarity. Thanks are due to Dr David Bland of Sheffield University for kindly commenting on this chapter, and to the Social Science Research Council for funding the work on which it is based.

THE MANAGEMENT OF THE ROYAL DOCKYARDS, 1672–1678
CORRESPONDENCE AND PAPERS

1 *Commissioner Thomas Middleton to Edward Gregory,*
the Clerk of the Cheque

Chatham,
12 September 1672

Whereas I am informed there are several shipwrights, caulkers, joiners and other workmen belonging to his Majesty's dockyard at Chatham which do frequently absent themselves from his Majesty's service without leave, or notice given to any of his Majesty's officers residing in his said yard, to the great hindrance and prejudice of his Majesty's service. These are therefore to pray and require you to cheque all such workmen which shall henceforth so desert the service without leave from myself or the Master Shipwright, for the first fault, two days, for the second four days, for the third six days, and if then they make not their appearance to make them Run[16] on your books . . .

2 *Middleton to John Owen, Clerk of the Ropeyard, and Robert Sliter,*
Master Ropemaker at Chatham

Chatham,
5 October 1672

Whereas it hath been observed that the ropemakers employed in his Majesty's ropeyard spinning their yarn by weight, without being limited to any certain length, do spin their threads bigger than they ought to be spun, or than is usual in merchants' yards, which may be of very ill consequence to his Majesty's service, for the prevention whereof for the future these are to will and require you that henceforth you enjoin those ropemakers under your charge that instead of the weight they have hitherto usually spun for a single day's work, they spin seventeen threads of ordinary yarn and sixteen threads of fine yarn the same length you usually warp your hales, which is about one hundred and seventy fathoms, from the second of February to the last of October both included, and fifteen threads and a half of ordinary yarn and fourteen and a half of fine yarn from the first of November to the first of February, both included, and so proportionately for a greater or lesser time than a single day. And if at any time you shall discover that they have spun short of that length, that then you cause them to spin so much more than the foresaid length as may make good all those threads the same length, as you shall find them to fall short, or else to prick[17] those men that shall refuse so to do, so much time as the said length you shall find them short, shall amount to, and if they shall notwithstanding persist in spinning their threads bigger than they ought to be, whereby their said day's work in length shall exceed the usual weight of a day's work, as they have hitherto spun, that then you cause them to spin so much more in length than their said day's work as may be proportionable to the excessive bigness and weight of their threads, or else to prick those men that shall refuse so to do, double the time that the said length shall amount to . . .

3   Commissioner Richard Beach to the Navy Board

Chatham,
15 February 1672/3

I did acquaint your Honours in mine of the 12th of a contest between the Master Shipwright[18] and myself about entering of men, who, in regard I had caused some house carpenters to be entered by my warrant (though he desired it before) threatened to turn them out of the yard and break their heads and will admit of none that shall be entered by my warrant and within these two days hath entered a considerable number of servants, as well as master workmen; the warrant which he acts by I am unacquainted with, and by the account that Mr Gregory gives me hath assumed this authority since the like difference happened betwixt Commissioner Cox and him (which your Honours may please to recollect). I say there are entered one hundred and sixty or seventy servants upon the list and divers of those that have servants by his favour are such as no merchantmen would entertain. I do assure your Honours I am not ambitious of trouble, but as it refers to his Majesty's service should omit nothing that may be advantageous thereunto. And further he will not have the Boatswain of the yard employ any labourers, but by his appointment, therefore many works must of necessity lie still that might be done, but if his power must thus be propagated I humbly conceive it is a diminution of your Honours' authority as well as mine and will be found in time to be an encouragement to him and others to go on in a contemptuous way against whatever the Commissioner upon the place shall determine. For if now I do see any negligent fellow that doth not perform his duty, as I daily see too many, I have no power to turn them out of their employments, so that by degrees his authority will be greater than the Commissioners' and indeed as he goes on is ahead . . .

4   Beach to the Navy Board

Chatham,
18 February 1672/3

Your Honours' letters of the 15th by an express have received and according to your directions therein shall govern myself, though I did desire nothing more than what you have generally agreed to, which was that I might have a sight of those people he entered that no more boys or decrepit persons might be entertained in the yard, the which the Shipwright refused and would enter whom he pleased, I have much to say but shall forbear till I have the honour to wait upon you.

I desire to know whether the Shipwright may build and rebuild without acquainting me therewith, therefore I humbly conceive when your Honours send any warrants to that purpose or for anything else to the officers here wherein I may be concerned, that you would please either to inclose them in my letter, or hint it to me, or else order them to acquaint me with it, it would be a means to avoid any future contest and that we set up our horses the quieter together for the future.

Yesterday we had a most extreme storm of wind the oldest man here never knew the like,[19] the *Charles*'s moorings gave way, so did the *St Michael*'s and *St George*'s but God be praised we got them off to their moorings again without any harm.

Several lighters and boats sunk which I hope to retrieve in a few days without any great damage, the *Henry*'s main top was blown off the head of the mast into the river, so in the dock the *St Andrew*'s spritsail top and spritsail yard was blown ashore, and the spindle of the weather cock over the gate blown off, and also great part of our houses and storehouses untiled, but God be praised that we escaped so well, pray God it be no worse in other places.

As soon as the men are entered and got their bounty money they are gone all to London we have had no assistance from any of them in the last storm.

We have had great want of oars in this extremity of weather, having been necessitated to make use of the officers' of the yard, therefore I humbly conceive that a certain store of oars might to remain here constantly for the use of the yard upon the like occasions.

Mr Chambers that contracted with the Surveyor for a quantity of reed, and received £20 imprest hath not sent in any yet. The purser of the *Old James* hath formerly contracted for a quantity of broom bavins and to be delivered in here, which he hath not performed, your Honours would do well to force him to comply with his contract in regard there is so little to be had and he can very suddenly furnish us.

This day I shall dispatch away the horseboat with those stores your Honours ordered to be sent up, which could not be done before by reason of foul weather.

Here enclosed [omitted] I send you copies of two contracts lately made for broom bavins, and also a letter from the Master of Attendants at Sheerness the consideration whereof I refer to your Honours.

Here is no tar in store for our use or the ropemakers, their being almost spent, the hemp also spends apace, here is neither oil, nor glue, and but little tallow, here will be wanting much old canvas for the covering of poops and cabins, as also oars of all sorts as the ships grow ready, and more especially barge oars, which I desire the Surveyor may supply us with, most of these stores, if your Honours please may be sent down in the horseboat.[20]

The major part of the money that was sent down is paid away therefore I desire your Honours would please to hasten hither a speedy supply as well for the satisfying what contracts I have made, lest my credit should suffer through the want thereof as for the contenting the volunteers, who are already very numerous here, and on Thursday next I intend to have them paid his Majesty's bounty . . .

5   Beach to the Navy Board

Chatham,
21 March 1672/3

. . . His Highness[21] being here this day hath been much importuned by the people of the yard to move for their salaries and board wages, which as soon as you can, I desire your Honours to take into consideration.

As soon as I see it convenient shall advise your Honours when it is fit to discharge any of the workmen here.

I am glad your Honours have taken into consideration the paying of the pilots here for the river of Medway. It will be a very great encouragement to them for the future.

As soon as the French shallop shall be launched and in a condition for the receiving of men, they shall be entered according to your order.

The first fair wind the *Prince, St Andrew, Henry, Triumph, St George,* and *Unicorn* will fall down.

This day we have launched the *St Michael,* and docked the *Victory;* tomorrow, God willing, we intend to launch the *French Ruby* and dock the *Montague;* Sunday we intend to launch the *Victory* and dock the *Revenge* with the *Montague,* and Monday next God willing we intend to dock the *Royal Sovereign* which is the last of the ships we have to dock.

The *St Michael* and *French Ruby* will suddenly fall down to Sheerness after the rest or at the first of the next spring all endeavours shall be used for a quick despatch of all things.

I suppose your Honours judge it fit as I give you an account of what ships are ready to fall down to Sheerness, that you would please to order them their provisions in time and that the officers of the Ordnance may do their parts for the speedy dispatch to hasten down their ordnance arms and ammunition.

6   William Collins, New Forest Purveyor to William Hewer, Navy Office Clerk

Portsmouth,
25 June 1673

These are to desire you to get an order for the pressing of carts[22] for the speeding of the timber into his Majesty's yard for here has been so much rain the forest ways are so bad that in summer the like has not been in an age and the harvest is coming on and without an order they will not come in notwithstanding I have paid them and promised to pay them for what they should carry. Since I have been with a Justice in the forest he tells me if the Commissioners send down a warrant to them they will order the carts of every Hundred to come in so that by this means his Majesty's service will be much furthered, pray fail not with all speed for the accomplishment of it . . .

7   *John Daniel, Storekeeper of Sheerness*[23] *to the Navy Board*

Sheerness,
5 July 1673

The experience I have had of late of his Majesty's damage by reason of the inconvenience I am under for want of stowage of provisions in safety here, puts me upon troubling your Honours at this time, that you will please to give order for some fit place to be appointed and built on shore, wherein all stores committed to my charge may be safely laid up and preserved. At present I am forced to divide them into two distinct places, keeping most of the outstores on shore at Sheerness and all instores on board the *White Fox*, and having no person appointed by your Honours to assist me in securing them while I am employed in the receipt or delivery of the one the other lies at the mercy of idle, pilfering persons (whereof here are many) which make it their business to steal and carry them away, besides the accidents of fire which we are in danger of, which, though I shall make it the chief of my care to prevent, yet, by the negligence of any on board the ship may too soon happen, to the great loss of his Majesty and the utter ruin of myself. According to my duty I have endeavoured to the utmost of my ability to be personally present at the receiving and issueing all stores, but I find the business to be too great for any one person to officiate singly of himself. Therefore have been forced to make use of one as an instrument who is at present with me, having great satisfaction in his ability and fidelity, I humbly desire your Honours will please to grant him the encouragement of 2s 1d per diem, upon the consideration of which he is willing to continue, and under which, by reason of the temper of the air and ill-accommodation the place affords, I doubt I shall not procure any to live here in such a capacity . . .

8   *The Navy Board to Edward Gregory, Clerk of the Cheque at Chatham*

14 July 1673

We are told by a late letter from Commissioner Beach that he hath found but little obedience from the officers of his Majesty's yard at Chatham to the orders of this Board, directing their attendance every morning upon the Commissioner, then upon the place, to acquaint him with what orders they had received from this Board, and to receive from him what directions he had to give them in relation to his Majesty's service, as also that yourself particularly hath in despite of him re-entered a boatwright whom he had not many days before discharged for misdemeanour, and that you have without his knowledge entered a clerk for the Master of Attendant which we are sorry to hear of.

We desire that you will forthwith let us know what you have to say touching these particulars, that we may be the better guided in our proceedings thereon . . .

9   Phineas Pett, Master Shipwright, Chatham, to the Navy Board

Chatham,
17 July 1673

I received your Honours' letters of the 14th and 15th instant and am most heartily sorry that your Honours should have further trouble given you, as touching any matter of complaints, knowing it to be very unpleasing to your Honours, relating to Commissioner Beach or myself, and do look upon it as my great unhappiness, that not only my life alone is made very uncomfortable with these proceedings of his, but also the rest of the officers by his strange kind of carriage to us all in general, not only to our faces but his continual threats and cursing of us behind our backs, and his much lessening of me in my command among the workmen, in his daily slighting of me, and his not only commanding those officers under me, but also the workmen of the yard to do what he pleaseth without taking the least notice of me, and his giving them what extra allowances he thinks fit for their work, and also his discharging of the ablest workmen in the yard, whom instead of such hard measure deserves better encouragement, when he pleaseth without my knowledge or any manner of cause. I do most humbly conceive that if this be permitted, which I in the least not doubt the justness of the Board in, there will be no need of a Master Shipwright, or I am sure he must stand but for a cypher, if not borne out in his command, and the King's service consequently much prejudiced thereby . . .

May it please your Honours having now given you a true account as near as I am able in this affair, do humbly acquaint you that rather than be thus continually obnoxious to such a man's tyrannical scourge and impositions having not formerly been accustomed to so wicked and a hellish living, I should desire to trust to God's providence in some other way, though my zeal to serve his Majesty would lead me to submit to anything reasonable for my own quiet, that I might have comfort for my said service and endeavour to sweeten my life, which I do hope I ought fairly to seek in the use of lawful means, and therefore do humbly refer myself and case to your Honours' favourable and just determinations, begging that you would please to find a way to allay and mitigate these extravagances, to put a stop to these growing evils, that more humanity and candour may sway us to a joint endeavour to do his Majesty's service, which is now much detrimented, if I can see anything, by these wretched unchristianlike proceedings . . .

10   *John Young, Surveyor of the new ship building at Bristol, to the Navy
Board*

Bristol,
23 July 1673

. . . these are humbly to give your Honours an account of his Majesty's ship
building by Mr Francis Bayley[24] near Bristol. Since the 12th instant that I
last gave your Honours' an account of her she hath had eight piece of fore
and aft knees to her gundeck beams and four breast hooks in the hold and
four transom knees . . . he hath not had any timber brought into his yard
since, we have now had ten days of dry weather and Mr Bayley is in hopes
in few days more that the ways will be hardened, so as that ploughs may drag
his timber and plank. His workmen half of them or more hath left him and
will not work above one month for him without their wages, neither will the
timber merchants let him have one foot of timber without ready money laid
down before it is moved from the place, the ploughs will not haul for him in
the country under seven shillings per ton for one mile. And as yet from the
waterside, being more than one mile they will not haul at all, and for that
which they do haul they will be paid every night, Mr Bayley being now short
of money to supply his workmen and other persons concerned, he is at a great
stand with his Majesty's ship . . .

11   *Admiralty Order to the Master Shipwright and the Clerks of the Cheque,
Stores and Survey at Chatham*[25]

Derby House,
23 August 1673

Whereas we understand that there is not such due care taken as there ought
to be upon the repairing of his Majesty's ships to prevent the wasting,
splitting in pieces of the timber and plank which is to be taken off from the
said ships, whereby some pieces which might be made fit for further service
are rendered altogether useless, which is directly contrary to the seventh
article of the Master Shipwright's duty and to the fifth article of the
Storekeeper's duty prescribed in the Lord High Admiral's instructions. We
do hereby strictly charge and require you and each of you according to the
respective duties of your places to take particular care upon the repair or
breaking up of any of his Majesty's ships that all possible circumspection and
industry be used in the taking off from the said ships every piece of timber
and plank without splitting or doing other injury to it, as also that you do not
permit or suffer any of the timber and plank taken off from any ship,
although the same be by you judged useless, to be cut out for firing or
removed from the place where it shall lie when taken off from the ship until
the same hath been viewed by the Commissioner upon the place, and he shall
have signified what part thereof he judges fit to be preserved for further
use, and what not, upon which, that which shall not be by him set apart for
further service and no other parcel may be employed according to former
custom . . .

12 *Phineas Pett, and Joseph Lawrence, Shipwright's Assistant, at Chatham, to the Navy Board*

Chatham,
26 August 1673

... That whereas your Honours are given to understand that the workmen here do frequently between the times of their musters absent themselves from their work in the yard, going out of it and coming into it by the Mast yard, we do assure your Honours we do not know of any such practice and have taken all the care imaginable to prevent it, not only by our often visiting that way ourselves, but also by our having given strict order and charge to the Porter of the yard[26] and to Christopher Bland, labourer, who was long since appointed to assist the Porter of the yard, for that very intent and purpose, for the preventing of those abuses to his Majesty, which if true we must needs own were insufferable, and also by our having given strict charge to the Master Mastmaker and his foreman for the detection of any such persons.

As to the latter part of your letter wherein your Honours are given to understand that there is not such due care taken, as there ought in the ripping up of old ships in order to their repair, to prevent waste and spoil in the timber and plank taken off from the said ships. We do assure your Honours of your being also very much misinformed as to that particular, we having been so careful in the preventing of any such like abuses to his Majesty that we have not, while ships have been ripping up, suffered any workmen whatsoever belonging to the yard, to carry out any old wood out of the gate, but have only allowed of the carrying of new lawful chips which have fell from the axe. And particularly gave strict order and suffered the carrying out of no old wood nor chips but what was new and such as fell from the axe, ever since we began to rip the *Revenge* and long before.

Therefore do assure your Honours of our being much injured by those false informations, in which we hope you plainly discover more malice than truth, having not been wanting in our duties as to these particulars nor never shall, but shall by all that in us lieth endeavour to be found faithful in the performance of our trust whatsoever is committed to our charge ...

13 *Beach to the Navy Board*

Chatham,
30 August 1673

In answer to that part of your Honours' letter of the 26th wherein any of the officers of the yard have failed in their instructions: be pleased to take notice that I have often times desired the Shipwright and his Assistant to take more care to perform their duties at the gate and not to suffer unlawful chips to be carried out, but I have never yet seen the Shipwright there since my first coming down, and very seldom his Assistant, but they may carry but what they please (except myself or the Porter hinders them) contrary to the tenth article of their instructions.

Then whereas I have often desired them to take more care to keep the men to their works (especially the Shipwright's Assistant) and to order the Quartermen [27] to take more care of their particular duties, according to the sixth article: the Shipwright's Assistant hath given me for answer that the Quartermen would tell him they were afraid to speak to them for fear they should beat their brains out, and I do assure your Honours that let me press them to their duties as much as I can I see no amendment, and I dare avouch that there is not ordinarily done above half a day's work in a day, by the generality, which is occasioned by the neglect of the Shipwright and his Assistant in not chequing them for it.

And as to servants did your Honours know certainly what servants are entered here and how many, you would never allow it, for I am never acquainted with what are entered, nor how rated, that latitude being given to the Shipwright to enter and discharge whom he pleaseth. As your Honours may find by the enclosed list [omitted] of the names of such which have absented themselves so many days as is therein expressed, which I know not of until I demanded this account from the Clerk of the Cheque's instrument which I suppose according to the sixteenth article of the Clerk of the Cheque's instructions those that had not answered to the third call having stayed away so many days ought to be made Run.

Neither do they perform the contents of the ninth article to observe the time of the appearance or departure of the men to or from their works, and if it were not more for the Porter's care than either of them, they might come and go at their pleasures.

In the last pay of the yard of Christmas quarter 1672 there were no less than 228 servants and a great part of them boys borne and paid in that quarter and I do believe there is no less than 190 servants and a great part of them likewise boys which are still kept in the yard, and have as much and more per diem than the labourers of the yard have.

There are likewise servants allowed to young fellows, whereas other men that have wrought in the yard many years and have a great charge cannot have that favour.

As to the latter part of your Honours' letter wherein you desire to know whether I have been necessitated to give several orders for the taking off of the hands from the *Montague* for the building and repairing of boats: I do assure your Honours that I have by several orders, viz., of the 22nd of July, 16th, 17th, 18th, 19th and 24th August all which were chiefly to hasten the building and repairing of boats, and finishing of masts according to your Honours' several orders, which were never punctually complied with there being several of the boats still to finish and several a-building, they not employing above three hands upon divers boats at a time formerly and yet I know there shall not want some critical excuses for their non-obedience, but had they not kept the sawyers at work about sawing timber for the *Montague* as they constantly did, (notwithstanding my several orders) the boats might have been finished long since as the masts also . . .

I cannot omit giving your Honours an account of those watchmen belonging to the yard, they being labourers and allowed a watch, it being a long custom, they going from their works at four in the afternoon and come in again at eight in the morning, so that there is four hours in a day loss to the King, being hours of work, and have 12d per man a night watching.

I humbly conceive it is impossible for men, especially as most of them are ancient, to pay their due service to the King in the day and watch in the night, for I have found them very often negligent and although I have threatened them to turn them out, yet I find them neglect their duties to [*sic*] too often.

I dare not meddle with altering the watch without your Honours' order, but leave the consideration thereof to your Honours' better discretion, but am confident that watchmen are to be produced for the same or less monies and the four hours labour a day saved . . .

14   *John Tippetts, Surveyor of the Navy,*[28] *to the Navy Board*

Sheerness,
9 September 1673

His Majesty ought by Michaelmas next have been furnished with two most useful graving places at Sheerness, one for second rate, the other for third rate ships and downwards, but that yesterday the few teams we have some time had, gave off, pretending business of their own, I presume the Act for carriage was large enough to compel them to it, and do believe it may be done to their advantage, being well paid for the same as hitherto they have been, did they not discourage one the other, those who have wrought have seemed very well content with their allowance, I have calculated what is yet to be filled and find that twelve teams with 24 carts will complete it in thirty days.

I desire you will please to send your warrant to the Justices whose names are in the margin [Sir George Sands, Sir George Moore, Sir William Hubleson, Thomas Suthers Esq.] to divert their warrants to the four parishes in the Isle of Sheppey and if they judge meet, to the places adjacent for the speedy performance of this service, being of so great concernment to his Majesty that it be done before the days grow short . . .

15   *Beach to the Navy Board*

Chatham,
12 October 1673

. . . now I do find that all those that have timber to sell know there is a necessity for our having of it, and will sell it at their own rates, however, if I can get them to part with it upon reasonable terms to be paid in course allowing them one quarter or one fifth advance according to the value I shall use my endeavours.

But if your Honours would please to take it into consideration and furnish us with one thousand or fifteen hundred pounds to be ready here upon all occasions, I doubt not but to make as good bargains for timber as any man else that your Honours doth employ, without which your Honours can never expect this yard can be well provided (in regard timber is so scarce in these parts) . . .

16   Beach to the Navy Board

Chatham,
10 November 1673

These are to acquaint your Honours that we are very much necessitated for men for the carrying on of those great works which are expected which are impossible to be done without a considerable supply of men.

I have therefore sent a warrant to Milton and another to Faversham to the chief Magistrates and officers of each place, to warn in twenty able men from each place, which they may very well do and have men enough remaining to carry on their fishing trade,[29] but I do fear they will serve us as formerly they used to do and not appear, I do therefore humbly leave it to your Honours' considerations, whether it will not be requisite to acquaint the Lords Commissioners of the Admiralty with our great straits and that an order may be sent down to the Governor of Sheerness to stop all fishermen from going out of this river to fish which have not protections, until we are supplied, so that when we have a list of their names and the places where they live if they neglect their duties after their being warned in there must be a messenger sent down for them. And being to be paid weekly according to the usual allowances, I suppose it will be no burden to them.

Here enclosed [omitted] I send your Honours a list of those ships whose officers were absent from them last night: and indeed it is grown so accustomary with them − neglect of duty and carelessness − that they neither value the orders in their own instructions nor the orders nor warrants they receive from me or the Masters of Attendants, and particularly the Boatswains . . .

And I do assure your Honours that they are grown so expensive and wasteful of his Majesty's stores and provisions (especially of boats) that it is insufferable. I do humbly desire your Honours therefore to make an example of some of them that his Majesty's service hereafter may be better complied with both in action and good husbandry, otherwise it will be worse . . .

Understanding there is a quarter's pay will be ordered down very suddenly for the workmen of the yard, the which I do humbly conceive will be but a very small matter towards their relief many of them being not much concerned in it and those which are, being much more in debt than that amounts to, and are at present in a starving condition; some of them having not eat one bit of flesh in a month or six weeks time together. I therefore humbly desire your Honours if it be possible to procure them another quarter's pay to be sent down with it . . .

17   *Beach to the Navy Board*

Chatham,
18 November 1673

The last winter I did prohibit the bringing of chips on shore by an order affixed to the gate which was derived from the order your Honours gave me, yet notwithstanding they were connived at and did bring their boats full of chips ashore, upon which I caused twelve or fourteen of them to be discharged for their contempt, but they were re-entered again not known to me.[30]

And now as I have formerly advised your Honours I affixed another order to the same effect and sent an order on board every individual ship, to the officers there not to suffer any chips to be brought on shore, but they all came clamouring to me and tell me plainly they cannot live without their chips by which your Honours may see what a loss his Majesty hath been continually at by the loss of their time splitting out timber, plank and board, and splitting down cabins, etc., for the making of chips. Therefore in regard the Master Shipwright hath spoken to me in their behalfs I have thought fit to acquaint your Honours therewith that you may either allow or not allow it, and that your Honours would please to acquaint the Shipwright whether you will allow it or no, for let a Commissioner make all the orders and take all the care possibly he can yet if the Master Shipwright will not do the like it will signify but little . . .

18   *Phineas Pett, Master Shipwright's Assistant, Woolwich, to the Navy Board*[31]

Woolwich,
28 November 1673

I am forced to acquaint you of a great obstruction to his Majesty's service at Woolwich by bailiffs arresting the workmen in the yard. As for instance this week John Digby arrested by Edward Pattison a bailiff of Deptford, and Thomas Edwards arrested by Thomas Edlay a bailiff of Lewisham. I doubt not but your Honours will find out some expedient to make these bailiffs exemplary that it may be a prevention of the affrightment of others from his Majesty's works . . .

19   *Thomas Bowyer, Anchorsmith, Woolwich, to the Navy Board*

Woolwich,
7 December 1673

By reason of my great straits for want of provisions and money to pay servants' wages in order to the furnishing his Majesty's ships with such provisions of iron that the present occasion of his Majesty's service doth and may daily require, and which by the duty of my place I am obliged if possible to provide, I am constrained to acquaint your Honours with my present

condition, humbly entreating that upon your Honours' considerations that
there is £2,900 due to me you will be pleased to grant me your assistance in
the obtaining the same, £1,145 due in the years 1666 and 1667, £400 more
being about two years since postponed, and £1,360 in these three last quarters
in which sum is contained not only my own particular stock but also my
uttermost credit being thereby made incapable of carrying on his Majesty's
service without a speedy supply to oblige my creditors to further trust . . .[32]

20 *Petition from Portsmouth workmen, to the Right Honourable the*
Principal Officers and Commissioners of his Majesty's Navy

Portsmouth,
[c. 12 December 1673]

The humble petition of the workmen belonging to his Majesty's yard at
Portsmouth sheweth . . .

That your petitioners hath almost five quarters' pay due to them and that
they cannot be trusted any longer by reason that the people who given us trust
hitherto are become themselves unable to buy wherewith to furnish us, their
stock being already decayed, likewise his Majesty's taxes are now collecting
for his Majesty; your poor petitioners know not what shift in the world to
make that unavoidably your Petitioners' household goods must be seized and
taken from them . . . [33]

21 *Phineas Pett, Master Shipwright's Assistant, Woolwich,*
to the Navy Board

Woolwich,
24 December 1673

. . . Not having an answer of my letter yesterday to your Honours and not
knowing what haste the works of the ships in hand might require, I have taken
the course that all our men shall be at their several works on Friday
morning,[34] upon penalty of losing a month's pay in which I hope I shall have
your Honours' approbation . . .

22 *Phineas Pett, Master Shipwright's Assistant, Woolwich,*
to the Navy Board

Woolwich,
27 December 1673

Yesterday in the forenoon I came up having been down the river on board
the *Greenwich* and *Mary Rose* and found upon my return that not one man
was at work notwithstanding the strict injunction that was laid upon them
for working; some of them did appear at the yard but they had notice from
Deptford that the men did not work there, and that very few of the men being
here they went all away.

This morning in again there came about six or eight men but no work would go down with them in regard the rest of the men about the town could not be prevailed withall, and not one of the foreigners were returned, although considering the badness of the weather his Majesty is a gainer by their not working yet I humbly conceive it fit those men who were most positive in their resolutions not to work but did discourage others should meet with some reproof at some convenient time when haste of work is over.

I shall go to Deptford to make choice of three fit trees for the new ships' masts and then shall acquaint your Honours with what they say about the delivering us the East country plank ordered to this place . . .

23 Captain Philip Lanyon, Navy Agent at Plymouth,[35] to the Navy Board

Plymouth,
11 January 1673/4

. . . I perceive your Honours have ordered a supply of four hundred pounds to my nephew John Lanyon, which for the tradesmen's encouragement I have communicated to them, but I find their disbursements are so large that this supply will give them but small encouragement to proceed further in so much that I cannot prevail with them for the *Swan*'s cables, sails and officers' stores until your Honours are pleased to order a more ample supply, which in their behalf I humbly desire for the despatch of the *Swan*, which otherwise I cannot hope to accomplish which I humbly leave to your Honours' consideration.

I desired one of the shipwrights usually employed on his Majesty's ships in this port to supply the master of the merchant ship (who lent his boat to Captain Wright for the security of the *Nonsuch* frigate) with a new boat to the value of twelve pounds which he refused to do without ready money so the commander is still unsatisfied, the *Nonsuch* and *Dartmouth* being at sea . . .

24 Beach to the Navy Board

Chatham,
7 February 1673/4

I have not more to advise your Honours of than that this morning our late prest shipwrights demanded their board wages of the Clerk of the Cheque, who told them he did not expect it very suddenly and that as soon as it came they should be paid who replied they would not starve (having no credit here) and therefore are all gone away, and I fear a great part of our riggers will likewise be gone (if monies comes not in time) which is what offers at present . . .

25 Commissioner Anthony Deane, Portsmouth, to the Navy Board

Portsmouth,
8 February 1673/4

. . . The many ships which has come hither of late has exhausted the monies which should be applicable to these ships to come about, I therefore pray that we may have the two hundred and fifty pound promised last week that we supply ourselves to go on with the works in hand.

It's hard to be imagined how the hearts of our poor workmen are sunk for want of money to subsist this piercing weather, going out into the bay and afloat where the work lies is very tedious and were it not for the continual hopes I give them of the Board's promise of care for them as well as mine, I do think there would be little or no work done it does so disorder them, to be so much behind in their pay, and a quarter more than all the other yards, makes me pray they may be thought upon for some speedy relief.

It being the King's only advantage to have men kept obedient and strict to their commands in despatch of works which other ways goes so heavy and careless as not to stir when commanded, it troubles me to see of what ill effects it will produce, if some remedy be not speedily supplied which I heartily desire may be moved on their behalfs and they humbly beg it to be made equal at least with the rest of the yards if there can be no further relief . . .

26   *Phineas Pett, Master Shipwright's Assistant, Woolwich, to the Navy Board*

Woolwich,
16 February 1673/4

. . . The clock belonging to this yard being very aged and too small, and now the days begin to lengthen it will be a very great loss to his Majesty not to have a good going clock in this yard which when the sun does not shine is the guide of so many workmen in their coming to and going from their labour and we having an excellent bell placed in the new turret a good clock there also would be of good consequence to his Majesty's service . . .[36]

27   *John Corbet, Rector of Woolwich, to the Navy Board*

Woolwich,
23 February 1673/4

I am sorry that I should be forced to trouble your Honours as now I do. I know you have a multitude of important businesses, and may not be at leisure to hear every complaint. But on the other hands I am sensible that I have too long foreborne to acquaint you in whose power it is to regulate the grievous misdemeanours of several persons belonging to his Majesty's dockyard at Woolwich. So it is, and I am troubled to write it, that several carpenters' servants and others belonging to the said yard have several times openly affronted me their Minister in passing and repassing to and from the Church on the Sabbath day, and at other times in their coming from work, their way being through the Churchyard, they have disturbed the company, while I have been burying the dead by their noises and reproachful language, and so they did at another time when I was preaching a funeral sermon and several times they have grossly abused me as they passed by my house with the like noises, and opprobrious words. And if it happen that I have any occasion to pass the streets, while they are coming from or going to work they do the like incivilities so that it hath been taken notice of by strangers, ministers and others to be most shameful and unsufferable, to the dishonour of God and religion and to the great scandal of his Majesty's service that those who are employed in the King's work should be so disorderly and be suffered openly to affront the established orders of the church and ministry. I doubt not but your Honours in your wisdom will take some order for the redressing these things which will engage me to pray for your Honours' long and lasting felicity . . . [37]

28   Admiralty, General Order

Derby House,
25 February 1673/4

His Majesty having yesterday been pleased to declare the ratification of the Treaty of Peace made between himself and the States of the United Provinces, these are to pray and require you forthwith to consider of all ways and means of retrenching his Majesty's present charge in the Navy as well by the reducing of all those extraordinary occasions of expense which have arisen by the war, as by the endeavouring to do the like in reference to any other abatements of charge, his Majesty's service will admit of it in time of peace, which so soon and as often as you can offer us any reasonable propositions in, we shall desire and expect your doing the same in writing in order to our coming to such further determinations thereon as upon debate shall appear most conducing to his Majesty's service.

In the meantime it is our desire that you do immediately proceed towards this great and important work by the present retrenchment[38] of his Majesty's charge in the particulars followeth, viz., . . .

(2)   The cutting off all night and tide works in his Majesty's yard and all extraordinary proportions of working, particularly in the ropeyards . . .

(4)   The discharging as many of the workmen in his Majesty's yards as the service in time of peace may without prejudice admit of and shall be contented to be dismissed therefrom upon promise, which we do hereby authorise you to make them, of having their arrears of wages duly paid from quarter to quarter as the remainder of the workmen which shall be continued shall from time to time be paid . . .

29   Beach to the Navy Board

Chatham,
28 February 1673/4

I am necessitated to send this express to your Honours to advise you that if no speedy course be taken for the paying of soldiers and riggers we shall not dare to look out of our houses, they threatening already to pull down my house, and tear me to pieces if they have not their monies. I have used all the kind promises I can both to their officers and them giving them an assurance of the first monies that came down they should be paid, and as for the riggers there is not one of these which lives in these parts and if we should discharge them before we have money to pay them their landlords would lay them in gaol but they threaten so hard and are such robustrous fellows that we know not what may ensue if we discharge them before we have money to pay them, therefore I hope your Honours will take it into consideration that either out of the money in Mr Gregory's hands (or elsewhere) we may have a speedy supply and indeed I am sorry that they have so much reason to complain and that the world should take notice (as they do) what necessities you are driven to for so small a sum . . .

30   *Deane to the Navy Board*

Portsmouth,
28 February 1673/4

Upon the receipt of yours of the 26th I have inquired amongst the workmen of the yard who live at other places if they will go to their several homes, and of the promises the Lords gives the Board they should be paid their wages at the several payments those in the yard were, and I do not find one man will go without his wages or constraint, for they allege before they get home they shall be clapt in gaol and that they have not a penny in the world to help themselves or buy bread; except they receive it here and to be put off without their pay they are utterly ruined this is what they allege under great calamity and therefore humbly pray their pay after which they are content to be discharged if thought fit . . . [39]

31   *Phineas Pett, Master Shipwright at Chatham, to the Navy Board*

Chatham,
4 March 1673/4

Mr Gregory this day communicated to me a letter from your Honours relating to his giving you an estimate of the wages of several workmen, in order to their discharge out of his Majesty's works here, such as were last prest and have least money due to them. When I gave your Honours the late account of the several numbers of each calling fit to be continued (now in time of peace) for the carrying on of the present works (excepting the rebuilding of the *Old James*) upon consideration had of purging the yard of a great many idlers and insufficient persons that hath been sent hither out of several presses from the river of Thames, and some others here intending to keep none in his Majesty's works but them that were fitly qualified, did reduce the number as low as possible, this yard having already been too much a receptacle for some persons to be sheltered in, because of the names of townsmen. I humbly pray your Honours would be pleased that there may be regard had to the keeping in of able men, here being some among the latter entered men that having now fitted themselves with houses in town, would be willing to reside here, and others who have longer sheltered themselves, which would be much more for his Majesty's advantage to have them discharged. I speak not this out of any prejudice I have to the townsmen, judging it but very reasonable that they should be continued in the works before others, provided they are as fitly qualified for the doing of his Majesty's service . . .

32   Admiralty Memorial for the Lords of the Council[40]

Derby House,
18 March 1673/4

That for the speedier retrenchment of his Majesty's present growing charge in the Navy by improving to that purpose as may be the monies which shall be provided for the paying off of such of his Majesty's ships and workmen in his yards which by the determination of the late war are now to be discharged, it may be ordered . . .

(3)   At the paying of the quarter's wages now to be satisfied to the several yards, to cause the numbers of the workmen therein respectively to be retrenched according to the report of the officers of the Navy to the Lords of the Admiralty bearing date the 6th instant, giving to those who are so to be discharged an assurance from his Majesty of their being paid their arrears quarterly in the same course and measure as the workmen to be continued in the yards shall be paid, with liberty in the mean time to be borne on the yard books or discharged by list, payable in the manner aforesaid, as the party concerned therein shall for their particular convenience desire, care also being taken that such workmen belonging to Portsmouth hereby to be discharged as are concerned in that one quarter wherein the said yard of Portsmouth is further in arrear than the rest of the yards be at the time of their discharge paid so much as is due to any of them upon the said quarter so as to bring the arrears due to them to be equal with what at the same time will be due to the remainder of the workmen which are to be continued and no more . . .

33   Phineas Pett, Master Shipwright at Chatham, to the Navy Board

Chatham,
20 March 1673/4

I am very sorry I am constrained to give your Honours any trouble on such occasions as these (which my duty enjoineth me) to acquaint you that we are now at such great a stop for want of provisions that we cannot employ one third part of our workmen we having not one piece of timber in the yard fit for the carrying on the works of the *Montague* (to fasten her gundeck) or the works of the *Prince*, some of her wale pieces and thick plank without board requiring to be shifted. I also wrote to your Honours some time since to acquaint you that the shipwrights' and joiners' works to his Majesty's new yacht here were very near finished and that we were at a stop for want of the carver, painter, plumber and locksmith's work which they are not about to proceed on without a supply of money. And the yacht if she be not speedily launched being liable to receive very great damage by the piercing winds (at this time of year) splitting and coursing her plank, she being wrought up with East country plank, which will receive much more damage by the weather than English oak by reason of the freshness of the wood; do most humbly beg your Honours' favours in these behalfs that the great prejudice his Majesty's yacht will receive by the weather (if not speedily launched) may be prevented. And that his Majesty's expectations may be answered as to her being launched the first spring tide in April next . . .

34   *Jonas Shish, Master Shipwright at Deptford,*[41] *to the Navy Board*

Deptford,
14 April 1674

This day being the 14th of this present we have launched his Majesty's ship *Europa* out of this dry dock at Deptford, and discharged 50 shipwrights; here is more shipwrights left in the yard than the number which your Honours appointed us, and as I have formerly acquainted your Honours that they may be continued till the ways of the new ship be laid and the ship struck into her cradle, which I judge will be done with the help we have now in the yard, in 24 days (if other works do not prevent us). I thought it convenient to acquaint your Honours what poor widows' servants are now left in the yard their Masters are all of them dead and slain in his Majesty's service, the greatest part of these widows have some three, others four and five children, the bread they eat is from the mealman, which trusts them from quarter to quarter, knowing that each widow hath a servant in his Majesty's yard. If it be your Honours' pleasure to give them an employment till further order from your Honours I will assuredly see that they shall earn their wages, for they are all lusty grown young men which have served some two, some three, some four and some five years, and are able to do his Majesty good service . . .

35   *Phineas Pett, Master Shipwright's Assistant, Woolwich, to the Navy Board*

Woolwich,
18 April 1674

I find the disposition of the men inclinable to keep the holidays; many of them have already pretended earnest business in the country for two days and if they should be commanded to work in case there be not a necessity it will be a heartless business, and no way profitable to his Majesty, however whatsoever your Honours please to command in this and all other matters shall be faithfully and cheerfully observed and obeyed . . .[42]

36   *Memorandum by Beach*

Chatham,
28 May 1674

Shipwrights	Their Age	Years in service here at Chatham	
Robert Giles	58	38	
William Martin	60	40	
Edward Allen	64	10 – 40 in all in public service	
Robert Mitchell	63	39	
Robert Podd	74	40	
Joseph Osborne	70	26	
William Burroughs	55	37	
Richard Watt	61	14	
John Oliver	67	24	
Thomas Eason, sen.	61	14	
Housecarpenters			
John Guire	60	40	
Peter Williams	55	35	
Sawyers			
James Danks	76	30	
John Kemsley	66	40	
Richard Hartrop	57	27	
Scavelmen			
Peter Darby	62	1	query: why he is continued
Labourers			
Christopher Bland	60	20	
Edward Deane	60	30	
Richard King	60	40	
John Howell	52	11	query if impotent
William Jaxon	50	9	
William Watson	62	7	
Edward Pollentine	53	6	
Thomas Sexstine	56	5	query if impotent
John Mitchell	49	2	
George Chowning	50	3	
Francis Cooke	47	1	
Nicholas Narrels	52	7	

37   Beach to the Navy Board

Chatham,
3 June 1674

. . . As to the objections your Honours desire to know concerning the ancient men you mention we never made any; it was your Honours made the objection and when the Shipwright (at his being at London) informed your Honours of them you then thought it very unreasonable they should be turned out of the yard, having served so long which no man could well do to a private servant without some regret therefore have nothing to say more but refer it to your Honours' consideration . . .

38   Deane to the Navy Board

Portsmouth,
12 July 1674

I have a long time been jealous by what I have observed in our ropehouse and of the leaving work of the men who pretend to do a day's work every day in five hours, that there was some disadvantage unto the King in the making of cordage, and that either through the length of time, hurry of business or willingness as well of the officers who were to cheque them and had both a benefit in the early leaving work as also a share in the extra work by servants that the King has a great injury by it, finding it very difficult to trace the error when so many men were employed, and a great store as formerly, I was resolved to take this opportunity to do it, and instant the example, which is here enclosed [omitted] to see the difference of cordage now of our making in stores, whereby it appears how four threads are put into our cables and cordage now in stores, how many the Dutch cables have now in our stores, how the Master Ropemaker says he gave the Board for a rule when he came into his employment, and how many I have seen of some ancient establishment . . .

39   Phineas Pett, Master Shipwright's Assistant at Woolwich, to the Navy Board

Woolwich,
22 July 1674

. . . I find by your Honours' letter of the 18th instant which came hither but this morning that your Honours have ordered to this place two-thirds of the remains of Mr Kingsbury's timber, but being to come from Deptford I expect no otherwise than their accustomed practice to cull out the best, and send their leavings to this place. I could heartily desire if your Honours saw fit (this being the only time of the year to procure timber at the easiest rates) that this yard might have some speedy supply which would give a great deal of life to the most profitable and quick despatch of the works in hand, and I cannot but humbly acquaint your Honours that a supply of about £400 or £500 worth of proper timber would save the King twice the value, not only in the timely despatch of the works, but also in making men's labour turn to the most advantageous account.

I find upon my giving your Honours an account in my letter aforesaid of his Majesty being damnified by men's running ashore to their meals when they work afloat, that your Honours require the dates of those letters or warrants for the giving of half-a-tide a day extra to the men working afloat. I have only this to say that the same having been a custom in this place, time out of mind, and although we cannot find the warrant which doubtless in former years hath been granted for the same which might have miscarried by the death of several officers in this place, yet I doubt not upon your Honours' serious consideration of the advantage his Majesty will reap thereby, you will see cause to give speedy directions to the Clerk of the Cheque in confirmation thereof, I did in my letter of the 16th briefly present your Honours with this evil of men's coming ashore to their meals and showed what hindrance it was to his Majesty's service in this open road and am confident upon your Honours' speaking with Sir Jeremy Smyth or the Surveyor herein, they will appear very sensible hereof . . . [43]

40 *Letter to Nathaniel Darrell, Governor of Sheerness, from his Ensign*

Sheerness,
6 September 1674

This morning finding many of our men which belonged to the yard drinking at the Porter's I took an occasion to beat them out, telling him that if he used the trade of making our men drunk as he had begun, when it was their duty to keep the guard, I would keep it in his house in regard I found more men there than on the yard.

I told him likewise that no porter in any of his Majesty's yards ought to sell above six shilling beer and that over the hatch except betwixt twelve and one of the clock, all the officers of the yard being by but none spoke a word except Mr Hunter and Mr Shish who told him clearly that if he did not decline his proceedings he would certainly be turned out. [44]

41 *Beach to the Navy Board*

Chatham,
13 October 1674

. . . I recommend to your Honours' consideration whether or no you please to approve of our workmen coming to work at 8 o'clock the mornings and to have no breakfast nor dinner times but to work till 4 the afternoon, and then to break off, this to begin November the first, and to continue till the last of January being the three darkest months in the year. I am confident and so are the rest of the officers that his Majesty's service would be advantaged by it for considering the mornings are so dark that they cannot see to work till near 7 their breakfast and dinner times, and that they cannot

see but till five in the afternoon so that in the vacant times they are studying
of roguery, cutting or splitting of timber board or filching and stealing some
thing or other which they cannot so well do if it were light, and several other
inconveniencies prevented . . .

42   Sir Samuel Moreland to the Navy Board

Whitehall,
22 October 1674

. . . I had before this time put the King in mind of a promise he was pleased
to make me upon my last return from Chatham, of giving a commission to
your Lordship [Lord Brouncker], the Surveyor of the Navy [John
Tippetts], and Sir Jonas Moore [Master Surveyor of the Ordnance] to join
with Commissioner Beach in viewing and examining those engines I set up
for clearing the Double Dock of the spring water, and to make their report
thence to his Majesty in writing under their hands, by which report I was
willing to stand or fall. And this I thought myself obliged to petition the King
for (and so soon as ever I am in a condition to take such a journey which I
hope may be within eight or ten days I shall still do) in my own defence, by
reason of the unkind and uncivil deportment of some, and the malicious
behaviour and foul play of others when I was last there to set the engines at
work (it being my misfortune to go down when Commissioner Beach himself
was absent from whom I must needs acknowledge I received all manner of
civility from time to time). And I doubt not but those persons were the
original authors of those reports which have been since spread abroad to my
disadvantage. But I hope when all things shall be rightly scanned and
examined by your Lordship and others who understand what engines are,
they may be forced to be more useful for his Majesty's service, than such
persons would willingly have them to be, who make it their business to decry
what they do not understand . . . [45]

43   Phineas Pett, Master Shipwright's Assistant at Woolwich, to the Navy Board

Woolwich,
12 November 1674

On Monday Commissioner Haddock gave a visit to this place and took
particular inspection of the state and condition of all his Majesty's works at
this yard, and also of the want we are in of the provisions lately demanded.
He also signified to us the pleasure and late commands of the Lords of the
Admiralty touching the prohibition of all chips or any other old unserviceable
wood whatsoever to be made use of for firing from that day forward,[46] and
laid command upon me forthwith to put the same in execution, which
accordingly yesterday I did see so fulfilled with the best care and
circumspection possible that the workmen by this discouragement might not
cease their cheerful carrying on his Majesty's works. I acquainted them that

I was a sharer myself with them in this suffering possibly by the miscarriages of some three or four particular persons misrepresented with several aggravations, the whole body of workmen is brought under this affliction. I endeavoured to quiet the minds of the men by several arguments and that we had Commissioners over us that would weigh and consider the poor condition and merit of honest workmen and wherein they might be damnified, in due time they might be recompensed.

Now may it please your Honours:

It falls out worse for myself and poor sickly family in this agueish air (which none yet ever experienced but found the ill circumstances of) than with the common workmen, there being not occasion to make chips at this time as at other times, the greatest part of our hewing work being over, for out of great desire that all such abuses should be prevented, which I have endeavoured ever since my coming to this place, I have carefully laid together under lock and key great quantities of old pieces of unserviceable stuff that I would neither use myself not suffer others, so I am not only unprovided with fuel, but for my care have contracted the ill will of my neighbours, that part which is good for nothing else (they say) might have been long since divided . . .

44 *Deane to the Navy Board*

Portsmouth,
21 January 1674/5

. . . As to that part of your commands of the 12th instant touching my opinion and reason of the smallness of the chips and loss of time, I could wish it were from other hands to confirm it, but in regard you are pleased to command it I do here give faithfully not only my own opinion but the proper officers' who command the men that they believe the King has not so much work done in a day by one fourth part as when the men had the chips, the reason is plain, for when the workmen had the chips so soon as the foreman appointed the work if but half an hour before the bell rings the coldest day in winter they would presently stript into their waistcoats and sweat until they dropped to get of the chips as large as possible, this was their interest and the King had the advantage where that was done in an hour and the chips lawful which takes up two hours to be hewed off, with more ease, there being no rule how a man should hew or how much strength or blows shall be bestowed on a piece but one man for strength and interest shall hew that in two hours another cannot do in six, especially if the weakest will not bestow his strength or reserve it by way of discontent, which I fear is so much amongst them as not to be forgot so long as merchant yards and all England gives the benefit and much more wages ready money every Saturday night . . .

45   *The Admiralty to the Navy Board*

Derby House,
29 March 1675

. . . Whereas by your report of the 2nd February you have represented to us that having in pursuance of our former orders in that behalf forbidden the workmen in his Majesty's several yards to carry out thence any chips, and have caused the chips to be gathered up, and lodged in places fitting for that use by persons appointed on purpose for it, which having been practiced for above two months there are so considerable a quantity of chips gathered together in the several yards as cannot be conveniently suffered to remain there either with respect to the room which they take up or with safety to the King's yards and stores in case a fire should happen among them, and that you having proffered the said chips to sale no persons do appear to offer anything for them. Which upon your attending at the reading of your said report you acquainted his Majesty you judged did arise from a combination among the parties interested in the advantage which did arise from the old practice of permitting the workmen to carry away chips from his Majesty's yards, upon consideration thereof had, his Majesty is pleased to direct and accordingly we do hereby signify the same unto you that you give order that the smaller chips and shavings made in his Majesty's yards which cannot without probable danger be kept in the yards, the greater chips which shall be fit for the pitch kettle being to be reserved for that use, be carried out of the yards by the labourers employed in the gathering up of the chips and there left to be taken away by the poor people of the neighbourhood either promiscuously or in such method as yourselves upon advising with the officers of the parishes nearest his Majesty's respective yards shall judge convenient . . .[47]

46   *Jonas Shish, Master Shipwright at Deptford, to the Navy Board*

Deptford,
6 May 1675

Your letter dated to me the 4th of this instant came to my hand the fifth day at six of the clock the afternoon. In answer to it by reason the whole suit of masts are yet to be made, and the ship to be sheathed, with several other works in hand which require expedition, and a weak company of shipwrights now at work in his Majesty's yard at Deptford I judge it will be 38 days before the work which is to be done to that ship will be finished, or if it be your Honours' pleasure to give an order that the shipwrights may work the Holy days[48] and now the days are long to work from five of the clock in the morning till eight at night, and to have but half an hour for their dinner, I judge we may launch the ship *Eagle* out of the dry dock, the next spring after this which is now coming, which will be 22 or 23 working days, and by reason the river is full of work, here is no shipwrights comes to be entered, that are strong laborious men, for our best shipwrights hath placed themselves in merchants' works and will not come into his Majesty's yard except compelled thereunto . . .

47   *Deane to the Navy Board*

Portsmouth,
12 June 1675

Some intelligences has sent our ropemakers word from Chatham last night that they spin but 17 threads a day nor will they do more, and ours it seems threatens to do the same[49] notwithstanding they begin every day at seven o'clock or after and the ropehouse doors lock and all men gone by one o'clock at noon, as I have observed every day since these instructions, if they do not do their duties as commanded I have ordered our clerks of the ropeyard to take no notice of their time, if they leave the works, or as many as does, I shall make them runaways by an R on the books, it being a time we can never spare them better and preserve the discipline of the Navy than now, for we have not much to do for if a confederacy should take from a yard to a yard I know the effect, they have not one word to plead for any thing, only they say other yards does it not, which I pray to be resolved of to convince them of their error, if they speak to me about it which they have not yet done, the clerk of the ropeyard informed me of the intention and asked to know how to be guided if they did not do their duty which I have directed as aforesaid if approved of, and they deserve it, we have had exceeding good work done ever since these rules came down and they spin for a day 62½ ell generally, in less than a week I shall be prepared to resolve any question which relates the whole matter of fact, I mean since the settlement.

His Majesty's intending to be here at launching next spring I do pray your good companies and assistance at the work and the launching dinner where a hearty welcome shall be the best dish of.

48   *The Admiralty to the Navy Board*

Derby House,
19 June 1675

. . . Sir John Narborough[50] having in one of his late letters taken notice of a great inconveniency which he apprehends to arise from the lead sheathing, upon occasion of his late careening the *Henrietta* at Livorne [Leghorn]. Namely that her ironwork was in an unusual manner and degree consumed with rust which he knew not what else to impute to than to this new sort of sheathing adding also that he finds that the sea doth by degrees wash the lead away by wearing it thinner and thinner till at length it leaves the ship bare, and thereby exposes it to the worm, a transcript of which letter has been sent you by Mr Pepys, these are to pray and require you to consider of the said observation of Sir John Narborough and how far this inconvenience discovered upon the *Henrietta* touching the rusting of her ironwork is confirmed by any like effects upon other ships sheathed with lead, and also whether the lead as it is now usually laid on be not drawn too thin, and therefore ought for the time to come to be laid on thicker, and what the consequence thereof will be either to the greatning of the charge, or occasioning any other inconvenience . . .

49   John Owen, Clerk of Chatham Ropeyard, to the Navy Board

Chatham,
12 July 1675

I received your Honours' of the 10th instant in which you are pleased to direct me to give notice to the ropemakers belonging to his Majesty's ropeyard here forthwith to return to their work upon the receipt of it, I presently gave them notice and they all made their appearance this morning, after I had made known unto them your Honours' commands. The Master Workman [Robert Sliter][51] bid them go to their work, and told them they must perform it according to the late rules, upon which they presently went all away. I have according to your Honours' directions discharged them from the works. I sent this day to several ropemakers about Chatham who have made it their request formerly to be entered, they sent me word without they might work as formerly they should not come into the service. I gave your Honours an account the 8th instant that there was then at work the Master Workman and foreman's servants and a servant of one Thomas Rose who makes the lines and twine, Mr Sliter told me they should work according to the late rules, but the first day being Thursday the 8th instant he commanded his servants to set on and to spin 18 threads for their day's work which is according to the new rules, but going home to dinner before he could return they had broken off at 17 threads (their old task). Whereupon he threatened them that unless they would spin 19 threads the next day (that is 18 for their day's work, and one to make good the threads they spun short that day) he would send them to the house of correction, whereupon they promised him that they would, and came to work the next day with a full intention to do it (as he told me) but meeting (as he conceives) with some of the workmen who had inveigled them they were off again and would by no means do 24, but told him they would spin 25½ threads which is a day and half according to the old rules, which they have done Saturday and today being mustered only a single day each day for the same, which Mr Sliter desires they may continue to do, till I know your Honours' further pleasure herein. The overplus serving to make good the work that was done short, since the late rules were made known . . .

50   John Moore, Master Attendant, and Hugh Salesbury, Clerk of the Survey at Portsmouth, to the Navy Board

Portsmouth,
21 September 1675

We are with yours of the 17th instant, for answer sails made of Ipswich canvas lying at the yard or in a storeroom and be not opened and aired in eight or ten days will mildew and rot in a month's time if not thoroughly dried when laid up, that sort of canvas being made of black hemp and is the worst sort, and makes the worst canvas used in his Majesty's service, we find small noyalls far befo[re(?)] for service and not so apt to mildew as your Ipswich canvas do.

We have not had much experience of that sort of canvas in this yard having none but the *Royal Charles*'s sails here made with that sort of cloth and we find her main and fore course to be a little mildewed for want of airing in the time that they were at the yard at sea, no sort of English canvas is so subject to mildew as Ipswich, this is all we can say relating to this affair . . .

51   *Captain John Tinker, Master Attendant at Deptford, to the Navy Board*

Deptford,
21 September 1675

In answer to yours concerning the judgement and of the observation I have made of the Ipswich canvas, I do not judge it so bad as it is reported to be as your Honours may see by the enclosed [omitted], neither did I find it so bad at sea, for I have worn it in double sails as courses, and by experience did find that it did outlast the best sort of single sails, what canvas soever they were of, and about twenty-five and thirty years ago, his Majesty's, and the biggest merchant ships, had their main and fore courses of the aforesaid Ipswich canvas, but it requires an exacter looking to than any other sort of canvas, being more subject to mildew, and my reason of that is, the making of it with greener hemp than other canvas, and the gumming of it is the cause of the mildewing, for I cannot judge it to be anything else, for in former times when that canvas was so much in use, it was of a good brown colour, and now it has a tincture of greenish, the hemp not being well cured which if remedied the canvas may be very serviceable, and the sails if well looked after, that is to say well and often dried, and I was with your Honours at the Board Master Surveyor did order me to wet a yard of Suffolk, and a yard of Ipswich to be wet, and laid by for a trial, and about a week hence I will send it to the Board that your Honours may judge of it . . .

52   *Admiralty Orders to the Master Attendant, Master Shipwright and Clerk of the Survey at Deptford*

Derby House,
29 April 1676

. . . Whereas upon the view lately taken by us at Deptford of the Storekeeper's books of issues of stores we find the quantities of the materials issued to be generally entered in figures and not in words at length, and that the said books are not withstanding signed by the Master Shipwright whereby an opportunity is given for alterations to be made in the said books after their being signed, greatly to His Majesty's prejudice: these are to pray and require each and every of you henceforth not to sign any warrant to the Storekeeper for the issuing of any provisions unless the quantities of all and every of the provisions thereby directed to be delivered be expressed in words at length and particularly the Master Shipwright and his assistant are hereby required to take especial care that neither of them do sign to any of the Storekeeper's books of issues unless the quantity of all the provisions therein entered, which by their signing are vouchers to the Storekeeper for the said issues be entered plainly in words at length . . .

53   *Robert Sliter, Master Ropemaker of the Chatham Ropeworks, to the Navy Board*

Chatham,
n.d.

I understand by Sir Richard Beach that before your Honours think fit to determine anything touching my reading the mathematics to the Navy, you desire to know what allowance hath been given formerly for that service, and in what method I intend to proceed in my reading.

As to the first I suppose Sir Richard Beach will give your Honours the best satisfaction he can, who with Mr Gregory's assistance can do it better than I.

As to the other the design being the advancement of navigation I intend and purpose to follow the method following, if it shall be approved of, conceiving it most proper and conducing to that end, viz.

Arithmetic
- Natural
  - Vulgar
  - Decimal
- Artificial
  - and therein the construction and application of the Tables of Logarithms

Geometry — So much of the principles and practice as is necessary for navigation

The doctrine and use of the Sphere or Globe
- Terrestrial
- Celestial
  - Spherically and in plano

The doctrine of triangles
- Plains
- Spherical
  - With the calculation and application of the tables of
    - Sines
    - Tangents
    - Secants
      - Natural
      - Artificial

Astronomy — The doctrine of the second motions and eclipses of the Luminaries with such other propositions touching the diurnal? motion, as are necessary in the Art of Navigation

Navigation
{
Propositions of sailing according to { the plain / Mercators / The Arch of a great circle } Chart

The construction and application of Instruments for the taking of Observations, heights, distances, plotting of countries, working of Traverses, etc., the making of maps and charts and reducing them to any assigned proportion
}

Some other things collaterally will occur, and if this method shall be accounted either preposterous or deficient any better that shall be prescribed shall willingly be submitted to and followed . . .

54   The Admiralty to the Navy Board[52]

Derby House,
17 February 1676/7

. . . We do herewith send you a copy of a proposal lately handed to us by Sir Richard Beach, Commissioner for his Majesty's Navy at Chatham, from Mr Sliter Master Workman of his Majesty's ropeyard there touching a mathematical lecture to be by him undertaken for the benefit of the youth belonging to the Ordinary at Chatham, at the allowance therein mentioned by him demanded from his Majesty for the same, upon debate whereof had at our late attending his Majesty on the affairs of the Admiralty it appeared that something of like kind was heretofore done by an encouragement given thereto from the Chest, which since his Majesty's Restoration hath been let fall by the Governors of the Chest as being a charge not proper to be borne by the same, but for as much as this motion now made hath the appearance of something useful for the propagation of navigation and the charge proposed to be borne by his Majesty, therefore not exceeding the allowance of an able seaman's pay per annum his Majesty is graciously pleased so far to incline to the encouragement thereof as to refer to you the due considering the said proposal and upon conference with Sir Richard Beach about it to report with all convenient speed to this Board . . .

55   Commissioner Sir John Kempthorne[53] to the Navy Board

Portsmouth,
17 April 1677

In answer to yours of the 14th we do attend your instructions as to the sheathing with lead the parts nigh the rother irons of the *Plymouth* as also the coming of the lead and nails for the completing said ship.

As to my own sentiment and judgement of his Majesty's ships to be sheathed with lead by the experience that other men have had thereof, and by what I have seen myself, my humble opinion is, it is no way profitable nor safe for his Majesty's service, but dangerous and destructive and may prove of very ill consequence. I humbly conceive the said lead and the nails together, will have the same operation and work the same effects on the bolt heads and all other iron work as it doth on the rother irons.

Since I wrote you last I have made observation with the Master Shipwright and his Assistant, of some of the sheathing lead that lay here in store which I conceive may have taken some wet, which hath caused it to appear of a cankerous and corroding substance, and I humbly conceive may be venomous to iron. Therefore I shall by the next coach send you a piece thereof for your own inspection and consideration . . .

56　Sir Richard Beach to the Navy Board

Chatham,
25 April 1677

Whereas you are pleased to inform me that at Portsmouth they make use of nothing but broom to bream ships with, I suppose the same is occasioned from their want of reed, for broom is a very dangerous fire to burn upwards under the wales and especially when the wind blows hard, however, we do make use of as much as we can with safety. I have ordered the Purveyor to buy what quantity he can ere it be bought up by the builders in these parts, for we find it very hard to procure as well as reed. He tells me that Sir John Banks[54] hath a parcel of eight thousand reed sheaves to dispose of, which I have directed him to endeavour the buying of, if the same may be had upon reasonable terms and that he desire Mr Kipping to forbear the disposing of his parcel of oak timber till such time as he hear further from me.

If there can be no course taken for the procuring of more workmen for the yard, the works will go on but very slowly the most and best of our workmen being now employed upon the yacht and the ships ordered to sea. And I am confident the Parliament will be necessitated to agree to the pressing both of workmen and seamen, if they expect that those ships intended shall be built in any reasonable time, and when ready to man them; for the workmen in these parts that have 2s 8d and 3s a day and the same paid every Saturday night, will never come into the King's works voluntarily for the wages allowed therein, and that only paid but once in twelve months' time, nor will able seamen come into the service for 23s per mensem when as they can have 28, 30 and 32 shillings in a merchant man without so much hazard of broken bones, but I beg your pardon for this digression . . .

57　Beach to the Navy Board

Chatham,
30 May 1677

. . . I am glad you are pleased to take notice of the great abuse committed by the pale makers in cutting all the best of timber both in these parts and other places, giving three pounds five shillings a load for it as Mr Kipping and others can justify. There is also another grand abuse committed in Essex, which I suppose little or no notice is taken of, and that is in destroying all their best timber to make oyster barrels of.[55]

I fear that I shall make but few contracts for timber. Mr Kipping has been this day with me but will not abate anything of fifty five shillings per load for his parcel of timber that I lately sent you the tender of, Mr Lawrence having seen it says that it is very large and sound and fit for building, and that there be some very considerable pieces amongst it . . .

58   *The Admiralty to the Navy Board*

Derby House,
27 June 1677

Whereas . . . it appears that the restraint sometime since laid upon their the said workmen's carrying chips out of his Majesty's said yards doth still remain upon them not withstanding the resolution which, upon a full debate upon that matter the 19th May last past, was taken for your suffering the said workmen without any written order to be given to that purpose to return to the practice anciently allowed them of carrying out of his Majesty's yards the lawful chips falling from the axe, which resolution we at our said attendance on his Majesty understood your expecting a written signification of from this Board, these are to let you understand that as well from the argument urged by yourselves of the great charge and little profit that hath attended the experiment by you for about three years made of the said prohibition to the workmen as out of his Majesty's inclinations to the giving at this time all reasonable encouragement to the said workmen in the performance of their service, in the repair of the old, and building of the new ships now designed. It is his Majesty's pleasure that the said workmen be permitted to resume their ancient practice of carrying out lawful chips at the accustomary hours with as little publication of any orders in writing to be given for the same as the nature of the affair will admit . . .[56]

59   *Beach to the Navy Board*

Chatham,
16 July 1677

Here enclosed I send you an account [omitted] of the neglects made since the first of this instant July by several workmen belonging to this yard, and forasmuch as no severe course hath been taken, neither with them that formerly absented themselves, nor with those that never appeared since they were prest, it hath encouraged these to take the same liberty and will animate a great part of the rest to do the like. So that whereas you may suppose we have such a considerable number of workmen daily employed as will expedite the works and accomplish the same in such a time, we come far short thereof and shall fail both in the work and time 'till there be a course taken to restrain them from this liberty, to which end I have caused several that wrought

without leave in merchants' yards to be chequed, and in regard the Master
Shipwrights of the said private yards hath induced our workmen to absent
themselves, by giving them extraordinary wages, I have sent an order to them
all that for the future they forbear enticing any of our workmen from the
works here or employing any of them at any time tho' out of the King's hours,
for as long as they were permitted the liberty of employing them in the
evenings after they left work here so long as they could see, and in the
mornings from daylight till the time that they came to their call, it occasioned
them either wholly to absent themselves the next day, or if they came to work,
to abscond and sleep in holes not being capable of doing any service . . .

60   *Beach to the Navy Board*

Chatham,
14 August 1677

. . . We have had so much rain fallen in these parts that horses in several
places can scarce pass much less carriages with timber which will very much
obstruct and hinder the progress we should make in the works of the new
ships . . .

The thousand of deals which came last are so bad that they are scarce fit
to make hog sties of and indeed we never have anything from Deptford but
the refuse and what is culled. I hope you will please to give orders it may be
remedied for according to the stuff so must the work be . . .

Here hath not been less than 572 neglects of the workmen and labourers
belonging to this yard in one month's time notwithstanding all orders hath
been given to the contrary as well to the shipwrights of the private yards in
the parts adjacent as well as to themselves, yet they make it their constant
practice before and after the hours of working here to tire themselves there,
so that when they come to work in the yard it is at a very easy rate and without
some punishment his Majesty's works will be retarded for neither fair means
nor threatening can reduce them. I do therefore think with your consents that
the easiest punishment that can be inflicted on them and which will take most
effect is to cheque them two days' pay for one day's absence which will be
no heavy burden considering what large allowances the Shipwright gives
them for their work and the farmers to the labourers to get in their harvest
. . .

61   *Beach to the Navy Board*

Chatham,
26 September 1677

. . . We are very much visited with sickness in the yard, and I fear will prove
pestilential there being at Mr Lately's 4 or 5 sick, at Mr Gregory's 6 or 7, at
Mr Pett's one dead and 3 or 4 sick, at Mr Kirk's one dead and one sick.[57]
The Porter and his wife sick, at the Storekeeper's one sick, at my house 2,
at the Joiner's 3 or 4, some others that are recovered, half the Ordinary sick,

not one house in five in Strood but is visited and many in Chatham and Rochester, and burials very frequent, God divert his heavy judgement from us . . .

62   *Nathaniel Richmond, Boatswain of the* Foresight,[58] *at Sheerness, to the Navy Board*

Sheerness,
20 October 1677

In obedience to your order I have used all endeavours to procure men for the rigging our ship, but can get none it being a time when the Queenborough men are all employed in dredging for oysters for the doggers from Holland, they will not stir from their present work which is so advantageous to them earning four, six and eight shillings a day. I desire but the help of ten or a dozen hands which I humbly beg may be provided and directed to come down, that the ship's despatch may not be hindered . . .

63   *Kempthorne to the Navy Board*

Portsmouth,
30 October 1677

. . . I do find that notwithstanding I have your press warrants for land carriage yet the excuses and the impediments that the owners of teams do make will retard his Majesty's service and be more detrimental to the same than if we did advance one shilling per load or thereabouts in the price to give them encouragement, especially at this time now our occasion doth require it, which I humbly represent to your consideration, in case you are not pleased to approve thereof. I humbly desire your supply of more press warrants, as also copies of the act of Parliament for that purpose . . .[59]

64   *John Mulliner to the Navy Board*

10 December 1677

I being under contract with your Honours to serve his Majesty with timber into the stores at Deptford and Woolwich, as I bring the timber from Maindham [Mendham] and Wingfield in Suffolk am necessitated (by the badness of the ways) to use sometimes six and seven horses to draw the same, in which I am opposed by Justice Benningfield in Hallesworth which town I bring the timber through, he takes away my horses (above five) caused me to pay 20s to redeem my two horses and threatens, if he takes me with more horses than five in my cart, I shall pay 40s a horse and he will indict me at Sessions. According to your Honours' direction upon my former complaint I showed the Justice a copy of my contract, to satisfy him that this timber and plank was for the King, upon which he said I care not for it, for I know what I have to do as well as the Commissioners . . .

I humbly beg your Honours would please to consider of it, and to use some expedient that I may have my liberty to use so many horses as I need for the better carrying his Majesty's timber and plank.

65   *The Lords of the Admiralty to the Navy Board*

Derby House,
28 March 1678

. . . Upon consideration had of your advice in your letter of the 25th instant touching your repeated observations of the evil wherewith the sheathing of his Majesty's ships with lead is attended in reference to the untimely destruction of the ironwork of their rothers, these are by his Majesty's command to signify to you his pleasure that you do not for the time to come sheath any of his Majesty's greater ships with lead, until a more certain knowledge can be had of the true ground of the said evil, and that therefore the *St Michael* and *Royal Oak* designed to the Straits and lately ordered to be sheathed with lead, be performed with wood sheathing, and that together with the performance thereof upon the *St Michael*, a girdling be brought upon her according to his Majesty's late discourse thereon with Sir John Tippetts, to whom referring you for more particular advice therein . . .[60]

66   *The Lords of the Admiralty to the Navy Board*

Derby House,
12 April 1678

. . . And whereas it hath been lately objected that the lead and nails which hath been used in the sheathing of his Majesty's ships are prejudicial to the rother irons, the Company of Milled Lead being confident that the fault is altogether in the iron, proposed to his Majesty at our late attending him on the affairs of the Admiralty, that upon the ordinary rates they would not only furnish such ships as shall be sheathed with lead with rother irons at present, but also carry such a reserve as shall answer any common exigency. These are in pursuance of his Majesty's further pleasure signified to us at the same time to pray and require you when any of his Majesty's ships shall be sheathed with lead, you do make use of such rother irons as shall be provided, and made for the said ships, by the order of the said Company of Milled Lead, causing the usual rate you now give to be paid them for the same . . .[61]

67   *Beach to the Navy Board*

Chatham,
16 April 1678

I am glad his Majesty is induced to believe that the sheathing of the ships with board is safer and more advantageous in several particulars for the ships than with lead[62], for here we find in the *Henrietta* inch bolts eaten to the thickness of a straw, the braces and stirrups of the false keel eaten to nothing, and so was it likewise in the *Antelope* occasioned certainly by the copper nails, lead and salt water making a kind of copperas that eats the ironwork very much in a short-time, which will not be found so in those ships that are sheathed with board.

Here inclosed goes an account [omitted] of those men which have been prest by the Master Attendant and warned in that will not appear belonging to Milton and other places; and hope your Honours will take some course that these fellows may be punished for their contempt of the King's service; and that hereafter when they are either prest or warned in by the Magistrates of the places they may not presume to desert the service; it having been their common practice from time to time to abscond when we have most occasion to make use of them; and if a Messenger be sent down I will give him the best directions I can; and when the ships are going I will advise some commander to take some course for the pressing or seizing of them, for these fellows never go to sea in the King's service except forced . . .

68   *Admiralty Orders to yard officers at Woolwich, Deptford, Chatham, Portsmouth, Sheerness and Harwich*

Derby House,
27 June 1678

Whereas it hath been lately observed in some bills brought to this office that a liberty is taken contrary to your instructions of bringing an extraordinary charge upon his Majesty for things that are unnecessary and such as have not heretofore been used in the Navy, as in particular the carving and sometimes also the building of boats, the adorning of ships, and also houses in the yard beyond what is convenient, these are to let you know that whatsoever extraordinary work is or shall be done for ornaments to ships, boats, or houses without particular warrant from this Board, the person or persons by whose direction any such extra work shall be done shall not only pay for the same but shall have his offence therein represented to the Lords Commissioners for executing the Office of Lord High Admiral, or to the Lord High Admiral for the time being in order to his being punished for the same . . .[63]

69   *Beach to the Navy Board*

Chatham,
7 August 1678

. . . I have several times since my coming hither both warned and ordered the Porter of the Gate to take more care than he did, and not to permit or suffer our workmen to come into his taphouse working times to spend and idle out their time in drinking and taking tobacco (as they frequently do to his Majesty's great prejudice in a year), but all will not do it being a daily practice. For which I did this day cheque him twenty shillings, which I thought fit to advise your Honours of that you may know for what reason it was and that for the future he may obey orders. Or that somebody else that will take more care may have his employment for he hath gotten a good estate therein, and it would be a good donation of his Majesty to some deserving person . . .

70　*Beach to the Navy Board*

Chatham,
31 August 1678

I have received yours of the 30th with the inclosed petition of John Browne, shipwright: wherein you desire an account why he is made Run which is as followeth. He being employed upon the new third rate at the boatslip did cause the rest of the men to neglect their work and spoke very scurrilously of the service and to my face in the Clerk of the Cheque's office gave me very opprobrious language before the rest of the workmen, and when I told him that when the new ships were built they would be more calm and glad to be entertained in the King's service, he (above the rest) vilified me; insomuch that he which mustered the men in the Office told him he was too saucy to give such language to the Commissioner. But I forebore chequing of him till a day or two after he affronted the Master Shipwright for finding several of them absent from their work (as they had been too often) he would have made a private cail, and this Browne swore he should not surprise them, but cried out a call, a call for all the yard, which made all the men come from their work when there was no such thing intended, and gave the Shipwright very saucy language. Upon which he came and complained to me, and told me those men which wrought upon that ship would do nothing but what they pleased themselves, for that this Browne was the mouth and ringleader of them, and that he was not a fit fellow to be employed in the yard, being too mutinous and stubborn, upon which for reducing the rest of the men to better obedience (which they have been ever since) with the Shipwright's approbation I made him Run. And in fine he is most certainly a very mutinous factious fellow and not fit to be employed in the King's service, 'tis true he came after and would fain have submitted himself, but I did not think it convenient because the other workmen would be scared into better obedience by his example, and I believe an old crooked tree may as soon be made grow straight as he to alter his disposition. Besides he hath hindered the King's service five times more than his money comes to. This is what account I can give you of the aforesaid Browne . . .

71　*Phineas Pett, Master Shipwright at Chatham, to the Navy Board*

Chatham,
4 October 1678

I have received yours of the 2nd instant and Mr Lawrence as I am informed being sick (to whom I have sent your Honours' letter), and that in regard of my assistants and also the foreman of the yard both of the old and new works being also very ill, and not able to come abroad to give me the least help or assistance in carrying on those (as I humbly contrive) more weighty affairs of his Majesty's under my charge and myself being but crazy at present, this sickly time, so that I am no ways able without great prejudice and hindrance to his Majesty's other affairs to undertake the task of clearing the hulk, of the stubb and dirt that is in her by the great to make her swim, and do believe it will be found a very hard matter to procure men at this juncture of time, the season for cold weather now so near approaching, and it proving in these parts to be so extraordinarily sickly as the like since my time was never known (except in the great contagion) and being very cautious of undertaking any affairs whatsoever that I am unexperienced or unskilled in (as I am wholly in this) having never in all my life undertook such a task do humbly pray that your Honours would please to have me excused in this matter, assuring your Honours that I shall ever to the utmost of my power at all times very readily obey your commands . . .

72   *Beach to the Navy Board*

Chatham,
3 November 1678

. . . What powder and shot was formerly allowed for the small arms on board the ships here (especially the powder) is all expended, of which I desire your Honours will please to procure us a supply.

Considering these dangerous conspiracies which are afoot at present[64] and not knowing what attempts may be made against us here (especially in the night), and there being so few of us in health in the yard to oppose any surprisal, the watchmen signifying but little, only the preventing of thievery and embezzlements. I think it worthy your Honours' consideration whether it is not requisite that some force should be appointed here in the yard till these fears and jealousies are a little past and I cannot think of any better way for our security (if your Honours approve thereof) that application be made to his Majesty that some of the soldiers which are quartered at Rochester and parts adjacent may by turns do duty here in the night, till we judge ourselves in more security, the duty which they do at Rochester being very easy (being only some few sentinels) which I leave to consideration.

The days being much shortened and growing shorter whereby the workmen cannot be kept to their duties no longer than they can well see, which is now from after 7 to 5 and now breakfast time ceasing and dinner time allowed I do humbly conceive it would be more advantageous for his Majesty's service and agreeable to the workmen that they might come into the yard to their calls at half an hour past 7 in the morning so that by that time they are called over it would be 8. And from that time working dinner time and until four will be eight hours complete so that considering how long it is before they set to work in the morning and likewise when they come in after dinner and that it will not be long they can see to work until five with the roguery and villany they commit when it begins to grow dark (which we cannot possibly take notice of). I am of the opinion it would be far better they work those eight hours (which they may do in the depth of winter) and so continue from the 5th of November (at which time they go away at 11 o'clock) till Candlemas day at which time they are allowed their breakfast time again.

Mr Gregory informs me that the Master Shipwright hath in discourse with him formerly approved thereof but he is so tender of himself at the present that I cannot consult him about it, if this may be with your Honours' approbation it will be requisite that an order be directed to that effect . . .

73   *Beach to the Navy Board*

Chatham,
2 December 1678

I have this day at the muster acquainted all the officers of his Majesty's ships here of the hazard they run in not receiving the Sacrament and taking the Test since they entered upon his Majesty's service, or had removes (as the Secretary of the Admiralty desired me to do), and have advised them that forthwith they comply therewith in receiving the Sacrament and taking the oaths and Test, at the next Quarter Sessions.

The Gunner of the *Restoration* hath produced a certificate from the Crown Office of his taking the oaths and Test, but did confess that he had not then received the Sacrament. But did, with about thirty more, receive it yesterday in order to his taking the Test. But as to the Gunner of the *St George* I have no further satisfaction from him than what I gave you an account of lately, since which I understand there hath been a priest taken in his house belonging to the Countess of Portland, whom the Mayor of Rochester detains still in prison and was found with several popish sermons about him. Captain Turner is at London, and what satisfaction he can give for being a Protestant I do not yet know.

Notwithstanding all the orders and threatenings that have been given to the officers of his Majesty's ships here for doing the day duties as well as the nights, they will not understand it, so that the King hath but half a year's service in a twelve month from them, and will never be rectified, nor they perform what is expected from them till some of them are dismissed from their employments . . .

Notes

1   The third Dutch war was formally declared by England on 17 March 1671/2, and the treaty of peace was signed on 9 February 1673/4.

2   Restoration Mediterranean naval policy was barely sufficient to cope with the minor states of the north African coast. The numerous treaties were usually shortlived; there were in fact no less than seven with the Algerians in 1664, 1668, 1669, 1671, 1682, 1683 and 1686, G. L. Beer, *The Old Colonial System*, Vol. 1 (New York: Macmillan, 1912), pp. 122–4. Though there were striking successes against Tripoli in 1675 by the squadron under the command of Sir John Narborough, the war against this state in 1677–8 showed how difficult the problems of supply could be.

3   These figures are taken from J. R. Tanner (ed.), *A Descriptive Catalogue of the Naval MSS. in the Pepysian Library*, Vol. I, 'Register of Ships . . . 1660–1686', N.R.S. Vol.

26 (1903), p. 266. National Maritime Museum MSS., Anderson 37, has a 'list of the Navy, 1672', which gives 7 first rates, 9 second, 21 third, 35 fourth, 16 fifth and 32 sixth rates. It was probably made out before the action of Sole Bay, 28 May 1672.

4   Occasional repair work was carried out to ships at numerous places around the country, and abroad. This encouraged the government to support requests for building new quays in England, and to extend the policy to the whole of Britain after 1707.

5   The most substantial source for the work of the dockyards 1672–8 is the Navy Board In-letters, ADM 106/273 ff. There are additional collections in the Admiralty papers at the Public Record Office, Kew; in the State Papers Domestic, before June 1673; at the National Maritime Museum; and in the Pepysian Library, Magdalene College, Cambridge, for which see C. S. Knighton (ed.), *Catalogue of the Pepys Library at Magdalene College, Cambridge*, Vol. 5, Manuscripts, Part ii, Modern (Brewer, 1982). There is a list and index for SP 46 Supplementary 136/137, and an extended list, financed by the Social Science Research Council, of ADM 106/273–314. J. R. Tanner (ed.), *A Descriptive Catalogue of the Naval MSS. in the Pepysian Library*, Vol. II, N.R.S. Vol. 27 (1904) and Vol. III, N.R.S. Vol. 36 (1909) reprints Admiralty Out-letters for 1673–7, and Vol. IV, N.R.S. Vol. 57 (1923) reprints the Admiralty Journal for 1673–9.

6   Recent work suggests that the Stop had a wider impact than has hitherto been thought, J. K. Horsefield, 'The "Stop of the Exchequer" revisited', *Economic History Review*, 2nd Series, Vol. 35, no. 4 (November 1982).

7   Figures for dockyard employment and pay are in ADM 42/143 (Chatham Extra, 1660–82); 42/485 (Deptford Extra, 1660–77); 42/1215 (Portsmouth Extra, 1660–85); 42/1601 (Sheerness Extra, 1673–82); 42/1846 (Woolwich Extra, 1660–82).

8   Basic payments varied from 2s 1d for shipwrights down to 1s 1d for labourers, with less for apprentices and boys; there were slight variations for some grades of workmen between yards. Overtime payments could add substantially to basic pay, a night was 5 hours, a tide 1½ hours.

9   There were attempts to by-pass the 'in course' system of payment, though the Navy Board considered that this only aggravated the supply of stores; ADM 3/275 fol. 22, 2 August 1673: reprinted in J. R. Tanner, *Cat. Pepysian* Vol. IV.

10 J. R. Tanner, *Cat. Pepysian*, Vols II–IV; B. Pool, *Navy Board Contracts 1660–1832* (London: Longman, 1966).

11 See ADM 106/294 fol. 186; for illness in the area, P. MacDougall, 'Malaria, its influence on a north Kent community', *Archaeologia Cantiana*, Vol. 95 (1979).

12 A. W. Johns, 'Phineas Pett', *Mariner's Mirror*, Vol. 12 (1926).

13 ADM 106/288 fol. 251, 22 October 1673.

14 *A Collection of the Statutes relating to the Admiralty, Navy and Ships of War* (London, 1778).

15 R. V. Saville, 'Some Aspects of the Role of the Government in the Industrial Development of England, 1686–1720', unpublished Ph.D. thesis, Sheffield University, 1978, ch. 8.

16 To make a workman 'Run' on the yard books meant he would lose all back pay due to him. Appeals against such a penalty were allowed.

17 To mark their names on the books as absent from work.

18 The Master Shipwright was Phineas Pett. For details of his career, see A. W. Johns, 'Phineas Pett'. Edward Gregory was Clerk of the Cheque, the boatswain was John Attewell. The correspondence between the Navy Board and Pett and Beach indicates the extent to which the dispute affected the work of the Chatham yard.

19 The storm of 16–17 February 1672/3 was widely reported.

20 The horseboat was a regular naval supply vessel that plied the Thames and Medway. The Master Attendant at Sheerness was John Rudd, succeeded in the summer of 1674 by John Perryman. The Surveyor was John Tippetts, appointed to this post from September 1672 in succession to Thomas Middleton; Tippetts was knighted on 3 July 1675 along with Anthony Deane and Richard Haddock (J. R. Tanner, *Cat. Pepysian*, Vol. III, pp. xlv, 78).

21 This was Prince Rupert, *Calendar of State Papers Domestic*, 1673, p. 73. The *Royal Sovereign* was to be docked by Monday 24 March.

22 The Navy had the right to take up carts and horses before 1660, and this was confirmed by 14 Car. II c. 20, 'An Act for providing carriage by land and by water for the use of His Majesties Navy and Ordnance'. Carriages and horses could be taken up for the Navy and Ordnance with notice given to two or more local JPs at rates of one shilling a mile, for each

load of timber and 8d a mile for other goods; paragraph 8 laid down extra payments of 4d a mile for moving timber in the New Forest to a place of lading. For details of this and other legal powers of the Navy, see R. V. Saville, loc. cit., pp. 451–8.

23   Sheerness was under the control of the Commissioner at Chatham, the yard tended to be neglected and there were frequent complaints by officers and artisans of the condition of storehouses, arrears of payments and shortages of supplies, as well as the problems of living in such an isolated place.

24   John Young was responsible for supervising the work done by Francis Bayley on the third rate ship, the *Oxford*, built near Bristol. Several letters have survived in the State Papers from Francis Bayley, in addition to those in ADM 106. Bayley had written on 14 July 1673 asking the Admiralty for the benefit of 14 Car. II c. 20. In their reply of 19 July, they decided not to extend the said benefit, since the timber for which it was required 'cannot be said to be the king's till it be wrought into the ship. Besides, the power of impresting land carriage if given would be for his private advantage and not the king's and would be open to abuse.' J. R. Tanner, *Cat. Pepysian*, Vol. II, p. 11.

25   The Storekeeper at Chatham was Thomas Wilson, the Clerk of the Survey Edward Homewood.

26   The Porter of the new dock, John Howling, derived part of his income from the taphouse he kept, the normal practice at the dockyards.

27   Quartermen were in charge of groups of workmen, and therefore supervised their work.

28   See note 20. The Act referred to in his letter is 14 Car. II c. 20, discussed above in note 22. Sir George Moore had previously offered help to Governor Nathaniel Darrell of Sheerness, *Cal. S.P. Dom.*, 1673, p. 260, 17 May 1673.

29   For the oyster fishery, R. H. Goodsall, 'Oyster fisheries on the north Kent coast', *Archaeologia Cantiana*, Vol. 80 (1965).

30   The men were re-entered by Phineas Pett, the Master Shipwright.

31   For the career of this Phineas Pett, A. W. Johns, 'Phineas Pett', loc. cit. p. 433. Pett arrived at Woolwich in 1672 as Master Shipwright's Assistant in succession to Daniel Furzur. Jonas Shish was the Master Shipwright for both Woolwich and Deptford at this time, and on his retirement in December 1675 Phineas Pett was promoted to Master Shipwright at Woolwich, and John Shish became Master Shipwright at Deptford. In this letter Pett was reporting the arrest of Royal Dockyard workmen which was illegal while they were listed on the yard books.

32   J. R. Tanner, *Cat. Pepysian*, Vol. I, p. 106, for similar problems with anchorsmiths.

33   The petition was sent with a letter from Commissioner Richard Haddock, 12 December 1673, to the Navy Board, ADM 106/292 fol. 94B. Haddock supported the petition, 'with my humble request in their behalf that they may have two quarters' pay ordered them, their case being lamentable if not paid so much'.

34   Christmas Eve fell on Wednesday 24 December, so the Friday was Boxing Day. The resistance to work on Boxing Day was widespread, and continued into the eighteenth century.

35   J. R. Tanner, *Cat. Pepysian*, Vol. II, p. 219, 15 January 1673/4, Pepys to Lanyon, 'Is sorry the departure of the *Swan* is like to meet with delay for want of money, which he heartily wishes he could tell how to remedy'.

36   On time and clocks, E. P. Thompson, 'Time, work discipline and industrial capitalism', *Past and Present*, 37 (1967); Peter Linebaugh, 'Crime in London, 1700–50', unpublished Ph.D. thesis, Warwick University, 1976.

37   The workmen were warned by the Navy Board to be more attentive to their behaviour for the future.

38   J. R. Tanner, *Cat. Pepysian*, Vol. II, p. 263, 27 February 1673/4.

39   The Navy Board solved the problem of the threat of arrest by allowing workmen to remain on the yard pay books [32].

40   J. R. Tanner, *Cat. Pepysian*, Vol. IV, pp. 25–6, 16 March 1673/4; [see also 30].

41   See note 31.

42   In 1674 Easter Sunday fell on the 19 April. By this time the Navy Board clerks were referring to this Phineas Pett as 'Master Shipwright' though the title was not formally acquired until the retirement of Jonas Shish in December 1675.

43   Sir Jeremy Smith was Controller of the Victualling Accounts from 17 June 1669 to 3 November 1675, when he was succeeded by Sir Anthony Deane. J. M. Collinge, *Navy Board*

Officials 1660–1832, Vol. 7 in *Office Holders in Modern Britain* (Institute of Historical Research, 1978).

44 J. R. Tanner, *Cat. Pepysian*, Vol. IV, p. 102, 28 November 1674, note of the 'hardships the officers and servants of the Navy do lie under from the Governor's imposing upon them the persons from whom alone they shall be at liberty to supply themselves with meat and drink within the said garrison'; see also ibid., pp. 156, 161. Samuel Hunter was Clerk of the Cheque, John Shish the Master Shipwright.

45 *Cal. S.P. Dom.*, 1673–1675, p. 185, 28 February 1673/4, warrant for a patent to Sir Samuel Moreland for the sole use of an engine invented by him for raising water, for fourteen years; *Cal. S.P. Dom.*, 1673–1675, p. 612, [?] February 1675, schedule of prices of his water engines including pumps for draining low grounds. J. R. Tanner, *Cat. Pepysian*, Vol. II, p. 60, 18 September 1673, Pepys to Commissioner Beach; ibid., pp. 66–7, 24 September; p. 91, 15 October 1673; p. 145, 2 December 1673, letters to Navy Board. ibid., Vol. IV, p. 234, 9 October 1675; p. 351, 16 September 1675, Admiralty Minutes.

46 The occasion for this attempt to restrict chips was encouraged by information supplied from an ex-workman of Woolwich, William Ward, who with his accomplices was allowed £100 by the Admiralty, ADM 2/1 fol. 172/3, 18 July 1674, fol. 179/180, 4 November 1674. J. R. Tanner, *Cat. Pepysian*, Vol. IV, pp. xci–xcii, 74–5, 31 October 1674, Admiralty Minutes.

47 J. R. Tanner, *Cat. Pepysian*, Vol. IV, p. 156, 27 February 1674/5, for the decision to allow the poor to have small chips and the larger ones to be used for heating pitch.

48 In 1675 Whitsunday fell on 23 May.

49 ADM 106/309 and 310 contain many letters on the strike, the cause of which was the Navy Board order of May 1675.

50 Sir John Narborough was commander of the squadron ordered to prosecute the war against Tripoli, an entirely successful campaign. Narborough's original letter was read at the Admiralty, 12 June 1675, J. R. Tanner, *Cat. Pepysian*, Vol. IV, p. 185, 12 June 1675; and see, ibid., Vols II–IV, for details of lead sheathing.

51 See documents **53** and **54** for his offer of a mathematical lecture.

52 J. R. Tanner, *Cat. Pepysian*, Vol. IV, p. 391, 20 January 1676/7, Admiralty reference of matter to the Navy Board; ibid., Vol. III, p. 376, 10 February 1676, discussion by the Admiralty.

53 Sir John Kempthorne succeeded Sir Anthony Deane as Commissioner at Portsmouth when the latter was made Comptroller of Victualling, 25 November 1675; the Master Shipwright was Daniel Furzur.

54 Details of the career of Sir John Banks in D. C. Coleman, *Sir John Banks, Baronet and Businessman* (Oxford: Clarendon, 1963).

55 Wood prices were generally on the increase from the 1650s, and a number of treatises, including that by John Evelyn, *Silva or a Discourse of Forest trees . . .* (1664) widened the knowledge of types of wood and their uses; B. Henrey, *British Botanical and Horticultural Literature before 1800*, Vol. 1, Sixteenth and Seventeenth Centuries (London: OUP, 1975); R. H. Goodsall, loc. cit., for the oyster fishery.

56 J. R. Tanner, *Cat. Pepysian*, Vol. IV, pp. 429–30, 19 May 1677 for the decision to reverse. The reluctance to put this decision on paper did not stop other groups of workmen subsequently demanding the right to chips.

57 Philip Lately and John Kirk were Master Attendants at Chatham.

58 The *Foresight* had been ordered to the Straits for Sir John Narborough's squadron, J. R. Tanner, *Cat. Pepysian*, Vol. IV, p. 501, 2 October 1677; ibid., p. 526, 17 November 1677, order changed to convoy for the herring fishery.

59 The Act referred to was 14 Car. II c. 20; see note 22.

60 J. R. Tanner, *Cat. Pepysian*, Vol. IV, p. 575, 6 April 1678, Admiralty Minutes, for the decision to allow the lead contractors to procede with sheathing for one of these ships.

61 Charles II persisted in his support for lead sheathing for some time after yard officers were certain of the mistake; and see J. R. Tanner, *Cat. Pepysian*, Vol. III, p. xlvii.

62 Beach was probably referring to the Admiralty decision of 28 March 1678 [**65**].

63 Sir Richard Beach had been long pressing for a stricter control of house and ship improvements.

64 There were numerous rumours at this time, one of which was to burn 'all the big ships at Chatham', *Cal. S.P. Dom.*, 1678, p. 563, 9 December 1678.

Sources of Documents

1	N.M.M. CHA/E/1A		38	ADM 106/298 fol. 163
2	P.R.O. ADM 106/310 fol. 47		39	ADM 106/307 fol. 346
3	P.R.O. SP 46/137 Part 5 no. 362		40	ADM 106/298 fol. 22
4	SP 46/137 Part 5 no. 364		41	ADM 106/294 fol. 461
5	SP 46/137 Part 6 no. 389		42	ADM 106/301 fol. 201
6	ADM 106/281 fol. 167		43	ADM 106/307 fol. 397
7	ADM 106/282 fol. 259		44	ADM 106/310 fol. 37
8	N.M.M. CHA/E/1A		45	ADM 2/1 fols. 186/7
9	ADM 106/283 fol. 21		46	ADM 106/310 fol. 300
10	ADM 106/283 fol. 137		47	ADM 106/310 fol. 113
11	ADM 49/132 no. 46		48	ADM 2/1 fol. 191
12	ADM 106/285 fol. 15		49	ADM 106/309 fol. 177
13	ADM 106/285 fol. 90		50	ADM 106/312 fol. 223
14	ADM 106/285 fol. 289		51	ADM 106/310 fol. 205
15	ADM 106/287 fol. 304		52	ADM 49/132 no. 52
16	ADM 106/290 fol. 22		53	ADM 106/321 fol. 94
17	ADM 106/290 fol. 242		54	ADM 2/1 fols. 208/9
18	ADM 106/291 fol. 117		55	ADM 106/325 fol. 55
19	ADM 106/291 fol. 320		56	ADM 106/321 fol. 128
20	ADM 106/292 fol. 94D		57	ADM 106/321 fol. 171
21	ADM 106/293 fol. 85		58	ADM 2/1 fol. 217
22	ADM 106/293 fol. 125		59	ADM 106/321 fol. 255
23	ADM 106/300 fol. 112		60	ADM 106/321 fol. 296
24	ADM 106/294 fol. 141		61	ADM 106/321 fol. 349
25	ADM 106/298 fol. 82		62	ADM 106/327 fol. 338
26	ADM 106/307 fol. 270		63	ADM 106/325 fol. 302
27	ADM 106/297 fol. 343		64	ADM 106/326 fol. 199
28	ADM 2/1 fols. 158/9		65	ADM 106/330 fol. 4
29	ADM 106/294 fol. 184		66	ADM 106/330 fol. 6
30	ADM 106/298 fol. 105		67	ADM 106/331 Part 2 fol. 213
31	ADM 106/297 fol. 146		68	ADM 49/132 no. 56
32	ADM 2/1 fols. 162/3		69	ADM 106/330 fol. 293
33	ADM 106/297 fol. 148		70	ADM 106/330 fol. 343
34	ADM 106/298 fol. 395		71	ADM 106/332 fol. 176
35	ADM 106/307 fol. 301		72	ADM 106/330 fol. 431
36	ADM 106/294 fol. 309		73	ADM 106/330 fol. 486
37	ADM 106/294 fol. 311			

4

Benbow's Last Fight

Documents relating to the battle off Cape Santa Marta
19–24 August 1702

Edited by

JOHN B. HATTENDORF

Introduction

Benbow's last fight has lived in song, legend and history as one of the most notorious cases of cowardice in naval warfare. Despite Admiral Benbow's gallant leadership, his numerically superior squadron failed to defeat a French squadron because the English captains ran away from the fight and refused to support their wounded admiral. As a result, a court martial convicted the captains and two were executed.

A close study of the documents relating to the battle and the court martial suggests additional factors which complicate the traditional story: a six-day running battle in light and variable tropical winds, tired sailors, diminishing ammunition, battle-damaged ships, a French squadron determined on carrying out its mission and not being led astray to fight, English ship captains with serious professional doubts about the possibility of obtaining a decisive victory under the circumstances, an admiral bent on having his way and proving his case.

The battle was fought on the Caribbean coast of present-day Columbia in South America between 19–24 August 1702 O.S. (30 August–4 September N.S.). The court martial records and evidence relating to it fill a fat volume of manuscript which is far too lengthy to print here in full. However, much of it is repetitive, consisting of journals and depositions documenting the same facts and incidents. In this selection, I have attempted to form the material into a coherent and more readily usable collection by dividing the documents into eight sections: one for the events leading up to the battle, one for each day of the engagement, and a final section for the aftermath, court martial and executions. This has entailed a severe editing process in which

segments of documents have been placed in various sections in order to build
a complete picture of the developing situation. In each section, I have used
Admiral Benbow's letters and deposition as the central piece of evidence,
then I have used additional material from other documents which expand or
contradict his view. This method removes the element of corroboration
which is provided by numerous documents repeating similar viewpoints, but
it seems a reasonable method to follow under publishing constraints. I have
also tried to avoid reprinting documents published in other collections, but
reference is made to them in the notes.

Throughout, I have transcribed the documents using modern forms of
spelling, punctuation and capitalisation. For permission to publish Crown
Copyright documents, I am grateful to the Controller, Her Majesty's
Stationery Office. For permission to publish two supplementary documents,
I am grateful to the Bodleian Library, Oxford, and the British Library.

I should like to thank the following for their assistance: Dr R. J. B. Knight,
National Maritime Museum, Greenwich; Dr N. A. M. Rodger, Public
Record Office; Miss Fiona Cory, St Antony's College, Oxford; Everett C.
Wilkie, Jr. and Susan L. Danforth, John Carter Brown Library; and the
Reprographic Department of the Central Library, National University of
Singapore.

I

EVENTS LEADING UP TO THE BATTLE

1 *Vice-Admiral Benbow to Lord Nottingham*[1]

The 7 July, I received his excellency's the Lord High Admiral's Declarations of War with France and Spain, as also her Majesty's Declaration which I have communicated as required.

The 11 July, we sailed from before Port Royal with her Majesty's ships, etc., in the margin [*Breda, Defiance, Windsor, Ruby, Falmouth, Greenwich, Colchester, Pendennis, Strombolo* Fireship, *Carcass* Bomb, *Cresswell* Tender, *Recovery* Sloop] with a design to join Rear-Admiral Whetstone, but having advice the 14th by the *Colchester* and *Pendennis* who that day joined us that Monsieur Du Casse was expected at Logann which is on the north side of Hispaniola,[2] I plied for that part; nothing of moment happened till the 21, then took a small sloop near Cape Tiberoone. On the 24 by accident the *Strombolo* fireship's gunroom blew up and broke several of her beams, shattered her bulkheads and disabled her so far that I was obliged to send the *Pendennis* with her to Port Royal as also the bomb vessel and her tender which sailed so intolerable heavy that we could get but little ground. The 27th we came into the Gulf of Logann and not far from the town we saw several ships at anchor and one under sail who sent her boat to discover who we were but she came a little too near. Our boat took her before she got on board. The people of this boat informed that there were five or six merchant ships at Logann and that the ship which they belonged to was a King's ship and could carry fifty guns but now had but thirty mounted. I pursued him and pressed him so hard that when he saw all hopes lost for making his escape, run ashore and blew up. It being now night we lay as near the shore as convenient.

The 28 in the morning came before the town of Logann where there was but one ship of about eighteen guns, the rest sailed from thence before day in order to secure themselves in a harbour called the Cue,[3] but we having some ships between them and home took three of them and sunk another. This ship of eighteen guns was hauled ashore under their fortifications, which was a battery of about twelve guns. We fired at their battery, sent our boats and burnt the ship aground which could not be got off. The ship that was sunk had sixteen guns and one brought away of sixteen the other thirty and one brigantine of six. These ships has in them some wine and brandy and some small matter of sugar.

The 29 we came before Petit Guavus[4] but finding no ships there we went not into the place. We saw three or four ships in the Cue, a harbour which lies much within the land and well fortified by nature, etc., did not think it safe nor convenient to run such a risk for so small a matter. We continued in this bay till the 2 August standing from one end of the part that is inhabited to the other fatiguing the inhabitants who expected our landing but our circumstances would not admit of it.

We sailed for Cape Donna Maria[5] where is a good bay and water where we arrived the 5th.

Having advices that Monsiuer Du Casse is gone to Cartagena and from thence to Porto Bello I design to sail on that coast with her Majesty's ships in the margin [*Breda, Defiance, Ruby, Greenwich, Falmouth, Windsor*].[6] Accordingly we sailed the 10th August 1702 and stretched over toward the coast of Santa Martha[7] near that place the 19th in the morning we spied ten sail to the eastward . . .

2   *Line of Battle*

The *Defiance* to lead with the starboard tack and the *Falmouth* with the larboard tack onboard.

Ships' Names	Commanders' Names
Defiance	Captain Richard Kirkby
Pendennis	Thomas Hudson
Windsor	John Constable
Breda	{ Admiral Benbow { Christopher Fogg
Greenwich	Cooper Wade
Ruby	George Walton
Falmouth	Samuel Vincent

For so doing this shall be your warrant. Dated on board her Majesty's Ship *Breda* July the 14th 1702.

Directed to the several commanders above mentioned.

II

19 AUGUST 1702

3 Benbow to Lord Nottingham

. . . little wind at east we made the best of our way to come up with them. About noon the wind came out of the sea then we could lie with them and soon perceived them to be Frenchmen some of our ships being three or four mile astern[8] I made the signal for battle and went with an easy sail to have them come up, and steered with the French who steered to the westward along shore under their two topsails. There was of them four sturdy ships from sixty to seventy guns, one great Dutch-built ship about thirty or forty guns and one small ship full of soldiers. The rest were a sloop and three small ships. I was very uneasy to see our ships so long a-coming up and in such disorder. Our line of battle was as per margin [*Defiance, Pendennis, Windsor, Breda, Greenwich, Ruby, Falmouth*]. The *Defiance* being to lead, whose commander I found did not make all the haste he might into his station as also the *Windsor*, I sent them to make more sail. The night approaching we steered along side of the enemy and endeavoured to get near them being to windward and steering large, but not with a design to attack them before the *Defiance* was abreast of the headmost ship, but before this was done the *Falmouth* in the rear attacked the Flemish ship, the *Windsor* the ship abreast of her, as also did the *Defiance* soon after we were obliged to do the same having received the fire of the French ship abreast of us. The *Defiance* and *Windsor* after they had received two or three broadsides from the enemy luffed out of the line, out of gunshot. The two sternmost ships of the French lay upon us, which very much galled us, our ships in the rear not coming up as they ought. It was four o'clock when we begun and continued till it was dark. We kept them company all night steering to the westward. I did believe that if I ordered a new line of battle and lead myself on all tacks (perceiving the French would decline fighting if they could) might do the better and that our people for shame would not fail to follow a good example . . .

4 Vice-Admiral Benbow's Deposition

Near Santa Martha on the coast of New Spain near the latitude of 10 degrees

North met with Monsieur Du Casse with four men-of-war, viz., *Laura* of 70 guns and 500 men, *Agréable* of 70 guns and 450 men, *La Pauline* of 68 guns and 450 men and the *Phoenix* of 68 guns with 450 men as also one large Flemish ship of about 40 guns and three transport ships . . .[9] We saw their ships as soon as it was day, being to the eastward of us we making the best of our way to come up with them. About one in the afternoon perceived they were French, then soon after the Admiral put abroad the signal for battle our ships being at some [distance] astern he going away with an easy sail, as did the French steering to the westward with little wind about the southeast and fair weather. The *Defiance* Captain Kirkby commander was to lead on that tack as the line of battle directed but he taking little notice of it came with an easy sail which was taken notice of by the Admiral sending his boat with his Lieutenant[10] who told him it was the Admiral's order to tell him that he should make more sail and get abreast of the enemy's van for that he would engage them as soon as possible. Upon this he set his main sail and loosed his topgallant sails, after this he was got into the Admiral's grain and very near the length of the van of the enemy. About 4 o'clock the *Falmouth* in the rear attacked the Flemish ship, the *Windsor, Breda* and *Defiance* then as believed within point blank, the fire began,[11] which did not last with the *Defiance* more than three broadsides or about half an hour before she luffed out of the line and out of gunshot of the enemy having received no manner of damage, keeping her foresail and topgallant sails set so it was thought she would have quite deserted. The Admiral continued engaging two of the French ships till it was dark without any assistance. After it was night the *Defiance* fell astern leaving the Admiral to pursue and to keep them company, which he did all that night . . .

5   *Deposition of John Taylor, Master, H.M.S.* Ruby

Wednesday 19 of August, fair weather, small gales and calms. At 5 this morning small gales and winds South to ENE we see 10 sail . . . At 11 we had a signal to draw in a line of battle which was observed. At half hour past 4 the *Falmouth* firing first we all engaged the enemy, but the *Pendennis* that could not come up. At 6 at night we left off. At noon Cape St Martha's bore SW½W 8 leagues. At ½ hour past 4 it [bore] SW 6 leagues. We chase the enemy all night.

6   *Deposition of Bartholomew Ordd, Master, H.M.S.* Breda

. . . about noon the wind veered to the South we then steering with them we then made the signal for the line of battle, they steering along the shore to the westward. About 4 this afternoon we came within point blank shot of the 2 of the sternmost of the French men-of-war, being on our starboard tack and they to leeward. Captain Kirkby in the *Defiance* on the tack to leeward and the *Windsor* next him and the *Falmouth* being sternmost of our line and abreast of our enemy she engaged her, but we being only abreast of the second of the French line, the Admiral desiring to be fair up with the headmost of their line, we did not fire, but the *Windsor* being ahead of us did fire a broadside into that ship which was abreast of us. The *Defiance* ahead of the *Windsor* fired likewise, then the enemy fired at us, we were forced to enter battle, but none of our guns could reach their commander or his second, but their shot reached the *Defiance* Captain Kirkby receiving not above two broadsides before he luffed out of the line, without gun shot of the enemy. The *Windsor* following him and left us to engage those 4 ships which at night did seize the rest of our squadron being much out of order and astern. We lost in this action several men and received a shot through the very heart of our mainmast, also had our sails and rigging much shot and disabled and several shot between wind and water, this being Monsieur Du Casse and being 4 men-of-war from 70 to 60 guns. The action being over, Captain Constable came aboard here very drunk we being about 12 to 13 leagues to the eastward of Santa Martha . . .

7 *Journal of John Martin, Master, H.M.S.* Defiance

. . . At 2 o'clock the Admiral hoisted a red pendant at the main topmast head, the ships made sail ahead towards the French with a small breeze. About 3 o'clock the Admiral filled, and hoisted the red flag at the foretopmast head. The *Windsor* shot ahead of him to fall into her station. At ½ an hour after 4 the French commodore braced to, he leading the squadron. The *Falmouth* in the rear of the line fired at two of these ships that was in the rear of them, ahead of which was four men-of-war, the Admiral and *Windsor* fired, the enemy's three ships firing at us at which time Mr Luck the 2nd Lieutenant received his mortal wound. We continued firing till 5 o'clock then desisted, our shot not reaching. They fired several shot afterwards at us, chain shot at the main mast just below the parrel 7 inches through the mainyard in the slings almost one half through the rigging, shot the larboard foretopsail sheet, both the fore jeers and the chains in 4 pieces and several ropes of the running rigging. The *Windsor* and *Breda*, shortening sail and not coming up to close the line, we did not bear down. The commodore of the French a point abaft the beam to eastward of us, the *Falmouth* kept firing at the sternmost ships, then the squadron lay by with their heads to the northward and we kept the way and sent a boat aboard the Admiral, we afterwards brought to with the head to the northward to lie for the boat, the Admiral's boat met her and they came aboard together. We had orders by the Admiral's boat to keep after him all night, and bear away when he did, which we did edging nearer to the French and steering with them.

8   *Deposition of Edward Palmer, Carpenter, H.M.S.* Defiance

. . . *Defiance* leading in the line of battle. About four o'clock in the afternoon
began to engage the headmost of the enemy and continued it about half an
hour or three quarters, about which time she edged out of the line, this
deponent then being upon the gundeck heard there was an order given not
to fire any more guns which was observed, the men crying out they should
be knocked in the head at their guns, and that if some few guns were fired
now and then 'twould prevent the enemy having so fair an object at 'em, at
the same time this deponent spoke to Lieut. Knighton and asked him the
meaning of not firing, who replied it was according to orders . . .

9   *Deposition of Francis Knighton, 3rd Lieutenant, H.M.S.* Defiance

. . . Deposeth that he does not know of the *Defiance* being out of the line of
battle the 19th nor knows not of any directions that were given for luffing
out of it, but that 'twas Colonel Kirkby's opinion unsafe to bear down upon
the enemy their ships not being near enough to him to bear down with
him . . .

10   *Deposition of Gavin Hamilton, Surgeon, H.M.S.* Defiance

. . . about five of the clock in the afternoon when the *Defiance* had left off
firing John Hazleurst, Coxswain of the barge, was brought down to this
deponent wounded by losing his right arm, who exclaimed extremely against
Colonel Kirkby his then Captain for ill conduct, saying it was God's just
judgement upon him for sailing with a person he knew to be a coward, that
the said Coxswain was reproved by Lieutenant Luck for his exclamation
(who was brought down wounded immediately after him) who told him it was
not then a time to rail, that the Coxswain replied they were destroyed at their
guns without making any resistance tho' required by the [men] . . . that the
men publicly and generally exclaimed and complained of barbarous usage
for standing still to be dashed at their guns without making any resistance
that commanding no gun should be fired . . .

11   *Deposition of Samuel Vincent, commanding H.M.S.* Falmouth

. . . At three in the afternoon the Red Flag was spread at our Admiral's
foretopmast head, which was a signal [to] every ship to use the utmost of
their endeavour to engage the enemy. At four we the nearest to and abreast
of the enemy's sternmost ships (and ordered to bring up the rear) engaged
them till half an hour past six; then we sheared off and desisted from firing,
intending the boat onboard the Admiral to acquaint him with our
proceedings and to ask him leave to engage in the night, but the gale

freshening, the boats could not get ahead of the ship but was forced to come aboard again . . .

12 Deposition of Jacob Tiley, Master, H.M.S. Windsor

. . . Captain Constable's directions to him was to keep the *Windsor* within half a cable's length of the *Defiance*, go where she would and not have regard to the station the Admiral was in.

13 Deposition of Edward Holland, 1st Lieutenant, H.M.S. Windsor

. . . after some time had been spent in firing, I observed that our shot did not reach, which I acquainted Captain Constable of, and he ordered to forbear . . .

14 Deposition of Henry Partington, 1st Lieutenant, H.M.S. Greenwich

. . . One thing I took notice of that by the Captain's orders, the day he [Captain Wade] saw the enemy or the day after, we bent an old foretopsail which is fit for nothing but to be cast it's so thin that if it had shivered in the wind it would have flown out of the bolt rope, which we chased with and a reef in the main topsail which I mentioned and objected against upon the quarterdeck before the Captain, Master and Pilot, but had no answer tho' I said the foretopsail looks more like a design than a chasing sail . . .

15 Deposition of Edward Eaton, Clerk, H.M.S. Greenwich

. . . about 5 in the afternoon being something nigh the *Falmouth* began to fire at a Dutch built ship which I could perceive had a great number of men some shot passing from the enemy, the *Defiance* to lead the van began to fire as did the *Windsor* at a great distance steered out of the line persistently from the enemy leaving the Admiral to lead we being next the Admiral we let some guns pass from us to the two small ships and then edged away and broke the line. My Captain instead of animating the men told them they were ships of great force and said 'twould make our hearts ache. 3 times successively, he did pretend to bear down to the hindmost ship, but when in gun shot luffed up into the line saying he was not to break the line. The first Lieutenant seeing of the Captain's ill management and that we were in a confused order came up to know what he intended to do whose opinion was asked about keeping the line he replied and said that he was not to break his line, but he being somewhat mellow or otherwise in drink as he was at Logann had no regard to any instructions but fired to no purpose without considering what distance we were from the enemy . . .

16 *Line of Battle*

The *Breda* to lead upon each tack and before the wind, etc.

Small vessels	Ships' Names	Commanders' Names	
Recovery sloop	*Breda*	{ John Benbow Esq., Admiral	
		{ Christopher Fogg	
	Defiance	Richard Kirkby	The same signal
	Windsor	John Constable	for each ship's
	Greenwich	Cooper Wade	Captain and Lieutenant as
	Ruby	George Walton	the line of battle
	Pendennis	Thomas Hudson	of the 25th July
	Falmouth	Samuel Vincent	last directs[12]

When the signal is made to draw into this line, each Captain is directed and required to keep her Majesty's ship he commands not further than half a cable's length from the ship he follows, and in the same parallel with the *Breda*, he is not to quit this line on any pretence whatever without first giving me notice, nor to keep at a greater distance than is directed, as he or they shall or will answer the contrary at their perils. And for so doing this shall be your warrant. Dated on board her Majesty's Ship *Breda* abreast of Santa Martha on the Main continent of America, August 19th 1702.

                                                                    Benbow

To Colonel Richard Kirkby Commander of her Majesty's Ship the *Defiance* and to all other Captains. If any ship falters the ship that follows is to supply her place.

III

20 AUGUST 1702

17   *Benbow to Lord Nottingham*

20th at daylight in the morning I found we were[13] near the enemy only the *Ruby* up with us the rest of our ships three, four and five mile astern. It proved little wind and we[14] were within gunshot of all the enemy. They were so civil as not to fire otherwise must have received a great deal of damage. At 2 this afternoon, the sea breeze came. The enemy got into a line making what sail they could. Our ships not coming up, we with the *Ruby* plied our chase guns on them till night then left off. Keeping them company all night . . .

18   *Benbow's deposition*

. . . This morning at day light the Admiral and the *Ruby* were fair up with the enemy and within shot of all their ships, the rest of ours being 3 and 4 mile astern. The Admiral seeing this backwardness altered his line of battle sent to each ship another wherein he signified that the *Breda* to lead on all tacks, etc., (seeing the enemy would make a running fight) hoping that our captains would follow a good example. The *Ruby* and the Admiral lay within gunshot of the enemy at two this afternoon, but the French was so civil as not to fire otherwise might have disabled them both. Then the sea breeze came up. The French put themselves into a close line making what sail they could to the westward, the *Ruby* and *Breda* plying their chase guns on the sternmost. This day the Admiral sent on board the *Defiance* to Captain Kirkby to keep his line and station which he said he would, but did not. The *Breda* and *Ruby* kept the enemy company very close all night, the rest of the ships two or three mile astern though the signal of battle was out night and day, but not regarded . . .

19   *Deposition of John Taylor, Master, H.M.S.* Ruby

Thursday 20 of August, fair weather, moderate and small gales, winds S by E to [S]. At 5 this morning the Admiral made a signal to draw in a line of battle which the fleet observed. At 6 this morning Cape St Marthas bore

ESE 6 leagues. We continued our chase at 12 noon Cape St Marthas bore
SE½E 5 leagues. At 7 this morning being ahead of the flag [endeavoured]
to follow the *Greenwich* but our Lieutenant[15] going aboard we were ordered
to keep ahead. At 6 at night Cape St Marthas bore E by N 7 leagues . . .

20   *Deposition of Samuel Vincent, commanding H.M.S.* Falmouth

. . . we endeavoured to get up with the enemy but could not by reason of light
wind and the *Pendennis* not making sail [or] closing the line as per the
Admiral's order tho' we called to them several times [so] to do . . .

21   *Deposition of Francis Knighton, 3rd Lieutenant, H.M.S.* Defiance

. . . that the 20th when the *Ruby* and *Breda* lay becalmed abreast of the enemy
the *Defiance* was astern and made what sail they could to come up with
them . . .

22   *Deposition of Edward Holland, 1st Lieutenant, H.M.S.* Windsor

. . . At another time when I was upon the quarterdeck (the day I cannot justly
fix) we happened to be abreast of the *Defiance*, he had his foresail and topsail
set and we our topsails half mast. The Admiral fired a gun to windward with
powder and a little after, another was fired with shot, upon which I told
Captain Constable, that it was my opinion the Admiral seeing the *Defiance*
sail heavily that he designed us to go ahead and close the line next to him. He
was then of my opinion and ordered the foresail be set and the topsails
hoisted, but Colonel Kirkby called to him and asked his reason for not
keeping his line, Captain Constable answered that those guns were a signal
for him to go ahead, but Colonel Kirkby told him that he mistook the signal
and that it was for him to keep his line, upon which the foresail was hauled
up, the topsails lowered and we fell astern of the *Defiance* . . .

IV

21 AUGUST 1702

23   *Benbow to Lord Nottingham*

... 21st − At daylight in the morning we being on the quarter of the second ship of the enemy's[16] and within point blank shot the *Ruby* being ahead of us, she fired at the *Ruby*, which the *Ruby* returned. The two ships which were ahead[17] fell off being little wind, brought their guns to bear on the *Ruby*. We brought our guns to bear on this ship which first begun and shattered him very much, which obliged him to tow from us, but the *Ruby* being so much shattered in her masts and sails and rigging that I was obliged to lie by her and send[18] boats to tow her off. This action held almost two hours, during which the rear ship of the enemy's was abreast of the *Defiance* and *Windsor*, who never fired one gun,[19] though within point blank. At 8 a gale of wind sprung up, the enemy making what sail they could; we chasing them in hopes to come up with them. Then abreast of the River Grande our ships then in good order for battle, which was more than I saw before, being then in hopes they would consider their duty, the *Ruby* being disabled lay astern. At 2 this afternoon I got abreast of two of the sternmost[20] and finding we got nothing of them, in hopes to disable them in their masts and rigging[21] I began to fire on them as did some of our ships astern, but we lying abreast of them they pointed wholly at us which galled us much in our rigging and dismounted two or three of our lower tier guns; this held about two hours. They got without shot, we making what way[22] we could after them, but they using all the shifts possibly they could to evade fighting (and when so, 'tis a very hard matter to join battle). This night we used our utmost to endeavour to keep them company ...

24   *Vice-Admiral Benbow's Deposition*

... the *Breda* being on the quarter of the second ship of the enemy's and the *Ruby* on her broadside very near, the *Breda* luffed up thinking to go under the second ship's stern and to cut the sternmost from the rest by laying her aboard or otherwise. The second ship of the enemy seeing that fired on the *Ruby* which lay within musket shot. The *Ruby* returned it, but the Admiral seeing their combat somewhat unequal and that the *Ruby*'s rigging began to fly about their ears altered his design, bore away and lay his broadside to the quarter of that ship which had engaged the *Ruby* and in a little time obliged him to tow away the other two ships. The French brought their broadsides to bear on the *Ruby* shattered her much which obliged the Admiral to send boats to tow her off, it being little wind that the ship could hardly be governed. At this time the *Defiance* and *Windsor* was abreast of the sternmost ships less than point blank. The Admiral ordered that the Captain of the *Defiance* should be called to, to fire on that ship on his broadside, but finding he did not, it was repeated again but to no purpose for he fired not one gun, which if he and the *Windsor* had done (as 'twas their duty) they might have disabled that ship. This action of the *Breda* and *Ruby* lasted about two hours and no ship fired else. About 8 this morning a gale of wind sprung up easterly, they making all the sail they could in a close line and good order, the Admiral pursuing came up with the two sternmost ships of the enemy's and finding he could get nothing of the van proving little wind he attacks them. The *Defiance* was then pretty near the Admiral not above two cables' length astern. This continued about two hours being little wind that the *Breda* did not govern with her helm, otherwise should have given a good account of those two ships for all our ships were within shot (only the *Ruby*). The enemy towed from us, their ships feeling their heavy boats. Soon after this a tornado came which obliged us to haul in our lower tier guns and reef. The Admiral's main topsail yard being shot away and his rigging much shattered, for the two ships pointed wholly at him. He continued his chase, but did not engage more this day . . .

25   *Deposition of Bartholomew Ordd, Master, H.M.S.* Breda

. . . The ship which engaged the *Ruby* is of force about 70 guns and she with their commodore and one more plied their guns very much upon the *Ruby*, we plying ours upon the ship that fired first upon the *Ruby* down came her main topsail and topgallantsail and down came the *Ruby*'s maintopsail yard being shot in the slings and her mast and yards with rigging very much shot and torn. We sent boats and towed her off from the enemy. The enemy that first engaged the *Ruby* also so disabled that she towed off . . .

[afternoon action]
. . . They two with the others ahead plied their shot so fast upon us galled us very much both in sails, rigging, mast and yard, also dismounted two of our lower deck's guns and sunk our long boat. They edging from us got without shot of our guns having all their sails set, we still holding on our chase and fitting our ship for the second encounter in all which time the sternmost of our fleet's shot could not reach our enemy.

At noon the River Grande bore SE distance 5 leagues.

26 *Deposition of Arthur DelGarno, 2nd Lieutenant, H.M.S.* Ruby

. . . at ½ an hour past 5, we were within pistol shot of one of the French ships of war having her stern painted blue. He first fired after we engaged him so hot that at 7 o'clock this morning he towed with his boats from us, the French commander in chief taking notice of it with another ship bore down upon us. About ½ past 7, we were obliged to be towed off by boats, which were the *Breda*'s, *Defiance*'s and our own, we having engaged three ships of the enemy until we were disabled by having our main topmast wounded a third through about half mast down, our topmast shrouds cut in several places, the maintopsail yard shot in two in the slings, the stays and backstays, standing and running, almost all shot, mainmast and foremast very much wounded, and in bracing our foreyard, our foremast cracked all round in the upper wound. That obliged us to shorten sail and to fish him, having nothing but the shrouds to support him and all our sails shot to pieces . . .

27 *Deposition of Francis Knighton, 3rd Lieutenant, H.M.S.* Defiance

. . . that the 21st when the *Ruby* and *Breda* were engaged with the enemy the *Defiance* fired some guns at the sternmost but one of the enemy's ships, but 'twas Colonel Kirkby's opinion they were not within point blank shot of the sternmost of 'em, and ordered that no shot should be fired at him nor were they . . .

28 *Deposition of Edward Palmer, Carpenter, H.M.S.* Defiance

. . . the *Defiance* was in the station close up the *Breda*'s stern and *Windsor* and the *Defiance* both within point blank shot of the enemy's sternmost ship yet neither of 'em fired any shot at her tho' called to from the *Breda* several times to engage her which the Boatswain acquainted the Captain with twice for which he was reproved by his Captain nor was it regarded by his Captain. About that time the Master acquainted him they were within shot for which he was reproved as he informed this deponent and Boatswain . . .

29 *Deposition of Thomas Mollamb, Boatswain, H.M.S.* Defiance

. . . the *Defiance* was in her station close under the *Breda*'s stern and *Windsor* under the *Defiance*'s, that the *Defiance* then being upon the bow of the enemy's sternmost ship and *Windsor* upon her quarter fired not one gun at her tho' called to from the *Breda* by direction of the Admiral to engage her which this deponent with the men upon the forecastle informed the Captain of as also the Master. A second time this deponent called to his Captain to acquaint him the Admiral commanded some fire and withall told him they had a fair prospect to destroy the ship, that thereupon his Captain reproved him bid him hold his tongue and told him to mind his own business and not intermeddle in that affair which if he did not regard he would run his sword into him or words to that effect, that at the same time the men at their quarters cried out they had as good throw the guns overboard as stand by them, notwithstanding all which the Captain commanded they should not fire . . .

30   Deposition of John Codner, 2nd Lieutenant, H.M.S. Greenwich

. . . he heard Lieutenant Langridge of her Majesty's Ship *Breda* say Captain Constable you must keep within half a cable's length of the *Defiance* and if the *Defiance* falters you are to make good the line and not to slacken sails tho' the Admiral does, for he does it for bringing the rear of the fleet up.

31   Deposition of Edward Eaton, Clerk, H.M.S. Greenwich

. . . About noon the enemy stood into the shore our Admiral doing the same, then tacking again and standing off the Admiral fired at the enemy we then being out of the line at a great distance. The enemy upon their tacking came pretty nigh us so that their shot over reached us. My Captain gave orders not to fire and when the enemy was out of reach we repaid them with one gun which was very nigh half a mile short . . .

32   Deposition of Edward Holland, 1st Lieutenant, H.M.S. Windsor

. . . in the morning of the third day, the Admiral and *Ruby* engaged the enemy. We had very small winds in stretching along the *Defiance* and we were pretty near a ship of the enemy's rear, who sailed heavier than the rest, and as I thought was within shot of us, I told Captain Constable of it and desired I might try some guns at him, our Gunner was of my opinion, his answer to me was that it was but throwing away powder and shot or to that effect . . .

33   Deposition of Samuel Vincent, commanding H.M.S. Falmouth

. . . About 2 in the afternoon we had a hard squall with wind and rain which put us by further engaging . . .

V

22 AUGUST 1702

34   *Benbow to Lord Nottingham*

. . . 22nd − This morning at daylight the *Greenwich* was about three leagues
astern, though the line of battle was never struck night nor day; the rest of
our ships indifferently near (except the *Ruby*), the enemy about a mile and
a half ahead. At 3 this afternoon, the wind came to the southward[23] which
before was easterly. This gave the enemy the weather gage, but in tacking we
fetched within gunshot of the sternmost of them (firing at each other) but our
line being much out of order and some of our ships three mile astern. This
night I perceived that the enemy was very uneasy altering their courses very
often between the West and North . . .[24]

35   *Benbow's Deposition*

. . . The *Greenwich* was about three leagues astern of the Admiral, the rest
of the ships as usual 3 or 4 mile astern, only the *Falmouth* whose station it
was to be in the rear, seeing the behaviour of some of the Captains of our
ships ahead, forsook that station and came up with the Admiral. The Captain
sent his Lieutenant on board and desiring that he might have leave to assist
him seeing nobody else would, which the Admiral accepted of and ordered
the Lieutenant to thank his Captain for his offer, after this the *Defiance* never
came near the Admiral but kept astern, he and the rest, as though they had
a design to see him ruined or had intended to desert, the *Defiance* leading the
van of them four ships as a separate division. This morning at daylight the
enemy was about a mile and a half ahead. The Admiral pursued with all the
sail he could and came very near the enemy and when it proved calm so did
not engage. About three this afternoon a small breeze came at west, the
enemy stood in for shore and fetched within Sambay,[25] we then keeping to
leeward of them. As they tacked, the Admiral fetched within shot of the
sternmost and fired several shot, tacked and stood after them, our ships being
a great distance astern and to leeward, night coming on the Admiral kept
them company. This night the Flemish ship left their company . . .

36   *Deposition of Bartholomew Ordd, Master, H.M.S.* Breda

Saturday . . . fair weather all night, only one squall of wind and rain, we making sail what we could to keep the enemy company . . . At 3 this afternoon, the wind veering to the SW the enemy having the wind of us, but in tacking we came within point blank shot of the sternmost of them, firing at each other as we past. Our line being much out of order as formerly 'twas. The *Greenwich* fired likewise in passing of them, but their guns reached not above half way.

At noon the island Sambo[26] bore SSE distance 2 leagues.

37   *Deposition of Samuel Vincent, commanding H.M.S.* Falmouth

. . . By daylight the Admiral made the signal for the line of battle, and we made what sail we could to get up with the enemy, the Admiral being near them, and the *Greenwich* about 3 leagues distant and astern of the Admiral, we made what sail we could from the rear to second her. And about two in the afternoon we stood to the northward to gain the wind of the enemy, the Admiral and ourselves fetched within gunshot of them and exchanged some broadsides with them. The *Greenwich* recovered the line of battle, but not within gunshot of the enemy, tho' they fired a considerable number of guns without doing any damage to them, the shot falling very short.

38   *Journal of William Herriott, 1st Lieutenant, H.M.S.* Falmouth

. . . this morning in time of action our pinnace being shot and not being able to free her, we were obliged to cut her away, but saved the men . . .

39   *Deposition of Peircy Brett, Master, H.M.S.* Falmouth

. . . our pinnace was shot in towing the ship and we could not keep her free we cut her adrift . . .

40   *Deposition of Henry Partington, 1st Lieutenant, H.M.S.* Greenwich

. . . That being upon deck after out of reach of our lower deck guns I heard him [Captain Wade] say, viz., if this be the Admiral's conduct by God it will be another Parliament business; why does he not bear down, by God. He bore down and give him a dose at which time we were astern of the enemy's sternmost ship, notwithstanding he put his helm aweather and stood steering with her which put us farther astern and from the enemy than at first and ordered me to stand by the guns below for he would be upon the enemy's quarter and once asked my opinion whether he could not answer bearing out of the line. I told him that he could not answer it, for the signal for the line

was a positive command to keep the line therefore could not answer his
bearing out of the line one way or 'tother, but without any regard to that put
his helm aweather and bore up and said he was sure it could be no harm to
bear to the enemy tho' he found bearing up occasioned our falling farther
astern and farther from the enemy. At another time finding that our lower
deck shot would not reach the enemy, I went up into the gangway and told
him that our shot below did not reach the enemy by a third of the way and
asked what I should do. His answer was that he could not help it, but
commanded me to fire away.

41   *Journal of John Codner, 2nd Lieutenant, H.M.S.* Greenwich

. . . at the same time, he [Captain Wade] being drunk with both Master and
Pilot and had been so every day since we first began to engage the enemy . . .

42   *Deposition of Edward Eaton, Clerk, H.M.S.* Greenwich

. . . Being nigh the enemy we followed the *Windsor* in our due line and
engaged two of their ships, but soon we did forsake the line and bore away
which the Master did persuade the Captain to who did readily condescend
thereto tho' he had sent orders down to the Lieutenant that he did design to
be on the enemy's quarter and continued bearing away and luffing again
which kept us very much astern. Then the Captain says to the Master what
if the Admiral should fire a shot at him. Oh says the Master we will tell the
Admiral the ship will not answer the helm. The Captain then begins to find
fault with the Admiral's conduct saying God damn it, it would be another
Parliament business and that he would not favour any one, and that
notwithstanding the several orders for keeping the line, he swore by God he
did not understand those damned verbal orders and did believe that he ought
not to follow them without a written order the Master being of the same
opinion at the same time. One of the Master's Mates had the impudence to
say that [he] had often heard of Admiral Benbow's bravery and conduct,
but when told him so again he would say were great liars . . .

43   *Deposition of Isaac Sun, Master, H.M.S.* Greenwich

. . . the 22 in the morning they [the *Greenwich*] were fallen astern
considerably by taking up their longboat and pinnace which were break away
from their stern . . .

44   *Deposition of Francis Cotterell, Boatswain, H.M.S.* Greenwich

. . . he said to the Lieutenant Codner, what do we fire these shot in vain for,
the Lieutenant said I do according to order, but said the Lieutenant I'll go

aft and ask the Captain again whether we shall labour firing and the Captain he replied to him again we must keep doing the Admiral won't believe we fight else and he (this deponent) says they was not within gunshot of the enemy all the time of the engagement except when we came astern of the blue stern ship, then fired some guns at her and shot ahead of her.

45   *Deposition of Edward Palmer, Carpenter, H.M.S.* Defiance

. . . during the time of the engagement, he does not know of any encouragement the Captain gave his men, but rather the contrary, for when application was made to him by his men in time of action for their victuals he replied let me see the man [who] dares say he deserves his victuals or to that effect . . .

46   *Deposition of Gavin Hamilton, Surgeon, H.M.S.* Defiance

. . . when they applied to him for their provisions which was their due he refused it them, and answered let me see the dog [that] says he deserves it in this ship, that the greatest [insult] this deponent heard his Captain give his men was abusing them by the names of dog and rogue . . .

47   *Deposition of John Spurr, Midshipman, H.M.S.* Defiance

Saturday the 22 the men applied themselves for their provisions not having received any meat during the time of engagement who instead of encouragement met with a repulse in very hard language . . .

VI

23 AUGUST 1702

48   *Benbow to Lord Nottingham*

23rd − At daylight this morning the enemy was about six mile ahead of us and the great Dutch ship separated from them, out of sight. Some of our squadron at this time more than four mile astern (viz., *Defiance* and *Windsor*) we making what sail we could after them. At 10 o'clock the enemy tacked, the wind then at ENE, but very variable. We fetched within point blank shot of two of them[27] passing our broadsides at each other, most of our ships could not come within shot. Soon after we tacked and pursued them what we could. About noon, we took from them a small English ship called the *Ann* Galley which they had taken off of Lisbon.[28] The *Ruby* being disabled could not keep company; I ordered her for Port Royal. At 8 this evening our squadron was all fair by us, being then distance from the enemy about[29] two mile. They steered SE and very little wind then at northwest and variable, we steering after them and all our ships (except *Falmouth*) falling much astern. At 12 the enemy began to separate we steering after the sternmost.

49   *Vice-Admiral Benbow's Deposition*

This morning the enemy at daylight bore northwest about 4 or 5 mile. The Admiral pursued all he could, though no ships nearer him than 3 mile (only the *Falmouth*). At 10 this forenoon, the enemy tacked, the Admiral and *Falmouth* fetched within point blank shot of two of the sternmost of the enemy where was passed two or three broadsides. After this the Admiral tacked as also did the *Falmouth*, [and] pursued the enemy, they making all the shifts and sail they could to get clear. About 4 this afternoon, it proved calm; the *Falmouth* very near the Admiral, but the *Defiance* and the rest 3 or 4 mile astern (though you are to take notice that there was not a ship of the English but sailed better than the Admiral, before and after this battle). It continued calm till about 7 this evening, then a gale of wind came up, the Admiral and *Falmouth* being about 2 miles from the enemy, our ships that were astern having the wind first . . .

50 *Deposition of Bartholomew Ordd, Master, H.M.S.* Breda

Sunday the 23 weather fair the enemy steering W and WNW till between 3 and 4 in the morning we keeping in sight of them, the moon setting under the horizon, at 4 the wind at ENE they altering their course and stood North . . . At noon Cartagena bearing about South distant about 16 leagues.

51 *Deposition of William Herriott, 1st Lieutenant, H.M.S.* Falmouth

. . . this deponent by order of his Captain called to the *Pendennis* near forty times severally to make more sail and let out his reefs to get nearer the Admiral and into his station as his line of battle directed, also for him to do the same to the ship ahead of him, but finding in three days they had no regard to it Captain Vincent made sail ahead and at two in the morning the 23rd August 1702 came close under the Admiral's stern, hailed him and asked whether he should keep close to him or fall into the rear of the fleet as directed by the line of battle and received the Admiral's order to keep close to him . . .

52 *Deposition of Isaac Sun, Master, H.M.S.* Greenwich

. . . when the *Breda* and *Falmouth* took the *Ann* Galley prize there was no ship nearer them than the *Greenwich* which he believes was about half a mile distance . . .

53 *Deposition of Edward Eaton, Clerk, H.M.S.* Greenwich

. . . was but little wind unless the former part of the morning which soon died away. The Admiral and the *Falmouth* fired several shots at the *Ann* Galley prize and being calm the Admiral manned boats as did the *Falmouth* and the said ship without any resistance struck . . .

54 *Deposition of John Taylor, Master, H.M.S.* Ruby

. . . At 3 o'clock afternoon the fleet being becalmed and at a great way off them there was a signal for Lieutenants. Our Lieutenant went aboard, returned with orders to carry a puncheon of water for the *Ann* Galley prize they had retaken that day and six barrels of powder for the Admiral and half 100 weight of match. At 8 at night our powder and match was returned and orders sent by the *Defiance* boat for us to part company with the fleet to convoy the *Ann* Galley prize for Jamaica which whensoever we had a gale as at 9 we did.

VII

24 AUGUST 1702

55   *Benbow to Lord Nottingham*

24th − At 2 in the morning we came within call of her, it being very[30] little wind, being all[31] clear fired our broadside with double and round alow and round and partridge aloft, which she returned very heartily. At 3 o'clock by a chain shot my right leg was broke to pieces and was carried down. This continued till day, then see seemingly the ruins of a ship of about seventy guns, her main yard down and shot to pieces, her foretopsail shot away, her mizzenmast shot by the board, all her rigging gone and her sides bored to pieces with our double headed shot. The *Falmouth* assisted in this matter very much and no other. Soon after day we saw the other part of the enemy coming[32] toward us with a strong squall of wind easterly. At the same time, the *Windsor, Pendennis* and *Greenwich* coming ahead of the enemy towards us, came to leeward of the disabled ship, fired their broadsides past her and stood to the southward[33] then the *Defiance* following them who came also to the leeward of the disabled ship, fired part of her broadside, then the disabled ship did not fire above twenty guns at the *Defiance* before she put her helm aweather and run right away before the wind lowered both her topsails and run to leeward of the *Falmouth* (which was then a gun shot to leeward of us, knotting her rigging) not having any regard to the signal of battle. The enemy seeing our[34] other three ships stand to the southward expected they would have tacked and stood with them, they brought to with their heads to the northward, they then being about two mile from us we being then within half gunshot of the disabled ship. The enemy seeing those three ships did not tack bore down upon us and run between the disabled ship and us,[35] giving us all the fire they had in which they shot our main topsail yard and shattered our rigging much we having none of our ships near us neither did they take notice of the battle signal but all in a confused hurry. The captain fired two guns at those ships ahead in order to put them in mind of their duty. The French seeing this great disorder of fear and confusion amongst us, brought to and lay by their own disabled ship, remanned her and took her in tow. Our rigging being much shattered, we lay till 10 o'clock. Our ship being again fitted the Captain acquainted me of it. I ordered him to pursue the enemy and told him I would give them battle; at that time the enemy was about three mile from us and to leeward having the disabled ship in tow steering North-East, the wind at SSW we making all the sail after them we could our battle signal always out notwithstanding our ships running confusedly amongst another which appeared much like fear and gave the enemy no small encouragement having before seen the behaviour of some of us. I ordered Captain Fogg to send to the Captains to keep their line and behave themselves like men. Captain Fogg sent this message by Captain Wade to Captain Kirkby and Captain Constable who told them I was very angry they did not behave themselves better. Soon after this message Captain Kirkby came on board me and before he asked how I did he repeated these words, that he wondered I would offer to engage the enemy again and said it was not requisite nor convenient after six days trial of their strength, and magnified the strength of the French, lessening ours. I did not believe there was a snake in the grass otherwise should not have met with so many misfortunes. I told him that was but his opinion; I would send for the rest of the Captains to know theirs. Accordingly ordered Captain Fogg to make the signal and their opinion was as enclosed.[36] When I saw this I was well assured that they had no mind to fight and that all our misfortunes heretofore came through cowardice and that the objections they made for not fighting was erroneous. I have thought it fit further not to venture for if the enemy could have disabled me, they would soon have dispatched them except those that had good heels which I believe would not have been wanting. When this opinion of theirs was given we were a-broadside of the enemy and the only opportunity we had to fight in six days. We were one seventy-gun ship, one of sixty-four, one of sixty and three of fifty. Our masts and yards, etc., in as good condition as could be expected and not eight men killed amongst them all, besides those of the *Breda*. Ammunition sufficient, I then and all our men willing and to refer this to a fitter opportunity which never could be expected to me was a perfect denial.

They likewise say that the French had five men-of-war from sixty to eighty guns which is false for there was but four from sixty to seventy and one of them in a tow, being all to pieces, and as to their numbers of men they are well thinned, believing we have as many good men as they. If this be allowed, there is no going to sea for a flag, etc., unless he carries his father, sons or brothers to assist in the day of battle. I thought always till now that a good example would have made anybody fight. This night we parted with the French but with no small regret to me and made the best of our way to Port Royal where we arrived the 31st with our ships where we found Rear-Admiral Whetstone with the rest of her Majesty's ships, only the *Dreadnought* is sailed for New England as per orders.

56   *Benbow's Deposition*

. . . about two o'clock the 24 in the morning the Admiral came up with the sternmost of the enemy within call, the *Falmouth* pretty near, but the rest of our ships about 4 mile astern which was more than half the ground we ran from 8 the 23rd at night (when they were all up with us to that time). The Admiral and the *Falmouth* engaged this ship at 2 in the morning and about 3 the Admiral was wounded and when day saw the ruins of a ship about 70 guns her mizzen mast shot by the board, her main yard shot in 3 or 4 pieces, her foretopsail yard likewise, her stays and rigging all shot in pieces, so she lay as a wreck. Soon after day our four ships being to windward of the disabled ship came down upon her but instead of lying by her, after they had fired their upper guns at her bore away and never came near her more, the *Defiance* came within pistol shot of her fired about twelve guns put her helm aweather and run from her and fearing the ship did not make haste enough to wear, the Captain ordered his mizzen yard to be lowered, the spritsail and the topsail and foretopmast staysail to be loosed in order to make the more haste from the fire of the disabled ship. The three French which were then about 4 mile from the disabled ship, when they saw the cowardly behaviour of our Captains in a squall came down upon the Admiral who lay close by the disabled ship getting in their spritsail yards gave him all their fire run between him and the disabled ship, remanned her and took her in tow, the Admiral's rigging being much shattered obliged him to lie till 10 o'clock then made sail after the French, but our ships when they saw the Admiral pursue followed in the greatest disorder imaginable instead of keeping their line. The Admiral gave orders to Captain Fogg to stand abreast of the van of the French and when so to attack them, the Admiral hearing the disorder our ships were in ordered Captain Fogg to send to the Captains to keep in better order and to behave themselves like Englishmen. Captain Wade being then aboard, this message was sent by him who delivered it (as is supposed) to the Captain of the *Defiance* who seeing the Admiral's resolution to engage came aboard the Admiral and came down where he was and before he ever asked how he did, he expressed these words, viz., that he wondered that he should offer to engage the French again, it not being necessary, safe or convenient having had six days trial of their strength, magnifying that of the French, lessening ours. The Admiral told him that was but his opinion only and that he would have the rest of the Captains'. Accordingly ordered the signal to be made for them to come aboard, at this time we were within shot of the enemy to windward and the only opportunity we had in six days chase to engage them when the Captain of the *Defiance* started this thing. The Captains being come aboard the Captain of the *Defiance* used all his art to poison the rest, which as many as he could come at, had been done before, otherwise should have succeeded better. He formed a writing with his own hand which was both cowardly and erroneous the substance of which was not to engage the French any more, brought to the Admiral for which the Admiral reproved him and told him that, that paper would ruin them all. So he went up again and writ another copy of which is here to the same effect, but to defer fighting till a better opportunity which never could be, for we had the weather gage, a fine gale of wind, six ships to four and one of them quite disabled, all our ships in as good a posture for fighting as could be expected and not eight men killed in all our ships (except the *Breda*) and to defer this to a fitter opportunity, to the Admiral seemed a perfect denial who having seen the cowardly behaviour of some of them before had reason to believe that they either had a design against him or to be traitors to their country if an opportunity happened that the French could have destroyed the Admiral.

57   *Deposition of Bartholomew Ordd, Master, H.M.S.* Breda

... About day sprung up a brisk gale at East or East by North, it being then fair for our fleet to come up to our assistance, they being then about 2 or 3 miles distant from us, we being engaged on our starboard side and the enemy on our larboard side at us our fleet coming briskly up to our assistance as we expected. The wind at the same time taking us on the starboard quarter and the enemy on the larboard quarter which caused both ships to yaw to each other, so coming very near the enemy within ship's length of him going out of head of the enemy gave him a dose with double and round in at his larboard bow which rent and tore him both in masts and yard, hull and rigging, then going close along his starboard side likewise loaded and fired as fast as possible we could still got astern then endeavouring to tack after her again the wind continuing for the rest of our fleet to come up and to take and leave of the said disabled ship. The *Defiance* Captain Kirkby then leading the rest of the fleet and in room of going to windward of the disabled ship went to leeward and fired some small quantity of guns and immediately bore up round before the wind, loosing spritsail, spritsail topsail, letting fly his maintopsail sheets and lowering them down to the cap so run right away to leeward, as if he were mad and so brought to in this condition out of shot of the enemy, and there lay. The *Windsor, Greenwich* and *Pendennis* run also t leeward of the disabled ship also out of shot on their starboard bow. Monsieur Du Casse seeing the disorder in our fleet bore down to the rescue of the disabled ship and took her in a tow, there being 2 ships more besides himself, we being then about and abreast of the said ship that we so much had disabled and within ½ gunshot of him. They all 4 of them then plying their guns all at us which rent and tore us more than in all time of engaging before, that we had scarce any sails or rigging left to command our ship. Then Captain Fogg ordered a shot to be fired at the *Windsor, Greenwich* and *Pendennis* for them to fall astern into their line, but all to no purpose they still keeping their topsails and foresail set to keep them ahead out of shot as they were, which was great discouragement to our men saying that they were all agreed to make us all a sacrifice, we making all dispatch possible we could to fit our ship. About 10 o'clock we were fitted again expecting to have the second encounter as we were absolutely resolved on it and all with courage. The line of battle being out all this time, the enemy then with their disabled ship in a tow had to get about 3 miles from us but our ships running so disorderly in a confused manner one abreast of another. It then being about noon, Captain Wade came aboard here and desired of Captain Fogg that he might follow us. Captain Fogg then ordered him to go onboard Captain Kirkby and Captain Constable to let them know the Admiral was very angry for their not keeping their line, then Captain Kirkby came aboard here going down to the Admiral told the Admiral that it was not reasonable to fight the enemy any more. The Admiral desired to know his reason, a signal being ordered immediately for all Captains, we then being fair abreast of the enemy.

Being a brave commanding gale and smooth water, the enemy seeing us fire a gun for the signal for all Captains, they thinking we fired at them, they fired several shot on board and over some of our sternmost ships.

The result of the consultation of the Captains was to refer engaging or giving battle to the French till a better opportunity, which in my opinion could never be, so good night.

58   *The Captains' Resolution*

At a consultation held on board her Majesty's Ship *Breda* the 24 August 1702 off of Cartagena on the Main Continent of America, it is the opinion of us, whose names are undermentioned, viz.:

First − of the great want of men, in number, quality and the weakness of those they have.
Secondly − The general want of ammunition of most sorts.
Thirdly − Each ship's masts, yards, sails, rigging and guns all being in a great measure disabled.
Fourthly − The winds are so small and variable that the ships cannot be governed by any strength each ship has.
Fifthly − Having experienced the enemy's force in six days battle following. The squadron consisting of five men-of-war and a fireship under the command of Monsieur Du Casse, their equipage consisting in guns from sixty to eighty and having a great number of seamen and soldiers on board for the service of Spain.

For which reasons above mentioned we think it not fit to engage the enemy at this time, but to keep them company this night and observe their motion, and if a fair opportunity shall happen (of wind and weather) once more to try our strength with them.

Richard Kirkby	Chr Fogge
Saml Vincent	Coopr Wade
John Constable	Thos Hudson

59 *Note from the Court Martial Proceedings*[37]

Memorandum: The Admiral was wounded about 3 in the morning of Monday.

Colonel Kirkby came aboard of the Admiral on Monday 24 August 1702 and went down in the cockpit to see the Admiral. The first word he said he was sorry to see his Honour in that condition, and said further that it was not requisite nor convenient to fight the French any more. The Admiral desired a signal to be made for the Captains to know their opinion and that was all the Admiral said after which Colonel Kirkby desired to take the Admiral by the hand which was refused him.

60 *Deposition of Robert Thompson, 1st Lieutenant, H.M.S.* Breda

. . . Captain Fogg called for me upon deck desiring my opinion we seeing the other three enemy ships bearing ESE of us distant 4 miles and our four ships, the *Defiance, Windsor, Greenwich* and *Pendennis* bearing N by E or NNE distant about two miles they all standing toward us with a strong squall at E or E by N. My opinion to Captain Fogg was that our ships might meet the enemy before they could come near us and our best way was if possible to sink this disabled ship and then there would be one less of their number. Captain Fogg immediately agreeing to this said that will do very well and let us at her in the name of God. I then went down to my quarters upon the gun deck and raised the metals of all the guns there as high as possible I could and bringing them pointing upon her. We were got within a ship's length of her starboard bow and firing a broadside into her bow double and round we having only our topsails set run alongside her starboard side loading and firing at her as fast as possible. We steered under her stern and alongside her larboard side her head lying to the northward we standing to the northward upon her lee bow then Captain Fogg called to me to bring the men from between decks upon deck to tack ship which I immediately did but when I came upon deck I see our four ships gone past us and running to leeward of the disabled ship I looking further about me saw the three French ships to windward lying by with their foretopsail to the mast and maintopsail full with their heads to the northward about two mile distant our helm being alee and ship astays the *Defiance* running alongside of the disabled ship and fired at her but I believe did not receive twenty shot from the disabled ship till she put her helm aweather run directly afore the wind lowered her topsails upon the cap and run to leeward of the *Falmouth* who was then lying knotting and splicing her rigging without gunshot which running away surprised our men so much that they could not keep their eyes from her nor to [keep] from expressing the coward parts of the officers on board her. I then looking farther about me saw the enemy coming afore the wind towards us we being about with our head to the southward set our foresail standing towards the *Windsor, Greenwich* and *Pendennis*, which was then to leeward of the disabled ship, with a [desire] to have brought them into a line with us to have received the enemy which was coming afore the wind, but our three ships having no regard to the signal kept the same sail set and would not fall into their line. We fired a shot at them but to no purpose they still keeping in a huddle upon our weather bow the enemy then upon our weather quarter fired each of them a broadside at us in which they shot down our maintopsail yard and shattered our rigging and sails more than all the time we were engaged before. They then brought to by their disabled ship putting men on board her and took her in tow towing her to the northward from us we making what dispatch we can in knotting and splicing our rigging.

. . . At 2 o'clock the enemy having fitted a small ship for a fireship out of a bravado sent her to let us see her newmade sally port but no shearhooks then immediately went back again ahead of their own ships. I being much grieved to see this out-braving of the enemy I went amongst the captains to put them in mind of the reputation of our country and said to them Gentlemen did you ever see such a sight before or read of the like in history they said no I further spoke to Captain Wade saying is not this a shame? He answered it was adding some more words but Captain Kirkby taxed him with not being a man fit to sit at a consult that would give ear to every single man's words at that rate. Then Captain Kirkby reading over their resolved consult he read referring battle to a better opportunity. I said Colonel Kirkby is now the time that we must turn Flemings and do as the proverb says: stay seven years for a fair wind and when it came are not ready for it. At this saying Captain Kirkby looked earnestly at me and laughed. I then wished them all well and to mind what they were doing having thus eased my troubled mind I came out upon deck. The headmost of the enemy being abaft our beam at 4 o'clock the consult being over they went onboard each to their respective ships we still sailing with the same sail. At 8 o'clock at night we were about two leagues ahead of the enemy they steered in for the shore towards Katergein[38] and we having no more to say to them steered along shore to the eastward.

61   *Deposition of John Spurr, Midshipman, H.M.S.* Defiance

. . . when the *Breda* and *Falmouth* had disabled a ship of the enemy's the *Defiance* being to windward bore down upon her and run to leeward of her within pistol shot of her fired at her in passing at which time the foot of the mizzen or mizzen yard of the *Defiance* was shot upon which the Captain ducked down his head and made a retreat aft, ordered more sail to be set . . .

62   *Journal of John Martin, Master, H.M.S.* Defiance

. . . about 6 o'clock we had a fresh gale at E by N, we made sail up with the French ship. The *Falmouth*'s rigging being much damnified forward of the Admiral stood to the northward, [thwart] the French ship's forefoot, we astern of the said ship could not rake him fearing to damnify the Admiral, the Admiral fired several shot at him as he [thwarted] his forefoot, as soon as the Admiral passed the wake of our shot, we engaged him, the courses up both topsails aback, to stop her headway close along his side. The commodore of the French bearing down to him after we had backed astern of him, we furled the foretopsails and lay with the maintops aback. *He damnified our masts and yards, viz., mizzen yards shot hanging* [in] *the splinters, the fore yard in the larboard ditto ½ way through, the main topmast under the main cap one third through, the forepart of the mainmast through the head in the wake of the rigging (we carried away his mizzen mast below the top). The rigging, viz., shot the main jeers and block, the main parrel to two parts the one of them stranded, the larboard maintopsail sheet, maintopmast stay, main lifts, main buntlines, maintop bowlines, the larboard leech of the maintopsail, the starboard maintopsail bowlines, two backstays of the maintopmast, two pair of main shrouds at the head of the mast, both foretopsail bowlines, both foretopsail runners, the starboard brace of the foretopsail, two main topmast shrouds, two foretopmast backstays and several ropes more of our running rigging.* The commodore of the French bore down directly upon us, our ships being astern, the rearmost of the French could aflung a shot over us (the commodore having his spritsail yard under his bowsprit). Having no ship nearer us, we wore to the northward *having weared from along the French ship's side (to prevent being boarded by the commodore of the French, etc.) we brought to upon the other tack firing our after guns as they came to bear,* upon which the commodore of the French came up close to the northward of the maimed ship and sprung his luff to the northward, then the *Greenwich, Windsor, Pendennis* and *Breda* (which had tacked to the southward) came up close to the leeward of her and passed their broadsides on the maimed ship and bore up to the southwestward. *In the space of the* Greenwich *and* Windsor, *we gave the maimed ship the starboard broadside, and then lay within point blank with our head to the northward till the Admiral passed his last broadside and bore up, then we bore up round to the southward to join him.* The French commodore wearing round, bore down to the leeward of the maimed ship and fired several shot at our Admiral who was in the rear of the said ships, the Admiral afterward laid his maintopsail aback and then formed a line to the southward, the *Falmouth* edged into the line, sometime after we followed (as we were coming in we knotted and spliced our rigging and clapped a fish on the fore and mizzen yard). The Admiral hauled up South by South by West (wind at ESE, a moderate gale). The French stood as we did with the other ship. At ½ an hour past 9 the French tacked to the northward. At 10, the Admiral tacked to the northward (wind bearing from the E by S to the westward till noon, for the most part calms). We towed with our boats to come into the line, from 10 to noon we kept our boats towing to the eastward, being almost calm. The French lying to the northeastward of us.

. . . At noon little wind, every ship having his boat ahead, the French to the westward abreast of us, standing as we do. About 3 o'clock a signal for all commanders. At the firing the signal gun, the French commodore, the headmost of the line, with his second ship in tow and the 3rd ship, fired some shot which reached us. The van of our squadron being a great way ahead. At 9 o'clock when we tacked, the French hauled to the westward. At 12 o'clock we see the French on the larboard quarter . . .

63 *Deposition of Thomas Mollamb, Boatswain, H.M.S.* Defiance

. . . during the whole time of the engagement, he did not know of any encouragement his Captain gave to any of his men, but the contrary rather from his own pusillanimity by walking and dodging behind the mizzen mast and falling down upon deck . . .

64 *Deposition of Edward Palmer, Carpenter, H.M.S.* Defiance

. . . on Monday the 24th in the morning when the *Breda* and the *Falmouth* were soon to have disabled a ship of the enemy's there was little or no wind, but a gale presently arriving the *Defiance* was to windward of her bore down upon her, and run to leeward of her within pistol shot never braced to firing about one broadside as she passed her, at which time the spritsails, spritsail topsail and foretopmast staysail were ordered to be set and so run to leeward of the *Falmouth*, nor did they come any more within gunshot range of the enemy . . .

65 *Journal of John Goodall, 2nd Lieutenant, H.M.S.* Pendennis

. . . About 5 [this morning] we came up and engaged . . . we received a shot through the head of the mainmast, the larboard arm of the main yard shot away, two of our main shrouds [several other] rigging cut, and killed one man in the main top . . .

66   *Journal of George Harwarr, 1st Lieutenant, H.M.S.* Pendennis

. . . At 4 afternoon a signal for all Captains. The Admiral being wounded on
both legs by a chain shot and abundance of his men killed and wounded and
had not 4 rounds of powder and shot left. Stood into the shore all night the
morning stood off, and several of our men declare positively that they saw
the French ship shot in the fight the day before sink about 6 or 7 o'clock in
the morning . . .

67   *Deposition of Samuel Vincent, commanding H.M.S.* Falmouth

. . . she damnified us extremely in our rigging, masts, yards, sails and hull.
There being little or no wind the rest of our ships were a great way astern.
Between 5 and 6 there happened a fine breeze of wind and the French bore
down to the assistance of their disabled ship, and at [the] same time the
Defiance, Greenwich, Pendennis had an opportunity of coming up with the
enemy and engaging them but they only fired some few guns at their disabled
ship and then bore away.

During the time of action, I have not understood that there was any
complaint for either men or ammunition, but only at the consultation, at
which time they all said they should want ammunition. I replied and said I
believed the *Falmouth* wanted more than any of them. For, I thought that
3 or 4 hours' fight would go a great way with the shot on board us as we
engaged in the morning, for I had not observed that from either of them there
had been such great expense either of powder or ball.

68   *Deposition of Edward Eaton, Clerk, H.M.S.* Greenwich

. . . Very early in the morning the *Falmouth* fell in with the French they being
in a promiscuous order having all night and the greater part of Sunday been
calm. Next to the *Falmouth* was our Admiral we being a great way astern but
having a fresh gale about 6 in the morning came up with the blue stern ship
which was much disabled by the *Falmouth* and *Breda*. The *Defiance* being
next ship fired some guns and then bore away and lowered her topsails and
we to follow next the Captain then began to be in fear and said he wished the
enemy had left us the night before. [I told the] Captain that we were within
gunshot and that we lie very [near] to rake the said ship which he made no
answer to and when [she] came abroadside of him, he said they were
preparing their lower tier for us and so would bear away and then he kept luff
and got ahead of the enemy, which when we were, fired some guns and said
that he must follow the Colonel [Kirkby] . . .

69 *Deposition of Henry Partington, 1st Lieutenant, H.M.S.* Greenwich

. . . The last day that we were engaged, after the Captain's [Wade] return
from the Flag, he spoke these discouraging words on the quarterdeck Oh
Lord if any of the enemy's ships boarded us we should be immediately taken
for he was not prepared to defend himself; upon which I answered, if he was
afraid of that he ought to lay his gratings fore and aft bar and bolt them but
gave me no answer but kept them open notwithstanding and that his windows
in the bulkheads ought to have been fitted with plank barred and loop holes
through them for small arms but took notice of any advice I gave him . . .

70 *Deposition of Christopher Fogg, commanding H.M.S.* Breda

. . . the reason of his signing to the consultation held on board her Majesty's
ship *Breda* the 24th of August 1702 was because he perceived by the ill
behaviour of the four captains of the squadron whose names are in the
margin [Captain Richard Kirkby, Captain John Constable, Captain Cooper
Wade, Captain Thomas Hudson] and their backwardness to engage the
enemy that if they had engaged the French any more either the *Breda* or the
Falmouth or both of them must have unavoidably been sunk or taken by the
French.

VIII

AFTERMATH, COURT MARTIAL

AND EXECUTIONS

71   *Benbow to Lord Nottingham*[39]

. . . I have confined those Captains which refused to fight and think to proceed as our Articles directs, or to send them home, where I humbly beg leave to be if recovered. For no body is safe to head any party if not stood by, I never met with the like misfortunes in all my life and hope never shall. But it is what I always feared[40] for the Captains that comes these voyages are reckoned as lost so it may be thought anything may serve in these parts, but that is a wrong notion for if good men are not sent here a worse thing may happen to us for I find that the French will defend their ships to the very last extremity. We are now at Port Royal with her Majesty's ships in the margin [*Canterbury, Dunkirk, Pendennis, Greenwich, Gloucester, Breda, Defiance, Kingston, Windsor, Falmouth, Ruby, Seahorse, Earle* Galley, *Harmon* Fireship, *Strombolo* Fireship, *Carcass* Bomb, *Serpent* Bomb, *St Antonio* Sloop].

The *Gloucester* is now careening, the *Seahorse* lately has, the *Bristol* cruises on the south side of this island, the *Colchester* on the north, the *Experiment* off of the east end. We are repairing our damages received by the French which we shall find very difficult as having no masts not yards in stores and very little of anything else. Our ammunition is two thirds expended.

If it please God I recover, and as soon as our ships are in a better condition will go in quest of Monsieur Du Casse, hoping for better success. I am, etc.

Breda in Port Royal Harbour,
24 September 1702

My Lord

The aforesaid is the duplicate of my last by the *Thomas and Mary* Captain Burges commander bound for Bristol. Since which I have advice that the Duke of Albuquerque did embark on Monsieur Du Casse's squadron at the Groyne as also fifteen hundred Spanish soldiers which was brought into these parts by eight French men-of-war and fourteen transport ships. The first place they came to was Porto Rico where they wooded and watered, cleared several of their transport ships sending them to Europe after three days stay in that place, then sailed to the westward, and off the east end of Hispaniola they separated which I judge must be about the 10th August. The Duke of Alburquerque with two men-of-war, one of sixty, the other of seventy guns with four transport ships having a thousand Spanish soldiers on board run down on the north side with five hundred Spanish soldiers and stopped at Santo Domingo but did not stay, but sailed for Rio de Hatch, lay before that place about six hours where he left two men-of-war, one of fifty, the other of forty guns to settle the asiento. From thence he designed for Cartagena and Porto Bello there to land his soldiers. This advice I have had from the commander of the ship I took from him which in my former had no account of.

The 20th of this instant arrived here her Majesty's ships *York* and *Norwich* as also the storeships and victuallers which came out with them, which to us were very welcome, also his Royal Highness the Lord High Admiral's order for sending a ship for New England to convoy home two merchant ships laden with masts, etc., which is complied with, likewise for sending a man-of-war to Barbados, there being a great number of merchant ships that requires convoy home. Yesterday came into this port a merchant ship which in great stress of weather lost her mast who sailed from Barbados about the 10 August the Master of which informs me that the merchant ships were all sailed in June last and that he left but three sail in that place, for which reason defer sending a ship that way. Also shall in all duty observe his Royal Highness's orders as to the impressing of men in these parts which has been with all care complied with as my instructions direct which he is pleased to refer me to. I have not imprest one man from the shore nor ordered any since my being in these parts nor nowhere else more than the orders from the Governor (for the time being) directs, which is to take one man in five out of all ships and vessels coming into this port, which has not been exceeded having given as strict orders as possible to that purpose and will use my utmost endeavour if alive to see them complied with. The people of these parts are very busy with their privateers, and 'tis by report what they generally write, is seldom true. If I had not more regard for the safety of the Queen's island and their goods more than they have themselves, this island would not be long out of the possession of the French, for I dare really believe that at this time (now their privateers are out) besides the soldiers which are not above three hundred fifty, there is not a thousand effective men on the island, so that their security must be forced upon them, for at this time here is neither law nor Governor, so that every man in a manner seems to do what is right in his own eyes, but I hope all will do well and things come into a right centre when her Majesty shall be pleased to send a governing soldier here.[41] We are using all the dispatch we can in fitting our ships which will be ready in a little time considering my circumstances and a shattered leg having lain at this time thirty-two days on my back in this torrid zone. I have not yet proceeded to try any of the Captains which are refused to do their duty, but hope in a little time to do it.

The *Gloucester* is careened, the *Kingston* and *Ruby* are fitting for it. Our powder decays mightily in these parts besides the consumption otherwise, so that I humbly conceive it absolutely necessary that there be fifteen or twenty rounds of powder, shot, parchment, paper, etc., sent here, if it is thought these ships shall continue in these parts. Those few men we have stands pretty well, but are so small in number that no great matters can be expected more than doing their endeavours when occasion may offer which I hope never to see wanting again.

I have ordered the *Dunkirk* to cruise off of the east end of this island . . .

72   *Indictment of John Arthur, Gunner, H.M.S.* Defiance

John Arthur, late Gunner of her Majesty's Ship *Defiance*, is indicted and accused (not having the fear of God before his eyes nor the duty of his allegiance to his sovereign Lady the Queen) of high crimes and misdemeanours tending to embezzlement of her Majesty's ordnance stores under his charge, in hiding of forty-three barrels of gun powder which these deponents found covered in the wad room, fore powder room and larboard wing of the said room, not exposed to view when a survey of the gunner's stores were taken on the 9th of September, but was discovered by a second survey the 10th September, which forty barrels of gun powder he positively denied having in the ship the first day of survey being the 9th of September. The covering preventing its being seen were old wads, cones, cases of wood, etc.

Francis Knighton
George Forster

73   *Rear-Admiral Whetstone to Josiah Burchett, Admiralty Secretary*

I dare not omit this opportunity of giving you a short account of our present state in these parts as I have by several before, which I hope are come safe to your hands, tho' presume you have it at large from Admiral Benbow. Not long since I returned from a cruise of about sixty-two days off the coast of Hispaniola, where I cruised with five ships of war, whose names are in the margin [*Canterbury, Dunkirk, Bristol, Dreadnought, Kingston, Harmon Fireship*], and a fireship in order to have met with Monsieur Du Casse, but he came not that way, but went over for the Main, and steering down that coast for Cartagena, was met by Admiral Benbow with seven ships of war. Between our Admiral and Du Casse was a sharp dispute for several days, as I presume he has given you an account at large, and of his own misfortune of his leg being broke and the complaint he makes of some Captains' backwardness in engaging the enemy, which not being an eye witness to I shall say no more of that.

We have had a sickly time since we came hither, having buried about fifty men. And most of our officers, myself and the rest of our ship's company have been extremely ill, but now, blessed be God, in better health.

In my cruise off Hispaniola, I met with nothing but a Spanish man-of-war of eighteen guns and ten pateraros, one French and one Spanish sloop which three I brought into this place. With most humble duty to his Royal Highness the Lord High Admiral, etc., and most humble service to yourself, I am

On board her Majesty's Ship
Canterbury at Port Royal
in Jamaica, October 17th 1702

The foregoing is a duplicate of a letter sent you the 10th September 1702 by the *Thomas and Mary* of Bristol, Mr Burges commander.[42]

74   *Court Martial Adjournment*

At a Court Martial held on board her Majesty's ship *Breda* in the evening on the 8th of October 1702:

It is agreed that this Court Martial be adjourned till tomorrow morning at seven of the clock or before, and accordingly they are adjourned, and that every gentleman of the court do repair on board their respective ships and not to go on the shore upon the forfeiture of five pounds till the court again meets, again Captain Russell excepted.

William Whetstone

75   *Evidence against Richard Kirkby*

The evidences against Colonel Richard Kirkby, commander of her Majesty's Ship *Defiance* [summed] up which are as followeth, as they deposed upon oath before the Court Martial held on board her Majesty's Ship *Breda* in Port Royal Harbour at Jamaica the 8th October 1702.

Thomas Mollamb Boatswain of her Majesty's Ship *Defiance* proves cowardice, breach of orders and neglect of duty against the said Colonel Richard Kirkby.
Edward Palmer Carpenter of the said ship proves the same as abovesaid.
Jno Spurr Midshipman of the said ship proves the same as abovesaid.
Mr Thomas Langridge 2nd Lieutenant of her Majesty's Ship *Breda* proves the same as abovesaid.

Captain Samuel Vincent commander of her Majesty's Ship *Falmouth* proves the same as abovesaid.

Mr James Lyonburge [Leijonberg] 1st Lieutenant of her Majesty's Ship *Ruby* proves the same as abovesaid.

Mr Arthur DelGarno 2nd Lieutenant of her Majesty's Ship *Ruby* proves the same as abovesaid.

Mr Jno Taylor Master of her Majesty's Ship *Ruby* proves the same as abovesaid.

Mr William Herriott 1st Lieutenant of her Majesty's Ship *Falmouth* proves breach of orders and neglect of duty.

Mr Peircy Brett Master of her Majesty's Ship *Falmouth* proves cowardice, breach of orders and neglect of duty.

Israel Sparks Master's Mate of her Majesty's Ship *Falmouth* proves the same.

Mr George Harwarr 1st Lieutenant of her Majesty's Ship *Pendennis* proves the same.

Mr Henry Partington 1st Lieutenant of her Majesty's Ship *Greenwich* proves the same.

Mr Isaac Sun Master of her Majesty's Ship *Greenwich* proves the same.

Edward Eaton the Captain's Clerk of her Majesty's Ship *Greenwich* proves breach of orders and neglect of duty.

Mr Robert Thompson 1st Lieutenant of her Majesty's Ship *Breda* proves cowardice, breach of orders and neglect of duty.

Captain Christopher Fogg commander of her Majesty's Ship *Breda* proves the same.

Mr Francis Knighton 3rd Lieutenant and Mr Jno Martin Master of her Majesty's Ship *Defiance* prove not much either for or against Colonel Kirkby, but Mr Francis Knighton 3rd Lieutenant upon oath before the Court declared that Colonel Kirkby did not keep his line, but was out of it, and farther than he ought to have been; and Jno Martin the Master declared upon oath before the Court that Colonel Kirkby made him make several alterations in his journal.

Mr Bartholomew Ordd master of her Majesty's Ship *Breda* proves cowardice, breach of orders and neglect of duty.

Admiral Benbow proves the same.

76   *Court Martial Report*[43]

AT A COURT MARTIAL held on board her Majesty's ship the *Breda* in Port Royal Harbour in Jamaica the 8th, 9th, 10th and 12th days of October 1702.

PRESENT

The honourable William Whetstone, Esquire, Rear-Admiral of her Majesty's ships of the West India Squadron, PRESIDENT

Samuel Vincent
Joseph Hartnell
Christopher Fogg   CAPTAINS
John Smith
John Redman
George Walton

William Russell
Barrow Harris
Hercules Mitchell
Phillip Boyse
Charles Smith

Arnold Browne, Esquire, Judge Advocate

who being duly sworn pursuant to the Act of Parliament,

OCTOBER THE 8th

PROCEEDED to the trial of John Arthur, Gunner of the *Defiance* on a complaint exhibited by Francis Knighton, Third Lieutenant of the *Defiance* and George Foster, Gunner of the *Canterbury*, for hiding and concealing 43 barrels of powder in the wardroom and covering them with wads, cones, etc., when a survey of her Majesty's stores of ammunition after an engagement were ordered and denying to the surveyors that there was any more powder on board than what was in the powder room and gunroom, viz., 100 barrels, which upon a second survey was discovered. It was proved also that he had two keys to the powder room, and that having lost or mislaid his own, he without application to the commanding officer then on board (who kept the other key), prevailed with William Baker, carpenter of the said ship, to break open the door.

IN mitigation of his offence, he alleged that, examining into the powder room, he found 3 barrels that had received rot which caused his removal of the 43 barrels, but had little to say for his concealing them from the surveyors, etc.

WHEREUPON the court adjudged that (the said offence falling under the 33rd article of war) the said John Arthur should be carried from ship to ship in a boat with a halter around his neck, the Provost Marshal declaring his crime, and all his pay as Gunner to be mulcted and forfeited to the Chest at Chatham, and be rendered uncapable of serving her Majesty in any other employment.

OCTOBER 8th, 9th

Colonel Richard Kirkby, commander of the *Defiance*, was tried by the aforesaid Court (except Captain Samuel Vincent and Captain Christopher Fogg who appeared as witnesses for the Queen) on a complaint exhibited by the Judge Advocate on the behalf of her Majesty of cowardice, neglect of duty, breach of orders and other crimes committed by him in a fight at sea commenced the 19th of August 1702 off of Santa Martha in the latitude 10 degrees North near the mainland of America, between the honourable John Benbow, Esquire, Vice-Admiral of the Blue Squadron of her Majesty's fleet and Admiral and Commander-in-Chief on board her Majesty's ship the *Breda*, Christopher Fogg commander, and six other of her Majesty's ships, viz., the *Defiance* Richard Kirkby commander, the *Falmouth* Samuel Vincent commander, *Windsor* John Constable commander, *Greenwich* Cooper Wade commander, *Ruby* George Walton commander and *Pendennis* Thomas Hudson commander, and Monsieur Du Casse with 4 French ships of war, which continued till the 24th August inclusive.

THE witnesses that were sworn on behalf of the Queen are, viz.,

The honourable John Benbow, Esquire, Admiral, etc.
  2 Captains
  8 Lieutenants
  5 Masters
  5 Inferior officers
  _____

  21 witnesses

WHO deposed that the said Colonel Richard Kirkby having the van in the line of battle on the 19th of August, about 3 in the afternoon the signal of battle being out, the Admiral was forced to send his boat on board of Kirkby and command his making more sail and get abreast of the enemy's van for that he was about to fight them. About 4 the fight began and the said Kirkby did not fire above three broadsides and then luffed up out of the line and out of gunshot, leaving the Admiral engaged with the two French ships till dark, and the said Kirkby fell astern leaving the Admiral to pursue the enemy.

THAT the 20th at day the Admiral and *Ruby* were within shot of all the enemy's ships, but Colonel Kirkby was 3 or 4 miles astern. The Admiral then made a new line of battle and took the van himself and sent to each ship, with a command to the said Kirkby, to keep his line and station, which he promised to do, but did not, keeping 2 or 3 miles astern, tho' the signal of battle was out all night. The French making a running fight, the Admiral and *Ruby* plied the enemy with their chase guns till night.

THAT the 21st at daylight the Admiral was on the quarter of the second ship of the enemy's rear and the *Ruby* on the broadside, very near, who plied him warmly and met the same return, by which he was so much disabled, tho' the Admiral came in to his assistance, that he was forced to be towed off, and this prevented the Admiral's design of cutting off the enemy's sternmost ship. This action lasted two hours, during which time the said Kirkby lay abroadside of the sternmost ship (as did also the *Windsor* John Constable commander). The Admiral then commanded the said Kirkby to ply his broadsides on him, but this having no effect, he a second time commanded the same, but he fired not one gun, nay his own Boatswain and seamen repeating the Admiral's commands to him were severely reproved and threatened that he would run his sword through the Boatswain. Had the said

Kirkby done his duty and Captain Constable his, they must have taken or destroyed the said French ship. The Admiral, though he received much damage in his sails, rigging, yards, etc., yet continued the chase all night.

THAT the 22nd in the morning at daylight the *Greenwich* was 3 leagues astern and the *Defiance*, Colonel Kirkby, with the rest of the other ships 3 or 4 miles, the *Falmouth* excepted whose station was in the rear. That the said Captain Samuel Vincent seeing the behaviour of the said Kirkby and the rest came up with the Admiral, sent his Lieutenant on board desiring leave to assist him which was accepted, the said Kirkby never coming up and by his example the rest did the same, as if they designed to sacrifice the Admiral and *Falmouth* to the enemy or desert. The enemy were now about a mile and a half ahead, standing into the shore with a small breeze at west and fetched within Sambay, the Admiral firing at the sternmost till night and continued the pursuit, and a Flemish ship that was then in Monsieur Du Casse's company on board of which was all the French and Spanish now Governors and other officers made her escape.

THAT the 23rd in the morning at daylight, the enemy bore north-west distant about 4 or 5 miles, the Admiral and the *Falmouth* pressed all they could to get up with them, which at 10 they did, and fired several broadsides at them upon which they made all the sail and shift they could to get clear. The Admiral and *Falmouth* pursuing them, but the said Colonel Kirkby with the rest of the ships being 3 or 4 miles astern (tho' there was not a ship, but before and after the battle sailed better than the Admiral). About 7 this evening, it having been sometime calm, a gale of wind sprang up. The Admiral and *Falmouth* were about 2 miles from the enemy, and at 8 the said Kirkby with his separate squadron was fair up with the Admiral. And this day the Admiral sent away the disabled *Ruby*, George Walton commander, to Port Royal and under his conduct the *Ann* Galley, retaken from the French, etc.

THAT the 24th in the morning about 2 o'clock, the Admiral came up with the sternmost of the enemy within call and the *Falmouth* pretty near, but the said Colonel Kirkby, with the rest of the ships according to custom, were 3 or 4 miles astern. The Admiral and *Falmouth* engaged the said ship and at 3 the Admiral was wounded, his right leg being broke, but commanded the fight to be vigorously maintained and at daylight the enemy's ship appeared like a wreck, her mizzen mast shot by the board, her main yard in 3 or 4 pieces, her foretopsail yard, the same, her stays and rigging all shot in pieces. Soon after day, the said Kirkby with the rest of the ships being to windward of the disabled ship, he, the said Kirkby, bore down (with the rest of his separate squadron) and fired about 12 guns at the said ship and fearing a smart return from her, he lowered his mizzen yard, his topsails on the cap, set his spritsail, topsail and foretopsail staysail and, having weared his ship, set his sails and run away before the wind from the poor disabled ship, the rest following his sad example, tho' they had but 8 men killed on board them all, except the Admiral. The other 3 French men-of-war were at this time of action, about

4 miles distant from their maimed ship, whereupon the enemy seeing the
cowardice of the said Colonel Kirkby and the rest of the 3 English ships in
a squall bore down upon the Admiral who lay close by the disabled ship and,
having got in their spritsail yards, gave them all their fire, and running
between him and the disabled ship remanned her and took her in tow. The
Admiral's rigging being very much shattered was obliged to lie and refit till
10 o'clock and then continued the pursuit, the rest of the fleet following in
the greatest disorder imaginable. The Admiral commanded Captain Fogg
to stand abreast of the enemy's van and then to attack them, having then a
fine, steady gale the like not happening during the whole engagement, and
further ordered that he should send to all Captains to keep the line of battle
and behave themselves like Englishmen, and this message was sent by
Captain Wade then on board the *Breda* that the said Colonel Kirkby on the
receipt of this message and seeing the Admiral's resolution to engage, came
on board him who then lay wounded in a cradle on the orlop and without
common respect of inquiring after his health he the said Kirkby expressed
these words of following (viz.) that he wondered that he (the Admiral) should
offer to engage the French again it not being necessary, safe or convenient
having had six days trial of their strength, and then magnified that of the
French and lessened that of the English. That the Admiral being surprised
at this speech said it was but one man's opinion and that he would have the
rest of the Captains' and accordingly ordered the signal to be made for all
the rest of the Captains to come on board and at this time the Admiral and
the rest of the ships were to windward and within shot of the enemy and had
the fairest opportunity that in six days presented to chase, engage and destroy
the enemy. That the said Colonel Kirkby had endeavoured to poison the rest
of the Captains, forming a writing under his own hand which was cowardly
and erroneous, the substance of which was not to engage the enemy any
more. He the said Colonel Kirkby brought it to the Admiral who reproved
him for it saying it would be the crime of all upon which the said Colonel
Kirkby went away but writ another in the following words, viz., . . .
[Document **58** quoted in full].

   THAT during the said six days' engagement he never encouraged his men
to fight, but by his example of dodging behind the mizzen mast and falling
down on the deck at the noise of a shot and denying them the provisions of
the ship, the said men were under great discouragement. That he amended
the Master of his ship's journal of the transactions according to his own
intimations.[44]

   ALL of which being fully proved as aforesaid.

THE said Colonel Kirkby denied the whole except the pretended written
consultation, which being shown to him he owned his own hand and name
to. He brought several of his own men to give an account of his behaviour
during the fight, but their testimony were very insignificant and his behaviour

to the Court and witnesses most unbecoming a gentleman, and being particularly asked by the Court why he did not fire at the enemy' sternmost ship, which he lay point blank with the 21st of August, he replied it was because they did not fire at him, but that they had a respect for him, which upon several occasions during the trial the same words he repeated three several times.

WHEREUPON due consideration of the premises and of the great advantage the English had in number of ships, being 7 to 4, of guns 122 more than the enemy, with all other his arts and behaviour as aforesaid, and more particularly his ill signed paper and consultation as afore[said], which obliged the Admiral for the preservation of her Majesty's fleet to give over the chase and fight, to the irreparable dishonour of the Queen, her Crown and dignity, and come to Port Royal in Jamaica, for which reasons the Court was of opinion he fell under the 11, 12, 14 and 20th articles of war[45] and adjudged accordingly that he be shot to death and further decreed that the execution of the said Colonel Kirkby be deferred till her Majesty's pleasure be known therein, but be continued a close prisoner till that time.

OCTOBER 9th, 10th

CAPTAIN John Constable, commander of the *Windsor*, was tried before the aforesaid Court on a complaint exhibited by the Judge Advocate on behalf of the Queen for breach of orders, neglect of duty and other ill practices committed during a fight commenced the 19th of August 1702, as aforesaid (refer to Colonel Kirkby's trial)

The witnesses sworn on the behalf of the Queen were, viz.,

2 Captains
7 Lieutenants
5 Masters
2 other officers
The Honourable John Benbow, Esquire, Admiral, etc.
_____
17 witnesses

WHO deposed that the said Captain John Constable never kept his first nor second line of battle, but acted in all things as Colonel Kirkby had done, that the Admiral had fired two guns to command him into the second line of battle, that he did set more sail to come into the line and his station, but upon Colonel Kirkby's calling to him to keep his line he accordingly did, that the Admiral sent his Lieutenant Langridge to command the said Constable keeping his line of battle within half a cable's length of the ship before him which was twice verbally delivered, and that he signed the said paper consultation as is inserted in Colonel Kirkby's trial aforesaid, tending to hindrance and disservice of her Majesty, etc., and was drunk during the fight.

ALL which being fully proved as aforesaid.

THE said Captain John Constable denied his breach of orders or neglect of duty, but owned his signing the paper or consultation prepared by Colonel Kirkby and did it at his request and for that he had received damage in his masts and rigging and owned no other article to be true that he signed to. He called several witnesses to his behaviour who all declared that he kept the quarterdeck during the engagement and encouraged his men to fight and sometimes gave them drams of rum, and as the verbal message delivered by Lieutenant Langridge was delivered in some heat and passion and was understood to be to keep the line within half a cable's length and to follow Kirkby, which he did, that he so understood it himself and several of his men, he prayed the mercy of the Court and so considered.

WHEREUPON due consideration of the premises, the Court were of opinion that the said Captain John Constable fell under the 12, 14 and 20th articles of war and adjudged the said Captain John Constable to be immediately cashiered and rendered incapable of serving her Majesty, be imprisoned during her Majesty's pleasure and be sent home to England a prisoner in the first ship the Admiral shall think fit and be confined a prisoner till then.

OCTOBER 10th, 12th

CAPTAIN Cooper Wade, commander of the *Greenwich*, was tried before the aforesaid Court on a complaint exhibited by the Judge Advocate on behalf of the Queen of high crimes and misdemeanours of cowardice, breach of orders, neglect of duty and other ill practices committed during a fight commenced the 19th of August 1702 as aforesaid (refer to that part of Colonel Kirkby's trial).

The witnesses sworn on behalf of the Queen were, viz.,

> The Honourable John Benbow, Esquire, Admiral, etc.,
> 9 Lieutenants
> 3 Masters
> 3 Inferior officers
> _____
> 16 witnesses

WHO deposed that during the six days' engagement he never kept the line of battle, fired all his shot in vain and not reaching half way to the enemy, that he was often told the same by his Lieutenant and other officers, that notwithstanding he commanded them to fire saying they must do so or the Admiral would not believe they fought if they did not continue their fire, that during the fight the Admiral was engaged in, the said Captain Wade received but one shot from the enemy, that he was in [drink] the greatest part of the time of action and that he signed the paper or consultation drawn up by Colonel Kirkby as aforesaid.

ALL which being fully proved as aforesaid.

THE said Captain Cooper Wade acknowledged the honour, courage and conduct of the Admiral during the whole six days' engagement, declaring the bravery and good management of the Admiral in this time of action and that no man living could do more or better for the honour of the Queen and Nation. He called some persons to justify his behaviour, who said but little in his favour, he begging the mercy of the Court concluded.

WHEREUPON the Court were of opinion that the said Captain Cooper Wade falls under the 11, 12, 14 and 20th articles of war and accordingly adjudged the said Captain Cooper Wade to be shot to death, but it is further decreed by the Court that the execution of the said Cooper Wade be deferred till her Majesty's pleasure be known therein, but to be continued a close prisoner till that time.

OCTOBER 12th

CAPTAIN Samuel Vincent, commander of the *Falmouth*, and Captain Christopher Fogg, commander of the *Breda*, were tried by the aforesaid Court on a complaint exhibited by the Judge Advocate for high crimes and misdemeanours and ill practices in time of Admiral Benbow's fight with Monsieur Du Casse as aforesaid in signing a paper called the consultation and opinion held on board the *Breda* the 24th of August 1702 which is verbatim recited in Colonel Kirkby's trial to which I refer, it tending to the great hindrance and disservice of her Majesty's fleet then in fight, and the said paper so written being showed to each of them, they severally owned their hands to the same.

BUT the said Captain Vincent and Captain Fogg, for reason of signing the same, alleged that being deserted during each day's engagement by Colonel Kirkby in the *Defiance*, Captain John Constable in the *Windsor*, Captain Cooper Wade in the *Greenwich* and Captain Thomas Hudson in the *Pendennis* and left as a prey to Monsieur Du Casse they had great reason to believe they should be captives to their enemy.

AND the honourable John Benbow, Esquire, Admiral, etc., coming into Court declared that during the said six days' fight the said Captain Fogg behaved himself with great courage, bravery and conduct, like a true Englishman and lover of his Queen and country and that the said Captain Vincent valiantly and courageously behaved himself during the said action and desired leave to come into the said Admiral's assistance then engaged with the enemy and deserted by all the rest of the aforesaid ships which he did to the relief of the said Admiral, who otherwise had fallen into the hands of Monsieur Du Casse.

WHEREUPON the Court, being of the opinion that the signing of the aforesaid paper brought them under the censure of the 20th article of war, accordingly adjudged the said Captain Samuel Vincent and Captain Christopher Fogg to [be suspended, but the execution thereof is hereby respited till his Royal Highness Prince George of Denmark, Lord High Admiral of England, etc., his further pleasure be known] therein.

CAPTAIN Thomas Hudson, commander of the *Pendennis*, died on board his said ship in the harbour of Port Royal the [blank].

> At five o'clock the 12th day of October 1702
> the President, etc., having finished all the
> business before the Court dissolved the same.
> William Whetstone
> Arnold Browne

77   *Verdict of the Court Martial on Captain Kirkby*

. . . it is agreed and declared by this Court that for his breach of orders in not observing and helping his line of battle and other the Admiral's commands, he falls under the eleventh article of war enacted the eighth day of May in the thirteenth year of the reign of King Charles the Second Anno Domino 1661. For his cowardice in that he withdrew, kept back and did not come into the fight and do his utmost to endamage the enemy or assist and relieve the Admiral and two other of her Majesty's ships then engaged, falls under the twelfth article of war. For his neglect of duty in that he did not pursue and chase the enemy nor did relieve or assist the Admiral and others his known fr[iends] in view to the utmost of his power, falls under the fourteenth article of war. For signing a paper tending to the great hindrance and disservice of her Majesty's fleet then engaged as aforesaid, falls under the 20th article of war. For the reasons aforesaid, it is the opinion of this Court that the said Colonel Richard Kirkby falling under the articles as aforesaid by which he is adjudged to be punished with death and is hereby adjudged to be shot to death, but it is further decreed by this Court that the execution of the said Colonel Kirkby be deferred till her Majesty's pleasure be known therein, but be continued a close prisoner till that time.

Wm. Whetstone	G. Walton
Jno. Hartnell	B. Harris
Jno. Smith	H. Mitchell
Jno. Redman	P. Boys
Wm. Russell	Cha. Smith

Arn. Browne Judge Advocate

78   *Rear-Admiral Whetstone to Burchett*[46]

I received a commission dated the 6th of October from Admiral Benbow to hold a Court Martial for the trial of Captain Kirkby in the *Defiance*, Captain Constable in the *Windsor*, Captain Wade in the *Greenwich* and Captain Hudson in the *Pendennis*, all accused of cowardice, breach of orders, neglect of duty in the engagement the Admiral and six ships more had with Monsieur Du Casse with four French men-of-war from 66 to 70 guns each. In this battle, the four Captains and ships did not use their endeavours to destroy or to take the enemy, but they followed Captain Kirkby and took no notice of the Admiral or his commands, but left him and the *Ruby* to engage the enemy by themselves. After the *Ruby* was disabled and forced to tow off, the *Falmouth*, Captain Vincent, came up to his assistance whilst the others seemed only or little otherwise than spectators. This appeared and sworn in court to by the best of those ships' own officers and a great many other ships' officers which beheld their actions. Colonel Kirkby used this expression in Court that the French out of respect to him, when they had an opportunity as himself related they had, did not fire at him nor make use of the advantage.

The 8th instant I began the Court Martial on board the *Breda* because of the Admiral's lameness, who was an evidence against Captain Kirkby and others. The first trial was the Gunner of the *Defiance* for concealing and hiding 43 barrels of powder and denying there was any such on board the ship when surveyed, for which he was made uncapable of the Queen's service, etc., as per decree of the said Court will appear. The same day, Captain Kirkby's trial came on, continued till next day at noon, for cowardice, breach of orders and neglect of duty. Sworn against by the Admiral, 10 commissioned officers, 11 warrants and inferior officers. Many more would have done the same, if required. His sentence, to be shot to death, but respited from execution till her Majesty's pleasure is known.

The next was Captain Constable for breach of orders, neglect of duty, but cleared by his own officers and men of cowardice. His sentence, cashiered from her Majesty's service and imprisonment during her pleasure.

The 4th was Captain Cooper Wade for the same as Captain Kirkby, sworn against by 16 commission and warrant officers of his ship and others. His sentence is the same as Captain Kirkby's.

The 5th was Captain Vincent and Captain Fogg for signing a paper with Captain Kirkby and others not to engage the French when they had a fair opportunity. But the reasons they gave for so doing was that seeing the cowardly behaviour of those Captains, they did believe that if they engaged again they would wholly desert and leave the Admiral and *Falmouth* a prey to the French and others. Great character given of their courage and behaviour in battle, the Court suspended them from their employs in her Majesty's service, but this suspension not to commence till his Royal Highness's pleasure is known. These trials lasted 4 days. With this comes all the affidavits sworn to in Court with the decrees of the Court Martial and other papers relating thereto accompanies this letter, which I humbly lay before his Royal Highness and Council.[47]

On board her Majesty's ship *Canterbury*
at Port Royal at Jamaica
October 20th 1702

79   *Vice-Admiral Benbow to the Commissioners of Ordnance*

Jamaica,
October 20th 1702

That her Majesty's service might not suffer for want of some fitting person to officiate as your agent and supply her ships with ordnance as necessity requires, I have appointed Mr Charles Hutchinson Storekeeper and Muster Master to discharge that duty who, not having any credit upon your account, has been obliged to make use of his naval credits for that service. I desire you'll please to reimburse the Commissioners what they have imbursed on your account and that you'll confirm Mr Hutchinson and take care for credit for him for the future.

I am further to observe to you that [half or] two-thirds of [our] ammunition is expended, particularly powder and shot and if we should be constrained to buy the same here, you'll be surprised at the prices. I desire you'll have regard thereto and take effectual care that we be supplied therewith . . .

80   *Whetstone to Burchett*[48]

25 November 1702

I humbly present his Royal Highness and Council our account that on the 4th of this month Admiral Benbow died, and by all indulged to be, by the wound of his leg which he received in battle with Monsieur Du Casse, it never being set to perfection, which malady being aggravated by the discontent of his mind, threw him into a sort of a melancholy which ended his life as before. All things relating to her Majesty's service that I can get notice of have secured. He left no directions in any matters with anybody before his death which occasions more enquiry . . .

81   *Captain Richard Kirkby to Burchett*

December the 11th 1702

By mine of the 9th of September,[49] I gave you notice of my confinement upon my return hither (with Admiral Benbow) from the coast of Cartagena, who as I told you respected not the 17th, 18th, 19th or 20th articles of our fighting instructions in all actions we had with Monsieur Du Casse his squadron, nor the 28th article of the same[50] in the matter of my confinement, he shamefully parting with Monsieur Du Casse on Tuesday the 25th of August last on the coast of Cartagena and my imprisonment was on the Monday following. After which he made use of his power to terrify some of the officers of the squadron and encourage others with hopes of preferment to form their affidavits to his desire. Which he having effected to his purpose, he brought me (with surprise) upon my trial (near six weeks after my confinement) having made a common lawyer, who knew nothing of the Civil Law, Judge Advocate, who proceeded contrary in all (respects) to the methods of naval trials. Regarding my defence and (with others of the Court which I beg you'll excuse me naming of at present) discountenanced my officers in giving their evidences to the truth, especially the Master and a Midshipman (whose business it was to observe transactions in time of service), threatening to order them into custody. These and many other gross proceedings passed at the Court Martial too long to be here related, but amongst the rest, they denied my proposal that the surveys taken of the *Defiance* and *Breda* (of the damages each ship had received in the late action with the said French squadron) might be produced and compared whereby the Court might have satisfied themselves, that if the damages received by a ship in fight were any token of her being engaged, I should have been found to have been as much engaged as the Admiral.[51] But his presence and influence in the Court carried everything as he would have it, except the immediate execution of the sentence of death, which point only I have a great deal of reason to believe he could not get the Court to comply, for Mr Collison his secretary, etc., came to me on [the] Poop, after the Court was risen, as a visitant and, amongst several things he discoursed, he told me it was an unseasonable thing that Mr Browne, the common lawyer, should have the allowance for Judge Advocate of the Court Martial who knew nothing of the matter, in so much that the sentence was brought to the Admiral several times for his approbation and he believed the Court could not have concluded the matter if the Admiral had not ordered him to assist the Judge Advocate, and so by his help, they finished the sentence (it being then sometime after four o'clock in the afternoon), the consideration of it and their dinnertime having taken up all the forepart of the day. Though Admiral Benbow assisted as well with advice as evidence, I have discovered since there is a false return made of my pleadings. The following instance having been seen by several gentlemen in the copies of the trial: where it is said that when I was asked the reason why I did not fire upon the enemy at some particular time or times, that I should answer, by reason of my acquaintance with Monsieur Du Casse, whereas my real answer was that I was not within shot of the enemy, and the Court demanding the reason of that, I told them the enemy sheered off from us, and the Admiral having taken the lead upon himself, would lead me no nearer, that by our usual distant fight, her Majestys ammunition was spent to no purpose. I hope that his Royal Highness, the Lord High Admiral, will

not doubt, but that (if I had owned myself a traitor as their words render me), they would not have troubled the Queen to know her pleasure concerning me, nor scrupled to gratify Admiral Benbow with a speedy execution upon me. Several accidents have discovered he did not think himself safe from the question at home while I lived, and 'tis thought, the trouble of his apprehensions hastened his death (the wound in his leg being only a common fracture) which has since happened, for which reason I shall urge no further concerning him than is necessary to maintain my own innocence of what is laid to my charge with all the scandal he could invent. As in this, I doubt not but I am misrepresented in his report home in many particulars to render me incapable of her Majesty's mercy. I desire you will please to take notice (also) if to fill up a complement of evidences' names (mentioned in the sentence),[52] they have inserted those of Mr Francis Knighton, Third Lieutenant, and John Martin, Master, as men upon whose evidence I was condemned when there is nothing in the tenor of their affidavits from which I could be esteemed guilty of any crime.[53] So that if I may be permitted to represent my case, it will be made evident that I was condemned upon the affidavits of Admiral Benbow and his officers, whose malice and partiality therein I can sufficiently prove. By which it will be made to appear that names of evidences were ennumerated only to outweigh me in the balance of the Queen's mercy, that so provoking her Majesty's resentment against me, he might (with expedition) obtain an order for execution upon me to acquit himself of his future fears. To prove this (I hope) needs no more than this following instance. Soon after I had received the sentence, I employed a gentleman to ask the Admiral leave for me to write home to acquaint my friends with my condition. Admiral Benbow was surprised at the motion and would give no consent to it, so that I was denied any means of paying my duty to his Royal Highness by desiring you (as now I do) that you will please to lay my unhappy circumstances at my Lord High Admiral's feet by acquainting him with the purport hereof which most humbly begs his Highness's favour to conduct it to her Majesty's gracious mercy. This is my prayer to him and request to you who am
Sir
Your most humble servant
Richard Kirkby

Upon better thought I have enclosed with this a copy of a journaler's account[54] of Admiral Benbow's transaction with Monsieur Du Casse, one of which I sent by mine of the 9th of September, this for fear the other should not come to your hands. There was a paper brought into Court against me which was signed by all the rest of the Captains of the squadron (then with Admiral Benbow) as well as myself, a vindication whereof I delivered into the Court in writing, which if not returned home with the affidavits against me (since I think it to answer all objections to the paper of accusations), I am very much wronged in that point.[55]

82   Minutes of the Prince's Council

7 January 1702/3

A memorial to the Queen in Council, that her Majesty will be pleased to empower his Royal Highness to direct Vice-Admiral Benbow to put in execution the sentence of the Court Martial held in the West Indies for shooting Captain Kirkby and Captain Wade for cowardice.

[Members present: Sir George Rooke, Sir D. Mitchell, Mr Hill, Mr Churchill]

83   Lord High Admiral's Memorial for her Majesty in Council

Whereas by the results of a Court Martial held at Jamaica by Captain Whetstone, who acts as Rear-Admiral of the West India Squadron, it appears to me, that Captain Richard Kirkby, who commanded the *Defiance*, and Cooper Wade, who was Captain of the *Greenwich*, are sentenced to be shot to death for not doing their duty in engaging the French ships commanded by Monsieur Du Casse, when met with by Vice-Admiral Benbow, but that the execution of the said sentence is respited till her Majesty shall signify her pleasure therein. And it appearing by the several depositions, as well of the said Vice-Admiral Benbow, as of great numbers of officers of the ships that were in this action, that they, the said Captain Kirkby and Captain Cooper Wade, were apparently guilty of cowardice, it is therefore proposed unto her Majesty that she will be pleased to empower me to order Vice-Admiral Benbow, or the officer commanding the squadron, in case of his death or inability by sickness or otherwise, to put the sentence in execution by shooting to death the aforesaid two Captains as a just punishment for their aforesaid crimes and as a necessary example to deter others from being guilty thereof for the future. And whereas Captain John Constable, who commanded the *Windsor*, was also tried by the said Court Martial and found guilty of breach of orders and neglect of duty, and for that and his signing a paper, through ignorance and drunkenness, tending to the great hindrance and disservice for her Majesty's fleet, sentenced to be cashiered and for ever rendered incapable of serving her Majesty, as also to be imprisoned during her Majesty's pleasure. It is further proposed unto her Majesty that the said sentence may be confirmed and that the said Captain Constable may be sent home a close prisoner in the first ship of war that shall come from the West Indies.

84   Burchett to Robert Warre, Under-Secretary of State

Sometime since there was sent to the Right Honourable the Earl of

Nottingham, the draft of instructions[56] to Vice-Admiral Benbow, as well as for his governing himself during his stay in the West Indies, as in his return from thence, but his Lordship not having yet signified her Majesty's approbation of the same, I am to desire you will move him therein because the time is affixed for the sailing of the men-of-war.

I send you herewith, for his Lordship's information, the copy of some part of a letter received yesterday from Vice-Admiral Benbow, giving an account of the present circumstances of the island of Jamaica, which I am to desire you will please to lay before his Lordship the first convenient opportunity.

85   Minutes of the Prince's Council

8 January 1702/3

. . . Upon a letter from Vice-Admiral Benbow to the Prince, in behalf of Captain Fogg and Captain Vincent;[57] resolved that pursuant to his Royal Highness's pleasure, orders be prepared for Vice-Admiral Benbow to take off the suspension on those two officers . . .

[Members present: Sir George Rooke, Mr Churchill, Mr Hill, Sir David Mitchell]

86   Lord High Admiral's Order to Vice-Admiral Benbow[58]

Whereas it appears unto me, that at a Court Martial held by your order, by Captain Whetstone, who acts as Rear-Admiral of the squadron of her Majesty's ships under your command in the West Indies, Captain Christopher Fogg, Captain of the ship wherein you bore your flag, as also Captain Samuel Vincent who commanded the *Falmouth*, when you met with and engaged the French ships under the command of Monsieur Du Casse, are suspended from their employments for signing with the other Captains of her Majesty's ships to a paper lending to the prejudice of the service for that they did advise not [to] renew the engagement with the enemy at a time when there was a fair opportunity of doing the same. But you having by your letter dated the 20th of October last,[59] represented to me, that the said Captain Christopher Fogg and the Captain Samuel Vincent did behave themselves with courage and zeal for her Majesty's service, during the time of action, and that they were ensnared into signing the said paper by Colonel Kirkby, who commanded her Majesty's ship the *Defiance* who, with Captain Cooper Wade, her Majesty hath ordered to be shot to death for their cowardice in the aforesaid action pursuant to the sentence of the Court Martial, and for which you will herewith receive my orders. I have considered of the character you have given of the behaviour of the aforesaid Captain Fogg and Captain Vincent and do hereby direct and require you to take off the suspension put on them by the Court Martial, that so they may be capable of serving her Majesty in the squadron of her Majesty's ships under your

command, in such manner as you shall think the most proper to employ them. Given under my hand this 9th day of January 1702/3. George.
[Initialled by members of the Prince's Council]
GR [Sir George Rooke]
DM [Sir David Mitchell]
GC [George Churchill]
RH [Richard Hill]

87   *The Queen to the Lord High Admiral*

Anne R.

Whereas you have represented to Us by your memorial of the 7th instant that Captain Richard Kirkby and Captain Cooper Wade have been deservedly sentenced by a Court Martial to be shot to death, but that the execution of the said sentence has been respited till Our pleasure be signified therein, and whereas you have also represented to Us, that Captain John Constable, who was also by a Court Martial sentenced to be cashiered and be forever incapable of Our service at sea and to be imprisoned during Our pleasure, should be sent a close prisoner from the Indies in the first ship that shall come from thence, We being fully satisfied of the above said matters do hereby signify Our pleasure to you, that We do not think the said persons do deserve any favour from Us to prevent or hinder the execution of the respective sentences. Given at Our Court at St James's the 13th day of January 1702/3 in the first year of Our reign.

By her Majesty's command
Nottingham

To Our most dear husband
Prince George of Denmark
Our High Admiral of England,
Ireland, etc., and of all Our
Plantations, etc.

88   *Nottingham to Benbow*

23 January 1702/3

I have received your letters of September 11 and 24 and October 20,[60] and other letters from Mr Browne of October 18,[61] and from Captain Whetstone of October 20[62] which I have laid before her Majesty, who is extremely well pleased with your conduct, and as much offended with the baseness of those officers who deserted and betrayed you.[63] Of these matters you will have a fuller account from the Prince's Council, as also instructions for your future proceedings, so that there is very little occasion for me to write to you, but I would not omit this opportunity of assuring you of my service, and that I truly lament your misfortune of losing your leg, as indeed all men do that I meet with. I hope that this will find you in other respects well, and that you are reserved to do her Majesty and your country yet greater services, of which no man is more capable than yourself.

89   Burchett to Commissioner St Lo, at Plymouth

20 March 1702/3

The *Bristol* being suddenly expected from the West Indies, I desire you will cause the enclosed orders to be immediately sent off to her commander, in case the ship should touch at Plymouth, and that you give me an account of your having so done.

90   Captain Edward S. Acton to Burchett

In obedience to an order from Rear-Admiral Whetstone for her Majesty's ship under my command to return for England, I parted from the keys of Port Royal February 14th in company with the said Admiral, and sailed with him up to Cape Tiburon, and took my orders and leave of him February 18th off Cape Tiburon, the cape bearing N½W, and saw him make sail with the fleet consisting of 12 men-of-war and fireships bound up the south side of Cuba, and arrived here last night between 9 and 10 of the clock and waited upon the Commissioner forthwith, who delivered me an order from his Royal Highness for putting the sentence in execution pronounced by the Court Martial: (viz.) by shooting Colonel Richard Kirkby and Captain Cooper Wade to death which I shall cause to be done as near to the time as possible may be, and give them notice to provide for the same, I humbly wish to know his Highness's pleasure about Captain John Constable who is here prisoner likewise, and to know his pleasure for my proceeding or stay.

At my departure the island of Jamaica was never more healthy and I thank God the whole fleet never better and the ship under my command very healthy (myself being the weakest and sickest in her).

I have sent what packets I had up this post; I do not doubt that his Royal Highness is informed of the total burning down of Port Royal[64] and of the people settling at a place called Kingston, if it be required to give my particular account, I shall do it to the best of my power. My ship hath been very leaky and defective for this long time, it being as much as we could do sometime to free, all of which shall be given in the account of her defects.

Bristol in Plymouth Sound,	I am in all respects your
April the 16th 1703	honour's humble servant
	E. S. Acton

This post not going so soon as I expected have joined this postscript to inform his Royal Highness that at six this evening I caused Captain Richard Kirkby and Captain Cooper Wade to be shot to death together upon the forecastle in the presence of several captains and commissioned officers and many other spectators. I do likewise think myself obligated to give this account of them that for Captain Kirkby, during the time of his being in prison, he behaved himself mannerly and very much like a Christian by continual prayer and reading of good books, and upon receiving notice of his approaching death seemed very easy, desiring of God to strengthen him and the night before his execution I sat up late with him and found him very calm and easy, not railing or reviling, but forgiving all the world and praying, for the Queen health and prosperity, and his Royal Highness the good and honour of his country. He received the sacrament with Captain Wade and after prayers spoke a quarter of an hour to all the people in general to forbear swearing and debauchery and be obedient to their superiors, but did not rail at his hard fate or any such thing to arraign his judges or the like, but Captain Wade could not forbear till I deferred him to retire. He is very timorous and of a low spirit. I delivered their bodies as desired to their friends to be privately interred.

At the time of Captain Kirkby's execution, he delivered to me a paper before the officers and gentlemen that was there to get printed, if I thought fit, but I shall get it copied and know his Royal Highness's pleasure before I proceed any further in that matter.

91 *Acton to Burchett*

The enclosed is the paper Colonel Kirkby gave me just as he was going to die which I have sent up just as he gave it to me having taken a copy, but shall do nothing therein until I know his Royal Highness's plea[sure there]in.

Rear-Admiral [Whetstone] gave me an order to bring home a French captain, Monsieur de la Courb by name, and 12 prisoners. Two are dead in the passage, the other ten and the captain I have delivered to the agent here. Prisoners they were taken by Admiral Benbow at Petit Guavas the first of the war.
Wind at North-West
Complement 174
From onboard her Majesty's Ship
Bristol in Plymouth Sound
April the 18th 1703

92 *Richard Kirkby's Last Statement*

An account of some passages relating to my trial on board the *Breda*, the 9th of October 1702 in Port Royal Harbour, Jamaica:

1 First I refer (for matter of fact) to the journals account of transactions between Monsieur Du Casse and Admiral Benbow.
2 Secondly, from the 24th of August 1702 to the 31st ditto, which was the

time we performed our passage to Jamaica Island (after Admiral Benbow had left Du Casse's squadron off of River Grande on the coast of Cartagena in America) where immediately upon my arrival I was made prisoner by order of Admiral Benbow, without any intelligible cause assigned, which truly did surprise me, not being conscious to myself of meriting any such thing, and reflecting on all things that had passed in the said expedition, I could not charge myself with any defect of my duty according to the best of my judgement so that I concluded he designed to cover his own defects with my destruction (for a signal from him in our passage would have done the same thing, or he might have interceded upon a fault committed) and I was soon convinced of the truth of my surmise, for as soon as I was confined, every place about the point of Port Royal and all the remarkable habitations of Jamaica were filled with all the slanderous reports imaginable reflected upon me by the said Admiral's emissaries, so that the Chaplain of the *Defiance* meeting with them on shore wherever he went, for about a week together after my confinement, in conscience to the truth, confuted them in many places (like a worthy man of his order) by his knowledge to the contrary of their allegations for which, he the said Chaplain was confined to the ship, from which he was not released till after my trial.

3   Thirdly, during my imprisonment, I had frequent notice of the continual managements of my own Boatswain and Carpenter's bartering with men on board the ship to give such evidence that they proposed against me, assuring them that they could secure them safe whatever they said against me, for I was never to command them anymore. One Munger Hardman, a Scotch gentleman volunteer, refused their overtures.

4   Fourthly, the Gunner of the *Defiance* being seized (before I was, the same day) for a heinous concealment of 40 barrels of powder, it being made plain that he and his accomplices had taken the lock off the powder room door, after that fitted the gun room door key to it, and clapped the lock on again, the true key of the powder room door being all the time in my Lieutenant's hands or mine. While this man was trying, the yeoman of the powder room (who was mainly concerned with him) being upon the Admiral's quarterdeck, Thomas Langrith, the Admiral's Lieutenant, came to the said yeoman of the powder room, who as I take it he is named Archibald Ballantine, and after he had told him he would certainly be hanged, thereby consternating the man, Langrith told Ballantine that there was no way to save his life, but by saying what he did was by my order. This came to me by several voluntary [illegible] from the said Ballantine.

5   Fifthly, I was brought to trial the eighth of October 1702: Rear-Admiral Whetstone sat as President, Captain Vincent, Captain Fogg principal evidence, Mr Browne Solicitor-General of Jamaica being Judge Advocate being commissioned a few days before the trial in the room of Mr George Collison, Admiral Benbow's clerk, who had acted in that station till he

had collected so much evidence against me, etc., as the Admiral thought for his purpose, the said Admiral's first Lieutenant, Robert Thompson, accompanying him for the most part or altogether, as I have been credibly informed, so that they had brought all the officers of those ships which accompanied Admiral Benbow in the expedition against Monsieur Du Casse to evidence against me, etc., by one means or another, I mean fair or foul. Then the President (i.e. Whetstone) with the rest of the Court proposed an indictment to be read against me after the manner of the Common Law, which was in the most gross language, and then read their affidavits which were of much such like language, and likewise very far from the truth in general, which I doubt not will be affirmed by many men in the squadron when they come home. Therefore, I shall only insert here some few particulars (viz.), the Court charged me with not making fire upon the enemy at some times when the Admiral was engaged. I answered [7 lines crossed out] that the Admiral having taken the lead on both tacks, he seldom brought me within reach of my shot to the enemy, and when I saw my shot would not go home, I forebore firing. The Court asked me why I did not engage the enemy, which they seemed not to understand I had done, so I requested then that they would please to send for the surveys lately taken of the damage done to the *Breda* and *Defiance*, and if that were any token of the engagement with an enemy, they would find I had been as much in the conflict as the Admiral, but (that's after I had many times pressed it) was denied me. On Lieutenant Partington of the *Greenwich* being brought into Court read his affidavit wherein they found nothing against me, the Admiral (who sat by all the time brow-beating of evidence) and the President and the Judge [Advocate] (not saying to the contrary) made him take pen and ink and write an affidavit against me.[65] I often repeated my desire that the Lieutenant, Master and Midshipman of the *Defiance* should read their affidavits, theirs having been taken upon oath by the former Judge Advocate, which I at last prevailed with the Court should be read, but as I remember a great dinner being said to be ready, adjourned the Court till that was over, which being about two hours after they begun, to read the Master's and Midshipman's affidavits, but to be short, one of them after several interruptions having read a very little, the Admiral who sat by cried out, he lied, he had sworn the contrary, and presently he and the President exclaimed (saying) a trick, a trick and the President proposed several times to clap them by the heels and to invalidate the Master's evidence. The Boatswain of the hulk came hastily into the Court [justifying] the . . . [torn] he swore that the Master had in the company of several he named, said (crying) that he was amazed and undone for I had made him add several things to his journal. The Master did not own the man's assertion nor did any of the company justify the man's affidavit, but a sentence or such like being found in the Master's journal when produced, the President called out upon it that it was [another] trick and knavery, whereupon I desired the Court to ask him if that writing they found fault with was not truth which acknowledged to be so from his oath,[66] but which [ignored] it was urged by the President and some others to confine him, but with much ado he escaped it, but his evidence and the Midshipman's were both disregarded.

I remember Captain Vincent and Captain Fogg swore against me concerning a paper which was signed by them, as well as myself, who writ it at their persuasion. I asked the first why he signed it. He answered he would have signed anything at that time and yet the countenance of the Court Martial stood respectfully towards him, as it did towards the second, when I having [taxed him] with a known negative to many in the squadron, he affirmed it immediately. But for the vindication of the said paper, I delivered a writing under my hand to the board, but they did not so much as seat it then, nor did I ever hear they considered it, for the next day (after they had dined) a little after four o'clock, the Court passed the sentence upon me for which I am about to suffer. I will now conclude with a billet I received from Mr George Collison, Admiral Benbow's Clerk and late Judge Advocate, wherein he consoled my misfortune, ridiculing the capacity of the Court Martial and Judge Advocate. He said that they had been all that day about drawing up the said sentence and had their drafts several times to Admiral Benbow for his approbation, adding that he believed they would never have made an end of it, if the said Admiral had not commanded him to do it for them, whereupon he showed them the method and dictated to them, but would not write himself, urging that it was a hard thing that the others should go away with the profits of the Court and he do the business for them. By this may be seen how a commander-in-chief in the West Indies may carry any matter against an inferior officer, of which I am a fatal example who humbly presents my hearty prayers to Almighty God to bless and protect his Church in England by law established, her Most Sacred Majesty and her dominions with peace, plenty and happiness. On board her Majesty's Ship *Bristol* in Plymouth Sound this 16th day of April 1703.

Notes

1   The original of Benbow's letter of 11 September has not been found. This transcription is made from a duplicate included as the first part of a letter sent on 24 September 1702. Benbow sent a second letter, dated 24 September, to William Blathwayt which is nearly identical to the letter dated 11 September. In this collection, I have used the entire Colonial Office copy of the letter to Nottingham, but I have given the major textual differences in the letter to Blathwayt in the notes. The Blathwayt letter may be found in the British Library, Additional Manuscript 18389, fols. 44–6.

Further letters giving information on the activities of Benbow's squadron leading up to the battle of 19–24 August have been published in the *Calendar of State Papers, Colonial – America and the West Indies*, Vol. XX (1702):

(a) Benbow to Secretary of State, 13 April 1702, pp. 216–18, no. 333, includes enclosure on the condition of ships.

(b) Benbow to Vernon, 13 May 1702, pp. 316–17, no. 473.

(c) Lt. Governor Beckford to Vernon, 15 May 1702, pp. 323–4, no. 489.

(d) Benbow to Vernon, 1 June 1702, pp. 367–9, no. 560.

(e) Lt. Governor Beckford to Council of Trade and Plantations, 10 July 1702, pp. 460–3, no. 743.

2   This is Léogâne on the north coast of the Tiburon peninsula of south west Haiti. According to a contemporary French account in a printed newsletter, *Relation de ce qui s'est passé entre une escadre du Roi de quatre vaisseaux commandée par Monsieur Du Casse* . . . (Bordeaux, 1703), [John Carter Brown Library, Brown University, Providence, Rhode Island], the French squadron departed Ferrol and the Bay of La Coruña in northwestern Spain on 24 June/4 July 1702 and arrived at San Juan, Porto Rico, on 29 July/8 August, departed there 9/20 August for Santo Domingo where it arrived on 13/24 August. En route to Santo Domingo, the French had divided their squadron and on 11/22 August, two warships were dispatched to the west to convoy the duke of Albuquerque and troops to Cuba and Mexico, while Du Casse with four warships proceeded south toward Cartagena from the coast of Hispaniola. Du Casse's letter to Pontchartrain, 6/17 August 1702, reporting his plans, is quoted at length in Le Baron Robert [Emmanuel Léon] Du Casse, *L'Amiral Du Casse, Chevalier de la Toison d'Or (1646–1715)* (Paris, 1876), pp. 254–6.

3   This may be Baradères Bay.

4   Petit-Goâve.

5   Cap Dame Marie, at the western tip of the Tiburon peninsula.

6   Add. MS. 18389 adds 'in quest of him'. In fact, Benbow was ahead of Du Casse who had not yet left the town of Santo Domingo on Hispaniola.

7   Santa Marta on the coast of present day Colombia.

8   Add. MS. 18389 omits 'astern'.

9   The French account [see note 2] identifies the French ships as *l'Heureux* commanded by Du Casse, *l'Agréable* le Chevalier de Roussy, *le Phénix* le Chevalier de Poudens and *l'Apollon* M. de Demuin. The large ship was named *Prince de Frise*, M. de St André. The account also mentions a fireship named *le Marin*. The French lookout sighted the English at sunrise and was able to identify them at eight o'clock.

10   Thomas Langrith (Langridge), 2nd Lieutenant, H.M.S. *Breda*.

11   The French account records that the English admiral was in the centre of the line firing against *l'Apollon* and *le Phénix*, while the others of his van against *l'Agréable* and *l'Heureux*. During the engagement, le Sieur Audumau, Sousbrigadier des Gardes de la Marine, was dangerously wounded on board *le Prince de Frise*.

12   This document has not been located.

13   Add. MS. 18389 adds 'very'.

14   Add. MS. 18389 replaces 'and we' by 'then'.

15   Arthur DelGarno, 2nd Lieutenant, H.M.S. *Ruby*.

16   *L'Apollon*.

17   *L'Heureux* and *l'Apollon*.

18   Add. MS. 18389 adds 'our'.'

19   Add. MS. 18389 reads 'who fired never a gun'.

20   Add. MS. 18389 reads 'abreast of the two sternmost'. These ships were *l'Agréable* and *l'Heureux*.

21   Add. MS. 18389 omits 'and rigging'.

22   Add. MS. 18389 replaces 'way' by 'sail'.

23   Add. MS. 18389 replaces 'came to the southward' by 'came about to the SW'.

24   The French account indicates that *l'Heureux, l'Agréable* and *le Phénix* replied to the English fire. M. d'Ypreville, Sousbrigadier des Gardes de la Marine was killed on board *l'Agréable*. *Le Prince de Frise* was ordered to proceed independently to Cartagena during the night.

25   Juan Lopez de Vargas, *Mapa Geographico de la provincia de Cartagena* (Madrid, 1787) shows a body of water, Bahia de Samba, enclosed by an island, Galera de Samba, and a point, Punta de Samba. On modern maps, the island and point appear only as a spit of land. One supposes that in over two hundred years, the Galera de Samba and the Punta de Samba were joined by the effects of weather. The spit of land is now called Galera Zamba.

26   ibid.

27   The French account reports that *l'Apollon* received this fire, then *l'Agréable* and *le Phénix* exchanged fire with the English.

28   The French account notes that this vessel was taken by Du Casse's squadron three days after
      they had left Ferrol.
29   Add. MS. 18389 omits 'about'.
30   Add. MS. 18389 omits 'very'.
31   Add. MS. 18389 omits 'being all'.
32   Add. MS. 18389 omits 'coming'.
33   Add. MS. 18389 adds 'not having any regard to the line of battle'.
34   Add. MS. 18389 replaces 'our' by 'the'.
35   The French account reports that during the engagement which began at 02.30 on 24
      August/4 September, *l'Agréable* and *le Phénix* came up, with Du Casse at the head in
      l'Heureux, to find the enemy surrounding *l'Apollon*. Upon seeing Du Casse, the men of
      the dismasted and disabled *l'Apollon* saluted their commandant three times with the cheer,
      'Vive le Roi'.
36   Document **58**.
37   Folios 10–17 of P.R.O. ADM 1/5263 are items which appear to be stray notes taken from
      oral testimony, probably in the course of the Court Martial proceedings, but possibly made
      during the deliberations by members of the Court. They are incomplete, scrappy notes which
      seem most unusual as part of an official record. Only this item from fol. 13 provides
      information not provided by other sources.
38   Cartagena.
39   Lieut. Gov. Peter Beckford reported to the Earl of Nottingham on 4 September with details
      of Benbow's encounter. He included a copy of the Captains' resolutions of 24 August and
      also a document which gave Benbow's reply to them. These are both printed in *Cal. S.P.
      Col. – America and West Indies,* Vol. XX, pp. 577–80, no. 936. Du Casse's short letter
      of 28 September 1702 to Pontchartrain noting the exemplary conduct of some of his own
      officers in the battle, along with the letter of the Chevalier de Galliffet, dated 18 October,
      describing the battle are printed in Du Casse, *L'Amiral Du Casse*, pp. 262–6.
40   Add. MS. 18389 replaces 'feared' by 'expected'.
41   Thomas Handasyde was soon to arrive as Governor of Jamaica. Perhaps Benbow had in
      mind an aggressive, military man such as Christopher Codrington, Governor of the Leeward
      Islands, 1699–1704. Benbow's concern for the security of the West Indies is reflected in
      the Queen's Order in Council, 27 September 1702, printed in *Cal. S.P. Col. – America
      and West Indies,* Vol. XX, p. 624, no. 1000.
42   This is the same vessel in which Benbow sent his letter to Lord Nottingham, dated 11
      September 1702 (Documents **1, 3, 17, 23, 34, 48, 55** and **71**). Neither of these originals has
      been found.
43   This document was published shortly after the trial as a pamphlet under the title, *An Account
      of the Arraignments and Trials of Col. Richard Kirkby, Capt. John Constable, Captain
      Cooper Wade, Captain Samuel Vincent and Captain Christopher Fogg on a complaint
      exhibited by the Judge Advocate on behalf of her Majesty, at a Court Martial held on board
      the ship* Breda *in Port Royal Harbour in Jamaica in America, the 8th, 9th, 10th, and 12th
      days of October, 1702, for cowardice, neglect of duty, breach of orders, and other crimes,
      committed by them in a fight at sea, commenced the 19th of August 1702 off of St Martha,
      in the latitude of 10 degrees North, near the Mainland of America, between the honourable
      John Benbow, Esq., and Admiral Du Casse with four French ships of war. For which, Col.
      Kirkby and Capt. Wade were sentenced to be shot to death. Transmitted from two eminent
      merchants at Port Royal in Jamaica, to a person of quality in the city of London* (London:
      Printed for John Gellibrand, and are to be sold by A. Baldwin, near the Oxford Arms in
      Warwick Lane, 1703). A similar text is printed in T. B. Howell (comp.), *A Complete
      Collection of State Trials and Proceedings for High Treason and Other Crimes and
      Misdemeanours . . . ,* Vol. XIV, *A.D.1700–1708* (London, 1812), no. 423, pp. 537–46. A
      summarised version appears in *Cal. S.P. Col. – America and West Indies,* Vol. XX, pp.
      674–8, no. 1003 i.
          The insertions within square brackets do not appear in the manuscript copy, ADM
      1/5263, but are included in the 1703 printed text.
44   The only document which directly relates to this matter is the deposition of Richard Gull
      dated 8 October 1702, ADM 1/5263, fol. 28: 'Richard Gull, Boatswain of her Majesty's
      hulk the *Lewis*, deposeth upon oath that Jno Martin, Master of her Majesty's Ship *Defiance*

said in the Boatswain's cabin of *Defiance* and before the Boatswain and Carpenter of the said ship, crying that they made him alter several things and would have it all upon him and he should be undone.' There is no indication of the date when this occurred. See also note 66 relating to document **92** and the italicised portion of document **62**.

45   13 Car. II c. 9, 'An act for the establishing articles and orders for the regulating and better government of his Majesties navies, ships of war and forces by sea':

XI   Every captain, commander and other officer, seaman or soldier of any ship, frigate or vessel of war, shall duly observe the commands of the admiral, or other superior or commander of any squadron, as well for assailing or setting upon any fleet, squadron or ships of the enemy, pirate or rebels or joining battle with them or making defence against them as all other the commands of the admiral, or other his superior commander, upon pain to suffer death or other punishments, as the quality of his neglect or offence shall deserve.

XII   Every captain, and all other officers, mariners and soldiers of every ship, frigate or vessel of war, that shall in time of any fight or engagement, withdraw or keep back or not come into the fight or engage and do his utmost to take, fire, kill and endamage the enemy, pirate or rebels and assist and relieve all and every of his Majesty's ships, shall for such offence of cowardice or disaffection, be tried and suffer pains of death, or other punishment, as the circumstances of the offence shall deserve, and the Court Martial shall judge fit.

XIV   Whatsoever person or persons, in belonging to the fleet, either through cowardice, negligence or disaffection shall forbear to pursue the chase of any enemy, or pirate or rebel beaten or flying, or shall not relieve or assist a known friend in view, to the utmost of his power, shall be punished with death, or otherwise, as a Court Martial shall find fit.

XX   No person in or belonging to the fleet shall conceal any traitorous or mutinous practices, designs or words, or any words spoken by any to the prejudice of his Majesty or government, or any words, practices or designs tending to the hindrance of the service, but shall reveal them to his superior, that a meet proceeding may be had thereupon, upon pain of such punishment as a Court Martial shall find to be just.

See Document **77** for the application of these articles to the captains. The text of the articles may be found in N. A. M. Rodger (ed.), *Articles of War: the Statutes which governed our fighting navies 1661, 1749 and 1866* (Havant, Hampshire: Mason, 1982), pp. 15–16.

46   A similar letter to the Principal Secretaries of State is printed in *Cal. S.P. Col. – America and West Indies*, Vol. XX, pp. 673–4, no. 1063.

47   These enclosures are not presently with this letter, but now comprise the 232 folios of ADM 1/5263.

48   A similar letter to the Principal Secretaries of State is printed in *Cal. S.P. Col. – America and West Indies*, Vol. XX, pp. 744–5, no. 1191. The remainder of the letter concerns naval operations in the West Indies under Whetstone's command.

49   This letter has not been found.

50   For the text of the articles which Kirkby accuses Benbow of violating, see J. S. Corbett (ed.), *Fighting Instructions, 1530–1816,* N.R.S. Vol. 29 (1905).

51   The text of this report has not been found.

52   The document to which Kirkby refers here is undoubtedly the proceedings of the Court Martial for 8, 9 October 1702. This was written out in two forms, one which related only to Kirkby's trial and another which incorporated the same information in the report of the Court Martial for 8–12 October. This second form is printed here as document **76**. The first form is not printed here to avoid duplication; the only significant difference is that the report for 8, 9 October lists the witnesses by name, while the longer report only gives the total numbers of witnesses. The names of the witnesses are printed in document **75** with additional comments as to what points their evidence was to prove.

The report for 8, 9 October is listed, but not printed in full, in *Cal. S.P. Col. – America and West Indies*, Vol. XX, p. 678, no. 1063 iii; it may be found in the Admiralty records in ADM 1/5263, fols. 8–9.

53   See documents **9, 21** and **27** for Knighton, and **7** and **62** for Martin.

54   This account has not been identified.

55 This document was not made part of the official record and is not referred to in any part of it; it has not been located.
56 The draft of these instructions, received 21 December from the Admiralty, is printed in *Cal. S.P. – Domestic*, Anne (1702), pp. 345–6.
57 Letter of 20 October 1702, not located among the Public Records.
58 This order was sent with a covering letter from Burchett to Benbow, 19 January 1702/3, with a summary of the orders; see ADM 2/406, fol. 108, not printed here.
59 Not located.
60 Documents **1**, **3**, **17**, **23**, **34**, **48**, **55**, **71**; see also note 57.
61 Printed *Cal. S.P. Col. – America and West Indies*, Vol. XX, p. 673, no. 1062.
62 ibid., no. 1063.
63 A similar letter was sent to Col. Beckford, Lieutenant Governor of Jamaica on the same date, in which Nottingham wrote, 'The escape of Du Casse was very unfortunate, and her Majesty does very highly and justly resent the behaviour of those officers who were the occasions of it . . .', SP 44/209.
64 For the history of this town, see Michael Pawson and David Buissert, *Port Royal, Jamaica* (Oxford: OUP, 1975).
65 The Court Martial record contains three depositions by Henry Partington. Two are dated 5 September (ADM 1/5263, fols. 144 and 145). A third is dated 8, 9, 10 October (fol. 214). The third was evidently made during the Court Martial, but the contents are the same as the earlier documents.
66 There appear to be no obvious alterations to the the manuscript of Martin's Journal in the Court Martial record, however several segments of the entry for 24 August have been marked with square brackets. It is possible that these phrases were the ones which Kirkby allegedly ordered Martin to add to his Journal. See document **62** in which these phrases have been italicised.

List of Documents and Sources

1 Benbow to Nottingham, 11 September 1702; P.R.O. CO 318/3, fols. 176–80.
2 Line of Battle, 14 July 1702; P.R.O. ADM 1/5263, fol. 218.
3 Benbow to Nottingham; continuation of document **1**.
4 Benbow's Deposition, 8 October 1702; ADM 1/5263, fols. 18–20.
5 Deposition of John Taylor, Master, H.M.S. *Ruby*, 4 September 1702; ADM 1/5263, fols. 30–1.
6 Deposition of Bartholomew Ordd, Master, H.M.S. *Breda*, 5 October 1702; ADM 1/5263, fols. 21–6.
7 Journal of John Martin, Master, H.M.S. *Defiance*; ADM 1/5263, fol. 49.
8 Deposition of Edward Palmer, Carpenter, H.M.S. *Defiance*, 20 September 1702; ADM 1/5263, fol. 55.
9 Deposition of Francis Knighton, 3rd Lieutenant, H.M.S. *Defiance*, 6 September 1702; ADM 1/5263, fol. 65.
10 Deposition of Gavin Hamilton, Surgeon, H.M.S. *Defiance*; ADM 1/5263, fol. 94.
11 Deposition of Samuel Vincent, commanding H.M.S. *Falmouth*, 8 October 1702; ADM 1/5263, fols. 79v–82.
12 Deposition of Jacob Tiley, Master, H.M.S. *Windsor*; ADM 1/5263, fol. 108.
13 Deposition of Edward Holland, 1st Lieutenant, H.M.S. *Windsor*, 9 and 10 October 1702; ADM 1/5263, fol. 171.
14 Deposition of Henry Partington, 1st Lieutenant, H.M.S. *Greenwich*, 5 September 1702; ADM 1/5263, fol. 145.
15 Deposition of Edward Eaton, Captain's Clerk, H.M.S. *Greenwich,* 8 October 1702; ADM 1/5263, fols. 198–9.
16 Line of Battle, 19 August 1702; ADM 1/5263, fol. 104.

17 Benbow to Nottingham; continuation of **1** and **3**.
18 Benbow's Deposition; continuation of **4**.
19 Deposition of John Taylor; continuation of **5**.
20 Deposition of Samuel Vincent; continuation of **11**.
21 Deposition of Francis Knighton; continuation of **9**.
22 Deposition of Edward Holland; continuation of **13**.
23 Benbow to Nottingham; continuation of **1**, **3**, and **17**.
24 Benbow's Deposition; continuation of **4** and **18**.
25 Deposition of Bartholomew Ordd; continuation of **6**.
26 Deposition of Arthur DelGarno, 2nd Lieutenant, H.M.S. *Ruby*; ADM 1/5263, fol. 156.
27 Deposition of Francis Knighton; continuation of **9** and **21**.
28 Deposition of Edward Palmer; continuation of **8**.
29 Deposition of Thomas Mollamb, Boatswain, H.M.S. *Defiance*, 15 September 1702; ADM 1/5263, fol. 66.
30 Deposition of John Codner, 2nd Lieutenant, H.M.S. *Greenwich*, 10 October 1702; ADM 1/5263, fol. 107.
31 Deposition of Edward Eaton; continuation of **15**.
32 Deposition of Edward Holland; continuation of **13** and **22**.
33 Deposition of Samuel Vincent; continuation of **11** and **20**.
34 Benbow to Nottingham; continuation of **1**, **3**, **17** and **23**.
35 Benbow's Deposition; continuation of **4**, **18** and **24**.
36 Deposition of Bartholomew Ordd; continuation of **6** and **25**.
37 Deposition of Samuel Vincent; continuation of **11**, **20** and **33**.
38 Journal of William Herriott, 1st Lieutenant, H.M.S. *Falmouth*; ADM 1/5263, fol. 159.
39 Deposition of Peircy Brett, Master, H.M.S. *Falmouth*; ADM 1/5263, fol. 161.
40 Deposition of Henry Partington; continuation of **14**.
41 Journal of John Codner, 2nd Lieutenant, H.M.S. *Greenwich*; ADM 1/5263, fol. 154.
42 Deposition of Edward Eaton; continuation of **15** and **31**.
43 Deposition of Isaac Sun, Master, H.M.S. *Greenwich*, 5 September 1702; ADM 1/5263, fol. 93.
44 Deposition of Francis Cotterell, Boatswain, H.M.S. *Greenwich*, 10 October 1702; ADM 1/5263, fol. 138.
45 Deposition of Edward Palmer; continuation of **8** and **28**.
46 Deposition of Gavin Hamilton; continuation of **10**.
47 Deposition of John Spurr, Midshipman, H.M.S. *Defiance*, 20 September 1702; ADM 1/5263, fol. 69.
48 Benbow to Nottingham; continuation of **1**, **3**, **17**, **23** and **34**.
49 Benbow's Deposition; continuation of **4**, **18**, **24**, and **35**.
50 Deposition of Bartholomew Ordd; continuation of **6**, **25** and **36**.
51 Deposition of William Herriott, 1st Lieutenant, H.M.S. *Falmouth*; ADM 1/5263, fol. 113.
52 Deposition of Isaac Sun; continuation of **43**.
53 Deposition of Edward Eaton; continuation of **15**, **31**, and **42**.
54 Deposition of John Taylor; continuation of **5** and **19**.
55 Benbow to Nottingham; continuation of **1**, **3**, **17**, **23**, **34** and **48**.
56 Benbow's Deposition; continuation of **4**, **18**, **24**, **35** and **49**.
57 Deposition of Bartholomew Ordd; continuation of **6**, **25**, **36** and **50**.
58 The Captains' Resolution, 24 August 1702; ADM 1/5263, fol. 44.
59 Note from the Court Martial Proceedings, undated; ADM 1/5263, fol. 13.

60   Deposition of Robert Thompson, 1st Lieutenant, H.M.S. *Breda*; ADM 1/5263, fols. 39–42.
61   Deposition of John Spurr; continuation of **47**.
62   Journal of John Martin; continuation of **7**, fols. 51v–52. Words in italics are marked within square brackets in the manuscript.
63   Deposition of Thomas Mollamb; continuation of **29**.
64   Deposition of Edward Palmer; continuation of **8, 28** and **45**.
65   Journal of John Goodall, 2nd Lieutenant, H.M.S. *Pendennis*; ADM 1/5263, fol. 74.
66   Journal of George Harwarr, 1st Lieutenant, H.M.S. *Pendennis*; ADM 1/5263, fol. 78.
67   Deposition of Samuel Vincent; continuation of **11, 20, 33** and **37**.
68   Deposition of Edward Eaton; continuation of **15, 31, 42** and **53**.
69   Deposition of Henry Partington; continuation of **14** and **40**.
70   Deposition of Christopher Fogg, commanding H.M.S. *Breda*, 8 October 1702; ADM 1/5263, fol. 109.
71   Benbow to Nottingham; continuation of **1, 3, 17, 23, 34, 48** and **55**.
72   Indictment of John Arthur, Gunner, H.M.S. *Defiance*; ADM 1/5263, fol. 132.
73   Rear-Admiral Whetstone to Josiah Burchett [10 September 1702], duplicate dated 17 October 1702; ADM 1/2641.
74   Court Martial Adjournment, 8 October 1702; ADM 1/5263, fol. 103.
75   List of Evidence against Richard Kirkby; ADM 1/5263, fols. 101–02.
76   Court Martial Report, 12 October 1702; ADM 1/5263, fols. 1–7.
77   Verdict of the Court Martial on Richard Kirkby; ADM 1/5263, fols. 8–9.
78   Rear-Admiral Whetstone to Burchett, 20 October 1702; ADM 1/2641.
79   Benbow to the Commissioners of the Board of Ordnance, 20 October 1702; Bodleian Library, MS. Montagu d.11, fol. 150.
80   Whetstone to Burchett, 25 November 1702.
81   Richard Kirkby to Burchett, 11 December 1702; ADM 1/2004.
82   Minutes of the Prince's Council, 7 January 1702/3; ADM 3/17.
83   Lord High Admiral's Memorial for her Majesty in Council, 7 January 1702/3; P.R.O. SP 42/7.
84   Burchett to Warre, Under-Secretary of State, 7 January 1702/3; SP 42/7.
85   Minutes of the Prince's Council, 8 January 1702/3; ADM 3/17.
86   Lord High Admiral's Orders to Vice-Admiral Benbow, 9 January 1702/3; ADM 2/29, fols. 413v–14.
87   The Queen to the Lord High Admiral, 13 January 1702/3; SP 44/170, p. 124.
88   Nottingham to Benbow, 23 January 1702/3; SP 44/209, fol. 4.
89   Burchett to Commissioner St Lo, at Plymouth, 20 March 1702/3: ADM 2/406, fol. 555.
90   Captain E. S. Acton to Burchett, 16 April 1703; ADM 1/1436.
91   Acton to Burchett, 18 April 1703; ADM 1/1436.
92   Richard Kirkby's Last Statement, 16 April 1703; ADM 1/1436.

5

Naval Aspects of the Landings on the French Coast, 1758

Edited by

A. W. H. PEARSALL

Introduction

Pitt's 'system' of harassing attacks on the French coast has always aroused controversy, both at the time and among commentators ever since. While the present series of documents makes no pretence to reaching a judgement on the strategic significance of the landings it will, it is hoped, show that these operations did mark a considerable advance in the technique of combined operations, and one that was to be employed with much effect in the following years.

The origin of these expeditions lay in William Pitt's belief that such diversionary campaigns could usefully contribute to the best 'system' of war for British circumstances. They would occupy French naval and military resources and find a useful role for the British home army without becoming deeply involved in continental commitments. Meanwhile, other British forces could operate against French overseas possessions.[1] With these ideas in mind, Pitt had initiated an attack upon Rochefort in 1757, which failed in such a fashion as to offer a standing example of how not to conduct such expeditions. While it may thus have been a useful lesson to those who took part, such as Howe and Wolfe, it equally added to the shadow which already hung over the whole concept as a result of previous miscarriages from Camaret Bay to Cartagena and Lorient.

The 1758 expeditions did, however, have a practical stimulus in their planning. Frederick II of Prussia was Britain's ally, fighting at the same time France, Austria and Russia. Long drawn-out negotiations were in progress for a more formal alliance and obviously British support was an important factor. Pitt was prepared to subsidise Frederick directly and also to support the German troops, under Ferdinand of Brunswick, but was opposed to sending British troops. Frederick also wished to see a British fleet in the Baltic, which was equally regarded by Pitt as a diversion of force, and which in all probability it would have been impossible in practice to provide, given the other calls upon the Navy. Eventually, an agreement was reached under whose terms Britain promised to employ a considerable force in attacks on the French coast during the summer of 1758, as well as to send a small force to secure Emden.[2] This agreement was concluded on 11 April and at once considerable preparations were begun with great urgency.

The new departure in such matters was the provision of special equipment. It is by no means clear who was responsible for this innovation, but presumably it must have been Ligonier, Anson or even Pitt himself, as the instructions came through the Admiralty [Document 1]. The principal item of this equipment was a special design of boat, where hitherto all that had been available would have been the boats belonging to the ships. These special boats were not only designed to beach readily and then to lie on a flat bottom so that equipment could be disembarked, but also to take a tactical unit of troops — a half company. The documents show that one of these was built at Woolwich and viewed by the Board of Admiralty on 26 April, after which another nineteen were ordered to follow from various builders in great haste [2, 3]. Such speed led, of course, to a number of minor clashes [8].

The 'flat-boats', as they came to be called, were large, and had originally been called 'launches', which were the largest type of boat normally supplied to warships. Special arrangements had to be made for their carriage by ships, and in addition various other items of gear had to be provided to facilitate transfer of troops from transport to boat [15].

It was also foreseen that bomb vessels would prove useful in providing covering fire, and three of the few remaining bombs in the Service, then serving as sloops, as was the usual practice, were ordered to take their mortars on board.[3] The value of such vessels was increased by another new idea, that of firing small 'pound shot' from the mortars in large quantities, as an early form of shrapnel.[4]

Meanwhile troops were assembling — sixteen regiments assembled in the Isle of Wight — and transports were gathering. It was usual to hold a number of transports ready for service, and many were already at Spithead or in the vicinity, but others had to come round from the Thames. Some had to be modified to take flat-boats, others to take horses and others stores. Preparations in all these directions reached such a pitch that both the Controller and the Surveyor from the Navy Board went to Portsmouth to direct affairs [14] — one result being an example of a Navy Board warrant signed by these two and the resident Commissioner, a relatively unusual event [15] — while shortages of beds and hammocks earned Portsmouth further reproof, and various other minor wants became apparent.

At the same time commanders had been selected for the forces concerned.

The land forces were placed under the third Duke of Marlborough, with Lord George Sackville as second-in-command. The strong naval squadron was to be commanded by a much more junior officer – Captain the Hon. Richard Howe, then aged 32, but already noted as an officer of ability. He was allotted a force of four small ships of the line, (another being added in July) and several frigates, sloops and bomb vessels [20]. The best known of his subordinates were perhaps Robert Duff, the second-in-command, and Hyde Parker.

All the preparations were complete by the end of the third week in May, and the troops were embarked between 25 and 27 May, this being the only use of the flat-bottomed boats before actual operations commenced, as they were only issued to ships about the 23rd.[5] After waiting some days for a wind, Howe was able to sail on 1 June, with his awkward collection of shipping, in company with the Channel fleet under Anson. The latter bore away down Channel to take up the blockade of Brest. Next morning the 'expedition', as it was usually called at the time, was between Alderney and the mainland, somewhat at the mercy of the strong tides, but nevertheless alarming the French, whose warning signals could be seen.[6] For two days the fleet worked through the Channel Islands, losing one transport, the *Wards*, on a sunken rock. On 5 June they worked into Cancale Bay where, despite the stout resistance of a small three-gun battery, a landing was successfully made [22, 23]. Next day the horse and artillery were got ashore, and the army advanced towards St Malo. They found the place too strong to be captured without a siege, and so they contented themselves with burning much shipping at St Servan and sending a scouting force towards Dol. Some of the warships were detached to watch St Malo and to support the army if possible by landing the siege train, but their positive activities were limited to the landing of bread for it at Fort Roteauneuf. News of approaching French forces disturbed the nervous Marlborough and the army retired to Cancale, where it was taken off on 11 and 12 June. The weather turned bad and the fleet was unable to leave the bay until the 21st. That day they were off Granville, where some action was contemplated but the commanders could not agree on what, so the fleet sailed round the Cotentin to threaten Caen and Havre, but still the weather was poor. Finally they tried Cherbourg on the 29th, and the troops actually embarked in the flat-boats, but the onshore wind increased and the enterprise had to be abandoned. Food and forage were running short and the fleet was obliged to return to Spithead, where the troops in due course disembarked.

Uncertainty followed. The commanders were summoned to London for further consultations about future operations. Ferdinand's successes had led to a decision to send more British troops to Germany and three regiments were taken from the 'expedition', while the military commanders also sought, successfully, to transfer their attentions to that more congenial theatre. After some searching, Lieutenant-General Thomas Bligh, called to take command in Germany, found himself at the head of the French coast expedition.

The troops re-embarked on 27 July and the fleet sailed again on the 30th, but had to put back when the wind changed. Next day it had more success, but light and changeable winds made for a long and tedious voyage and it was 5 August before the force reached the French coast. Cherbourg was again the objective and on 7 August the troops were landed a few miles west of the town. Meeting little opposition thanks to the fire from the ships, the army moved eastwards and came upon some of the principal citizens, ready to surrender the town. Terms were agreed upon and on the 8th the place was occupied. The fleet moved in support of the army. For the next few days there was great activity demolishing the harbour and piers, until on 15 and 16 August the troops were taken on board again, and the fleet returned to Portland [32, 36].

Howe was anxious to maintain the pressure and set off again on the 25th, but weather compelled him to put back. They finally got away on the 31st and headed once again for St Malo. There has always been an unexplained mystery about this second raid on that locality in that the landing was made to the west of the river Rance, although St Malo was the stated objective. It was soon realised that the river with its fierce tides was an unsurmountable obstacle, and that the intended bombardment of the port was highly hazardous. Moreover, the onshore winds which had already proved so unhelpful again set in, so that, after landing at St Lunaire on 3 and 4 September, Howe told Bligh that he could not keep the fleet there, but must find a safer anchorage. Bligh therefore had no alternative but to march his army through the country to the new anchorage [38]. This was found at St Cas, a few miles to the westward, and here on 11 September took place the only serious fight in the whole campaign, under most disadvantageous conditions for the British troops. Strong French forces under the Duc d'Aiguillon followed the retreating British. The majority of the invaders were taken off but the rearguard, the Guards Brigade, were closely pressed. Though well supported by fire from the sloops and bombs, eventually they became so closely engaged that the ships could no longer fire, and they were overwhelmed on the beach. Many were killed, drowned or captured, while the four naval captains in charge of the four divisions of flat-boats were also taken [39]. Howe gathered up the remnant and returned to Plymouth, and later Spithead.[7]

Although Howe evidently expected to continue, this reverse exhausted what little military enthusiasm existed for these coastal attacks, and the increasing calls from Germany in any case drew off more troops, so that no further ventures took place in 1758. In 1759 operations on the French coast were confined to bombardments. Despite the fact that the defeat of the French fleets and of the invasion plans had made these attacks less necessary by 1760, Pitt was still convinced of their utility as diversions, and in 1761 he at last achieved his hope of a permanent lodgement on French soil by the capture of Belleisle. The 1758 operations therefore did not lead to any sustained line of policy, but they did achieve some success in withdrawing French troops from other theatres and in relieving the pressure upon Prussia, as well as inflicting a certain amount of damage on French ports and shipping.

A wider naval significance attaches to them, however, in the light of the character of the Seven Years' War as a maritime war against overseas colonies. A succession of important combined operations followed, all of which owed much in their organisation and equipment to Howe's and Duff's work on the French coast in 1758, and it is to this aspect that the following collection of documents pays most attention. Previous combined operations undertaken by the British services had only been occasional and no established doctrine existed. The last major ones had been Vernon's and Wentworth's attack on Cartagena in 1742, and the Lorient fiasco of 1746. Although a failure, the landings and close support of the army at Cartagena were well conducted by Vernon.[8] Boscawen who distinguished himself there, came to command in 1758 the attack on Louisbourg, the other source of experience which coalesced with that of the French coast to provide a body of knowledge on which were based the operations against Guadeloupe, Goree and Quebec in 1759, Belleisle and Martinique in 1761 and Havana in 1762. The contribution from the French coast was particularly in the special equipment, to be used in all the subsequent landings, and in the sets of orders produced by Howe [17, 25] soon to be printed in a similar style to the Sailing and Fighting Instructions [29] upon which the printed orders used by Rodney in 1762[9] were closely based. Furthermore, although the successes of combined operations between 1758 and 1762 did not appear to make them any more popular with the services, the arrangements and equipment evolved in 1758 continued to be their basis for many years to come, and so merit attention here.

The present collection of documents does not attempt to give any account of the proceedings of the troops, nor does it enter into the questions of policy behind the expeditions. It hopes to give an impression of the naval problems concerned with the hurried preparation and execution of Pitt's ideas. The documents are all drawn from the Public Record Office and the National Maritime Museum, and are almost entirely official in character. Although a number of journals of military men who took part in the raids are known to exist, no such journal by a sea officer has come to light, except for two printed in the *London Magazine*.[10] To some extent, however, the deficiency has been remedied from ships' logs, where occasionally one can find useful descriptions of events. Another serious deficiency is the disappearance of the journal which it must be presumed that Howe kept, since this was normally required for all flag officers. Such journals usually enter into more detail than do his often inadequate letters to the Admiralty.

The documents fall into three groups. There is first a number of papers drawn from Navy Board and dockyard papers describing the preparations and particularly the building of the flat-boats. Secondly are the orders issued by Howe for the governance of his force and for the landings. It will be seen that these came out piece-meal and, indeed, one apparently essential order is dated some days after the first landing [25]. Evidently its necessity must have been discovered by hard experience. Thirdly, but interspersed with the second group to form a chronological record, are documents giving an account of events.

The usual rules of the Society have been followed concerning spelling and punctuation, but it may be noted that the extracts from ships' logs run, as was then the practice, from noon to noon, and hence p.m. entries come first. The afternoon would be the day before that given in the log, the succeeding morning would be the actual civil day. Most of the orders concerning signals repeat the description of the flags in the margin to aid the user in finding the meaning quickly, but these have either been omitted, or inserted in square brackets within the relevant paragraph wherever the text directs one to the margin [25].

NAVAL ASPECTS OF THE
LANDINGS ON THE FRENCH COAST,
1758
DOCUMENTS

1 *Admiralty to Navy Board*

Admiralty Office,
7 April 1758

We do hereby desire and direct you to cause two boats to be built, in the most expeditious manner, agreeable to the plan which we herewith send you, with this difference only, that instead of fixed rowlocks, they are to have only one ash thole, with a grommet to it, for each oar.

2 *Admiralty to Navy Board*

Admiralty Office,
27 April 1758

We do hereby desire and direct you to use every means in your power to building with the utmost expedition as many launches of the same nature with that lately built, and viewed yesterday at Woolwich, as can be got completed and ready at Portsmouth by the 17th of next month.

3 *Navy Board Minute on the letter of 27 April*

28 April 1758

Direct Portsmouth Officers to build ten of them or as many as can be completed by that time – desire Commissioner Hughes to send for Mr Ewer and Mr Adams in his neighbourhood to build one each – direct Deptford, Woolwich and Chatham Officers to build one each to be completed in twelve days or sooner if possible. Agree with Mrs Winter, Mr Alexander and Mr Burr for one each to be built in twelve days and to allow 1s per foot more than for the last built by Mrs Winter if it appears she lost by that – and write to Mr Clevland that the captains of the ships of war in the river may have orders to carry to Portsmouth such of these launches as shall be completed by the time of their sailing.

4 *Navy Board to Officers of Portsmouth Yard*

Navy Office,
28 April 1758

Pursuant to an order from the Right Honourable the Lords Commissioners of the Admiralty of yesterday's date, these are to direct and require you to cause to be built with the utmost expedition ten launches according to the draught plan and scantlings which were sent to the Master Shipwright by last night's post, or as many thereof as can be completed and ready by the 17th of next month. For which this shall be your warrant.

5 *Navy Board to Portsmouth Officers*

Navy Office,
28 April 1758

These are to direct and require you to provide for the twelve launches ordered to be built in your yard and the neighbourhood of it, round loomed ash oars, twenty-four in number for each launch of the dimensions undermentioned and for such part thereof as you cannot procure from the contractor or make in the yard to demand them from Deptford so timely as that the whole number may be ready by the time the launches are completed.

	ft	in.
Whole length	12	10
of which within the Gunwale	3	5
Breadth of the blade		5¾
Diameter of the loom within the Gunwale		3⅝
close to the outside of the Gunwale		2⅝
To row with a single ash thole		

For which this shall be your warrant.

6 *Navy Board to Portsmouth Officers*

Navy Office,
29 April 1758

Having agreed with the undermentioned boatbuilders, bred up altogether in the clench-work way, to go to Portsmouth to assist in building the launches directed to be built by our warrant of yesterday, who have agreed to be there by Monday night and to work a day and quarter, the quarters of a day to be reckoned two hours and a half more than the common working hours of the Yard, viz.

Robt. Lovewell	Willm. Ripplingham
Robt. Stockbridge	Ambse. Rose
Willm. Mathews	Richd. Cooper

These are to direct and require you to employ the said men on the said launches accordingly; and the Clerk of the Cheque is to pay them weekly after the rate of five shillings a day, the same to commence tomorrow and to be continued two days after they are discharged from the said works; and likewise to pay the expense of the carriage of their chests and tools to and from Portsmouth and a guinea to each man for his expenses to London. For which this shall be your warrant.

7 *Navy Board Minute*

29 April 1758

Ordered that the Deptford Officers be acquainted with the sort of oars to be used in the launches and directed to demand 24 for each of the six building in the river to be completed in twelve days — that they be directed to receive the launches building by Mrs Winter, Mr Burr and Mr Alexander and that they send by the *Albina* storeship the two they have already received, one to be stowed on the booms and the other towed to the Downs, the latter of which is to be put on board the ship appointed to convoy her if she can take it on, but if not then she is to tow it round to Portsmouth and deliver them both to the Storekeeper of the Yard — the launches not to be put on board till the storeship is on the point of sailing and to send us an account of what the Master asks for carrying them.

8 *Navy Board to Portsmouth Officers*

Navy Office,
3 May 1758

Gentlemen,

We have received your letter of yesterday wherein you acquaint us that you have discoursed the oarmaker, and that he has convinced you he cannot make the oars which you were directed by our warrant of the 28th past to provide for the launches building in your Yard and in the neighbourhood, he being fully employed in supplying barge and boat oars for the current service. Such a loose and careless behaviour in a matter of so much concern gives us great displeasure, and we are sorry to find you so wanting in judgement as not to know that all your attention to what relates to the equipping the launches should be given in preference to any other consideration. You were directed likewise to demand of the contractor what number he could make, which you have not thought proper to take any notice of, but have demanded the whole from Deptford not considering whether they may be able to comply therewith. In short, it is absolutely necessary that as many of these oars as possible should be provided at Portsmouth, and therefore direct you to put them in hand, and to work all the extra thereon that can be done with advantage, and send to the contractor to make as many as he can timely provide, letting us know the number you are likely to get ready by these means, having desired Commissioner Hughes to agree for the remainder that may be wanted, to be made by any person in the neighbourhood, and you are to demand what other oars may be wanted for the current service of your Yard.

We are

Your affectionate friends

G. Cokburne T. Slade D. Devert W. Bateman

9   Navy Board to Portsmouth Officers

Navy Office,
6 May 1758

Having ordered Andrew Johnson and Robert Metcalf, two oarmakers belonging to his Majesty's Yards at Deptford and Woolwich to set out tomorrow for your Yard, to assist in making the oars you have our directions to provide for the launches building in your Yard and its neighbourhood; these are to direct and require you to employ the said men and supply them with proper tools for that purpose, and to allow them the same extra as was allowed the artificers lately sent from Chatham to your Yard, the same to commence from this day, or if they are inclined to make them by the pair, as your oarmaker does, to employ them in that manner. For which this shall be your warrant.

10   Rt Hon. William Pitt (Secretary of State) to Admiralty

Whitehall,
8 May 1758

I am commanded to signify to Your Lordships his Majesty's Pleasure that you do forthwith give the necessary orders for putting under the command of the Honourable Captain Richard Howe, at Spithead, three ships of the line and twelve or thirteen frigates and sloops together with the fireships, transports and all other vessels whatever, that have been prepared for a secret expedition; and Your Lordships will direct Captain Howe to follow such orders and instructions as he shall receive from his Majesty by one of his Principal Secretaries of State.

11   Navy Board to Portsmouth Officers

Navy Office,
10 May 1758

As it is expected that the transports for carrying horse will be ordered into Portsmouth Harbour, and finding it will be necessary that ten of them should take each of them one launch, these are to direct and require you to cause the ships named in the margin, on their arrival in the harbour, to be fitted in the most convenient manner with booms for stowing the said boats thereon, and if their own topmasts are not sufficient for that service, to supply them with what may be proper for it and send us an account of what you shall do herein. For which this shall be your warrant.

[Marginal list:]		
	True Briton	*Ranger*
	Anne and Mary	*Exchange*
	Eagle	*Mary (5)*
	Loving Friends	*John and Mary*
	Amity's Assistance	*Ruby*

12   *Navy Board to Admiralty*

Navy Office,
11 May 1758

We desire you will acquaint the Right Honourable the Lords Commissioners of the Admiralty that the six naval vessels named on the other side hereof, with six of the launches, (the other two being on board the *King of Prussia* hospital and the *Maidstone*) will sail for the Downs this evening and tomorrow morning, we having given directions to the masters to make the best of their way thither, that they may take the opportunity of this easterly wind to proceed to Portsmouth, which we hope their Lordships will approve of, and that they will be pleased to appoint a convoy for them upon their arrival, as their continuance in the Downs may be hazardous, the vessels not having room to hoist in the boats.[11]

[The vessels were:]   *Lyon* hoy, *Supply* hoy, *Woolwich* transport, *Royal Escape*, *Woolwich* lighter, *Chatham* lighter.

13   *Secretary of the Admiralty to Navy Board*

Admiralty Office,
13 May 1758

I have communicated to my Lords Commissioners of the Admiralty your letters of the 11th instant, giving an account that six naval vessels with six launches are on their way to the Downs, and in return I am commanded by their Lordships to acquaint you that Sir Peircy Brett is directed to keep the *Flamborough* and *Savage* sloop in the Downs till those vessels arrive there, and then dispatch them away immediately to Spithead under convoy of that ship and sloop.

14   *George Cokburne (Controller) to Secretary of the Admiralty*

Portsmouth,
15 May 1758, 11 o'clock p.m.

I arrived here this afternoon. I had the good fortune to meet Captain Howe on the road, by whom I found some difficulties had started about the transports carrying the flat-bottom boats. On my arrival here I immediately inquired into what would be the inconveniences attending them in a more particular manner than I could be informed from Captain Howe, who I met between towns and only conversed with as we stood in the road.

Their booms must be raised so high for their windlass to work that, when these boats are in, they will not be able to set a mainsail, in case they should have occasion, and the boats will always be in danger of being stove, whenever got in or out, from the weakness of the ship's companies and their yards not being square enough to keep them, of so great a breadth, clear of their sides. However, as ten of the ships are in this harbour, I shall order them to be fitted immediately for the reception of the boats, which will be done in twenty-four hours. They will then be ready and may either carry boats or not for the booms will not be in their mainsails' way, unless the broad boat is upon them, but may serve to carry a narrower boat if found necessary, and shall then send these ships out of the harbour as fast as possible together with those taken up here, which will be all completed tomorrow, for at present the harbour is greatly crowded with them, and will be more so when all the horse ships are ordered in, which must be done some little time before they embark. Whilst transports are in a harbour, there can be no dependence on them.[12]

I have sent to Captain Brett, who I hear is at Lymington, to desire a meeting with him. Tomorrow I shall inform myself about the small vessels I am directed to procure and will let you know what I do therein.

I shall forward the other things Captain Howe mentioned (which you will hear of from himself).

I write this in haste only to let you know that the ships shall be prepared to carry boats or let it alone, and I know them too well to let them stay a moment longer in the harbour than absolutely necessary.

I should be glad of Lord Anson's commands with regard to laying a platform on the casks of some of the transports where their holds will admit of it, which will make them stow more men, and is easily done, and I think will be better than hammacoes.

15   *Navy Board to Portsmouth Officers*

Portsmouth Yard,
17 May 1758

There being wanted for the use of the transports and ships of war under the command of the Honourable Captain Howe the several particulars mentioned below; these are to direct and require you to cause the same to be provided with all the dispatch you possibly can, and issue them to such of the transports or ships of war as shall be appointed to receive them, charging the masters therewith, viz.

Brows for landing or embarking men	Six
Floating Stages, in length 26 feet, and in breadth 10 feet each	Two
Punt, in length 28 feet, breadth 8 ft 6 in. and in depth 3 feet	One
Ladders of 30 feet in length	Sixty

For which this shall be your warrant. Dated at his Majesty's Yard near Portsmouth this 17th of May 1758[13]
G Cokburne T Slade R Hughes

P.S. For giving dispatch to these particulars, you are to employ the people thereon such extra as may be absolutely necessary.
G C, T S, R H.

16   *Regulations respecting the Order of Sailing and Anchorage of the Transports*

Essex, Spithead,
25 May 1758

The transports, etc., are to be separated into two divisions as specified in the order of sailing hereafter described: the one to be led by the Commander-in-Chief: the other by the *Brilliant*, the Officer Second-in-Command on board the *Rochester* being to close the rear of the whole.

The *Brilliant*, distinguished by a blue pendant at the main topmast head and lights as commander in the third post, is to repeat signals from the Commander-in-Chief to the *Rochester* (distinguished by a white pendant at the main topmast head and lights as commander in the second post) and the ships in the rear, and all signals made from this last for the conduct of the transports or their defence are to be complied with in the same manner (by the ships of war likewise when the Commander-in-Chief is not upon the spot) as if made from the Commander-in-Chief.

As the Commander-in-Chief, though meaning in general to be placed in the centre of the fleet, may find it necessary on some occasion to remain anchored in the van, when therefore he would have the *Brilliant* to move on to the van, meaning to take his place in the centre of the fleet on his arrival at any anchorage, he will make the signal by hoisting a flag striped red white and blue at the main topmast head with the ship's signal as for changing place when in order of battle, after the signal has been made for the fleet to prepare to anchor. At all other times it is to be understood that he means to remain in the same station as pointed out by this Sailing Order.

For the better guidance in choice of anchorage, upon this occasion when a sufficient number of pilots are not to be procured, it is to be noticed that three cutters (wearing each at their mastheads a pendant of the same colours with the distinguishing colours worn by the three commanders' ships that they are meant to represent) will be placed according to the extent thereof near the points of anchorage chosen for those commanding ships, by which the rest of the fleet are to be therefore guided in the choice of their respective stations accordingly.

It is moreover to be observed that the Order of Sailing delivered herein is not meant to confine the frigates stationed here on either quarter of the fleet to keep always on that same quarter, particularly on the change of tack when working to windward, but that division of them happening to be then to windward when the signal is made for tacking are to remain still to windward of the body of the fleet, till opportunity offers (by changing of wind or otherwise) to regain without inconvenience or loss of time their destined stations; the intent of the distribution of the ships of war in sailing order being only to secure the transports, etc., against any hazard of insult from the sudden arrival of an enemy on either quarter of the fleet during the night.

Neither is it required of the different corps of transports to observe on the change of tack their present destined stations in respect to the Commander-in-Chief, this appointment having been only made to prevent as much as possible an irregular mixture of the transports of the different regiments. Nevertheless, when the weather, extent of anchorage and their circumstances will admit thereof, they are desired to take their stations upon occasion of anchoring, as near as possible in the order above described.

Order of Sailing

	Diligence	*Swallow*
	Essex	
	Transports of the First Division	
Maidstone	Kingsley's 3rd Guards 2nd Guards 1st Guards	*Active*
Richmond	Wolf's Lowden's Bentinck's Holmes's Manners's	*Pallas*
	Fireships, Bombs and their Tenders	
Portland	Ordnance Transports	*Deptford*
	Baggage and Train Horse ships	

	Brilliant	
	Transports of the Second Division	
Rose	Richmond's Hay's Welsh Fusiliers	*Flamborough*
Tartar	Effingham's Cornwallis's Lambton's	*Success*
	Light Horse	
	Speedwell	*Saltash*
	Rochester	

17   *General Order to Squadron*

[25 May 1758]

If upon the arrival or approach of the fleet to the point of their destination, the Commander-in-Chief would have all the troops to be held in readiness (in respect to their accoutrements, provisions, etc.) for being disembarked, he will hoist a flag chequered red and white at the fore topgallantmast head, and if he would have any particular regiments only to do the same, the signal pendant expressive of those particular regiments will be hoisted at the same time as mentioned in the second article of the Distinguishing Signals delivered herewith [18]. But if from circumstances or weather or otherwise, it should be judged proper to defer the disembarkation, and it is therefore intended that the troops should be disarmed till further order, the same flag will be hoisted at the mizen topmast head.

When the Commander-in-Chief would have the troops under orders for a descent to be embarked in the boats and small vessels and kept in readiness to proceed upon the shortest warning to the shore, if by day he will hoist a flag chequered blue and yellow at the fore topgallantmast head and by night two lights of equal height in the fore topmast shrouds, and two of equal height in the mizen topmast shrouds, and fire a gun if necessary. But if from circumstances of weather, etc., as before, it should be judged proper to re-embark the troops again from the boats in contradiction to this order, if in the daytime the chequered blue and yellow flag will be hoisted at the mizen topmast head and by night the Commander-in-Chief will show the same signal lights as before and fire two guns.

When after the embarkation of the troops in the boats and arrival at the appointed rendezvous, the Commander-in-Chief would have them proceed in the order prescribed to the shore chosen for the descent, if by day he will hoist a flag blue pierced with white at the fore topgallantmast head, and in the night two lights one under the other in the fore topmast shrouds and two more in the same manner in the mizen topmast shrouds and fire one gun if necessary. But if in contradiction to this order he would have the boats to return with the troops back again to the appointed rendezvous, the pierced flag will be hoisted at the mizen topmast head by day and by night the same signal lights shown as above with two guns.

18   *Distinguishing Signals for calling Officers on Board*

Essex at Spithead,
25 May 1758

(1)

When I would speak with the Captains of any ship of war of the squadron, the signal will be made as against that ship's name expressed; if with a Lieutenant the same signal and a weft of the ensign; but if for a boat without a commissioned officer, the weft will be hoisted only half staff up.

Red	White	Blue	Yellow	Place where	
Rochester	Brilliant	Deptford		Main	⎫
Maidstone	Essex	Richmond		Fore	⎬ topmast head
Rose	Tartar	Portland		Mizen	⎭

Pallas	*Active*	*Success*	Starboard	Main-topsail
Flamborough	*Swallow*	*Furnace*	Larboard	yard arm
Saltash	*Salamander*	*Diligence*	Starboard	Fore-topsail
Speedwell	*Granado*	*Pluto*	Starboard	yard arm

(2)

When the Colonel or Commanding Officer of any particular regiment or other officer in the first division of the transports is wanted on board the Commander-in-Chief, the signal pendant as underneath, to specify the particular regiments will be shewn, and a white broad pendant hoisted at the same time over the distinguishing pendant at the main topmast head, but if the Adjutant only of such particular regiment of that division is wanted the signal will be made as for the Colonel of that regiment and a yellow pendant hoisted at the ensign staff.

Red	*White*	*Blue*	*Yellow*	*Place where*
Ist Battalion of Guards	2nd Battalion of Guards	3rd Battalion of Guards	Major of the Brigade of Guards	Main
Kingsley's	Bentinck's	Home's	Major of the First Brigade of Foot	Fore \}topmast head
Lowden's	Manners's	Wolf's	Major of the Second Brigade of Foot	Mizen

Second Division

If the Colonel or Commanding Officer of any particular regiment or other officer of the second division is wanted on board the ship of the Commander-in-Chief, the signal as underneath (expressive of that particular regiment) will be shewn, and a blue broad pendant hoisted at the flagstaff at the main topmast head, with the distinction as before if for the Adjutant only of the regiment.

Red	*White*	*Blue*	*Yellow*	*Place where*
Welsh Fusiliers	Lord Chas Hay	Cornwallis's	Major of 3rd Brigade	Main \} topmast head
Effingham's	Richmond's	Lambton's	Major of 4th Brigade	Fore

Respecting the Tenders, etc., of the Fleet

A yellow pendant will be hoisted on the flagstaff at the main topgallantmast head to paricularise the same when any of the signals are meant to regard the armed cutters, tenders, etc., of the fleet or others as undermentioned.

Red	White	Blue	Place where
Prince George cutter	*Tartar* cutter	*Lurcher* cutter	Main topmast head
Standard	Mizen topmast head		For all the General Land Officers to repair on board the ship of the Commander-in-Chief
White flag	Mizen Topmast head		For all the Colonels or Commanding Officers of Regiments
White flag	Mizen topmast head with Yellow Pendant at Ensign Staff		For all the Adjutants of the Army
Red pendant	Mizen Peak and on		For the Colonels or
White pendant	Flagstaff at Main topmast head		Commanding Officers of Regiments in the First Division
Red pendant	Mizen Peak and on		For all the Adjutants of the
White pendant	Flagstaff at Main topmast head and Yellow Pendant at Ensign Staff		First Division
Red pendant	Mizen Peak and Main topgallantmast head		For the Colonels or Commanding Officers of Regiments of the Second Division
Red pendant	Mizen Peak and Main topgallantmast head and Yellow Pendant at Ensign staff		For all the Adjutants of the Second Division
Yellow flag	Mizen topmast hounds		For the Chief Engineer to repair on board the ship of the Commander-in-Chief
Blue flag	Mizen Topmast hounds		For the Commanding Officer of the Artillery
Yellow flag	Mizen Peak		For all the Majors of Brigades in the Army to repair on board the ship of the Commander-in-Chief.

19   *Howe to Duff*

Essex, Spithead,
27 May 1758

My dear Duff,

I am most sensibly concerned to find by yours of the 23rd that your ship has been ordered into the dock, as I much fear it will be the means of depriving me of your assistance, and yourself of an opportunity of shewing the world how justly I have so placed my confidence.

It is upon an occasion, my dear Duff, that no two officers so young *in*

Rank as ourselves had ever before left to their management. The troops are all embarked, but the wind being westerly will prevent our sailing; perhaps whilst it continues to the westwards of the NW, I have therefore some faint hopes of meeting you still. I am obliged to act in the manner I have done in respect to the rendezvous, but as soon as you open it, if you think from the substance of it and what I have now said, that there is a possibility of your joining me before I leave the British coast, I beg you will come up to the eastward in quest of me so far as to look into St Helen's. If you do not join us before our arrival at our point of destination, you will be in danger of losing a share in the reputation everybody here seems most ambitious to acquire. I say not this to quicken your dispatch, but to condole with you in your ill-fortune should any obstruction intervene.[14] Adieu.

Believe me to be
what I shall remain ever
most truly yours
Richd Howe

P.S. It may perhaps be believed but nobody has authority to declare that I am to command on this expedition as yet. You will therefore please not to say it is confirmed by you whilst we [illegible] in England.

Enclosed: Order to rendezvous off St Malo.

20   *Line of Battle*

Essex, St Helen's,
30 May 1758

Order of Ships of War in the Line

Frigates	Ships' Names	Guns	Men	Captains' Names	Division
Maidstone	Deptford	50	350	Jno. Hollwall	
Active	Essex	64	480	Richd. Dorrill	
Pallas	Portland	50	350	Jervis Maplesden	
Flamborough	Rochester	50	350	Robt. Duff	
Richmond					
Rose					
Brilliant					

Order of Battle of Frigates when separated from the Ships of the Line

Commodore Howe

	Frigates' Name	Guns	Men	Captains' Names
Tartar				
Success	Maidstone	28	200	Dudley Digges
Saltash	Active	28	200	Richd. Hughes
Swallow	Pallas	36	240	Archd. Clevland
Furnace	Flamborough	20	160	Archd. Kennedy
Pluto	Richmond	28	220	Thos. Hankerson
Granado	Rose	20	160	Benj. Clive
Salamander	Brilliant	32	240	Hyde Parker
Infernal	Tartar	28	200	Jno. Knight
Diligence	Success	20	160	Paul Henry Ourry
Speedwell				

The *Deptford* to lead on the Starboard Tack and the *Rochester* the Larboard Tack of the Ships of War. And the *Maidstone* to lead on the Starboard Tack and the *Success* the Larboard Tack of the Frigates.

21   *Signals given in addition to the former delivered*

Essex, St Helen's,
31 May 1758

Blue Flag	Mizen topmast Hounds and Yellow Pendant at Ensign Staff	For Adjutant of Artillery
White Flag	Mizen topmast Head and Yellow Pendant at Ensign Staff	For the Brigadier of Light Horse
Yellow Flag	Mizen Peak	For all the Majors of Brigades in the Army to repair on board the Commander-in-Chief
Red Flag White Cross [*sic*]	Mizen topmast Head	For the Artillery Transports to draw nearer to the shore appointed for the place at which their stores are to be disembarked.
Red Flag White Cross [*sic*]	Mizen topmast Head	For Transports carrying Light Horse to move nearer to the shore as before.
White with Red Cross	Mizen topmast Head with Blue Pendant over it	For the Light Horse to disembark
Pendant striped Blue and White	Mizen topmast Head	For the Comptroller of Artillery
Yellow and White	Mizen topmast Shrouds	Agent of Transports

22   *Log of the* Essex *by Lieutenant James Cranston*

5 June 1758   Winds ESE, SE, SSW, WbS

First part little wind and cloudy, latter moderate and fair. At 1 p.m. brought to the *Fly* privateer belonging to Jersey. At 5 made the signal and anchored with the best bower in 25 fathoms, Cape Frehel SSW 5 or 6 leagues. At ½ past 2 a.m. made the signal and weighed and came to sail, 109 sail in company. At 6 made the signal for the troops to prepare for landing. At 8 made the signal for the transports having Grenadiers on board to come up to the van of the fleet. At ½ past 8 made the signal for the horse transports to come up to the van of the fleet. At ¾ past 8 made the signal for the ordnance ships to do the same. At ½ past 9 made the signal for the rear of the fleet to make more sail. At noon working into Cancale Bay, 109 sail in company.

Noon. Working into Cancale Bay, Cancale Point W½S 2 miles.

6 June   Winds NE, East

Little wind and fair. At 2 p.m. made the signal for ships having flat-bottomed boats to hoist them out. At ½ past made the signal and anchored in Cancale Bay with the best bower in 6 fathoms. At 3 made the signal for the flat-bottomed boats with troops on board to come on board us. Ditto for the Chief Engineer to come on board. At 6 Commodore Howe struck his pendant on board us and hoisted it on board his Majesty's ship *Success* and went in her with the *Rose* and *Flamborough* and *Swallow* and *Diligence* sloop near the village of Cancale to cover the landing of the troops. At 7 the enemy began to fire on them from a battery of 3 guns. At ½ past the *Success* and other frigates returned their fire and soon drove them from their battery. At 8 the Grenadiers of the army were landed and by noon all the Infantry were landed.[15] The broad pendant was hoisted on board us again. At 7 a.m. his Grace the Duke of Marlborough was landed.

Noon. At an anchor in Cancale Bay, Cancale Point NNW 4 miles.

23   *Log of the* Flamborough *by Lieutenant George Burdon*

6 June 1758   Wind W. Little winds and calm.

At 1 p.m. anchored in Cancale Bay in 13 fathoms. Veered to ¼ of a cable. do. the *Swallow* sloop stood inshore and was fired at from a fort at Cancale town, the *Swallow* returned the fire, but falling little wind the Commodore sent several boats to tow her off. At 5 do. we was ordered to weigh to go in shore to attack the fort. do. weighed and rowed in with the *Success* and *Rose*. At 7 do. we engaged the fort and fired several rounds till such time as we drove all the people from both fort and town do. run our ship aground on the mud abreast of the town in order to cover the landing of the men. At 8 they began to land and continued landing all night. At ½ past 8 a body of men fired at our men from the top of the hill. do. sent a party of our soldiers and drove them all away. do. employed getting our guns over to starboard and shored our ship to keep her upright. a.m. warped our ship into 9 fathom water and anchored with our small bower and veered to ½ a cable, Cancale town WbN½N and St Michael's Nunnery EbN½N. Broke down the bulk heads of the cabin and steerage and cabin [*sic*] and threw them overboard. do. hove overboard several spars from the booms in clearing away for the topmast to shore the ship. do. came on board from the Commodore Mr Andrew Enouf a pilot.

Noon. Laying on shore at single anchor in Cancale Bay.

24   *Howe to Duff*

Essex, Cancale Bay,
6 June 1758

You are to take under your command the ships and vessels named in the margin [*Active, Richmond*, cutter][16] with which you are to proceed without loss of time and cruise off of the port of St Malo; placing them in such stations as you shall judge to be most convenient, so as best to intercept any vessels of what nation soever attempting to pass into that harbour, whilst the event of the present intended operations of the troops against this town is still depending. But in all other respects you are to observe the attention as customary to his Majesty's Allies. You are to continue on this service till further order, sending me information from time to time (at intervals not exceeding three days) of your proceedings in every respect; and in case you should gain any intelligence relative to the motions of the enemy wherein the success of the present destined operations against the town of St Malo is concerned, or that you think is proper for me to know, you are to take the most expeditious method to acquaint me therewith, either by returning yourself to this port if necessary or by dispatching any of the smaller cruisers under your command with such informations.

25   Instructions respecting the Disposition of the Flat-boats on the Disembarkation of the Troops

Essex, Cancale Bay,
8 June 1758

When the fleet anchors next after the signal has been made, as in the margin [Flag chequered red and white at the fore topmast head], for the troops to prepare for the disembarkation, that opportunity is to be taken for hoisting out the flat-boats and getting them in readiness for immediate service.

The flat-boats are to be sent for at the same time from the transports, and kept alongside of those ships of war from which they are to be manned.

As when the signal a white flag with a red cross at the fore topmast head has been made, the transports carrying the Grenadiers of the different regiments (distinguished on that occasion by having their Navy Jacks[17] hoisted at their fore topgallantmast heads) will move up to the van of the fleet; the flat-boats, upon the signal made as in the margin [Flag chequered blue and yellow at the fore topmast head] for the troops to be disembarked, are to repair to and take in the Grenadiers of the different companies (half a company in each) from the transports as underneath expressed, the officer carrying off the last platoon from each being to cause the Navy Jack to be struck when he leaves the transport. [See table on following page]

Each boat having taken in the half company of Grenadiers as above is to assemble at or near the ship of the Commander-in-Chief that they may be able to move forward together to the shore, upon the signal made as in the margin for that purpose [Blue pierced with white, fore topmast head, or Lights (two) one under the other, fore topmast shrouds, mizen topmast shrouds]. They are then to form in line abreast, observing particularly that those of them carrying the different platoons of the same companies do always keep together, leaving sufficient space between each other for the convenient management of their oars. And as they will be commanded on this occasion by the captains of the ships of war, in the proportion of one captain to 4 boats, when it is intended that the line should advance, the signal will be made by a red flag, when to halt a white flag, and when to retreat backward from the shore in order to deceive the enemy or otherwise a yellow flag, shown from the boat in which the senior sea officer is embarked, and the several inferior officers commanding in the other boats are strictly required to be watchful for, and act conformable to those signals.

Boats Manned from the	Take from the Transports	Colours	Place	Grenadiers of Regiments
Essex	Anson	White Flag	Fore topmast Head	Company of Kingsley's
	Amity's Assistance	Blue Flag	Fore topmast Head	Company of Home's
Rochester	Lyon	Red and Blue Flag	Main topmast Head	Company of Manners's
	Isabel and Mary	Red and White Flag	Mizen topmast Head	Company of Welsh Fusiliers
Deptford	Mary (5)	Red and Blue Flag	Fore topmast Head	Company of Lambton's
	Ranger	Red and White Flag	Main topmast Head	Company of Effingham's
Portland	Ann and Mary	White Flag	Mizen topmast Head	Company of Lowden's
	Exchange (1)	Red and White Flag	Fore topmast Head	Company of Wolf's
Richmond ⎫				(½)
Pallas ⎬	Mary (6)	Blue Flag	Mizen topmast Head	company of Hay's
				(½)
Brilliant ⎫				(½)
Tartar ⎬	Eagle	Red Flag	Mizen topmast Head	company of Cornwallis's
				(½)

If any number of the transports should be advanced at the same time to the shore in line abreast likewise, the boats are to be kept in the rear of them ready to pass on forward to the shore through the intervals by divisions of a captain's command or otherwise on a signal made to advance as above.

So soon as the Grenadiers have been landed, or the first disembarkation made from the boats, each captain with his command of boats is to return to either one of the transports lying most conveniently and disembark the troops from that transport and the others of the same regiment, so continuing to do till the whole number of troops ordered have been disembarked; he is then to wait near the shore with his boats lying off upon their oars for further orders.

The captains of the different ships of war carrying, or having orders to man any of the flat-boats are to give copies of the abstract hereunto annexed to the different officers to be placed in each boat.

Abstract of the Instructions to be observed by each particular Officer commanding a Flat-bottomed Boat

When the half company of Grenadiers or other troops to be disembarked in the boat under his care is the last that are to go from the transport he attends, he is to direct the master of that transport to strike the Navy Jack he will have hoisted on this occasion at his fore topgallantmast head on his departure as aftermentioned.

He is next to repair and wait at or near the ship of the Commander-in-Chief, ready to take his place in the line amongst the other boats, when the signal as in the margin [Flag blue pierced with white fore topmast head or lights two, one under the other, fore topmast shrouds, mizen topmast shrouds] is made for the boats to proceed on to the shore chosen for the descent, observing to keep by the other boat carrying the remaining half company of the same regiment, leaving only between each a space sufficient for the convenient management of the oars.

He is to obey the orders of the sea captain in whose division he is placed. And when a red flag is shown from the boat carrying the commanding sea officer directing this service, he is to advance onward to the shore; when a white flag is shown he is to wait upon his oars, or move up into his station if needful; and when a yellow flag is shown, he is to retire backward from the shore or otherwise as he sees the boat carrying the signal flag to do.

When any transports are appointed for this service at the same time, as they will then sail also in line abreast, he is to keep with his own division ready to pass on forward to the shore through the intervals upon the signal made to advance as above.

Having landed the first disembarkation of the troops from his boat, he is to return back for the conveyance of the other troops as the captain of his division shall direct, and act in other respects according to the captain's orders.

26   *General Order to Squadron*

13 June 1758

A stool is to be made according to the form which is to be seen on board the *Essex* for embarking the troops in the flat-bottomed boats and the Carpenters of ships charged with conveyance or manning any of those boats is to be sent to demand from the proper officer in the *Forrester* hoy the stores requisite for this purpose. Each stool will take three deals, four foot of elm board and one pound of tenpenny nails.

The names of the pilots now on board the different ships of the fleet are to be returned, and a report made of what knowledge they have of the navigation into or near any of the ports of France, or particular parts of the coast between any certain points of land between Calais westward to the port of Bayonne.

The ships stationed on either quarter of the *Essex* are to carry each one light at the stern during the night, as a guide to the transports that they may keep in sailing within the circle of the ships of war.

The *Rochester* is to keep two flat-bottomed boats, No. 4 from the *True Briton*, blue flag at the main topmast head, No. 2 from the *King of Prussia*, red vanes mizen topmast head.

The captains of ships having them on board, or charged with the service of manning any of the flat-bottomed boats, are to send to see that they are put in due repair in respect to benches, sails, oars, etc., as necessary and report the state thereof and what supplies of each kind may be wanting consisting [*sic* − consistent?] with the purpose of the order.

The *Rochester* to man the extra flat-bottomed boats from the *Ruby*, a white flag at the main topmast head, *Loving Friends*, blue at the fore topmast head, when wanted on service.

27   *Additional Signals*

Essex in Cancale Bay,
17 June 1758

A mistake having been made in the appointment of the flag blue with a red cross at the mizen topmast head for the pilots of particular ships to come on board to the Commander-in-Chief, it is to be observed that a flag striped blue and white will be hoisted instead thereof at the same place on that occasion.

If the Commander-in-Chief should judge any of the ships of war to be out of the station assigned by the sailing orders or would have the captain of such ship to keep the transports nearest him within the circle of the ships of war, the signal will be made as for speaking with the captain of that ship and a flag half blue half white hoisted at the mizen topmast head; which signal will be kept abroad till the Commander-in-Chief judges it to have been duly observed.

When the Commander-in-Chief would have the transports either from circumstances of bad weather or otherwise to bear up for the nearest port, the signal will be made by hoisting a flag striped red white and blue at the ensign staff with 2 guns.

For all the Armed Cutters to come within hail under the Commander's ship's stern − Blue pendant, flag staff mizen topmast head. For all the Sloop Tenders to do the same − Yellow pendant, flag staff mizen topmast head. [The pendants and place of hoisting in the left margin]

When action shall be ordered for covering the descent of the troops by signal from the Commander-in-Chief, the ships joined with him on this same service are to continue firing from time to time only whilst the signal for battle remains abroad, but to keep everything in readiness in the mean time for beginning again the action as soon as the signal shall be repeated. And when the white flag shall be hoisted at the fore topmast head, the whole detachment or the ships whose signals are made therewith are to be retired back from the shore to a proper place of anchorage.

28   *Disposition for the Attack of Cherbourg*[18]

Essex off of Cherbourg,
29 June 1758

The *Essex, Rochester, Deptford* and *Portland* are to be kept in readiness for anchoring before the forts and town of Cherbourg, and forming a general attack upon the port when it shall be judged necessary: being to have a cable in abaft and springs on forward and abaft.

The *Brilliant, Pallas* and *Richmond* are to be prepared in like manner for the same occasion.

The boats of the two decked ships and frigates not appointed for immediate service are to have transporting hawsers in them ready to give such assistance to the frigates or bombs as necessary.

29   Regulations respecting the Conduct of the Transports and Disembarkation of the Troops

Essex at Spithead,
24 July 1758

[Summary: most of the clauses have already appeared, but this is the first *printed* set of regulations with the above title.]

I   Necessity of establishing such regulations; masters of transports to observe them and inform commanders of the troops.
II   Transports with the different detachments of the same regiment to keep together.
III   Transports with Commanding Officers of regiments to keep in station, following motions of commanding sea-officer of division.
IV and V   The first two paragraphs of [16].
VI   Similar to the last paragraph of [16].
VII   Pilot vessels wearing union jacks at the mastheads will be placed when particular care in navigation is required.
VIII   The third paragraph of [27].
IX, X and XI   The three paragraphs of [17].
XII   In case of separation, masters of transports must apply to the senior officer of troops for a sealed rendezvous.

30   List of the Troops and the Transports

[? July 1758]

			Troops	
Regiments	Ships	Tons	for each Regiment	Distinguishing Colours
1st	*Seaflower*	326		
Guards	*Thomas and Mary*	256	782	Red
	Success (2)	200		
2nd	*Ruby*	331	777	White
Guards	*Amity's Assistance*	446		
3rd	*True Briton*	360	689	Blue
Guards	*Magnanimity*	329		

Main topmast head

4th	*John and Ann*	423			
Bentinck's	*Adventure*	200	773	Red	
	John and Sarah	150			Fore topmast head
5th	*Eagle*	346	705	White	
Cornwallis's	*John and Mary*	359			
6th	*Ann and Mary*	348	683	Blue	
Lowden's	*Concord*	335			
7th	*Mary (5)*	383			
Hay's	*Betty*	207	779	Red	
	Success (1)	189			Mizen topmast head
8th	*Ranger*	356	730	White	
Effingham's	*Fell*	374			
9th	*Lovely Sukey*	129			
Manners's	*Lyon*	333	795	Blue	
	Elizabeth (2)	333			
10th	*Exchange (1)*	370	649	Red and White	
Wolfs's	*Constant Jane*	279			Main topmast head
11th	*Isabell and Mary*	321	662	Red and Blue	
Lambton's	*Friend's Goodwill*	341			
12th	*Anson*	403			
Richmond's	*Macclesfield*	221	751	Red and White	Fore topmast head
	Providence	127			
Grenadiers	*Richard and Ann*			Blue vane pierced with white	Fore and main topmast head
	Exchange (2)				Main topmast head
	Loving Friends				Fore topmast head
	Spencer				Mizen topmast head

31   *General Order to Squadron*

[late July 1758] [19]

Disposition for Manning Twenty-four Flat-Bottomed Boats for the Landing
the Grenadiers of the Army separate from the Frigates and names of the
Transports from whom they are respectively to take their Extra Flat-Boats,
which they are to see properly fitted. [See table on following page]

The state of the flat-bottomed boats are to be examined into, and it is to
be by an officer of each of the ships of war to which the manning is assigned,
and that they are provided with their several requisites for the disembarkation
of Foot only; and a return made to the *Essex* as soon as may be, with the
number marked on the stern of each flat-boat, carried on the different ships
of war and transports. The ships of war are to take those flat-boats fitted for
the disembarkation of the Horse occasionally.

When the Adjutants of the particular brigades are wanted to receive orders
from their respective Brigade Majors, the signal is to be expressive of each
Brigade from the different ships of war, wherein the several Brigade Majors
are embarked as follows:

Ships of War	No. of Boats	Transports' Names	Colours		Place where
Essex	Three	Ruby Amity's Assistance True Briton	White vane White vane Blue vane	}	Main topmast head
Rochester	Three	Eagle John and Mary Ranger	White flag White flag White flag	}	Fore topmast head Mizen topmast head
Montague	Two	Ann and Mary John and Ann	Blue flag Red flag	}	Fore topmast head Fore topmast head
Portland	Three	Anson Exchange (1) Mary (3)	Red and White Red and White Red	}	Fore topmast head Main topmast head
Jason	One	Loving Friend	Vane blue pierced with white		Fore topmast head

Brigade from the different ships of war, wherein the several Brigade Majors are embarked as follows:

For the	Brigade of Guards	Union Jack	Main topgallant shrouds
Adjutants	1st Brigade of Foot	Union Jack	Fore topgallant shrouds
of the	2nd Brigade of Foot	French Jack	Main topgallant shrouds
	3rd Brigade of Foot	French Jack	Fore topgallant shrouds

All Lieutenants. As the numbers are judged sufficient in fair weather, or for a short distance, the flat-boats therefore may be manned with sixteen men, unless otherwise particularly ordered.

It is to be noted that in future the transports carrying the several Grenadier companies of the Army will be distinguished by vanes blue pierced with white, and that instead of the transports before allotted, each ship of war, from which to take the several companies of Grenadiers, as specified under that head in the Instructions respecting the Disposition of Flat-boats in the Disembarkation of the Troops [25] – a second appointment, suitable to the change since made in the allotments of the transports, etc., will be hereafter issued.

32   Howe to Admiralty

Essex off Cherbourg,
8 August 1758

The wind serving on the evening of the 30th past, I sailed thereupon with the fleet from St Helen's Road for this coast. But disappointed in every other attempt by the frequent calms and unfavourable changes of the wind, did not arrive in with the shore till the fifth.

The Lieutenant General continuing however in his former resolution, the landing of the three first brigades of foot and one troop of light horse complete, covered by the fire of the frigates and bomb ketches, was effected in the Baie de Marais 2 leagues westward of Cherbourg on the next evening, and the remaining corps of infantry, light horse and artillery this morning.

The boats commanded by Captain Duff, with the Captains Maplesden, Rowley, Paston and Elphinstone under him, arrived at the shore without opposition from the enemy posted there, till after the disembarkation of the grenadiers.

The *Richmond* striking on a sunken rock on her passage into the bay, and remaining aground till the change of tide, by which accident some material damage is to be apprehended, I therefore judged it requisite to send that frigate back for the necessary repairs to England, the captain being directed to report the further particulars thereof to Their Lordships upon his arrival.

As soon as the troops are ready to advance onward to the town of Cherbourg, I shall proceed off of the port to give such countenance to their operations with the ships of war as from future circumstances may appear necessary.

33   *Log of the* Rochester *by Captain Robert Duff*

Monday 7 August 1758

First and middle parts moderate and cloudy, the latter little wind and fair. ½ past 1 [p.m.] double reefed the topsails. At 6 repeated the signal. ½ past 7 anchored with the small bower and a whole cable in 25 fathoms water, Cherbourg S, Cape La Hague NWbW½W, Querqueville Fort SWbW½W, Eastmost land in sight SEbE½E, a signal for Lieutenants on board the Commodore. At 9 received a flat-boat from the *Tartar*. At ½ past 2 a.m. saw the bombs firing at the town of Cherbourg. At 4 received three more flat-boats from the transports and two of our own in all six which we manned from our ship. At 8 repeated the signal and sent the boats to disembark the troops and all went to the *Pallas* where the Commodore was, and lying inshore with all the frigates and bombs to cover the landing. At 9 made the signal, ½ past anchored with the best bower in 17 fathoms water, Querqueville Fort SSE½E, extremes of the land from WNW to SEbE, distant from the shore about 2 miles. Saw the French troops to the number of 1000 or more of Horse and Foot coming to hinder our landing. Saw them draw several pieces of cannon along shore.

Noon. Querqueville Fort SSE½E, extremes of the land from WNW to SEbE, distance off shore 2 miles.

Tuesday 8 August

Little wind and fair weather. ½ past noon new berthed with the small bower in 13 fathom water and ½ a cable . . . At 1 p.m. the signal was made from the *Pallas* for the frigates to fire upon the shore to cover the landing and

directly the flat-boats put for the shore and landed without opposition and
continued landing till 9, the bombs playing and frigates firing till dark. At
4 a.m. sent the flat-boats to disembark the Horse.
Noon. The extremes of the land from NWbW½W to ESE, Querqueville Fort
SSE½E.

Wednesday 9 August

Ditto weather. At 1 p.m. the boats returned from disembarking the Horse.
At 7 weighed and drove further to the eastward and anchored at 8 in 17
fathom water, Querqueville fort SbW, extremes of the land from EbS to
NWbN. At 6 p.m.(?) repeated the signal and weighed and came to sail, at 8
anchored in Cherbourg Road in 9 fathoms, moored a cable each way . . . At
9 a signal for Lieutenants, unbent the sheet cable.
Noon. Moored in Cherbourg Road, the pier heads SbW. Pelee Island ESE,
extremes of the land from EbS to NW½W.

10 August

. . . at ½ past 4 sent 45 seamen and 14 marines on shore to work at the pier
heads and fortifications . . .

12 August

. . . at 9 this evening the gates of the basin and part of the pier heads were
blown up. a.m. some more of the works were blown up . . . [similar entries
on 13 and 14 August].

Tuesday 15 August

First and middle little wind and fair, latter rain. p.m. several vessels were
filled with stones at the east pierhead and set on fire to stop the channel. At
7 a signal for Lieutenants. This evening several mines were sprung at the
pierheads, forts and adjacent places. a.m. the frigates, bombs and sloops
formed themselves along shore to cover the embarkation. At 9 Querqueville
fort was blown up . . .

Wednesday 16 August

First and middle little wind and rain, latter fair weather. At 3 p.m. a signal
for Lieutenants, received three flat-boats from the transports, manned them
all and sent them ashore to embark the Horse. At 5 ditto a signal for
Lieutenants. At dark all the Horse were embarked. At 4 a.m. the barge with
2 cutters and 6 flat-boats went on shore to embark the Foot and were all on
board by 11 o'clock. This morning at daylight the Commodore's pendant
was shifted to the *Pallas*. ½ past 11 it was hoisted on board the *Essex* again.
The frigates, sloops and transports shifted their berths further from the
shore.

34   *Log of the* Infernal *kept by Commander James Mackenzie*

Monday 7 August 1758   Wind SW, WSW, W

Ditto weather. At 4 p.m. tacked to the northward and ½ past ditto to the southward, running into Cherbourg Bay. At 5 the Commodore made the signal to anchor. Ditto hoisted out boats cleared the bomb beds and got ready the mortars for firing. At 8 anchored with the best bower in 11 fathoms water Cherbourg SW½S 1½ mile distance. Ditto the signal on board the Commodore for all Lieutenants. At 2 a.m. weighed and came to sail, at 5 do. run by the fleet. Do. wore ship to the westward, the signal on board the *Essex* for our captain. Do. tacked and stood in again, the French began to fire at us from a small battery. At 11 do. anchored with the best bower in 5 fathoms at high water. Do. carried out a cadge [*sic*] and stream anchor, one on our starboard and one on our larboard quarter, cleared ship for action.
Noon Cherbourg SE 6 or 7 miles distant.

Tuesday 8 August   Winds WSW Calm WNW

Ditto weather. At 1 p.m. began to fire our mortars, sometimes with shells and others with 1 pound shot in order to disperse the enemy and cover our troops when landing, the *Pallas, Active* and *Richmond* employed on the same duty, the *Richmond* got upon a rock where she lay one tide. In firing one of our mortars carried away our main runner and tackle and starboard main brace block. At 5 do. got on board the stream and cadge anchors. During this action fired away shell 12 and pound shot 4,000. At 5 a.m. weighed and ran farther out from the shore.
Noon as before.

Wednesday 9 August

At 9 p.m. received on board 15 boxes of small shot and some caps for the mortars . . .

35   *Disposition for covering the Retreat of the Troops on their Embarkation from Cherbourg*

Essex, in Cherbourg Road,
14 August 1758

The flat-boats are to be manned and commanded as specifed in the order of the 28th past, and to proceed to the shore for the embarkation of the troops upon the signal made a flag blue pierced with white at the mizen topmast head.

The *Swallow, Saltash, Diligence* and *Speedwell* sloops are to be anchored from the Fort Gallet westward to the Hommet Point, as near to the shore as the Commanders see prudent, so as not to subject them to any hazard of danger from the fall of the tide.

The *Furnace* and *Granado* bomb vessels are to be placed in stations off of the Fort Gallet westward, so as to command with their fire the passage of the enemy from the southward towards the entrenchment formed round the Hommet.

The *Infernal* bomb vessel, the *Flamborough* and *Success* are to be anchored westward from the Fort nearest to the Hommet on that side; in order to prevent the approach of the enemy by a fire crossing in the front of the entrenchment that from the ships abovementioned. A particular attention is to be had on this occasion that the ships on either part be so laid as not to hazard any possibility of injury to each other respectively from the cross fire proposed.

The *Rose* is to be anchored westward of the Hommet, to cover the retreat of the last corps that will be embarked from that Fort.

The other frigates are to be moved nearer the shore on either part between the Forts Gallet and Hommet into such stations for covering the embarkation of the troops as shall appear most convenient after those before mentioned have taken their appointed stations.

The different ships are to be moved with the first opportunity to such stations as are judged most commodious in every respect so as to be arrived in the shortest time at those above named for covering the embarkation when the signal a flag striped red and white at the ensign staff has been made from the ship of the Commander-in-Chief, and proper warping anchors are to be laid in time, in readiness for transporting them to those stations, from the more distant anchorage at which it may be convenient for them to remain till the retreat commenceth.

36   *Howe to Admiralty*

Essex in Cherbourg Road,
16 August 1758

I received yours of the 11th by Lieutenant Young on the Sunday and that of the 12th by Lieutenant Chads (mentioning the honour of Their Lordships' congratulations on the success of his Majesty's Arms on this occasion) yesterday.

Since my last of the 8th, the troops encamped near Cherbourg having remained in quiet possession of their ground, detachments of the seamen commanded by the Captains Rowley, Ourry and Elphinstone have been assisting in the destruction of the port and piers under the direction of Captain James of the Artillery; a more particular report of which I shall forward by the next opportunity [not found].

Of the number of ships found in the port amounting to 35 of different sorts, I have reserved the *Tartar* privateer of Bristol taken some time since, and the *Eyderstaede* – Peter van Campen reputed master, said to be Danish property, and to have been detained at this port on suspicion till the result should be known of a suit yet depending in the Courts of Paris concerning the legality of the seizure. Into this last I have loaded the brass ordnance mentioned in the enclosed report [omitted], and if it is deemed proper, should recommend to have that ship fitted and employed as a transport on this service, in place of some of the smallest vessels now with the fleet. Captain Ourry in the *Success* is ordered to take these ships under convoy, and to be further governed in the disposal of them and the stores contained in them, as he shall be directed by instructions in consequence of his Majesty's Pleasure from Mr Secretary Pitt, or as ordered by the Lords Commissioners of the Admiralty . . .

Having taken off the light horse and artillery on the preceding evening at the General's request, the destruction of the port being completed, the infantry have been embarked this morning without obstruction, and as soon as the Lieutenant General has distributed the necessary orders for putting the troops into a proper state for service, I shall proceed further in the execution of the remaining part of my Instructions as the wind and weather will permit . . .

37   General Order to Squadron

27 August 1758

Lieutenants of Ships carrying flat-boats

The flat-boats in the next disembarkation, those carried in the frigates included, are to be manned from the two decked ships, and the Grenadiers first landed, as upon the last occasion.

A Union Jack to be hoisted at the ensign staff, in the different ships, the *Rochester, Montague, Portland, Jason* and *Salamander*, the captains commanding the flat-boats when all the boats of each division are assembled alongside after the embarkation of the troops, and that they are in readiness to proceed with them to the shore, as directed by the orders of the 21st [not found], which signal is to be kept abroad in those ships until the boats are called from them.

38   Howe to Admiralty

Essex, St Cas Bay,
8 September 1758

Since my last of the first instant, wherein I informed you of my departure from Portland Road on the 31st past, the fleet arriving off of this coast in the evening of the third, all the foot and a part of the light dragoons were landed next day without opposition in the Bay of St Lunaire. But the badness of the weather not permitting since that time, of carrying into execution the attempt upon the town of St Malo the chief object of this descent, in the manner proposed, and likewise interrupting the necessary communication with the army on that part, I moved the fleet yesterday to this more secure anchorage, where I purpose to remain till the arrival of the troops, or as may be otherwise consistent with the Lieutenant General's further resolutions.

A detachment of the troops hath been sent to destroy the coasting trade in the river of St Briac, said to amount to between two and three hundred sail in time of peace but in which only twenty vessels of different kinds were now found.

The *Fowey* having joined the fleet on the third, and being a ship more particularly suited for one part of the service proposed as least liable to injury on taking the ground, I was induced to detain Captain Phillips on that occasion, and further, till from a more equal state of the weather, I might be able to relate the determination taken for the future conduct of the fleet thereupon, from which step I hope no inconvenience will arise to the service in other respects.

That ship will follow the armed cutter charged with these dispatches as soon as the empty transports that are to go under convoy of Captain Phillips are in readiness to accompany him.

39   Log of the Infernal, *kept by Commander James Mackenzie*

Monday 11 September 1758   Wind NE quarter

Ditto weather. At 8 p.m. the signal on board the *Essex* for all lieutenants. At 6 a.m. weighed and came to sail per signal and ran close inshore in order to cover our troops' re-embarkation. At 7 do. anchored with the best bower and ran out the kedge anchor to steady her. At 8 do. our troops marched down to the beach and began to embark with all expedition. At do. the French army appeared upon a hill about 2 miles distance; we saw them drawing up their men in form. Do. fired a 13 inch shell at the enemy which seemed to fall with great effect, broke their ranks and caused great confusion. We kept a continual fire upon them with our mortars and at 10 do. they began to play upon us with their field pieces, soon after which they divided into parties and ran scullering amongst the woods in order to bushfight us. At 11 do. they appeared in sight and ran down upon the remaining part of our army upon the beach. Here a very hot engagement ensued, we playing our mortars upon them loaded with pound shot and some swivels. We saw the French fall down prodigious fast but were often reinforced, so that after a continual fire for about 2 hours, our few troops being overpowered by numbers were obliged to retreat, some got into boats and several took the water where they swam to save their lives; the enemy firing very hot upon them, some were drowned, some taken prisoners and several taken by boats sent for that purpose. Part of our people employed fixing our rigging which was shot away in the action. Noon. St Malo East about 4 leagues distant.

12 September 1758   Winds E, NE, NNE

Fresh gales and hazy weather. At 1 p.m. we left off firing the mortars, our troops being all embarked that could be got off. Do. got on board our kedge anchor, employed in warping out of the bay with our stream anchor. At 2 do. weighed and came to sail. At 8 anchored with the best bower in 10 fathom water . . . we fired during the engagement shells 32 carcass 8 small pound shot 3,000 and swivels 50.

Notes

1 For Pitt's general policy and the European background, see Sir Julian Corbett, *England in the Seven Years' War* (London: Longman, 1907), Basil Williams, *The Life of William Pitt, Earl of Chatham* (London: Longman, 1913), Brian Tunstall, *William Pitt, Earl of Chatham* (London: Hodder & Stoughton, 1938), O. A. Sherrard, *Lord Chatham: Pitt and the Seven Years' War* (London: Bodley Head, 1955).

2 Corbett, op. cit., Vol. I, p. 264.

3 Admiralty to Navy Board, 26 April 1758, N.M.M. ADM A/2485.

4 Contemporary accounts describe the firing as if a novelty [**34**], and no earlier examples have been traced.

5 Noted in log of *Essex*, N.M.M. ADM L/E 140.

6 The fullest narrative of events of the campaign upon which the following is based, is in Corbett, op. cit., Vol. I, pp. 275–302. There are several contemporary pamphlets containing accounts from the military viewpoint but the only naval officers' contributions are those in *London Magazine* (1758), pp. 305–6, 518–9.

7 Both Howe's and Bligh's dispatches are perfunctory. Some printed accounts are included in the sources mentioned above, as well as in *Gentleman's Magazine*, Vol. 28, pp. 443–4, and *London Magazine* (1758), pp. 435–6, 516–21, and these include the dispatches.

8 See B. McL. Ranft (ed.), *The Vernon Papers*, N.R.S. Vol. 99 (1958).

9 A copy may be found in the Duff Papers, N.M.M., DUF/9.

10 See note 6.

11 'Naval vessels' at this period denoted vessels under the control of the Navy Board, these being employed in and near dockyards or for conveying stores between the yards. It is evident from the above letter and another, not printed, that the launches were towed.

12 Eventually, on 17 May, the Admiralty ordered the two deckers of Howe's squadron to be fitted to carry three launches each, N.M.M. ADM A/2486.

13 This order was signed by two members of the main Navy Board at Portsmouth together with the resident Commissioner to form the necessary quorum.

14 Duff succeeded in joining Howe on 3 June.

15 Cranston runs together the evening, night and morning. The Grenadiers went ashore at 8 p.m.

16 The cutter was not named in the original. She was the *Prince George*.

17 The 'Navy Jack' was the flag of the Navy Board, red with three gold anchors, used by the transports.

18 Although this order relates to the abortive attack of 29–30 June, it is included to illustrate the preparations made by the ships.

19 This order was evidently issued in July, after the *Montague* had joined the force, and may be the order of 28 July mentioned in document **35**. The final paragraph may have been wrongly copied, for it implies that the Grenadiers' transports will be separately distinguished and that a fresh allocation of boats to transports will soon be issued. The latter has not been located by the editor.

List of Documents and Sources

1758

1	Admiralty to Navy Board	7 April	N.M.M. ADM A/2485
2	Admiralty to Navy Board	27 April	N.M.M. ADM A/2485
3	Navy Board Minute	28 April	P.R.O. ADM 106/2567
4	Navy Board to Portsmouth Officers	28 April	N.M.M. POR/A 19
5	Navy Board to Portsmouth Officers	28 April	N.M.M. POR/A 19
6	Navy Board to Portsmouth Officers	29 April	N.M.M. POR/A 19
7	Navy Board Minute	29 April	P.R.O. ADM 106/2567
8	Navy Board to Portsmouth Officers	3 May	N.M.M. POR/A 19
9	Navy Board to Portsmouth Officers	6 May	N.M.M. POR/A 19
10	Pitt to Admiralty	8 May	P.R.O. ADM 1/4122
11	Navy Board to Portsmouth Officers	10 May	N.M.M. POR/A 19
12	Navy Board to Admiralty	11 May	N.M.M. ADM B/159
13	Admiralty to Navy Board	13 May	N.M.M. ADM A/2486
14	Cokburne to Secretary of the Admiralty	15 May	N.M.M. ADM B/159
15	Navy Board to Portsmouth Officers	17 May	N.M.M. POR/A 19
16	Regulations respecting the Order	25 May	N.M.M. DUF/8
17	Howe to Squadron	[25 May]	N.M.M. DUF/8
18	Distinguishing Signals for calling Officers on Board	25 May	N.M.M. DUF/8
19	Howe to Duff	27 May	N.M.M. DUF/8
20	Line of Battle	30 May	N.M.M. DUF/8
21	Signals given in addition . . .	31 May	N.M.M. DUF/8
22	Log of the *Essex* by Lieutenant James Cranston	5–6 June	N.M.M. ADM L/E 140
23	Log of the *Flamborough* by Lieutenant George Burdon	6 June	N.M.M. ADM L/F 111
24	Howe to Duff	6 June	N.M.M. DUF/8
25	Instructions respecting the Disposition of the Flat-boats . . .	8 June	N.M.M. DUF/8
26	General Order to Squadron	13 June	N.M.M. DUF/8
27	Additional Signals	17 June	N.M.M. DUF/8
28	Disposition for the Attack of Cherbourg	29 June	N.M.M. DUF/8
29	Regulations respecting the Conduct of the Transports . . .	24 July	N.M.M. DUF/8

30	List of Troops and		
	Transports	[— July]	N.M.M. DUF/8
31	General Order to Squadron	[late July]	N.M.M. DUF/8
32	Howe to Admiralty	8 August	P.R.O. ADM 1/91
33	Log of the *Rochester* by		
	Captain Robert Duff	7–16 August	N.M.M. DUF/2
34	Log of the *Infernal* by		
	Commander James		
	Mackenzie	7–9 August	N.M.M. ADM L/J 125
35	Disposition for covering the		
	Retreat of the Troops . . .	14 August	N.M.M. DUF/8
36	Howe to Admiralty	16 August	P.R.O. ADM 1/91
37	General Order to Squadron	27 August	N.M.M. DUF/8
38	Howe to Admiralty	8 September	P.R.O. ADM 1/91
39	Log of the *Infernal* by		
	Commander James		
	Mackenzie	11–12 September	N.M.M. ADM L/J 125

Biographical Notes

Brett   Two references are made to people of this name. One is clearly to Captain Sir Peircy Brett, commanding in the Downs. The other, in document **14**, may be to him, or possibly to Timothy Brett of the Navy Office, an extra Commissioner.

Burdon, George, Lieutenant 1756, in the *Flamborough* 1758, Commander 1762, killed in action 1778.

Cranston, James, Lieutenant 1755, in the *Essex* 1758, Commander 1760, Captain 1760, died 1790.

Duff, Robert, Lieutenant 1739?, Commander 1744, Captain 1746, commanded the *Rochester* 1757–60, and was in command of the inshore squadron before Quiberon Bay. Rear-Admiral 1774, Commander-in-Chief Newfoundland 1775–7, and Mediterranean 1778–80, Vice-Admiral 1778, died 1787.

Elphinston, John, Lieutenant 1746, Commander 1757, in the *Salamander* 1758, captured at St Cas, Captain 1759, later entered the Russian service. Died 1785.

Howe, the Hon. Richard, 1758 4th Viscount Howe, 1790 1st Earl Howe. Lieutenant 1744?, Captain 1746, in the *Essex* 1758, later distinguished himself in blockade of Brest and Rochefort, at Quiberon Bay. Rear-Admiral 1770, Vice-Admiral 1775. Commander-in-Chief North America 1776–8. Admiral 1782, commanded Channel Fleet and relieved Gibraltar 1782. First Lord of Admiralty 1783–8. Again commanded Channel Fleet 1790 and 1793–5, including Battle of 1 June 1794. Admiral of the Fleet 1796. Died 1799.

Mackenzie, James, Lieutenant 1744, Commander 1757, commanded *Infernal* 1757–60. Died 1789.

Maplesden, Jervis, Lieutenant 1739, Commander 1746, Captain 1756, commanded *Portland* 1758, captured at St Cas. Captain of Greenwich Hospital 1770, Lieutenant-Governor 1778. Died 1781.

Ourry, Paul Henry, Lieutenant 1742, Commander 1756, Captain 1757, commanded *Success* in 1758. Commissioner at Plymouth 1775–83, died 1783.

Paston, William, Lieutenant 1755, Commander and Captain 1757, commanded the *Jason* 1758, captured at St Cas. Died 1774.

Phillips, Henry John, Lieutenant 1742, Commander 1756, Captain 1757, commanded the *Fowey* 1758. Took the name Towry 1760, died 1762.

Rowley, Joshua, Lieutenant 1747, Captain 1753, commanded the *Montague* 1758, captured at St Cas. Rear-Admiral 1779, Vice-Admiral 1787, baronet 1786, died 1790.

6

The Douglas Papers, 1760–1762

Edited by

N. A. M. RODGER

Introduction

James Douglas was a younger son of George Douglas of Friarshaw, a senior member of the Scottish bar, and like many another younger son of good family and poor expectations he made his career in the Navy. Patronised by Pulteney as a young officer,[1] he remained politically well-connected all his career. From 1754 to 1768 he was MP for Orkney in the Earl of Morton's interest.[2] In spite of this his professional advancement was not remarkably swift. He was nearly 30 before he received his first commission, and on the outbreak of the Seven Years' War in 1756 he was, aged 53, a post-captain of twelve years' seniority. During the early years of the war he had a successful and fairly profitable career, and having distinguished himself at the taking of Louisbourg and Quebec, was chosen to bring home the despatch announcing the capture of the latter place, and received the customary reward of a knighthood.[3] Early in the next year, 1760, he was ordered to hoist a broad pendant as a commodore 'with a captain under him' (in modern terms a first class commodore), and proceed to relieve Commodore Moore as commander-in-chief in the Leeward Islands.

Since the French maintained no permanent squadron in the West Indies, the chances of a general engagement there were low, but Douglas's new command presented many, and in some respects unique problems.[4] That part of the station which actually lay in the Leeward Islands, and included the dockyard at Antigua, was nearly three hundred miles to leeward of the principal British possession, Barbados in the Windward Islands. Between the two lay islands which were either French (Martinique and Guadaloupe) or 'neutral' but settled by Frenchmen (St Lucia and Dominica). The capture of

Guadaloupe in 1759 had gained for Britain the single richest colony in the Americas, but the acquisition added to the Navy's duties an extensive commerce, including much coasting trade, to protect from the French privateers whose bases lay close at hand in Martinique. These privateers were mostly sloops and schooners; small, fast, numerous and weatherly, with an intimate knowledge of the intricate local navigation, largely invulnerable to the pursuit of the large ships which formed the bulk of Douglas's squadron, and which were necessary in case a French squadron should appear in those waters [Document 4]. 'Large men of war', as a colonial governor wrote, 'cannot secure us against those small sloops who sail like the wind and find shelter behind every shoal and rock.'[5]

The obvious answer was for the Navy to acquire similar vessels, and this Douglas was to some extent empowered, indeed ordered to do. It was, however, a process fraught with delicacy. Suitable vessels could only be bought in the West Indies, which meant that the commander-in-chief would have to find their officers and men. To allow him to commission as many as he desired was to allow him power, not only to spend a great deal of money, but to make a great many officers. This power of patronage was the key to the eighteenth-century Admiralty's authority, the one element which counterbalanced weakness to command and near inability to punish. No right was more jealously guarded, nor more closely circumscribed when it was delegated — as it had to be —' to commanders-in-chief overseas. Consequently Douglas had to 'exercise great caution, and sometimes deception, in commissioning sloops [16, 22, 28].

It was easier to acquire private tenders, and Douglas soon acceded to the requests of his captains that they might be allowed to buy sloops to cruise against the enemy. These vessels were not the king's but the private property of the captains — Douglas himself owned two in succession [8, 51] — manned as tenders from their parent ships, and cruising to the profit of their owners and crews. Indeed one of the advantages of tenders was to provide prize money for the men of the line of battle ships who otherwise had little prospect of it [37, 41]. These little vessels were able to take on enemy privateers on their own terms with considerable success.

The prisoners thus brought in presented Douglas with a problem. If exchanged by cartel according to the usual practice, they soon manned other privateers (the vessels themselves being cheaply and quickly built) and were at sea again. It was alleged that they regarded capture as a joke.[6] Douglas therefore decided to start sending his prisoners to Britain, a prospect certain to appal the privateersman.[7] Unfortunately it soon appeared that the action had other effects, in particular that the French having retaliated, an important supply of seamen to the squadron dried up. Douglas found that he needed returned prisoners at least as much as the French did, and was obliged to reverse his policy [7, 10, 17, 22, 26, 37].

The problem of manning was always acute in the West Indies, where the demand for European seamen was very high, and wages equal to a year or even two years in the Navy were offered for a two-month voyage home to England.[8] Naturally this promoted desertion, and many of the remedies available to the Navy at home were inapplicable in the West Indies. Pressing at sea so far from home was out of the question, in port was difficult, and on shore was possible only with the consent of the local authorities. The planters, and consequently the colonial legislatures, were decidedly ambivalent towards the Navy which protected their commerce, but at the same time raised the cost of shipping their exports by competing with the merchant ships for an inadequate supply of seamen, and discouraged the American ships which brought their most vital imports. Colonial governors tended to be caught between orders from Whitehall to support the war effort, and the reluctance of local interests to make sacrifices, so that even the strongest found it difficult to make concessions to the Navy. In these circumstances the naval commander-in-chief needed tact and patience, and it is a tribute to Douglas that he was able to persuade colonial authorities to man sloops dedicated to their protection, and to permit pressing on shore [3, 55].

Just as important as manning was the physical maintenance of the ships, and this too presented unusual difficulties. The facilities of the dockyard at English Harbour were inadequate, and the large ships drew too much water even to enter it. It lay at the extreme leeward end of the station, so that ships sent there, even when they had been refitted, could take weeks to beat back against wind and current. Moreover when Douglas arrived the Storekeeper had recently died, leaving a deputy aptly named Mr Supple, who required constant watching, as did the Master Shipwright, who was moreover ill, and in July 1760 had to be invalided home. To complete Douglas's troubles the Master Attendant was detected selling his stores, and the new Storekeeper, when he arrived in August, proved to be 'so great a stranger to business that his Majesty's service is greatly perplexed'.[9] It is the more creditable that Moore had been able to keep the yard working efficiently [5] but, as Douglas pointed out, only by spending much of his time there. This Douglas could not do and the affairs of the yard were a constant worry to him [13, 14, 21]. He was for much of the time extremely short of naval stores of all sorts. The destructive heat of the sun, the tireless boring of the shipworm, the difficulty of keeping ships – especially the larger ones – in repair without a dock, and the very long periods spent at sea all resulted in a far higher consumption of stores than the same squadron would have required in home waters. In the West Indies the smaller cruisers could spend as much as four-fifths of their time at sea, double the average in the Service as a whole.[10] For all these reasons, compounded by distance from the sources of supply, there were never enough naval or ordnance stores, and at times Douglas was afraid he would have to lay up some of his larger ships [5, 12, 19, 20, 34]. Finally his troubles with the dockyard were mirrored and compounded by the maladministration of the naval hospital at Barbados [11].

All these vexations added to the administrative load which an overseas commander-in-chief could not escape in the best of circumstances; the constant stream of requests for surveys on stores [6, 9, 29, 52, 56], the complex and often troublesome business of victualling by agents and contractors remote from the supervision of the Victualling Board [2, 15, 59], the organisation of convoys [18], the discipline of the squadron [24, 27], and the procuring of intelligence [30]. Prizes and prize money were always a source of dissension as well as profit [8, 31, 32, 41]. The delicate business of making officers, so full of opportunities for an unscrupulous flag officer, required careful management and even more careful explanation to the Admiralty if the Board was to be convinced that the vacancies were genuine, and the promotions to be confirmed [1, 10, 25].

Politics and diplomacy were as much a part of Douglas's duties as administration, and one subject in particular was productive of endless difficulty. Many merchants in the British colonies of the West Indies and North America were in peacetime heavily involved in trade with the French West Indies, and disinclined to allow a state of war to interfere with so profitable a commerce, especially when fraudulent 'flags of truce' and neutral ports like the Dutch island of St Eustatia or the Spanish port of Monte Cristi (on the north side of Hispaniola near Cape François) offered a convenient means of circumventing the blockade.[11] Douglas's efforts to suppress such illegal trade involved much unproductive correspondence with the governor of St Eustatia and other neutral authorities [26, 37, 38, 47] who had no reason to co-operate with him, and naturally aroused the opposition of those elements in the British islands who were most interested in the trade. This was a further cause of friction between the Navy and local interests – Commodore Moore, though a zealous and successful defender of British trade, had actually been burnt in effigy in Barbados by a mob led by the son of the Attorney-General of the island because of his efforts to suppress illegal trade.[12] It is interesting to observe that Douglas, who was not less zealous, seems to have maintained much more cordial relations with the colonial authorities.

So far Douglas's responsibilities have been described largely in static terms, of the defence of trade and the maintenance of the British position, and these were indeed a large part of his cares. With an administration led by Pitt, however, British commanders-in-chief were not expected to stand on the defensive, and when Douglas sailed in the spring of 1760 he must have known that he would be expected to carry on the work Commodore Moore and General Barrington had begun with the capture of Guadaloupe, and that Martinique, their original objective, would be his also. The success of the campaign in Canada freed the necessary forces, and early in January 1761 Pitt drafted orders to Sir Jeffrey Amherst, commander-in-chief of land forces in North America, to detach an initial 2,000 men in the spring, followed by a much larger force after the hurricane season. The first objective would be Dominica, and if possible St Lucia, while the main campaign in the autumn would attack Martinique.[13] Because of various delays the first troops and their commander Lord Rollo did not reach Douglas until June, and though they moved swiftly and seized Dominica within a few days, it was all that could be achieved before the hurricane months. During the summer Douglas learnt officially of the larger reinforcements coming to make the attack on Martinique. Both the secret orders, dated 22 July 1761, and Pitt's letter of 5 August,[14] were quite explicit that Douglas was to command by sea, and an officer to be selected by Amherst (in fact General Monckton) by land. In the autumn Douglas threw himself into the preparations for the assault, making ready for the troops from North America and the naval reinforcements from home [36, 37, 39]. On 17 September he received Pitt's letter of 5 August. By early November all was ready, and Douglas must have felt that at last nearly two years of constant effort, with no more glory than the occupation of a largely undefended island, were to have their reward. Here at last was his chance of fame. But on 22 November, unforeseen by Douglas or anyone else[15] and unaccompanied by the squadron with which he had sailed, Rear-Admiral Rodney arrived at Barbados to take command of the station. It must have been a hard blow to Douglas to be superseded just at that moment, and it is not at all clear why it happened. Rodney's biographer[16] treats the decision as the natural consequence of his hero's greatness, and implies that it had been planned for most of the year. Unless Pitt was deliberately deceiving him, however, he had no thought of relieving Douglas when he wrote in August, and as late as 6 October, the day before Rodney's orders were issued, captains were being instructed to put themselves under Douglas's command.[17] There was no reason why a commodore should not command on such an expedition; Moore had done, and at that moment, on the other side of the Atlantic at Belleisle, Commodore Keppel was commanding the largest seagoing squadron of the Navy. Douglas had been a successful commander-in-chief; persistent and effective against privateers,[18] swift and decisive in the attack on Dominica, tactful and accommodating in his relations with colonial authorities. With some justice he must have felt that he had a right to the opportunity Rodney had come to take from him.

Moreover there were few men less likely to be conciliatory in these awkward circumstances than Rodney. A superb natural leader of men, always easy and thoughtful with junior officers and ratings, he could be haughty, suspicious and devious in his dealings with officers more nearly his equal in rank, especially those like Douglas who, he felt, enjoyed social advantages which he lacked. Making full use of Douglas's preparations (without any acknowledgement) Rodney moved swiftly against Martinique. As the operations neared their successful conclusion Douglas was left to blockade unimportant ports well away from Fort Royal; when the capital fell he was allowed to run the port and raise sunken ships while Rodney's favourites, Commodore Swanton and Captain Hervey (both his juniors), were despatched to sweep up the remaining French islands[19] [**40, 44**].

Meanwhile Rodney was planning to move on to fresh conquests. In January he had learnt that Spain had entered the war; early in March, soon after the surrender of Martinique, he heard of a French squadron imminently expected in the West Indies. This squadron discovered the fall of Martinique in time to avoid action with Rodney, and disappeared to leeward. From that quarter came anguished pleas for assistance from Jamaica, where a Franco-Spanish invasion was hourly expected. Moreover the naval commander-in-chief at Jamaica, Commodore Holmes, had lately died. Clearly it was necessary to send reinforcements to Jamaica, and Rodney had discretionary orders to do so in such a case, giving Douglas the command.[20] With the prospect of a general action, and mindful, no doubt, that Jamaica was 'the most profitable station in a Spanish war' [**45**], Rodney determined to go himself and leave Douglas to command in the Leeward Islands, where there was no longer any prospect of glory or profit.[21]

In the course of all these preparations Douglas, for all his forbearance, had been unable to avoid a breach with his superior. Rodney sent him unverified orders under his secretary's hand, and Douglas's tactful reply to this irregular and off-hand approach provoked a characteristically uncompromising rebuke – though Rodney was careful not to make the same mistake again[22] [**42, 43**]. To rub salt in the wounds Rodney insisted on taking all Douglas's best ships, including his flagship and most of his frigates [**45, 46, 47**].

On 23 March Rodney wrote to the Admiralty reporting his intentions. On 26 he received orders from England which overturned them all. Early in April he was to expect Admiral Pocock with a large squadron; all other operations whatsoever were to be abandoned and Rodney was to hold himself in instant readiness to join Pocock's flag.[23] It was now Rodney's turn to suffer the same disappointments he had inflicted on Douglas, even to being deprived of his flagship. Douglas meanwhile was despatched to Jamaica to replace Holmes.

He must have been glad to get away from Rodney, but his command at Jamaica was temporary and far from independent. All his work there was effectively in support of the great amphibious assault on Havana which Pocock commanded[24] [**54, 57, 58, 60**]. Nevertheless it was not easy, and immediately on his arrival Douglas found himself with a delicate problem. On the death of Commodore Holmes the next senior officer, Captain Forrest, had naturally taken command. This was entirely proper, and he would have been justified in hoisting a broad pendant to signify as much. He went further, however, in appointing himself a captain under him. This was a direct assault on the Admiralty's powers of patronage, and more than even a commander-in-chief might do on his own authority. Douglas was bound to disallow it, and it required all his tact to do so without causing a divisive quarrel[25] [**48, 49, 50**].

The incident further complicated his relations with the Jamaican authorities, traditionally hostile to naval commanders-in-chief. The omission of the customary salute from the forts on his arrival made a poor start, and Forrest was not only a sea officer but also a substantial planter, naturally popular as a local man. Having supplanted him, Douglas had a difficult task to restore good relations with the island authorities.[26] It is to his credit that he not only obtained the negro labourers needed for the Havana attack, but also gained permission to press ashore for the squadron [**54, 55**].

When Douglas finally returned to England in September 1762 [**61**] he had some reason to be a disappointed man. In spite of nearly three years' service on two stations, most of it in sole command, he had participated only on the sidelines of the two principal operations, the conquests of Martinique and Havana, and others had reaped glory and wealth where he had sown effort. The interest of his papers is therefore not so much for the light they throw on great events, but for their unusually complete view of the daily business of an overseas commander-in-chief of the eighteenth century. Since the documents of the Havana expedition (including many from the Douglas papers) have already been completely printed, and the Martinique attack well described elsewhere, I have made no attempt here to give a complete account of these operations. The object of this selection is simply to show a cross-section of the affairs of an officer in Douglas's position, and of the squadron he commanded.

The documents here quoted come largely from three letter-books among the Douglas Papers in the National Maritime Museum, supplemented by a few from the Public Record Office. They are quoted in modern spelling, capitalisation and punctuation, following the Society's usual practice, though no punctuation could make perfect syntax of Douglas's prose. The spelling of proper names has been regularised, but the distinct forms which Douglas and his correspondents freely mixed, such as Martinique and Martinico, have not been altered. The formal beginnings and endings of the letters are omitted throughout; other omissions are indicated thus . . . , and editorial additions [thus]. All letters are either to or from Douglas. All those from the letter-books are copies, but a number of the more private are in holograph, as presumably the originals were.

THE DOUGLAS PAPERS, 1760–1762

1 *To Lord Anson*

Portsmouth,
2 March [1760]
[holograph]

There is an order come down for the purser of the *Devonshire* to change into the *Dublin*, to which the purser of that ship is not willing. As I am informed he was made by Admiral Boscawen, I beg he may continue, for as I differed with him in the St Michael's election four years ago[27] (which I was told he took ill), I would by no means be the occasion of forcing one of his people out of the ship to make room for my secretary. I beg again your Lordship's favour in letting a commission be made out for Stewart Brisbane[28] as 5th Lieutenant of the *Dublin*.

2 *From the Victualling Board*

Victualling Office,
11 April 1760

Having made a new contract with Mr John Biggin of London, merchant, for the victualling such of his Majesty's ships and vessels as shall come to Barbadoes and the Leeward Islands and be in want of provisions, we herewith send you a copy of the contract for your information, and desire you will receive from him or his agent what provisions his Majesty's ships under your command may be in want of, and that you will also be pleased to communicate the contents of the said contract to the rest of the commanders of his Majesty's ships in those parts as opportunity shall offer, and are further to desire you will give yourself the trouble of leaving the copy of the contract with the next Commander-in-Chief that may happen to succed you on that station.

3 *To Lieutenant-Colonel Robert Melville,*
Lieutenant-Governor of Guadaloupe

Dublin,
3 May 1760

As the calms will not let us get out of your sight, and Captain Innes[29] has joined me, and knowing how necessary it is to get the troops on shore, I have directed Captain Innes to take them under his convoy to the different places you design them for, and as I am directed to send the officers home that came with them in the transports, have therefore sent you an order for the masters of the transports to receive and victual them. As I could not recollect their names, have left the order blank, which you will please to fill up with the names of the masters of the transports that may be most agreeable to the officers. You are sensible how distressed I shall be for small vessels, so that it will not be in my power to give your island so much protection as my inclination leads me to do, but as you have been so zealous for the public service to get a good many seamen, I pray therefore to beg your further assistance, and if you will procure men I will send a sloop for the protection of Guadaloupe; you will please to let me know as soon as possible.

4   To John Clevland, Secretary of the Admiralty

Dublin, in St John's Road,
11 May 1760

. . . [Commodore Moore] is to sail the 12th, when I shall take the command of the squadron upon me, which will be reduced when the two convoys of June and July leave these islands to four ships of the line, as I propose sending the *Buckingham* and *Nassau* with the first, and *Lion* and *Chesterfield* with the last, which will be the largest. Their going away is no loss to the squadron, as Mr Moore informs me that they are all four much decayed and must have gone home. As soon as I can conveniently have room in English Harbour, design to clean the *Lancaster* who has been eighteen months off the ground, then the *Raisonnable* who has been sixteen months; both go so ill now that they are only fit for convoys. I can think of no way of making line of battle ships useful in these seas against privateers but by sending a sloop to cruise with each, for the islands are so close together that a large ship alone has not the least chance of taking one of them. Mr Moore has also informed me that the enemy had so infested Guadaloupe with their small privateers that even a boat coasting alongshore was not safe, therefore he was obliged to purchase a one-mast sloop[30] and commission her for the service of that island, but she was unfortunately taken a month ago.

5   To the Navy Board

Dublin, in St John's Road,
11 May 1760

Since my arrival here which was the 14th instant, I have been at English Harbour with Mr Moore, where I found (entirely owing to his care) everything in good order. He informs me that the keeping of the officers there to their duty and to prevent them from defrauding the government, has taken more of his time than he could well spare from other duties, and given him more trouble than everything else. As Mr Moore has wrote often on that subject, and [his report] is confirmed to me by every captain who has been at English Harbour, I hope the Board will redress that grievance to me by sending out a sufficient person to supply the place of the officer he has complained of. The *Pill Frigate* is arrived in English Harbour, and the stores are now getting out as fast as possible. Mr Moore has showed me the letters he has wrote to the Board, which are much more to the purpose than I could have wrote on the occasion, and therefore have only to inform the Board that cordage seems to be mostly wanted (for the heat wears it out very fast) and leave the rest to the proper officers, whose business it is to acquaint you of the deficiencies of each species of stores, which they have not yet communicated to me as I do not take the command of the squadron till he sails, which will be the 12th.

6   From Captain George Balfour[31]

Bienfaisant, in St John's Road,
19 May 1760

Whereas the purser of his Majesty's ship under my command has represented to me that there is a quantity of butter and cheese on board, rotten, stinking, and not fit for men to eat, desire you will please to order a survey thereon.

7   To Clevland

Lion, off Antigua,
4 June 1760

My last was by Mr Moore, and on his leaving this island I took command of the squadron upon me, and disposed of them in the manner you will find in the enclosed [not found], which seemed to me the most effectual method for guarding the tracts the enemy's privateers cruise in for intercepting our trade, and also for retaking any they might send in to Martinico, which last shall be my principal view, for while the prisoners taken in the privateers are directly returned to Martinico, their being took does not diminish their numbers. Although Mr Moore while he was upon this station took sixty, they have still increased, and there is now more than ever; they have at this time forty-seven at sea, besides what are in port. If any of the squadron should take any of them before the convoy sail, I intend to distribute them amongst the merchant ships, as they remain in my power until they are landed. As this is the only method I can think of to break the spirit of privateering which reigns at Martinico, I hope their Lordships will approve of it. The only reason given for not having sent them to Europe before was a fear of its preventing the North American vessels from coming here; that reason scarce subsists now, for finding a much more beneficial trade with the French at Monte Christo and other places, few of them come to our islands . . .

8   *To Mr Walter Pringle at Basse Terre, St Christopher's*

> Basse Terre,
> 5 June 1760
> [holograph]

As I have appointed you my agent for all prizes that are brought into St Christopher's, and my tender having brought a small sloop, dispose of her to the best advantage, and as the tender will want a mast (having hers wounded) let one be got and charge it to my account.

9   *From Captain Molyneaux Shuldham*[32]

> *Raisonnable*, in Carlisle Bay, Barbadoes,
> 22 June 1760

The purser of his Majesty's ship under my command having acquainted me by letter of 10th instant that there is on board the said ship a quantity of rank and stinking butter, and a cask of pork which has been ate through by rats and destroyed several pieces of pork, as well as let the pickle from the remainder which has rendered it unfit for men to eat, I beg you will please to order a survey thereon.

10   *To Clevland*

> *Dublin* at St Christopher's,
> 25 July 1760

Please to acquaint my Lords Commissioners of the Admiralty that as Captain Cornwall[33] has been ill almost since he has been in the country, and could not get change in any of the ships going home, he has desired my leave to quit and go to England for the recovery of his health. I have appointed Captain James Innes the senior Master and Commander to be captain of the *Arundel*, Captain Middleton[34] into the *Emerald*, Mr Bagster[35] First Lieutenant of the *Dublin* in the *Barbadoes* sloop, and Captain Nott[36] removed into the *Antigua*.

You will also please to inform their Lordships that as privateers now from Martinico dread being sent to England, to damp the spirit of privateering have sent thirty of them in the merchant ships here that wanted assistance, the masters of the merchant ships giving receipts for them.

11   *To Mr Coverdale, Agent of the Naval Hospital, Barbados*

> *Dublin* in Carlisle Bay,
> 20 August 1760

From an inquiry made into the condition of the hospital for sick men sent on shore at this place, I find they have not the allowance agreed upon by contract. It is reported to me that they have fresh pork, with the broth thereof given them, which often occasions a flux (much oftener than any other meat) — which ought to be constantly either beef or mutton. Nor have they ever any Madeira wine, but raw rum in lieu of punch. They have no bedding but what they take with them from the ships they belong to, no sheets allowed them, nor any of their body linen washed at the expense of the hospital, money sometimes given them to buy themselves provisions, and but one woman to attend the whole hospital, wherein there is now twenty-seven people. These irregularities are so much to the detriment of his Majesty's Service that I am obliged to make it known to the Commissioners for the Sick and Hurt.

12   To the Navy Board

Dublin, Courland Bay, Tobago,
16 September 1760

I am to represent to you the great want of boats' oars in the squadron under my command, and as there are none in store at Antigua, nor none to be purchased either at that island or Barbadoes, beg you will by the first opportunity send out a proper supply particularly as the service may require the assistance of the boats of the squadron. I must also observe to you the great necessity there is for a supply of sheathing board, having very little in store and none to be purchased here, of which the ships begin to be in want of [*sic*] from the effect of the worms.

The captains of the squadron under my command having represented to me that the quick work of their ships suffers greatly from the violent heat of the sun, which might in great measure be prevented by being more frequently painted, therefore in order the better to preserve their upperworks am to desire you will be pleased to give directions for their being painted as often as there shall be found a real necessity, and for that purpose, that you will send out a further supply of oil and paint. By his Majesty's ship *Lion* was transmitted a report of the survey on the remains in store at Antigua, by which you will the better judge of every necessary that may be wanting, particularly cordage for running rigging, which there is a great expense of in the squadron from their being kept continually at sea, and which I hope there will be soon a sufficient supply of, as well as the stores before mentioned.

13   To Captain William Williamson, [37] H.M.S. Montague

Dublin, Carlisle Bay, Barbadoes,
6 October 1760

I desire you will give strict instructions to your carpenter to over look the caulkers that are employed in caulking the *Montague* in such manner that no time may be lost, as I want to know the difference of time in the performance of that work between this place and Antigua.

14   *To the Navy Board*

Dublin, St John's Road, Antigua,
16 October 1760

From my frequent representations to the Admiralty as well as to
your Board of the want of several stores for the use of the squadron
under my command, I have the greatest reason to believe a supply will
very soon be sent from England which will be more than the storehouses
can contain, as the stores remaining are very bulky and not of the qualities
most in demand; therefore have represented to their Lordships the
great necessity there is for additional buildings in and about the Yard
at English Harbour, particularly a masthouse, as the large masts are
now exposed to the sun which will perish them very soon, and is a means
of putting the Government to a greater expense by the decay of those
particular stores in a few years than double the charge of erecting
a proper building for that purpose – a plan and estimate of which (as
well as another storehouse that is much wanted) I herewith enclose, and
hope you will be pleased if it meets with your approbation to give
directions for their being put in hand as soon as possible, for as the stores
that may be ordered from England will be more than the present buildings
can contain, they must very soon go to decay for want of shelter
to keep them from the effects of the weather, which in this climate
is extremely searching and destructive to everything that is exposed
to it.

15   *To the Victualling Board*

Dublin, St John's Road, Antigua,
17 October 1760

By an article of my instructions from the Lords Commissioners of
the Admiralty I am to cause his Majesty's ships and vessels under my
command to be victualled, when in port, twice a week with fresh beef, if
it shall be found necessary for the healths of their companies, who have
been a long time on a salt beef diet which has much reduced their
strength and occasioned their being of a scorbutic habit of body; and
as I judge it absolutely necessary and for the good of the Service
that they should receive all possible refreshments to keep them in a
proper state of health, I have therefore given an order to Mr George
Lawrence to purchase from time to time as he may have opportunity
such quantities of fresh beef as shall be sufficient for that purpose,
on the most reasonable terms he can, and have directed him to draw bills
for the amount thereof on your Board, which are to be attested by me,
and hope when they come to hand you will be pleased to give directions for
their being honoured.

16   *To Clevland*

Dublin, St John's Road, Antigua,
17 October 1760

I beg you will be pleased to inform the Lords Commissioners of the Admiralty that in April last his Majesty's sloop *Virgin* was taken by three of the enemy's privateers off Guadaloupe, in which action Captain St Lo[38] with some of her men were killed, and as she was a very fine vessel the French fitted her out as a privateer immediately, and last month Captain O'Bryen[39] in the *Temple* (having the *Griffin* under his command), being on a cruise to the southward, received information that seven sail of vessels were at an anchor at the Granadoes, laden with provisions, etc., for Martinique; to which place he immediately proceeded, and after silencing their batteries cut out the vessels amongst which was his Majesty's sloop *Virgin* who had one hundred and fifty men in her; and as the Governor of Guadaloupe had represented to me the island was so infested with privateers the coasters were not safe in going from one port to the other, and as there was likewise Grand Terre and Marie Galante to guard, one sloop was not sufficient for that purpose and a large ship could not venture amongst the shoals, therefore desired as the *Virgin* was taken who was designed by Mr Moore to cruise for their protection I would pursue his intention and send her over again. In consequence thereof, as the French had altered her into a brigantine and fitted her out very well, I gave orders to the Naval Officer at English Harbour to purchase her, have commissioned her again, and am fitting her out for the service of the island of Guadaloupe and its dependencies, where the Governor and merchants have promised to man her. Had she not been in his Majesty's service before I should not have presumed to have taken this step, which I flatter myself from that consideration will meet with their Lordships' approbation.

17   *To M. Vassor de la Touche, Governor of Martinique*

Dublin, St John's Road, Antigua,
18 October 1760

Having received certain information that a tender belonging to the *Temple* (one of his Majesty's ships of this squadron I have the honour to command), who had on board thirty-seven men with an Inferior Officer, was taken and carried into Martinique some time last month, I have therefore directed Captain Nott who commands his Majesty's sloop *Antigua*, and who has the honour to present this to your Excellency, to take on board as many prisoners as he conveniently can and tender them to your Excellency, that the prisoners on both sides may be exchanged – which I flatter myself will be agreeable to every party, and have ordered Captain Nott to deliver the prisoners he brings with him to the officer you may think proper to send for them, and he will receive (agreeable to the rules of war) the like number in return.

18   *To Mr [Patrick] Maxwell, merchant, at Guadaloupe*

English Harbour, Antigua,
2 November 1760

I have received the petition from the merchants at Guadaloupe and the masters of the ships at that place, setting forth that four ships will be ready to sail from Basse Terre to Europe the 6th instant, and desiring convoy to proceed with the said vessels to the northward for their security from the enemy's privateers. In answer thereto desire you will acquaint the petitioners that the service will not admit of my sending a ship so soon as the 6th, but that I shall order them a ship for convoy who will be at Basse Terre on or about the 16th of this month.

19   *From the Officers of Antigua Yard*

English Harbour,
5 November 1760

We humbly beg leave to acquaint you that we are in immediate want of the undermentioned particulars for carrying on the current service of this port, and beg your Honour would give us your order for purchasing the same, viz.

Coils of 3½ inch	20	Locks cupboard	2 dozen
3 inch	28	plate	1 dozen
2 inch	20	hanging	2 dozen
1½ inch	20	settle	1 dozen
1 inch	30	Red Ochre	1 cwt
¾ inch	15	Brushes paint	36
Kersey Red	1 boll	tar	36
Lines Deep Sea	12	Sail Needles	60
Hand	2	Glue	12 lb
Tarred	12	Cabin Lines	12
Oil Linseed	30 gals	Thimbles	24
Lumber Board	5,000 ft	Leather liquored	3 backs
Tacks	20 lb	Twine fine	300 lb
Nails 3d	28	Bunting red	40 yds
Tallow	10 [cwt?]	blue	40 yds
Oars barge	36	white	40 yds
boat	36	Hoops for Mast Hoops	36
Shovels	36	Shingles	20,000
Fearnought	1 bolt	Candles	10 boxes
Locks Stock	2 dozen		

20   *From Mr John Stanley, Storekeeper of Ordnance*

Antigua,
22 November 1760

His Majesty's sloop *Antigua* have demanded the undermentioned Ordnance stores which are not in store, and must pray your directions for the purchasing the same, viz.

Sweet Oil	1 gallon
Sponge Tacks	400
Nails 6d	200
Fine Paper	8 quires
Rope of 2 inch	50 fathoms
Marline	6 skeins
Grape Shot 12 pdr	400
Linseed Oil	4 gallons

21   *To General George Thomas, Governor of Antigua*

English Harbour,
24 November 1760

I beg leave to represent to your Excellency the great inconvenience arising from public or suttling houses being permitted near English Harbour, which is not only a means of the seamen neglecting their duty, but is so prejudicial to their healths that I may venture to say not a ship comes into this port whose crew is not made sickly by the quantities of liquor vended to them by the people whose names I have mentioned in the margin [Coakley, Warren, Brown, Carpenter]. I am therefore to desire your Excellency will be pleased to cause the people I have named to be deprived of their licences, as I flatter myself you will be likewise of opinion it will be a means of preventing sickness and disorders amongst the seamen, and in many other respects for the good of his Majesty's service.

22   *To Clevland*

Dublin, St John's Road, Antigua,
29 November 1760

As his Majesty's squadron in these seas are greatly short of complement, a good deal owing to sickness and desertion, and whereas formerly we had a chance of being supplied by the flags of truce that brought over the English prisoners taken by the enemy, but for a long time they have disappointed us of that channel by encouraging our seamen to go to Curaçao and St Eustatia whose sloops are now chiefly manned by British subjects, and carry on a trade with the enemy; in consequence thereof I sent his Majesty's sloop *Antigua* over to Martinique with sixty French prisoners to exchange for an equal number of English, where they detained her three weeks, the governor and inhabitants of the island behaving with the greatest unpoliteness to Captain Nott; however as that is the best means of getting squadron supplied with men, shall continue it from time to time. I have also applied to the governors of the different islands for their assistance in getting men for the squadron.

Agreeable to their Lordships' directions I have purchased a very fine brigantine and given the command of her to Captain Williams.[40] She I think is much more convenient than a sloop, as such vessels require so large a mast and boom that when wanted are not only a great expense but difficult to be met with, besides when so large are very unhandy and liable to more accidents than vessels with two masts, who have tops for small arms which makes them much dreaded by the enemy's privateers.

I beg you will be pleased to represent to their Lordships that when his Majesty's hulk the *Kinsale* came from England she had on board an established number of men which were to be continued in her, but I am informed by the Master Attendant that Mr Moore, being in want of seamen, took them from her and distributed them to such ships of the squadron that were most in want of men, and in order to supply their places an equal number of negroes were hired, some of which have been employed on board the hulk these eighteen months past whose owners have not received the least pay for their hire, and as the Naval Officer here has not received any orders for their payment nor no advice on this head, beg their Lordships will be pleased to signify their directions to the Commissioners of the Navy to give orders for their being paid here by the Naval Officer every six months, otherwise their proprietors will not suffer them to continue any longer in the service.

I have only to acquaint their Lordships of the arrival of his Majesty's ship *Stirling Castle*.

23   *To Governor Charles Pinfold of Barbados*

Dublin, Carlisle Bay,
11 December 1760

I sincerely condole with your Excellency on the death of his Majesty King George the Second of glorious memory. I have as yet received no information of that from home; if you received the proclamation, beg you will be pleased to let me have one of them, and I should be glad [to know] when your Excellency proposes to have the ceremony performed, as I would have it performed on board the squadron the same day. Ours is every ship fires twenty minute-guns for the death of our sovereign, and twenty-one on the happy accession of his present Majesty King George the Third.

24   *To Clevland*

Dublin, Carlisle Bay,
14 December 1760

I acquainted you in my last for their Lordships' information that desertion was grown so frequent in the squadron that examples were absolutely necessary, and as three were condemned to death I designed to have had one of them executed, but the ship I put them into not meeting with her they deserted from I deferred their execution until there was more ships present; but as I am informed on his Majesty's (King George the Third) most happy accession to the throne of Great Britain it is usual for persons under sentence of death to be pardoned, I have therefore taken upon me to forgive them. And as there has been seven tried for desertion since that event, five of which were condemned to death, I intend to put the sentence into execution on two of them, one of which has deserted three times and the other four, to cast lots, as they are all foreigners entered volunteers into the service, received the King's Bounty, and have been taken fighting against us in the enemy's privateers.

25　*To Mr Richard Walsh, Master of the* Lancaster

Dublin, Carlisle Bay, Barbadoes,
27 December 1760

I have received your letter of 26th instant, acquainting me that by the death of your father, to whom you are heir, something considerable has been left you, and his affairs in trade being left very intricate cannot possibly be settled without your personal attendance, which if it is not very soon will be greatly to your prejudice, and desiring my leave to quit, towards which you have obtained Captain Man's consent.

I therefore, in consideration of the state of your affairs, do give you leave to quit your employment as Master of his Majesty's ship *Lancaster* in order to proceed to Europe to regulate and settle your concerns.

26　*To Clevland*

Dublin, Guadaloupe,
6 February 1761

. . . Soon after the hurricane season was over, the enemy's privateers put to sea, and as I had disposed of the ships under my command to the best advantage for the protection of our trade and annoying the enemy, which they soon discovering altered their usual stations and have lately cruised at great distances to the eastward of the islands, by which means they have taken some of the trading vessels, and as we have put them to great difficulties of getting their prizes into port, it has put them also into more ways of doing it and makes it difficult to intercept them − which the people here see is impossible to prevent therefore they are satisfied with my endeavours, which I beg leave to assure their Lordships has not been wanting, and that every method in my power shall be exerted to succour the trade of his Majesty's subjects and annoy and distress the enemy.

In order to damp the enemy's spirit of privateering I have sent a few prisoners to Europe, which has been of some service, but many of the masters of merchant ships refusing to take them, and the fear if they could be conveyed to Europe and America of sending all that might be taken, as the enemy consequently would in that case send such as might fall into their hands to France, which would intimidate the Americans and prevent them bringing the produce of their colonies, to the great distress of the islands; in consideration thereof I was induced to alter my former resolutions by sending the men of war with the prisoners in our possession to Martinique, and insisting on the governor's returning all that might be in his custody, which has hitherto proved to my wishes, having received from thence one hundred and ten men, which has helped to man the *Virgin* and *Guadaloupe*, two very fine vessels which I hope will be of the greatest service. I am sorry to say the *Barbadoes* is of very little, for although I have tried every method to make her sail it will not answer the purpose, and the *Dublin, Foudroyant, Belliqueux, Bienfaisant* are now so foul that they are in no condition to act as cruisers, and as their draught of water is too considerable to attempt the risk of entering English Harbour, shall be glad to know their Lordships' pleasure concerning them, for if they do not careen or dock in a few months their bottoms will greatly feel the effect of the worm.

By the list of captures which I will transmit to their Lordships by the next conveyance it appears how much the Dutch supply our enemies, and I am sorry to add they are likewise assisted by our own subjects; a circumstance as a proof of it I beg leave to inform their Lordships of. A privateer belonging to St Christopher's had agreed to convoy a ship and a brigantine from Martinique to St Eustatia, pretending they were her prizes. The ship was seized by the *Culloden* and the brigantine by a privateer. They are now to be tried at St Christopher's, and it is not in the least doubted but they will be condemned, being collusive captures. The owner of the two vessels concerned in this undertaking was taken by the *Crescent*, but has since made his escape to St Eustatia . . .

27   *From Captain John Barker*[41]

Culloden in Carlisle Bay,
15 February 1761

One John Elliot belonging to his Majesty's ship under my command being accused by William Richards of taking the key of his chest out of his pocket and stealing out of it some money, and on my inquiring into it it appeared to me he was guilty, and being a notorious thief and often whipped for thieving on board, I ordered him to run the gantlop, but he desired to be tried by a Court Martial, and I beg you will order him to be tried accordingly.

28   *To Pinfold*

Dublin, Carlisle Bay,
17 February 1761

As I had not time yesterday to look over the papers your Excellency gave me, which I have since perused, am to beg you will be pleased to make my acknowledgement to the Legislative Body of the island of Barbadoes for their favourable opinion of my services, and the trust they have reposed in me in voting £800 to give in exchange for a cruiser in the room of the *Barbadoes*, which I will lay out whenever a proper vessel can be found. Till then there will be no occasion for the money being paid, and must beg leave at the same time to acquaint them through your Excellency's means that I cannot make any application at home, should it be laid out, to have it replaced to this island, because I cannot acquaint the Admiralty of my having taken upon me to exchange one of his Majesty's vessels, as it would not be approved of – therefore if such a step is taken, it must be done in the most private manner.

29   *From Shuldham*

Raisonnable, Carlisle Bay,
7 March 1761

The gunner of his Majesty's ship under my command having represented to me that on account of fire having been discovered the 6th instant in the fore sailroom adjoining to the fore magazine, several barrels of powder were thrown overboard and others damaged, together with some cartridges, by throwing water and playing the engine to extinguish it, and desiring a survey, I beg the favour you will please to order that a survey may be taken of the remains of powder and cartridges on board, that the quantity damaged and thrown overboard may be known.

30   *To All Captains*

Dublin,
20 April 1761

Having employed Mr Pieter de la Chace, a Dutchman and inhabitant of the island of St Eustatia in procuring intelligence from Martinique, I desire if he falls in your way between the island of St Eustatia and Martinique you will suffer him to pass in his vessel with her lading free and unmolested, and the better to be assured of the identity of the said Mr Pieter de la Chace he will write his name in your presence, which to prevent imposition you are required to compare with that enclosed, to which I must enjoin you to the strictest secrecy, and whatever intelligence he may give you necessary for my information you are to come yourself with if convenient, or cause it to be communicated to me by the most speedy conveyance.

31   *To Jonathan Blehnman, Judge of the Vice-Admiralty Court of Barbados*[42]

Dublin, Barbadoes,
12 May 1761

I am favoured with yours enclosing the Register of the Admiralty's memorial concerning Captain Bagster's refusing to libel a vessel he had retaken, by which he was deprived of the fees his office entitles him to. In answer to which, must beg leave to inform you that as the captains' interest is greater than mine in all prizes am satisfied of their acting for the best, nor do I ever interfere into what port they send them or who are their agents. Therefore as Captain Bagster acts from a principle of humanity and no view of interest to himself, I can never dissuade him from behaving in so generous a manner; and whether it is absolutely necessary that a vessel retaken should be libelled when neither party desires it cannot pretend to give my opinion. But this I know; that it is contrary to the opinion of one of the ablest Counsel in the West Indies, who affirms that it is putting people to a needless expense − and since the article of fees is on the carpet, must beg leave to acquaint you that the charges of condemnation are greater here than in any other island in the West Indies, which may greatly induce (as the prizes are generally small) the captors not to bring them here − but this I flatter myself you'll cause to be remedied. Have therefore enclosed you the charges of the Advocate and Proctor on each prize; whether it is necessary to have either when a prize is not disputed, and how much, I leave to your determination as you are Judge of the Admiralty and the only person who can tax their bills.

32   To Mr [Benjamin] Southwell, Agent at Barbados

Dublin, Guadaloupe,
9 June 1761
[holograph]

Some time ago, to discourage the French from sending their free negroes and mulattos into their privateers, it was thought advisable by the Judges of the Admiralty at the different islands to condemn them all,[43] and as at Barbadoes where they have such a short run both to St Lucia and Martinique, that several of those negroes and mulattos have carried some of the wherries off and made their escape, which made the people of your island shy of buying them that were taken by some of the ships of the squadron at Tobago; that they might not go off so cheap I desired you to buy me eight of them, amongst which was a buck negro. However, I must desire you would never buy me any more, for I shall not be able to sell them at any of our islands, and must send them to Jamaica when an opportunity offers.

33   To Major-General Sir Jeffrey Amherst, Governor-General of North America

Dublin, in Roseau Bay,
16 June 1761

It is with the greatest pleasure I embrace the opportunity of acquainting you that as Governor Dalrymple had given me to understand in December last an expedition might be attempted, I had stationed a number of the squadron round the island of Guadaloupe so that they might be easily collected together to act in conjunction with the forces you might send from

America, and it was very lucky I happened to be upon the spot myself when the *Sutherland* arrived, she having only three transports with her, which with a detachment from Guadaloupe, together with the Marines *if wanted*, I thought was a sufficient force to take possession of the island of Dominique before succours were thrown in from Martinique. And as I well knew a reinforcement might be sent in twenty-four hours, and having information that an express was directly sent from Guadaloupe of the arrival of our troops, I advised sailing immediately, which we accordingly did, and beg leave to refer you to Lord Rollo for the particulars of our success.

My having been in the West Indies some time, has given me an opportunity of experiencing the vast difference of a rendezvous being to windward instead of to leeward, it having taken most of the transports a week getting up from Guadaloupe to this island, although but seven leagues distance. I therefore hope you will excuse my taking the liberty and advising Barbadoes as the properest place of rendezvous in case of any further designs upon the enemy's settlements here, where the transports can not only be better supplied with everything they want, but the enemy longer getting intelligence of their arrival, and will give us the great advantage of running down upon them with a fair wind in about thirty hours – and it shall be my particular care to have ships timely there to escort them, as well as pilots to conduct them . . .

34   *To Commodore Lord Colvill,*[44] *Commander-in-Chief in North America*

Dublin, St John's Road, Antigua,
6 [July] 1761

The letter you intended to honour me with by Captain Legge[45] was washed overboard when the *Sutherland* was pooped, which mortified me greatly, but found by his orders that his ship and the other three were to stay with the transports until the expedition is over. The hurricane months are now coming on, and they have been satisfied with the acquisition of Dominique.

We are greatly in want of stores here of all sorts, masts especially and likewise artificers, so that it is with great difficulty that we can keep the frigates and sloops so clean as they ought to be, and your Lordship has I will venture to say undesignedly added to my distress by sending the *Falkland*, who is so leaky she must be hove down to keep her above water, and the *Sutherland* as soon after as possible, being in the same condition, which it seems she has complained of ever since she came from England, the *Repulse* with both main and foremasts wounded, and the *Lizard* with a sprung bowsprit, all which the Builder[46] at Halifax knew were complained of but would not give them new ones although they have such plenty there, and merely for the sake of his remarkable words told their captains he would *introduce* a piece of each into one and a fish on the other, and that would make them *entirely* serviceable – but to my misfortune I do not find them so.

They have sent me from home several large ships that can't go into English Harbour to clean, therefore without orders am sending them to England as it is a pity good ships should be spoiled by the worms, and as they have not sent me out a ship for myself to relieve the *Dublin*, and as I must heave down some of your squadron here, have in revenge sent my own ship to careen and refit at Halifax, which I beg your Lordship will suffer to be done with the utmost despatch that she may be here again by the middle or end of September when something here is intended, and trust it will be considerable. The governor of Martinique told an officer I sent there lately he had certain advice from France the island would be attacked, therefore you will oblige me very much by giving Captain Gascoigne[47] all the assistance you can spare, as I want very much to have my ship back again where my lieutenants (all but the First who I keep with me in case of a vacancy) and all my people are.

35 *To Thomas*

Levant,
1 September 1761

I had the honour to acquaint you some time past of the ill behaviour of a privateer to a French lady, sending you the description of the person transmitted me in a complaint against such usage. I now have the pleasure to inform you that the said privateer was the *Hawke*, Lecraft master, who has your Excellency's commission. I am informed by Mr Pringle his behaviour at St Christopher's was so notorious that his owners are ashamed of it.

I make no doubt your Excellency will have a proper example made of the offender by having him prosecuted for his misbehaviour, the consequence of which I hope will be the loss of his commission, which may for the time to come be a warning for others not to follow his example.

36 *To Major-General the Hon. Robert Monckton*

19 September 1761

I had the honour of a letter from the Secretary of State Mr Pitt of 5th August acquainting me that you was to command the forces that were to come here about the end of October, intended for an expedition against Martinique. The honour of your acquaintance at Quebec gives me leave to wish you joy of your command, and that you may be assured it gives me the greatest pleasure to have an opportunity of convincing you that both duty and inclination lead me to assist you, Sir, and the army in everything in the power of the squadron I have the honour to command.

I am now going down to see and concert with Lord Rollo, Governor Dalrymple and General Thomas when and where the troops they can spare (and what number) may join your army, and to send transports for them, and hope to be here in Carlisle Bay, which I think the best place of rendezvous for the ships and transports that come from England and America, and Prince Rupert Bay on Dominique for those to leeward, and will also endeavour to collect persons (if to be found) that may be able to give us some intelligence of the inland part of Martinique. At Carlisle Bay the transports can get everything they may want better than anywhere else, and be sooner down on the enemy without fear of separation.

I have given orders to the commanding officer of his Majesty's ships here to give all the assistance you shall desire in everything relative to the expedition, and to co-operate with you in whatever shall be thought to forward it.

37   *To Anson*

Stirling Castle, English Harbour,
3 October 1761

I have the honour to inform your Lordship that as soon as possible will endeavour to put the orders of 22nd July by the *Amazon* in execution. As I am going up to Barbados to meet the ships and transports from America, have left orders for the ships when they come in here to follow as fast as they can.

By the same opportunity I had the honour of a letter from Mr Secretary Pitt informing me of his Majesty's approbation of my conduct at the reduction of Dominique. As your Lordship was the means of my being in this post of honour, and must have represented my conduct in so favourable a light as to occasion his Majesty's approbation, give me leave to assure you of my gratitude for it. He also informed me of the design against Martinique, and referred me for a more particular information to the orders of 22nd July from the Lords Commissioners of the Admiralty. Your Lordship may be assured that everybody here as well as myself will endeavour to show their zeal and concur with the army in everything that shall be for the success of the expedition – which has been expected at Martinique as soon as the hurricane season was over, which the general there told an officer I sent him of, and showed him a list of the force; and for your perusal I enclose a letter sent from a New England man, one Fletcher, who lives at St Eustatia, which was intercepted lately; we took him once and hope shall again, they have lately called in also some of their privateers.

By the first frigate shall send one of the Engineers to reconnoitre and judge what places may be properest to disembark at, as also shall carry up to the General Colonel Melville, who by his having been so long here, and on both expeditions, will be able to be of great service to them.

The squadron is now full manned, having at different times received three hundred men from Martinique. I assure your Lordship that four cohorns I took on board the *Dublin* has made the governor of Martinique very civil, for he not only sent me the *Temple*'s men I demanded, but also one hundred and fifty prisoners on my parole to return the like number, which were all he had, but also that he would suffer the cruisers off there to send a boat ashore to get refreshments — this I had desired of him, and thought we had a right to that indulgence, as we would not molest their fishing or passage boats.

As the Dutch still continue to supply the French with everything in sloops that are not easily taken, even by the frigates, the large ships had no chance. Therefore, as their captains represented to me that their men were quite disheartened and had no money to buy refreshments, while the frigates and sloops were often bringing in prizes, and that they might have leave to fit out and man tenders, which I consented to, and some of them have done great execution (but now shall call them in) one of them having taken twenty-four prizes.

38   To Johan de Windt, Governor of St Eustatia

Antigua,
8 October 1761

I had the honour of yours by Captain Buckner,[48] and should think myself extremely happy in being the instrument of keeping up that harmony which ought to subsist betwixt two nations so united in their interests, but am very sorry to inform your Excellency that it is like to be broke off by the subjects of the States, for every day gives us fresh proofs of vessels loaden with supplies of every kind going from your islands to the French our enemies, and returning with the produce of their colonies. Can you think, Sir, that while his Britannic Majesty is taking every measure that the most humane heart can think of to bring our enemies to reason and give peace to Europe, that we can look on and not endeavour to suppress this illicit trade? — which can be done by no other means than bringing all those we find trading with the French into our ports, where they are tried by our laws, and if the subjects of the States find themselves aggrieved by the sentence, they know they can appeal to England.

I am to represent to you that there is a late instance of a sloop called the *Mary Louisa* under Dutch colours from Martinique, belonging to St Eustatia, the 14th of last month firing on his Majesty's sloop the *Virgin* for near three-quarters of an hour. The captain, Christopher Martinburgh, who lives at St Eustatia or St Martin's, with thirty of his men after they run her ashore at Grand Terre escaped. They took in her five Dutch, as they call themselves, but all speak good English, who I keep in confinement until I know the fate of one of the *Virgin*'s people who they wounded. If he dies justice requires their being tried for their lives for murder.

Another instance I am to represent to you is of the subjects of the States firing at his Majesty's colours in a sloop from St Eustatia called the *Two Brothers* the 19th September, going into the Grenades (and by the confession of the people at the trial at St Christopher's, bound in there) who fired on the lieutenant of his Majesty's ship *Raisonnable*, who was in a tender of hers, and killed two Englishmen; who had they been detained there as they ought to have been, it is the opinion of the Attorney-General of those islands they must have been tried for murder. This you'll please to make known to the subjects of the States under your government; that as we have an undoubted right to and search for our enemies' effects in whatever neutral vessel they may be in, or whoever supplies them with provisions and stores, the neutral subject that makes resistance we can look on in no other light but pirates, being well persuaded neither the Lords the States nor their governors will ever countenance them in resisting. And if it had not been for the prudence of the lieutenant who commanded the *Raisonnable*'s tender much blood must have been shed, for it was as much as he could with all his authority prevent his people from boarding and putting them all to the sword. And as I cannot answer for seamen when they have such provocation, notwithstanding the utmost endeavours of their officers, and I my orders to prevent it, therefore I am now under the necessity of insisting upon your Excellency's exerting your authority and giving the most strict orders to prevent a repetition of such indignity to his Majesty's colours, as a continuance of it must be attended with the most fatal consequences.

As three of the owners of the sloop, who are English and live in St Eustatia, have appealed, I must beg leave to observe to you, and desire you will make it known, that as there are a great many English who have settled in St Eustatia, St Martin's, and Saba under the government of the States, who with their children are entitled to the privileges of an English-born subject, yet are daily taken in vessels supplying the enemies of their country; certainly, Sir, they ought to be informed that as they are entitled to the privileges, they must consider that they are also liable to the punishments of an English subject who betrays his country.

I have now only to add that as two of his Majesty's subjects were killed in this affair, I am obliged to represent it home, but flatter myself your own good sense and humanity will induce you to give such orders as will prevent the like offence being committed for the future.

39   *To Clevland*

Dublin, Carlisle Bay,
7 November 1761

Please to acquaint the Lords Commissioners of the Admiralty that his Majesty's ship *Greyhound* was dispatched from New York with Sir Jeffrey Amherst's dispatches of 8th October, wherein he acquaints me that three of the transports were arrived that sailed from England under the convoy of the *Alcide*, and as the rest were daily expected he had given the troops designed for the expedition orders to be ready to embark; have therefore sent two frigates to convoy the transports with the troops from Antigua, Guadaloupe and Dominica up to Barbadoes, and hope they will arrive here by the time the fleet comes, which I don't expect will before the end of the month. In exchange for the governor of Dominica and two other gentlemen I sent up by the *Woolwich* taken there to the governor of Martinico, he has delivered 100 prisoners, all they say then there.

On 3rd instant arrived the *Dublin* from Halifax, and I would be doing my Lord Colvill injustice if I omitted desiring you to acquaint their Lordships that she is come back careened, new sheathed, extremely well fitted-out in stores and in every other respect, and knowing that topmasts were scarce here, has sent in her two topmasts for ships of 74 guns, which is lucky as the *Greyhound* is come in with her foremast sprung in two places.

40   *To Rear-Admiral George Bridges Rodney*

St Anne's Bay,
4 February 1762

As the calms and lee currents prevented me from going to windward since I have been here, have sent boats to sound all round the bay, which with the countenance of the squadron has made the principal inhabitants of the quarter of Sac Marine send off a flag of truce to inform me that yesterday they had dispatched deputies to General Monckton to capitulate for this quarter and desire I would not commit any hostilities against them till an answer comes from him, which I judge necessary to acquaint you of immediately, and that I do not doubt as soon as the squadron appears off Trinité a deputation will come from thence also. I wish you joy of this series of success. I have sent the *Roast Beef* tender with this, who is only fit to go to leeward from her very bad sailing and being very badly fitted with sails, hardly fit to bring her up here. You will please therefore to send the answer by something that goes better. I did not choose to destroy here till I heard you had begun. Please to favour me with your answer as soon as convenient. The boats of the squadron have taken up the spare anchor and two of the *Raisonnable*'s guns.[49]
P.S.   Enclosed I send you the letter from the principal inhabitants of Sac Marine.

41   *To Mr Maxwell, Agent at Guadaloupe*

Dublin, in St Anne's Bay,
7 February 1762
[holograph]

The seamen in the tender I have lent to Governor Dalrymple have complained to me that they have not been paid their prize money for some prizes they took in her. I am to desire you would send me an account of them, as well as the shares they, myself and every officer are entitled, for you know as she is the *Dublin*'s tender it is to be divided amongst the ship's company as they are relieved by turns.

42   *To Rodney*

Dublin, Port Royal Bay,
21 February 1762

This evening by the *Culloden*'s tender received a letter of this date signed Thos. Atkinson, wherein he informs me that it is your direction I should send the *Granado* and *Thunder* bombs with their tenders to join Commodore Swanton[50] off the Grenades, but you forgot to send me your order for it, for I cannot think myself justifiable in detaching two ships of the squadron without a sufficient authority signed by yourself. Therefore, as it must be a mistake, I have sent an officer for it, and no time will be lost as I have given orders for the bombs and their tenders to get under sail in the morning as soon as they are ready; you'll therefore please to despatch the officer immediately with your orders which will come before they can be ready.

43   *From Rodney*

22 February 1762

. . . I believe Sir that if you had reflected one moment, or perused the former orders you had received from me, you would have found the said Thomas Atkinson was public secretary to me as Commander-in-Chief of this part of his Majesty's fleet, and that whatever letters are wrote by him in my name on his Majesty's service are to be complied with in the same manner by the officers under my command as those which are sent from the Secretary of the Admiralty. It may frequently happen during the service on which I am employed that verbal orders may be sent by officers; you know too well the consequence of their not being complied with, and I am sure upon recollection you will find that you have much mistaken this affair. I therefore desire the bombs may be immediately dispatched to join Mr Swanton at Grenada, and the *Basilisk* bomb be immediately sent to join me here . . .

44   *To Rodney*

Dublin, Cas Navire Bay,
23 February 1762

This will be delivered to you by Captain Brice[51] agreeable to your order, but wish he could have been spared, for as he has been employed at getting up the sunken vessels I don't know who to employ in his room that is fit for it, besides he was so well acquainted with the tricks of those that came with a view to plunder − which is no less than almost all the transports and trading sloops. They steal at noonday, and have robbed the vessel that has the sugar on board. I wish that one of the agents was here to sell it, for in spite of all the care that can be taken it will diminish. Amongst the spars in the sloop there are some topmasts ready squared for any ship. I fancy you would not have those converted to any other use as they may be wanted by some of the squadron; already the *Temple* has one, and had given one to the *Norwich* before your order came. I hope an answer to this will be by Captain Brice's returning here. Enclosed I send you an abstract of the weekly accounts by which you will perceive the great want of provisions.

45   *To Rodney*

Dublin, Cas Navire Bay,
2 March 1762

I had the honour of yours, and give me leave to assure you you will at no time find me captious or apt to stand upon punctilios. If you had answered mine when I desired to go to the Grenades I should have been satisfied, but the multiplicity of business and difficulties I suspect you labour under while you are united with the army will make me very readily excuse your forgetting that, and shall to the utmost of my power endeavour to carry on the service with the same harmony and friendship that has always subsisted since we were acquainted.

On receiving a letter last night from Captain Forrest wherein he acquaints me only (referring me to yours for the particulars) that the Spaniards have a strong squadron in those seas, made me recollect a copy of an order left me by Mr Moore which I send enclosed, as also the time the convoys are directed to sail from these islands. I don't write this with an intention of going from under your command, for as Mr Holmes's death is known another commanding officer will be sent there soon, so that I should have the command for a few weeks only at most, were you to send me there, although it may be the most profitable station in a Spanish war the Admiralty can give, but as I told you on your first coming here that I was desirous of going home, therefore as I mentioned it some time ago I should be glad of doing so by the first convoy if the service will allow it.

46   *To Rodney*

Dublin, in Cas Navire Bay,
17 March 1762

I must beg leave to acquaint you that in my letter of 2 March I mentioned that I preferred staying here rather than go to Jamaica, but as I knowed nothing of the Admiralty order you was since please to communicate to me, wherein they mentioned sending me there with the reinforcement, I therefore think it my duty to inform you that I am very willing to go to Jamaica or wherever the service may require, but if you are resolved to go, and think it necessary to carry my ship the *Dublin* with you, I hope my request will not be thought unreasonable in desiring to have her again when she returns, she being the ship the Board of Admiralty appointed me to.

47   To Rodney

Culloden, St Pierre Bay,
21 March 1762

Captain Keith[52] is just come in who I am sending to English Harbour to clean. He tells me that he wrote you a letter of complaint of the governor of St Eustatia's behaviour in firing a hundred guns at least at him and hulled the *Amazon* three times. Without losing of time, you'll have an opportunity of demanding satisfaction for that affront, which his forts have done at several of the men of war as they pass by. If you was to send one of the line of battle ships with your letter the day before you sail from St Christopher's, it would make him very humble to hear you was so nigh him, and might have a good effect for the future.

You have taken no less than three of the best sailing frigates, so that I have only the *Amazon* and *Actaeon* left. You must be sensible that the Spaniards as well as the French will have many privateers out, and I have many islands to guard, and few good sailing frigates to do it with. They have seven frigates at Jamaica already, and although the enemy may have many line of battle ships if the information is true, but I have not heard of their having many frigates. I hope also you'll leave me one of the bomb ketches, for I know the dread they carry with them has a very good effect, and I think you have not much occasion for them, as you have no land forces with you.

The *Actaeon* is coming in with the Spaniard from Barbadoes; the Marseilles ship he has left at Barbadoes to be sold there.

48   To Captain Arthur Forrest[53]

Dublin, off Port Royal Harbour,
12 April 1762

I received your favour of 11th, and am extremely sorry you should see things in the light you do. I am doing what I can in your favour, and you seem to think otherwise. You have only to read over the opinions of the captains (if that was necessary for me to follow) – does it not mention 'till a senior officer arrives, you are to hoist a broad pendant and have a captain under you'? And I do assure you, both admiral and captains where we came from thought you was doing what would not be approved of, for as senior officer you had the same authority that any commanding officer had except that of appointing a captain, and there was no occasion for their advice. I should not have come here had not the Admiralty sent orders, for as I had been long enough abroad I was to have gone home with the June convoy. Knowing an admiral is coming to command here I was not ambitious to be the second, for as Sir George Pocock will go home after the expedition, shall desire that favour also. If I had not come here, Captain Swanton must, and without a captain under him. This I hope will convince you that I don't act by you but what I think, as well as some others who are no bad judges, I can in no shape deviate from without being liable to censure from the Admiralty.

Our long acquaintance and friendship will I flatter myself convince you that no private reason could anyways induce me to do anything to hurt you, and Sir George Pocock's orders will be here soon, that interest could not do it.

49   To Forrest

Dublin at Port Royal,
12 April 1762

Since you went I have seriously considered what has passed, and am sorry you will oblige me to give you an order to strike your broad pendant, and hope you will hoist it again in the *Centaur* agreeable to the order. It is what everybody expects, and to let you continue it would be giving up a point of discipline I should be blamed for. For my justification and to show I have done all in my power I think, I thought it necessary the order should be worded as it is.[54]

50   To Admiral Sir George Pocock

Dublin [Port Royal],
[8 May 1762]

I had the honour of acquainting you of my arrival here, where I found Captain Forrest with a broad pendant and a captain appointed under him by his own authority, which he informed me he did in consequence of the opinion and advice of the captains then present, till a senior officer should arrive. Therefore as soon as I came off the port I acquainted him that he must be sensible that I could neither suffer the one he had made to continue, nor did I think I had any authority to appoint him one; therefore he must return to the command of the *Centaur* for which ship he had a commission from the Lords Commissioners of the Admiralty. But as the squadron was considerably increased and ought to be in two divisions, as he was the next in command I gave him an order to wear a distinguishing pendant, his answer to which was that on my order he would most readily strike his pendant, but did not chose to reassume the command of the *Centaur* with [out] a captain under him, and that his health requiring some relaxation from business, desired I would give Captain Goostrey[55] an order to discharge himself, his secretary and servants from the *Cambridge*'s books, which I accordingly did. All this was done with the greatest cordiality on both sides, as we have been long acquainted, for although he thinks I ought not to have done it, and I think I could not avoid behaving in the manner I did to him, we are still good friends, and although it may happen that you may bring out some orders in regard to him, for I must do him the justice to say that I believe no officer knows more of the nature of the service in these seas than himself. I have not appointed anybody yet into any vacancy he has filled up, although I think I had a right because I have authority to appoint officers and he could have none but by order. This is what I thought necessary to inform you of in regard to this affair.

51   To George Paplay, Esq., at Kingston

[*Dublin*, off Cape Nicola],
[24 May 1762]
(*holograph*)

As a sloop called the *Experiment* belonging to me in the King's service was taken going express to Sir George Pocock by a French privateer, as you are my agent at Jamaica remember and demand payment of the Storekeeper Mr Paterson at Port Royal for the same; I believe she was valued at £1,000. I had five negroes in her besides, however that was my own loss.

52   Order to the Masters of the Centurion, Alcide and Boreas

Centurion, Port Royal Harbour,
2 June 1762

Captain Boteler[56] of his Majesty's ship *Penzance* having represented to me that the outer cable of the small bower and old vyol, with sundry other rigging on board the said ship, are much worn and decayed and judged unfit for their proper use; you are therefore hereby required and directed to repair on board his Majesty's said ship and take a strict and careful survey of the cable, vyol and rigging complained of, and report to me from under your hands the condition thereof.

53   Order to Captain Thomas Lemprière[57] of the Centaur

Centurion,
2 June 1762

You are hereby required and directed to send a careful petty officer with twenty men to assist in unloading the *Nancy* store ship at Greenwich, for which this shall be your order.
Memorandum: The masts out of the store ships are to be got out of the sun as fast as they are landed.

54   To Pocock

Centurion, Port Royal Harbour,
6 June 1762

This comes by the *Alcide*, who I have sent as soon as we could get some of her men from the hospital. She has now fifty there still, and has buried upwards of thirty, and the sickness in her not quite abated, although every method has been used to stop it. She brings ninety negroes and thirty of Major Fuller's company of free negroes, which is all that will come. The weather has been so bad, and the sea breezes blown so fresh, that has prevented us from getting the transports watered and victualled for the negroes, but shall be able to send them in two or three days hence, under the convoy of the *Glasgow*. The *Penzance* will be ready by the same time, which I shall keep here, being the only frigate then in port ready for the sea. The *Centaur* got her mainmast in this day, and will be hove down with the greatest expedition they can do here. She is a good ship, but she has had now all her three masts shifted, and new sheathed as the worm had ate all her old sheathing off. She has given us a vast deal of trouble and has taken up most of the artificers. I have not yet heard anything of the *Deptford*, but hope no accident happened to her. Enclosed is a copy of the orders Captain Digges sailed under as also an abstract of the state and condition of the ships here. The *Sutherland* has on board eighteen of the *Centurion*'s men, which please to remove into any ship you may think I may be most likely to meet with.

55   *To Captain Samuel Uvedale*[58] *of the* Boreas

8 June 1762

Whereas his Majesty's ships are in great want of men from sickness and desertion, and as Governor Lyttleton through an application has given orders to Mr Furnell Custos of Kingston to press straggling seamen, which was done about twelve days ago, but as that was not found sufficient to get the number wanted I have applied to Mr Furnell to have another trial. You are therefore to go to Mr Furnell and acquaint him you are come from me, and to concert with him the time and manner the pressing should be, desiring he will give you the assistance of the constables, and the men so pressed are to be sent to gaol or on board the *Glasgow* till they are inspected by a magistrate. A lieutenant with a boat's crew will be sent from each ship, who you and Captain Carteret[59] are to give orders to assemble at the time and place shall appear most convenient, as men are wanted for the transports to carry negroes for the expedition.

56   *To the Pursers of the* Centurion, Penzance, Boreas *and* Fowey, *or any three of them*

9 June 1762

Mr James Forrester, purser of his Majesty's ship *Centaur*, having represented to me by his letter of this date that he has not passed an account for the said ship since she has been commissioned, and that to obviate any inconveniencies that may arise to him and his family should any unforeseen accident befall the said ship, he requests a survey on the provisions, necessaries, etc., on board: you are therefore hereby required and directed to repair on board his Majesty's said ship and to take a strict and careful survey of the provisions, casks, iron hoops, biscuit bags, slops, beds, portable broth and necessaries on board, reporting to me from under your hands the remains of each species in the charge of the said Mr James Forrester.

57   To Captain Dudley Digges[60]

Centurion, Port Royal Harbour,
18 June 1762

As soon as his Majesty's ship *Deptford* is completed with water and provision and is in every respect ready for the sea, you are hereby required and directed to proceed off Cape François where you are to cruise betwixt the Tortudas [and] Mariguana [MS. Mayaguana] for the protection of our trade that comes on the north side of Hispaniola, as also to prevent vessels from North America under pretence of flags of truce going to supply our enemies with stores and provisions; and as there are some ships of the line in at Cape François you are to be very careful not to run risk of being surprised by them when you are cruising either to windward or to leeward of the Cape to intercept any of our enemy's vessels going in there, or going through the Old Straits to the Havanna. You are from time to time to fill your water and at the end of six weeks to repair to Port Royal for further orders.

58   To Digges or the Senior Officer in Port

Centurion,
21 June 1762

As it may be some time before Commodore Keppel arrives here to take the command of the squadron, the senior officer in port is to direct the *Ferret* and *Port Royal* to be employed in cruising for the protection of the trade of this island, which may be infested from the Spanish and French privateers. The *Port Mahon* is to be ordered to heave down as soon as she has been sent off Cape François to demand the officers and men of the *Hussar* lost at Cape François, if they are not sent before, and the other ships that are not under any other orders from Sir George Pocock to be kept cruising to windward of this island, the south side of Hispaniola, and the north side of Cape François and Tortuda − if that can be done with safety, as the enemy has a squadron in that port − and in case they shall meet at any time with any material intelligence relating to any attempts the enemy may design against this island, to proceed down to Port Royal to inform the commanding officer and governor of it. The ships that are foul are to be cleaned, but as artificers are scarce only two at a time are to be kept in for that purpose. As the general of Hispaniola has sent some English prisoners down, on application from the merchants you are to give them some of the French prisoners to go to Hispaniola, and to return with English prisoners giving the masters strict charge to deliver the seamen to the first man of war they meet with and to deliver them to the commanding officer at Port Royal; and as there is a Spanish flag of truce come from St Iago who must be a spy, you are not to let him go away until Friday next, and as the governor of that place did [send] some English seamen here, and as I am informed that there are about twenty Spaniards here who are inhabitants of that place, to let the officer carry them with him; also to let a small French sloop that came here with the *Dublin*'s men from Port Lewis go away on Saturday next with as many of the French officers and men as she can take, and as the next great convoy will sail from this the 25th July, to direct the Commissary Mr Mathison to let the masters of the merchant ships take as many Spanish prisoners as they can with safety.

As the Commissioners of the Navy have made complaints of the great expence of stores here, you are to be particularly careful that you make no demands of stores but what are absolutely necessary, and to sign no demands but what are regular and agreeable to the first indent; and after taking a copy of these orders the originals to be left with the next senior officer till Commodore Keppel arrives, for which this shall be your order.

59   *To Mr Hall, Agent-Victualler at Greenwich*

Centurion in Port Royal Harbour,
21 June 1762

Whereas it has been represented to me by the different captains of the squadron that the rum sent on board by the contractors' agent here is not only very new but also ill tasted, and has been the occasion of giving the seamen the flux, I have therefore given directions that the masters should be particularly careful in tasting all rum, as well as other provisions sent on board, and not to receive any rum that is less than three months old, as the contractors' price is very high, and they can well afford to give a price for rum proper for the seamen to use: you are therefore hereby required and directed to send no rum on board of any of the ships of the squadron but what is three months old, and to be particularly careful in getting the species of provisions directed by the contract, that the health of the men may not suffer by their being deprived of provisions so proper for their nourishment; and as there is wine in some of the prizes, whenever it is good and the captains desire it, if within the contractors' price to send some of it to the ships in port, for which this shall be your order.

60   *To Pocock*

Centurion, off Cape Antonio.
4 July 1762

This serves to inform you that I sailed from Port Royal 20th June, and as

I had sent the *Boreas* to collect the ships that were to load at the northward and western ports of the island, she joined me off the west end the 25th, and sailed from thence with 123 sail that took orders, and about eighteen that did not. As the number of ships are more numerous than I was made to believe, could not spare the *Boreas* to send you an account of our arrival and I had no other frigate ready at Port Royal but the *Rose*, which I found necessary to send to windward of the island as I heard of a privateer being off there. I now send this by the *Alarm* to give you the earliest intelligence of my coming that you may prepare your letters for England. The *Penzance*, who is much out of repair, is the ship that has the charge of the convoy that sails the 25th July for Europe, till she joins the other ship you design to go with them for the Channel agreeable to the petition the merchants sent you for that purpose.

The *Centaur* in attempting to heave down sprung her mainmast in two places, who with the *Fowey* and *Deptford* will soon be ready for the sea. She is to convoy whatever transports for the fleet and army may be ready; the other two are to go to windward for the protection of the trade.

As I left the *Viper* at Port Royal to convoy part of the fleet, could not get out that day we did. In the afternoon the *Hampshire* arrived there who brought in a French ship loaded with sugar from Cape François, but the captain brought no intelligence of any kind.

It gives me the greatest satisfaction to hear by Captain Elphinstone[61] of the success you had in getting through the Old Straits, as also in landing the troops so safe and so near the town, and flatter myself by the time I get off I shall be honoured with the accounts home of our being in a fair way of being masters of the Havanna.

I am told that the fleet and army are in great want of rum, and am informed there is a considerable quantity on board the ships in this convoy, and apprehend you may be supplied from them at a cheaper rate than having it from the contractors, the government price being 4s 4d sterling per gallon, besides the charge there will be of sending it from Jamaica to the Havanna. As Captain Elphinstone informs me you are anchored at the mouth of a river, and as the convoy would be glad to stop twenty-four hours to take in water, the taking the rum out may be effected in that time.

61   *To Clevland*

[Draft copy,
7 September 1762]

This is to inform the Lords Commissioners of the Admiralty of my arrival here this day with the trade from Jamaica who sailed under the convoy of his Majesty's ships *Centurion, Boreas* and *Viper*, which consisted of 126 sail who took sailing instructions, and about eighteen that did not, when I left that island the 25th June.

As my orders were from Sir George Pocock to call off the Havanna, we stayed there a week, and left it 19th July, and in the passage met with a ship from Philadelphia who informed me a French squadron had taken Newfoundland, which information comes enclosed.

On the 2nd, about 160 leagues to the westward of Scilly, I met with Captain O'Bryen in the *Woolwich* and the *Falkland* with the trade from Barbadoes and the Leeward Islands under their convoy, so for the better protection of the whole, I gave him orders to sail in company to the Downs, but on 3rd in the evening there came on a very hard gale of wind at SW which lasted twenty-four hours and then came to the NW, by which means many of the convoy separated. On 5th the *Falkland* joined me again, as did the *Boreas* on 6th with about twenty sail, and as the *Viper* left me on 21st July I made the *Boreas*'s signal to separate and see the ships out of danger that were bound to the ports in Ireland and St George's Channel, and am now arrived in the Downs with about fifty sail, who are part of the two different convoys.

Please to acquaint their Lordships, agreeable to orders from Sir George Pocock I have brought home seventy invalids from the hospital at Port Royal in the *Centurion, Boreas* and *Viper*, and also eighty-six men from the army, mostly French, who had listed as volunteers at Portsmouth to serve in Major Fleuron's corps, but as a great many of them had deserted to the enemy and the rest behaved so ill they were not to be trusted, therefore Lord Albermarle broke that corps, and desired they might be treated as prisoners.

Please also to acquaint them that when I left Jamaica there were in the prison there 1,100 French and Spanish prisoners, which were more than it could conveniently hold, therefore as the spirit of privateering had prevailed so much since the Spanish war that not only his Majesty's ships had lost many of their men, but the merchant ships also, so that they could not have come home with this convoy without my assistance, in consequence thereof I gave orders to the Commissary for Prisoners at Jamaica to deliver as many Spanish and French prisoners to each master as they wanted and they could take with safety, and left the same orders for Captain Boteler of the *Penzance*, who was to sail with the next convoy the 25th July from thence to the Havanna, where an addition would be given to the strength of it from Sir George Pocock.

Since the above I see the *Woolwich* appearing in sight with more of the convoy, and enclosed is a list of those that came out with me from Jamaica.

Notes

1   B. Mc L. Ranft (ed.), *The Vernon Papers*, N.R.S. Vol. 99 (1958), p. 149.

2   Sir Lewis Namier and John Brooke, *The History of Parliament: House of Commons 1754–1790*, 3 vols. (London: HMSO, 1964), ii, p. 331.

3   John Charnock, *Biographia Navalis*, 6 vols. (London, 2nd edn 1796), v, p. 290.

4   See in general Richard Pares, *War and Trade in the West Indies, 1739–1763* (Oxford: OUP, 1936).

5   Governor Dalrymple of Guadaloupe to Pitt, 14 April 1761, in G. S. Kimball (ed.),

THE DOUGLAS PAPERS, 1760–1762

Correspondence of William Pitt . . . with Colonial Governors, 2 vols. (London and New York, 1906), ii, p. 418.

6   See Commodore Moore to Clevland, 26 February 1760, in P.R.O. ADM 1/307.

7   Governor Dalrymple adopted a similar policy at the same time; see note 5 above.

8   On manning in general, see Richard Pares, 'The Manning of the Navy in the West Indies, 1702–1763', *Transactions of the Royal Historical Society,* 4th Series, Vol. XX (1937), p. 31.

9   Moore to Clevland, 20 December 1759, Douglas to Clevland 23 and 24 July 1760, all in ADM 1/307. Douglas to Navy Board, 24 July 1761, N.M.M. DOU 4 p. 145.

10 ADM 7/573 pp. 299, 300, 310.

11 Pares, *War and Trade,* Ch. IX.

12 Moore to Clevland, 26 February 1760, ADM 1/307.

13 P.R.O. PRO 30/8/98 fols. 65–70, printed by Kimball (op. cit., ii, p. 247) without correcting the date of January 1760, which by an obvious slip appears in the original.

14 ADM 2/1331 p. 407; Kimball, op. cit., ii, p. 457.

15 'Coming in a single ship he surprized everybody, but none more so than Sir James Douglas, who I believe did not expect it', Capt. J. Legge to Amherst, 29 November 1761, P.R.O. WO 34/55 fol. 39.

16 David Spinney, *Rodney* (London: Allen & Unwin, 1969) pp. 175–6.

17 ADM 2/1331 pp. 411, 413.

18 Dalrymple spoke of his 'active and well-disposed squadron' (note 5 above).

19 For the Martinique operation see Spinney, op. cit., Ch. X, and J. S. Corbett, *England in the Seven Years' War,* 2 vols. (London: Longman, 1907), ii, Ch. VII.

20 ADM 2/1331 p. 447.

21 Spinney, op. cit., pp. 191–6.

22 PRO 30/20/8 p. 72.

23 Spinney, op. cit., pp. 196–201.

24 See David Syrett, *The Siege and Capture of Havana, 1762,* N.R.S. Vol. 114 (1970).

25 Further documents on this affair are printed by Syrett, op. cit., pp. 86–90.

26 George Metcalf, *Royal Government and Political Conflict in Jamaica, 1729–1783* (London: Longman, 1965), p. 155. Metcalf seems to be in error in attributing the delay in sending the negroes to a quarrel between Lyttleton and Douglas (see Syrett, op. cit., pp. 122, 137) and does not mention the Forrest affair.

27 On the disputed election of 1754 for the borough of Mitchell in Cornwall, see Namier and Brooke, *House of Commons,* i, p. 234.

28 Lieutenant 1758. He was Douglas's nephew.

29 James Innes; Lt. 1746, Captain 1761.

30 Not a sloop in the naval sense of a cruiser below the 6th Rate, (usually ship, brig or ketch rigged), but a 'West India' sloop, i.e. a very large cutter. In a West Indian context it is not always easy to know which sort of sloop is meant.

31 Lt. 1745, Cdr. 1756, Capt. 1758.

32 Later Lord Shuldham; Lt. 1739, Capt. 1746, Rear-Admiral 1775, Vice-Admiral 1776, Admiral 1787.

33 Thomas Cornwall of the *Emerald*; Lt. 1749, Cdr. 1756, Capt. 1757. His complaint was gout, according to Charnock (op. cit., vi, p. 222), on whose reckoning he was then only twenty-eight.

34 Charles Middleton, later Lord Barham; Lt. 1745, Capt. 1750, Controller of the Navy 1778–90, R-Adm. 1787, V-Adm. 1793, Adm. 1795, First Lord 1805–6.

35 John Bagster; Lt. 1744, Cdr. 1762.

36 John Neal Pleydell Nott; Lt. 1756, Cdr. 1759, Capt. 1761.

37 Lt. 1744, Cdr. 1748, Capt. 1758.

38 Edward St Lo; Lt. 1755.

39 Lucius O'Bryen; Lt. 1738, Cdr. 1744, Capt. 1745, R-Adm. 1770.

40 Roger Williams; Lt 1756, Cdr. 1760.

41 Lt. 1735, Cdr. 1744, Capt. 1745, R-Adm. 1770.

42 He was also the Attorney-General whose son had led the riot against Moore, an old enemy of Government and of the Navy. See Pares, *War and Trade,* pp. 204, 214, and 'Manning of the Navy', p. 52 n. 1.

43 On this see Pares, 'Manning of the Navy', p. 32 n. 1.

44   Alexander, Lord Colvill; Lt. 1739, Capt. 1744, R-Adm. 1762.
45   Julian Legge; Capt. 1746.
46   i.e. the Master Shipwright.
47   Edward Gascoigne; Lt. 1742, Cdr. 1755, Capt. 1760.
48   Charles Buckner; Lt. 1756, Cdr. 1761, Capt. 1766, R-Adm. 1793, V-Adm. 1794, Adm. 1799.
49   The *Raisonnable* had been lost on a reef going in close to engage a battery.
50   Robert Swanton; Lt. 1735, Capt. 1744, R-Adm. 1762.
51   Robert Brice, later Sir Robert Brice Kingsmill; Lt. 1756, Cdr. 1761, Capt. 1762, R-Adm. 1793, V-Adm. 1794, Adm. 1799.
52   Basil Keith; Lt. 1756, Cdr. 1758, Capt. 1760.
53   Cdr. 1741, Capt. 1745.
54   The order is printed by Syrett, op. cit., p. 86.
55   William Goostrey; Lt. 1744, Cdr. 1757, Capt. 1759. He was killed soon afterwards attacking the Morro Castle.
56   Philip Boteler; Lt. 1756, Cdr. 1761, Capt. 1762.
57   Lt. 1741, Cdr. 1757, Capt. 1759.
58   Lt. 1747, Cdr. 1758, Capt. 1760.
59   Richard Carteret of the *Glasgow*; Lt. 1744, Cdr. 1745, Capt. 1761.
60   Lt. 1745, Capt. 1753.
61   John Elphinstone, commanding the *Richmond*, whose skilful pilotage was largely responsible for bringing Pocock's fleet safely through the Old Bahama Channel; Lt. 1746, Cdr. 1757, Capt. 1759.

List of Documents and Sources

		1760	
1	Douglas to Anson	2 March	P.R.O. ADM 1/307
2	Victualling Board to Douglas	11 April	N.M.M. DOU 8 p. 8
3	Douglas to Melville	3 May	DOU 4 p. 1
4	Douglas to Clevland	11 May	DOU 4 p. 2
5	Douglas to Navy Board	11 May	DOU 4 p. 4
6	Balfour to Douglas	19 May	DOU 8 p. 5
7	Douglas to Clevland	4 June	ADM 1/307
8	Douglas to Pringle	5 June	DOU 4 p. 9
9	Shuldham to Douglas	22 June	DOU 8 p. 6
10	Douglas to Clevland	25 July	DOU 4 p. 18
11	Douglas to Coverdale	20 August	DOU 4 p. 27
12	Douglas to Navy Board	16 September	DOU 4 p. 32
13	Douglas to Williamson	6 October	DOU 4 p. 33
14	Douglas to Navy Board	16 October	DOU 4 p. 42
15	Douglas to Victualling Board	17 October	DOU 4 p. 53
16	Douglas to Clevland	17 October	DOU 4 p. 44
17	Douglas to Vassor de la Touche	18 October	DOU 4 p. 36
18	Douglas to Maxwell	2 November	DOU 4 p. 40
19	Officers of Antigua yard to Douglas	5 November	DOU 8 p. 25
20	Stanley to Douglas	22 November	DOU 8 p. 22
21	Douglas to Thomas	24 November	DOU 4 p. 49
22	Douglas to Clevland	29 November	DOU 4 p. 50
23	Douglas to Pinfold	11 December	DOU 4 p. 55
24	Douglas to Clevland	14 December	DOU 4 p. 60

25	Douglas to Walsh	27 December	DOU 4 p. 66

1761

26	Douglas to Clevland	6 February	DOU 4 p. 74
27	Barker to Douglas	15 February	DOU 8 p. 42
28	Douglas to Pinfold	17 February	DOU 4 p. 79
29	Shuldham to Douglas	7 March	DOU 8 p. 48
30	Douglas to All Captains	20 April	DOU 4 p. 99
31	Douglas to Blehnman	12 May	DOU 4 p. 115
32	Douglas to Southwell	9 June	DOU 4 p. 123
33	Douglas to Amherst	16 June	P.R.O. WO 34/55 fols. 7–8
34	Douglas to Colvill	6 July	DOU 4 p. 137
35	Douglas to Thomas	1 September	DOU 4 p. 150
36	Douglas to Monckton	19 September	DOU 4 p. 152
37	Douglas to Anson	3 October	DOU 4 p. 156
38	Douglas to de Windt	8 October	DOU 4 p. 162
39	Douglas to Clevland	7 November	DOU 4 p. 174

1762

40	Douglas to Rodney	4 February	DOU 4 p. 190
41	Douglas to Maxwell	7 February	DOU 4 p. 192
42	Douglas to Rodney	21 February	P.R.O. PRO 30/20/8 p. 69
43	Rodney to Douglas	22 February	PRO 30/20/8 p. 70
44	Douglas to Rodney	23 February	DOU 4 p. 196
45	Douglas to Rodney	2 March	DOU 4 p. 201
46	Douglas to Rodney	17 March	DOU 4 p. 202
47	Douglas to Rodney	21 March	DOU 4 p. 204
48	Douglas to Forrest	12 April	DOU 4 p. 210
49	Douglas to Forrest	12 April	DOU 4 p. 212
50	Douglas to Pocock	8 May	DOU 4 p. 220
51	Douglas to Paplay	24 May	DOU 4 p. 239
52	Douglas to Masters of various ships	2 June	DOU 6 Pt. 2 p. 3
53	Douglas to Lemprière	2 June	DOU 6 Pt. 2 p. 4
54	Douglas to Pocock	6 June	DOU 6
55	Douglas to Uvedale	8 June	DOU 6 Pt. 2 p. 9
56	Douglas to Pursers of various ships	9 June	DOU 6 Pt. 2 p. 10
57	Douglas to Digges	18 June	DOU 6 Pt. 2 p. 16
58	Douglas to Digges	21 June	DOU 6 Pt. 2 p. 19
59	Douglas to Hall	21 June	DOU 6 Pt. 2 p. 19
60	Douglas to Pocock	4 July	DOU 6
61	Douglas to Clevland	7 September	DOU 6

7

Letters of Captain George Miller Mundy, 1797–1809

Edited by

P. K. CRIMMIN

Introduction

George Miller Mundy (1777–1861) was the third son of Edward Miller Mundy of Shipley, near Ilkeston, Derbyshire and his first wife, Frances Meynell. Mundy entered the Royal Naval Academy on 9 July 1789 for the maximum three years. After brief service in the West Indies he served nearly three years as a midshipman in the Mediterranean, at the capture of Toulon, the reduction of Bastia and Calvi and in a small squadron, under Captain Samuel Hood, protecting British trade in the Greek archipelago. His father was one of the two Members of Parliament for Derbyshire, from 1784 to 1822, and the friend and colleague of the third Duke of Grafton. Grafton, who had been First Lord of the Treasury, 1766–70, was a cultivated man with a wide circle of friends, among them his Northamptonshire neighbour, Earl Spencer, First Lord of the Admiralty, 1794–1801. Such influence and his own merits secured Mundy his promotion to lieutenant when only 19, on 11 March 1796. Thereafter his rise was steady; first to third lieutenant in H.M.S. *St George*, then to a similar position in H.M.S. *Blenheim*, in which ship he fought at the Battle of Cape St Vincent, 14 February 1797. *Blenheim* was in the thick of the action. She had 105 round shot embedded in her hull and expended 180 barrels of powder. At one time she was engaged with five of the enemy at once, yet she had only ten seamen killed and forty-five officers and men wounded. The Spaniards, by contrast, suffered considerably, losing approximately 1,000 men killed and wounded. Spanish surgeons were without adequate medical or surgical supplies, due to the inadequacies of their government, and their distress was only partially relieved by the assistance of the British surgeons. Doubtless Mundy heard this from his friend, Mr Reynolds, the invalid surgeon for whom he invoked his father's help.

Mundy's move to the *Victory*, as fourth lieutenant, was sudden, but he did not remain in her long, transferring to H.M.S. *Goliath* and serving in her, as fourth lieutenant, at the Battle of the Nile. Only two months later, in October 1798, he was made acting commander of the *Transfer* brig, being confirmed in her on 24 December. He achieved post rank 10 February 1801, while in the *Swan* sloop, thereafter serving in the Channel and off the northern French coast in various ships until appointed to the thirty-eight-gun frigate *Hydra* on 21 October 1802. He remained in her for eight years.

At first he watched the French coast during the build-up of Napoleon's invasion fleet. In 1804 he joined the fleet off Cadiz and during Nelson's pursuit of Villeneuve, he remained in the Mediterranean, protecting Sardinia and Sicily, and earning the commendation of Vice-Admiral Collingwood as 'a clever young man' for his 'exemplary vigilance and activity'. A few days before Trafalgar he was detached, with others of the blockading squadron, to get water, stores and provisions at Tetuan and Gibraltar. He thus missed the battle, to his bitter disappointment. It was possible for a commander to send a favoured captain on a cruise in hope of prizes, though from what we know of Collingwood it seems unlikely, if Mundy was so favoured, that his aunt's influence was responsible. One must assume he was indulging in kindly teasing in his letter to her [4]. Whatever the cause he was successful. In February 1806, while off Cadiz lighthouse, Mundy took a French brig, *Le Furet*, during pursuit of the frigates he mentions, and in the following months he took more prizes. For the next two years he remained off the southern coast of Spain, capturing a variety of brigs, schooners, polacres, etc., in a series of daring expeditions, frequently reported in the *Gazette*. The necessity of a refit brought *Hydra* to England in July 1808, convoying a large merchant fleet. When Mundy returned to the Mediterranean, in December, he was sent, with H.M.S. *Leonidas* and some smaller vessels, to the Catalan coast, to help the patriots in their resistance to the French invasion.

Vice-Admiral Collingwood was attempting to assist the Catalans by cutting off coastal trade and blockading Barcelona. The French had occupied the town in 1808, but barely controlled it, and it was almost constantly under siege from the *somatenes*, the Catalan guerrillas, who frequently cut communications between the French army and the rest of Spain and France. General Duhesme's attempts to break out and occupy the hinterland ended in humiliating defeat, from which his inexperienced Italian troops in particular, returned to Barcelona demoralised. Like his chief, Mundy found enthusiasm and spirit among the people and lethargy among their leaders. He attacked the coastal roads, driving the French columns inland, where they were harassed by the *somatenes,* whom Mundy supplied with arms and ammunition. He issued proclamations to the foreign troops in the French army, promising them the protection of British ships if they deserted. But he failed to rouse the authorities to vigorous prosecution of the siege of Barcelona and received no co-operation from the enfeebled Spanish navy in his attempt to put a stop to all coastal traffic. Yet his operations were generally successful and warmly commended by Collingwood.

In October 1809 *Hydra* was sent to watch Toulon and in February 1810 went for a refit to Gibraltar, where Mundy served as senior naval officer. On his return to England the following August, *Hydra* was found totally unfit for further service and put out of commission. During the Hundred Days Mundy served off Marseilles and in 1816 he formed part of Admiral Lord Exmouth's expedition to Algiers. This was the end of his active service. Made a Companion of the Bath in June 1815 and promoted to Rear-Admiral 22 July 1830, he was knighted seven years later and made Vice-Admiral of the Red 23 November 1841. He became Admiral of the Fleet 24 December 1849. He had been elected Member of Parliament for Boroughbridge in 1818, retaining the seat until 1831. He died, unmarried, at his house in Grosvenor Square on 9 February 1861, aged 84.

These six letters form part of a larger collection, ranging from 1795 to 1809, and are deposited among the Miller Mundy papers, D517, at Derbyshire County Record Office. The majority are addressed to Mundy's father at his house in Piccadilly and written in a clear hand with few obscurities. I have modernised the spelling and punctuation, omitting repetitions and, where a page is torn but the sense is clear, inserting missing words in square brackets. The occasional French and Spanish words have been italicised.

CAPTAIN MUNDY'S LETTERS, 1797–1809

1 *George Mundy to Edward Miller Mundy*

Blenheim, R. Tagus,
8 March 1797

My dear father, – Your kind letter of the 13th January accompanied by one from Fanny and four others enclosed for Mr Walpole, General Caldwell and Mr Burn, came into my possession three days ago by the arrival of the *Adamant* and convoy, for which I thank you very much and am greatly indebted and obliged to Fanny for her kind exertions.[1] It is unfortunate that the quarter from which you conceived I should receive the most civility and find the most serviceable and pleasant acquaintance, proves the contrary by the departure of Mr Burn for England. I judge, from what Mr Walpole told me, they must be in England at this time. I shall keep the letters till I hear further from you. I did myself the pleasure of calling upon Mr Walpole the day before yesterday. Both him and his lady were very civil and inquired much after you and Fanny. I almost dread their invitation, the palace is so far distant from the river that on foot it is quite a journey, and through the most filthy and dirty streets that can be conceived, and carriages, which in every respect are as bad, are difficult to be procured.

Mr Walpole informed me that General Caldwell is on the frontiers. According to Sir John Hort's request I shall take the first opportunity of sending his letter.[2] The twelfth regiment of dragoons is in the convoy. They are now disembarking, a very fine sight for the Portuguese. The contrast between their *Rosinantes* and them, with their activity and neatness, will not a little astonish them. You don't mention anything of Godfrey. I expected to have heard of his promotion.[3] Fanny tells me he is at Exeter and likes his quarters much. Really your family accounts are vastly pleasing, excepting of poor Lady Newdigate. However I hope to God the next will be better; it must distress Sir Roger very much.[4] It gives me great pleasure to hear my aunts Nelly and Barton are in good health; the happy state of Jim and his little family must be very gratifying to Mrs Barton.

What a fortunate lot of fellows we have been of late. After giving those great fellows a slight drubbing, to get all our prizes and fleet safe in without the smallest accident.[5] Since we have been here it has been blowing hard and we hear, by a gentleman who arrived from Cadiz yesterday, that when he left it, they had not had accounts of their fleet for some days. Therefore we may conclude they must have suffered very much, not only in their masts and from sickness, but for want of provisions. I really now begin to pity their distresses and wish they were in port. When one considers the great numbers of wounded, without the least refreshment, together with their natural uncleanliness and the want of surgical assistance, their situation must be truly shocking. I hope the Admiralty will not hesitate a moment in sending out a reinforcement. We certainly require at least ten sail of the line in addition to our fleet. Then, should fortune once more throw the Spaniards in our way, there would be no doubt of success. We understand the Spanish court have demanded the [navy?] of the Portuguese and in case of a [refusal] will march their way to Lisbon. I think they are great proficients in the species of gasconade which they are learning from their honourable allies the Republic, but unfortunately for them they are not so able to execute.[6]

This moment I parted with young Mr Hart, brother to Mr Walpole. He has been so good as to promise to forward the letter to General Caldwell. Lisbon is at this period particularly dull, no amusement whatsoever is permitted. Sir John Jervis lives on shore, he has been very unwell.[7] At this time I think it may be of great service to push the business of promotion, the action may have great weight. But you must certainly know better the situation of affairs in that quarter than me and I am sure, dear father, you will do every [thing] for the best. I send this by the *Jason*. Pray remember in best love, etc., and believe me as ever

Your sincere and dutiful son

G. Mundy.

2   *George Mundy to Edward Miller Mundy*

R. Tagus,
29 March

Dear and honoured father, – I am, you see, still belonging to the *Blenheim*, though in doubt yet whether I am to continue or not. However today we expect the arrangements will take place. Admiral Parker has his flag in this ship and all his followers are arrived in the *Ville de Paris*.[8] They are very numerous; so much so that should I remain, I must stand in the light of some of them. Therefore it will be much more pleasant to quit. Sir John Jervis hoists his flag in the *Ville de Paris* today and I think will certainly be at sea by Sunday. I fear you will consider me a very troublesome fellow, but I really can't resist trespassing once more on your kindness. It is a request in favour of an old messmate and particular friend, Mr Reynolds, the former surgeon of the *Blenheim* who, on account of a complaint of the liver, has been under the necessity of changing with the *St Joseph* to go to England, finding himself unequal to the task of a second rate. What he looks for is either a prison, slop or receiving ship, where he may still be serving his time and where there is but little practice. Now, if you are acquainted with any one of the Commissioners of the Sick and Hurt Board, such as Dr Blair, Mr Gibbons, etc., it may easily be accomplished.[9] It is not for many that I would ask such a favour, but being a great friend and having paid particular attention to me when indisposed, I am by gratitude bound to serve him. He is very clever in his profession and has served the whole war, which certainly entitles him to a little indulgence from the service.

Victory at sea, 6 April

Duty interfering was the cause of my not finishing. I did not return to the ship till between 7 and 8 at night, when I found myself completely turned out of that, Admiral Parker's people had taken possession and a commission for me, for the *Victory* with orders to join her instantly. I am very happy, contrary to your kind suggestions, Sir John has not taken me into the ship with him, as I can assure you for an officer there is not a more disagreeable station in the fleet. Indeed I have not the least doubt when he promotes me it will not be from the *Ville de Paris*.[10] We left Lisbon last Friday and looked into Cadiz the day before yesterday. There were not more than ten or twelve of their ships ready for sea, that we saw. It is reported on board the Commander-in-Chief today that they certainly will come out in a very short time, but I must say I doubt it much, if we continue so close to their port. However, should they honour us with a visit, I have not the least doubt that some of them will be so kind as to follow us into Lisbon. We now have twenty-two sail of the line, eight of which are three-deck ships, I think strong enough for anything they can bring to oppose us.

I deserve to be hung for not mentioning to you before, that the eldest son of Mr Walpole is just arrived from the West Indies in the *Ariadne*, in order that you might find him out and pay him every civility in your power, which I am sure you would have done with pleasure, had you known it before. He lives with Mr Burn, but in which part of the town I don't remember. It distresses me very much, as I fear he must have left England before this arrives. I will be much obliged to you, should you send anything out to me, to direct it to Williams's Hotel, Lisbon.

The next letter you receive from me will, I hope, be on as good an occasion as the last you received, dated at sea. Till then, believe me

Yours dutifully

Remember me kindly.   Geo. Mundy.

3   *George Mundy to Edward Miller Mundy*

Victory off Cadiz,
15 May 1797

My dear father, – Still on the same scent, but I fear have neared the chase but little. The Spaniards appear more inclined to defend their anchorage than their trade, though of late I must give them the credit to say they have made every endeavour to appear more formidable. They are dropping their ships down to the mouth of the harbour daily and have, at this moment, twenty-four sail of the line, to external appearance, ready for sea. We understand today they proposed coming out to give us a drubbing, but don't find it convenient, though a very charming day. I think it will require some compulsion to part them from their anchors, excepting to return up the harbour.[11] The fishermen are the only creatures we have any friendly communications with; they now and then supply us with the fruits of their labour. Since I wrote last we have taken one Spanish frigate and one we have destroyed. The latter was of very large dimensions. There never was a blockade more completely formed. The several consuls at Cadiz have sent a very severe remonstrance to Sir John Jervis concerning it; since which we have permitted vessels to leave the port. Our prizes are but few in number this cruise. I fear the Spaniards are rather too knowing for us in that respect. We hear the French are very much enraged with the King of Spain. They have abused him in the grossest terms. They say the Spaniard, once an honourable and brave people, are now the most dastardly, with various compliments of the kind, and threaten to use force if he does not show himself more hearty in the cause and send the fleet to sea. I hear little Walpole came out in the *Ville de Paris*. I was very sorry I had not an opportunity of seeing him. I shall ever regret your not knowing he was in London.

It is a long time since we had any vessels from England. I am very impatient for a letter, not only the pleasure of hearing from you, but the present politics are particularly interesting to people who have the least love or concern for their country.[12]

The next conveyance, I hope, will [arrive] with the garments. I have [wanted them] lately. What they were I declare I [have] forgot, but this I must say, there is scarce an article of my wardrobe that does not want replenishing and particularly the linen. Remember me kindly to all inquiring friends and consider me, dear father, yours dutifully,

G. Mundy.

4 *George Mundy to Mrs N. M.*[13]

Hydra off Cape Blanco, Coast of Barbary,
10 November 1805

My dear aunt, – Being once more embarked on a quiet cruise in search of that which all the moralists and philosophers that ever have been can never persuade me is not a necessity, *l'argent competant*, or that which will produce it, and really feeling myself indebted to you for this said moment of quiet and independence, being all alone; whether it turns out as one would naturally wish, and fortune deign to smile upon the weary *Hydra*, or whether she does not, still I must consider myself put in this happy state of tranquillity and ease, with all the etceteras, by you behaving so prettily and making yourself so agreeable to the friends of our present Commander-in-Chief, Admiral Collingwood.

Indeed, had I not discovered that the good man had long tied the connubial knot, I say had I not fortunately made the discovery, perhaps I should have been induced to have turned his warm commendations to rather a scandalous account and begun to imagine that he, who had the credit of contending with the elements off the Black Rocks for the last two years, might have been somewhere else and otherwise employed.[14] But that's neither here nor there. Therefore I must now explain why I have troubled you with the long side of a preface which is thus to be accounted for; that finding myself so comfortably situated in my emigration from the bustle of fleets and squadrons and the painful task of blockades, which has been my sole occupation for these last two years, I think it would be very unbecoming were I not to devote a few moments in scribbling over a sheet of paper, the history of your being the patroness of this selfsame cruise, in which I may become a rich man, and my many thanks! Besides, it would be extremely selfish in me to enjoy all the fruits of your worthiness, my dear aunt, and you to receive none of them. You will, I fear, find me more dull, if possible, than usual as a correspondent, being in rather a feeble state, though certainly a convalescent, from an ugly cough and cold, which has reduced me to a mere thread. But in justice to the cough, I ought to say that the severe exertions I naturally made, but without effect, to join our fleet on hearing of the enemy's being out, and the distress of mind I have suffered ever since, at not being an humble assistant on that glorious day, which was my birthright, etc., etc., to the end of the chapter, and which I won't trouble you with, have acted with much the greatest force against my shattered constitution.[15] But I have this satisfaction, that if any species of service at sea can agree with me and put me at all to rights, it is the one that I am upon. Should it not however, I must then endeavour to get a month's drift on shore at Lisbon.

No letters have reached me since one from my good father of the 6th of September, from which I learn of you having migrated to Wales and having spent two most delightful months with Mrs O. From thence you had taken flight to Lancaster, and was to meet him at the old, dear rendezvous, Shipley, where no doubt this will find you, surrounded by the sprigs and younger branches of the family. I have it in mind to order Godfrey's regiment out to Lisbon, on Portugal's joining the coalition.[16] But what a selfish animal I must be, to make the poor fellow bring out his little wife, his little son and his little – , I am not yet master of that part of the history, and, in short, all his household furniture and forsooth to please me. No, no, let them stay where they are in God's name! I hope they have not got into a cold house at Nottingham, the Shipley fireside will be much better. Then comes citizen [?] and the happy Waltons and my best of babes, Maria, to sum up Fanny Willoughby in the armchair and Fred in his shooting jacket; heavens! what an agreeable scene. But pray tell the selfsame Fanny, to beware of a large hole in her right-hand pocket and *mon père aussi*, although he is a particularly neat man in his habiliments, no man more so!

The *Hydra* is in the latitude of Madeira and if only the sight of one of the French frigates now in Cadiz, should but be acquired and lead the said *Hydra* a short dance to the westward, the deed will be effected and the purse strings must be drawn wide yawning. A few days ago I met, that is to say, Nesbit Willoughby came board the *Hydra*, when off Cadiz. He, poor fellow, was actually belonging to one of the ships that took part in the glorious action, but had been left behind in England and arrived off Cadiz ten days too late. I quite forget whether I mentioned him to my father a few months ago, when he was in the *Acasta*. If I did not, let me say that Nesbit is in high reputation with Admiral Duckworth and Captain Dunn, his captain, and was first lieutenant with that Admiral in the West Indies until he was called home. Captain D tells me he is a very excellent officer, very zealous and ready at all pieces of service. I was quite pleased to hear this of him and I trust and hope he will get forward. It is said Admiral D will have again the West India station, in which case, no doubt, W. will go to him, if possible.[17] Pardon me for this long story! Indeed I'm sure you will, as it is with the hope to put one who has erred, but which he has long done away, in the light he deserves to be seen in, which piece of common justice you would most naturally have done, and have not boasted of it, as I have.

It is from the many and frequent hints I receive in bad weather of the damage done to my pericranium, that I must learn how to commiserate the sufferings of poor dear Augusta in her sympathetic accident. But I have the highest opinion of the magnanimity and patience of mind with which such disasters are born by the more tender sex, therefore do not doubt of her evincing a perfect cure, at least if she follows the advice of the *tenderest of nurses* and best of mothers which, had I done, must inevitably have been my case. But for my non-compliance it must be allowed, that I could produce four or five as *fair* and *pretty* and most *agreeable* excuses, as any moderate man would wish to be served with. But it is high time for me to be very serious! This is past all bearing you will say! Here's a fellow has commenced with a story of husseys and has been longer winded than a defendant's counsel. But never mind, my dear aunt; as the post, I think, arrives in the evening at Shipley, complain that your eyes cannot read such stuff at that time of night and let one of your nieces or nephews or grandchildren or other of the numerous descendants, and pray bear in mind that I promise to perform equally as dutiful and becoming an action when it comes my turn again to take post alongside the Shipley fire. Remaining ever most affectionately

Your nephew
George.

5   *George Mundy to ?Edward Miller Mundy*[18]

. . . This must be executed with all possible speed and *pray send the bills to my agent*.

Bye the bye, during my employment in harassing and disturbing the peace of mind and body of the *gabachos*,[19] as we Catalonians term the French, in the middle of the night, I was awoke by the sound of music, and soon, on escaping from the clutches of Morpheus, discovered the patriotic tune of God Save the King, played by a very good band, which I found to be the band of the first Neapolitan regiment, which had deserted from Barcelona that eve, and had come out in a fishing boat. They have now been with me near two months and seem so contented and are such delightful musicians and such an alleviation from the sufferings of war and a seafaring life, that I am inclined to go to a little expense for them. I will therefore trouble you to lay out 100 pounds in instruments for me, viz.: *a serpent, a French horn, an F trumpet and seven tones, an octave flute and two clarinets*, and if there is any thing left, lay it out in the best music for a band.[20] I should not have troubled you with this commission were I certain Jeffrey was in England. To his little wife, his brats and particularly my sturdy godson, I beg many salutations, as well Nelly and her amiable chickens, not forgetting my child Maria, and tell Henry, *Hydra* is no longer *Hydra* but Pickle junior. Again, heaven bless you

George   Love to my aunt.

We have just learned that you have voted a large army for this country. I am delighted to hear it, but you must be rapid in execution. There is a good deal of good to be done yet and particularly while Austria is untouched. To be sure a patriot is a very rare thing in Spain and traitors are common, and those principally among the higher classes. But still the country can be saved by immediate and active exertions. Now my lamented friend Moore is gone, I hope Wellesley will command.[21]

G.

6   *George Mundy to Edward Miller Mundy*

Hydra at anchor off Barcelona,
5 April 1809

I have just received your most welcome letters, my dear father, of the 23rd December and the 24th of the following month, and as I wrote you but a few days ago, I can have little to do but answer them, a most agreeable task. But if I am *courte* in my remarks, you must not be surprised, as my friend Staines of the *Cyane* is just taken from me, and is already under weigh.[22] You will be happy to learn at the same time, that the Lord has not taken her unto himself, because I have made a bad use of her. *Au contraire!* He has written me a very handsome letter on the exertions of my little squadron and praising my first lieutenant, Hawkins, much. So far, so good. But your letter of December, I must observe, did give me somewhat of a chill, without looking at the date. The colonel of the King's Own and the disasters of my poor friend Moore came to my recollection. Thank heaven Godfrey has got clear of his brigadier; may he never be exposed to such temptations to rebel again.[23] I trust he has recovered his looks. I am not surprised at any impression that the lovely Maria may have made even on a heart of granite.

The thing of all others that I wanted to hear of, you tell me; that dear Frederick has undergone the operation he promised me he would, and with success.[24] Now to the next paragraph, the statement of your own health: God of his infinite mercy keep you so, and pray do not let one moment's pang disturb your kind heart on my account. Thank heaven I am most actively and honourably employed and having learnt to philosophise a good deal during my long services for my country, I think I can bear with disappointment as well as most. I agree with you in wishing Georgiana P possessed the heart of F, but I fear it is detained in the north, at least so it appeared to me. However it is possible a little estrangement from the Tees may alter, by degrees, his attachment, but 'twill never do even to hint Ga. to him, it must come of itself. Radford and Hassels are both well.[25] The latter has just recovered from a most dangerous accident, a blow in the head. He [is] a most amiable, spirited, brave lad as can be, quite an ornament to Derbyshire, and I trust, will shine in the service of his country. Your enclosed in the letter of the 24th January, was from our friend, Bob Sewell, and I am sorry to learn they have refused him leave of absence. Pray congratulate Nelly and Ned on the production of little Alfred.[26] May he follow the steps of his namesake of old, even the misfortunes I could almost wish, for they made him the more distinguished. I am most delighted to hear of the changes with respect to Clumber,[27] and I hope to hear of the total recovery of the little Duchess. Pray remember [me] most kindly to her and the Duke.

I am expecting still more active employment soon and I shall be superseded in my command no doubt. However it will be by my friend Benjamin Hallowell in the *Tigre*. If indeed we are to have a disposable force of ten thousand troops to act as a flying camp, I wish they were here.[28] I would answer for our possessing Barcelona in a fortnight and of putting them in a situation to *attrape* more than twice their number of the enemy. Excuse the scratches and rents in this epistle, but I have been up all night, writing a description of the present state of Catalonia for the Chief, no trifling affair. Adieu, kindest love to you all, ever most affectionate and dutifully,

George.

Notes

1 Frances, his elder sister b. 1773, who married Lord Charles Fitzroy, second son of the third Duke of Grafton in 1795. Walpole was possibly the Hon. Thomas Walpole (1727–1803), friend of the third Duke of Grafton, a City magnate with connections with a Lisbon banking house. Sir John Caldwell (1756–1830), fifth baronet of Castle Caldwell, co. Fermanagh and lieutenant colonel of the Fermanagh militia. His first wife was Harriet Meynell, Mundy's aunt.

2 Sir John Hort, first baronet of Castle Strange, co. Middlesex. He had been consul general at Lisbon in 1767.

3 His elder brother, Godfrey Basil (1776–1848), lieutenant in the Third Dragoon Guards, the King's Own, 23 December 1795, he was promoted to captain 24 August 1797. In 1801 he married Sarah, youngest daughter of Admiral Lord Rodney and was the author of the first biography of his father-in-law, published 1826.

4 Sir Roger Newdigate (1719–1806), fifth baronet of Arbury, co. Warwick, founder of the Newdigate Prize for English Poetry in the University of Oxford. Hester Miller Mundy, George Mundy's aunt, was his second wife.

5 Four prizes were taken at the Battle of Cape St Vincent: the *Salvador del Mundo* (112), the *San Josef* (112), the *San Nicholas* (80) and the *San Ysidro* (74).

6 France and Spain had signed the first treaty of San Ildefonso 19 August 1796 but Spain did not declare war on Britain until 8 October. An increasingly reluctant French ally, though Spain made threats against Portugal she did nothing more positive at this time.

7 Created Earl St Vincent 23 June 1795.

8 Rear-Admiral William Parker had joined Jervis on 6 February, with five sail of the line. He was created a baronet 24 June 1797 for his part in the battle. The *Ville de Paris* (110) was the largest ship in the British fleet.

9 A slop or quarantine ship held infectious seamen, a receiving ship held men recently pressed or joined before they were allocated to other vessels. A surgeon's duties, properly performed in such ships, were frequently onerous. In 1795 the Commissioners for the Care of Sick and Wounded Seamen, commonly called the Sick and Hurt Board, consisted of Dr R. Blair, Dr J. Weir, Dr J. Johnstone, Sir W. Gibbons, the only non-medical commissioner, and Sir Gilbert Blane, the distinguished physician, recently appointed by Lord Spencer.

10 Jervis's exacting professional standards and reputation as a disciplinarian were well known. He considered the Royal Naval Academy a 'sink of vice and abomination' so Mundy might not have expected to find favour with him.

11 The Spanish fleet, between twenty-six and twenty-eight sail of the line, was under the command of Admiral Masseredo. Jervis cruised off Cadiz from 4 April to 19 May. In early July, in an unsuccessful attempt to force the Spaniards out, he twice bombarded the port.

12 In February there had been a financial crisis when the Bank of England suspended payments in gold. The mutiny among the Channel fleet at Spithead broke out on 15 April.

13 His father's unmarried sister, Nelly Mundy.

14 The hazardous in-shore position for blockading Brest, where Collingwood had served under Admiral Cornwallis 1803–5.

15 The Battle of Trafalgar, news of which had only just been received in London on 5 November.

16 Pitt's attempts to form a coalition against France with Austria, Prussia and Russia, in the autumn of 1805, were shattered by Napoleon's victory at Austerlitz on 2 December.

17 Josiah Nesbit Willoughby (1777–1849), lieutenant 13 January 1798, post captain 5 September 1810. He was appointed to H.M.S. *Prince* 11 August 1805. When Admiral

Duckworth was sent to the eastern Mediterranean, flying his flag in H.M.S. *St George*, Willoughby was appointed lieutenant to her, 15 January 1807.

18 Part of an undated and unaddressed letter, written between February and April 1809.

19 A derisive Spanish term for French sympathisers.

20 Several captains maintained a band. Hallowell did so on H.M.S. *Courageux* in 1796, Thomas Fremantle had hopes of acquiring one in 1805 though he found musical instruments too expensive, and Collingwood had one of 'twelve very fine performers' in 1807. The Neapolitans probably learnt the national anthem when Naples was a British ally and Nelson's ships were often there.

21 In the spring of 1809, war between France and Austria again seemed possible. The Cabinet were considering whether to send forces to northern Europe or the Scheldt to divert French attention from the Danube. Sir John Moore, commander of the British army in the Peninsula since August 1808, was killed at Corunna, 16 January 1809, covering its evacuation. Sir Arthur Wellesley landed in Portugal as commander of British forces there, 22 April 1809.

22 The *Cyane* (26) was assigned to cruise off the Italian coast from June 1809.

23 The reference is obscure. The colonel of the King's Own or third regiment of dragoons was William Cartwright. Godfrey Mundy had been promoted to lieutenant-colonel 2 July 1803.

24 His younger brother, born 1778, rector of Windlestone, co. Durham 1803–46.

25 William Radford, born 1780, entered the Navy 1803 as an A.B., midshipman in 1805, joined *Hydra* in 1807. He was captured in a felucca he had helped to take and remained a French prisoner until 1815 when he was promoted lieutenant.

26 His eldest brother, Edward (1774–1834) married Nelly Barton, possibly his cousin, in 1800. Their third son, Alfred, was born 9 January 1809.

27 The Nottinghamshire estate of the Duke of Newcastle. The Duchess was Mundy's half-sister by his father's second marriage. She married the fourth duke in 1807.

28 In 1808, hearing of Napoleon's occupation of Madrid and Moore's retreat to Corunna, the British government attempted to secure Cadiz as a base in southern Spain. In January 1809 a force of 4,000 men was sent from England for this task but the Central Junta rejected the idea and the troops eventually returned to Lisbon. There had been suggestions that this force be sent to take Barcelona.

Bibliography

Fremantle, A. (ed.), *The Wynne Diaries*, 3 vols., II (London: OUP, 1937), III (London: OUP, 1940).

James, W., *The Naval History of Great Britain*, 6 vols. (London: Harding, Lepard & Co., 1837).

Lloyd, C., and Coulter, J. L. S., *Medicine and the Navy 1200–1900*, 4 vols., III, *1714–1815* (London: Williams & Wilkins, 1961).

Marshall, J., *Royal Naval Biography*, 12 vols., II (London, 1824).

Newnham Collingwood, G. L. (ed.), *A Selection from the Public and Private Correspondence of Vice-Admiral Lord Collingwood*, 4th edn (London, 1829).

O'Byrne, W., *A Biographical Dictionary of Naval Officers*, 3 vols. (London, 1849).

8

Documents Relating to the Copenhagen Operation, 1807

Edited by
A. N. RYAN

Introduction

The British operation against the city and naval dockyard of Copenhagen in August–September 1807, which ended in the seizure of the Danish fleet, is of interest to historians on both sides of the North Sea.[1] Some of the abundant documentary evidence is already in print. On the British side it includes private correspondence between Lord Mulgrave, first lord of the Admiralty,[2] Viscount Castlereagh, secretary of state for war and the colonies,[3] and the commanders of the land and sea forces, General Lord Cathcart[4] and Admiral Gambier,[5] concerning particularly the government's belated decision to attempt a permanent occupation of the Danish island of Zealand.[6] On the Danish side there is a rich collection of material, printed by the general staff, dealing with the situation on Zealand and inside Copenhagen during the campaign, which reveals the insuperable problems facing the defenders.[7]

The purpose here is to print other correspondence, both public and private, which is essential for an understanding of the origins and conduct of the operation. It contains George Canning's[8] hurried scrawl in the early hours of 22 July 1807 to Granville Leveson-Gower, the British ambassador to Russia,[9] reporting the receipt of intelligence 'directly from Tilsit' about the proposed creation by France and Russia of an anti-British maritime league to which the northern powers and Portugal would either consent, or be compelled to adhere [document 10]. Later, when asked in parliament to disclose the grounds on which it had violated Denmark's neutrality, the government claimed to have had private information concerning secret engagements in the Franco-Russian treaty of Tilsit 'to employ the navies of

Denmark and Portugal against this country' and refused to disclose its source for fear of endangering the informant.[10] In fact by 22 July preparations for drastic action against Denmark were already well advanced [6, 7, 8, 9]. The decision to send a fleet to the northern seas had been taken no later than 14 July; the decision to employ an army, no later than 17 July, the day on which the first written allusion was made to the possible seizure of the Danish navy.[11]

These decisions had not been prompted by a single item of information, but by a variety of considerations: the allegedly forward state of the Danish men-of-war,[12] the reported strength of anti-British sentiments at Copenhagen, the vigorous Danish protests, through J. G. Rist, *chargé d'affaires* in London, against the British order-in-council prohibiting trade between one enemy port and another (January 1807) and the blockade of the Elbe estuary (March 1807) and, more recently, the possible consequences of the Russian defeat at Friedland (14 June 1807), including the prospect of a continental peace to be followed by the alignment of Denmark, through force or persuasion, against Great Britain [1, 2, 3, 4, 5]. Some pieces of the jigsaw of intelligence were defective and some were missing; but, such as it was, it yielded when assembled so menacing a picture of the state of Denmark that it looked like a playback of 1801.[13] As for the missing pieces, a careful search seemed entirely inappropriate. If the navy had to go in, it had to go in with time in hand to complete its mission before winter edged across the Baltic and drove the warships back to their bases in Britain.

The interlocking timetable of the initial military and diplomatic moves, with an alarm system set to go off on the expiration of a fixed number of days, freed the commanders from uncertainty as to their actions should any restraint be placed upon the persons of the diplomats or should communications with them be interrupted [12]. The first step in the operation was the isolation of Zealand, Copenhagen and the naval dockyard from the rest of the Danish dominions through the occupation of the Great Belt by a powerful squadron in the early days of August [7, 8, 16, 20, 21]. Simultaneously Francis James Jackson[14] arrived at Kiel, where the prince royal of Denmark was in residence, and presented the Danes with choices of alliance with Britain, a condition of which would be the deposit of the fleet in British hands, the voluntary surrender of the fleet or its forcible removal. Once the Danes rejected Jackson's demands, the fate of their fleet was sealed, for the disparity in the strengths of the opposing forces in and around Zealand were such that prolonged resistance was out of the question. The British were able to throw in over 16,000 regular troops from England and another 10,000 hastily withdrawn from the island of Rugen, where they had recently arrived under Cathcart to assist Britain's ally Sweden in the defence of Swedish Pomerania [9]. The defenders of Copenhagen numbered 5,500 regular troops, six battalions of the Zealand *landevaern*, the citizen militia and the student corps: a total of about 13,000 regulars and auxiliaries.[15] Zealand was weakly defended because the bulk of the regular Danish army was stationed on the Holstein frontier as a pledge of Denmark's determination to defend her neutrality against the French.[16]

The British army landed unopposed at Vedbaek, north of Copenhagen, on 16 August and moved steadily towards the investment of the city, the only remotely effective resistance being the harassment of its left wing by Danish gunboat flotillas operating in the shallow coastal waters [21, 22, 28, 30]. Investment led, after an appeal to surrender had been rejected, to bombardment and bombardment to capitulation on 7 September [26, 27, 30]. Under the terms of the capitulation the Danes agreed to surrender the fleet; the British, to evacuate Zealand 'as soon as the ships shall have been removed or within six weeks of the date of this capitulation'. The agreement to evacuate gave rise, when it became known in London on 16 September, to a flurry of activity designed to achieve its reversal and a permanent occupation of Zealand.

There is no doubt that the government was shocked by the Danish declaration of war, of which it had learned on 4 September, and the terms of the capitulation. It was all the more sensitive on these subjects, because during the operation it had made a series of miscalculations. To judge from their actions, ministers had been more confused than enlightened by the dramatic intelligence of 22 July from Tilsit. It seems, in retrospect, that the obvious conclusions to be drawn from it were that a hostile confederation was in the making which would bring on a maritime war in the Baltic with Denmark likely to make common cause, as in 1801, with France and Russia. The commanders, however, were left with the impression that their task was to return as soon as possible with the Danish fleet as a trophy. Castlereagh, it is true, made tentative inquiries on 3 August about the possibility of holding Zealand; but on 27 August he dispatched conditional instructions for the early return of part of the forces with the intention, as we now know, of employing them in a similar operation at Lisbon [24, 25, 28]. Since this dispatch was in their hands when the capitulation was being drawn up, the commanders were under some pressure to terminate the operation as quickly as possible. In any case the naval and military officers, including Sir Arthur Wellesley, commander of the reserve, did not believe that the forces available could hold Zealand, especially as the protective screen of warships in the Great Belt was likely to be broken up by the northern winter [23].

The operation was therefore finally wound up in October with the Danish fleet in British possession, but with the stage set for an all-out maritime war in the Baltic with Denmark and Russia in the ranks of the enemy.

THE COPENHAGEN OPERATION, 1807

1 *Unsigned and undated memorandum by Captain Dunbar, R.N.*[17]

On my first going to Copenhagen in December 1806 the state of the Danish fleet immediately struck me; and I reported it to Mr Garlike[18] by letter which I know was sent at the time to Lord Howick[19] and afterwards to Mr T. Grenville.[20] On my return to England in January *both* had been received, for Mr Grenville observed to me that I laid much stress upon the Danish fleet. I told him I could assure him that they were 20 sail-of-the-line, 12 frigates, mostly first class and a proportion of sloops, which the Danes told me could be ready in less than a month. They were obviously much more ready for commission than ours are when reported to receive men. I think I saw and reported five new floating batteries and many gunboats building. Many of the former had even their mortars in. These I noticed and on hinting it only to Captain Grover (whose duty it was to attend to my wants and who held a situation in the Admiralty) he observed, 'My dear sir, these are meant to oppose the Swedes in Norway and the junks (meaning the batteries) are to receive stores in the manner the one does alongside your ship'. This attempt at disguise could not escape me. Indeed so desirous were the Danes to get me out of dock and out of the way that they worked by torchlight all night for five nights and even during mealtimes when fresh hands were employed.

On my return to Copenhagen in May following, no less than seven sail-of-the-line had been docked in the *only dock* they have and it takes three days to pump the water out each time. The *Waldemar* was rigged, Lindholm to command her to take the Duchess of Weimar to Russia; all the flotilla and praams rigged and *all this in May*, the marine batteries greatly strengthened and exercised every day. Not a step had been taken to equip proper vessels (such as small frigates and sloops) to cruise in the Belt and keep out the French, while nothing had been left undone to hasten the kind of vessel most fit to oppose the English.

In all companies in which I was, it clearly appeared to me they had at that time determined to side with France. The pilot, who is no small man there, declared to me when I parted that in *20 days* the whole fleet could be ready if required.

It may be material to observe that on seeing Grover a second time, in going up to Memel, it was with the utmost reluctance he allowed me to go into the arsenal.

2 *Canning to Gower*

9 June 1807

. . . The occasion of dispatching a messenger to Copenhagen is a complaint . . . against the style and tone which Mr Rist's notes have lately assumed and, as I am almost afraid, not without the special instruction of his court.[21] It is, however, much best to take it as the indiscretion of the individual, in the first instance, rather than as the ill-disposition of the government. If the allies have gained a victory when our messenger reaches Copenhagen, Mr Rist will be disavowed and recalled. In the contrary event, I suppose he will be supported and I must look for a tedious controversy here to be terminated by nothing but a peace (which God forbid) or a fleet in the Baltic. But it was really impossible to bear Mr Rist any longer without affording ground for a suspicion that we were half-beaten already. And I am afraid the disposition at Copenhagen is so unfriendly as to want nothing but the appearance of being able to insult us with impunity to break out into open defiance. Such too seemed to be Lord Pembroke's[22] impression in a few lines which I had from him yesterday, written after he had been almost 4 and 20 hours at Copenhagen.

3 *Thornton[23] to Canning*

Received 10 July 1807   Altona,
                                                          1 July 1807

. . . Within these few days, and on yesterday more particularly, a very general idea has got into circulation that some demand has been made to the court of Denmark by the French minister at Copenhagen relative either to the occupation of Altona and Glückstadt, as being depots for English merchandise and the residence of persons disagreeable to the French government, or to the more general occupation of the duchies and to the exclusion of the English commerce and navigation from their other ports. I have had private intimations sent to me from persons, of whose good intentions I cannot have the smallest doubt, though I might suspect the accuracy of their intelligence or the firmness of their nerves, and the latter still more, if the apprehension had existed only within these few days and had been excited by recent events. But I have been informed from a perfectly authentic source that about a month ago some pressing orders were sent to the French minister at Copenhagen from Bonaparte's headquarters; and insinuations relative to their contents, similar to those above mentioned, were thrown out by M. Bourrienne.[24]

However this may be, His Majesty's government must be prepared to look forward, in any event of a continental peace or even of a continental armistice dictated by Bonaparte and depending upon his will, to the occupation of the duchy of Holstein and to the exclusion of the English navigation and to deliberate upon such measures as remain absolutely within the power of England to secure a footing upon the rest of the Danish dominions and a connection through them with the continent of Europe. Under this point of view I should regard the arrival at Stralsund, even at this hour, a very considerable body of English troops as a fortunate and most desirable circumstance. And the co-operation of Sweden with the acquiescence of Russia (in case the latter should be obliged to make a continental peace not absolutely hostile to us) would render the Danish islands and the northern kingdoms of the Baltic absolutely invulnerable to the attack of the French . . .

4 Thornton to Canning

Received 12 July 1807

Altona,
5 July 1807

. . . There is some variation after all in the account of the courier [bearing a letter dated Tilsit, 29 June 1807, from Alexander I of Russia[25] to the hereditary prince of Mecklenburg-Schwerin] whether the messages of Bonaparte related to an armistice or an interview with the emperor of Russia. The latter certainly took place in the middle of the Niemen in the first instance and afterwards at Tilsit where the emperor came accompanied by his officers and the first regiment of his guards. Two days after this interview the king of Prussia also had an interview with Bonaparte and (as the courier declares) the two sovereigns were at Tilsit with Bonaparte when he was dispatched.

5 Thornton to Fitzharris[26]

Received 12 July 1807

Altona,
5 July 1807, 11½ o'clock p.m.

. . . The reports (but I have already observed that they are *but* reports and from no very high authority) are that France will hardly be induced to treat with England, but will concede everything to Germany; but though I think it appears plain from the emperor's own phrases in his letter to the hereditary prince *(l'heureux rapprochement entre l'empereur des français et moi)* that peace is resolved on, I cannot so well think that at the first instant Russia will abandon her allies.

6 Castlereagh to the Lords Commissioners of the Admiralty

Downing Street,
18 July 1807

The unfortunate events which have recently taken place in the north of Europe and which have led to an armistice between Russia and France, and the avowed designs of the enemy, by the unrestrained exercise of his power in contempt of the rights of neutral nations, to exclude as widely as possible His Majesty's subjects from all intercourse with the continent, have determined His Majesty forthwith to send a fleet into the Baltic; and I am to convey to you the king's pleasure that your lordships do instruct the officer in the chief command of the said fleet to direct his attention on his arrival in those seas to the following objects:

Firstly to cooperate with His Majesty's ally the king of Sweden for the security of his dominions.

Secondly to protect any reinforcements which it may be necessary to send to Pomerania or to cover the return of His Majesty's troops in the event of its being thought expedient to withdraw them from thence.

Thirdly to secure against all annoyance the large mass of British property which is now afloat in the Baltic and to reserve to this country an uninterrupted intercourse and supply of naval stores from the Baltic.

I am also to convey to your lordships the king's pleasure that you do direct the officer in the chief command of the above fleet to obey such orders as His Majesty may from time to time command me to convey to him for the direction of his conduct in the service on which he is employed.

7   Castlereagh to the Commander-in-Chief of His Majesty's in the Baltic

Downing Street,
19 July 1807

In addition to the orders which you have received from the lords commissioners of the Admiralty I have received the king's commands to convey to you the following instructions, most secret, for the direction of your conduct on your arrival in the Baltic.

In the present predominant state of the power of France on the continent, and exposed as a principal part of the Danish dominions are to the grasp of the enemy, His Majesty cannot but entertain the most anxious apprehensions that the maritime power, position and resources of Denmark may shortly be made the instrument in the hands of France not only of excluding our commerce from the Baltic and of depriving us of the means of naval equipment, but also of multiplying the points from which an invasion of His Majesty's dominions may be attempted under the protection of a formidable naval force.

However painful it is to His Majesty's mind to distrust the future conduct of any neutral power, in justice to the clearest interests of his own dominions His Majesty feels himself irresistibly compelled to adopt adequate measures of vigilance and precaution till he can be fully assured that the power of Denmark may not be made the means of inflicting a most fatal blow against the interests of this country.

His Majesty feels himself additionally compelled to adopt this line of conduct from the state of forward equipment in which the Danish navy has been of late kept and which can alone [be] done in contemplation of being compelled by France at no distant period to adopt a course of conduct which must involve her in hostilities with Great Britain.

Under these circumstances His Majesty feels it necessary as a measure of precaution to authorise you to prevent the Danish government from sending any military reinforcements into the island of Zealand from any other parts of the Danish dominions till you receive further instructions from home, it being of the utmost consequence in the event of a rupture with that power that the island in which the Danish naval arsenal is situated should not be strengthened to such a degree as might place it beyond the reach of a combined attack by His Majesty's sea and land forces.

It is probable the Danish government upon the arrival of your fleet in the Baltic, more especially should you have occasion to carry this instruction into execution, may be induced to accelerate the equipment of their fleet for sea.

His Majesty, anxiously wishing to avoid, if possible, any unnecessary act of hostility or rigour towards this power, directs that you do give no interruption to frigates and lighter vessels, still less to the trade sailing to and from the Danish ports, unless you should have reason to suppose they are employed in carrying troops to Zealand in breach of the measures of precaution above directed to be taken; but should any Danish ships-of-the-line attempt to put to sea, as it can only be with an intention of giving interruption to the regulations you are ordered to enforce, you will in the first instance aforesaid represent in the most amicable manner to them of the necessity of their returning into port; and upon refusal it will be your duty to consider their proceeding to sea as intended for purposes hostile to His Majesty's interests and you will in that case use your best exertions to capture or destroy them.

8 *Castlereagh to Gambier*

Downing Street,
19 July 1807

In executing the instructions conveyed to you in my letter of this date, marked most secret, it is of importance to the king's service that the measures of precaution therein enjoined to be adopted should be understood by the Danish government as proceeding in the first instance from yourself and not as having been previously authorised by the government at home.

. . . Should you be pressed to declare the grounds on which you have thought fit to give any interruption to the passage of troops going to

Zealand or to visit vessels which you may suspect to have troops on board, you will declare that, from the intelligence you have received, you have the strongest reason to believe France is determined immediately to force Denmark to act hostilely against Great Britain; that under these circumstances you feel yourself called upon (as a measure of precaution) to object to her altering the existing distribution of her army or fleet, but that in the execution of this determination you are anxious to avoid any hostile proceedings, that you will confine yourself, in the first instance, to causing any vessels you may meet with troops on board to return into port and will only proceed to detention upon their persisting in the attempt to pass over into Zealand; and you may at the same time express your earnest hope that, until communication can be had with England, the Danish government will not permit its troops to make any movement which might give occasion to any unpleasant occurrences between the forces of the two powers.

9   *Castlereagh to Cathcart*

Downing Street,
19 July 1807

. . . Admiral Gambier has been ordered to proceed forthwith to the Baltic with a powerful and numerous fleet; and a land force consisting of the regiments stated in the margin [in all 16,700 troops] will follow as speedily as they can be embarked. The co-operation of the British troops now at Stralsund is deemed so indispensable to the effectual execution of this service that His Majesty feels himself called upon, however reluctantly, lest any prejudice might thereby be occasioned to the interests of His Majesty's ally the king of Sweden,[27] to order the troops now at Stralsund to be forthwith embarked and to proceed with the least practicable delay under your lordship's command to the rendezvous which Admiral Gambier will point out and where you will be joined by the land forces from hence, the whole to assemble under your lordship's command.

Mr Pierrepont[28] will be instructed to confide to the king of Sweden personally, in the strictest confidence the general nature of the service which has compelled His Majesty at this moment to call for the assistance of that corps which, under different circumstances, he had, with so much satisfaction to himself, placed at the disposal of His Swedish Majesty. But that no premature alarm at Copenhagen may be created, it is material that the ostensible cause of the re-embarking the corps should be understood to be with a view to their return to England.

His Majesty is persuaded the king of Sweden will feel the interests of his crown not less concerned than those of His Majesty that the power of France should not be interposed at the entrance of the Baltic between His Majesty and his allies. Were France enabled to turn the maritime resources of Denmark against Great Britain, they would beyond all question soon be directed with not less malignity against Sweden.

It is also satisfactory to His Majesty to reflect in withdrawing his troops that the late extension of his subsidiary engagements with the king of Sweden will have furnished His Swedish Majesty with an ample garrison (namely 14,000 effective men) for the defence of the fortress of Stralsund and that any advantage that might have resulted from the services of the British troops, in enabling the king of Sweden to undertake a forward movement, has unfortunately been terminated by the facility which France will now have, in consequence of her armistice with Russia and Prussia, of rendering her army decisively superior on the frontiers of Pomerania.

10   *Canning to Gower*

Foreign Office,
21 July 1807

. . . If it be true, as we hear from all sides, that Bonaparte has determined upon occupying Holstein and ultimately forcing the Danes to take part against us, we have not much time to waste in speculation, but must take measures of vigilance and precaution without delay. My dispatch, enclosing Taylor's[29] instructions, will lead you to look for a fleet in the Baltic. It will sail, I hope, tomorrow, some two and twenty sail-of-the-line. The language which you will hold about it will be the same as is suggested in the dispatch to Taylor. But I think you will find no disposition in Russia to question the propriety of an act, which, if they continue to hold opinions respecting the designs and conduct of Denmark like those which their minister at Copenhagen has been professing for the last three or four months, they may censure as tardy (as they do all our measures) but cannot consider as violent or unprovoked. Indeed I am of opinion that the measure has been deferred too long; but we must now make it effectual . . .

22 July 1807

Since I concluded my letter to you at two o'clock this morning I have received intelligence which appears to rest on good authority, coming directly from Tilsit, that, at a conference between the emperor of Russia and Bonaparte, the latter proposed a maritime league against Great Britain to which Denmark and Sweden and Portugal should be invited or forced to accede. The emperor of Russia is represented not indeed to have agreed to the proposition but not to have said anything against it. He preserved a profound silence which is attributed in the report made to me to the presence at the conference of persons before whom he probably would not like to open himself. I think it right to give notice to you [of] this information; but it is strictly in confidence for your excellency alone, as the knowledge of it would infallibly compromise my informer. If this be true our fleet in the Baltic may have more business than we expected. Ascertain the facts, if possible, and write by the quickest mode; and by more than one.

11   *Garlike to Canning*

Copenhagen,
27 July 1807

Enclosure:

Hanchett[30] to Garlike

2 May 1807

. . . The generality of the ships appear to be in good repair. The frigates and smaller vessels are coppered, excepting the schooner and the sloops. Four of the line-of-battleships are coppered from the keel to within about six feet of the line of floatation. The others have no copper on. All the vessels have their ballast in and spars of every description on each side of the lower deck. No other stores of any kind are on board them.

Their rigging, sails, guns, etc., are all complete but in storehouses in the dockyard. The floating batteries have their guns mounted. You may place confidence in this report, as I have not only been in the holds of some of them, but have seen their stores of every description in their respective places in the dockyard.

12   *Castlereagh to Cathcart*

Downing Street,
29 July 1807

(Copy to Gambier)

The troops enumerated in the margin of my letter to your lordship of the 19th inst., having been embarked in four divisions at Hull, at Harwich, at the Nore and in the Downs, are ordered to proceed under their respective convoys and to assemble off Elsinore under the protection of His Majesty's fleet, which has already preceded them to the entrance of the Sound.

It is to be hoped that, by the time the several divisions above alluded to shall have been concentrated off Elsinore, or at such other anchorage as the admiral may have chosen, that the troops from Stralsund will also have arrived in conformity to the orders forwarded to your lordship to this effect on the 19th inst., duplicates of which were sent to Lord Rosslyn.[31]

I am now to convey to your lordship the king's pleasure with respect to the ulterior measures to be adopted by your lordship and which you will proceed to carry into execution, without waiting for the whole of your forces being collected, so soon as your lordship may deem the force actually assembled under your orders fully adequate to the effectual accomplishment of the proposed service.

His Majesty has thought fit to send a minister properly accredited to Kiel, where the crown prince[32] now is, there to enter into such explanations with the Danish government as are considered applicable to the present conjuncture, and upon the result of which must depend how far His Majesty may hope to receive that degree of security with respect to the conduct of Denmark which, in justice to the safety of his own dominions, he considered it indispensable to require.

But while His Majesty is anxious to avail himself of any opening which may afford a prospect of Denmark being prevailed on to enter into such amicable arrangements as His Majesty might deem satisfactory, it is necessary, where so much is at stake and where the difficulty of vindicating in case of necessity his own rights may be so much increased by delay, to guard against the consequence of an excessive forbearance by adopting such precautionary measures as may be adequate to the exigency and importance of the case.

So soon therefore as your lordship considers yourself in sufficient force to effect a landing and to proceed, if necessary, to the attack of Copenhagen, you will apprise His Majesty's minister, Mr Taylor, of the same and Mr Taylor will be instructed, upon receiving such notification from your lordship, if he has reason to suppose that the Danes are taking measures either for improving the defences of Copenhagen, for equipping their fleet, for assembling any part of the militia of the island [Zealand] or for receiving reinforcements of regular troops from the army in Holstein, to represent to the Danish government on the spot that, although a mission has been sent from the king to Kiel in the confident hope that every ground of jealousy or distrust between the two powers may be amicably adjusted, yet that, until it is distinctly ascertained that these friendly overtures have been met on the part of the Danish government with corresponding dispositions, the instructions under which His Majesty's naval and military forces act will not allow of their witnessing with indifference military preparations carrying forward which may eventually be directed against them; that he is therefore compelled to declare that, unless the government of Copenhagen will immediately agree to suspend all military and naval preparations within the island of Zealand, including any efforts to organise or assemble the militia or to pass reinforcements of troops into the same from their continental provinces, it will be the duty of those to whom the command of His Majesty's forces has been entrusted immediately to effect a landing and to proceed to acts of hostility both by land and sea.

Should on the contrary the Danish government be disposed to desist from any species of preparation and be prepared to afford to those entrusted with the care of His Majesty's interests satisfactory proofs that it is not their intention to convert that period, which His Majesty is anxious to appropriate to the friendly discussion of mutual interests, to hostile preparations, the officers in the command of His Majesty's forces will abstain from any act which can be painful to the feelings of the Danish government and will await their decisions (if not unduly protracted) upon the proposition which His Majesty's minister dispatched to Kiel has been instructed to open on the part of the Danish government, with an anxious hope that the result may confirm and improve the friendly connections between the two states.

Mr Jackson, to whom the mission to Kiel has been entrusted, has been directed to bring the Danish government to an explicit decision with the least possible delay and to apprise you of the result by the most expeditious channel of communication. Time is in itself of so much value in the successful execution of the service with which you are charged, more especially as the difficulties, which our fleet and army could have to encounter, would be much increased were operations against Copenhagen to be protracted to a late season of the year, that it becomes indispensable to bring the whole question to an issue within the shortest practicable space of time. It is therefore indispensably necessary not only to guard in the manner above mentioned against any hostile preparations being carried on within the island of Zealand in presence of His Majesty's land and naval forces, but also to provide for the case of any interruption being given to the execution of the mission with which Mr Jackson is entrusted.

Should your lordship therefore have any well-grounded reason to suppose that any constraint has been put on Mr Jackson's person, or any interruption given to his intercourse with Mr Taylor at Copenhagen, your lordship will in that case consider yourself authorised to proceed, in conjunction with His Majesty's naval forces, to the immediate reduction of Copenhagen and the seizure of the Danish fleet.

I am further to convey to your lordship the king's commands that, in the event of no communication whatever being received at Copenhagen from Mr Jackson within eight days of his landing at Tonningen (of the precise times of which measures have been taken for informing your lordship), you are in that case to consider this circumstance in itself as affording so strong a presumption that the means of communication have been denied to His Majesty's negotiator by the Danish government as to call on your lordship's part, as a further measure of precaution, for the immediate landing of the army; but you will in that case notify the Danish government that it is not done with a view to immediate hostilities, provided no measure either of preparations or hostility be taken on their part. But should your lordship, after the landing of your army in sufficient force to undertake hostile operations, still remain at the expiration of twelve days of Mr Jackson's landing at Tonningen without any information from that minister that the demands of the British government have been acceded to, your lordship will forthwith proceed to hostilities unless the Danish government on the spot should agree to the immediate removal of the Danish fleet to a British port, to be restored, in case of amicable surrender, to the Danish government upon a peace.

I cannot conclude without recommending your lordship the most cordial and confidential intercourse with the officer to whom His Majesty has entrusted the chief command of the fleet destined to co-operate with your lordship in this important service.

13 *Taylor to Gambier*

Copenhagen,
2 August 1807

I have the honour to acknowledge the receipt of your letter of the 1st inst., in answer to which I have to acquaint you that I was this morning introduced to Count J. Bernstorff[33] who declared to me that he could not hold any official communication with me until I had presented my credentials to His Danish Majesty, which he supposed would not be before Friday next [7 August]. The cause of this delay is owing to the necessity of referring to the prince royal, who resides at present at Kiel, as well as the Danish minister, Count Bernstorff's brother.[34] I thought it right however to state to Count J. Bernstorff that, however unwilling I felt to depart from established forms, that having received His Majesty's commands since my arrival at Copenhagen to demand an immediate conference of the Danish minister in consequence of some intelligence of importance which had been received by His Majesty's government, viz. that a proposal for a maritime league against Great Britain had been made by Bonaparte to Russia, I could not omit that opportunity of requesting that he would inform me whether any proposition of this nature had been made to their court. Count J. Bernstorff immediately declared to me distinctly that no such proposition had been made to Denmark by France or by any other power whatever and that he could assure me that this was the first time he had heard this report.

The declaration made to me by Count J. Bernstorff that he could not immediately communicate officially with me persuaded him also, I imagine, from adverting to the subject of the presence of His Majesty's fleet under your command in the Baltic.

With respect to General Bernadotte's[35] army, the nearest of the enemy to the frontiers of Holstein, I have been assured that it is not in sufficient force to cause any immediate apprehension to the Danes of his march into that country.

14 *Castlereagh to Gambier*

Downing Street,
3 August 1807

. . . I should wish to know, regard being had to the temper of the inhabitants of Zealand and the means of keeping any naval forces in the Baltic, even of the lighter description, to watch the Belt in the winter, how far the permanent occupation of that island can be looked to as practicable and with what extent of means it might be rendered tenable against France in possession of the adjacent ports; first upon the supposition of the Danes being parties to its defence, secondly of the Swedes being put in possession of it as a security for the restoration of Swedish Pomerania and thirdly of our attempting to hold it ourselves as a position commanding the entrance to the Baltic . . .

15   *Gambier to Pole*[36]

Elsinore,
4 August 1807

I herewith transmit to you for their lordships' information a copy of a letter from Captain Beauman[37] of the *Procris* to Benjamin Garlike, Esq. reporting the state of the Danish navy at Copenhagen.

Enclosure:

Beauman to Garlike

Procris, off Elsinore,
25 July 1807

I have the honour to inform you that in pursuance of your wishes I this day inspected the dockyard and ships at Copenhagen. I found lying there in a state of ordinary 18 sail-of-the-line − one of 90, two of 80, eleven of 74 and four of 64 guns; one of the 80s rigged, all the rest with their lower masts and part of their ballast in; eleven frigates from 40 to 30 guns each, ten sloops, seven of which are brigs, four floating batteries of 24 guns and several small gunboats of one and two guns each; three 74s building of which one I think may be launched in three months, another in about five or six months, the other at a very distant period.

I went on board the greater part of the line-of-battle ships and found them in the most perfect state of repair; their rigging, sails, etc., etc., all fitted and each ship's stores placed separate in the storehouses in the completest order. There is not the most trifling article for fitting a fleet wanting, everything in the best possible condition. And I am of opinion the whole of the Danish fleet might with the greatest ease, provided they had seamen, be at sea in six weeks from the commencement of their equipment. There are two of the 74s and two 64s rather old, but by no means in a state to prevent them going to sea. They are all fine men-of-war. There is an abundance of timber and every species of stores in the dockyard.

I observed they were constructing rafts for the purpose of sinking on the ground and in the harbour, one of which is finished. It is built similar to a cat, the middle part of which is to contain the ballast for sinking. It stands always with three points upwards and should a ship strike on it, it will be scarcely practicable for her to disengage herself. It is built exceedingly strong and pointed at the end of each leg with heavy sharp iron. These rafts, I am informed, began building immediately after the battle of 2 April 1801.

I beg you will not conceive from this statement that I mean to insinuate that a fleet is fitting out at Copenhagen. To the best of my judgement and belief there is not the least sign of any unusual or active preparation. From what I could learn it has been the usual state of the fleet ever since Lord Nelson's battle of the 2nd of April. And I may venture to assert there is not at present the shadow of appearance for the equipment of a fleet, as it is impossible it could be hid from the eye of any naval officer.

16   Gambier to Pole

Prince of Wales, Elsinore,
4 August 1807

I have the satisfaction to acquaint you for the information of the lords commissioners of the Admiralty of my arrival at this anchorage yesterday with the ships and vessels named in the margin [*Prince of Wales, Pompée, Captain, Spencer, Maida, Brunswick, Ruby, Dictator, Hercule, Alfred, Goliath, Centaur, Cumbrian, Surveillante, Thunder, Fury, Zebra, Vesuvius, Halcyon, Sappho, Combatant, Forward, Minx, Turbulent*].

A statement of the disposition of the fleet under my command accompanies this letter which, together with the enclosed copies of my orders to Commodore Keats[38] will give their lordships full information on my proceedings.

I have thought it right under the present circumstances to order the vessels that were stationed at Kiel for the purpose of carrying dispatches from thence to Memel to join me, the necessity for which their lordships will not fail to see.

Enclosure 1:

Instructions by Gambier to Keats

27 July 1807

You are hereby required and directed to take the ships and vessels named in the margin [*Vanguard, Orion, Nassau, Franchise, Sybil, Nymphe, Cossack, Leveret, Alert, Mosquito, Goshawk, Alacrity, Acute, Tygress, Urgent, Desperate*; since added, *Superb, Dictator, Ruby* (recalled), *Leda, Banterer, Combatant, Halcyon, Procris, Sappho, Fearless, Turbulent, Flamer, Mariner, Intelligent*] under your command and, when the signal shall be made for you to part company on the service appointed, you are to proceed with them into the passage called the Great Belt and place them in the most advantageous stations for intercepting all vessels that may attempt to pass into the island of Zealand, or the islands contiguous thereto, from the opposite shores, taking such position with the ships-of-the-line at the entrance of the Belt from the Baltic as you may judge most effectual for protecting the frigates and small vessels therein from any of the Danish ships-of-war that may attempt to resist or oppose the service which you are hereby directed to carry on.

And whereas it is of the utmost importance towards the attainment of the object for which the fleet under my command is employed that no troops or other reinforcements of men whatsoever shall be suffered to land in the islands abovementioned, you are to direct the commanders of the ships and vessels under your orders to board every vessel passing the Belt and, if the officers who board such vessels shall find any troops or any considerable number of men on board them, above the compliments necessary to navigate them, which may serve to reinforce the troops on the island of Zealand, they are to desire the masters of such vessels to return to the ports whence they came; and if they should refuse to do so and persist in passing to Zealand, or any other of the islands contiguous thereto, the vessels are to be detained and the men put on board the larger ships under your command until you shall have acquainted me therewith and received my directions for their further disposal.

You are to give the most positive directions to the captains and commanders of the ships and vessels under your command not to molest or intercept any trading or fishing vessels belonging to Danish subjects which may be passing the Belt, provided they shall not be found as abovementioned carrying troops or other reinforcements of men to the islands aforesaid, but, on the contrary, you are to afford them every assistance they may stand in need of.

As you will without doubt already understand the object of the service on which you are employed, you will take care to give directions to the captains and commanders under your orders to cause a most vigilant look-out to be kept, rowing guard in the nights and using all other precautions to carry effectually into execution the purposes of this order.

During your employment on the above service you are to use your endeavours to obtain the best information respecting the Danish forces and transmit to me the earliest intelligence thereof. You are also, as often as possible, to communicate your proceedings to me and inform me of the precise stations which you may assign to the several ships.

Enclosure 2:

Instructions by Gambier to Keats

30 July 1807

In addition to my orders of the 27th instant you are hereby required and directed in case you should meet with any Danish frigates or smaller vessels of war not to give them any interruption, unless they shall appear to be employed in carrying troops to the island of Zealand or the islands contiguous thereto, in which case you are to proceed with them in the manner prescribed in my orders aforesaid. But if any Danish ships-of-the-line should oppose your carrying my orders into effect, you are in the most amicable manner to desire their commanders to return into port; and if they shall refuse to do so you will use your utmost endeavours to capture or destroy them.

17   Canning to Gower

Speaker's Chamber, House of Commons,
5 August 1807

. . . Now surely, if that combination is so far advanced, if, as I believe, it is eventually stipulated for in the Russian treaty, the consenting to go into a negotiation at once under the Russian mediation, without asking a question or betraying any of that jealousy which we must be known to feel, would be so like a confession of being beaten − which we are not − or at least frightened, which I think we need not be, as to ensure the demand of all the sacrifices and the imposition of the hardest terms which we can possibly be called upon to agree, even after an unsuccessful struggle.

At the same time you may be assured (and my former letters will have contributed to assure you) that I have no passionate or unreasoning objections to negotiation – nothing like it, though I think the Russian mediation the most inauspicious mode of negotiating to which we could be compelled. It is in fact only a contrivance to bring the maritime question into discussion with two to one against us. A direct negotiation with France singly might not avoid that question; but it would at least not bring it against us with the weight of an authority pretended to be impartial, but really inimical . . .

But at the present moment I really do not think the acceptance of it would have been justifiable, even with the Danish fleet on our coasts – and less with ours in the Baltic.

You may judge with what anxiety we wait the result of our expedition. Succeed or not, I am satisfied we should have deserved to lose our heads if we had not attempted it; and, as far as naval and military exertions go, I think everything has been done to ensure success, if unfortunately the previous negotiation should not prevent the necessity of having recourse to hostility. I had written that I am afraid the failure of our negotiation was too probable. But that is *not my* opinion. I think the presence of such an armament may produce an acquiescence – a very cheerful one certainly not – but an acquiescence that will save extremities.

Do not fail to let the emperor know that this armament, one of the most formidable I believe ever left this country, was prepared with other views and would have been applied in a manner to afford the allies the most benevolent assistance. And do not let us forget that it is not *our* fault that it was not ready sooner . . .

18   *Gambier to Pole*

Prince of Wales, off Elsinore,
7 August 1807

. . . The *Leyden* and *Inflexible* are this moment arrived and many of the transports under their convoy are already at anchor, the rest working up.

19   *Gambier to Castlereagh*

Prince of Wales, off Elsinore,
8 August 1807

I yesterday received the honour of your lordship's private letter of the 30th July with the copy of the instructions to Lord Cathcart.

Everything has been prosperous with us hitherto and there is every appearance of its continuance. All the accounts we receive agree in stating that there are not more than 5,000 men at most in Zealand, exclusive of the militia. No movements whatever have been made with the troops in Holstein; and, if they were to attempt to embark, I trust the number of ships and vessels I have stationed in the Belt will completely obstruct their passage. Mr Nicholas[39] arrived here last night and brought letters to me from Mr Jackson allowing [sic] the time proposed to expire before we begin our operations. Friday next [14 August] is the day fixed for landing the army, which I have no doubt we shall be able to do without any opposition at the most favourable spot. Lord Cathcart is not yet arrived here, but I look for him every moment. The northerly wind, which brought the transports through the Cattegat [Kattegat] has delayed him on his passage. The weather has been the most favourable for the transports that could be and we now have 15,400 troops present. The Danish government took alarm the moment it was known that some of our ships were in the Belt. The arrival of the transports has caused an alarm among the people of the country today. The works at Copenhagen are strong towards the sea, but we have so much zeal and activity among us that I hope by God's help to overcome every obstacle that may be opposed to us.

20   Gambier to Pole

Prince of Wales, Elsinore,
10 August 1807

I have the honour to transmit you herewith for the information of the lords commissioners of the Admiralty a copy of a letter which I have this instant received from Commodore Keats and anticipate the satisfaction their lordships must feel from the squadron under the commodore's orders having, by means of his judicious precautions, passed up the Belt without meeting with the slightest accident. And I have no doubt that the surveys and remarks, which the commodore has directed to be made, will prove a valuable acquisition to our knowledge of the navigation of that passage.

Enclosure:

Keats to Gambier

Ganges,
9 August 1807

I have the honour to inform you of the arrival of the ships and vessels named in the margin (*Ganges, Vanguard, Orion, Mosquito, Desperate, Urgent*) off Dars Head [Darsser Ort], having disposed of the others conformable to your directions and according to the accompanying statement [not here]. No accident whatever was experienced in the passage of the Great Belt or other delays than what unavoidably arose from calms, light or contrary winds and currents; which latter particularly affected and considerably retarded the ships-of-the-line, whilst its operation on smaller vessels was scarcely perceptible. Some advantage was derived from a pilot obtained by the *Desperate* at the Grass Holmes who accompanied us to Aysborg, where three others of little knowledge were procured to the south end of Langeland. But the services of Captain Jackson[40] of the *Mosquito*, who with three active gunbrigs preceded the squadron and marked, without occasioning the smallest delays, most of the banks and projecting shoals, were highly useful and advantageous.

The charts with which we were supplied, though not always correct, were very serviceable. The navigation is far from difficult, cannot anywhere be commanded by cannon and is abundantly spacious for any fleet. And when the surveys and remarks, which I have enjoined the different captains to cause to be made at such times as they are not occupied on the more important of their instructions, shall be collected, I apprehend the whole navigation of the Belt may be laid down with extreme conciseness. The principal difficulty appeared to me to arise from currents, the set and velocity of which being frequently a few fathoms down very different from what it is on the surface, resists in large ships particularly the effect of the helm and sometimes, in what we think very commanding breezes, renders them quite unmanageable.

21   *Gambier to Pole*

Prince of Wales, Elsinore,
14 August 1807

Since my letter of the 7th instant by the *Orestes* I have been joined by the ships and vessels named in the margin [*Minotaur,* Rear-Admiral Essington,[41] *Mars, Valiant, Defence, Hussar, Africaine, Astraea, Comus, Bonnette, Pelican, Lightning, Tartarus, Aetna, Richmond, Indignant, Safeguard, Gallant, Gloria, Quail, Pigeon*] and have transmitted orders by the *Pelican*, which I have sent with Mr Garlike to Memel, for the *Valorous, Arrow* and *Surly* to leave their station off Danzig and join me without delay.

Having sent occasional reinforcements to Commodore Keats, the force now under his orders consists of six sail-of-the-line, seven frigates, seven sloops and nine gunbrigs, stationed as described in the enclosed copy of the disposition he has sent me [not here]. Having received intelligence that the enemy is about to embark troops at Rostock for the purpose of attacking Rugen, I have sent the commodore this information directing him, if he shall ascertain it to be true, to station vessels off that port to prevent their sailing.

Lieutenant-General Lord Cathcart arrived here on the 12th instant in the *Africaine*. And the *Dispatch, Bellette, Paulina* and *Mutine* are appointed to convoy the British troops from Rugen to this place. The *Rosamund* is to remain in Port (Peerd) Bay to attend Mr Pierrepont . . .

22 *Gambier to Castlereagh*

Prince of Wales, in the Sound, Off Wibeck [Vedbaek],
16 August 1807

I have the honour to inform your lordship that Lieutenant-General Lord Cathcart joined me off Elsinore on the 12th instant. Every disposition being made for the disembarkation of the army, the service was intended to be carried into execution on the evening of the 14th instant, but the wind not allowing the transports to move towards Copenhagen, it was not till last evening that I arrived off Wibeck, a village situated about midway between Elsinore and Copenhagen. And at this place the army was disembarked this morning without the smallest opposition.

23 *Gambier to Castlereagh*

Prince of Wales, off Copenhagen,
20 August 1807

I have received the honour of your lordship's letter of the 5th [*sic*] instant, which I have communicated to Lord Cathcart, and lose no time in making my reply to the several points on which your lordship desires my opinion . . .

The Belt and other passages with the Cattegat are so liable to be filled with large masses of ice in winter, and sometimes frozen over, so that the navigation of them, which is at all times difficult, is during the greater part of that season altogether impracticable.

To keep possession of the island of Zealand appears to me to require a much larger army than that which His Majesty has at present before Copenhagen. Indeed, so far as I am capable of forming an opinion on this subject, I do not think it practicable by any means that Great Britain possesses to defend the island against the immense bodies of troops which France might bring against it . . .

24 *Castlereagh to Cathcart*

Downing Street,
27 August 1807

Since my dispatch to your lordship of the 3rd instant intelligence has been received with regard to the designs of the enemy of such a nature as to make it necessary for me, without waiting for the report of your operation in the Baltic, to send your lordship, with a view to save time, such conditional orders for the direction of your conduct as may be applicable to the case hereafter supposed.

In conveying to your lordship His Majesty's pleasure you are to understand that the execution of these orders is not to be suffered to interfere with the effectual accomplishment of the important service on which your lordship has been employed. Subject to this reservation, the application of which to the state of circumstances as may exist on the spot is left to your lordship's discretion, I have to acquaint your lordship that it is deemed of the highest importance to His Majesty's service that at least 10,000 men and, if possible, one half of your whole corps, reckoning your force at 25,000 men, should be detached with the utmost possible expedition with a view to a particular service, this force to proceed to the Downs there to receive further orders.[42]

In selecting the particular corps to be detached, I am to desire your lordship will include the Brigade of Guards and the Light Brigade under the orders of Major-General Sir A. Wellesley.[43] The selection of the other regiments is left to your lordship's discretion to be decided according to circumstances.

You will send back as large a proportion of the engineers' and artillery equipment as you may deem prudent and also of the cavalry tonnage. The latter point is of particular importance in order that a considerable proportion of the horse transport may be applicable to the intended service.

It is also of great moment, with a view to the embarkation of the troops to be employed from hence in conjunction with those which your lordship is ordered to detach, that you should send home such a proportion of the troop and store ships, now in the Baltic, as can be spared consistently with the retaining the necessary means of embarking and bringing away the remainder of the troops and horse when requisite.

In carrying this part of my instructions into execution, I have to request that your lordship will take into consideration what number of troops can be conveniently brought away in His Majesty's ships of war and also in the Danish line-of-battle ships, assuming them to be placed at our disposal, presuming that the crews of our men-of-war must be weakened in order to navigate the Danish ships, their capacity of carrying troops for so short a distance will be proportionately increased . . .

The above instructions, as your lordship will perceive, are framed upon the supposition that the main object of the expedition to Copenhagen has been accomplished, either by consent or force, without the necessity of protracted operations against the place. Should this happily have been the case although His Majesty's ministers are prepared to expect that the equipment and removal of the Danish fleet may require some time in execution and that it may be highly imprudent to look to the completion of this service except under the protection of a commanding naval and military force, yet they do entertain a confident hope that in the event of the removal of the Danish fleet having been previously decided, it will not be requisite (more especially if the Belt continues to be guarded by the lighter cruisers) to retain the same amount of force to complete the service as it was originally considered expedient to employ in order to enforce, if necessary, compliance with His Majesty's demands . . .

25 *Castlereagh to Gambier*

Downing Street,
27 August 1807

I have the honour to enclose for your information the copy of a dispatch which by the king's command I have addressed to Lord Cathcart and I am to convey to you His Majesty's pleasure that you do co-operate with his lordship in carrying the instructions therein contained into execution.

I am further to signify to you that the pressing demands for naval force, connected with the state of affairs to which the above instructions relate, render it highly desirable that you should detach six or seven sail-of-the-line with such proportions of frigates as can be conveniently spared to act in conjunction with the force which it is proposed to employ on a particular service, subject however to the same discretion which has been confided to his lordship with respect to the army, namely that this detachment shall not interfere with the effectual execution of the service with which you have been already charged by my former orders.

I am further to state that the return of the naval and military force to England should be considered as resulting from the services in the Baltic being deemed no longer requisite and not from their being destined to any ulterior service.

26 *Gambier and Cathcart to Peymann*[44]

British H.Q., before Copenhagen,
1 September 1807

We, the commanders-in-chief of His Majesty's sea and land forces now before Copenhagen, judge it expedient at this time to summon you to surrender the place for the purpose of avoiding the further effusion of blood by giving up a defence which, it is evident, cannot be long continued.

The king, our gracious master, used every endeavour to settle the matter now in dispute in the most conciliatory manner through his diplomatic servants.

To convince His Danish Majesty and all the world of the reluctance with which His Majesty finds himself compelled to have recourse to arms, we the undersigned, at this moment when our troops are before your gates and our batteries ready to open, do renew to you the offer of the same advantageous and conciliatory terms which were proposed through His Majesty's ministers to your court.

If you will consent to deliver up the Danish fleet and to our carrying it away, it shall be held in deposit for His Danish Majesty and shall be restored with all its equipment in as good state as it is received as soon as the provisions of a general peace shall remove the necessity which has occasioned this demand.

The property of all sorts, which has been captured since the commencement of hostilities, will be restored to the owners and the union between the United Kingdom of Great Britain and Ireland and Denmark may be renewed.

But if this offer is rejected now, it cannot be repeated. The captured property, public and private, must then belong to the captors and the city, when taken, must share the fate of conquered places.

We must request an early decision because in the present advanced position of the troops, so near your places, the most prompt and vigorous attack is indispensable and delay would be improper.

27   Peymann to Gambier

Copenhagen
1 September 1807

Our fleet, our own indisputable property, we are convinced is as safe in His Danish Majesty's hands as ever it can be in those of the king of England as our master never intended anything against yours.

If you are cruel enough to endeavour to destroy a city that has not given any the least cause to merit such a treatment at your hands, it must submit to its fate. But honour and duty bid us reject a proposal unbecoming an independent power. And we are resolved to repel every attack and defend to the utmost the city and our good cause for which we are ready to lay down our lives.

The only proposal in my power to make in order to prevent further effusion of blood is to send to my royal master for learning his final resolution with respect to the contents of your letter if you will grant passports for this purpose.

28   Gambier to Castlereagh

Prince of Wales, Copenhagen Road,
5 September 1807

I have received the honour of your lordship's letter of the 27th ult. directing me to send home some of the ships-of-the-line under my command, if in so doing it should not interfere with the effectual execution of the service with which Lord Cathcart and myself are charged. In the present state of our operations here and the uncertainty of our getting possession of the Danish fleet, I am sorry it is not in my power immediately to comply with this discretionary direction. If the Danes do not destroy their ships before the town is surrendered, it will require the whole of the force now with me to equip and navigate them to England. But the moment I can spare any ships from hence, I shall not fail to fulfill His Majesty's commands.

The bombardment of Copenhagen, which was the unavoidable

consequence of General Peymann's refusal to comply with the terms proposed to him, as mentioned in my letter of the 2nd instant, commenced with great activity and effect on the evening of the same day and has continued, with occasional interruptions, ever since. The city was set on fire very soon after the batteries were opened and has continued burning in different parts. For the last two days the conflagration has been very considerable and at this moment rages with great violence.

29   *Castlereagh to Cathcart*

Downing Street,
5 September 1807

Since my instructions to your lordship of the 27th August intelligence has reached this country that a formal declaration of war has been issued by the Danish government, accompanied by letters of marque and reprisal against the ships and property of His Majesty's subjects.

These proceedings on the part of the Danish government appear to His Majesty not only to have essentially changed the ground on which the former instructions was [*sic*] given but to preclude the possibility of any final pacification being concluded between the two crowns without previous reference home or fresh powers being given to that effect; it being concluded that the full powers entrusted to Mr Jackson on his departure from hence have been vacated[?] by the declaration of war so made by the court of Denmark.

Under these circumstances, referring to my dispatch to you of the 3 August with respect to the importance which is attached by His Majesty's government in the event of force being had recourse to and the unconditional surrender of the fleet being required, I am to convey to you the king's pleasure that in any capitulation you may hereafter enter into, you do confine yourself to the surrender of the Danish fleet and fortress of Copenhagen as a military question falling strictly within your province and that of Admiral Gambier as commanders-in-chief of His Majesty's military and naval forces to decide on; but that you do refer any other points to be discussed between the two crowns to Mr Jackson who is instructed not to conclude and sign any treaty with the Danish government which shall not be subject to the subsequent approbation of his own court.

Should you have concluded any capitulation with the Danish commander previous to the receipt of this dispatch, His Majesty will be disposed to give effect to the stipulations therein so far as the terms may be compatible with the state of war in which the two powers have been placed towards each other by the act of the Danish government above referred to. But it is desirable that the final execution of any such capitulation should await His Majesty's further orders.

30 *Gambier to Pole*

Prince of Wales, Copenhagen Road,
7 September 1807

The communications which I have already had the honour to transmit to you will have made the lords commissioners of the Admiralty acquainted with the proceedings of the fleet under my command down to the 2nd instant. I have now to add that the mortar batteries, which had been erected by the army in the several positions they had taken round Copenhagen, together with the bomb-vessels which were placed in convenient situation, began the bombardment on the evening of this day with such power and effect that in a short time the town was set on fire and, by the separate discharges of our artillery, was kept in flames in different places till the evening of the 5th, when, a considerable part of it having been consumed and the conflagration having arrived at a great height threatening the speedy destruction of the whole city, the general commanding the garrison sent out a flag of truce desiring an armistice to afford time to treat for a capitulation. After some correspondence had passed between the Danish general and Lord Cathcart and myself certain articles were agreed upon, of which I have the honour to transmit you a copy.

From these their lordships will perceive that all the Danish ships and vessels of war (of which I enclose a list), with the stores in the arsenal, were to be delivered up to such persons as should be appointed to receive them on the part of His Majesty. I accordingly appointed Sir Home Popham[45] for this purpose; and having made the necessary arrangements for equipping them with the utmost dispatch, I have committed the execution of this service to Vice-Admiral Stanhope[46] in whose ability and exertions I can place the fullest confidence. As few of the ships are in any considerable progress of equipment, it will require some time to complete them for sea, but not a moment will be lost in bringing the whole of them to England.

[*Marginal note:* 16 September. To be inserted in the Gazette Extraordinary except the words within   .]

I am happy on this occasion to express the warm sense I entertain of the cordial co-operation of the army by whose exertions, with the favourable concurrence of circumstances, under divine providence, ever since we left England, our ultimate success has been more immediately obtained. I would also convey to their lordships in terms of the highest approbation and praise the conspicuous zeal and earnest endeavours of every officer and man under my command for the accomplishment of this service. And, although the operations of the fleet have not been of a nature to afford one a general and brilliant occasion for adding fresh testimony to the numerous records of the bravery of British seamen and marines, yet the gallantry and energy displayed by the advanced squadron of sloops, bombs, gunbrigs, etc., which were employed under the command of

Captain Puget[47] to cover the operations of the left wing of the army from the Danish flotilla, ought not to be passed over in silence. I have beheld with admiration the steady courage and arduous exertion with which, on one occasion in particular, they sustained for more than four hours a heavy and incessant cannonade with the Danish batteries, blockships, praams and gunboats in a situation where, from the shallowness of the water, it was impossible to bring any of the larger ships to their support . . .

31 *Canning to Gower*

Foreign Office,
2 October 1807

. . . I will not enter with you at large into the question of peace. But I will fairly state my opinion to you that there never was a moment at which it was less attainable nor [*sic*] less desirable, though I feel a thousand times less objection to it now than I did before the success of the expedition.

A peace in the making of which our maritime rights should have been questioned, would have utterly undone this country, stamped with ignominy the characters of those who made it. Yet before the Copenhagen operation, could we have hoped to have avoided these questions? Would they not have formed the very basis of any negotiation into which Bonaparte would have consented to enter? With a northern confederacy formed against us, we should have had to contend with fears at home as well as with the enmity of all Europe (for we must not disguise the fact from ourselves – we *are* hated throughout Europe and that hate must be cured by *fear*); not to mention America who will *now* probably listen to reason.

We have now, what we have had once before and once only, a maritime war in our power unfettered by any considerations of whom we may annoy or whom we may offend. And we have (what would to God poor Pitt had ever resolved to have) determination to carry it through. Not but what we have croakers enough amongst our own circle – not in the cabinet but in those around it. But we do not listen to Sturges-Bourne[48] and, thank God, Lord Carrington[49] is in opposition, and so is Lord Auckland.[50]

32 *Canning to Gower*

Hinckley,
5 November 1807

. . . I am by no means surprised or angry at your feeling some little disappointment in the evacuation of Zealand. I wish we could have kept it; *could,* morally, that is to say – that our commanders had not admitted the article stipulating to evacuate into the capitulation; *could*, physically or militarily speaking, but against that the opinions of our officers, both by land and sea, was so peremptory that no government could publicly have taken upon itself to act in contradiction to them. I am not without suspicion that the prospect of an uncomfortable service had not something to do in framing their opinions. The article of the capitulation certainly was admitted at a time when they thought us indifferent to the retaining the island and when they were under orders to send home as soon as possible a considerable part of their force with a view to another operation. That operation was Lisbon.

Notes

1 C. T. Sørensen, 'Den Politiske Krise i 1807', *Dansk Historisk Tidskrift*, I (vi) (1887–8); J. Holland Rose, 'Canning and Denmark in 1807', *English Historical Review,* xi (1896); Rose, 'Canning and the Secret Intelligence from Tilsit', *Transactions Royal Historical Society*, new series, xx (1906); E. Møller, 'England og Danmark – Norge i 1807', *Dansk Historisk Tidskrift, VIII* (iii) (1912); W. F. Reddaway, 'Canning and the Baltic in 1807', *Baltic Countries*, ii (1936); C. J. Kulsrud, 'The Seizure of the Danish Fleet, 1807', *The American Journal of International Law*, xxxii (1938); A. N. Ryan, 'The Causes of the British Attack upon Copenhagen 1807', *E.H.R.,* lxviii (1953); Ryan, 'The Navy at Copenhagen in 1807', *Mariner's Mirror,* 39 (1953); Sven Trulsson, 'Canning, den hemliga Kanalen till förhandlingarna i Tilsit oeh invasionsföretaget mot Köpenhamn 1807', *Scandia*, 29 (1963); Trulsson, *British and Swedish Policies and Strategies in the Baltic after the Peace of Tilsit in 1807* (Lund, 1976). For the impressions of a participant see W. G. Perrin (ed.), 'The Bombardment of Copenhagen, 1807: The Journal of Surgeon Charles Chambers of H. M. Fireship *Prometheus', The Naval Miscellany (Vol. III)*, Navy Records Society, Vol. 63 (1928), pp. 367 ff.
2 Henry Phipps, 1st Baron Mulgrave of Mulgrave (1755–1831) entered politics as a follower of William Pitt to whom he became a military adviser; first lord of the Admiralty, 1807–10; 1st Earl of Mulgrave and Viscount Normanby, 1812.
3 Robert Stewart, Viscount Castlereagh (1769–1822) was secretary of state for war and the colonies from March 1807 to October 1809; secretary of state for foreign affairs, 1812–22.
4 William Schaw Cathcart, 10th Baron Cathcart (1765–1843) served in the wars of the American and French revolutions; lieutenant-general, 1801; 1st Viscount Cathcart, 1807; ambassador and military commissioner with the Russian army, 1812–14; Earl Cathcart, 1814; ambassador to Russia, 1814–21.
5 James Gambier (1756–1833), described by William Dillon as 'a strictly devout, religious man, bordering upon the Methodist principles', was a nephew of Margaret Middleton (née Gambier), wife of Lord Barham; lieutenant, 1777; captain, 1778; rear-admiral, 1795; vice-admiral, 1799; admiral, 1805; admiral-of-the-fleet, 1830. Commanded the *Defence* (74) on 1 June 1794; commander-in-chief and governor of Newfoundland, 1802–4; member of Board of Admiralty, 1795–1801, 1804–6, 1807–8; raised to the peerage, November 1807.
6 Lady Georgiana Chatterton, *Memorials Personal and Historical of Admiral Lord Gambier: Edited from Family Papers*, 2 vols. (London: Hurst & Blackett, 1861), ii, pp. 42 ff.; *Correspondence, Dispatches and Other Papers of Viscount Castlereagh, Second Marquess of Londonderry: Edited by His Brother Charles, Marquess of Londonderry*, 2nd series, 12 vols. (1848–53), vi, pp. 176 ff.

7 Dansk Krigsministerium, *Meddelelser fra Krigsarkiverne*, utg. af Generalstaben, ii and iii (Copenhagen, 1887–8).

8 George Canning (1770–1827), secretary of stage for foreign affairs, March 1807–October 1809 and September 1822–April 1827; president of the board of control, 1816–21; prime minister, April–August 1827.

9 Granville Leveson-Gower (1773–1846), ambassador extraordinary to Russia, 1804–5 and 1807; 1st Viscount Granville, 1815; ambassador to France, 1824–41; 1st Earl Granville, 1833.

10 Wendy Hinde, *George Canning* (London : Collins, 1973), p. 171. For evidence pointing towards Prince Adam Czartoryski, a former Russian foreign minister, as the informant, see Trulsson, *Scandia* (1963), and Trulsson, *British and Swedish Policies and Strategies*, pp. 41–2.

11 Mulgrave to George III, 14 July 1807; Castlereagh to George III, 17 July 1807, A. Aspinall (ed.), *The Later Correspondence of George III*, 5 vols. (Cambridge: CUP, 1968), iv, pp. 604–7.

12 As early as 30 December 1806, Viscount Howick, then foreign secretary, had written to Benjamin Garlike, ambassador to Denmark, that 'you will not neglect to transmit the earliest intelligence of any preparation which may seem to be made with a view to resist the power of England rather than that of France' (FO 22/49). For reports on the Danish navy which suggest that it was not in as advanced a state of preparation as the British government believed, see documents **11, 15** and especially, **30**.

13 The best study of Denmark's role in the anti-British northern confederation, backed by France and Russia, of 1801 is Ole Feldbaek, *Denmark and the Armed Neutrality, 1800–1801: Small Power Policy in a World War* (Copenhagen, 1980).

14 Francis James Jackson (1770–1814) had held a number of diplomatic posts including that of minister in Berlin (1802–6); ambassador to the United States of America, 1809–10.

15 J. T. von Raeder, *Danmarks Krigs-og Politiske Historie fra Krigens Udbrud i 1807 til Freden i Jonköping den 10 December 1809*, 2 vols. (Copenhagen, 1845), i, pp. 83 ff.

16 E. Holm, *Danmark – Norges Udemrigske Historie under Den Franske Revolution og Napoleons Krige fra 1791 til 1807*, 2 vols. (Copenhagen, 1875), ii, pp. 269 ff.

17 James Dunbar (1770–1836), commander of the *Astraea* (32) employed in the transport of diplomatic missions, 1806–7; lieutenant, 1790; captain, 1802; knighted, 1810; baronet, 1814.

18 Benjamin Garlike (died 1815) was ambassador to Denmark, 1805–7.

19 Charles Grey, Viscount Howick (1764–1845), secretary of state for foreign affairs in the Grenville ministry, September 1806 – March 1807; 2nd Earl Grey,1807; prime minister, 1830–4.

20 Thomas Grenville (1755–1846), first lord of the Admiralty, September 1806–March 1807.

21 J. G. Rist, Danish *chargé d'affaires* in London, was the spokesman for Denmark's case in the conflict with Britain over neutral and belligerent rights, 1807.

22 George Augustus Herbert, 11th Earl of Pembroke (1759–1827), lieutenant-colonel, 1783; M.P. for Wilton, 1784–94; served in Flanders, 1793–4; travelled via Copenhagen on a special mission to Vienna, 1807; general, 1812. F. J. Jackson comments upon the importance attached by Canning to the impressions formed by Pembroke ('An Account of the Last Two Months of My Life . . . October 1807', F. O. 353/56).

23 Edward Thornton (1766–1852), resident in the Hanse towns and ambassador to the Circle of Lower Saxony, 1805–7; ambassador to Sweden, 1808 and 1812–17; ambassador to Brazil, 1819–21; to Portugal, 1823–4; G.C.B., 1822.

24 Louis Antoine Fauvelet de Bourrienne (1769–1834) was French minister to the Hanse towns.

25 Alexander I (1777–1825) succeeded his father, Tsar Paul, as tsar of Russia,1801; concluded the treaty of peace and alliance, including secret clauses, with Napoleon at Tilsit, 7–9 July 1807.

26 James Edward Harris, Viscount Fitzharris (1778–1841), under-secretary of state for foreign affairs, March–August 1807; 2nd Earl of Malmesbury, 1820.

27 Gustavus IV Adolphus (1778–1837) succeeded as king of Sweden after the murder of his father, Gustavus III, in 1792. Autocratic and unstable he was dethroned in 1809 and became a stateless wanderer known variously as Count Gottorp and Colonel Gustafsson; died at St Gall.

28 Henry Manvers Pierrepont (1780–1851), ambassador to Sweden, 1804–7.

29 Brook Taylor (1776–1846) received orders on 21 July 1807 to replace Garlike at Copenhagen and to survey the situation there; ambassador to Württemberg, 1814–20; to Bavaria, 1820–8; to Prussia, 1828–30; G.C.H., 1822.

30 John Martin Hanchett, lieutenant, 1804; commander, 1807; captain, 1809; said by W. L. Clowes, *The Royal Navy : A History from the Earliest Times to the Present* (London : Sampson Low, 1900), v, p. 272n. to have been reputed a natural son of the future George IV.

31 James St Clair Erskine, 2nd Earl of Rosslyn (1762–1837), commissioned, 1778; major-general, 1798; lieutenant-general, 1805; 2nd in command to Cathcart; general, 1814.

32 Frederik, crown prince or prince royal of Denmark, was regent during the insanity of his father, Christian VIII; succeeded as King Frederik VI, March 1808; died 1838.

33 Joachim Bernstorff, the Danish foreign minister.

34 Christian Bernstorff, the Danish minister of state; elder brother of Joachim.

35 Jean Baptiste Jules Bernadotte, later King Charles XIV John of Sweden, (1763–1844) was at this stage of his long and remarkable life commanding a French army in northern Germany. Neither Taylor nor the Danes could know that on 2 August Napoleon sent conditional instructions to Bernadotte for an invasion of Holstein (*Correspondance de Napoléon Ier* (Paris, 1864) xv, p. 467.

36 William Wellesley-Pole (1763–1845), second son of the 1st Earl of Mornington, was secretary to the Admiralty, 1807–9; succeeded to the earldom of Mornington, 1842.

37 Francis Beauman, lieutenant, 1796; commander, 1805; captain, 1807.

38 Richard Goodwin Keats (1757–1834), lieutenant, 1777; captain, 1789; rear-admiral, September 1807; K.B., 1808; later appointments included the governorships of Newfoundland and of Greenwich Hospital; vice-admiral, 1811; admiral, 1825.

39 Edward Nicholas, lately vice-consul and *chargé d'affaires* at Hamburg.

40 Samuel Jackson, lieutenant, 1796; commander, 1801; captain, 5 November 1807; C.B., 1815.

41 William Essington, lieutenant, 1777; commander, 1781; captain, 1783; rear-admiral, 1804; vice-admiral, 1810.

42 See exchange of correspondence between Castlereagh and George III, Aspinall, *op. cit.,* pp. 620–2.

43 Major-General Sir Arthur Wellesley (1769–1842), later Duke of Wellington, commanded the reserve in the Zealand operations; was influential in persuading the government to abandon the idea of permanent occupation of Zealand.

44 Ernst Peymann, a 73-year-old general of engineers, was commander-in-chief of the land forces defending Copenhagen.

45 Sir Home Riggs Popham (1762–1820), captain-of-the-fleet in the Copenhagen operation; lieutenant, 1783; commander, 1794; captain, 1795; achieved fame and notoriety through unauthorised attack on Buenos Aires, 1806; rear-admiral, 1814.

46 Henry Edwin Stanhope, lieutenant, 1777; commander, 1779; captain, 1781; rear-admiral, 1801; vice-admiral, 1805; admiral, 1810.

47 Peter Puget, commander of the *Goliath* (74); lieutenant, 1790; sailed with Vancouver and gave his name to Puget Sound; captain, 1797; C.B., 1819; rear-admiral, 1821; died, 1822.

48 William Sturges-Bourne (1769–1845), a lord of the treasury, 1807–9; commissioner for the affairs of India, 1814–22; home secretary, April–July, 1827.

49   Robert Smith, 1st Baron Carrington (1752–1838), MP for Nottingham, 1779–97;
     a friend and private financial adviser of William Pitt.
50   William Eden, 1st Baron Auckland (1744–1814) negotiated Anglo-French
     commercial treaty, 1786; ambassador at the Hague, 1790–3; joint postmaster
     general, 1798–1804; president of board of trade, 1806–7.

List of Documents and Sources

All these documents are in the Public Record Office.

1	Memorandum by Captain Dunbar	Undated	FO 22/52
2	Canning to Gower	9 June 1807	PRO 30/29/8/4
3	Thornton to Canning	1 July 1807	FO 33/38
4	Thornton to Canning	5 July 1807	FO 33/38
5	Thornton to Fitzharris	5 July 1807	FO 33/38
6	Castlereagh to Lords Commissioners of the Admiralty	18 July 1807	WO 6/14
7	Castlereagh to C-in-C. of H.M. Squadron in the Baltic	19 July 1807	WO 6/14
8	Castlereagh to Gambier	19 July 1807	WO 6/14
9	Castlereagh to Cathcart	19 July 1807	WO 6/14
10	Canning to Gower	21 July 1807	PRO 30/29/8/4
11	Garlike to Canning	27 July 1807	FO 22/52
	Enclosure: Hanchett to Garlike	2 May 1807	
12	Castlereagh to Cathcart	29 July 1807	WO 6/14
13	Taylor to Gambier	2 August 1807	WO 1/187
14	Castlereagh to Gambier	3 August 1807	WO 6/14
15	Gambier to Pole	4 August 1807	ADM 1/5
	Enclosure: Beauman to Garlike	25 July 1807	
16	Gambier to Pole	4 August 1807	ADM 1/5
	Enclosure 1: Instructions to Keats	27 July 1807	
	Enclosure 2: Instructions to Keats	30 July 1807	
17	Canning to Gower	5 August 1807	PRO 30/29/8/4
18	Gambier to Pole	7 August 1807	ADM 1/5
19	Gambier to Castlereagh	8 August 1807	WO 1/187
20	Gambier to Pole	10 August 1807	ADM 1/5
	Enclosure: Keats to Gambier	9 August 1807	
21	Gambier to Pole	14 August 1807	ADM 1/5
22	Gambier to Castlereagh	16 August 1807	WO 1/187
23	Gambier to Castlereagh	20 August 1807	WO 1/187
24	Castlereagh to Cathcart	27 August 1807	WO 6/14
25	Castlereagh to Gambier	27 August 1807	WO 6/14
26	Gambier and Cathcart to Peymann	1 September 1807	WO 1/187
27	Peymann to Gambier	1 September 1807	WO 1/187
28	Gambier to Castlereagh	5 September 1807	WO 1/187
29	Castlereagh to Cathcart	5 September 1807	WO 6/14
30	Gambier to Pole	7 September 1807	ADM 1/5
31	Canning to Gower	2 October 1807	PRO 30/29/8/4
32	Canning to Gower	5 November 1807	PRO 30/29/8/4

9

The Letters of Midshipman E. A. Noel, 1818–1822

Edited by
ERIC POOLE

Introduction

Edward Andrew Noel, the writer of these letters, was born on 2 January 1802. His mother, Diana Noel, was the only daughter of Vice-Admiral Sir Charles Middleton, who in 1805 became Admiral of the Red Squadron and First Lord of the Admiralty and was elevated to the peerage as first Lord Barham. His father, Gerard Noel Noel, nephew and co-heir of Henry Noel, the last earl of Gainsborough of the original creation, succeeded to his father-in-law's baronetcy on the death of Lord Barham in 1813, while Diana Noel succeeded to the peerage as Baroness Barham. Edward was their eighteenth, and youngest, child. He joined the Navy in August 1816, and served in H.M.S. *Eridanus* from then until June 1817, when he transferred to H.M.S. *Tigris*, being paid off from that ship in January 1818. In the following April he entered H.M.S. *Liverpool*, a vessel of the fourth rate, with 50 guns, and it was during his five years' service in this and other ships on the East Indian station that the letters were written, mostly to his mother and to his sister Julia, but including a few of a more formal nature to his mother's cousin, Captain Robert Gambier Middleton of the Navy Office in London.

Some account needs to be given of others of the children of Sir Gerard Noel Noel and Lady Barham:

(a) Charles, the eldest, born in 1781, was created earl of Gainsborough in 1841. He married four times, but only his second and third marriages need to be mentioned here. The former was on 13 May 1817, to Elizabeth, daughter of Sir George Grey, baronet. She died on 20 September 1818 shortly after bearing her first and only child, Charles George Noel. She is referred to by Edward as 'my sister Bessy', and her death evidently caused him much grief. It is from her that the present earl of Gainsborough is descended. The third marriage, on 29 June 1820, was to Arabella, daughter of Sir James Williams of Clovelly, baronet. After bearing five children she also died, shortly after giving birth to the last of them in 1829.

(b) Gerard Thomas Noel, born in 1782, married Charlotte Sophia O'Brien, the daughter of Sir Lucius O'Brien of Dromoland, in 1806.

(c) Emma Noel, born in 1788, married Stafford O'Brien in 1808. He was the son of Henry O'Brien of Blatherwycke Park, Northamptonshire, and a third cousin of Charlotte Sophia O'Brien.

(d) Augusta Julia Noel, born in 1796, married Thomas Gisborne Babington in 1814. They lived at Holly Hill, Hampstead, and had three daughters, Augusta, Julia and Louisa. Julia, who was born about 1818, is mentioned in the letters. She died in 1831.

(e) Juliana Hicks Noel ('Julia') was born in 1800 and was Edward Noel's favourite sister and the recipient of many of the letters. She was unmarried at this time, but married the Reverend Samuel Phillips in 1834, dying a few months before her husband in 1855.

All the signs are that Lady Barham was a person of imperious character and a harsh piety, and it is hardly surprising that she and her husband were living apart, or that he re-married less than four weeks after her death. She had moved to Fairy Hill, on the Gower Peninsula, shortly after her father's death in 1813. There seems no doubt that she was able to maintain a tight, and even cruel, emotional grip on her son, whether he was at home or on the other side of the world. His letters to her are filled with lengthy protestations of affection, most of which have had to be excised from this collection for reasons of space and of consideration for the reader's patience, but it is difficult not to suspect that he found the relationship a tyrannical one. Her attitude to him may have influenced the contents of his letters in a subtler way. Certain of the letters addressed to her contain bitter complaints about his conditions of service, his dissatisfaction with life in the East, and his eagerness to get home; and yet the general impression from the letters as a whole, and especially those to his sister, is of an intelligent and observant young man enjoying an adventurous and interesting life among agreeable companions. The letters which his mother wrote to him are not extant, but his replies to her make it clear that she indulged in much carping at him for supposed faults of extravagance and impiety, even though she cannot have had the smallest knowledge of his actual conditions of life at the time. It seems likely that he felt under some pressure to gratify her also by declarations that he was not really enjoying himself. Perhaps the most telling passage in this respect is in his letter of 21 August 1822 [23]. We see him, on receipt of a letter from his mother, going straight to the Admiral and asking for a passage home, but immediately abandoning this request on having it explained to him that it would involve the loss of three months' seniority; and this despite his having repeatedly expressed to his mother his impatience to come home to her and to get out of the Navy altogether. Like the protestations of affection, most of these passages have been excised from the present text, both for reasons of space and for their dubious relevance to an understanding of actual conditions of service at the time.

Edward left Fairy Hill on 16 February 1818, riding over Cefn Bryn, the main ridge of the Gower Peninsula, to Swansea. There, he took the overnight boat to Bristol, and after calling on family friends in that city he went on to London, where he stayed for some time with Augusta and Thomas Babington at Holly Hill, Hampstead. On his arrival, he at once called on Captain Middleton, who was at the Navy Board's office at Somerset House, and was apparently the officer responsible for instructing him as to his further movements. He did not, however, join his ship until 20 April, as she was refitting at Chatham. It seems that it was during this period of waiting that he fell in love with Thomas Babington's sister Mary, and this speedily led to a close friendship between Mary Babington and Edward's sister Julia. Mary was slightly older than Edward, having been born in 1799, and he was not the only young man to fall in love with her. When she died in 1858, her cousin Thomas Babington Macaulay, the historian, noted in his journal that 'when I was seventeen or eighteen I was half in love with her, but her conversation soon healed the wound made by her eyes'. Her niece, Eliza Conybeare, put the matter rather differently, saying that Macaulay once 'laid himself out, with all his powers, to captivate Aunt Mary. She was a year or two older, and did not take the matter seriously, but they carried on largely, and the folk present then say he never through life was so brilliant as during those few months.' She certainly seems to have been a person of greater mental calibre than Macaulay's schoolboyish taunt would suggest, and whatever she may have thought of Edward, he remained devoted to her throughout his time abroad, despite his mother's evident hostility. It would be interesting to know what passed between them on his homecoming. In 1829 she married James Parker, a Scottish lawyer who made for himself a distinguished name in the history of English law, particularly in the field of the Chancery reform, being made Vice-Chancellor of the Court of Chancery a few months before his regrettably early death in 1852.

While waiting to join his ship, Edward was studying with a Dr Patrick Kelly who ran an 'academy for gentlemen' in Finsbury Square. It is also probable that it was at this time that his portrait was painted, for in June 1818 Julia wrote to Mary Babington:

> You seem to intimate that Augusta will come here this year. That is indeed delightful, as I am sure she wishes it no more than Mama and myself do . . . I hope Augusta will bring Edward's picture with her. I dare say it will be a great temptation to me, however . . .

H.M.S. *Liverpool* sailed from Spithead on 19 July 1818, under the command of Captain F. A. Collier, and Edward was not to see England again until July 1823. After calls at Madeira and the Cape, she arrived in Trincomalee on 11 December. From there, her first voyage was to Mauritius, with a call at Colombo from 18 to 24 February 1819. She took with her into exile a number of Kandyan chiefs. The kingdom of Kandy had been annexed by the British in 1815 after the king, Sri Wickrema Rajasinha, had been defeated and captured with at any rate the connivance of some of the chiefs. The chiefs were, however, disappointed at the arrangements then made by the British, and at the end of 1817 a revolt broke out which lasted almost exactly a year. Two of the leaders were executed, and it appears from Edward's letter of 1 February 1819 that a considerable number of the others were transported to Mauritius.

Since Mauritius had been taken over from the French in 1810, the British had with no great encouragement been trying to prevent the importation of slaves there. In the words of R. W. Beachey, the trade 'was carried on by desultory smuggling rather than by open-scale methods. Slave vessels lay ashore, landed their slaves at night in fishermen's boats and by raft, while lookouts on shore turned a blind eye to their operations', while 'the attempt to maintain a vigilant and effective blockade . . . was weakened by the hurricane season, when the British naval patrol withdrew to the north.' In this thankless task, *Liverpool* relieved the frigate H.M.S. *Magicienne. Magicienne* had not been altogether unsuccessful, for at just about this time, on 20 February 1819, Philippe Caday, Joseph Amand Tregrosse and Louis Amand Cleransac were standing trial at the Old Bailey in London for having brought from Mozambique to Mauritius a number of Africans to be sold as slaves. Their schooner had been intercepted by *Magicienne* on 21 February 1818, and three days later their storehouse had been found to contain shackles for men, women and boys. Ninety-two Africans, male and female, had been found in the huts, mostly naked and suffering from a skin infection. One was dead, another dying, and nine too weak to be moved. On conviction, all three prisoners were sentenced to three years in the House of Correction, with hard labour. *Liverpool* took over operations against the slave traders from April 1819 until 8 September of that year. Her efforts, or rather those of her boat crews, also met with some success, at least three slavers being intercepted in addition to the two mentioned in Edward's letter of 7 August 1819.

She then sailed for Bombay, to join a fleet which was being assembled to put down piracy in the Persian Gulf.

The naval force arrived in the Gulf on 24 November 1819, *Liverpool* being its largest ship. Her officers made a reconnaissance of the coast near Ras al Khaima on 28–29 November, and troops were landed there on 3 December. Ras al Khaima itself was bombarded by *Liverpool, Curlew* and *Aurora* two days later, and the place was captured on 9 December. On the same day, Edward was formally advanced from 'volunteer first class' to the rank of midshipman. Zaya was captured on 21 December or 22 December, and shortly afterwards Edward wrote an account of the campaign to Captain Middleton. On 8 January 1820 a 'general treaty of peace' was signed with the 'Trucial Shaikhdoms' as they afterwards became known in consequence. In the same month, *Liverpool*, with the cruisers *Ternate, Teignmouth* and *Aurora*, cruised along the Gulf coast, destroying fortifications, and was still in the Gulf towards the end of March 1820. She arrived at Bushire on 6 March, and was off Ras al Khaima again on the 25th. However, she was back in Bombay on 2 April. Between then and June she sailed to Madras by way of Cochin and Trincomalee, and from there she made a nine-month cruise further east, with a long stay at Macao from September to December and visits to Penang and Manila. Unfortunately, only one of Edward's letters from this period has survived.

He transferred to H.M.S. *Dauntless*, a sloop of 18 guns, at Trincomalee on 13 March 1821 to take part in a voyage to South America, to fetch treasure from there to Calcutta. Leaving Trincomalee on 23 March, she put in to Sydney Cove from 23 June to 1 August, and made landfall at Valparaiso Bay on 19 September. While she was on her way, the situation in South America had radically changed. A Chilean fleet, under the command of Lord Cochrane, had been conducting a successful campaign against the Spanish since 1818, including a blockade of the coast of sufficient rigour to arouse the protests, in particular, of Sir Thomas Hardy, the British commander in the eastern Pacific, as a result of which the provisional Chilean government issued a decree modifying the blockade on 22 June 1821. Meanwhile, the Spanish viceregal authority collapsed, and in a pattern of events unhappily familiar in the history of Latin America a group of royalist officers had on 29 January 1821 deposed the viceroy, Pezuela, and appointed one of their number named Lacerna to take his place. After a defeat of the Spanish land forces by the Chileans near Pasco in May, Lacerna evacuated Lima on 6 July, taking with him, it was said, a considerable amount of bullion, and San Martín, the insurgent leader, entered the city on 10 July and proclaimed Peruvian independence five days later. Callao, the port of Lima, surrendered to San Martín on 22 September. *Dauntless* therefore arrived off the coast of South America after the fall of Lima, and just three days before the fall of Callao. This must have materially affected plans for the picking up of the cargo. Whatever the full purposes of the voyage were, Edward cannot have been in the secret, for in a letter which referred to 5 October as 'the other day' he was writing to his mother that the ship was now on her way back to India. His expectations were repeatedly disappointed: there was much coming and going off the coast of Peru, and in fact *Dauntless* did not finally set off across the Pacific until 26 November. During this period in South America, and probably in late October, he was robbed of sixty dollars. It seems that these belonged to a friend, and not to himself, though the evidence of his letters that the robbery put him personally into financial difficulties suggests that he honourably recompensed his friend for part at least of the loss.

The return voyage was not uneventful, with some rather odd manoeuvrings in Polynesia. Over Christmas, the ship was off the island of Christina (Hiva Oa in the Marquesas group). The captain's log records that on the morning of Christmas Day, as a result of two natives 'annoying us with a musquet', a gun was fired at them, and that that afternoon several broadsides were fired at a village. After calling at Tahiti from 10 to 19 January 1822, the ship cruised for thirteen days in a northwesterly direction, but then turned in a direct southwesterly course for Sydney. Supplies ran desperately short, perhaps as a result of the loss of time among the islands; though in view of Edward's harrowing account of the privations on board, it is fair to mention that there was still a 348 lb barrel of pork to be opened when they were six days from Sydney.

On his arrival in Sydney, Edward lost no time in going to visit his friends there, the Blaxland family of Newington, Parramatta. John Blaxland had emigrated to New South Wales with his brother Gregory in April 1806, and had taken up an estate of 1290 acres on the Parramatta River, naming it Newington after his former home in Kent. He had four sons and six daughters. There may have been a long-standing family friendship, in that Barham Court, Teston, where Edward's father was living, is also in Kent, but it is also possible that he had come to know of the family on his first visit to Sydney, through Mrs Harriet Blaxland, who was the daughter of Jean Louis de Marquett, a merchant of Calcutta; it was for certain Calcutta merchants that the cargo of bullion was being fetched from South America. Unfortunately, Edward's letter explaining these matters, which he apparently wrote in Santiago de Chile in September 1821, is not extant. This is the more to be regretted in that Santiago is well inland from Valparaiso, and the letter might have thrown light on what Edward, and no doubt others of the ship's company, were doing there.

No letters have come down to us from the rest of the voyage. *Dauntless* made her way through the East Indies, and moored at the mouth of the Hooghly on 23 June 1822, doubtless discharging her cargo of coins and bullion there. She then proceeded to Trincomalee, and the next news that we have of Edward is that he was transferred from H.M.S. *Dauntless* to H.M.S. *Glasgow* there on 21 August 1822, and that in September he was in Bangalore, visiting Henry and Harriet O'Brien. We have an account of him in a letter which Harriet wrote to his cousin, Sophia Mackworth, and which she in turn quoted at length in a letter dated 11 May 1823:

> We have had a truly delightful visit from dear Edward Noel; on the 20th September he came to us and stayed till the 27th . . . It was a most happy thing for us that he obtained leave, for you may easily imagine the joy of seeing the face of a *Friend* in this land of strangers. About the beginning of next year or perhaps sooner he sails for England . . . I scarcely ever met with any one possessed of a more *refined* and *interesting* mind, during the week he spent with us, his great delight was to sit with me in my own quiet little room and read his journal together with some beautiful poetry which he had composed on passing circumstances during his long voyage . . . He has far too sweet a mind for the boisterous life of a sailor . . .

He joined H.M.S. *Curlew* on 31 October, and her whole crew was transferred to H.M.S. *Termagant*, a newly-built ship which was to be taken to England and was then at Cochin, on 18 November. She sailed from Cochin on 15 December and, after being fitted out at Trincomalee and Madras, set out for England on 26 February 1823. The Cape was reached on 28 April, and St Helena on 23 May. She stayed there for five days and Edward composed a 'Fragment written at Napoleon's grave' and made a drawing of the site. Portland Bill was sighted on 7 July, *Termagant* anchored at Spithead next day, and Edward and the rest of the ship's company were paid off on 4 August.

He was therefore not back in England when his mother died on 12 April 1823. She left a last note to him, preserved among the letters:

> To my beloved Edward with an earnest and *last request* from his fond mother, Barham.
> Read your Bible and do at least offer daily an ejaculation for mercy.

The note bears the date 17 February 1818, probably not in his mother's handwriting and certainly erroneous, for the paper is watermarked 1821. There is therefore no reason to doubt that it was written shortly before she died. According to a family legend, Edward only learned of her death when, on disembarking, he went to his tailor to order a new suit, and the tailor asked, 'I suppose you want black, sir?'

Edward remained at Portsmouth, awaiting his examinations, and was still there on 3 September, when he received his passing certificate. He did not live long to enjoy the comforts of his homeland and his freedom from the tyranny of his mother. It seems from one of his sister Julia's letters that he had contracted a fever, probably malaria, during his time in the East, and that there was a recurrence of this. He died on 11

November 1823, and was buried on 29 November at Exton, Rutland, the home of his father.

His letters have descended from his sister Julia to her great-granddaughter, Mrs Gwenllian Day of Ponsanooth, Cornwall, with whose kind permission and encouragement they are now being published. Belated gratitude is also due to Mrs Nora Austin, who typed and sorted the letters, making the task of editing them a great deal easier, but unhappily did not live to see the work finished.

THE LETTERS OF MIDSHIPMAN NOEL, 1818–1822

1 *To Lady Barham*

Hampstead,
20 February 1818

My grief at parting with the two whom I most love on earth, for so long a time as I feared, was excessive. When Julia left me in the lane, or rather, when I left her, having then lost *both*, my tears flowed fast, and I was insensible for some time to everything but sorrow; till, on the Swansea road over Keven Brin, Mab started at seeing (as I did afterwards) two wretched, ill-looking women sitting on the ground wrapped up in a cloak in that lonely place, and trotted down the mountain leaping over furze bushes for about twenty yards, and three further she would have been in a deep bog. However, being then past the women, she was tractable when I arrived in Swansea. I walked on the sands till nearly dark, and then called upon Mr Kemp and tea'd with him. I set off at nine, and arrived at Bristol next morning about 10 . . .

I am happy to say that I was waiting a *quarter of an hour* at Somerset House for Captain Middleton before he came. He seemed very well pleased at my coming so soon, but he expects that Captain Collier will not wish me to join for ten days or a fortnight. The *Liverpool* is fitting at Chatham and is going to the East Indies, as I expected and hoped. Also, C. M. expects that she will be out between *four and five years*. If so, I *hope* I may finish my servitude in her.

I am just going to speak to Dr Kelly about attending him for the few days I am here. I will in future endeavour to write a better hand, as you advised me.

I had a rough passage over the water, and the major part of my fellow travellers, having good eyes, perceived every now [and] then a wave coming that would fill us, and a deal of danger in carrying so much sail. I, having not such good eyesight, did not perceive these dangers, and prevailed upon the coxswain to shake another reef out. He did, which added one knot to our way through the water, and as we landed the breeze died away to hardly a breath, and we were at least ¾ of an hour sooner, and I caught Mr Cooke as he was going from his office, which was fortunate.

I must now finish, as I am going to Finsbury Square . . .

2 *To Juliana Noel*

Hampstead,
Tuesday, 23 February 1818

I study at Dr Kelly's during the day, and spend the rest of my time with dear Augusta. Now I will tell you about my new ship, which I cannot join until Captain Collier's return from somewhere or other, which I rather think will be about a fortnight. Her name is the *Liverpool*. She is fitting for foreign service at Chatham. She is going to the East Indian station, I believe is to be in commission for between four and five years, and her ship's company and officers will then leave her and bring home two other ships built somewhere there. So then I hope to have served my time in her, and may have some chance of promotion on our return to England . . .

You see that my letter is not *quite* so badly written as some former ones, though not *much better* . . .

3 *To Lady Barham*

H.M.S. *Liverpool*, Portsmouth,
18 July 1818

Tomorrow, my dearest Mother, we shall sail from dear England, in expectation of three years' absence, perhaps more. During that time, I hope to be consoled by frequent intercourse, by letters from my darling Mother and all my dear family . . . Will my dearest Julia write to me once two months regularly. But pray do not tire yourself with writing, because to hear from one under the same roof will be quite as satisfactory, when I know that it saves you fatigue . . . I am required on deck now as we are unmooring . . .

4 *To Juliana Noel*

H.M.S. *Liverpool*, Trincomalee, Island of Ceylon,
27 December 1818

We must really correspond, yet by what method I do not know. When I left England, I hoped to hear from you half-yearly, but alas I now find that instead of half-yearly I am likely to be *another twelve months* ignorant of every occurrence which can interest me, knowing just enough of many important probable events to cause anxiety, which is a most unhappy state. I am thus continually conjecturing and musing upon my unhappy fate, while others round me are free from every care, floating along the tide of life with uniform indifference, passing the present hour in walking, talking, riding, shooting, fishing, eating, drinking, joking, and unless sleeping always merry. Day after day rolls on unmarked, unnoticed by these sons of Neptune. Whether or not I am of that race, I am of another build. I eat, drink and shoot, fish, ride, walk, talk, laugh and joke, but still my mind is otherwise employed, for ever brooding on uncertainty. I must forget a deal, and I must not indulge in raising visions. I must be free as they.

28 DECEMBER

I will . . . give you a sketch of accidents, incidents, occurrences, etc., which has passed since that unfortunate morning when we loosed our sails to the breath of Aeolus, and left Spithead three hours before the usual welcome visit of the postman. That morning was the 19th July. On the 29th we saw Madeira, and being within six miles of Funchall had the pleasure of frying in a slack calm for about seven hours. Towards midnight, we were visited by a breeze, which carried us to our anchorage by candlelight which appeared through the cabin windows of H.M.S. *Topaze*. Next morning, we found ourselves close under the land, which was very high. I confess I was much disappointed in the idea I had formed of this island. I went on shore, and with two messmates hired mules, and proceeded up the mountains by a perpendicular paved road, walled in on each side, and about three yards wide. Now and then the luxuriant vine overhung these walls and afforded us a temporary respite from the scorching rays of Phoebus, but this was only now and then, and by the time we arrived at anything like a level we were incapacitated for enjoyment of the scene. After this first resting, we still proceeded on our pilgrimage, and for three miles we had not even the shadow of a leaf. When we had undergone this purgatory, our glazed eyes were delightfully refreshed by the sight of a grove of Spanish chestnuts, under which we reposed for a short time, having before us a most extensive view of the town, bay and shipping of Funchall, which certainly is truly grand and beautiful. We entered a cottage in a vineyard, and were regaled by the pleasant and good-natured hostess with the produce of her own vineyard. We returned the way we came in a smart canter (as we thought, in imminent danger of our lives) but however though the road was horribly steep, our faithful mules at length landed us in Funchall again. We sailed from here 3rd August, and arrived at the Cape of Good Hope on 17th September, only eight weeks from England, which to me unhappy appeared an age, though a short passage. Simons Bay (our anchorage) was bounded by high craggy mountains which hid their summits among the clouds. Returning from the low shores of India we shall, I hope, anchor in Table Bay, a picture of which would be worthy of the pencil of my dear Mother. *Then, then*, when we return − alas, how distant may be that wished for time! When it arrives, however, I will endeavour to get a copy of the majestic Table Mountain, which I have only seen from its base, but which from the anchorage is, as I said before, very grand . . .

N.B. If you are determined upon being an old maid, let me know in time, and I will supply you with a large variety of monkeys, cats, rats, ugly parrots and muskittoes . . .

5   *To Lady Barham*

H.M.S. *Liverpool*, Trincomalee, Island of Ceylon,
1 January, 1819

. . . For four hours in darkness and in still silence I muse upon the past and anticipate the future. Yet this room, or rather dirty den or cell, in which I have existed six months away from England, among wild beasts, and looking forward to three years more, absent from all I love, present with those whom I wish absent; to find myself in this room is indeed enough to make me sad. However, the worst is past, and I already picture to myself sometimes the happy day of my return to England.

1 FEBRUARY

We are going to relieve the *Magicienne* at the Isle of France, as soon as we can get provisions, and I rather think we shall be there eight months at least, so that if letters are sent direct to the Isle of France I may have the inexpressible pleasure of receiving them three months after their leaving England. Those which have already left, I may receive some twelve months hence, perhaps not then. I have seen nothing of India yet, and I am afraid I shall not see China. We expect to visit the Persian Gulf after we're relieved from the Isle of France, and shall finally leave the *Liverpool* at Bombay, and bring home a new eighty-gun ship, the *Ganges*. This island is a very valuable possession, chiefly on account of its situation, being just off the coasts of Malabar and Coromandel, where there is not a single harbour, while here there is a remarkably spacious and secure one for the largest ships to anchor in, and so situated that in either monsoon ships can arrive at or depart from it. It is the first and most important naval station in the Indian Seas. In the interior the natives are occasionally very troublesome. They rebelled about a year ago, and destroyed an immense number of our troops by harassing and fatiguing them which, together with the sickness which prevails six months in the year, almost extirpated the English regiments; when, another regiment arriving, the Rebels or Natives (poor fellows, it's very natural that they should love liberty as well as all of us) were got under. We are to convey into banishment forty or fifty chiefs and leaders, who were taken during the late war, which lasted just one year. This is a most unhealthy climate; the sooner we sail the better.

1 MARCH   Latitude — . Longitude — .

On our way at last for the Mauritius. How I envy the happiness of the officers of the *Magicienne*. They have just completed three years from England, where they will arrive probably in three months.

1 APRIL   Port Louis, Mauritius.

Now, my dearest Mother, we are moored for perhaps a year in this harbour, and as soon as the *Magicienne* has recovered from the effects of a hurricane which we experienced a few days ago, she will sail for England. When *shall* I hear from you? . . .

3 APRIL

Yesterday I saw a paper of October. I saw the death of my dear sister Bessy. Poor Bessy, whom I saw last smiling and happy in her fond husband's arms! . . .

6   *To Lady Barham*

H.M.S. *Liverpool*, Port Louis, Isle of Mauritius,
14 June, 1819
June 16

Tomorrow sails a fast ship for England. Probably three months will bring her to her destination. In four months we shall (according to the present intention of our Admiral) be relieved from this station, and another two months will bring us to the Persian Gulf, among the numerous pirates which infest that Gulf and the Red Sea . . . If . . . such is the event, the termination of it will, I hope, send us at once to fit the new ship which we expect to convey home; the *Ganges*, 84, at present building at Bombay . . .

7   *To Lady Barham*

Mapon, Isle of France,
Thursday, 7 August 1819

I am now writing . . . in a French fisherman's hut on the windward coast of this island. We are cruising in open boats here, to prevent the landing of slaves. We go down to the frigate at Port Louis, every fortnight or three weeks, for provisions. I am in a very good sailing-boat, though not the most comfortable for to live in altogether. I was thinking the other night that our group would afford you a very good subject for a picture. The boat was hauled up on the beach; at a short distance from her, we had erected a temporary shed, outside of which, under some high rugged rocks, we had a large blazing fire. Round the fire were seated your son, his messmates, and the boat's crew. They had not been shorn for about a fortnight, and all of us, but for the naval button, you would have thought Gypsies, being a good deal sunburnt, habited in shabby blue with which we dressed for the night, the day being very hot, and during the last, present and next month, the nights very cold. Our boats have taken two vessels with slaves on board, whose masters will be sent to England, and afterwards, most likely, to Botany Bay. Immediately the wretched slaves perceived Englishmen on board, they set up a general shout, and were released from their horrid confinement: 97 of them, all huddled into the holds of a little vessel not near so big as a commissioner's yacht. The slave dealers are, I am sorry to say, encouraged by most of the *English* as well as French on the Island, in consequence of which they will risk a great deal to land a cargo of slaves, and we expect some armed vessels soon. If we meet with resistance from any of them, on their capture they will be hung instantly – Rascals, Mr Wilberforce.

8   *To Juliana Noel and Lady Barham*

H.M.S. *Liverpool*, Port Louis, Isle of France,
21 [August 1819]

I have visited the tombs of Paul and Virginia lately, but though I have been shown two cottages *said* to have been theirs, yet I do not think they are to be found, the nature of the buildings on this island being so slender that, unless frequently repaired, they soon decay and fall to pieces; which I doubt not has been the fate of those cottages . . . We were off that part of the island, to which Virginia walked to request of a planter the pardon of his slave. The Mountain of the Three Peaks is remarkable, and so wild, steep and rugged that they never could have climbed its summit. I have not had a near view of it, therefore I cannot believe but that it is the regular way from the northward of the island. It looks rather formidable to a European.

I am collecting shells, but I have a vast deal of trouble in getting them clean, the fish being so very obstinate that one is obliged to bury them in the earth for a fortnight, at the end of which time they require seven or eight warm-water thorough washings of each individual shell, so that the washing of three hundred is not a minute's work, but a great deal more tiresome, and almost suffocating . . .

I must close this letter as the ship that will convey it is now getting under weigh. 'I have nothing in the world to say' is an old finish, yet it is likely to be one now if nothing happens in five minutes, when I leave to board the *Lady Boningdon*, which ship will be in dear England in all probability in four months at the outside. Then, when you are burning large fires to keep you warm, you will probably see the outside of this letter. You will see that it is from foreign. I believe you know my hand – you will open it and not understand it. You will think it hardly worth a sixpence, yet if I can provoke you to write an answer, I shall think it worth *anything*. The last two pages are almost unintelligible, even to me. The fact is that I have been in the hot sun, and am suffering a temporary fever from its fierceness . . . I hope to hear from you soon now, for long, long, has

been the first year's absence, and not a word since July 18 have I heard
from anyone except dearest Mama. Thank her again for writing. Direct
to me at Bombay . . .

9   To Lady Barham

H.M.S. *Liverpool*, Bombay,
20 October 1819

. . . We are going to conduct an expedition to the Arab pirate coasts
of the Gulf of Persia, which will occupy 5 months. We expect to sail in
a few days, with a convoy, containing about 3,000 land forces. On our
return, I shall expect some letters – which I believe are here now! but
directed to the Admiral, whom I have been anxiously looking out for
during the last three weeks . . .

10   To Commissioner R. G. Middleton

H.M.S. *Liverpool*, off Ras al Khyma, Persian Gulf,
December 1819

I have the pleasure to inform you that we have had the conduct of the
naval part of a expedition fitted out at Bombay against the pirates of the
Persian Gulf, in which (you will agree with me) we have been fortunate,
for in no other station in India has there been anything to do, and almost
every frigate on the station for the last five or six years has been expecting,
and been disappointed. You have perhaps heard that for our active and
vigilant conduct during our station at the Mauritius, Captain Collier
received warm acknowledgement from the Governor, so that we may
reasonably expect, that it will [be] esteemed creditable to have served in
the *Liverpool*, and for a situation in her, I feel much indebted to your
kind interest in my welfare, for which I assure [you], my dear Sir, I am
grateful. You will perhaps have heard before this reaches you, that the
two principal fortresses on the Arabian coast of the Gulf have been
reduced. At both places we landed and mounted two of our 24-pounders,
which knocked their walls about in style. At this place, which we attacked
first, we certainly expected to find some treasure, but the crafty rascals
stowed it away in the woods. We came down here before the convoy, with
the Commander-in-Chief of the Forces, who lives on board, and one night
before the convoy arrived, we discovered in the middle watch a fleet of
boats steering for the town. We got under way immediately to prevent
them getting in, but there was no wind and they were a long way off, so
that all except one got in. The men jumped overboard and set the vessel
on fire. Some days after, we heard that these boats had made several rich
prizes in money, which led us to expect that we should find some of it.
It is expected that all the other chiefs of the fortresses along the coast will
not stand fire. We shall however visit them all and destroy their forts and
vessels.

I have received my letters more regularly than any one on board –

usually, upon an average, twelve months after date. I will be much obliged to you if you will continue to send them in the same manner, and take this opportunity of thanking you for the trouble you have already taken. I shall be very happy to get under way twelve or fourteen months hence in H.M.S. *Bombay* for England, for I wish very much to see you all again. Kind remembrances to Mrs Middleton. I hope to hear a good account of her health, which was so delicate when I left England. In great haste, for the boat is going to shove off.

Your much obliged and affectionate cousin.

11   *To Juliana Noel*

H.M.S. *Liverpool*, off Margadene, Coast of Arabia Felix, January 1820

. . . I cannot as formerly complain of *the heat*, being just at present in such a climate as would make the dairymaid's nose look red and raw . . .

. . . I am . . . at a loss for words – quite at a loss – not so an old cow upon the main deck, who has annoyed me excessively for some time by groaning. She only came on board today, and is growling at her new style of living. Well she may, poor creature! And well may everyone who comes on board for residence! . . .

At 8 o'clock p.m., 29th January 1820. The wind blew cold from the NE, and according to the custom generally prevailing among the midshipmen of the first watch, I mixed a glass of grog, and having ascertained the state of the weather, very naturally asked my servant for a cloth dress. In about a quarter of an hour he brought it me. You know what dress a midshipman puts on when the thermometer is as low as 40°. In the first place, a pair of shoes which (ten chances against one) are neither wind, nor water tight; a pair of socks which without a doubt want darning; a pair of trousers, which if they were new and whole would be much warmer; a coat which, if it had two skirts instead of one, and two sleeves instead of one and a half, would certes be more perfect; and a waistcoat! The waistcoat which I put on last night was (in kind compliance with my request) altered and refitted, reduced, and afterwards by you completed, with strings, etc., etc. It was a kind action! that it was! It certainly might have been altered by the tailor, but then I should have been quite careless of its fate – it would never have reminded me of those most happy days I passed at home! . . . If you recall not, you reduced its size. Now it has so happened that in the course of two years I have increased in size. Therefore I found it absolutely necessary to make a rent from top to bottom. Then I recollected the kind hand which fashioned it, and my thanks (the sincerity of which the uncommon length of this letter proves) must vent themselves in words. Now, if the waistcoat had been reduced by Tailor Williams, I should have been quite out of humour with the poor man, called him thick-headed and stupid, a lubber and a lout, unfit for his profession. I should likewise have been much vexed with myself for giving directions for the reduction − whereas I am now in a good humour with myself and all the world; all which are the happy consequences of this kind action! . . . The waistcoat is in a good state of preservation, and being a favourite from henceforth will be taken great care of, so that you may again see it, and again receive my thanks, when I return home . . .

We have for the last three months had the conduct of an expedition against the pirates of the Persian Gulf. Having reduced two of their most formidable fortresses, the rest of the Arab chiefs sent in their submission quickly. We however have paid them all a visit and destroyed their towns and towers, and vessels. Our loss has been only one man − but from sickness very many, and those our stoutest seamen. With an anxious eye, soon after dawn I daily sweep the distant horizon in hopes of the approach of a sweet 'Sylph', a cruiser who has letters and dispatches for us, and the Commander-in-Chief of the Forces, who lives on board. I have some fears as to the fate of this poor Sylph, for she is (though not of sylphid form) a small vessel, and I believe weakly manned and ill provided; and there are still pirates cruising in the Gulf, which all sail well and contain (some of them) three or four hundred men . . .

Query − will the cocoanut oil which has now been spilt upon this paper be visible when it arrives in possession of the fair hands of Julia? I hope not − yet I must provide an excuse for not writing this over again − and here is one, pat − the *Nautilus* will sail before it can be done. I wish the purser would provide candles instead of these horrid oily lamps . . .

12   *To Lady Barham*

H.M.S. *Liverpool*, Gulf of Persia,
4 March 1820

My ever dear and honoured Mother, with what pleasure do I embrace this opportunity of writing again to you! And first I will tell you how this opportunity has offered. We have (as a former letter which will not reach so soon, will inform you) had the convoy and naval direction of an armament from Bombay, and in the space of two months have destroyed or reduced all the pirate fortresses on the shores of Arabia, which have afforded their cruising vessels a safe retreat from the cruisers of the East India Company. The Commander-in-Chief of the expedition has been on board of us during the whole time, and having dismissed the troops and transports we are now going to Busheer, that he may make certain arrangements − which however are nothing to us − What an official kind of dispatch I have written! However, the Commander-in-Chief has been so kind as to offer a conveyance of two letters (overland) with the dispatches which he will send in a few days, so I will have mine ready for him. I think you must keep this letter as a curiosity, and here I am half inclined to tell you of the mode of carriage – but that and many other things I will amuse you with while you knit, Mama; in a short year and a half . . .

BUSHEER, MONDAY

We arrived here yesterday. This is a fine healthy place: thermometer between 50° and 60°. The sight of snow upon the Persian mountains is novel and pleasing. I think that we have been extremely fortunate in being concerned in this expedition, for it has been expected by every frigate on the station for the last six years, and been so delayed from time to time that we had given up the hopes. However, it is now completed, and I have been engaged in active service where only it has been going forward, and my cheeks have been regaled by the temperature of an *English* breeze, which has brought to them the northern colour. We shall, alas, in a fortnight be hot as ever!

MONDAY MORNING, BUSHIRE

I have a great inclination to drawing, and amuse myself with attempts now and then. I wish I were near enough to receive lessons from your masterly hand, Mama . . . I missed a great chance the other day, having unfortunately no money in my pocket. A dollar would have bought a pair of woven Persian shoes whose make and everything else would have been exactly to your taste. I shall have other chances, though. I have . . . by the by, a most curious camp stool which I got at Ras al Khyma. It came from Mecca . . . I will say adieu – May no Arab intercept the messenger!

TUESDAY

As this will go overland, it will be interesting to know how long from its departure will be its arrival. I will mark the former and I will thank you to make a memo. of the latter . . .

13   *To Juliana Noel*

H.M.S. *Liverpool*, Madras,
29 June 1820

. . . Captain and your dear Mrs O'Brien arrived here four days before the *Liverpool*, whose arrival they heard of two days ago. Dear people, they were not long in sending for me, but I could not come till yesterday . . . They had the finest voyage possible – not four months at sea, and fine weather always . . .

14   *To Lady Barham*

H.M.S. *Liverpool*, Macao,
November 1820

. . . Captain Collier said the other day that I should *positively* remain in India when he goes home. Now if I had fifty voices I'd stun him with 'No! No!' My heart is seldom joyful, but when I think of speedily returning home it bounds and leaps with pleasure. Now the whole business may be completed by an answer to this question: Can I be *sure* of a commission as lieutenant by the end of the year '22, provided that I remain in India? If not (and I see *no* chance of getting it out here, for Admiral Blackwood has as many followers* as a man covered with honey, after plundering a beehive, or a midshipman in London, and he will be Commander-in-Chief till 1824) − if not − if I cannot be *sure*, I would not remain a day longer in this unfriendly climate than I could possibly help. I have hitherto, thank God, had tolerable health, but I always feel *inanimate* in India. We have delightful weather here now, like the autumn in England. It has already been of wonderful service to me, and illustrates so clearly that a northern country is my constitutional element, that I shall have no hesitation in flying from the burning Tropic − not to mention the *very* strong attraction that binds dear England's children to their native isle. In August next, the *Ganges* (our new ship) will trip her anchors, and unless I have your express desire that I shall stay out, I'll sail in her for England! I shall bring with me plenty of work for you, my mother, and for Julia. The implements and materials − the produce of this country. The implements are about a score of different knitting needles of ivory in a pretty ivory case, and the materials − fine silk of every colour . . . Now having seen all that is to be seen of Asia, excepting the capital Calcutta, I long to return home. I have therefore written to Captain Middleton upon the subject . . .

* By followers, I mean midshipmen whom he has promised to promote by the first opportunity.

15   *To Lady Barham*

H.M.S. *Dauntless*, Madras,
20 March 1821

I have only time, dearest Mother, to inform you of my change of situation − that we are bound upon a most interesting voyage to South America. The object is an enormous freight which is at Lima, the capital of Peru blockaded by the insurgents, and they want a British man-of-war to convey the treasure to Calcutta. But our orders are yet sealed, and not to be opened until we sail and see the south of Ceylon. We shall however certainly be absent from this station for about nine months, so that I may venture to beg for an answer directed as I have dated. Will you have the kindness to inform Captain Middleton of my situation, in case that my letter to him should possibly be miscarried. I have been obliged to provide myself with blue clothing (for the cold weather which we shall meet with) which is both expensive and bad.

I am now under the command of Captain George Cornish Gambier. My bills will therefore bear his signature. The ship that is to carry this is on the trip. Her sails are loose. Would that I were bound in her for England, but this new arrangement is so decidedly advantageous that with all my longing to return to happy England I did not hesitate to quit the *Liverpool* . . .

16   *To Lady Barham*

> H.M.S. *Dauntless*, Sydney Cove, Port Jackson,
> July 1821

. . . In my profession I could nowhere be more happy than under the command of Captain Gambier. All professional advantages I here enjoy, and I make the most of them, so that when I return home (how the thought thrills through me!) I shall be prepared to pass both examinations and thus become eligible for promotion if in England by the middle of October in the next year 1822, which I trust I shall be . . . But I must tell you, my Mother, why I have drawn so largely upon Captain Middleton, I hope not too largely, for I have exceeded much what would be necessary, and therefore I fear you may think that I have been squandering foolishly; but I have met with curiosities which I thought so well worth purchasing as specimens and remembrances of the manners and customs, etc., of the countries which I have visited.

We are going to South America and expect much incivility – but of that I will speak hereafter . . .

17   *To Juliana Noel*

> H.M.S. *Dauntless*,
> 5 October 1821

I have sent you some Botany Bay seeds, which I hope you will find good and pleasure in rearing – likewise some scarves which you must call 'mantelias', commonly worn by the ladies of Chilé. Your taste will fit them as they ought to be, but bind them with a broad satin ribbon. I offer them to my Mother, to Augusta and yourself.

Your fond brother, Edward.

18   *To Lady Barham*

> H.M.S. *Dauntless*, West coast of South America,
> October 1821

. . . The consolation which I consider most is this: that whereas there must be some gentlemen who serve their country in the line which I have chosen, so, though it is the least of all professions eligible, yet its discomforts may be recompensed one day or other by the gratification of rendering my country worthy service. I hear reports of war, but I do not credit them, though I think that there will be some disagreement soon – but this is not the purpose. My Mother! I may see you in twelve months. It must be so. I will positively *not* stay out . . .

We are now on our return to India, having personated your antipodes! So that I have the satisfaction of knowing that I cannot be any further from my native land than I have been. I sent to Julia the other day by a safe hand some mantelias which I begged her to fashion after the manner of this country, viz. Chilé, and as they pleased my taste I hope that you may like one. I need not say that the fleecy side is worn outermost . . .

19   *To Commissioner R. G. Middleton*

H.M.S. *Dauntless*, Callao Bay, Coast of Peru,
November 1821

It is with pleasure that I address you now (I hope for the last time) under the consideration that but a few months after the receipt of this I shall be myself in England, for I do not see any advantage whatsoever in remaining out in India, and the *Dauntless* will go directly home from thence October next, and I shall have completed time. Within a little of that I certainly expect to be in Portsmouth, so that nothing could have been better planned than my exchanging for this cruise, which has renovated my health and given me an opportunity of seeing these interesting countries, New Holland and South America, together with those in our way back, the Marquesas and Otaheita, which have been visited by no man-of-war since the *Briton*. Upon this voyage we sail tomorrow. The whole west coast of South America is now free. This place, which has a number of strong fortifications, fell into the hands of the Patriots six weeks ago, after a two months' blockade – Lord Cochrane on the sea, and San Martín by land. The latter has assumed the title of Protector of Peru, and has a right to it.

You must think me, as I think myself, extravagant, but not, when I am considered as on my travels, *very* much so. All Englishmen are so cheated, so systematically cheated that whenever they appear the rascals (natives) raise their prices. Add to which, robbery (which I experienced but a few days ago, of sixty dollars belonging to a friend, which I was conveying to him), etc., etc., and you will, my dear Sir, excuse me . . .

20   *To Juliana Noel*

H.M.S. *Dauntless*, Matavai Bay, Otahaite,
12 January 1822

The few moments that I have to spare will be sufficient to inform my beloved Julia that I am at length returning. In a few days we shall pass the meridian of 180°, and afterward be continually lessening our longitude until we are in no longitude at all. Id est, the Observatory at Greenwich . . .

. . . I write in haste from off the beautiful island called Huahine, where we touch merely to deliver letters. I defer the mention of the interesting state of the far distant islands, and progression from horrible idolatry to the knowledge and worship of the true God, which I am happy to say rapid as could possibly be expected . . .

21   *To Juliana Noel*

H.M.S. *Dauntless*, Sydney Cove,
13 March 1822

Shall we *never* meet, my Julia? How often shall I breathe my longings from the Southern Hemisphere, and fondly fancy they're the last to be expressed? But two months past, and I was certain that I should be *now* in India, and for that country we were bound until distress, sheer famine compelled us to steer hither, as the only port within our reach, at that time distant more than 1100 leagues! Providentially we had afterwards no long calms, and not much bad weather. For the last six weeks, we have existed upon the following short allowances: half a pint of cocoa and half a pound of scarcely eatable flour (which your pigs in England would have spurned), cooked without leaven and hard as a musket ball, composed our pitiful breakfast. Two-thirds of a pound of rancid beef our dinner. From that time (noon) until the next breakfast time, we had nothing but a little arrowroot, which most fortunately we got out of a vessel just arrived at Tahiti when our sails were hoisted upon leaving it. These were our three meals, with the prospect of having even them reduced. For the first three weeks, our rum lasted on a short allowance. Yesterday morning the last chip of firewood was consumed, and the last drop of oil expended in our glimmering lamp! Conceive our joy when, on the night preceding, the beautiful revolving flame of Sydney lighthouse beamed on our delighted eyes! And further when you remember (if you have received my letter dated September from Santiago de Chili) that here in this sweet beautiful spot I have *more* sisters! Then you may picture to yourself my joy. Immediately our sails were furled, I rode up to their residence called Newington, and at that moment if they *had* thought of me they would have supposed I was in England! . . .

22 *To Lady Barham*

H.M.S. *Dauntless*, Sydney Cove,
23 March 1822

You will be surprised to hear that we were compelled by dire necessity (after we had proceeded from Tahiti on our voyage to India for thirteen days) to bear up for the nearest port, at that time distant 3,500 miles – a greater distance than from England to the West Indies! We were then reduced from *half* to *short* allowance. For the day we had two-thirds of a pound of rancid beef and half a pound of scarcely edible flour, and half a pint of cocoa – and for the last seventeen days, no rum. A kind Providence favoured us, and we arrived (mere skeletons*) on the 12th inst.

Now we are all hearty, and shall sail (D.V.) upon the 31st. I hope with more certainty than I have hitherto expressed, that I shall be home in the first month of 1823, as we shall make no stay in India, our relief being already out there . . .

I seize this opportunity by an officer who has left us and will sail immediately for England. He is a worthy and pious man whom I am sorry to lose. Adieu, my Mother.

P.S.   I have just heard a most melancholy account of the death of *twelve* officers of the *Liverpool* which took place within a few months after I quitted her, when she proceeded to the Persian Gulf a second time. They died by the terrible distemper, the epidemic cholera. The hand of Providence directed me hither . . .

   *(Words deleted)

23 *To Lady Barham*

H.M.S. *Glasgow*, Trincomalee,
21 August 1822

. . . Yesterday I received your most kind letter of January last . . . I cannot tell you how my heart rose within me when I read the affecting term by which you called me . . . I went immediately to the Admiral and requested him to take me home with him as he sails today for England. He told me there was not a single vacancy in the ship, and consequently I should lose three months' servitude, which in justice to my prospects I could not think of. However, he said the *Glasgow* will be in England soon after the *Leander* and you may join her, which I did accordingly. We sail this evening for Madras and Calcutta to put the *Glasgow* under the orders of the Marquis of Hastings, whom we take home. I am in great hopes that he will go directly, according to report, though some say that he will not leave until November. I have left the *Dauntless* because she will remain in India twelve months longer, which I cannot think of particularly because of my health, which I esteem the greatest earthly blessing, and mine has suffered much though not severely.

My late voyage in the Southern Hemisphere has been of the utmost service to me. I see the hand of Divine Protection over me in the direction of my way, particularly lately as the *Liverpool* in two months after I left her last lost nearly all her officers – three in one day! I feel the utmost anxiety – more than I can express – to return to my most beloved Parent, which is the great reason of my application to Sir Henry Blackwood . . .

I must say that I have been very extravagant, but pray consider the occasions. My journal will, I am confident, convince you that if I have been rather careless, *that* is all. I was robbed of a large number of dollars in South America, besides finding everything wherever I have been enormously dear. I have now not a single article of apparel English, and all that we get out here is amazingly expensive and so bad that it does not last one fifth the time that English would.

Captain Middleton has written to Captain Gambier to limit my allowance to £50. He has not sent a word to *me, which would have been preferable*. I am sorry for this – I *would have made shift with it if it had been your wish without* such a procedure. Forgive me, my Mother, for this sort of writing, but I feel very much . . .

24   *To Captain Middleton, from Captain Gambier*

H.M.S. *Dauntless*, Bombay Harbour,
28 November 1822

Edward Noel has passed his examination with much credit to himself, and upon consideration I have permitted him to proceed to England in the *Termagant*. I was induced to do so in order that he might have an opportunity of passing at the College, and as nothing yet is done with respect to promotion, he would then be quite ready to attend to the wishes of his friends on that subject. I can assure you I have found him always a young man very deserving of esteem and consideration, and [he] has given me reason to be entirely pleased with him, for his attention and activity in his duties, and as you are pleased to take an interest in him, you cannot but be gratified to hear that he is a youth of spirit, and possessing an excellent disposition which has gained him the regard of all on board this ship.

25   *To Lady Barham*

H.M.S. *Termagant*, Cochin,
November 1822

At *length* I am bound home! D.V. I shall be in England by the end of June . . .

I send this by a ship now in the Roads and under weigh for England – would that we were also! But we were only launched last week, and have all the tedium of fitting out. Forgive my haste.

10

Sir Henry Keppel's Account, *Capture of Bomarsund, August 1854*

Edited by

A. D. LAMBERT

Introduction

When he came to write his memoirs Admiral Sir Henry Keppel declared:

> It is not my intention to trouble my readers with a sailor's opinion of the capture of Bomarsund. Experienced officers, both French and English worked well together.[1]

However, Keppel had originally formed a very low opinion of the organisation and conduct of the operation, and had taken the trouble to make a full record of what he saw. It is this paper, handwritten in one of the *St Jean d'Acre's* log books, that is printed here.[2]

After two commissions in eastern waters fighting pirates with the Rajah of Sarawak, Henry Keppel, the diminutive fourth son of the fourth earl of Albemarle, was selected for the prize appointment of captain of the new 101-gun screw steam battleship *St Jean d'Acre* in 1853. The winter was spent working up in the Tagus and then he joined the first squadron of the Baltic fleet under Vice-Admiral Sir Charles Napier. They left Spithead on 10 March 1854.[3]

Keppel soon became disillusioned with the conduct of the campaign. After the excitement of boat action with Malay pirates he found the need to drill his ship for a fleet action which few expected, almost as tedious as the constant, fruitless cruising. Since he had no experience of regular warfare, Keppel's view of the situation was much the same as that of the general public. He thought that all the problems of the campaign could be solved by a liberal display of individual dash and courage. When the Russian fortress of Sweaborg (near modern Helsinki) was considered too strong for the fleet to attack he proposed taking the sailing battleship *Cumberland* (70) in tow and steaming directly into the main approach channel on the grounds that if they were sunk the two ships would at least block in the Russian forces.[4]

It was hardly suprising that Keppel, bored and frustrated, came to detest Napier, whom he considered over cautious. Like his fellow battlefleet captains he spent much time and ink abusing the admiral to his friends at home. By the time the allied governments had decided to capture Bomarsund and made the necessary preparations his view had become so jaundiced that he criticised everything he saw. In this respect his position during the operation was ideal; his ship was held in reserve at Ledsund and he employed his leisure visiting either the ships in Lumpar Bay or the siege works ashore. Consequently little escaped his notice, or his caustic commentary.

The basic theme of Keppel's narrative was that the whole operation had been unnecessary. He considered that ships could overcome forts, and this fact alone can explain his violent criticism of Napier who, from his greater experience, did not share Keppel's optimism. Keppel also objected to the fact that Rear-Admiral Chads's old blockships *Edinburgh, Blenheim, Ajax* and *Hogue* were placed before the enemy while his fine ship was kept out of harm's way. This was all the more galling since his distilling galley was constantly in use to replenish the small water tanks of the blockships. He did not realise that Napier had been specifically instructed to use the old ships for any attack against forts,[5] and foolishly fancied that Chads was able to dominate Napier.

While the violent and inaccurate complaints of Keppel might appear to have been harmless they actually carried great weight. He was a popular officer, with influential friends and relatives; his comments and similar letters from other battlefleet captains provided the First Lord, Sir James Graham, with an ideal excuse to dismiss Napier.[6] Half-a-century later Keppel admitted to Napier's daughter that he had caused her father a great deal of trouble, and implied that he had been in the wrong.[7]

Bomarsund and the Baltic Campaign

Faced by the possibility of war with Russia Sir James Graham dispatched Captain John Washington of the Hydrographer's Department to inspect the Russian positions on the Baltic coast during the summer of 1853. At the direction of the venerable Hydrographer, Sir Francis Beaufort, Washington visited the little known fortress of Bomarsund in the Aland

Islands. He was impressed by the size of the fortress and noted the foundations for an even larger work.[8]

The Aland Islands had been captured from Sweden by Russia during the winter of 1808–9, and by the Treaty of Frederickshamn they were declared to be demilitarised. However, Tsar Nicholas I (1825–55) ignored the stipulations of the treaty and began work on the fortress of Bomarsund in the 1830s. He intended that it should exert a powerful influence over the direction of Swedish politics.

The isolated position of Bomarsund made it an obvious target for the Baltic fleet in 1854, for it could be cut off by naval forces and captured by an overwhelming land force. The very ease of the operation led the First Lord to consider it as a bait to lure Sweden into the alliance against Russia.[9] Indeed his early letters to Napier had so deprecated the idea of an attack that it was not until late in May that Captain Sulivan, the brilliant fleet surveying officer, was sent to investigate the islands.[10] His masterly report gave Napier the most comprehensive account of the islands and the size of the force needed to capture them. Sulivan favoured a land attack; the difficulties of navigation would prevent the fleet from bringing its full weight of artillery to bear.[11] Napier favoured an immediate attack, using the marines of the allied fleet to besiege the fortress, but his co-Commander-in-Chief, Vice-Admiral Parseval Deschênes, rejected the plan. This forced Napier to call on the First Lord for instructions, and caused much of the delay which Keppel later criticised.

While Graham considered Napier's request Captain William Hall attacked the main fort at Bomarsund on 21 June without orders. The paddle frigates *Hecla*, *Odin* and *Valorous* bombarded from long range with their 10 inch shell guns, but despite expending all their ammunition they achieved nothing.[12]

The government had attempted to bring Sweden into the alliance, but King Oscar (1844–59) was too cautious and the negotiations broke down at the end of May. At the same time there was a growing need to find a strategic role for the allied army then lying on the defensive at Varna on the Turkish shore of the Black Sea. The Cabinet of 28 June decided in favour of an invasion of the Crimea, with the object of destroying the Russian fleet and the arsenal of Sebastopol; at the same time a French army would be requested to capture Bomarsund.[13] Graham, a leading advocate of the Crimean operation, had no time for the Bomarsund attack as he remained convinced that all the efforts of the allies should be concentrated in the east.[14] The French army offered by Louis Napoleon rapidly expanded from an original force of 5,000 to almost 10,000, but the mere numbers were deceptive for many of the troops were raw recruits. At the Admiralty Captain Alexander Milne, Third Naval Lord, had to find transport for this enlarged force; a situation only partly eased by the use of the reserve battle squadron as troopships. The delays consequent upon the arrangement of transport and embarkation prevented an early start, and it was not until 7 August that all the troops and their equipment were in position. Meanwhile Napier had invested the islands and sent the blockships under Chads into Lumpar Bay, the sheltered anchorage within the Aland group. A squadron of ten battleships under Rear-Admiral Henry Martin stood guard at the entrance to the Gulf of Finland against the unlikely possibility of a Russian sortie.

The French general, Baraguay d'Hilliers, was an exceptionally difficult man. He was too dangerous as a political rival to the Emperor to be employed with the main army in the east, yet by the same token he was best kept out of the country. His engineer, General Niel, was a favourite of Louis Napoleon and there can be little doubt that he had been sent to report on Baraguay's movements. The entire French contingent had been placed under Baraguay, who was at some pains to exclude the French Navy from any part on shore. He would also have preferred to keep the British forces off the islands, but that was something which Napier would not countenance. General Jones, the British engineer, had originally been sent as a liaison officer, specifically to keep the quarrelsome Napier away from Baraguay, but finding this task impossible he took a more active role in the siege.

Keppel's factual account of the operations that ended with the surrender of Bomarsund is the most complete available, but it must be read in the light of his hostility toward the amphibious style of the attack, and also toward the French, and toward Napier and Chads. Apart from the personal friction between Baraguay, Parseval and Napier, who all detested each other, the operation was well conducted. The only unnecessary loss occurred when the *Penelope* hit an uncharted rock. Having been forced to wait for a large army by the governments of Britain and France it was wise to conduct regular siege works against the weaker landward side of the main fort, rather than the seaward face that had been designed to beat off a powerful naval attack. The result was inevitable and therefore the cautious approach ensured that allied casualties were light. The advantages of this careful policy were wasted when the sanitary arrangements of the French army broke down and they had to hurry home, decimated by cholera.

The whole operation demonstrated in miniature all that the Crimean descent should have achieved. It was a valuable success to open the allied account and pointed the way forward for the development of a war strategy. The decision to invade the Crimea and the capture of Bomarsund were the first offensive moves of the Russian War. The miscarriage of the former ensured that the half-thought-out limited war strategy of peripheral attacks, inspired by Palmerston, became tied down to a protracted siege that drained the allies' resources. The effort eventually required to capture Sebastopol was out of all proportion to the value of the city; it dislocated allied strategy and starved the Baltic of troops for the 1855 campaign.

The capture of Bomarsund was the highlight of the Baltic campaign of 1854, and has hitherto been considered the only noteworthy occurrence in that theatre during the Crimean War. However, the strategic value of the Baltic grew as the Russian War progressed, and after the fall of Sebastopol, in September 1855, the allied governments, led by Palmerston and Louis Napoleon shifted their view to the north. Preparations were put in hand for a naval attack on the fortress/arsenal of Cronstadt and military campaigns in Finland and the Baltic provinces. These indications of allied resolve brought Sweden into the alliance in November and forced Austria to shift from her ostentatious neutrality in the following month. This three-pronged threat brought Russia to accept the mild terms of the Austrian ultimatum in January 1856. Bomarsund had been a valuable first step in the learning process that led to the plans for the Baltic campaign of 1856.

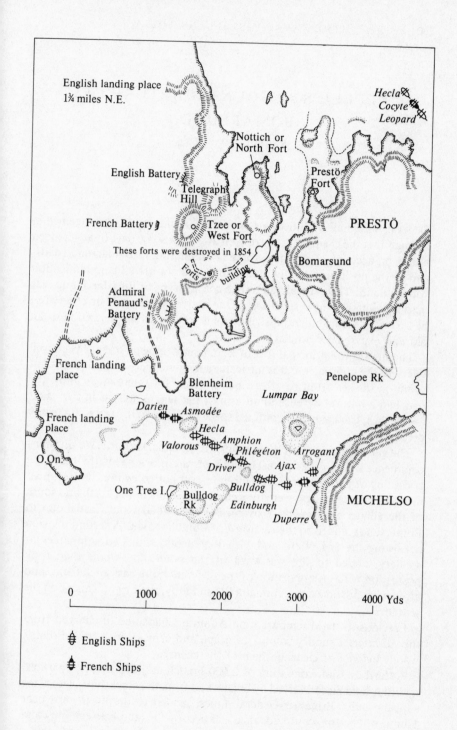

English landing place
1¾ miles N.E.

Hecla
Cocyte
Leopard

Nottich or
North Fort

Prestö
Fort

English Battery

Telegraph
Hill

PRESTÖ

French Battery

Tzee or
West Fort

These forts were destroyed in 1854

Forts
building

Bomarsund

Admiral
Penaud's
Battery

French landing
place

Penelope Rk

Blenheim
Battery

Lumpar Bay

French landing
place

Darien

Asmodée

Hecla

O.On.

Valorous

Amphion

Phlégéton

Arrogant

Driver

Ajax

One Tree I.

Bulldog
Rk

Bulldog

Edinburgh

Duperre

MICHELSO

| 0 | 1000 | 2000 | 3000 | 4000 Yds |

⊕ English Ships

⬥ French Ships

KEPPEL'S ACCOUNT, CAPTURE OF BOMARSUND, AUGUST 1854

General Baraguay d'Hilliers was not long in making his arrangements, he knew that the enemy must have been aware for some days of an intended attack on account of the large force accumulating in Bomarsund roads, and of the position taken by our steamers to cut off all communication with Finland. The general had only a coast survey of the island, and was ignorant whether the disposition of the natives was hostile or otherwise, he therefore arranged and distributed his force with the discretion of an old and experienced soldier.

The site for the principal fort of Bomarsund appears to have been well selected, the approach to it is intricate, and while there was not sufficient room on the sea front to afford ball practice for many large ships, the rear had a natural defence in an arm of the sea, as well as in two lakes or marshes, leaving only a confined space for an invading force, and easily defended.

The general decided on three points of disembarkation. Two divisions commenced landing at an early hour on the morning of the 8th. One consisting of the Chasseurs de Vincennes, supported by the 2nd Regiment of Light Infantry (these were to occupy the heights to the north and south of the village of Tranvik, crossing the main road from Castleholm to Bomarsund) landed to the eastward of Point Tranvik. A second division consisting the 3rd, 48th, and 57th Regiments, with two companies of artillery landed to the westward of the point, the whole then took possession without opposition of the different points assigned them, and afterwards advanced on Nora and Sodsa Finby, their right leaning on the seashore.

Previous to the disembarkation Admiral Chads had discharged from the *Edinburgh* sundry rounds of grape and canister into the adjoining woods by way of clearing them of the enemy.

A third division consisting of 2,000 French and 672 English marines, and four field pieces, served by bluejackets from the blockships, with some sappers under Brigadier-General Jones, landed to the northward near Hulta, whence he was to advance and occupy the land between Siby and the sea, putting himself in communication with the French at Finby.

These arrangements having been carried out, the forts became completely invested, by land, viz. to the westward by the main body of the French army, and on the north by the French and English marines.

The allied fleets being within sight to the southward were supposed to guard that side, while the east being awkward to approach, either by land or water was left open for the [French] army to extend their communications as far as Presto, the other parts of which island were, however, continually being visited by the steamers and boats of the fleet, rendering any attempt to cross beyond dangerous.

Admiral Plumridge arranged his steamers to the northward so as to cut off all communication with the mainland, as well as to prevent any surprise or reinforcement from Finland.

Sir Charles Napier's flag was hoisted in the *Bulldog*. At 3 a.m. just before the disembarkation, the *Amphion* and the French steamer *Phlegethon* took up a position to demolish an earth battery near the point of landing that had previously opened fire on Admiral Chads's arrival in the *Edinburgh*, thereby pointing out how near he might venture without getting within range, it was the same fort that had annoyed Captain Hall in *Hecla*, when on the 21st June he, with *Odin* and *Valorous* opened fire on the main fort. After an hour's well-directed fire from the *Amphion* with shot and shell Captain Key got into his boat, and having hailed the *Phlegethon* to cease firing landed and found the fort deserted while three guns of about 95 cwt. each were discovered some paces from their carriages and half buried in the earth, a fourth, on its carriage was found loaded to the muzzle by which the conclusion arrived at was that the guns had been dismounted and the battery evacuated at about 1 a.m. as at that time three distinct explosions were heard and seen to have been fired from that fort. By firing these guns with a slow match the garrison were enabled to decamp in safety, judging from the manner in which the gun mounted was found loaded, bursting as well as dismounting must have been their object. The Commander-in-Chief, looking on from the *Bulldog* made anxious inquiries by signal to *Amphion*; 1st, 'Are you in want of assistance?', Answer, 'No!'; 2nd, 'Well done!'; 3rd, 'Have you been hit?', Answer, 'No!'. While the landing was being effected on the south, Sir Charles Napier proceeded with Admiral Chads and the Captain of the Fleet in another steamer to see how the marines got on to the northward, leaving his flag flying in the *Bulldog*; her captain in turning his vessel grounded well within range of the forts, had they opened fire he would have signalised the blockships to his assistance, and Captain Hall, although junior captain, would have had the satisfaction of demolishing the Bomarsund forts, for which exploit he would have been placed under arrest. The spot selected by Baraguay d'Hilliers for his headquarters was on a rising ground in the village of Finby, out of range but commanding a view of the forts as well as of the ships in the anchorage, with which he established, from a windmill a communication by signal flags. The French artillery and chasseurs were in advance under the cover of trees and hills. A rearguard of 300 men were encamped on the extreme western side of the island, near the village of Castleholm.

The ground chosen by General Jones for the English camp was much nearer and well within range of the enemy guns but hid from them by a hill covered with large stones and fir trees, more convenient for riflemen than for the conveyance of artillery.

The French marines formed two camps, one a little further to the northward and the other as a rearguard near Siby.

To the southward a more convenient landing place near the camp was soon established where the French built a bakery, from which 11,000 loaves of bread were issued within 24 hours of their landing.

An entrenched camp was formed and the French engineers immediately commenced making fascines and gabions, while Generals Niel and Jones with Brigade-Major Ord of the French and English engineers, and Colonel de Rochebouet of the French artillery selected the point where the first batteries were to be erected.

It was determined that the westernmost circular fort, 'Tzee', from its commanding position should be the first reduced; to do which it was necessary to throw up sandbag batteries, the admirals having apparently decided on doing as little toward the reduction of Bomarsund as they possibly could.

The first French battery was to mount four 16 pdr. guns and as many mortars (brass) with which the general proposed to unroof the fort, and afterwards to breach it by the French heavy siege train on the west and by the English 42 cwt. guns, landed from our ships, on the north. The chasseurs, with their minié rifles were, by constantly playing on the embrasures of the enemy forts, to protect the works in progress on their side while the marines were to do the same on the north.

On the 5th, the Russians burnt a village near the NW side of the main fort, which had the appearance of having been residencies of the civil and military officials, this was apparently done to prevent any cover to the invaders.

Nothing particular occured on the 9th beyond the advancement of the marines and chasseurs as skirmishers, and preparations on the part of the French for getting their guns into position, while the enemy continued to exchange shots with the advance posts.

On the 10th, a large party of both French and English were employed filling their respective sandbags.

At day the 32 pdr. guns were landed from the ships and placed on sledges cleverly constructed and shod with iron, these were drawn up to the English camp over a distance of three miles by 200 seamen to each gun, with comparative ease, many hands making light work, they were headed by the bands of their respective ships and were loudly cheered on passing the French camps.

Some doubt having existed in the mind of the Commander-in-Chief as to whether any guns were mounted in certain embrasures of the main fort, at 11 a.m. the *Penelope* was ordered to proceed, piloted by the Master of the Fleet, in that direction so as to draw the fire, if there were any guns mounted, on her. The consequence was that the *Penelope* grounded within range of the fort, which opened fire with hot shot and did her considerable damage. To lighten her the guns were thrown overboard and several steamers (*Bulldog* not included) were ordered to assist, as well as to draw the fire off the *Penelope*, and a signal was made for the boats of the fleet to go to her assistance. Signals from *Amphion* for permission to fire, she being within range, and from the *Leopard* to engage the fort in the rear, she being stationed to the northward, were both negatived. While this was going on Admiral Chads went to the Commander-in-Chief on board the *Bulldog*, Sir Charles, getting a little excited stated to Rear-Admiral Chads that the time had arrived for moving the ships in and bombarding the forts, but this the Rear-Admiral was not prepared for, being unable to work the guns on shore and on board at the same time, and as it was too far to send to the ships that were kept down at Ledsund, nothing was done. If not the ships, their launches fully manned should have been from the beginning moved up, the blockships could then have been made use of and an effectual blockade established by a cordon of boats to the northward and the fleets placed in a less contemptible position. The *Penelope* was, after having been on shore for a couple of hours eventually towed off by *Hecla* and *Pigmy* having had two men killed and two wounded, three men wounded in *Hecla* and one Frenchman killed in a boat alongside. The *Valorous* was the only ship that fired and she threw a shell into one of the closed embrasures.

During the 10th, 11th and 12th, the troops were employed night and day filling and carrying sandbags, as well as ammunition and advancing the guns for getting into position, during which time the forts Tzee and Nottick kept up a fire on the operations, as well as throwing shot and shell over and into the English camp; we heard of numerous narrow escapes, but one marine only was killed in camp a round shot striking him in the chest as he lay asleep in his tent, he, poor fellow, little thought when he closed his eyes that he was not to awake again in this world.

On the night of the 11th it was thought that the Russians might make sortie and attack the parties employed on the works in progress, a larger force both French and English were ordered up; everything went on quietly on the side occupied by the marines, where there were 200 English advanced with 100 in reserve, and a larger proportion of French with 500 in reserve. On the west side in addition to the chasseurs, a portion of the 67th Regiment were advanced, just after midnight a party of the chasseurs had advanced close enough to the embrasures of Fort Tzee to hear the Russians carousing and singing inside, on creeping back they were mistaken by a party of the 51st Regiment for Russians and fired on, by which Lieutenant Nolfe and three of the chasseurs were killed, the chasseurs fired in return and then rushed on the 51st with their bayonets and killed 13 of them, not caring whether they were friends or foes but bearing in mind that they had shot their officer and men. It would hardly be fair to imagine that the chasseurs supposed their 51st to have been English, God help them had such been the case, this affair drawing the attention of the Russians they opened a smart fire of grape and canister in both directions, which lasted a couple of hours. A whole company of French marines, part of their reserve were seized with a panic when the forts opened fire and bolted clean into the English camp where they were met by General Jones and ordered back to their posts. The General, however was very anxious that their exploit should not get wind.

Baraguay d'Hilliers had informed General Jones that his *unroofing* battery would not be ready before the 15th, which would give more time to prepare his (Jones's) breaching battery. The French unroofing battery, however, opened fire at 3 o'clock on the morning of the 13th, as the French general must or ought to have known that it would do so. At noon the fire from the Russian fort slackened and at 4 p.m. a flag of truce was hung out, which was announced by loud cheering and everybody rushed forward, as well from the English camp as elsewhere to learn what it was about. General Niel who was in the French battery at the time caused a cordon of chasseurs to be posted to prevent a near approach, advanced with one officer to parley. A few individuals, among them Captain Eardley-Wilmot and Lords Clarence Paget and Dufferin who had proceeded direct to the fort on seeing the flag of truce when first hung out, and before the line of sentries had been posted were civilly accosted by a Russian officer from the inside who assured them that the fort had not surrendered, and giving his word that they would not fire until the officers were out of danger advised them to be off without further delay, a hint they immediately availed themselves of. On General Niel going up they asked for two hours to communicate with the Governor in the main fort, one hour only was offered, which, when Baraguay d'Hilliers heard of, said that it was just 59 minutes too long. As soon as the short parley was over the French artillerymen quickly retook their stations in the battery, and the chasseurs again spread themselves out among the rocks. The artillery men were at their guns and the officers with their watches in their hands waiting the expiration of the hour when a shot fired from the Nottick fort passed over their heads the order was given and the guns went off but when it was discovered that the shot was not fired from Fort Tzee no other shot was fired from the French battery until the hour given had expired when the firing recommenced on both sides, which was kept up until 6 o'clock when the Tzee fort ceased firing altogether. By misleading Jones as to when the breaching batteries would be required, Baraguay d'Hilliers, who is an older soldier, had an opportunity of trying what could be done by his battery and chasseurs without the assistance of the English, a dodge in which he succeeded, but more from the precision and quickness of the chasseurs minié firing than from the damage done by his battery. It was observed that in loading the rammer and sponge used by the Russians was frequently five or six minutes sticking outside before the cartridge could be rammed home.

In the navy department an attempt was made in the afternoon to land and mount a 10 inch 84 cwt. gun from the *Blenheim* and to raise a turf fort near the position of the one fired at by the *Amphion* and which was partially hidden from the enemy's guns, but the sheer heads showing above the rise of ground that at first intercepted the view of the work in progress brought on them such a shower of shot and shell as to oblige Captain Pelham to desist until darkness covered their operations when they redoubled their exertions. Just before daylight they masked their night's work with branches of trees.

At four o'clock on the morning of the 14th, the French unroofing battery recommenced by firing four guns at Fort Tzee to which no return was made. A volunteer party was then formed consisting of Lieutenant Gigot of the chasseurs and Lieutenant Gibon of the 51st with a small but determined body of men selected from the volunteers of both regiments to storm it, they moved up silently and then scrambled in without meeting any opposition. Some of the 51st found their way into the quarters of the Commandant, who drew his sword to defend himself, refusing to surrender except to an officer, when a French soldier thrust his bayonet into his side, and having pinned him down wrested his sword from him. On proceeding through the different apartments of the fort they found the Russian soldiers down on their knees. In the hospital were a number of wounded, being treated by their own surgeons. The Commandant was then marched, wounded as he was, to the quarters of the General-in-Chief, both English and French officers saluting him as he passed with the respect due to a brave soldier, he was subsequently embarked on board the French hospital ship where he died of his wounds; there were 32 other prisoners taken and some wounded. Strange reports were spread of some fifty bodies having been found in casks mixed with lime, this the Russian officers denied. One of the casks which looked as if kept for holding fresh water certainly contained the body of a man who had been placed in it heels uppermost and the whole fort had a strong odour of putrid bodies, the facts however, could not be satisfactorily established as at about 11 a.m. in the following day the captured fort blew up, but whether it was fired by one of the Russian shells that were thrown into it, or by accident is not known. On Frenchman probably seeking for plunder was blown up with it, and two others badly hurt.

As Fort Tzee commanded all the others, it was thought that they would not long hold out, nevertheless General Jones, whose breaching battery was quite ready on the morning of the 14th, immediately made preparations for changing its front, so as to bring his guns to bear on the northern or Fort Nottick which was at about 800 yards distance, while the French pushed their approaches to the right preparatory to shelling the Main Fort.

Afloat during the afternoon of the 14th, some rather indifferent firing took place from the *Edinburgh, Amphion, Driver* and a French ship of the line until sunset, a few only of their shot striking the Main Fort, while none of those returned reached the ships.

On the 15th, General Jones having succeeded during the night in changing the front of his breaching battery, at 8 a.m. Captain Ramsay with the bluejackets of the *Hogue*, opened fire on Fort Nottick, which together with that on Presto had kept up an active fire on both French and English camps, as well as on the then forming battery and [recently] captured Fort Tzee. Four 12 pdr. field pieces served by bluejackets and under the charge of Lieutenant Burgess of the *Edinburgh*, with Robinson and Orr mates of the *Ajax* and *Blenheim*, and Prince Victor of the *Cumberland* were getting into position, under cover of some rocks at about 50 yards to the left and at about the same distance from Fort Nottick, while 50 marines were stationed in a hollow in advance ready to repulse any sortie from the fort.

Soon after noon a Russian round shot knocked off the trunnion of one of the guns in the breaching battery mortally wounding at the same time the Hon. Cameron Wrottesley, a promising young engineer officer. At about 2 p.m. Fort Nottick showed evident symptoms of distress and before a large breach had been made, and shortly after a white flag was displayed, when the firing ceased and intimation thereof sent to General Jones.

Particulars of the Battery Practice in attacking Fort Nottick, August 15th, 1854.
Guns used Three 42 cwt. 8 ft. 32 pdrs.
Charge of Powder 6 lb.
Distance about 800 yards. Tangent Sight elevation 1¾ inches.
Firing commenced at 8 a.m. and lasted 10 hours.
Total quantity of ammunition expended 532 rounds.
Average rate per hour for each gun 18 rounds.
Quantity expended first eight hours 505 rounds, average 21 per hour.
During first hour and a half average 26 each gun, but on account of the guns getting hot the firing was slackened, otherwise the firing could have been kept up at an average of 26 rounds per hour and the breach sooner made.
Number of shot expended 487, shells 43 total 532.
During the last hour, as resistance on the part of the enemy had ceased an occasional shot only was fired.

The first 8 and ½ hours the guns were served by bluejackets, the last 1 and ½ hours by marine artillerymen.

General Jones ordered his Brigade-Major Ord to take possession of the fort, in the meantime Captain Elliot of the marines had marched in with a party and received the sword of the Commandant. Major Ord considering that it would not be practicable to keep open his communication after daylight with the advanced party, on account of the proximity of the Main Fort, and Colonel Graham arriving with two companies of marines, some sappers and a few bluejackets, the prisoners consisting of 1 lieutenant of engineers, 1 captain of infantry, 1 sub-lieutenant, 129 men, artillery and line, were marched down to the English camp, and subsequently embarked on board the *Termagant*. They had six men killed and 7 wounded. The contrast between the treatment in the two forts after capture was striking, in that taken by the English there was no unnecessary bloodshed, the Russian soldiers were kept sober and in order, and the Commandant after resigning his sword, sat down and treated his captors to a friendly cup of tea.

While the above was going on, the French were progressing with a breaching battery that was to take the Main Fortress in the flank and rear, and the ships in the anchorage distracted the attention of the Russians by keeping up a fire from their long range guns, the nearest English steamer being 2,400 yards and the blockships over 3,000 yards distant. At noon it being the fete day of Louis Napoleon a general salute was fired, the ships shotting the inshore guns. Two French steamers, the *Darien* and *Asmodee*, had gallantly taken up berths inshore of the English ship, being then about 2,300 yards distant from the Main Fort. Whether the Russians had any predilection for the tricolor is not known, but they appeared to direct their chief attention towards that flag so much so that the steamers were several times struck and showed their discretion by shifting their berths out of range.

By the morning of the 15th, Captain Pelham with Lieutenant Close and Mr Wildman, mate, and the seamen of the *Blenheim* had raised a barrier of turf, to supply which the fort lately made by the Russians was very convenient, 15 feet thick and 9 feet high and 35 long, with their ponderous gun of 4 ton weight ready in position. This gun during the day did more execution than all the desultory and distant firing of the ships all together, at sunset the firing ceased on both sides. At daylight on the 16th, the unfortunate Bomarsund Main Fort was attacked from different points, the French opened fire in rear, from a mortar battery, the English hill battery likewise directed its attention that way, while during the night the French had thrown up a breaching battery with [in] 380 yards and preparations were in progress for mounting it with 30 pdr. from their ships. In the north too Admiral Plumridge was firing on the Presto Fort and having got that fort in line with the Main Fort such shot as passed over the one would drop into the other. The ships again opened from their long range, and Captain Pelham's 10 inch was worked with considerable effect, it was in this state of affairs that a white flag was about noon displayed on the sea front of the Main Fort.

The flag of truce having been first seen from the shipping Sir Charles Napier despatched Captain Hall, his temporary flag captain with Mr Crowe, the interpreter to ascertain what was wanted, the French admiral sending his A.D.C. After landing at about 300 yards from the fort they walked towards the portal, Mr Crowe holding up the flag of truce while Captain Hall and the French officer carried their national colours. When they reached the gate some Finland officers addressed them through the loopholes, informing them that they would have to be detained until the sandbags were removed to enable them to open the gate, they were joined by Colonel Goujon belonging to General Baraguay d'Hilliers's staff. When they entered the court of the fort they found it full of soldiers in marching order, sentries had been placed along the passages by which they passed on their way to the general's apartments. General Bodisco received them in full uniform, he had Major Grahu and other Russian officers in attendance, he stated that after having done his best to defend the place he, at the earnest solicitation of his men, had come to the resolution to treat for terms.

Captain Hall gave him to understand that he represents Sir Charles Napier, and that no terms could be listened to short of unconditional surrender, in fact if this was not accepted the ships would recommence firing in the course of half an hour.

The French naval officer said that he was merely sent to demand the object of the flag of truce, and was not authorised to take any steps without communicating with his admiral.

The French colonel spoke much to the same purpose, and said it would depend on General Baraguay d'Hilliers as to what sort of terms could be accepted, and insisted on proceeding at once to ascertain the general's wishes.

Captain Hall who saw at once how very impolitic it would be to admit of any delay refused to listen to any postponement, and affirmed that he would in the name of Sir Charles Napier accept the surrender 'unconditionally'. After the quantity of talk naturally to be expected from the representatives of the French General Commanding in Chief on shore and the French Admiral Senior Naval Officer afloat, Captain Hall carried his point, and the interpreter was directed to make the same known to the parties concerned, at which they went through the form of expressing themselves satisfied.

It was resolved that the troops should lay down their arms, and that the French and English troops should immediately march in and take possession.

The French and English flags were then displayed from the walls of the fort. While this was enacting General Bodisco came forth from his chamber, Sir Charles Napier had found his way into the yard of the fort, and the two chiefs commenced to parley. The Russian general not appearing to be at all aware how much both he and his master were indebted to Sir Charles's 'discretion'! Shortly afterwards Baraguay d'Hilliers galloped up, attended by his staff and settled matters as if he had been in the habit of capturing forts. Bodisco on tendering his sword, which was politely declined, stated that he had the means of defending himself longer, although at an unnecessary loss of life, and he hoped his honour was without blemish. The French general, who thought otherwise, said that Bodisco had done all that a brave man could do, and then accompanied him back to his apartments.

The Russian soldiers who had previously rigged themselves in their best clothes got as drunk as they could in a short time, and plundered their own officers, at which work they were soon relieved by the entrance of the French soldiers.

Arrangements having been made, the generals and admirals with their respective staffs and other officers took up a position on either side, outside the gate, while the road to the mole was lined with troops, the English marines and marine artillery on one side and the French Chasseurs de Vincennes on the other, the prisoners then came forth, two and two headed by drums and fifes and marched down as well as they could. Those who were sober enough to know the difference shook hands with the English and made faces at the French, they looked as men might do who had had no repose for five days, except by the side of their guns. After they had passed, General Bodisco attended by his A.D.C., a drunken priest, a servant and a French orderly came out. On arriving at the mole he inquired for an English boat, but the French had taken possession of him, having embarked in one of their boats he pulled to the island of Presto probably to inquire after Madame Bodisco, and then embarked on board the *Tilsit* in which ship he subsequently sailed for France.

Thus fell the forts of Bomarsund, after much ado, bother and unnecessary expense. The manner in which the guns of the *Edinburgh* subsequently destroyed a portion of the main fort, shows what might have been done had our ships been near enough months before, as it was the injury done to the interior of the fort was trifling and ought not to have induced the governor with such a strong garrison, no breach, and a well casemated work, to have surrendered when he did. However there was a goodish close in store for him, his advanced works were taken, a formidable breaching battery ready and no prospect of relief. General Bodisco had besides arrived at years of distinction.

Since she took possession of the Aland Islands Russia has been constantly engaged in increasing the fortifications of Bomarsund, and no expense has appeared to be spared in their construction, and if we may judge from what already exist and those in course of execution it was intended for a first rate fortress and the principal port of Russia in the Baltic. The three towers of Tzee, Nottick and Presto were its advanced posts, and together contained a garrison of 2,400 men; it was mounted with 180 pieces of cannon, and furnished with considerable quantities of stores, and would in a few years have become an immense entrenched camp for land and sea forces the approaches to which would have been difficult, and whence Russian vessels of every size might have extended their operations to the several coasts of the Baltic. These Aland Islands form a chain of stepping stones across the Gulf of Bothnia, and the importance attached to them by Russia clearly shows the influence they are supposed to have exercised over the adjacent states. Stockholm lies almost within the radius of this fortress, and the coast of Sweden would have been at the mercy of its powerful neighbour while Denmark would have fallen yet more into dependence.

With Bomarsund was destroyed the prestige attached to these fine and threatening fortifications of granite, and there is nothing to secure them from the effects of a well directed fire. While inside however numerous the garrison, the wretched serfs under such a government can have but little heart to fight.

Notes

1   Admiral Sir H. Keppel, *A Sailor's Life under Four Sovereigns*, 3 vols. (London: Macmillan, 1899), Vol. II, p. 235; see also Vivian Stuart, *The Beloved Little Admiral* (London: Hale, 1967).
2   National Maritime Museum, Keppel MSS. HTN/6.
3   D. Bonner-Smith, *Russian War 1854: Baltic and Black Sea*, N.R.S. Vol. 83 (1943).
4   Keppel to Captain Stephenson, 9 June 1854, Keppel MSS. HTN/52a.
5   Rear-Admiral Berkeley (Second Naval Lord) to Napier, 4 May 1854, British Library, Add. MSS. 40,024 fol. 175.
6   The complaints of Captain Lord Clarence Paget of the steam battleship *Princess Royal* (91) reached Graham via the Duke of Newcastle, Secretary at War. Newcastle to Graham, 30 August 1854, Graham MSS. Bundle 120, microfilm at the University Library, Cambridge.
7   Keppel to Mrs Joddrell, 9 June 1901, N.M.M. NAP/10.
8   Washington to the Board of Admiralty, 1 October 1853, B.L. Add. MSS. 40,022 fol. 408.
9   Graham to Napier, 20 June 1854, B.L. Add. MSS. 40,024 fol. 310.
10 H. N. Sulivan, *The Life and Letters of Sir B. J. Sulivan* (London: John Murray, 1896), p. 123.
11 Sulivan to Napier, 10 June 1854, in G. B. Earp, *History of the Baltic Campaign of 1854* (London, 1857), pp. 333–6.
12 Sulivan, op. cit., pp. 190–1.
13 Palmerston Diary entry, 28 June 1854, National Register of Archives, Broadlands MSS. D.15.
14 Graham to Prince Albert, 20 June 1854, Graham MSS. Bundle 120.

11

Selections from the Phinn Committee of Inquiry of October–November 1855 into the State of the Office of Secretary to the Admiralty

Edited by
C. I. HAMILTON

Introduction

Thomas Phinn, the Second (or Permanent) Secretary of the Board of Admiralty, in effect set out the main lines of inquiry of his committee at their first meeting by proposing certain reforms in the organisation of his office, the Whitehall department of the naval administration. The clerks were one subject of his concern. He wanted them to be promoted not on the basis of seniority, as was the practice, but according to merit. He also wanted to move their hours of attendance to somewhat earlier in the day, so that papers could be the better prepared for the daily Board meeting at noon. And he argued that the Chief Clerk, supreme in the Whitehall Admiralty below the Secretary, involved himself in too much of the petty administration, somewhat demeaning his high position. Such a man should involve himself only in the higher questions of discipline and supervision, Phinn thought, thus taking some of the burden carried by the Secretary himself.

Phinn also expressed dissatisfaction about the keeping of records. One of his points was to do with the General Minute Book, in which the important minutes of each Lord of Admiralty were recorded (not to be confused with the Board Minute Book, which contained copies of Board decisions). Phinn said there was no definition of 'important', nor was there a single person responsible for the selection of minutes to be entered, but each departmental head made his own choice: consequently, some trivialities were entered whilst some weighty decisions were not. The system of dealing with correspondence also drew his fire, certain radical changes being suggested. He thought it a grave failing that there was no register of all incoming letters, arguing that some papers got totally lost as a result. Furthermore, he wanted departments to fill in chits as they passed on documents. For only after they had been acted on and sent to the departmental Record Office were papers noted in the indexes and made easily traceable: before that point they could wander from office to office willy-nilly, as good as lost, for months on end.

The Record Office itself was also said to need reform. The duties of the staff were arduous: not only had they to enter in the Index volume a brief reference to each letter deposited, but − a job demanding great application and accuracy − also compose a *précis* for the separate Digest Book. Phinn thought that most of the Record Office clerks were too young, and were attached to the office too briefly, to do such work well. Only older men, on permanent attachment, were said to have the seriousness and commitment to take the necessary pains. And Phinn wanted to reform the system as well as the staff. There were separate Index and Digest Books for each year. Thus, to find all the correspondence on a given subject, many volumes might have to be searched through. General indexes and digests were therefore desirable. Fortunately, as Phinn admitted, such searches were not very common: the great majority of papers called for from the Record Office were under a year old. This led to another suggestion for reform: that the various branches should keep by them all correspondence for twelve months after receipt, thus saving time when documents were needed and taking pressure off the Record Office.

Phinn's most radical suggestion was to do with the distribution of business, implicitly striking at the basis of the great Admiralty re-organisation of 1832. In that year Sir James Graham, the First Lord, swept away the boards of detailed administration − the Navy Board and the Commissioners of Victualling − which had been accused of being too independent of the Lords of Admiralty and thus too wasteful. Instead, administration was concentrated more than ever on the Board of Admiralty, through the principle of individual responsibility. Instead of the old boards, there were henceforward five departments, the Civil Departments of the Admiralty at Somerset House (as against the Naval, or Secretary's Department at Whitehall). Each of the five was headed by a Principal Officer: the Surveyor, the Accountant-General, the Storekeeper-General, the Physician of the Navy (or Medical Director-General), and the Comptroller of Victualling and Transports. (A sixth was added later, the Director of Works, though, as will be seen from Houghton's evidence, his status was somewhat inferior.) Each officer was responsible for his department to one of the Lords of Admiralty, the Superintending Lord of that department, and he, in turn, was responsible to the Board. Henceforward, it appeared, the lines of authority and accountability were clear.

But there was a flaw, according to Phinn, in that the Lords bothered themselves with far too much of the day-to-day administration of the Civil Departments. Much of the correspondence that went to them, he said, should go instead to the Principal Officers. He thought them quite competent to deal with most of it themselves, and if a letter had to be referred up for a decision then all the relevant papers could be submitted as well, permitting the Lord to resolve the matter with more despatch than if the unsupported letter had been sent to him initially. In essence, Phinn was proposing that more power should be devolved onto the Principal Officers, thus returning in some degree to the pre-1832 position.

He made another proposal about the distribution of work to the Lords, although this was a comparatively minor one. The Lords of Admiralty also had responsibility for work within the Naval Department. But, unlike with the Civil Departments, they were responsible not for particular offices, but for work of a particular kind, whatever the office or offices it was carried out in. The First Naval Lord, for instance, was usually responsible for all orders to do with the manning of the navy. This meant that one Lord's authority could spread to several of the Whitehall branches, overlapping with that of his colleagues'. (Henry Wolley, Head of the Commission and Warrant Branch, asserted in his evidence that he had to deal with six of the Lords.)[1] Phinn's sense of order was troubled, and he suggested that each Lord should supervise an entire branch, this effectively becoming his secretariat.

The Second Secretary made some other suggestions, concerning franking and the treatment of legal questions, but these are not of particular interest, and can be left aside. Instead, two obvious questions should be raised: what prompted Phinn to propose reforms, and why did the Board set up an inquiry into them.

Among Phinn's motives it would be unjust not to include the desire to promote administrative efficiency; but one must add that the desire was coloured and shaped by certain personal factors. Phinn was not happy in his post. He had been appointed on 22 May 1855 to succeed W. A. B. Hamilton. But his previous career as a barrister and an MP had not prepared him for Admiralty administration, although he had had a short apprenticeship, serving since May 1854 as Counsel to the Admiralty and Advocate of the Fleet. In consequence, he found Whitehall ways alien and confusing. As he confessed in a letter of 19 June 1856 to Sir Charles Wood, the First Lord:

the anxiety and harassing nature of the duties here, and the difficulties consequent upon the present condition of the office, and the almost momentary interruption in business, have frequently caused me more fatigue than the united attendance in my profession and in Parliament.[2]

Phinn must have hoped that an inquiry, by persuading the Board to specify more strict rules of business and by removing some of the Secretary's duties to the Chief Clerk's shoulders, would reduce his cares and confusion.

One suspects strongly that one of Phinn's main aims was to have firmer limits set between his own duties and those of his colleague, the First (or Parliamentary) Secretary. As the name implies, the Permanent Secretary had tenure. The other Secretary lasted only as long as his party was in office – or rather, as long as the Prime Minister willed it. However, in their duties there were great similarities and some considerable overlap. This was doubtless of slight importance when the two men concerned were flexible and amiable, but Phinn was not the former, nor was his colleague – Richard Osborne – the latter. Osborne was capable of great asperity: indeed, one of the causes of Hamilton's retirement appears to have been friction with him – a friction well displayed by the evidence they both gave before the inquiry. We know that Phinn also suffered from Osborne's abrasive tone. In 1856 he fell into an argument with his colleague about their respective duties: this in large part prompted the letter to Wood cited earlier. And it is reasonable to assume, considering the generous interpretation of the prerogatives of the First Secretary advanced by Osborne in his evidence before the Phinn Inquiry, including claims for a degree of primacy over the Second Secretary unprecedented since Graham's reforms, that there was already some conflict between the two men in 1855.

If the personal element helps explain Phinn's reform proposals, it is the impersonal, the institutional, that must be stressed in an explanation of the Board's sanction of an inquiry. The Board was responding to the pressures growing in the early 1850s that favoured administrative reform. These pressures chiefly emanated from the Treasury, which at this period was gradually extending its powers over other departments of government, chiefly by sponsoring joint committees of inquiry into their working. There were fourteen such inquiries in 1853–4, none of them into the Admiralty,[3] but it was apparent that the Lords of the Treasury would sooner or later scrutinise the administration of what was almost the heaviest charge on the Exchequer, being exceeded only by the Army. The Army administration laid itself open by the incompetencies it displayed during the Crimean War. The war did not similarly tarnish the Admiralty's reputation, but the Treasury still had a skeleton key with which it might hope to open the jealously independent department to outside scrutiny – the famous report drawn up in 1853 by Sir Charles Trevelyan (the permanent head of the Treasury) and Sir Stafford Northcote.

Their chief recommendations were these: that entry to the Civil Service should be by competitive examination; that the promotion of clerks should be based on merit; and that some sort of division should be made between what was called *intellectual* and *mechanical* work, between, that is, work such as drafting and digesting, and mere copying.[4] Given that the common practice was for applicants to be faced with only a simple qualifying examination, after their appointment to be promoted by seniority, and to spend long years as copy clerks before being allowed themselves to draw up memoranda and letters, the Trevelyan-Northcote recommendations were clearly radical. As such, they needed many years – some two decades – to be fully implemented, although May 1855 saw a beginning made when the Civil Service Commissioners were set up to give certificates to those candidates who passed approved, though non-competitive examinations, and who were otherwise qualified (by age, health, and character) for their duties. But the Trevelyan-Northcote proposals probably made their presence most felt in the 1850s by the way they dominated the discussions – often polemics, that went on about the future of the Civil Service. The *Civil Service Gazette* for instance, carried on a determined campaign in favour of the seniority principle.[5] And Anthony Trollope, still employed at the Post Office, wrote a whole novel, *The Three Clerks* (1857) to show the invidious and corrupting influence of the merit principle. More pertinent here, the proposals gave the Treasury room to ask questions about the organisation of other departments, and to suggest new means to promote efficiency and, naturally, economy.

Of course the Admiralty might have hoped to be able to ignore such questions; but in one way the Crimean War increased the Treasury's ability to extract an answer. The extra demands of war forced the Admiralty to make more promotions, and to take on some temporary clerks, for which Treasury sanction had to be obtained. Having sanctioned increases in the establishment, the Treasury was more entitled than before to ask about total staffing levels. And questions of number could easily lead to ones about efficiency and administrative reform. In short, even simple questions lacked innocence, and the Admiralty appears to have realised that Treasury inquiries had to be dealt with quickly, before they developed into anything more dangerous. Thus it was, when in June 1855 a Treasury circular was received asking for a return of the establishment levels over the previous few years,[6] some determined action was taken. First, the various Branch Heads in the Naval Department were asked by the Chief Clerk to propose ways of increasing efficiency. Secondly, in October 1855, Phinn was given his head, and a committee of inquiry set up under his name. As was usual, the Treasury was asked to send a representative to sit on the inquiry, and Henry Brand, one of the Treasury Lords, was appointed.[7] To counter him, the Board had appointed not only the Second Secretary but also, as chairman, Alexander Milne, the most experienced administrator among the Naval Lords. All in all, the Board had done what it could to ensure that an Admiralty viewpoint had been prepared and would be well articulated. Reform might have to be accepted, but on the Admiralty's terms, pre-empting truly radical change.

What were the immediate consequences of the inquiry? Minimal, is the answer. There was not even a report. One senior Treasury official noted in a letter in 1860 that the Phinn committee had been overborne by departmental difficulties and given up its task.[8] However, the strength of the evidence presented was sufficient to inspire a few changes. Phinn himself was to be disappointed: the Board did not lay down the new rules of business he wanted, and he resigned in 1857. But the Record Office did benefit: the complaints about the youth and transience of its staff led in 1857 to the permanent attachment of some junior clerks to that office, a measure confirmed and developed in 1863.[9] Moreover, attempts were made to prevent papers not yet processed by the Record Office being lost 'in circulation'.[10] And, perhaps as a result of some comments made before the committee by John Barrow, the Head of the Record Office, an Admiralty Librarian was appointed in 1856. At first the post was temporary, but it was put on the establishment in 1862.[11]

To these three cases where the lines of cause and effect appear comparatively direct and clear, yet one more can be added, illustrating what was suggested earlier, that an inquiry, properly managed, could actually limit reform and Treasury interference. In August 1860 Gladstone, then Chancellor of the Exchequer, expressed concern to the First Lord, the Duke of Somerset, about the recent growth in the Admiralty establishment. He said that no Treasury approval for further increases of staff could be granted unless some inter-departmental inquiry should look into the whole question of Admiralty staffing. Somerset trumped him by replying that there *had* been a recent inquiry, concluding:

> It seems probable that another inquiry would reproduce much of this evidence, while from the actual state of the departments no great economy appears to have resulted from that last joint inquiry.[12]

The defence could be only a temporary one, given that Treasury pressure continued. But even had it been more effective, it and the other possible arguments against change were being undermined by a gradual realisation within the Admiralty, fed by evidence from other government departments where the Treasury had been more successful, that reform could be salutary. By 1866 the Admiralty can be found approaching the Treasury to ask sanction for a new class of clerks − writers − simply to deal with copy work, so that a division could be made between intellectual and mechanical work within the naval administration. Naturally, the Treasury agreed.[13]

Even more changes occurred over the following years, and these ought to be noted, not because one may argue that they directly resulted from the Phinn Inquiry, but because they show which of the questions put before that inquiry continued to be of importance, and the date of their resolution.

One development the Admiralty shared with other government departments. In the 1870s recruitment by competitive examinations was established, along with the principle of promotion from one class of clerks to another by merit. Other changes, however, were peculiar to the Admiralty, and the most obviously beneficial was the centralisation of the naval administration at Whitehall. Previously, the Civil Departments had been at Somerset House, half a mile from the Whitehall Admiralty. In 1855 the Surveyor's Department had been brought in. And, at last, between 1869 and 1873, the other departments followed, ending a division – as Hamilton and others testified in 1855 – which caused great delay and duplication of effort.

The 1870s was also a time of reform of the system of correspondence. A registry for in-coming mail was instituted in 1870, and departments were allowed to keep papers for twelve months before sending them to the Record Office. Moreover, transit books were introduced, in which the movement of papers from office to office could be recorded: despite previous measures, it seems that on occasion 'in circulation' had still really meant 'lost'.[14] Thanks to firm resistance from most of the senior clerks, this new system applied only to some departments: however, their resistance was sapped in 1871 by an incident that showed only too well the dangers of the old system. The transport *Megaera* was chosen to take some supplies to Australia, but she proved unseaworthy, sinking *en route*. The subsequent inquiry discovered the Admiralty's ignorance of the ship's poor state to be due in part to the loss from sight of certain pertinent reports. It was suggested that a registry of in-coming correspondence, had one been established several years before, might have prevented this loss. Moreover, doubt was cast on the practice of indexing and digesting by the year. Before the decision to commission the *Megaera* was taken, a previous report on her had been called for from the records. But the request specified a particular year; the wrong one, as it transpired. The searcher looked through the appropriate Index and Digest, failed to find the report noted, and did not bother to look through the volumes for the previous year, where the reference would have been found. The volumes in question were in the Controller's Department which, like those of the other Principal Officers, had its own Record Office; but the main Whitehall Record Office had the same system of yearly indexing, and was thus open to the same kind of error.[15] The inquiry did not lay all the blame for the *Megaera* loss on record systems; but enough was said to ensure in 1872 a more thorough reform than that instituted in 1870, including separate branch registries for in-coming correspondence in the Secretary's Department.[16]

Phinn would have been particularly pleased by two other reforms. In 1879 the status of the Chief Clerk was recognised by a change of title: he became the Principal Clerk and Assistant Secretary. And in 1872 a Third Secretary was appointed, called the Naval Secretary, to bring a greater element of professional expertise to the Admiralty administration, and to share some of the burden of the other Secretaries. But the effect of at least this last change was temporary. Only until 1877 were there three Secretaries: in that year the Permanent Secretaryship was abolished. Five years later the old order returned in full, when the post of Naval Secretary disappeared, supplanted by a revived Permanent Secretaryship.[17]

One could suggest that in another case – to do with the over-burdening of the Superintending Lords – changes made years afterwards satisfied complaints made before the Phinn Inquiry, albeit perhaps temporarily. In 1860 the Surveyor (now Controller) was given greater personal authority over the dockyards, without continually having to work through the Superintending Lord. In 1869, however, a significantly different approach was attempted. In the Admiralty reform of that year, the 1832 system was altered radically. The burdens on the Superintending Lords were reduced, but this was done by cutting drastically the time spent at Board meetings, and by turning all the Lords (bar the First Lord) into the executive heads of the various departments. The Board was in effect abolished, and its directing and centralising power vested in the First Lord alone. However, the arrangement did not work well, too much weight being put on one man, and in 1872 the previous system was largely reverted to, with the same old fault that the Board and the Lords, absorbed in administrative matters, had little time to consider general policy questions.[18]

The fifteen years and more separating the Phinn Inquiry and the series of reforms just discussed surely confirms what was implied earlier, that there was no serious causal connection between them. Indeed, since there was no report, it would be surprising had the Inquiry been very influential. But this scarcely means that it is of no significance to historians. It is important as a point of reference on the rising curve of mid-nineteenth-century Admiralty – even governmental – reform. It is a perspective glass into a particular stage of development.

The resistance of most of the witnesses to the merit principle is particularly interesting. Their task was made more difficult by the Order in Council of 30 January 1816, which stated unequivocally that promotion from one class of Admiralty clerks to another had to be based on merit alone. It was also embarrassing that a more recent order, that of 11 August 1854, though applicable only to the Civil Departments, went so far as to state that even promotion *within* a class should be by merit.[19] Since both orders were the result of bargains with the Treasury, exchanges for establishment increases, the Phinn witnesses perhaps thought themselves fully entitled to argue their way around them.

They were able to appeal to the authority of a minute of 10 November 1842 drawn up by Sir John Barrow himself, Second Secretary for most of the first half of the nineteenth century (and the father of the John Barrow who gave evidence in 1855). The minute stated that the Admiralty staff were so generally excellent that there had hardly ever been a need to act according to the 1816 regulation, and that the seniority principle was just, as well as admirable from the point of view of office morale. The only acceptable dilution of the principle, Barrow thought, was if the senior was clearly incompetent: only then should the junior man be promoted. This minute was the Holy Writ of the senior clerks, and they each echoed it, adding further glosses of their own. The end result was the highly refined illogicality characteristic of a last ditch defence against necessary change; perhaps temporarily victorious, but ultimately doomed.

The Inquiry is also interesting because it shows a *small* bureaucracy at work – much like the gigantic ones of the present day in certain respects, though quite unlike in others. And we are presented with many of the details of that work, the *minutiae* of the office, from how letters were treated on arrival, down to how needle and thread were introduced into the office. Indeed, these details are perhaps the most valuable aspect of the Inquiry, being the sort of facts that the researcher finds it most difficult to unearth. The administrative historian is too often in the position of Averroes commenting on Greek drama, with almost the same degree of error possible.

Yet the Inquiry can mislead the reader, and a word of caution is required. One might sense from the various witnesses that two elements rubbed shoulders uneasily with each other in the naval administration, the one of order, hierarchy, and the six hours of work proper to a gentleman; the second, represented by Bromley, of self-help, meritocracy, and obsessive hard work. This antithesis must not be overly stressed, certainly not to the degree of representing one side as the incompetent and indolent gentlemen, the other as the vulgar if efficient players. Admittedly, Bromley's behaviour was not entirely gentlemanly. He leaked information about potential naval economies to the Treasury: when Disraeli was Chancellor in 1858–9 one of his correspondents wrote: 'We want a Treasury spy – a Bromley – in each department'.[20] However, his beginnings were not as humble as, Bounderby-like, he suggested in his evidence: he was the son of a naval surgeon, and he traced his ancestry back to a Lord Chancellor under Edward I.[21] His fellow witnesses, on the other hand, were not *fonctionnaires- fainéants*. Earlier in the century the pace of business at the Admiralty had usually been leisurely. Even during the Napoleonic Wars, Lord Palmerston, Civil Lord 1807–9, had duties he described as 'passing a couple of hours in the Board Room doing little or nothing'.[22] And the life of a clerk had not necessarily been much more hectic. In his evidence in 1855 H. F. Amedroz recalled that twenty years before, as secretary to the First Naval Lord, he was employed so little that he had had nearly all his time to spare.[23]

Perhaps life at the Admiralty at this time had much in common with Thomas Love Peacock's experiences at the East India Company Office:

> From ten to eleven, ate a breakfast for seven:
> From eleven to noon, to begin 'twas too soon;
> From twelve to one, asked, 'What's to be done?'
> From one to two, found nothing to do;
> From two to three began to foresee
> That from three to four would be a damned bore.[24]

By the middle of the century much had changed. The Principal Officers and Superintending Lords were particularly burdened, as is suggested by the rate of sudden deaths in office and retirements due to ill-health. Even the ordinary clerks did not escape. The responsibilities of the Admiralty had increased greatly since the 1820s and 1830s, and the amount of correspondence had increased even more quickly. But there had not been a commensurate staff increase, so the old leisurely habits of business had begun to alter. However, the attitudes and language that had matched those habits did not alter at the same rate. One only has to recall the way that the Admiralty in 1855 was administering a war-level navy with what was virtually a peacetime staff establishment (by the time of the Phinn Committee a mere five extra clerks had been taken on, all temporaries), to see that, in a somewhat shabby genteel way, the witnesses were keeping up a facade of the old ways whilst working hard behind it. When all else is lost, certain superficialities of language and manner remain, but these should not disguise from us that by 1855 the nineteenth-century revolution in government was somewhat more established in the Admiralty than Bromley's apparent isolation suggests.

The reader may find useful the following guide to the separate branches in the Secretary's Department. After each branch is shown the number of its permanent clerks at the time of the Inquiry, including the branch heads.

Secret and Political (5)   Commission and Warrant (4)
Military (4)   Pension and Pay (4)
Civil (4)   Legal (4)
Steam, Packet, and Transport (5) Manning and Miscellaneous (3)
Commission and Marine (4)   Record Office (4)

The total number of permanent clerks in the branches was 41. Appendix III shows that the number of such clerks in the Secretary's Department as a whole was 51. The ten not accounted for were the Chief Clerk, the Reader, his assistant, the Précis Writer, the two private secretaries to the

First and Second Secretaries, the three private clerks to three of the Sea Lords, and the clerk who, with the private secretary to the First Lord, made up the latter's private office. This private secretary was not one of the established clerks.

Note that the above table reflects the changes brought by the Crimean War. The burdens of naval mobilisation meant that certain branches could no longer cope with their work. The answer could not be simply to increase the number of temporary clerks, largely because, given the relatively small offices in the Admiralty building, expansion would have meant branches using more than one office each, making it difficult for the Branch Heads to exercise 'proper supervision'. The course adopted was to create more branches (which meant promotion to headships for a fortunate few). Thus in April 1854, the Military, Secret and Political Branch was split in two. And in the following January two Commission Branches were created out of one, and a separate Legal Branch was hived off from the Manning and Miscellaneous Branch.

The duties of the various branches are clear enough from their names, with perhaps two exceptions. First there are the two Commission Branches. The Commission and Marine Branch dealt with the promotion of executive and R.M. officers. The Commission and Warrant Branch dealt with Warrant officers, and with others, such as senior engineers and surgeons, who had once been appointed by mere Warrants, but who by the 1850s were commissioned officers. Secondly, there is the Civil Branch. An outline of its duties may be found in the selection from the evidence of J. H. N. Houghton.

It ought to be mentioned that also at Whitehall, though not part of the Secretary's Department, was the Surveyor's Department, moved over from Somerset House in 1855, and the department under the Hydrographer, of which the Harbour Branch effectively formed an autonomous part, and finally, the Royal Marines Office, headed by the Deputy Accountant General.

The original manuscript drafts of the Phinn Inquiry do not seem to have survived, but a limited and confidential edition was produced, of which a copy exists in the Public Record Office (ADM 1/5660). It is from this copy that the present selection has been made.

The printed version comprises ten pages of Phinn's opening remarks, 153 pages of evidence (1936 paragraphs of question and answer plus various memoranda and letters), eight appendices, which take up another ten pages, and finally, eight pages of index. Only about one-fifth of the whole is reproduced here, but the real loss is less than this implies, given the redundancy natural to such inquiries. The general principle on which material has been included is that it should either shed light on the daily running of the Admiralty, or show the reaction to the reforms proposed by Trevelyan and Northcote. Square brackets denote editorial glosses.

A word about nomenclature: one of the more irritating aspects of the history of not just the Admiralty but of almost any long-standing British government office is an excessive lack of precision in the use of certain terms. In the case of the Admiralty, the words 'department', 'branch', 'office', and even 'section' and 'bureau', can be found used interchangeably in official returns. The editor has been consistent in his use of 'branch' to mean sub-department, but the reader has to be warned that no such consistency can be expected from the Phinn witnesses. Their meaning is, however, clear enough on inspection.

In conclusion I must thank the Public Record Office for kindly allowing me to quote from the Phinn Inquiry and to cite other papers in their collections. I am also grateful to my colleague, Dr Michael Bratchel, for his valuable remarks on a draft of this introduction. And I cannot omit mentioning the generous help given by the general editor of this volume. He was an invaluable source of information on Admiralty developments in the late nineteenth century, and guided me to important P.R.O. documents that otherwise I should have missed.

THE PHINN COMMITTEE OF INQUIRY, OCTOBER-NOVEMBER 1855

Witnesses who appeared before the Phinn Inquiry,
31 October–29 November 1855, with the numbers
of the paragraphs of their evidence
(only those marked with an asterisk appear in
the present selection from the Inquiry)

* Henry Amedroz, Head of the Manning and Miscellaneous Branch, 1391–1515.

* John Barrow, Head of the Admiralty Record Office, 230–335, 1640–94.

* J. Henry Briggs, Reader to the Admiralty, 115–183.

* R. Madox Bromley, Accountant-General of the Navy, 1754–1841.

Waller Clifton, Head of the Steam and Packet Branch, 557–649.

* Jno. Jones Dyer, Chief Clerk, 1–114.

Robert S. Evans, Head of the Pension and Pay Branch, 844–958.

* Edward Giffard, Secretary to the Transport Board, formerly Head of the Legal Branch, 1279–1390.

* W. A. B. Hamilton, Phinn's predecessor as Second Secretary, 336–435.

* J. H. N. Houghton, Head of the Civil Branch, 1052–1149.

John Jackson, Précis Writer, keeper of the Board and General Minute Books, 1516–42.

J. Heneage Jesse, Head of the Commission and Marine Branch, 782–843.

* Sir John Liddell, Medical Director-General of the Navy, 1605–39.

Fredk. Locker, Deputy Reader and Deputy Précis Writer, 1560–1604.

M. W. Midlane, Head of the Legal Branch, 1150–1278.

* R. Osborne, MP, First Secretary, 1543–59.

* C. H. Pennell, Head of the Secret and Political Branch, 436–556, 650–74, 1051.

O. B. Piers, Searcher in the Record Office, 1707–53.

W. F. Robson, Solicitor to the Admiralty, 1842–69.

Captain Vetch, R.E., in charge of the Harbour Branch, 1920–36.

Captain Sir Baldwin Walker, R.N., Surveyor of the Navy, 1695–1706.

* Captain John Washington, R.N., Hydrographer to the Admiralty, 1870–1919.

Henry Wolley, Head of the Commission and Warrant Branch, 675–781.

Thos. Wolley, Head of the Military Branch, 959–1050.

Evidence of John J. Dyer, Chief Clerk

4   Will you state to the Committee what are your special duties as Chief Clerk of the Department? – I have the superintendence of the whole discipline of the office, and of everybody belonging to the establishment under myself.

6   At what hour do you come in the morning? – I am generally here about twenty minutes before 11.

7   What do your duties commence with? – I immediately sort the letters which have come down in the box from the Board. I divide them according to the duties of the several departments, and send them to the different departments for execution.

8   Does that go on throughout the day? – It goes on so continuously that it very seldom relaxes till 2 o'clock.

9   Do the letters which pass through your hands in that way return to you? – After the minutes are executed, all the letters that are written are sent to me; I collect them together, and send them to the Secretary for his signature; having signed them, he sends them down to me again, and I distribute them to the several rooms.

10 Do you take any charge of the correspondence itself, and of the way in which the letters are written upon the original minutes? – Not at all. I only transmit them. If I were to see anything wrong it would be my duty to point it out, but I am not responsible for doing so.

11 You do not consider it to be any part of your duty to examine the letters? – No; nor could it be.

12 What other duties do you perform during the day? – I have to keep a register of all the gentlemen's time of attendance, which is sent to me from every room in the office.

13 What do you do with that? – I enter it in the book.

14 In one general book? – In one general book, which is kept by me.

19 What other duties do you perform during the day? – I am the paymaster of all the contingencies of the office.

25 Do you pay . . . in cash? – Sometimes in cash, and sometimes by cheque. The disbursements amount sometimes only to a pound or two, and that I pay in cash; generally, I pay by a cheque.

26 Upon whom do you give the cheque? – Upon the London and Westminster Bank, who are my bankers [in my public capacity].

29 Is there a sum of money paid in to your account there? – Whenever I ask.

30 From whom? – I ask the Secretary, and an order is given to the Accountant-General to place so much to my account. [31] . . . I am not allowed to ask for more than £500.

37 Do you give security? – Yes. [31] [To the amount of] £1,000 myself and two others.

60 You have known the office for a great many years; has there been a great increase of business thrown upon it? – A very material increase; it has much more than doubled; it has trebled, I should think.

61 What has been the increase in the number of clerks; has the number of clerks doubled, or anything like it? – No.

69 Are the duties assigned at present to each Lord pretty much the duties which are generally assigned to them? – No; a new Board of Admiralty might come here, and they might divide the labour differently among themselves . . .

70 Is there generally, in point of fact, a great difference made in the distribution of the business when a new Board succeeds to office? – There is sometimes a change.

71 Is it an extensive change? – Sometimes it is, and sometimes it is not.

72 Does not it depend upon the Lords themselves? – Yes.

80 Do you ever go into the rooms to ascertain whether there is any arrear in the different branches? – I go into the rooms, and I make certain inquiries, but I do not interfere with the duties of the room unless something calls my attention to them.

83 Is . . . [the head of the room] responsible to you, or directly to the Secretary? – He is responsible [directly] to the Secretary for the conduct of his room.

85 As you carry on the discipline of the office, do you exercise any general superintendence of the way in which the rooms are managed? – There is a general superintendence.

86 What do you do to carry out that general superintendence? – If there is any complaint of the work not being properly executed, it is my duty to make an inquiry into it. If the gentleman at the head of the room has any remonstrance to make in the case of any gentleman serving under him, it is my duty to interfere.

87 Supposing a gentleman does not carry out his duties satisfactorily, would the report be made to you by the head of the room, or to the Secretary? – To me.

88 Would you in all such cases go to the Secretary, or in minor cases would you warn the gentleman yourself? – I should warn him on my own account; I never come to the Secretary unless I think his interference in necessary.

89 Is there any instruction from the Board for the guidance of the Chief Clerk in his duties? – None.

90 Or for the general guidance of the office? – No.

91 It is all regulated by custom? – Yes . . .

99   Is there any minute fixing the hours of attendance of the gentlemen here, or does it merely rest on custom? – I do not think there is any minute.

100   What are the regular hours of attendance? – From half past 10 to 5. Since the war one gentleman in each department has been desired to be here at 10 o'clock.

101   Has that been found sufficient for the transaction of the business? – It has always been found so; indeed at one time there was a proposition to make the hours much later – to make them from 12 till 7.

106   Have you anything to suggest with reference to any improvement which you think could be carried out in the business of the office? – Nothing, as a general principle.

107   Have you any suggestion to make in regard to details? – I might possibly suggest two or three things: if the Précis Book is to be indexed, the Précis Writer must have some assistance given to him . . .

108   When was that Précis Book established? – In the year 1847.

109   What was the custom before that? – No [Board or General] minutes were entered in any way, at least none for the last half-century.

110   There are old books with minutes entered, are there not? – Yes, upwards of half-a-century ago.

111   Previous to that there was a long-continued practice of entry? – Yes, but they were very short entries. There is nothing in the book which can be relied on.

112   Can you trace why the system was given up? – No, we never knew. We have tried to ascertain, but we cannot.

113   Who is responsible here for the state of the office as regards its cleanliness, and so on? – The Housekeeper.

114   Is she under you? – She is.

Evidence of John H. Briggs, Reader to the Admiralty

117   What are the duties of Reader? – I come here at half-past 8 in the morning. I make abstracts of the movements of the ships in the preceding day. I then, with the Secretaries, open the letters, and arrange with them what are to be sent to the Lords, and what are to be sent to the heads of the Departments to be prepared for the superintending Lords, and also take out the more important ones which are to be brought before the Board. Having done that I attend the Board.

121   Do you know if there is any record kept of the letters which are daily received? – The only record, or register, which is kept of the letters received is of those which come from foreign Admirals,

and Admirals at home ports. Every letter received from an Admiral
. . . has a number affixed to it — that is entered by me in my books,
so that I can identify it . . . All their letters are numbered day by
day, and acknowledged in the Military Branch Department. With
regard to other letters, they are not so. The more important ones
are those from the Secretary of State, the Treasury, and other Public
Departments. Those are comparatively few during the day. They
are placed before Mr Osborne or Mr Phinn in the morning, and
brought before the Board . . . and disposed of immediately, sooner
than . . . in some other Departments they would be registered. —
The only flaw I see in our system is this: it is at times difficult to
prove a negative . . . I should be disposed to say, that out of 500
letters which came here you would have no difficulty in getting 499
produced, but you might have a difficulty about a letter which it
is supposed has been sent . . . I think, if it was desirable to keep
a register for all letters, there would not be much difficulty about
it . . . however, the business would be very little simplified by it.

123   At what time do the members of the Board get their letters? —
. . . at half-past 9 o'clock. I commence opening the letters at a
quarter to 9, generally speaking. The letters which they then get
are those which are forwarded from the departments at Somerset
House . . . and as fast as I open the letters which relate to the
departments of the Lords, who I know are in their rooms and
anxious for them . . . I send them in to them so as to supply them
from time to time as fast as possible . . .

124   Does the distribution of the letters to the Lords rest with you? —
Each Lord superintends a distinct Department; therefore, directly
I see that a letter relates to the Department of that Lord, I send
it to him . . . [125] . . . It is part of my duty as Reader to distribute
the business properly. Of course the more confidential letters I never
think of distributing without bringing them under the notice of the
Secretary. — I say to him, 'Do you think this is a letter of sufficient
importance to bring before the Board, or would you send it to the
superintending Lord of the Department in the first instance?' But
generally, however important it is, you send it to the superintending
Lord that he may be master of the subject, and bring it before the
Board himself in due form. With regard to the most important
despatches, they are always delivered to the Secretary . . . Mr
Osborne or Mr Phinn.

131   Are you aware of any instances in which a letter has been lost?
— I can scarcely tax my memory during fifteen years with an
instance . . . [133] . . . [but] it is very difficult to prove the
negative. The only complaint I recollect was one of Admiral
Hamilton, a short time ago, by some inventor. He said he wrote

a letter but received no answer.

136   From your knowledge of all the departments during the . . . years you have been Reader, has the correspondence of the office increased, independently of the pressure occasioned by the present war? – Yes . . . The amalgamation [of 1832] brought here an immense mass of business, and I confess, in some respects, a description of business which I was very sorry to see entailed upon a Cabinet Office. It brought here the appointment of officers of the more subordinate branches of the profession. Formerly, Masters, and all the subordinate ranks in that branch . . . were appointed by the Navy Board. All Surgeons, Assistant-Surgeons, and so on, were appointed by the Commissioners of Victualling. The same applies to Paymasters, Assistant-Paymasters, Clerks, and Clerk's Assistants. That brought an immense mass of detail at once to this office. You are perhaps not aware that every appointment of any one of those officers entails a warrant, to which is affixed the signatures of two Lords and a Secretary. That change was combined with the introduction into the service of other classes of officers which did not then exist, namely, Engineers, with all their different classes and Naval Instructors, and others . . . The next great addition was the *Excellent* [gunnery ship]. It may be asked, how could that entail upon the office any great deal of business? Every officer of the navy is obliged to pass an examination in gunnery. You note in the Commission Branch whether he is of the first class, the second class, or the third class, and those who pass particular examinations are put on a separate rosta [*sic*] . . . You then have the examination of all the Gunners, and their certificates . . . That is the first branch. Then come all the experiments incidental to gunnery, involving shot, shell, gun-carriages, sights, and everything appertaining to naval science. A third great addition was the Packet Service . . . an immense service, entailing the expenditure of a very large amount indeed.

137   It comprises the making of all the contracts? – Yes. That brings me at once to one of the great causes of the increase of business. I referred just now to the arrival of despatches . . . when I was first Reader they arrived once a month [from the Mediterranean] or once in six weeks; now [thanks to the regular Packet Service] there are two Mediterranean mails a week . . . and what applies to . . . [that station] . . . applies to all the others. You never can have rapidity of communications without an increase of correspondence . . . Another great item arose from the introduction of steam . . . First of all we had the paddle-wheel; after the paddle-wheel came the screw; that necessarily involves again the question of high pressure engines . . . ; then comes the question of all the

appointments of Engineer officers; then come steam factories for dockyards; then the great supply of coals. When you follow those out in all their ramifications you will see that they must involve a very great addition to the business of the office. The next item I will mention is that of the Department of the Director of Works: Formerly if a work was undertaken in a dockyard it was done by a private contractor, but now the works which are undertaken . . . are of so vast a character that it is indispensably necessary to have an officer [*sic*] of our own, and an exceedingly important branch it is . . . We have had the subjects of Harbours of Refuge brought to us . . . [25] There is also a considerable increase of business, though it is not so much now as it was formerly, occasioned by railways. Railways involve the question of Tidal Harbours. There is not a river which can be crossed without the Admiralty sanction. All this leads to litigation and complicated business . . . Then there is the system of railway passes. There is likewise the Electric Telegraph: formerly we did our business in the morning; now we are never safe, day or night, for five minutes. We have had the organization of the dockyard battalions.[26] Then there is the Naval Coast Volunteers.[27] Then come all the educational questions: education, I believe, was not thought much of in the Navy formerly – now it is; there are Naval Instructors, Naval Schoolmasters, Seamen's Libraries, Dockyard Schools, Greenwich Hospital Schools, Royal Marine Schools, and all these are under the superintendence of the Lords of the Admiralty, and they require a great deal of supervision, and respecting them questions are being constantly put in the House of Commons. Another item, which is likely to increase, is that of war medals and gratuities. There is compensation for loss of clothing, and allotments of monthly allowances. Then we come to the great question of the Transport Services, and various other matters, such as inventions . . . [141] . . . The greatest increase of all, perhaps, is inventions, which is now almost a department of itself. The number of letters I open daily, upon every conceivable subject, is almost incredible.

138 In your office as Reader, being of course cognisant of all the correspondence which takes place with the outports . . . do you know of any subjects which could . . . be carried on at the outports, either by the Commanders-in-Chief or by the Superintendents of the yards? – . . . there is one subject which gives rise to a great deal of correspondence, that is, the discharge of seamen. I think the Commanders-in-Chief at Portsmouth, Plymouth, and the stations generally might be permitted to exercise a discretion on that subject.

140 Might . . . [one give] general instructions to the Admirals, leaving them to refer exceptional cases to the Board? – Yes. We have had entailed upon us of late years a very considerable correspondence with reference to dockyard appointments. Mr Osborne has very handsomely given up all that patronage. It was very desirable to get rid of it from the Admiralty, and it has proved a great relief.[28]

145 You have stated the increase of business which has been thrown upon the Admiralty since 1832; can you state what increase has been made in the establishments? – The Chief Clerk will be able to give that information.[29] I consider the pressure upon the Lords and the Secretaries to be such that it is very difficult to get through the current business.

147 Are you of opinion that in any way the correspondence might be simplified? – I think in one respect it has been simplified: a great many of the minutes are written in a much more condensed form than they were formerly . . . [148] . . . I cannot see any [further] means of either condensing or simplifying the correspondence . . . If you were to compare the orders now for the sailing of ships with the orders formerly, you would see that we do not write a page where formerly we wrote three or five. All the verbiage of a bygone age has been dropped . . .

164 It has been suggested that the office might be so constituted as that each branch should form a Secretariat to one of the Lords. Do you think that would be an improvement? – I think it would be very desirable, but the difficulties would be very great. Admiral Berkeley, as First Sea Lord, superintends the Secret Branch, which embraces all the orders, and everything which is political. He has also the armaments and complements, which are in the Military Branch, and he has the appointing of officers to gun-boats in . . . the Commission Branch. The only mode of doing it would be to make a different distribution of the business among the different Lords.

165 The business being distributed according to agreement among the Lords themselves, and not according to any rule, supposing there is a change of Government, involving a change of the Lords, and a particular Lord said, I am not acquainted with such a part of the business, and would rather take so and so; would not that interfere with the proposed arrangement? – I think it would. There are five Lords, and if you were to decide that the First Sea Lord should take such and such business, and the Second Sea Lord such and such duties, and make that dovetail in with your distribution of the business, that would be perfectly practicable. Whether the incoming Lords would like it I cannot say.

170 Have you had much experience of the working of the Record

Office? – I was for several years in it . . . I do not wish to make any personal remarks, but I think that gentlemen who have been placed at the Indexes and also at the Digest have not from their standing in the office been equal to the performance of the duties required of them . . . the gentlemen who are engaged upon the Digest, instead of being . . . young in office, should be experienced clerks . . . They ought to abstract just those points which are deserving of attention, and those should again be put in condensed and clear language, and be well written . . . With regard to the indexes, I entertain the opinion . . . that they ought not to be kept (if I may use the expression) by intellectual clerks; it is mere drudgery, but it does require very great attention, and I think if the two gentlemen who are placed at the Index were persons who were to spend their lives there, and according to their care, attention, and good conduct, were to have a rise every five years, similar to that given to gentlemen at the Treasury, the books would be much better kept than they are at present. Now they are handed over to young men who have just come into the office.

178 Was it not considered in the year 1836, that this was the best record of any public Department in England? – I should be disposed to say so; but there is this difference, that though the system may have worked admirably when it was a small Department, and when the business was all of an important character, since the immense influx of business has brought such a mass of detail into the office, that which is important is smothered in that which is unimportant.

186 Has the number of decisions of the Board very much increased? – [187] [they have] very nearly doubled, for this reason – that we have Boards now every day, whereas formerly we had sittings only every other day.

188 How long has the Board sat every day? – Since Admiral Sir James Deans Dundas came here in the year 1846 [as Second Naval Lord]. That entails a great deal of additional work both upon the Secretaries and upon the Reader, for this reason – that on the non-Board days we were formerly able to prepare all our letters for the following day.

189 When the Board was only held every other day, was not that found to be a check to the speedy despatch of business? – Certainly. I think the present system is very superior to the old . . . at the same time the business is more difficult of accomplishment, as it has to be done against time.

211 During your experience in the office, has the rule of promotion been by seniority, or [in] exceptional cases . . . by merit? – The rule has been generally – I may say, almost invariably – to promote by seniority . . . there was one case of a gentleman who

was irregular in his conduct, and was passed over . . . It operated as a warning, and he felt the disgrace so keenly that he tendered his resignation.

212   Is that the only instance in your experience in which a gentleman has been passed over? – The only instance.

214   . . . do you think it desirable that . . . gentlemen should be selected for merit and assiduity? – . . . I am, I must say, opposed to what may be called competitive emulation, and I am so upon this ground, that I am afraid it will destroy the harmony and good feeling which I consider so essential to the efficient performance of the public service. I think, however, that the object you have in view can be effected by a less violent course. I think by the judicious distribution of what I may be allowed to designate staff offices, a great deal may be done to encourage and reward merit in the junior classes. There are at present the private Secretaryships to the First and Second Sea Lords, and to the Secretaries; extra allowances are granted to the head of the Private Office [of the First Lord], and to the two gentlemen who correct the Quarterly Navy List. Then in the Second Class there is the Précis Writership, and I should in future be glad to see the Deputy Reader, who is now a junior, filled by a Second Class Clerk, and it would afford me great pleasure to see appointed a Paymaster of Admiralty contingencies, relieving the Chief Clerk of that duty . . . Then with regard to the First Class there would be the Reader and the head of the Secret Branch.

215   . . . do you think it desirable, supposing a vacancy occurs in the First Class, to take a gentleman to preside over a Branch who is inferior in capacity and intelligence, when you could find a superior though a junior? – It would depend upon a great many circumstances. The question would be whether the gentleman is, or is not, equal to the discharge of the duties required of him.

216   So that if there were a gentleman very superior in the discharge of his duties you would not promote him over one who you thought would be equal to them? – No. I think it would be attended with heart-burnings and jealousies that would more than counteract the benefit. At the same time I am for encouraging merit in every possible way.

Evidence of John Barrow, Head of the Admiralty Record Office

234   Will you be kind enough to explain the principle upon which any public document after leaving the Board and the Branch to which it belongs comes to you . . . ? – In the usual course, it ought to come up to me, in a box, the following morning, after it has been

executed in the branch. Frequently, however, it happens that a letter does not arrive possibly for a month or two months, and frequently, I fear, not at all: it is in circulation − it is difficult to say where − according to the number of persons who have been named in the despatch. For instance, Sir Edmund Lyons [Commander-in-Chief Mediterranean and Black Sea] sends a despatch, inclosing one from Captain Osborn in the Sea of Azof. He mentions several officers in his despatch. It goes to the Commission Branch to be noted, if any Lieutenant is mentioned: it then goes to the Commission and Warrant Branch, should any Master be mentioned: after that it goes to the Marine Office, if Marine officers are mentioned in it: if there is a Surgeon mentioned it will go to Somerset House . . . Perhaps some of the squadron . . . might get on shore, or their engines damaged, and [the Admiral] might mention that such a vessel had broken down: the same letter would then go to the Surveyor's office. I mention this to show that a letter is very widely circulated before it comes to me. In the meantime an application may be made by the Board for the letter, but I am unable to produce it.

236 When it does come to you what course do you pursue? − I then read the letter, and mark it, according to the variety of subjects . . . [it] may contain; that is to say, I mark every name of every officer and of every ship mentioned in it, and I put figures at the top, according to the subjects which go into our digests . . . The letter then receives a stamp, indicating the date of its receipt in the Record Office . . . and it is passed through the Index . . .

237 Is it only the names of officers and ships which you index? − That is all; and of any persons that may be mentioned . . . [238] When it has been entered through the Index and Digest it goes away to the pigeon-holes.

239 Supposing that the letter we have now been tracing was No. 100, does it go into the same pigeon hole with No. 99? − It follows it, if it is from the same station . . .

240 All the letters from Sir Edmund Lyons would be kept together for the year? − Yes.

241 Is your subdivision entirely according to stations? − Yes.

243 Does the Index itself contain anything besides the name; does it refer to the subjects which are contained in the letter? − Very slightly; a single word, perhaps, will indicate the subject, and the Digest numbers are also inserted.

247 Who enters the detail of the letters in the Digest? − Two . . . gentlemen. That requires considerable mental energy and experience.

248 The Digest is in fact a *précis* of the letter, is it not? − Yes, it ought

to be as concise as possible, but to convey all the information required.

251   Are they second or third class clerks who are employed at the Digest? – Third class.

252   Are they second or third class clerks who are employed at the Index? – Third class; at present they are temporary clerks . . .

253   . . . are you satisfied with the gentlemen who are employed [for] . . . indexing and digesting . . . ? – No, I am not. [254] I think these two temporary clerks, and all young gentlemen coming into the office, are not calculated for the work: I speak now of the Index. I think it requires people who are older in years, who will be alive to the importance of the names being very carefully entered. Few young gentlemen, as far as my experience goes, have ever given much attention to the books . . .

255   Are not the gentlemen employed permanently attached to the Record Office? – They are not; that is another great evil . . . This very year I have had several gentlemen employed upon the Index, which causes great confusion.

256   What are the circumstances which cause a change in your Staff in the Record Office? – Sometimes the shifting of gentlemen from one department to another, according to the exigencies of the office.

259   What is the strength of the department at present? – There are seven [gentlemen] . . .

260   What are their duties? – The reading of the whole of the correspondence, the searches, and delivering papers out.

262   What are the daily average number of entries in the Index and in the Digest? – . . . we have about 170 letters to record every day . . .

265   Have you any paper to put in with reference to the commencement of the practice of recording the public documents in this office? – There is an Order in Council in 1809 which establishes the Record Office.

266   Has it not been very much enlarged of late years? – I think not.

267   Have there not been a great many letters which were not registered bound up, which were brought to light by yourself? – Yes, a vast number. I have bound a great many into volumes, and have had an index made of them; – all the Admirals' despatches prior to the year 1792 [from 1688]. They were up in the garrets, without any index whatever to them, and I had them carefully bound into volumes and indexed.

268   What are the principal papers which are required for the use of the Board? Are they documents upon which a correspondence has been going on during the previous six or twelve months [or longer] . . .? – Generally speaking they are documents which have occurred during the last twelvemonth, or . . . perhaps . . . the last

year or two. Frequently we have to refer also to papers of previous years, but generally . . . the letters asked for are letters of the current year, and of the last.

270 . . . Would it be better . . . that a letter should be recorded in the department, and kept there . . . (say [for] twelve months) till all correspondence has ceased on it, than that it should be sent back to you? − I think it would be better if it could be so arranged . . . the particular department could keep those letters till the correspondence terminated, and then send them in to me as a whole.

276 How do you trace a document on which there has been a large correspondence going on for a series of years. Take, for example, the question of coal depôts, on which a large correspondence has taken place with respect to sites at the principal yards, which has now been going on since 1847; suppose I send for the last document which has reached this office, in what mode do you record all the other documents which have taken place upon the same subject? − They are all entered under one head in the Digest for different years.

277 For different years? − For different years only.

278 Then to trace a paper which is called for for the purpose of seeing what has been done, it is necessary to go through the books of five or seven years? − Yes, but all under one head in those digests.

281 You have nothing in your office which, when the last letter is received, can be ticketed with it as a digest of the whole? − No.

282 Has it ever been proposed? − No, not to my knowledge.

284 Do you think it feasible? − I should think not. It is of course a question of numbers; it would be quite feasible if you had one or two gentlemen to attend to that duty. In such a case as had been mentioned, having a large bundle of letters of that description, I should keep them together and bind them into a volume. The subject which has just been mentioned is one in which the papers are all together, in a single volume, or, as I should call it, a 'case', and if you asked for those papers they would be presented to you complete . . .

300 Do you enter every letter in the Digest? − No, not every letter.

301 Ordinary routine letters are not included in the Digest? − No; personal letters only go in the Index.

302 How are you guided in the introduction of letters into the Digest? − It depends entirely upon myself whether I consider a letter of sufficient importance to be inserted in the Digest . . . [303] . . . not less than seventy or eighty [are digested daily].

322 Do you see that any advantage would be gained by . . . constituting the head of the Record Office the Librarian of the establishment? − He is nominally the Librarian now, but we have no library.

323   Have you found disadvantage occasionally result from not having
       a proper library of reference? – Occasionally, but latterly that
       difficulty has been removed, because Sir Francis Beaufort [the
       previous Hydrographer] established a good library upstairs, and
       you can find there most of the books which you require. At one
       time I suggested the establishment of a naval library, but it did not
       seem to meet with much encouragement . . .

324   Do you not consider it a great defect that there is no General Index
       and Digest in the office? – I consider it a very great defect, and
       I consider also that it would be difficult, if not impossible, to
       establish a general Index . . .

328   Have you turned your attention to the question of registering letters
       on their first being brought into the office? – I have often
       considered it, and I think it most desirable that it should be done.

329   Would it at all facilitate the discharge of the duties of the Record
       Office? – It would in this respect – we should have some clue
       to a letter, whereas at present we have none. Frequently I am at
       a loss to consider where a letter may be which has not come to me,
       and I endeavour to call to mind where it may possibly be.

1662   Have you turned your attention to the mode of recording papers
       in other Government offices? – Yes; I have examined the system
       at the Foreign Office and at the Colonial and other offices, but
       I have found no office which is under similar circumstances to this
       . . . [1663] . . . the arrangement is, generally speaking, more simple,
       but then the correspondence, I may say, is more simple, too, than
       ours. The correspondence of the Admiralty is exceedingly
       diffuse.

1674   When a letter refers to two subjects, is it digested under one head
       or under two? – When it is questionable under which head it ought
       to be placed, it would go under both.

1683   Have you turned your attention to the subject of a register of letters
       when received? – I have considered it. I think it could be done;
       but it would probably require the assistance of three gentlemen in
       order to be done quickly.

1684   Have you traced out any form of a register? – The more simple
       the better. It should consist of three or four columns perhaps. The
       date of the letter, from whom it is received, the subject, and the
       disposal of the letter.

1685   At what time does the Record Office close? – At 5 o'clock.

1686   Searches made afterwards are made by the messenger, are they not?
       – They are made by the clerk in attendance, whoever he is . . .
       [1687] 'Former papers' are very seldom asked for after 5 o'clock:
       the business of the office is supposed to be at an end.

1688   Do you make it a point in the office that the whole of the business of the day shall be closed before the clerks leave? – In my department, no; it ought to be so, but it is not.

1689 Why is it not so? – Because the gentlemen at the Digest, for example, do not get through their day's work in the day. The consequence is, that there always has been latterly an arrear at the Digest . . . [1691] [of] probably a day and a-half, or a couple of days.

[The twin themes of under-staffing, especially during wartime, and the particular strain of digesting, are again to be found in the Appendix to Barrow's evidence, a letter written to the First Secretary on 16 July, before the Committee of Inquiry met.]

APPENDIX

. . . With respect to the proper strength of the Record Office, I beg to state that I have been endeavouring for some time past to carry on the work with seven, and occasionally with six gentlemen; and when they have been all present the business of the Department has gone on smoothly enough. But whenever there happened to be an unusual pressure, or from any cause one or two of the gentlemen have been unavoidably absent, great inconvenience has arisen, and has been experienced throughout the office generally, by the work being consequently thrown into arrear. At the present time the arrear of work in the Record Office is considerable, and there are now only five gentlemen actually employed in the Department, four of whom (two being extra clerks) are very inexperienced.

I am therefore of opinion that during the war the strength of the Record Office should consist of not less than nine gentlemen, viz:

> One Senior Clerk, First Class.
> Two Second Class Clerks . . .
> And six Third Class Clerks.

Of these the Department should never, under any circumstances, be left with less than seven actually present during the war, six in peace . . .

In regard to the Digests, I have always been of opinion that two gentlemen of some experience and standing in the office should be employed on those books. And during the war this is more than ever necessary, when the correspondence is not only voluminous but often very intricate, requiring considerable skill and care in making the abstracts of the various subjects contained in each letter, for entry under the corresponding heads of the Digest. To keep a Digest well, not only method, but a considerable amount of mental exertion is required; and the work when conscientiously performed is both laborious and unremitting; so much so that few gentlemen like to be employed on a Digest if they can avoid it. And I would therefore suggest (what I have long desired to do) that some addition should be made to the salary of the two gentlemen so employed, say £50 a-year to each . . .

Evidence of Admiral W. A. B. Hamilton

336 You were [Second] Secretary to the Admiralty for a series of years? − I was . . . [337] For rather more than ten years; ten years and four months [January 1845–May 1855].

338 Before that you held the office of Private Secretary to the Earl of Haddington [First Lord, September 1841–January 1846]? − Yes, for three years and a half [from September 1841].

340 . . . Can you give any information as to the advantage which you think would be derived from a registry of letters? − I do not think letters could be practically registered unless they were sent in the first instance to such a department as the Record Department . . . For although it is very easy to register a letter received, the trace of that letter even if registered may be as easily lost as the letter itself . . . I do not think an efficient register for practical purposes can be established without having the means of entering . . . the contents of any letter, whether as to its purport or actual inclosures . . . [341] In order in some measure to obviate the mischief which, when I first became Secretary, I observed from papers becoming detached, and plans being lost, or the inclosures not forthcoming, I directed that all inclosures should be sewn in. I imagine I was the first to introduce needle and thread into the office, for which I believe the gentlemen are now obliged to me, though at first they thought it a trouble. It may appear trifling, but if there were some one present and ready at once to attach every inclosure, there would be a vast deal of trouble saved. Mr Briggs has alluded in his evidence to a letter which had been said not to have been answered. That was a case in which the complaint was not from the want of an answer, but that the plans could not be found.

354 . . . should [letters] go down to the heads of the branches before coming to the Superintending Lords; do you conceive that that would work advantageously for the office? − I do not think that in all cases it would. I think with the business of the Senior Naval Lord [above all] . . . it would not answer. Most of his papers

... require immediate despatch; they relate to business with which he is fully cognizant, and he can generally make his minutes without reference [to the branches].

355   It is not by the submission of all letters and papers to the members of the Board in the first instance, that they are kept informed of all which has taken place upon the various subjects under their supervision? – Certainly ...

365   You know what the hours of attendance in the office are; do you think any benefit would arise to the public service by an alteration of those hours, and by getting the gentlemen to attend here at 10 o'clock? – I think that a certain number, say two from each branch might attend at 10, but they ought, I think, [to] be allowed, at the discretion of the head of the branch, to leave at 4. I do not think with the pressure of work there is at this office, that any gentleman can permanently stand at work with advantage to the public service for more than six hours a-day when it comes to the business of his life.

366   Do not you very often find that the Lords want assistance before the gentlemen who could afford that assistance have arrived? – Yes.

367   From your experience of Boards of Admiralty have not you found that the Lords were generally here at or before 10? – Always some of them.

368   Were not there frequently decisions to be taken and even letters written as early as 10 or half-past 10? – Letters were to be written as early as half-past 10, and decisions were made upon letters before half-past 10.

377   What has been the number of hours' attendance which has been established at Whitehall? – Six hours is the nominal period of attendance; as it is, I believe, at all offices.[30]

383   Are the letters all brought to the Board Room? – A large portion are ... All that come from the Secretary of State's office and from Commanders-in-Chief abroad or at home. But those letters that look like mere applications, or which from their handwriting are supposed not to come from our own officers, are opened by a gentleman in a room adjoining the Board Room, who assists the Reader in opening the letters.

381   Was it a practice while you were Secretary that all [Board Room] letters should be opened by the Secretary? – ... the practice was constantly changed. For instance I might begin by opening all the Secretary of State's letters. There may be a change of Secretaries, and the new Parliamentary Secretary may say, 'Let me have the letters of the Secretary of State'. There is an end to my seeing any more of them. But when he goes away I may see the whole of them again. Occasionally the First Secretary has wished to have particular letters opened by himself.

404   Do not you think a General Index would be of value to the office? – Very great value indeed. Great progress has been made in that direction, and partial indexes have been established, and they have been of the greatest advantage . . .

405   I think you were in the office when the system of the Board Minute Book was established? – Yes.

406   It was a mere revival of a practice which had fallen into disuse? – Yes.

408   Were not you thereby enabled . . . to recur to the very words of a decision of the Board when they happened to be a matter of question at the Board? – I never used it for that purpose; nor do I think the minutes are sufficiently reduced to rule to make a reference to the Board Minutes serviceable for all which may appear analogous cases . . . [410] The value of the Board Minute Book is to substantiate that such an order has been given, or to enable any member of the Board to see what business has been transacted.

411   Was the General Minute Book established when you were here? – They were both established together.

412   Did you find that the Lords had frequent recurrence to the General Minute Book to see what was being done in other Departments? – I think the Lords were frequently in the habit of looking at those books.

420   Did you find when you were Secretary that you had great difficulty in reading all the letters which were submitted to you? – It was impossible to read all, and it was not necessary to read all . . . I could not say mistakes were general, yet at any rate my supervision was such that . . . there was hardly a day in which I had not to send down a letter containing some little clerical error, or something requiring slight correction . . . I was able, notwithstanding the rapid way in which I signed the papers, to make a kind of supervision of them; but it was impossible, looking to the number of letters, to be answerable for the right spelling or diction of the whole of them; nor did I think it necessary to look to those which I knew to be mere routine cases of information. Any letter which is signed by command of the Lords must be a mere transcript of the minute of a Lord, and therefore it would not require anything but the superintendence of the gentlemen in the branch.

430   What is your opinion with reference to promotion in the office . . . ? – I think that seniority should be the rule, and that there should be a clear case made out of another person being preferable before you pass over the senior.

431   Are you aware of the Order in Council of the 30th of January, 1816; and that these words are to be found in it: 'That the removal from a lower class to a higher shall be the reward of qualifications for the duties of the higher class, without any reference whatsoever to the

seniority the person may hold in the lower class'? − Yes; but the rule of the office has been to promote by seniority, and although I think there may be cases in which it had better not have been so, yet the rule might remain, and wherever there was a clear case for exception, such exception should be acted on . . . [432] I have never known any rule of promotion adopted but that of seniority since I have been here; but then it has happened that the senior has been the person recommended by the Chief Clerk.

APPENDIX

[From evidence submitted by Hamilton after the Committee had interviewed him]

. . . I have no hesitation in giving it as my opinion that urgent necessity exists for strengthening the hands of the Secretary . . . The amount of business to be transacted daily at the Admiralty, and for which the Secretary is supposed to be responsible, has become so great as virtually to invalidate that responsibility. He cannot read properly all the letters he has to sign . . . [and] the consequences of an error in a letter of seeming unimportance may nevertheless be serious . . . [Moreover, there does not] remain to him the time . . . for the exercise of any suggestive faculty, or for giving effect to any practical view for which concentration of the mind is necessary. Talent and energy must alike be swamped by the increasing stream of daily routine, which still flows on in the old contracted channel.

As a remedy for this defect . . . I would suggest the appointment of an Assistant Secretary, to be selected from the office for his ability and capacity, his integrity, and his thorough acquaintance with the Admiralty business, and on him might devolve a large portion of the work now done by the Second Secretary, to whom he should be entirely subordinate, though equally with him responsible to the Board . . . So assisted . . . the Second Secretary would be able to devote more of his time to the higher duties of his office, and by a frank communion and intercourse with his assistant, and with the comparative leisure that each would acquire, the views that either might entertain for the better working of the establishment would be consolidated and so framed as to admit of their being brought before the Board from time to time for its approval . . .

It may seem as though too great stress were laid on the advantage to the Second Secretary, to the exclusion of the relative aid to be derived by the First Secretary, in the appointment of an assistant; but it is to the thoroughly efficient working . . . of the Second Secretary's Office, that chief regard must be had; for, burdened as the Second Secretary now is, he would be infinitely more overcharged if the First Secretary had the entire representation of the navy in the House of Commons − a state of things which, in the course of the last fifteen years, has been the rule rather than the exception.[31]

The Parliamentary business that would then devolve upon the First Secretary, would leave him little time for the regular business of the Admiralty, and the Second Secretary could expect but a small share of his assistance in the daily duties of his office; and it is to such a contingency that regard has been had, in speaking of the aid required for the Second Secretary . . .

There is one other point I venture to touch upon, though most reluctantly, fearing as I do that the Board will not go along with me. I have often entertained a doubt as to the expediency or well working of a daily Board. The practice is comparatively a recent one, and although introduced, if I remember rightly, about the year 1850 or 1851 without any minute or resolution of the Board, has become an established rule . . . [However,] with a Board pending or in haste to meet . . . [the Secretary] must be content to get at the greater part of [the correspondence] . . . by the process of reading at the Board, and I could appeal to any Secretary to say whether, with the heavy charge devolving upon him of making the minute on the letter just read, he can always attend properly to the one that follows . . . It would be an advantage in some respects that there should be time to prepare a subject for the Board; and it cannot be said that delay in operations would be a consequence of the Board not sitting daily, since the practice, as I have stated, is of comparatively modern date, and it is not at the Board that the ordinary orders relating to the movements of ships are usually given. Whenever there is great pressure of business, there may be a tendency to confound hurry with despatch; and it may be a question whether this tendency has been sufficiently guarded against in the natural desire to have the business brought before the Board with the least possible delay . . .

In conclusion, I need hardly observe to the Committee, that one of the most effectual steps towards simplifying and reducing the business of the Admiralty would be the concentrating the whole of the Departments in one spot. The present separation of the offices occasions serious delay, and Somerset House has been spoken of as the fittest place for the concentration of the Admiralty; but such arrangement would give rise to inconvenience and delay of another description. It is indispensably necessary that the First Lord should be upon the spot, the centre round which the whole machinery of the offices revolve. He should be accessible for constant and instant reference so far as the Admiralty business is concerned; but it is equally essential that he should be near his colleagues in the Cabinet, and within immediate reach of the offices of the Secretaries of State and Commander-in-Chief of the army, to say nothing of a proximity to the Houses of Parliament, and these requirements are only attainable by means of a general office at Whitehall.

Plans by Mr Scamp, the Deputy-Director of Engineering Works, adapted to this purpose, have been in existence at the Admiralty for the last four or five years, and might be well worthy the examination of the Committee.

Evidence of C. H. Pennell, Head of the Secret and Political Branch

452   In 1853 the Department which you now superintend was called the Military and Political Department? – The Military, Secret and Political Department.

453   For what cause was there a separation made? – The pressure of the war necessitated it. [454] . . . the division took place on the declaration of war.

461   In your opinion from your knowledge of the department as it then stood, it was not possible to go on without such a division of the department as was then made? – Assuredly not; it was a complete scramble to get through the business. Some gentlemen entertained the opinion that war would not be declared, and I was, therefore, unwilling to put forward the question of an increase of the establishment till it was shown that war would take place; but as soon as war was declared the office was put on a proper footing. The Board was perfectly willing to do anything at any time upon the necessity being pointed out.

537   Do you think a great deal of manual or mechanical labour might be saved by adopting the system of a copying machine? – I do not see any very valid objection to it.

538   Does it not give you, better than any mere transcript can do, the very *fac-simile* of the letter, erasures and all, if there be any? – It is again a question of a balance of advantages and disadvantages; there are disadvantages in having flimsy and detached sheets of paper . . . On the other hand you save clerical labour . . . On the whole, except as a question of economy, I should infinitely prefer the present mode, as being more secure and certain.[32]

539   Is it not also a question, to some extent, of mental education of the younger gentlemen in the office; are not you obliged to detain gentlemen for ten or fifteen years as mere copyists of letters? – Yes.

540   Suppose a gentleman comes into this office, is not he for ten or fifteen years a mere copyist? – Frequently.

541   Do not you think that has a pernicious effect to some extent? –

To a certain extent, I think it dwarfs the capacities of men.

542 If you had a more mechanical mode of copying, might not you employ the young gentlemen in making précis and abstracts of papers, so preparing themselves to discharge the higher duties of the office? – Yes.

548 From your experience here, what is your view as to the system of promotion by selection according to merit? – I have seen both systems acted on; and after long consideration of an exceedingly difficult question, I have come to the conclusion that the best working principle is that of rigorous rejection for incompetency, rather than selection for merit.

550 An incompetent person ought not to be in the office at all? – Certainly not; and that is the very result of promoting a man on the ground of presumed merit, and those men who are passed over are to a certain extent discredited . . . [554] If I may be permitted to say so, I think there is a fallacy underlying the argument on the subject of promotion by merit. It is assumed that there are persons whose merits are so patent and preeminent as would justify their being promoted over the heads of others; those giants have never crossed my course . . .

555 Have you ever known your principle of the rejection of an unfit man carried out? – A gentleman who was passed over because of his demerit would have been chosen if it had not been for his being really an incompetent clerk.

556 During the changes which have taken place here during the last thirty years, do you believe that in every case the senior has been perfectly fitted for the duties of the new situation in which he has been placed? – No; I think in some cases there has not been a due appreciation of the particular powers of the individual; he might have been well fitted for some departments, but not for others. But I confess that I have not myself seen those intellectual giants which are sometimes spoken of; whether it be that the field is a circumscribed one, or that the average capacities of educated men are nearly the same, or the operation of both cases come together, I certainly have not met with men who might be supposed to be entitled to carry everything before them.

Evidence of J. H. N. Houghton, Head of the Civil Branch

1055 Will you look over the duties mentioned in the table [of duties] as belonging to your branch, and state whether they are the general duties in which you are employed? – They are; I may say that this head, 'Offices, Dockyards, and Civil Establishments', does not only involve the *matériel* and the buildings, but all the *personnel*, the salaries, and the discipline of the establishments, etc.

1068 I see you are charged with the Navy Estimates. Do you attend to the whole of the business of the Navy Estimates? – As far as the Whitehall Office is concerned. They are principally prepared at Somerset House, and an extra allowance made for it. When they come here they require the signature of the Lords, and we submit them to the Treasury, and in many cases we have to get Orders in Council to carry them out. For instance, if a new situation is made it is put in the Estimates, and it requires an Order in Council to establish the situation. A number of details are done here, but the real work of the Estimates is done at Somerset House as a matter of account.

1069 Works under the Director of Works are with you? – That is an extensive part of our business. Perhaps the Director of Works is in a different situation to the other officers. He is not called a principal officer of the Navy, and he gives no orders to hospitals or dockyards; but every order is made on a submission from him, which is approved of, and we have to write to the different departments accordingly.

1071 Would not it be desirable that the Director of Works, his being strictly a technical and professional business, should write the letters to carry out his submissions, sending them for signature to the Secretary? – I do not see the necessity for that; knowing that it is technical we follow *verbatim et literatim* what he submits.

1072 Often without understanding it? – Very often.

1074 Supposing a scheme to be propounded for improving a slip at Keyham, will you tell the Committee the various steps it goes through, and the letters you have to write? – The shipwright officer would submit it to the Superintendent of the Yard; he would refer it to the Clerk of the Works on the spot. The Clerk of the Works would make his report to the Superintendent. The Superintendent would forward it here addressed to the Secretary. The Secretary sends it to Sir Robert Peel [Civil Lord]. Sir Robert Peel refers it to the Director of Works for his report. The Director of Works, if he requires further particulars, sends a request to the Superintendent of the Yard that he will direct the Clerk of the Works to report upon the following subjects in detail . . . That comes back to the Director of Works without coming through this office. The Director of Works then makes his submission, stating the case to the Board, explaining how it originated, and saying that the expense will be so much, forwarding a plan, and submitting that certain directions be given to the Superintendent accordingly.

1075   That submission goes to the Superintending Lord [Peel], does it not? — Yes.

1077   Then assuming the Board to approve the submission, you write the letter? — Yes, embodying the submission of the Director of Works.

1078   Supposing it involves expenditure, then whom do you notify? — The Accountant-General and the Director of Works; and if it is connected with machinery, the Surveyor of the Navy is acquainted with it, and the Storekeeper-General if a matter of contract.

1079   Then the letters to be written would be to the Admiral Superintendent, to the Director of Works, the Accountant-General, and possibly to the Surveyor of the Navy? — Yes; the three last would all be on the same paper. The Director of Works invariably obtains from the Record Office what he terms the groundwork of the 'acquaint'. I think that is the practice with most of the principal officers at Somerset House. Consequently the Board's decisions are often revised after those decisions are made, the minute made here by the Superintending Lord or the Board put into a different shape, and the decision is altered.

1080   Of course it is re-submitted to the Board? — Yes, it ought to be.

1085   If a purchase is to be made by the Admiralty, or there is a sale of land to be effected belonging to the Admiralty, would you have anything to do with it? — I should think we should have something to do with it.

1086   During the progress of the negotiation do you have frequent reference to the Solicitor? — Certainly.

1087   At the stage of business when letters are to be written, do you write them, or does the Solicitor . . . ? — We should direct him to make the purchase, and I think he would carry out the details.

1088   You were a considerable time in the Record Office, were you not? — About two years.

1098   Have you any difficulty now in getting papers from the Record Office? — Most of the papers have been collected before they reach my office.

1099   Do you never go yourself to search for papers? — When anything is pressing I do.

1100   When you have called for previous papers yourself, have you found difficulty in obtaining them? — Sometimes I have.

1104   When you acted as a searcher, did any delay of that kind occur? — I think not; the business was much less in point of quantity that it is now.

1106   Do you think it desirable that gentlemen should go and search themselves in the Record Office? — I do not think it is a good practice.

1107   Then if it is not desirable as a practice, is not much of the advantage of having gentlemen pass through the Record Office taken away? —

In that point of view; but on Sunday, for instance, when I am in attendance here, or in the evening, I can go to the Record Office and find a paper which I could not have found from the Digest, if I had not understood the way in which the papers are put away.

1111   You have been Précis Writer, have you not? – Yes, I have.

1113   Was the [Board] Minute Book first commenced by you? – I suggested it to Lord Auckland in the year 1847 . . . it was in consequence of Captain Hamilton having mentioned to me that a great want was felt in consequence of not having the business previously done by the Board brought in a concentrated form before them. The original minutes at one period came direct from the Secretary at the Board to be inserted in the book before being executed; but, after a time, complaints were made that it delayed the business, and they went through the Departments for some time. They were sent down to the Chief Clerk, and he distributed them to the Departments, and I used to have great difficulty in getting them from the Departments, and very often I did not get them at all. Then another change was made, and they were ordered to come direct to the Précis Writer. I am now speaking of a period extending over six years, during which changes were frequent.

1115   Have you any doubt that, while you were Précis Writer, from the nature of the system, many minutes made by the Board escaped being entered in the Board Minute Book? – Certainly, many escaped.

1117   Have you seen the working of the new system? – As far as my own room is concerned.

1119   Do you think it is an improvement on the system adopted when you were Précis Writer? – Certainly, it is more of a system.

1130   What principle do you adopt, as head of the branch, as to the entry of General Minutes? – I send everything, except such things as 'own receipts', or the refusal of a ridiculous inquiry, or anything of that kind.

APPENDIX

[Letter to Captain Milne, the Chairman of the Committee of Inquiry, from Nelson Houghton]

With reference to my evidence given before the Committee this day, I beg to lay before you the following memorandum on the subject of promotion, agreeable to your directions.

I observe that the printed report on the organization of the Permanent Civil Service [Trevelyan-Northcote], and the remarks of Mr Phinn at the opening of the proceedings of the Committee, both point to promotion by merit as contradistinguished from promotion by seniority. It appears to me that a middle course might be pursued with advantage both to the public service and the individuals concerned; and which would combine both systems, without impairing the principle of either.

I may exemplify it thus: On a vacancy occurring in one of the upper classes of the clerks, it would be for the consideration of the Board whether the gentleman next in seniority was qualified to fulfil the duties of the post, and if he is so found, I think his character and seniority combined ought to give him the strongest claim to it; but if on investigation he is not found qualified, then the claims and character of the gentleman next below him in seniority should be considered in a similar way; and so passing through the list regularly downwards . . .

It is felt to be a great discouragement to official zeal, and always liable to be attributed to sinister motives, when a person very low down on the list is selected for preferment over the heads of those who have perhaps instructed him in his duties, and taught him to acquire that very skill which accidental circumstances have brought more immediately under the personal knowledge of his chief – his seniors at the same time possessing equal skill, with far greater experience, acquired by years of toil, which they naturally expect to have rewarded in the course of office, if they are not known to be disqualified.

If a public officer has shown merit in any particular duty or work, he is, no doubt, deserving of reward; but it ought not to be given to him at the expense of other public servants, possessing equal merits, but unfortunately without the opportunity of displaying them.

The adoption of a plan of this description would be a *juste milieu* between the two extremes, and be an inducement for the younger members of the service to establish an official character early in their career . . . [33]

Evidence of E. Giffard, Secretary to the Transport Board,[34] *formerly Head of the Legal Branch*

1284   As a junior in the Record Office what duties did you perform? – First of all I was at the Index, and then I was promoted to the Digest. Mr Bedford was the head of the room.[35]

1285   Had you any difficulty with regard to the mode of conducting the business there then? – Not the least; it was the most perfect system possible.

1286   Had you any difficulty in getting papers? – Never. Mr Bedford was an invaluable gentleman in that respect. I do not think he ever missed finding a thing, however complicated. The papers, of course, have increased in number since then.

1294   Did you find any difficulty in getting letters from the Record Office [as head of the Legal Branch, when Mr Barrow headed the Record Office]? – A good deal . . . [1295] From the want of working the [record] system properly.

1301   From your experience of the Record Office, what do you consider to be the value of the Digest? – I do not think the work of the office could go on without the Digest at all.

1304   If a 'previous paper' is asked for, and only the subject is given, it is to the Digest you would refer, and not the Index? – It is the only way you would have of getting it.

1312   Did you ever find the want of a General Index in the Record Office? – The Digest is made up year by year at present. – There are in the Record Office two most valuable books, called 'Mr Rouse's Digest', embracing a period of twenty years each.[36] If you would make a Digest of the present Digest up to this time, it would be the best thing you could do for the office . . .

1320   Do you think it would be desirable to establish a General Register of the letters which come into the establishment? – No, it would delay the work. When the War Department was formed, I took the trouble, in consequence of having one or two serious delays, to ask how they did their work. I was told, 'We do it on the Colonial Office Plan'. I said, 'It may be very good for the Colonial Office, who only answer their letters at fixed intervals by the regular mails, but for a department which has to do its work *de die in diem*, it will not answer'. According to that plan, on a letter coming in the morning, it is opened by the registering gentleman. If there be a heavy correspondence it may chance not to go to the department which it concerns until late in the day . . .

1359   How is the promotion from one grade, and from one rate of pay, to another, made in the [Transport Department] . . . ; is it by selection or seniority? – . . . I have generally gone upon the principle of taking the seniors and setting their names down, and marking their qualifications by each. I think it would be very desirable that you should carry out the present system of promotion by merit and seniority very stringently. I do not think it has ever been acted on sufficiently.

1360   Which do you understand to be the rule of the office at Whitehall – promotion by seniority, or by merit? – Neither the one nor the other; but rejection for incompetency.

1361   You are aware of the Order in Council in 1816; has that ever been acted upon in the office in your time? – Not in my time. I only know one instance in which it was ever acted on.

1362   Have you known the senior invariably promoted? – Ever since I have known the office.

1363   Do you know what the rule at Somerset House is? – It is guided more by merit than seniority.

1364   Are you aware that the Order in Council applies both to Whitehall and Somerset House? – Certainly.

1365   But the practice at Somerset House has varied from that at Whitehall? – Recently it has done so. I do not think it did so formerly.

1366   Can you suggest, from your experience at Somerset House, any objection to the system of promotion by merit? – The inconvenience that the public service suffers, and which must be expected where all is rivalry, is, that clerks who have the means of obtaining information from their position . . . keep such information in their own breasts, or in private memoranda, with the natural desire of standing first with their superiors and keep back others who might be dangerous rivals.

1367   Are the Committee to understand you that that is a book which is not required by the rules of the office to be kept, but which is kept by way of extra diligence by a particular gentleman who desires to perfect himself in the business of the office? – Yes; and supposing he is away, no one knows anything of the information which has been so obtained.

1368   Have not you known a similar system pursued where promotion by seniority prevails? – No.

1369   Have you not known any gentleman keep a private memorandum book in order to perfect himself in the discharge of his duties? – Not a private memorandum book which is kept from other persons. In Mr Houghton's room one of the most valuable books is the Index to the Lords' Letter-books, and there is more information to be found in that single book than you would obtain from the Digest by very long searches.

Evidence of Henry Amedroz, Head of the Manning
and Miscellaneous Branch

1401   Have you any suggestion to make with regard to the registration of letters? – It will probably be found that in those Government offices where letters are registered before anything is done on them, rapidity in replying is not in general much an object; I would allude to the Secretaries of State and the Treasury, not perhaps with all but with a great part of their correspondence. In the Admiralty the large amount of letters received (averaging 170 a-day), besides returns in large numbers, must constitute a very considerable, if not an insuperable, difficulty in registering all the letters before they are sent to the members of the Board for minuting, and to the departments for execution, considering that almost all the letters, or at least a very large number, are answered the very same day they are received. Absence of delay in correspondence has always been a marked feature in the mode of conducting business at the Admiralty. If registering the letters could be done without material delay, or without requiring too expensive a staff to do it, the Register would certainly be of use in tracing a letter before it reaches the Record Office (for here its use would cease entirely); but the question is whether the labour and delay would not exceed the advantages.

1406 The next suggestion made by the Second Secretary is with respect to the distribution of business. – To a certain extent the plan there proposed might work well, but it had better not extend beyond comparatively unimportant or routine letters, or the continuation of a correspondence already commenced, where the intentions of the Board are clear. In such latter cases the heads of departments might, by knowing what had previously passed, be able to save the Board some trouble, besides in some instances preventing wrong minutes being made by the Board, from their not having before them what had previously taken place. In important cases, however, or where any subject is first originated, it would probably be much more desirable that the member of the Board should receive the document at once; and this would also save time, as the head of department must (only later) adopt the same course of sending it to the individual Lord to whom it appertains, the former not being able (nor would it be right he should) to take the initiative, and, as it were, exercise the duties of one of the Board . . . A judicious selection of some [letters] to be sent to the departments might, at times, no doubt be a good plan; but the present system does not in general, work badly, and the Board's wishes must decide this question . . .

1417 Do you not think the Chief Clerk should have some general knowledge of what is going on in the Admiralty? – Yes, and I do not think he can discharge his present duties without having it.

1418 Supposing that were withdrawn from him, and the letters were assorted by a junior clerk instead of the Chief Clerk, would not he be comparatively ignorant of what was going on? – It would diminish his knowledge.

1419 Are you aware that he disclaims any control over the correspondence at present? – I was not aware of that.

1420 Are you aware of the Chief Clerk exercising any control over the execution of the minutes, or anything of the kind? – Not over the execution of the minutes, but over the distribution of the work he exercises control.

1421   Captain Milne asks whether it is not desirable that he should be acquainted with the tenor of the correspondence? – He cannot be that.

1422   But he could be acquainted with the general nature of the duties going on in the office? – With the general subjects he would be; he must know the subjects conducted by each of the different branches; but he cannot enter into the mode in which the duties are done.

1447   Mr Phinn alluded [also] . . . to the reorganisation of the business – that is, the redistribution of it, so as to bring the departments under the supervision of each Lord. Have you gone at all into that question? – That is a point I have not looked into. I know the division of the work in the different rooms of the office at the Admiralty is found to be very difficult, from the very varied and involved nature of the correspondence of the Admiralty; and if there were an attempt not only to arrange the correspondence between different rooms, but again to make it tally with individual Lords . . . the difficulty would be very great.

1448   It approximates to that already in some of the branches, does it not? – To a certain extent. In most of the branches it would be found that the majority of their correspondence is under one particular Lord; but most of the branches will also have a great deal of business which is under several Lords.

1484   The next subject is with reference to the Chief Clerk. Have you anything to say with regard to Mr Phinn's remarks on that subject? – I agree with the first portion of his remarks entirely [about the Chief Clerk involving himself too much in the details of office business]. It was, I believe, formerly the rule, or at least the custom, for the Chief Clerk to control the discipline, and distribution of work, in the office, and this appears to be the proper course. Heads of departments are answerable for their own work, and for those under them. If any difference occurs, or his wishes are objected to, reference should be made to the Chief Clerk, and the Secretary should not be applied to unless the decision of the Chief Clerk should be deemed objectionable to such an extent as to justify such further step. At the same time, the Chief Clerk should not be considered as a final authority, but appeal should be readily allowed to the Secretary. With respect to any control of the Chief Clerk over the work as done in the branches, I should be very sorry to see it laid down too closely. Much harm might accrue from dividing the responsibility as to the state and efficiency of each department from its head. He must be answerable to the Board direct for the proper execution of their orders, and the control which the Chief Clerk already exercises is perhaps sufficient for him, namely: the proper attendance of all the gentlemen, their leave of absence; the distribution of all the work; deciding differences between heads of departments as to their proper duties; assisting a weak from one stronger at the time; and, in short, superintendence over the office generally, but not into each department.

1495 Your father was the Chief Clerk here? – Yes, for seventeen years [1832–49].

1496 Was not it his custom to take the supervision of the branches? – Not more than I have described. He never interfered in the internal working of the rooms.

1497 Did he never visit the rooms? – Not to look into what was being done.

1498 Had he any returns submitted to him with regard to the state of the business in the different branches? – Yes, very often; but I believe it was generally when the Board or the Secretary called for it. Also he may have asked for it in conversation with the heads of the departments; but not as an obvious known interference. He would not come into the rooms and say, Let me see your entry books.

1499 Have you paid any attention to the subject of the General Minute Book, and the Board Minute Book? – The heads of the departments must exercise considerable moderation in sending letters for the General Minute Book, since if all, or even a great part only, of the letters executed were sent to the Précis Writer, it would be quite impossible for him to get through the work. In fact, his labours would amount to very nearly that of the two Digests in the Record Office, which the Minute Books to a certain extent resemble. Whilst on this subject, I should be very glad to draw attention to the distinction between the Board Minutes and General Minutes. Letters for the former are to be executed first, and the letters sent the same day to the Précis Writer; but, unfortunately, it very frequently happens that the most trivial subjects are Board Minutes, and really important ones are not. I have had an exchange of dockyards between two shipwrights made a Board Minute. Any plan by which Board Minutes might be restricted to really important matters, would be a great advantage.

1509 Have you been in the habit of keeping current papers in your branch? – Yes. Mr Phinn's proposition, I see, is that each branch should keep its own record for six or twelve months, or during the currency of the correspondence. In my opinion no branch could, with its present staff, keep, and properly sort and index, all the letters belonging to it for anything like the time stated. The letters received are over 1,000 a-week, not reckoning returns and bulky inclosures; each of the nine departments would have, therefore, about 3,000 for six months, and 6,000 for the year. This would give from twelve to fifteen feet of closely pressed papers laid flat without folding. Each department would then require to contain within itself a minor Record Office. Now one objection would be that as the work of the Admiralty is so extensive and varied, and yet the subjects are at times so involved and connected, one department with another, as frequently to make the most experienced doubt where a subject may have been done, it will be readily seen how much labour, loss of time, and confusion would be created, if former papers of this uncertain nature had to be searched for in each of these nine little Record Offices. But the strongest point of view seems to be that, in fact, the Record Office will be found expressly and admirably adapted by its very nature to receive and supply the current papers . . . Letters to which immediate answers are expected, may indeed, and with advantage, be kept in the branches; but it must be a well-understood rule that, when the reply arrives, it should be sent direct to the branch, and not, as is often the case, to the Record Office for former papers. I have already tried the plan, but discontinued it because I found that the Record Office was searching for the papers which I had kept, and I was waiting for the reply, which they had got in their department . . . Strengthen the Record Office, remove young and inexperienced hands from the Indexes and Digests, and the Record Office ought to supply readily whatever papers it may have received.

1511 Have you anything to say with respect to the question of promotion in the office? − Sir John Barrow once said upon that subject what struck me as very true, which was, that rejection might be necessary, but selection never.

1512 Are you aware that that is a question past discussion by Her Majesty's Order in Council, which is express on the point? − I have heard of it, but I am very sorry for it. Promotion is so slow in this office that it is a very cruel thing to pass any one over when it comes to his turn, unless he is clearly unfit for the duties.

Evidence of Ralph Osborne, MP, First Secretary of the Admiralty

1544 Have you seen the observations which have been submitted to the Committee by Mr Phinn, with regard to certain suggested improvements in the office? − I have read them with great attention . . . Mr Phinn in his observations alludes first to the subject of the registry of letters. My idea is that such a registry is not practicable. As far as my experience goes I have never in the course of three years, except on one occasion, known any letter which has been lost or misplaced, and I doubt, therefore, whether a registry of letters would be worth the expense and trouble it would occasion. I do not think you can do better than at present . . .

As to the hours of attendance of the clerks, I think the arrangement we have lately made, that one gentleman in each department should attend at 10 o'clock, a very convenient one; while, on the other hand, great inconvenience would be occasioned if the gentlemen left earlier than they do now. Mr Phinn's proposal does not take into account that there is now a late post arriving at 4 o'clock, and that a great quantity of Secretaries of State's letters also come in at that hour. Whether the Lords come here early or not they usually work up to half-past 4. When the House of Commons is sitting of course I have to be in attendance there . . .

[Another] point of importance is the state of the Record Office. I think the system of the Record Office is an admirable one if properly carried out, but I think the blame which attaches to it now is owing to its not having a sufficient staff. I think men have been put into it too young . . . In consequence of the war there has recently been a much greater pressure upon the department than there ever was before, while the staff has been left as it was before the war . . . [However] the fact that papers are not to be obtained, is sometimes not the fault of the Record Office so much as of ourselves and the Lords; they get mislaid among other papers. No document is left for them except in the first instance; they are handed about from man to man without any further receipt being given for them, and the Record Office has to answer for everything . . . When a gentleman takes a paper from the Record Office I would not only make him give a receipt to the Record Office, but inform them when he passes it on to another party, which is not done.

1547   Are you of opinion that the Chief Clerk should exercise any control over each branch in the way of seeing that there is no error? – Certainly; he should guard against arrears and take any means he thinks fit to set things right . . . [1546] . . . under the First Secretary, [he ought] to exercise a general supervision of the office, but I do not think he ought to interfere unnecessarily with the heads of departments, who are men receiving, some of them, £700 or £800 a-year, and who ought to be held responsible, each for his own department. Upon any complaint, from whatever quarter it comes; he should go into the department to inquire into the behaviour of the gentlemen, and, if necessary, report to the Secretary . . .

[1547] the next point referred to [by Phinn] is the promotion of clerks . . . I cannot say that I have been quite satisfied with the working of the Order in Council of August 1854 in the dockyards and Somerset House. I have found that each promotion out of the usual course of seniority has led to a not entirely satisfactory correspondence; this has occurred more frequently since the Order in Council came into force. I have always required the chief of a department to explain his reasons whenever he has passed over a particular man. I have every reason to fear that whenever there has been any extraordinary departure from the rule of seniority it has caused a great deal of ill-feeling, not only in the person passed over, but in the whole office in which it has occurred. It is very hard to prove the absence of favouritism, and still harder to prove to the satisfaction of those passed over and the rest of the clerks the superior merit and usefulness of the man who is preferred. Nevertheless, I think a strict scrutiny should be made as to the efficiency of each person before he is promoted. If it be shown that he is unfit I would pass [over] him without scruple; but a man may be of superior ability in passing an examination, and yet make a very bad clerk. We are expecting, I think, too high a standard of merit in the case of clerks, who are not paid very high salaries . . .

1548   You are, no doubt, aware of the Order in Council of 1816? – I have read it; but I should always be very much inclined . . . to give seniority great weight, retaining of course the power of rejection if a man be unfit. After all, the prizes in the office are very few. Staff appointments may be regulated by the merit or the peculiar fitness of the individual. I have invariably said in the case of all these appointments which have been in my gift, that I should not give them to the seniors as a matter of course, although it has frequently so happened that the senior was the best man, by the testimony of Mr Dyer and Mr Pennell, and the heads of department whom I consulted.

1550   When Admiral Hamilton was on leave did you find that you were able to discharge the duties of Secretary to the Board? – Perfectly. He always took his leave during the session of Parliament, and I found I was perfectly able to take his duty and attend a Parliament also.

1551   Did any delay occur in the office with regard to the despatch of letters? – None whatever.

1552   Of course the labour falling on the First Secretary would be much greater when he represented the Admiralty in the House of Commons? – Of course; I am only speaking of what happened to myself: but I am clearly of opinion that a person of business habits in the situation of Second Secretary would not require an Assistant Secretary.

1553   Is there any recognised division of labour between the Secretaries? – It is entirely arranged between themselves. I sign all the Secretary of State's letters, and all which are called the more important letters. The Chief Clerk makes the distribution, and sends those up to me.

1554 You are responsible for those letters? – I am. I believe if Mr Phinn wanted to go out I should sign all the letters; if I wanted to go out Mr Phinn would do the same.

1555 With regard to your duties at the meetings of the Board, is there any understanding upon that point? – I always take the Board when I am present. During the whole of the session of course I take the Board always. All letters from the Secretaries of State, all despatches arriving from Admirals, are sent to my house[37] or my private room, and I open them with my own hands. All the other letters – I am speaking, of course, of when I am present – are opened in the morning, in my presence, by the Reader. Those are letters of the common sort – reports from Admirals at the stations and the dockyards; the importance of those letters is now much diminished, by telegraphic messages anticipating their contents.

APPENDIX

[As in the case of Admiral Hamilton, the appendix to Osborne's evidence comprises suggestions drafted after he had testified.]

. . . [Concerning the proposed Assistant Second Secretary] It is almost unnecessary that I should inform the Committee that I dissent entirely from both the hypothesis [of overwork] and the remedy, inasmuch as the proposed plan is virtually to supersede the office of the First Secretary.

The Chief Clerk and the Office have always been under the First Secretary; and I cannot allow that in consequence of the First Secretary's Parliamentary duties the whole of the work must necessarily fall upon the Second. My practice has been to take all political and important letters . . . besides attending frequently at the opening and disposal of less important papers. I have taken the larger portion of the attendance upon Boards, notwithstanding the interference of Parliamentary and other public engagements. I sign all the important letters daily, not only up to the hour of meeting of the House of Commons, but often also at the House, and frequently for weeks together I sign all the letters written in the office.

I have my own regular apportioned duty besides, but I do not arrogate anything to myself for the performance of what has always been the First Secretary's duty. I only mention it to show that a First Secretary exists, who, even in the absence of his colleague, does not require an assistant.

I might add to this that it has been the practice – and I see no objection, when there is a pressure of business, though I seldom or never availed myself of this assistance – for the Chief Clerk sometimes to sign a portion of the letters . . .

I should be the last to deny that the business of the Admiralty has been increasing year by year, and we are now conducting war duties on a peace establishment. The responsibility of the Secretary . . . is therefore very great . . . He should be present at, and take a part in, the opening of letters, and he has his own special duties to attend to; but the great mass of the correspondence, as soon as its nature is ascertained, is forwarded to the Lord or the department to which it may relate. To what degree, in attending to his own duties, a Secretary may exercise his 'suggestive faculties' must depend on the disposition of the individual.

I must also dissent from those who would return to the old system of occasional Board days. A daily Board must be a considerable addition to the duties of all concerned, but the advantages are commensurate, and the necessity of the immediate consideration of all matters which may come before it in wartime is so obvious, that I trust we may never revert to the old system . . .

From my own experience of the office, and after reading the evidence, I would submit, with all deference to the Committee, that we should leave well alone, not giving the gentlemen of the office a plea for relaxing their exertions by the imposition of petty restrictions, but rather encouraging them by all means to work cheerfully and with energy, and to prove themselves worthy of the responsibility which has been placed on them.

Evidence of Sir John Liddell, Medical Director-General of the Navy

1606 Can you give the Committee any information with reference to the system which is adopted in communicating between Whitehall and your office [in Somerset House]? – It is all documentary, and there is a constant circle of reference and noting. I do not know that I can give the Committee a better idea than by producing one of our papers that for the last eight months has been going backwards and forwards. It has twenty-five references upon it, and I do not know that it has quite finished yet.

1607 When communications come to you from this office, do you receive a written order? – Yes; a written note . . .

1608 The letter is turned down, 'Refer to Medical Director-General to report'? – Yes.

1609 What are the steps which are taken? – In the case of the Assistant Surgeons, for instance, I transmit applications from candidates

. . . to the Secretary of the Admiralty, which are referred to the departmental clerk at Whitehall, who notes and takes them to the Medical Lord. He orders a schedule to be sent to the candidate, which is returned to the Secretary, to be again referred to the Lord, who sends the schedule to me to examine and report. It goes back to the Secretary, and the same formalities and directions are again gone through, when the candidate is ordered to appear for examination before me, and I am ordered to examine him, or if there are three candidates, five letters are written for the examiners to meet at Somerset House, who report the result of the examination through me to the Secretary . . . at length, a submission is made by me to the Secretary for appointment of the candidate to a ship, and he becomes an Acting Assistant Surgeon in the Royal Navy; thus employing Clerks, Lord of the Admiralty, Inspectors of Hospitals, Messenger, and Director-General, no end of times, for what must necessarily be done by one man, the Director-General of the Navy, who is alone responsible for its proper performance . . .

1614   Is there anything connected with the correspondence of the hospitals which you think might be improved? – I think so. As an illustration of the working of the present system, I will state what occurred yesterday. Application is made by the Deputy Inspector of Haslar Hospital to the Captain Superintendent for a nurse to accompany a blind man to the railway station, which application is sent to me by the Captain Superintendent. I recommend that it should be complied with and send it on to the Admiralty. I hear no more of it till about a week afterwards. I get a second application from the Superintendent requesting an answer to his first. I again refer it to the Admiralty, requesting an answer may be given, and I am informed that it has been given; but as they do not say that I was to inform the Captain Superintendent or whether they have done it, I have to send a messenger to the Admiralty to know whether they have or not. That arises from my being bound to send everything to the Admiralty. I have no power not to do so in the simplest matter.

1615   Are there many cases of a similar nature to that which you have just mentioned? – That is the regular routine.

1616   What is the remedy you would propose for that inconvenience? – I think all those simple routine matters ought to be done either on the spot or sent to me, or to the Admiralty, but not to both.

1617   The difficulty is to determine what is simple and what is not, is it not? – Any [Principal Officer] . . . would be the best judge of that; he would, for his own sake, in the case of a new or doubtful matter, seek the security which the Admiralty application would give him.

1619   Do you think the correspondence could be simplified in carrying out the details of your department? – I do. Most of the transactions in my department, of the most insignificant kind, are carried through a circuitous process of submission, consideration, and record; where the most trifling correspondence is multiplied into a voluminous collection of papers, in which needless formalities constitute more than half the work performed.

Evidence of R. M. Bromley, Accountant-General of the Navy

1757   In your department at Somerset House what is the extent of the daily receipt of letters and documents? – The number of orders, letters, etc., recorded this year, up to the 30th of June, is 28,158; at which rate for the whole of the year, they would amount to 56,816.

1758   With reference to the receipt of letters in your department have you any general register? – I have.

1759   How is that carried out? – It is a daily register of papers as they are received in the office, numbered consecutively.

1760   Is that in the Record Office? – It is in the Record Office; but the Record Office in my department, and the Record Office at Whitehall, differ very materially in this respect. The papers as they are received ... are opened ... [and] classed; that is to say, the wheat is separated from the chaff; papers of more than ordinary importance are entered in a register, which is called the 'Black Ink Record Register', and they number about 7,000 in the course of the year. The remainder pass through what is called the 'Miscellaneous or Promiscuous Register', and are numbered in red ink. My object for that is, that all the black ink records may be returned to the Record Office. The red ink numbers are not of sufficient importance for that; they form vouchers to the accounts, and they are placed away as vouchers to the accounts in my department. My predecessor, Sir John Briggs, established this simple system of registry.[38]

1762   Does not ... [registering] cause delay in the commencement of business? – Not at all; the Record Clerk is usually there as early as from 9 to half-past 9. I require that the more important of the orders shall be gathered together and first recorded and brought to my table. In the course of an hour from that time I get the remainder of the papers. The promiscuous letters are entered very rapidly and very briefly in the Promiscuous Book, and separated into baskets for the different branches of my department to which they relate, so that by 11 or half-past the whole of those papers have been read by the gentlemen to whom they relate in the different branches of the office. The important letters which I have had under my consideration I either make my minutes on at once, or turn up the corner, and mark the name of the head of the branch to which that paper relates for him to act on it. Generally by half-past 11 in the day the whole of those papers . . . are circulated.

1763 Does the register of the letters contain a digest of the subject? – No; attached to the Register is a nominal index, but I have a Digest in my office. [Moreover] Each branch of the office is required to keep a Digest or Notation Book of its papers . . . by having an immediate daily register I am able to detect . . . where a paper has gone to, and I hold the head of each branch responsible for keeping a digest of all those papers under the particular heads or subjects to which they relate.

1764 Then there must be a very clear division of subjects for each separate branch? – No doubt; nevertheless . . . I have 160 clerks now employed under me, there being eleven branches to which these papers are referred, and I will venture to say that I would find any paper as rapidly as any department could which keeps a Central Index.

1765 Do you consider that that principle is equally applicable to a Department like Whitehall, embracing such a voluminous and extensive system of classification? – . . . I do not hesitate to say that there is no department in which you could not have a proper and complete subdivision of labour in recording papers, as in my department.

1766 You are aware that Mr Finlayson's system is adopted here, which differs from the one you have in use? – Yes, very materially.[39]

1767 Do you consider that Mr Finlayson's system is equally applicable to the record of letters as the one you adopt? – I have always been under the impression that Mr Finlayson's system would break down under any great pressure. In the time of Mr Bedford [Barrow's immediate predecessor], it was the common remark at his office and at Somerset House, that papers frequently could not be found. There was a very considerable arrear in digesting the papers in the Record Office, in Mr Bedford's time. There was a box in the Record Office into which papers used to be cast till they had time to sort them; and they used to accumulate there to a considerable extent.

1768 The system you adopt establishes eleven Record Offices instead of one Central Record Office? – Yes; by that subdivision of labour I am able to separate my papers into branches, and have established in each branch a Digest or Notation Book, under particular heads, so that I can see at one view the whole subject for a given series of years, instead of having, as you have, one enormous, bulky

Digest Book, which only lasts for a year, and has not the value of a continuous Digest for a series of years.

1771 How long are the registered papers retained in the branches? – I am very particular respecting that; it must in some measure depend upon illness or absence. Particular gentlemen like to make their own notations, and if that gentleman is absent for any time, papers may be kept a week or two in the branch, but, generally speaking, I require them to be returned within forty-eight hours to the Record Room; but then many of the papers I allude to will be permanent vouchers, and will never return to the Record Room. Still there is always a clue to the paper by reference to . . . [my] nominal index. I refer to the particular gentleman or branch to which it has been taken, and there I can find out where the paper is.

1776 From day to day, is there a consecutive series of numbers in the Register? – From the 1st of January to the 31st of December, the numbers are consecutive.

1777 Is every letter, no matter of what description, registered? – No. In addition to the 56,000 letters I have mentioned, I have a great many letters from poor women and others, who are daily applying to know if their husbands are alive or dead . . . I receive between 20,000 and 30,000 letters of that description in a year, of all characters of writing. I require them to be disposed of daily, and I have not one remaining in my office unanswered.

1778 Assuming that one of those letters happens to be mislaid, and a party writes a second time, you have no means of tracing the original letter? – Only by the fact of its having passed before the First Clerk of the branch, and his entry that he has received seven letters, or whatever might be the number, during the day, and there were none remaining. You could not trace any particular number. In addition to that 20,000, I suppose I have about 3,000 persons come to a window in the course of a-year, asking, for example, 'Is John Smith, of the *Volcano*, alive or dead?' The clerk at the window turns to the ship's book, and replies, 'Alive on the 31st of December'. It is that character of an inquiry of which the letters are not registered.

1780 Do the 56,000 letters of which you speak include those which come from the Admiralty at Whitehall? – Yes; every description of letters of the higher character.

1781 What staff is requisite to register those 56,000 letters? – I dare say I shall astonish you by my answer – two clerks; but I have added a third clerk within these last few months, because I have thrown upon that department a very important duty . . . that is, the despatch of letters and the . . . [registering of outgoing] correspondence. The number of letters sent out of the office from the 1st of February to the 30th of June was 9,908; and the proportionate number for the year would be 23,772 letters . . .

1782 How many hours a-day do those three clerks work? − I am afraid I am a hard taskmaster; but in war time I consider seven hours is a very fair attendance for gentlemen, but six hours is the usual and common period of attendance. I am quite satisfied, however, that the gentlemen in my department, since the war broke out, have not worked as a rule less than seven hours, and there are very honourable exceptions where they have put their shoulders to the wheel in a very extraordinary manner.

1785 What takes place when a letter is opened; who reads it? − It is the rule that any letter addressed to me by name is brought to me to open. Any letter addressed to me as Accountant-General of the Navy and on Her Majesty's service, is opened in the Record Room. The person employed upon that duty is a very confidential gentleman [Mr Bentley] who has been employed upon such business a great number of years, and I should not place a gentleman in that position unless I had the utmost confidence in him. The letters being collected upon the table, he and two gentlemen with him tear them open and sort them. Those with the names of ships are all put together; the Junior Clerks open them, throw the covers into a basket and spread them open. Those which are important letters, coming from the Admiralty, Mr Bentley opens; he then sorts them, runs his eye over them to see the most important, and puts them on the top. As soon as he has entered them, he takes them into my room immediately if I am there. If I am not there, he is informed the moment I come, and he brings them and puts them into my hand.

1786 Who reads the heading of the letter or gives the number of it to the Registrar? − . . . [Mr Bentley] does that business himself; he goes from opening these important letters and takes them immediately to the Registrar Book for entry. The number is first entered, the date of receipt, the date of the paper, the name of the correspondent, Admiralty or War Office, and so on. Then in the subject-column he very briefly gives the subject, and if he sees that it is a paper which relates to Mr Walker's branch, for example, he turns up the corner and writes 'Mr Walker' upon it, and in a column of his Register he marks 'Mr Walker'. Those papers are brought to me as soon as I come to the office.

1791 Are you acquainted with any Record Office which carries on the same system of register as the office at Whitehall? − The War Office does to a certain extent, with this difference: the papers that are received in the War Office are numbered according to the regiment, and sub-numbered consecutively according to that regiment; but although there is an opinion at the War Office, of those who have grown up with the system, that that is the best way of keeping the Records, a Report was drawn up by Lord Chandos, Sir Charles Trevelyan, and myself, in 1852, condemnatory of that system of Record. To a certain extent it has been modified since that time, but I do not know of any department where the papers do not bear some number, with the exception of the Admiralty.

1792   How do they manage at the War Office with their miscellaneous letters which refer to no regiment at all? – They deal with their branches by letters of the alphabet, and they deal with their correspondence by numbers, and they ask you to do a thing which I know is impracticable – this is, always to quote the number of the letter in your reply. The public will not do it, and the public departments do not do it, and I know they are constantly at fault in consequence . . .

1798   You have under you the department of the Accountant-General . . . and the other principal officers have each his separate department, but the whole is concentrated at Whitehall, is it not? And therefore we require to have a more general record here, as it must embrace all the subjects to be dealt with in those separate departments, whereas you would only deal with one. – . . . I believe . . . there would be a great simplification of the business, first of all, if the Board could come to Somerset House . . . The Board for some time – I believe since 1848 – were in the habit of coming to Somerset House weekly. If papers were brought before the Board at Somerset House, they would be stamped at Somerset House, but they would be taken charge of immediately by the principal officer who submitted them to the Board; they would never go to the Record Office here, and therefore if the Board cannot come to Somerset House to deal with those papers, I am of opinion very many of the documents we send to Whitehall, to be adjudicated upon by the Board, need not be recorded at Whitehall, but might be returned to the Department at Somerset House with the Board minute upon them. It does not appear to me to be necessary for the Board of Admiralty to record all those various documents here; but it is a question whether it is not necessary and politic to hold the principal officers responsible for those documents, and for bringing them before the Board as occasion may arise. In that way it appears to me your Record Book is choked up with matter which is not of a description that need go into it. There is a mass of documents passing through this office which should be at once sent on to the principal officers, and dealt with by them.[40]

1799   Assuming that the Secretary of War writes an official letter here addressed to the Secretary of the Admiralty, as that may relate either to pay or to pension, do you think that letter, coming from a principal officer of the Government to this department, should go to your department and be recorded? – I think so. There are two ways of avoiding it. One is that you should at once sanction your principal officers corresponding with the principal officers of other departments, and that you should notify to the Minister of State, whoever he may be, that that is the rule you mean to adopt, or if you do not think fit to repose that confidence in your principal officers, that you should receive the letter at Whitehall, and pass it on at once, without record, to the principal officers at Somerset House.

1801 Did not Sir James Graham specially seek to provide against the possibility of a principal officer asserting his independence of the Board of Admiralty? – To this extent, there has been always an objection to the principal officers of the navy corresponding with a Secretary of State, or an Under-Secretary of State; but I believe no injury would accrue to the public service from a principal officer corresponding with the principal officers of departments under a Secretary of State . . . [And] I believe a Superintending Lord would more readily obtain information concerning any matter if papers were sent direct to the principal officers at Somerset House, and he would have the advantage of consulting with the principal officers upon a question in all its details before he brought it before the Board, if he thought it necessary to do so.

1802 Letters addressed to the Secretary of the Admiralty marked 'Accountant-General' in the corner are sent to your office unopened, are not they? – They are. [However] There are a great many references which are constantly being made to Whitehall which I think might be avoided, if it were possible for the principal officers to see the original correspondence . . . [For example] You see my reports daily of naval officers coming home, asking whether I am to pay the mess allowance of those officers. The Board have already had that under consideration, and they have laid down certain general rules for messing officers on returning home. I am bound to adhere to those rules; all I want is to see whether a certain officer has been allowed to come home with leave . . . The steamer or ship which brings the officer home, in a few weeks sends in a claim to me to pay this officer's passage-money. I know what the regulations are, but I do not know whether the officer himself has got the permission of the Board to return home. Within four months I have reported 254 cases, whereas if I had seen the sanction of the Board to that officer coming home . . . I could have saved the Board all reference and consideration in the 254 cases, and, moreover, I could have saved 254 reports from my office to this office, and 254 replies . . .

1809   What are the hours of attendance at Somerset House? – Nominally from 10 till 4; a line is drawn, or presumed to be drawn, at a quarter-past 10. At 11 o'clock the Attendance Books are brought up into my room, and although I do not look at those books daily, I do occasionally, and put my initials to them; and that very moral check, if I may so term it, upon the young men, I have no doubt has the effect of insuring greater accuracy of attendance, in addition to the heads of the branches watching them as they do.

1810   When gentlemen come at a quarter-past 10, do they find any of the business of the day ready for them to commence? – There is always work remaining . . . over to be done; more especially during the war, there is plenty to do . . . With respect to attendance, I might mention that . . . [in the] Attendance Book – there being one for each branch – I have a column for the time of departure, which each gentleman, when he signs the book on the following morning, inserts, that is, if he leaves the office after 5 o'clock; if he leaves the office before 5 o'clock, I do not allow him to insert the time of his departure, but if he stays, which I think upon reference to my books you will find a great many gentlemen do to a later hour, he would put in the time he left. Some of my gentlemen have been in attendance from 8 o'clock one morning to 8 o'clock the next morning to get ready the Crimean medals . . . [1812] . . . The Committee are aware that, prior to my joining the department, there was a great deal of extra-money paid for extra-attendance at Somerset House. Within a very short time after my appointment as Accountant-General, I proposed to the Board that that should be stopped. It amounted to thousands a-year. From a short time after my coming there, not one shilling has been paid for the extra-attendance of clerks; but it has been thrown entirely upon the honour of gentlemen to exert themselves as they have done, and I must say it has succeeded beyond my expectation.

1818   Are there not a great many letters which might be disposed of by Superintending Lord without the necessity of [a reference to the Board] . . . ? – There is the blot . . . It has always appeared to me that the members of the Board have endeavoured to grasp at too much detail . . . You, Captain Milne, are fully aware, from your long experience here, how, just as you are going away from Somerset House, a principal officer lays hold of you and asks you to approve a certain paper. You have not time to consider it, and you must after all take it upon his representation.

1819   Do you conceive that any great delay would arise in the conduct of the public business by papers being sent in the first instance to the heads of the branches? − No; I think that [it] is an erroneous idea to suppose otherwise. I know the Lords of the Admiralty . . . wish to have papers immediately, but my belief is, if they will only place confidence in the principal officers at Somerset House and the heads of the branches here, there will be no delay; it would encourage them to bring those papers more rapidly before them and in a more complete shape.

1820 Of course you would exclude the consideration of personal matters, such as the qualification of particular officers for command or appointments? − They are of a higher character altogether, and should rest with the Board.

1821 Must not you also exclude letters of a professional naval character? − It has always struck me that if the discipline, the equipment, and the movement of the fleet were more specially considered by the Board, and the details connected with pay, stores, provisions, and other matters, were left to the principal officers the public service would be advanced . . . the old practice has been unsettled, first [in 1832] by throwing over the subordinate Boards, which did much of the work now thrown upon the Admiralty, and subsequently by adding new business to the Admiralty year by year . . . That . . . is the real cause of the machine being thrown out of gear . . . The Navy Board was broken up. The system of principal officers was established by Sir James Graham, intending to carry out the details of the Navy Board practice, but by degrees attempts have been made to grasp or dispose of those details at Whitehall, instead of being left, as they should be, at Somerset House . . . [1824] . . . I think if it could be done with satisfaction to the Board, supposing you were to hark back, I will not say to the system of the Navy Board, but to the system of letting your permanent principal officials deal with details, having confidence in them that they will not take upon themselves the higher character of business which the Board ought to deal with, and which could be marked out by instructions, you would, in my opinion, lessen the labour here very materially, without interfering with the general powers of the Board of Admiralty.

1832 There is an Order in Council in reference to the system of promotion at Somerset House; how have you found the system which is laid down in that order work? − I am a very staunch advocate for promotion by merit and fitness. I trust I am somewhat an example of having worked harder than most men, but having risen as I have done I feel proud of it, and I have held it in view in dealing with all the gentlemen who have been placed under me . . . There are only one or two instances in which I have taken gentlemen by seniority since I have been Accountant-General of the Navy, and

I believe I have made a mistake. It was not exactly incapacity that I had to complain of, but the absence of a certain degree of fitness for the duty, which is readily observed when placed in charge of a higher duty. The classes [of clerks] have been formed with this view, that the progressive rise from the minimum to the maximum shall be the reward of service. But the promotion of gentlemen from one class to another is to be the reward of merit and admitted fitness, and I think by passing them through the various sieves of classification, gentlemen in the lower classes may be found qualified for the Second Class; but when you get them into that second class you require a very superior man before you can allow him to go into the First Class. The Board and the principal officers have all to rely upon that first class for carrying on the public service.

1833 You have found . . . the principle of seniority to prevail . . . [in
/4 some of] the different offices into which you have been commissioned to inquire, have you not? − Yes; whenever I have found the principle of seniority prevailing, I have found, if I may use the common expression, the department in a dead-lock, that is, the juniors are disheartened, and the seniors have no cause to exert themselves . . .

1835 Have you found the system of promotion by merit produce any feeling of dissatisfaction on the part of those who have been passed over? − Certainly. You cannot expect a gentleman to admit that his merits are inferior to those of a gentleman who may be raised above him . . . [However] Whenever it is necessary to make a promotion, I am enjoined by the words of the Order in Council to select those persons 'who in the opinion of the principal officer are most deserving of such promotion, and whose promotion would be best for Her Majesty's service; and in making such selection and recommendation, such principal officer is enjoined not to suffer himself to be influenced by any other motive whatever than the advantage of Her Majesty's service, on full consideration of the merits, abilities, and services of the person so selected.' I maintain that if any one at the head of a department has moral courage sufficient to act upon that Order, the public service must be advanced; and much as I regret wounding the feelings or vanity of any one, I prefer doing so to inflicting a lasting injury upon the public service.

1836 Do not you find that the person recommending has always a very valuable assistance in the public opinion of the office generally, which is an almost unerring guide? − It is the true guide, and the only safe guide . . .

1837 Have you adverted to some evidence given by Mr Giffard, to the effect that in Somerset House it was found that the system of promotion by merit led gentlemen to keep information private which was necessary for the public service, in order to use it for the advancement of their own individual interests? – . . . With regard to my own department, I must say that Mr Giffard is not quite correct in that statement, and for this reason: the moment I find that any gentleman in my department is collecting public information for his own personal advantage, as to the mode in which the business should be conducted, it is my invariable rule to remove him to a new duty. When I joined my present office as Accountant-General of the Navy, Sir James Graham [then First Sea Lord] made this observation . . . He said: 'It is a delicate and difficult task for you to undertake, for among other things the Wages Office is in a state of insubordination.' It was upon the face of it a very difficult thing to work the department. But why? Because at the head of the branch of that section of my office, there were gentlemen who had been bred in a certain mode of conducting the business. My first step was to remove what I considered to be one of the greatest obstacles in the way of improvement, and to put into that office a gentleman who had never been in it before. That very step enabled me to undermine, as it were, the previous insubordination, and the objection that would have been taken to every step of mine in altering the mode of paying the navy . . . I venture to affirm that the success which has attended the whole system, in the course of two years, has astonished me.

1839   Is there any other remark you have to make upon the suggestions of the Second Secretary? –

[As might be supposed, Bromley had several remarks, and not always on topics other than those dealt with in his previous evidence. Notably, he returned to the point about giving more independence to the principal officers, arguing that the Superintending Lords were in part prevented from attending 'to the higher question of Naval Reform' by their engaging so much in the general details of business. He made another, more novel point, in his suggestion that senior government clerks were engaging in too much mechanical work as a relief from responsibility. He went on: 'You are paying gentlemen at the Treasury £1,000 a-year as Chief Clerks for doing, in a great degree, Copying Clerks' work.' Furthermore, agreeing here with Hamilton, he urged strongly that the Somerset House and Whitehall administrations should be brought together in one place. Another remark of his deserves quoting]:

[1841] . . . When I went to my department I called upon every gentleman to favour me with any suggestions, or any opinion, upon the mode of conducting the business of the office. I have collected them, and very valuable material they contain. I have established a book in my department for entering these suggestions, with a column for my minutes upon them, either carrying them out or not. My object is this: the old rule . . . was to keep all the young men in the background, and not to allow them to make any suggestion whatever. If the Chief Clerk or the Head Clerk of a branch received any suggestion as to the mode of conducting the business, it was very common for him to 'Pooh, pooh!' that suggestion; but by the means I have adopted the Chief Clerk is forced to bring before me the suggestion of a junior, and it is placed upon record so that he can refer to it hereafter in connection with his promotion or otherwise . . .

Evidence of Captain John Washington, Hydrographer to the Admiralty

1916 Are you inconvenienced by the want of room? − Dreadfully so; the want of space is very great, and so is the want of assistance, and the want of a Librarian. We have 19,280 MSS. and other charts (a great part of them original documents), so crammed into presses from want of sufficient space, that it is almost impossible to get at them to consult them, which is a great hindrance to business. There are also 10,000 books up stairs, and 5,000 down stairs, of which no accurate catalogue exists. We are now forming a complete catalogue and printing it. At Paris and Petersburgh [*sic*] the space allotted to the Hydrographer alone is as much as the space allotted to the whole of the Admiralty in England.

1917 At Paris are they prosecuting as many or more surveys than you? − Very few indeed. I believe that they only published two new charts last year.

1918 At St Petersburgh, is there a corresponding provision for the Hydrographer's Office? − Yes, it is very complete indeed; it is even a larger building than that at Paris.

1919 Compared with the work executed in your department is the Russian greater or less? − It is not one-twentieth of the work which is executed in England. So great is the want of space that we are in arrears with all our work, and with our Sailing Directions particularly . . .

Appendix I

Memoranda in Explanation of the Increase of Official Business in the Admiralty, Whitehall

	Years					
						To 30 June
	1835	*1845*	*1847*	*1850*	*1854*	*1855*
Number of Men voted	26,500	40,000	43,000	39,000	63,000	70,000
Number of Her Majesty's Ships and Vessels in Commission:						
Sailing-vessels	155	159	160	133	118	136
Steam-vessels	12	75	96	67	144	192
Total	167	234	256	200	262	328
Number of Ships and Vessels on the following Stations:						
Mediterranean	24	21	33	21	56	80
Coast of Africa	—	28	28	26	13	14
Cape of Good Hope	14	9	9	8	7	8
East Indies and China	14	25	25	19	22	23
North America and West Indies	26	16	15	13	21	16
South America	—	13	13	12	8	9
Pacific	16	13	13	12	10	11
At Home, Packets and detached services	73	109	120	89	125	78
Baltic	-	-	-	-	-	89
Total	167	234	256	200	262	328
Number of Artificers employed in the Dockyards at Home, including hired Men and Convicts	7,884	12,194	13,219	12,161	12,382	14,976

Number of Seamen and Marines admitted to the Out-Pension of Greenwich Hospital	709	996	1,243	1,121	1,235	885
Number of Appointments of Officers issued from the Admiralty	1,736	2,701	3,479	3,225	5,949	3,349
Number of Letters received in the Admiralty	25,973	39,275	50,970	32,921	53,194	26,651
Number of Pages of Entry in the several Departments of the Office	10,132	15,872	21,068	11,617	18,544	11,912

Admiralty, 13 November 1855.

Appendix II

Return of the Gentlemen of the Establishment at Whitehall, with the period of Entry into the Establishment; their Servitude in each Class; and their respective Salaries
(Prepared in pursuance of their Lordships' Order of 1 November 1855)

Name	Rank	From	To	Present Salary £	Remarks
John J. Dyer	Junior Clerk	22 Jan. 1822	14 May 1832		6 years' previous service in Greenwich Hospital.
	2nd Class Clerk	15 May 1832	19 April 1838		
	1st Class Clerk	20 April 1838	17 Nov. 1853		
	Chief Clerk	18 Nov. 1853	—	1,000	
John Barrow	3rd Class Clerk	17 Nov. 1824	21 July 1832		
	2nd Class Clerk	22 July 1832	3 May 1844		
	1st Class Clerk	4 May, 1844	—	820	
Chas. H. Pennell	3rd Class Clerk	4 July 1825	21 Jan. 1833		
	2nd Class Clerk	22 Jan. 1833	23 May 1847		
	1st Class Clerk	24 May 1847	—	760	£100 per annum, additional, for conducting the secret and confidential correspondence.
Robt. S. Evans	3rd Class Clerk	1 Jan. 1827	2 May 1833		
	2nd Class Clerk	3 May 1833	8 Oct. 1847		
	1st Class Clerk	9 Oct. 1847	—	740	
J. H. Briggs	3rd Class Clerk	19 Apr. 1827	14 Dec. 1834	—	Employed in Victualling Office, 8 June 1826, to 18 April 1827.
	2nd Class Clerk	15 Dec. 1834	4 Jan. 1849		
	1st Class Clerk	5 Jan. 1849	—	720	A sum in addition, to make up £850 for service as Reader; and £100 in addition to maximum of the class.
John H. Jesse	3rd Class Clerk	26 Oct. 1829	30 Mar. 1835		
	2nd Class Clerk	31 Mar. 1835	31 Mar. 1850		
	1st Class Clerk	1 April 1850	—	700	
John H. N. Houghton	3rd Class Clerk	15 May 1832	4 April 1837	—	Employed in Victualling Office, 11 February 1830, to 14 May 1832.
	2nd Class Clerk	5 April 1837	17 Nov. 1853		
	1st Class Clerk	18 Nov. 1853	—	670	
Henry Wolley	3rd Class Clerk	11 June 1832	19 April 1838	—	Employed in Victualling Office, 1 June 1828, to 10 June 1832.
	2nd Class Clerk	20 April 1838	31 Dec. 1853		
	1st Class Clerk	1 Jan. 1854	—	620	
Waller Clifton	3rd Class Clerk	11 June 1832	16 Feb. 1841	—	Previous service at Deptford Victualling Yard, and Admiralty, Somerset House, 18 May 1829, to 10 June 1832.
	2nd Class Clerk	17 Feb. 1841	31 Dec. 1853		
	1st Class Clerk	1 Jan. 1854	—	620	
Thomas Wolley	3rd Class Clerk	3 May 1833	12 Mar. 1841		
	2nd Class Clerk	13 Mar. 1841	6 April 1854		
	1st Class Clerk	7 April 1854	—	665	
Maurice W. Midlane	3rd Class Clerk	1 Oct. 1833	6 Nov. 1842		
	2nd Class Clerk	7 Nov. 1842	21 Feb. 1855		
	1st Class Clerk	22 Feb. 1855	—	630	
John Jackson	3rd Class Clerk	18 Oct. 1834	3 May 1844		
	2nd Class Clerk	4 May 1844	—	515	£100 per annum as Précis Writer to the Board.

Name	Class	From	To	£	Notes
H. F. Amedroz	3rd Class Clerk	15 Dec. 1834	24 July 1846	—	Employed in Admiralty, Somerset House, 12 June to 14 December 1834.
	2nd Class Clerk Acting	25 July 1846	30 April 1855		
	1st Class Clerk	1 May 1855	—	600	£100 per annum as French and Spanish translator.
W. F. Evans	3rd Class Clerk	31 Mar. 1835	23 May 1847	—	Employed in Plymouth and Deptford Victualling Yards, and Admiralty, Somerset House, 15 May 1829, to 30 March 1835.
	2nd Class Clerk	24 May 1847	—	470	
R. W. Hamilton	3rd Class Clerk Acting	1 May 1837	8 Oct. 1847		
	2nd Class Clerk	9 Oct. 1847	4 Jan. 1849		
	2nd Class Clerk	5 Jan. 1849	—	440	
Thos. James	3rd Class Clerk Acting	5 May 1837	4 Jan. 1849	—	Employed at Admiralty, Somerset House, 31 January 1833, to 4 May 1837.
	2nd Class Clerk	5 Jan. 1849	30 Sept. 1849		
	2nd Class Clerk	1 Oct. 1849	—	440	
John H. Hay	3rd Class Clerk	5 May 1837	31 Mar. 1850		
	2nd Class Clerk	1 April 1850	—	425	
O. B. Piers	3rd Class Clerk	24 May 1837	17 Nov. 1853		
	2nd Class Clerk	18 Nov. 1853	—	365	
John Sheridan	3rd Class Clerk	22 Aug. 1840	31 Dec. 1853		
	2nd Class Clerk	1 Jan. 1854	—	365	
Alex. W. Innes	3rd Class Clerk	5 Nov. 1840	6 April 1854	—	4 months' previous service as extra clerk.
	2nd Class Clerk	7 April 1854	—	365	
Robt. Bell	3rd Class Clerk	9 Feb. 1841	15 Aug. 1854		
	2nd Class Clerk	16 Aug. 1854	—	365	£20 per annum for assisting Captain Milne.
Chas. J. Proby	3rd Class Clerk	17 Mar. 1841	19 Oct. 1854	—	6 months' previous service as extra clerk.
	2nd Class Clerk	20 Oct. 1854	—	350	
Thos. G. Grant	3rd Class Clerk	18 Mar. 1841	21 Feb. 1855		
	2nd Class Clerk	22 Feb. 1855	—	350	
Fras. Graves	3rd Class Clerk	26 Aug. 1841	31 Mar. 1855	—	1 year's previous service as extra clerk.
	(1st section)	1 April 1855	—	250	£50 per annum as Private Clerk to Second Secretary.
John Perrier	3rd Class Clerk	11 Nov. 1842	31 Mar. 1855	—	1 year 6 months' previous service as extra clerk.
	(1st section)	1 April 1855	—	250	£50 per annum as Private Clerk to Sir M. F. F. Berkeley.
Fredk. Locker	3rd Class Clerk	12 Nov. 1842	31 Mar. 1855	—	1 year 7 months' previous service as extra clerk.
	(1st section)	1 April 1855	—	250	£50 per annum as Deputy Reader to the Board.
Robt. M. Jones	3rd Class Clerk	10 May 1844	31 Mar. 1855	—	1 year 9 months' previous service as extra clerk.
	(1st section)	1 April 1855	—	250	
Wm. O. S. Gilly	3rd Class Clerk	17 Dec. 1844	31 Mar. 1855	—	3 years 2 months' previous service as extra clerk.
	(1st section)	1 April 1855	—	250	
Wm. C. Miller	3rd Class Clerk	25 July 1846	31 Mar. 1855	—	4 years 9 months' previous service as extra clerk.
	(1st section)	1 April 1855	—	250	
Henry C. G. Bedford	3rd Class Clerk	27 Feb. 1847	31 Mar. 1855	—	4 years 3 months' previous service as extra clerk.
	(1st section)	1 April 1855	—	250	£50 per annum while placed at the head of the First Lord's Office.
Henry E. C. Stapylton	3rd Class Clerk	24 May 1847	31 Mar. 1855	—	2 years 4 months' previous service as extra clerk.
	(1st section)	1 April 1855	—	250	£100 per annum as Private Clerk to First Secretary.
John R. Paris	3rd Class Clerk	9 Oct. 1847	31 Mar. 1855	—	2 years 9 months' previous service as extra clerk.

Name	Class					Remarks
Clarence Braddyll	(1st section) 3rd Class Clerk	1 April 1855 5 Jan. 1849	— 31 Mar. 1855	250 —		Acting 3rd Class Clerk, Admiralty, 15 March, 1848, to 4 January 1849. 2 years 7 months' previous service as extra clerk.
Chas. P. F. Berkeley	(1st section) 3rd Class Clerk	1 April 1855 1 April 1850	— 31 Mar. 1855	250 —		2 years 10 months' previous
C. S. Kennedy	(1st section) 3rd Class Clerk	1 April 1855 1 Oct. 1850	— 31st Mar. 1855	250 —		service as extra clerk. 3rd Class Clerk, Admiralty,
	—	1 April 1855	—	250		Somerset House, 14 January, 1846, to 28 May 1847. 3 months' previous service as extra clerk.
Walter Drummond	3rd Class Clerk	1 Jan. 1854	—	110		£50 per annum as Private Clerk to Rear-Admiral Eden. 6 years 2 months' previous service as extra clerk.
Chas. N. Kempe	3rd Class Clerk	1 Jan. 1854	—	180		Clerk and Draughtsman in Department of Director of Works, 1 April 1847, to 31 December 1853. 8 months' previous service as extra clerk.
Henry C. Pennell	3rd Class Clerk	1 Jan. 1854	—	110		3rd Class Clerk, Admiralty, Somerset House, 18 June 1852, to 31 December 1853.
Fras. J. Alderson	3rd Class Clerk	1 Jan. 1854	—	110		1 year 1 month's previous service in Audit Office.
A. E. West	3rd Class Clerk	1 Jan. 1854	—	110		2 years 8 months' previous service as extra clerk.
Astley P. Cooper	3rd Class Clerk	1 Jan. 1854	—	110		3rd Class Clerk, Admiralty, Somerset House, 14 January to 24 July 1846. 8 months previous service as extra clerk.
Edwin N. Swainson	3rd Class Clerk	1 Jan. 1854	—	110		2 years 8 months' previous service as temporary clerk.
B. A. Fonblanque	3rd Class Clerk	1 Jan. 1854	—	110		
Jas. G. Noel	3rd Class Clerk	13 April 1854	—	110		3rd Class Clerk, Admiralty, Somerset House, 21 March 1853, to 12 April 1854.
James Scott	3rd Class Clerk	13 April 1854	—	110		Ditto. 11 January to 12 April 1854. 1 year 6 months' previous service as extra clerk.
Robt. J. Callander	3rd Class Clerk	13 April 1854	—	110		Ditto. 20 January to 12 April 1854.
Alfred Buckley	3rd Class Clerk	12 May 1854	—	110		
Hon. W. P. Moreton	3rd Class Clerk	16 Aug. 1854	—	110		
Joseph Senior	3rd Class Clerk	16 Nov. 1854	—	100		Ditto. 17 August to 15 November 1854. 3 months' previous service as extra clerk.
A. F. M. Spalding	3rd Class Clerk	24 Feb. 1855	—	100		Ditto. 24 January to 23 February 1855.
Chas. E. S. Cooke	3rd Class Clerk	14 April 1855	—	100		

Admiralty, Somerset House, 2 November 1855

For Accountant-General,
(Signed) E. Gandy

Appendix III

Admiralty, Somerset House, 2 November 1855

Return of the Number of Clerks on the Establishment of the Admiralty Office, Whitehall, specifying each class, in the years 1830, 1840, 1850, and 1855
(Prepared in pursuance of their Lordships' Order of 1 November 1855)

	1830	1840	1850	1855
Chief Clerk	1	1	1	1
Clerks, 1st Class	7	7	7	10
Clerks, 2nd Class	6	10	12	12
Clerks, 3rd Class	12	18	19	28*
Total number	26	36	39	51

* 1st Section, 12; 2nd Section, 16.

Between 1830 and 1840 ten Clerks were added (viz., four 2nd Class and six 3rd Class), under Orders in Council of 1 August 1832, and 5 April 1837, the latter caused by the transfer of the business of the Packet Service from the Postmaster-General.

Between 1840 and 1850 three Clerks were added (viz., two 2nd Class and one 3rd Class), under Orders in Council of 11 February 1841, 2 November 1842, and Board's Order of 4 June 1850.

Between 1850 and 1855 twelve Clerks were added (viz., three 1st Class and nine 3rd Class), under Orders in Council of 29 December 1853, and 7 April 1854; these, consequent on the formation of a body of Naval Coast Volunteers under Act 16 & 17 Victoria, cap. 73, and the increased duties thrown upon the office by the present war with Russia.

Under Order in Council of 31 March 1855, the 3rd Class was divided into two sections.

For Accountant-General,
E. Gandy

Notes

1 The Phinn Inquiry, P.R.O. ADM 1/5660, p. 9.
2 Halifax Papers, British Library Add. MS. 49532, fols. 323–6.
3 Maurice Wright, *Treasury Control of the Civil Service 1854–74* (London: OUP, 1969), pp. 194–6.
4 P[*arliamentary*] P[*apers*], 1854 XXVII.
5 Wright, op. cit., p. 287.
6 Treasury to Admiralty, 14 June 1855, P.R.O. T5/2, pp. 44f.
7 Admiralty to Treasury, 16 October 1855, P.R.O. T1/5953A; and the reply dated 22 October, T5/2, p. 67.
8 George Arbuthnot to W. E. Gladstone, 15 August 1860, P.R.O. T1/6128A, brochure 11789.
9 J. H. Briggs to Vernon Lushington, 5 July 1869, P.R.O. ADM 116/3193.
10 Circular to the Principal Officers, 28 May 1860, P.R.O. ADM 114/1.
11 J. C. Sainty, *Admiralty Officials 1660–1870*, Vol. 4 in *Office Holders in Modern Britain* (London: Institute of Historical Research, 1975), p. 64.
12 Gladstone to Somerset, 14 August 1860, P.R.O. T1/6128A, brochure 11789. Reply of 15 August, Gladstone Papers, B.L. Add. MS. 44304, fols. 60–2.
13 Admiralty to Treasury, 13 January 1866, P.R.O. T1/6668B, brochure 19988. See also Wright, op. cit., pp. 186f.
14 *Instructions for opening, numbering, and recording the papers . . . on and after 1st January 1870*, P.R.O. ADM 116/3192.
15 *Megaera* Inquiry, *PP*, 1872 XXIII, pp. 512, 551, 575. Whitehall branches also kept some records of their own, consisting of some digests, perhaps even letter books; but they relied principally on the departmental Record Office. The Controller, after 1860, was the new title of the Surveyor.
16 P.R.O. ADM 1/6235 pt. 2, folder dated 2 July 1872. Not that the new system proved ideal. Further changes had to be made in the 1880s. Even so, Dr Rodger informs me, severe faults remained, and only in the 1920s did the Admiralty get an adequate record system, with efficient cross-referencing between the records of the various departments.
17 *PP*, 1888 LXXX, pp. 5–23.
18 Sir Oswyn Murray, 'The Admiralty', part VI, 'Naval Administration from 1832 Onwards', *M*[*ariner's*] *M*[*irror*], Vol. 24 (1938), pp. 458–78. N. A. M. Rodger, 'The Dark Ages of the Admiralty, 1869–85', part I, ' "Business Methods", 1869–74', *M.M.*, Vol. 61 (1975), pp. 331–44.
19 1816 Order, P.R.O. PC 2/197, pp. 439–55; 1854 Order, PC 2/240, pp. 160–4.
20 Henry Parris, *Constitutional Bureaucracy: the Development of British Central Administration since the Eighteenth Century* (London: Allen & Unwin, 1969), p. 251.
21 D[*ictionary of*] N[*ational*] B[*iography*], Vol. VI (London: OUP, 1886), pp. 399f.
22 N.A.M. Rodger, *The Admiralty* (Lavenham: Dalton, 1979), p. 95.
23 The original Inquiry, ADM 1/5660, p. 113.
24 David Garnett (ed.), *The Novels of Thomas Love Peacock* (London: Hart-Davis, 1948), p. xiv. Peacock joined the East India Company in 1819.
25 A series of harbours, of which Dover and Portland were the chief, begun in the 1840s to act as refuges for ships in times of storm and as centres of naval operations.
26 A force recruited from dockyard workers, and trained to defend the yards in case of attack, see C. J. Bartlett, *Great Britain and Sea Power 1815–1853* (London: OUP, 1963), pp. 243f.
27 A seaman reserve set up in 1853, recruited from full and part time coastal fishermen and merchant seamen.
28 Overtly political manipulation of dockyard appointments by a previous First Secretary, in 1852–3, had led to a serious scandal, see Robert Blake, *Disraeli* (London: Eyre & Spottiswoode, 1966), pp. 321–2.
29 See Appendices I and III.
30 Some offices worked a seven-hour day. Only in 1889 was a seven-hour day introduced for all the lower ranks of the Civil Service, Wright, op. cit., pp. 296–7. Somerset House was one of the offices where seven hours was worked even in 1855, which is doubtless

not unconnected with what Trollope tells us at the beginning of chapter 2 of *The Three Clerks*: ' . . . Somerset House is a nest of public offices, which are held to be of less fashionable repute than those situated in the neighbourhood of Downing Street . . .'

31 Hamilton means that the First Lord had usually been a member of the House of Lords.

32 A copying machine was not installed at the Admiralty until February 1869.

33 Houghton's willingness to accept some compromise between merit and seniority is perhaps in part explained by the fact that the Précis Writership, usually offered to the senior second class clerk, had been offered to him when he was a little way down the list in that grade.

34 Because of the special needs of the war, responsibility for transports was taken from the Comptroller of Victualling, and vested in a Board of Transports in February 1855. The Board was dissolved in 1857.

35 Bedford retired in 1844, to be succeeded by Barrow.

36 Presumably the work of John Rouse, Admiralty clerk 1809–34 (Sainty, op. cit., p. 148).

37 The First Secretary had one of the houses adjoining the Admiralty.

38 John Thomas Briggs (1781–1865), Accountant-General from 1832 until he retired in 1854, to be succeeded by Bromley. He was knighted in 1854, and was the father of the J. H. Briggs who gave evidence in 1855, *DNB*, Vol. VI, p. 329.

39 Presumably John Finlaison, Keeper of Records August 1809–February 1816 (Sainty, op. cit., p. 124).

40 It appears that the Board continued to meet regularly in Somerset House, *PP*, 1861 V, pp. 192, 289.

12

De Robeck and the Dardanelles Campaign

Edited by

PAUL G. HALPERN

Introduction

John Michael de Robeck, second son of the third Baron de Robeck, arrived rather unexpectedly in his dramatic, if somewhat controversial, position in naval history. He began the war in a thoroughly unexciting job, Rear-Admiral commanding the 9th Cruiser Squadron on the Cape Finisterre station. He seemed fated to spend long dull weeks in his flagship, the old cruiser *Amphitrite*, searching for German raiders which never appeared. 'One has not to feel bored and think one is doing good work. But it does come a little trying at times', he wrote to his future Chief of Staff Roger Keyes in September, 1914.[1] It was obviously a welcome relief when he became in January 1915 second-in-command of the Eastern Mediterranean Squadron under Vice-Admiral Sir Sackville Carden. De Robeck, flying his flag in the battleship *Vengeance* when the bombardment of the Dardanelles Forts began in February, found all the action he desired when the *Vengeance* was heavily engaged and well splashed on the 19th. But he was only second-in-command and still likely to remain merely a footnote in history. This changed suddenly when Carden's health broke down and he was forced to relinquish his command just before the major attack on the Narrows. De Robeck, who is described as a gentleman in most accounts, was probably genuinely dismayed that Carden would be denied the fruits of months of preparation, and he tried to have Keyes, then Carden's Chief of Staff, dissuade him.[2] Rear-Admiral Rosslyn Wemyss, Senior Naval Officer at Mudros, was actually senior to de Robeck and should have had the command, but generously agreed to step aside in favour of someone so closely engaged in the preparation and execution of the naval plans. De Robeck was made an acting-Vice-Admiral by the Admiralty, and unexpectedly found himself in a position of great responsibility.

The sequence of events at the Dardanelles is well known. The Anglo-French attack of 18 March was a failure, largely because of the undetected line of recently laid mines which led to the loss of 3 battleships and the near loss of the battle cruiser *Inflexible* [Document **1**]. De Robeck was at first ready to renew the attack and believed the Turkish batteries could be sufficiently dominated after a few hours bombardment to enable sweepers to clear the minefield. He was enthusiastically supported, some have even suggested over-persuaded, by Keyes, now his Chief of Staff, and Captain William W. Godfrey, Royal Marine War Staff Officer.[3] But on 22 March he reversed himself, and advised it would be preferable to wait for the Army gathering on Lemnos to land and seize the heights dominating the Narrows. De Robeck remained firm in his decision despite pressure from Winston Churchill, First Lord, to renew the attack [**1**]. The landings at Cape Helles and Anzac on 25 April did not achieve the desired results. The Army was soon hung up and unable to progress. This raised the question of another naval attack. Keyes had reorganised the sweepers and thought the prospects for success were bright. De Robeck was less sanguine and his cable to the Admiralty on 9 May portrayed the situation in a way Keyes considered an invitation to relieve him of any responsibility for failure if they ordered him to attack.[4] There are, unfortunately, relatively few private letters written by de Robeck extant for this period, but he obviously had little opportunity to write in that hectic time.

In England, Churchill and Lord Fisher, the First Sea Lord, fell out over the Dardanelles; Fisher resigned and Churchill himself was soon forced out of office.[5] Arthur Balfour became First Lord and Admiral Sir Henry B. Jackson, First Sea Lord [**5**]. Fortunately for the historian de Robeck and Jackson were friends (something not true of de Robeck and Fisher), corresponded with each other, and many of these letters survive in the de Robeck and Jackson MSS. The same is true of de Robeck's correspondence with Vice-Admiral Sir Arthur Limpus, now Admiral Superintendent at Malta and the senior British Flag Officer in the Mediterranean. The role of Limpus is a rather unglamorous one, but the support services he provided were vital and did much to keep the Dardanelles expedition going.

In May the Navy seemed to mark time at the Dardanelles, supporting the Army certainly, but waiting for the Army to achieve the breakthrough. De Robeck's anxieties increased many times when German submarines were reported on their way [**4**]. The new super dreadnought *Queen Elizabeth* returned to the Grand Fleet, too valuable to risk in operations of that nature. De Robeck switched his flag to the pre-dreadnought *Lord Nelson*, and eventually to the converted yacht *Triad*, which was less valuable and much handier for shuttling between the bases at Lemnos, Imbros and the beachheads, and had the advantage of being able to berth his whole staff. New weapons arrived at the Dardanelles in the form of blistered cruisers and shallow draft monitors. By the end of May the submarine threat became a reality and the battleships *Triumph* and *Majestic* were lost. Now major surface vessels had to be protected and nets – actually double nets or much heavier ones than the ships had been provided with – became the great necessity [9, 10]. Paradoxically submarines also gave de Robeck what he recognised as the most effective weapon the Navy had out there [7]. The handful of British submarines that managed to pass through the tricky currents of the Dardanelles operated effectively in the Marmara, and the Turks were heavily dependent on sea communications because of poor roads. But it was doubtful if the submarines alone could really starve the Turks out of the Peninsula, and by autumn improved net defences in the Narrows made the passage increasingly hazardous.

In August the second major landing attempt was made north of Cape Helles and Anzac at Suvla Bay. The troops failed to exploit their initial surprise; the result was again a stalemate; and the long deferred question of another naval attack reappeared. Its leading advocate was Keyes. De Robeck, who was well aware of the limitations of naval gun fire against targets on land, was cool [16]. He himself favoured another landing with fresh troops, on the Asiatic shore [12]. For a time it seemed as if this would take place with French forces, the French anxious to have their Army independent of British command [18, 21]. Later, British reinforcements were considered, but the plans were fought in both Britain and France by the 'Westerners', those who opposed any diversion of forces from what they regarded as the main and decisive theatre of the war, the Western Front [19, 20, 22]. These plans were all frustrated when Bulgaria entered the war on the side of the Central Powers and troops which might have been used at the Dardanelles were diverted to Salonika in an abortive attempt to rescue Serbia [23, 24, 26]. The success of the Central Powers in overrunning Serbia posed a major threat to the Dardanelles campaign for it meant that rail communications between Germany and Constantinople would be opened, and the British and French expected the Turks, whose reserves of ammunition had been slender, would now be well supplied [24, 29]. The Salonika expedition also opened yet another front and added to de Robeck's responsibilities and problems, as did the uncertain attitude of the Greek government [30].

The establishment of direct communications between Constantinople and Germany, along with the approach of bad weather which threatened supply of the Army over open beaches, raised serious questions about the future of the Dardanelles campaign. This in turn made the question of a renewal of the naval attack an acute one. Keyes and his supporters, notably Captain Godfrey, kept pressing the idea. Thanks to his own memoirs he has had a strong influence on the historiography of the campaign, and to a certain extent de Robeck has been seen through his eyes. After the war Keyes also provided Sir Julian Corbett with material, notably letters he had written from the Dardanelles to his wife, when the historian was engaged in writing the official account of the naval campaign.[6] Moreover, the author of the official military account, Brigadier Cecil Aspinall-Oglander was also a friend who shared some of his sentiments and would later be Keyes's biographer.[7] There was also never any love lost between de Robeck and Churchill, and the latter eloquently defended his position in *The World Crisis*.[8]

Keyes certainly has a tempting position, that of risking essentially old and expendable ships (but unfortunately their crews as well) in an operation which might yield great results, perhaps even the withdrawal of Turkey from the war. It seemed all the more attractive given the alternative of futile blood-letting on the Western Front. De Robeck, who bore the responsibility, was more cautious. Certainly no one doubted he would have acted energetically if ordered to renew the attack. But he could see beyond the problem of actually forcing the Dardanelles and he was not optimistic. Even if a few ships broke through, after moderate to heavy losses, what could they accomplish in the long run as long as the Narrows remained dominated by enemy artillery which threatened the passage of the essential but vulnerable support, the storeships, oilers and colliers? What if the Turkish Army did not retreat or the Turkish Government did not collapse even with Constantinople under the guns of the British fleet? De Robeck's views are presented in these documents [**27, 30**].[9] It is also extremely interesting to note that when Keyes was himself C.-in-C. Mediterranean at the time of the Mosul crisis in 1926, his own plans for military operations against Turkey clearly included securing the Gallipoli Peninsula with a military force as an essential part of any protracted operations by the Fleet in the Marmara.[10] De Robeck had the less glamorous position, but as Limpus, who agreed with him put it, he was thankful they had a man strong enough to say 'no' [**31**]. The debate is an endless one naturally, because like all 'what if' questions it can never be answered. The renewed naval attack was never tried.

The relationship between de Robeck and Keyes is a fascinating one, a mixture of admiration and reservations about judgement with de Robeck, senior in rank and ten years older, more restrained, and Keyes in private moments later on, letting himself go from time to time with more uncharitable sentiments.[11] It seems incredibly sporting today for De Robeck to allow Keyes to go back to England to plead his case, stressing that there was no ill will between them and that he encouraged subordinate officers to speak their mind. Keyes's trip is vividly portrayed in his letter diary published in *The Keyes Papers*.[12] But one cannot escape the feeling that he had perhaps less influence than he thought at the time [**29**]. De Robeck was, after all, the senior and a few letters quietly undercut his Chief of Staff's position, even if they must have added to the difficulties a vacillating government had in making a decision [**27**].[13]

By now de Robeck's own health was breaking down: his responsibilities were growing, especially with the Salonika expedition [**34**]; the summer climate had taken its toll; and by October he suffered from insomnia and neuralgia [**32**]. Those who lean towards a psychological interpretation might find much to comment on here, as indeed they could find much to speculate on in the illness of Carden before the March attack.

De Robeck left for a short leave in England in late November and in addition to resting, he undoubtedly did at least something in a quiet way to undo the arguments of Keyes. In the end it was the military in the person of Lord Kitchener (who had been out to the Dardanelles on a tour of inspection), and General Monro, commander of the Army at Gallipoli, who came down on the side of evacuation. Wemyss was acting commander in de Robeck's absence and together with Keyes conducted a last ditch attempt to stop the evacuation and renew the naval attack. De Robeck must have been surprised at Wemyss [**32**], but certainly not Keyes. Once again, he generously allowed Keyes to remain as Chief of Staff [**36**], even though, as Keyes later remarked, things were never quite the same again between them, and he himself suffered a guilty conscience over de Robeck's tolerance and magnanimity.[14] De Robeck's position, however, was supported by a number of senior naval officers on the scene, notably Rear-Admiral Christian[15] and Captain Heathcoat Grant as well as Limpus at Malta [**31, 37**].

De Robeck had expected to return before the actual evacuation. Instead he got back just after the evacuation of Suvla and Anzac. He favoured retaining the beachhead at Cape Helles [**32**], but the government decided to evacuate that too. He remained in the Aegean, preoccupied with the Greek imbroglio but with his responsibilities obviously contracting, until the summer of 1916. De Robeck's next command was that of the 3rd Battle Squadron at Sheerness. It consisted of the *Dreadnought* and pre-dreadnought 'King Edward VII' class, and after the Aegean must have seemed a come down. In November he received a more powerful command, the dreadnoughts of the 2nd Battle Squadron in the Grand Fleet. It was a thoroughly subordinate position with little scope for individual initiative.

Whatever the controversy over de Robeck, there is no doubt that he had the ability to inspire his subordinates and fellow officers. He was respected and well-liked in the French and Italian navies as well as in the Royal Navy. In 1918 his name was mentioned in Allied circles as a possible 'Admiralissimo' in the Mediterranean. Freed of his Dardanelles responsibilities he became a new man. After the war he was C.-in-C. Mediterranean from 1919 to 1921, and High Commissioner Constantinople from 1919 to 1920. He ended his career as C.-in-C. Atlantic Fleet from

1922 to 1924. But while command of Great Britain's two major fleets were positions of great responsibility, particularly in the turmoil in the Mediterranean and Black Sea following the world war, it is nevertheless true that de Robeck's real opportunity to influence history had been at the Dardanelles. Like Keyes he is forever linked to the Dardanelles campaign, and he was not unaffected by the controversy in the writings of others, notably Churchill. He died in 1928, perhaps before he might have been moved to reply to his critics in print, although there is no evidence he was temperamentally inclined to do so. There was even a clause in his will that none of his papers which might cause bad feeling were to be made public until the death of all concerned, and the family did not deposit the papers at Churchill College until after Sir Winston's death.[16] The eternal question remains. Did de Robeck miss his great opportunity through fear of taking responsibility for recommending a renewed naval attack or did he indeed have the moral courage to resist the temptations and pressures to which he was subjected and say no to an action which he felt would lead to a costly disaster?

DE ROBECK AND THE DARDANELLES CAMPAIGN

1 *De Robeck to Vice-Admiral Sir Arthur H. Limpus*[17]

[Holograph]   H.M.S. *Q.E.* [*Queen Elizabeth*],
                                              26 March [19]15

You are a real marvel the way you get the work done, how do you manage it?

Hope *Inflexible* will get the flexible mat in place today and will then proceed direct to Malta. Your constructor thinks there is a thousand tons less water in ship now than when she got back to Tenedos, probably about a thousand still in ship, this however should be much reduced if mat is a success! The bulkheads appear to be now well secured, of course usual thing happened, water got in through ventilation trunks and glands of electric wire leads. It will always be the same as long as we allow the holes in bulkheads below the main deck! *Inflexible* was drawing 32 ft. yesterday as against 36 ft. after she struck the mine! Will send *Dublin* and *Agamemnon* down if possible to make good their urgent defects! Others must wait. *Vengeance* is in a very bad way as regards engines and boilers but she may last to see the business through!

We were very unlucky on 18th March in losing ships but were on contrary wonderfully fortunate in saving life. The actual bombardment went well enough, it is the old story, we suppress the fire of forts but fail to actually destroy guns. My view is to [?] now have a combined attack which should succeed and not throw our ships and ammunition away until both the Army and Navy can strike at once! W. C.[18] is urging one to go on and strike. Much as one may like to obtain one's own glorification I prefer to go on my considered opinion and not be hurried! Good luck my dear friend and many thanks for your great efforts. Excuse my scrawl. Work is great and no time for letters . . .

[P.S.]   Trust Carden[19] is better?

2 *De Robeck to Limpus*

[Holograph]   H.M.S. *Queen E*[*lizabeth*],
Secret   11 April [19]15

Thanks to you we are well on with our arrangements and hope to be ready as soon or before the Army can move, of course the final jump must be made when the weather is at its very best! It is unfortunate losing so many lighters, but between *ourselves*, it is proposed to put one or two ships full of troops on the beach, it will be quicker and insure a large number getting on shore very quickly. If we are lucky and the Turks get taken off their legs all will be well, though we are bound to lose men and have hard fighting. The *Q.E.* [*Queen Elizabeth*] had a successful trial of her engines today and now all right, we did 23½ knots with 57,000 H.P. and they say they can get 75,000 if required in which case we ought to catch the *Goeben*,[20] though Russian Admiral Black Sea says she went 22 knots in day and 25 at night when he chased her last week; but do not quite understand how he could estimate her speed with his old ships; fear it has put him off embarking the Russian Army. But if we succeed, so much the better for us if we take Constantinople before the Russians, as we shall have more voice in the matter and these Balkan States all look to us to keep the peace! The arrival of the *Inflexible* at Malta came as a blessed relief to me and no doubt to everyone concerned, hope now you will be able to put her in safe condition to proceed to Gib.? My greatest difficulty now is finding officers and men sufficient for the landing of the Army and only that we have the crews of *Ocean* and *Irresistible* it would have been out of the question.[21] Good luck, you are indeed a wonder in the way you produce everything we want. Thanks old friend for it all . . .

3   *Limpus to de Robeck*

[Holograph]   Admiralty House, Vittoriosa.
                                                   Friday night, 7 May 1915

Splendidly done. Well done indeed. Perhaps I really knew more than most other people what a task had been set you. The actual *landing* alone in its organization and prearrangement with the scanty − scanty − and rough means we could send you from here − and the weather possibilities.

The steady and thorough preparations of the Germans warned by the bombardments of November and February/March that the blow was coming − My word but I knew what it must mean − and then the landing − the grit − the hardihood − the endurance [?] and the self sacrifice of that gallant [?] advance party and its followers. And you have succeeded − I mean by you − you *all*. Well done indeed by George. I am proud this day to be of the same race.

Landed, firmly established on shore at two places − well they won't shift them now. The question is now one of steady, persistent, patient pressure − plenty of ammunition − and − I am afraid another 50,000 or 78,000 men. Yet one must remember that the Germans and Turks have had a fearful surprise and a terrible hammering − and difficult though the ammunition supply of the attack may be, that of the defence is precarious − almost bound to fail. They must be in terrible straits for more ammunition − and while they can make but little locally and probably now *import* no more − for every indication shows Bulgaria and Roumania now disinclined to give any more underhand help of that kind. Ours − though it has to come over sea − is coming and *will* come. Of course their hammering plus the ammunition difficulty may cause a complete collapse of the defence. It is not likely in that case the men whom I believe to be later [?] joining you or well on their way − though not the 50,000 I spoke of − may do you − will do you as far as Bulair. But even then some patience will be needed [?] before the Peninsula and the Fleet can quell all action [?] from the opposite side and permit steady thorough sweeping by day in that current. I hope the Fleet sweepers came through the landing unharmed for I think they will be invaluable to you in the Marmara.

I hope the Admiralty have managed − through Fitzmaurice[22] and other agents to provide local guards against the burning and destruction of the Golden Horn Dockyard and plant and the small repair work and 8000 ton floating dock at Stenia (in the Bosphorus).

Remember also that *if* you can save the repair ship *Tir-Y-Muzghen* − you will find a nearly brand new distilling plant on board for 80 tons daily of water − and you must not trust local water. It *must* be boiled at all times.

Now I foresee a determined effort on the Germans' part to cause a serious diversion in the Mediterranean against our Transports, ammunition ships − couriers and commerce.

The French have *no* fast light cruisers − and their destroyers can't stand the work that ours can. So I have taken upon myself to warn the Adm[iral]ty and to suggest lending − from Home − light cruisers to the French C.-in-C. and sending 8 sturdy destroyers to sweep and hunt the submarines that are − and will appear − in the Western Mediterranean. It's a minor danger − but a troublesome one and best foreseen and met before any harm is done. Of course the Italians may come in immediately and save us the trouble of withdrawing such useful craft from the North. But I cannot be sure of that and I felt bound to utter the warning.

Play the game steadily − do not overdo yourself. Remember what I said about the boss of the show − he at all costs − *must* have sleep and rest enough to let him run the show through with a clear brain and a quick eye.

It is the finest landing ever done in history. No doubt about *that*. I am certain the Germans thought it absolutely impossible, and its accomplishment is a fearful jar for them. But they are dogged fellows like we are and they will try to hit hard in reply − in the Carpathians − towards Riga − and if they can in the Mediterranean and in Serbia. Well − they may delay the end a bit − but they won't change it.

Good night old chap and God speed you through the rest of your task . . .

[P.S.] When you are established through and have swept your way up to and into it Artaki Bay is a fine base at the SW corner of the Marmara and Ismidt Gulf at the Eastern end − though the latter is generally deep.

Pasha Liman a ripping place for small craft though the adjacent sponge fishery robs it of real privacy.

4 *De Robeck to Limpus*

[Holograph]   H.M.S. *Lord Nelson*,
                                            Sunday, 16 May [19]15

Ever so many thanks for your letter[23] and excuse me for being such a bad correspondent, but these are anxious days and I have little time even to write on a matter of business, but I will try and give you a general idea of what is going on.

(a) The Army at Cape Helles have dug themselves in and are making small advances by night towards Krithia, they have not sufficient room to prevent the beach being shelled at long range. It is necessary to take the line Achi Baba [?] to make that secure and give the Army room. However they seem comfortable and full of confidence, though they are up against a very stiff proposition.

(b) Australians north of Gaba Tepe are very well dug in, but apparently cannot advance and get more room, they also get their beach heavily shelled at times. Their chief anxiety is water so send along as many iron tanks as possible and they will be dug in under the cliff. I would like to see them have a good reserve of water always, say 300 tons and then there would be no anxiety; now they depend on water lighters each night, not very satisfactory. Otherwise Army have all they want and my chief trouble has been to get Wemyss[24] and Thursby[25] to clear away their transports, however the submarine scare has helped me over that and there will not be a great many left as a target.[26]

Now as to the future.

(a) Main base Port Mudros, all transports will go there and *no* further; troops to take to Gallipoli peninsula each night by fleet sweepers, 500 each, 6 of them, 3000 a night. That will reduce the risk of submarine attack.

Supply ships will go if necessary to Helles or to Kephalo. The latter bay I am making into an advance base, but I want a net defence and boom to make it secure. It is well situated and protected on three sides against attack and much better anchorage than the chart shows.

Ammunition ships to discharge at Mudros and forward their cargoes by fleet sweepers and trawlers. I don't want to risk an ammunition ship more than is necessary, especially as the Army is now really hung up for ammunition and would push on here if they had it!

(b) Naval base Port Mudros, all supply and naval ammunition ships there.

Ships standing off to go to Mudros.

Ships required as 'covering ships' for Army only being at sea and they are to cruise at night if possible; anchoring in their position at daylight and when they have nets to get them out at once on anchoring. It is absolutely necessary for them to anchor while firing, otherwise ammunition is thrown away. Now my *most important requirement* are nets and lighters on which to hang the nets and place them round these ships, when that is done we can feel some confidence that the ship will not be done down by a submarine.

I want a good net defence for Kephalo and hope the one coming out from England will do for that, as I keep 'water ship' and several supply ships there, also this ship, *Blenheim, Ark Royal* and several more important units who must be on the spot.[27] *Q.E.* [*Queen Elizabeth*] went off and in a way it was best, as she was really too valuable for this work and if they send me the new monitors they will do me much better. Now the great thing is to secure our bases and by that our communications from submarine attack and then we may look for a steady advance, but remember it will all be siege work now and fear heavy losses, unless the Turk suddenly throws his hands up.

As regards other matters, I have no further news of [the Australian submarine] *A.E.2* and fear she has gone,[28] what damage she did beyond one gunboat sunk no information! *E.14* has fired all torpedoes and hope to order her down tonight. She has got as far as we can make out one large gunboat, one small ditto, one transport, one large military transport, one steamer. Not a bad bag for 10 torpedoes. *E.11* should be ready tomorrow to go up and a submarine in the Marmara now is worth an Army Corps. The *Goeben* is still alive and fear while she is in being, the Russians will not embark; they have two Army Corps ready at Odessa to start and if landed could probably walk into Constantinople as there are few troops there now! As regards the *Goliath*, I fear she was a good ship thrown away and ought *not to have been sunk*.[29] She was in a dangerous position. Shelford [?] anchored and though they saw the destroyer did not fire at her; but made the challenge, hence she was torpedoed. Officer of watch too *old*! A promoted W.O. Suppose one ought not to have risked a ship there, but it was at the repeated and earnest request of the French general!

You must excuse bad writing and worse spelling and English but have not time to read it over as there is much to do!

I continue lost [?] in admiration of Malta dockyard and the way you keep us going. If I can I will send *Albion* to you at once. Then I should like *Agamemnon* to go and get put right, she is a good deal knocked about. Fyler[30] has been splendid, the *very* best of all, a real bruiser and never happy unless he is fighting somebody. We never know one's man until war begins.

Some of the T.B.D.s badly require refit and wish they would send me a few more from England! The French C.-in-C. took four of his away and left us one, which is hardly playing the game.

Private. Have they told you about the future and the new formation of the squadrons out here? Don't like it at all! They are sending a French V.A. up here senior to Guépratte[31], which is a great mistake; dear old soul he is the most loyal friend one could have and hate anybody coming between us!

Goodnight my dear old friend and more power to your elbow! . . .

5   *De Robeck to Limpus*

[Holograph]   H.M.S. *Lord Nelson*,
                                                        Saturday, 22 May 1915

You continue to do great work for us here and indeed without you I don't know where we would be, it will be a little hard and take time to straighten out matters now, after the removal of so many ships. Thursby's loss is a great one and he was really splendid the way he worked with the Australians, but of course this show with the Italians is the more important for him. I suppose you know him, his bark much worse than his bite! He always begins with a grievance against somebody; but as long as he imagines that he is putting matters right, he is perfectly happy!

The more I read of [the] *Goliath* case, the worse it is and fear poor Shelford[32] had no sort of arrangements made to meet a torpedo attack, it is all quite incomprehensible to me and am recommending a C.M. later on! Of course these old Third Fleet ships are badly officered and the O.W. aboard *Goliath* was quite unfit for the work in hand.

Things are all right here, but do not look forward to the first enemy's submarine visit and apparently there is one now at Smyrna; though it is not absolutely certain and I get reports by the dozen of their presence in the Aegean; so hope her arrival is postponed on account of Italy? The Australians have been doing big things lately and been fairly giving the Turks *hell*. The 1st Corps from Constantinople came down to the Dardanelles with orders to drive them into the sea, result Turks have probably lost well over ten thousand men, as after first day there were over two thousand dead Turks in front of part of our trenches and there have been three more attacks since, so the estimate is very low. Turks tried the white flag game without result. The Turk has now asked for an armistice and in a way it will be good for our people; as otherwise they would be stunk out of their trenches. It is a capital thing for us these attacks, as these are the Turks' best troops and there will be fewer to deal with later on! *E.14* came back all safe, had bad luck with his torpedoes, but got one very large transport (2 funnels, three masts) full of troops. *E.11* is now up there and has got 12 torpedoes onboard, so I have great hopes he will do big things! We are busy with a certain number of ships each day covering the Army, who have very little ammunition, though we have not much ourselves, we have to help! I am therefore anxious to get different ships down to Malta as soon as possible for you to put them right, before we make a big push! Sorry I couldn't wire you about *Q.E.* [*Queen Elizabeth*] I was ordered to inform nobody, I hope the Admiralty will always inform you for these important moves. Our French C.-in-C. really takes the cake and will make no further remarks, I am more than sorry that they have sent a French V.A. to be in charge instead of dear old Guépratte, who is the most loyal of men. I hope the new man Nicol[33] will be equally so!

Hospital ships are a nuisance and have had to give very definite orders regarding them and this is how it stands at present. One H.S. for serious cases always off Gaba Tepe & Helles (two altogether). All slightly wounded taken by fleet carriers to Mudros each day, where they are having a hospital started; later there will be one at Kephalo Bay; it was such a mistake sending them all to Egypt or Malta.

I had to send *Soudan* to Malta with some military cases, as they were out of ships! Please send me a Naval Hospital Ship as soon as possible. The Admiralty are playing up again and sending me some light craft and it is what I want to deal with submarines, etc., in these parts! Then with mines we should make the use of Smyrna, Vourlah [?] and Chesme nearly impossible for the enemy, wish they would give me plenty of mines.

What do you think of affairs at home, evidently J. F.[34] took the opportunity to resign over the Dardanelles question, but he does not appear to have succeeded in his actions [?], as I suppose W. C. will go C. Sec^ty to Ireland now and stay in Cabinet. A chance for us all in the future now and honest men may come by their own. God bless you old friend and good luck to you and yours . . .
[P.S.] Excuse scrawl, English and spelling!!

6 *Thursby to de Robeck*

[Holograph]   H.M.S. *Queen*,
                                                        24 May [19]15

Just a line to let you know of my doings and to say how sorry I was to leave your flag and to thank you for all you did for me when I was with you. For the present until the Gallipoli peninsula is taken it seems to be a military job but as soon as it is possible to pass the Narrows the Navy will come to the front again and I shall hope to hear of your flag flying off Constantinople. I hope you will not mind my making a suggestion to you on a matter of minor detail and that is with reference to stores, etc. It would be a good thing if when ships arrive at Mudros or elsewhere if when it has been ascertained what is on board them it was communicated to the ships concerned, and the ships ordered to report when they have got the goods. If this is not possible perhaps the senior officers of squadrons might be informed so that they could take steps to see their ships got the gear.

I came across several cases where merchant ships with gear for ships *present* had had it on board for 5 or 6 weeks and had even gone backwards and forwards between Malta and Mudros with it still on board altho they had several times anchored within a few hundred yards of the ships the gear was for. When *London* was at Mudros she was coaling from a collier full of gear for *Queen* and other of my ships and knew nothing about it altho she was told to get all gear for *Queen*, etc. This is a small matter and easily put right so I hope you do not mind my mentioning it.

I have now got all my little squadron together, *Amethyst* and *Sapphire* will require 2 or 3 days in Dy. hands but all will be ready by 26th. All battleships have been in dock.

Admiral Gamble[35] is expected today or tomorrow from Italy with my orders and instructions. Capt. Richmond[36] will represent me on board the Italian Flagship. In reply to my application for a Flag Commander and a wireless expert they have appointed Lieut. Poë and a Captain of Marines.

I called on the French C.-in-C.[37] He is a decent old chap but I think feels he is rather left out in the cold as operations frequently take place in his command without his knowledge, vide the bombardment of Smyrna. I think he would do anything he could with the material at his disposal if it were put to him what was expected of him. He is at present much put out because under the Convention he has to supply *12* Destroyers to the I[talian] fleet. I rubbed into him his responsibility for the presence of the German submarines. According to him his destroyers ought to have got one of them and it was due to the stupidity of his destroyer captain that they let him get away. I *do* hope you will circumvent them up at the Dardanelles. If only you could get your nets you would be alright. They have got 4,000 of our wounded here now and expect another 2,000, you should get most of them back before very long.

Limpus as you know is splendid here. Everything possible is done with the least possible fuss or paperwork.

Again thank you very much for all you have done for me . . .

P.S.   My best chin chin to Keyes and wishing you a speedy success.

7   *De Robeck to Limpus*

[Holograph]   H.M.S. *Triad*,
                                                            3 June [19]15

You are still keeping us going and more power to you and please God the submarines have not yet torpedoed any of our transports, but how long they will leave them alone heaven only knows! They torpedoed S.S. Ship No.14 '*Tiger*'[38] and old Willy Forbes[39] who is now nearly seventy behaved splendidly and the old man wants another job out here, but think he had better go home and see his wife and get some new clothes! A grand spirit in the old men sometimes, fear in *Majestic* it is rather the other way and a large proportion of these men are much shaken and will not be much use afloat. Of course many of them were Grandfathers and should hardly have been out doing a 'show' of this sort! *Triumph*'s behaved very well and the loss of life has been wonderfully small.[40] Now as for the future.

The Admiralty wired for all our available ratings so we are down to bed rock in regard to men again. They are sending me:

(a) 2 Cruisers − *Theseus* and *Endymion* with outer [?] skins and they should prove useful vessels for this work − 12 6″ guns each.

(b) Monitors − about six of different sorts including two with 14″ guns. Should all reach here by end of June.

(c) Four light cruisers, new pattern, 2 12pdr guns, light draft, etc.

(d) A few various small steamers.

What I want in addition to these are:

    4 'E' Class submarines
    8 T.B.D.s at least.

I believe at present I will get neither though perhaps the former may come along when more submarines are ready! Our submarines in the Marmora are the most valuable weapon that the Navy has at present. Our destroyers up here are all in need of seeing 'Dr Limpus' and having their insides put right! How we can man any extra small craft I don't know, the calls are so numerous, we want more tugs and more steamboats.

Our steamboats are about finished and many will soon be beyond repair, though *Reliance* and *Blenheim* do what they can to keep them going. We are anxious to have some small steamers which draw 10 or 12 ft., about 500 tons, to take stores, etc., from Mudros to the Peninsula and hope that the Admiralty can find us some. I hate the idea of a valuable store ship being torpedoed and sunk off the beach. If we have a small steamer that can run alongside the pier unloading will go twice as quick! Also the number of lighters required will be greatly reduced! We cannot get the military to build proper piers and am now going to talk seriously to Sir Ian[41] about his C.R.E. [Commanding Royal Engineer] who will not get on. The water supply is always a serious one and again the military will not face the situation. There is plenty of ground water at Imbros [?] that only requires boring [?] and pipes laid down to a pier and it could be put direct into the water lighters! and taken over at night the ten miles! Soldiers will not help themselves and we have done too much for them and they lean on us always now! However here we have no friction and they cannot complain of our assistance!

As regards our anchorages and their protection. Mudros may be considered fairly secure but by no means perfectly so! Two nets are in place though the net gate would be easy for a good submarine officer to get through and attack inside.

Kephalo is an open anchorage to the north otherwise protected on three sides, perhaps if six old steamers were sunk x [across] the bay, a moderate breakwater would be formed and also with nets hung from lighters, submarine attack would be difficult! The anchorage off Helles will always be exposed to torpedo attack, ditto Gaba Tepe, though in case of latter, there is a harbour called Suvla Bay to the north of the landing which might be used if we held a little more of the Peninsula! Though we may lay nets and have temporary measures for the protection of ships, they will not last if we get a southerly gale! If you can buy me some old craft that could be sunk please do so, they will all come in useful for making protection. I dare not use these transports or supply ships! The Army is to make another attack tomorrow and hope they may prove successful, fear they are up against some very stiff entrenchments, much wire and many machine guns. Still they are in good heart, have a lot of artillery and plenty of men. There are many rumours as to the Turk being tired of the war, but I see no sign of it at present and he fights away hard every day! Enver Pasha[42] out of the way, then perhaps we would see a quick change!

These submarines are the devil and are cramping one's style very much and until we can sink them there will be no peace. A change in Greek government would be our greatest help, the present Greek Minister of Marine is reported as being in German pay. Which seems very true. Good luck and kind regards. Excuse scrawl . . .

8   *Admiral Sir Henry B. Jackson*[43] *to de Robeck*

[Holograph]   Admiralty, Whitehall.
Private   9 June 1915

I have often intended writing to you but have invariably missed the bag and put it off, but one goes tomorrow and I seize a few spare moments.

I have been with you in the spirit during the whole time you have been carrying out our only really offensive movement of importance, and longed for your success; as Dardanelles was one of the numerous jobs I had to watch before I had to take up this very onerous task I have now entered into. We all underestimated it, I fear, but not to the extent that those who ordered it in the manner it has been attempted. I must say this to excuse myself, as I always advocated combined operations from the time the first trial shot was fired by Carden last year.

You must be overworked and find but little time to tell us details, which we should much appreciate especially as to artillery used on shore, 15″ how[itzer], etc. Is it to [be] used or about to be. What I should personally like to know is the organisation of your command, duties of flag and senior officers not in ships, base arrangements, organisation of transport, munition and water supplies to the troops and those minor but important details which are not included in the fighting part which I know you are in the thick of.

We are sending you some smaller but possibly more suitable (being less vulnerable) vessels, but we shall shortly have to ask you to spare all naval ratings not in ships as we have a large programme of small vessels nearing completion which must be manned. The R.N.D.[44] can probably be drawn upon to supply individuals fit for subsidiary shore jobs or else the military can do so. Please think this over pending the official intimation. I wish Bulgaria would come in *now*. I think she will later; she wants as much as possible for as little as she can give. Your submarines have done wonders and six more are on the way to help you. The cry everywhere is for small fast vessels, and we have an enormous number on order but they'll take time to materialise.

I can't criticise military strategy but have often wondered why you don't try and exert more military pressure from Gaba Tepe.

Write me a note if you can spare time or telegraph if you prefer it but remember we all wish you success and luck and with best wishes . . .

9 *De Robeck to Jackson*

[Holograph]

H.M.S. *Triad*,
15 June 1915

A line to congratulate you and you have all my best wishes and feel sure everybody is delighted at the change, which will give the service a chance of settling down even though it is war time! I have intended to write to you often, but the day is never long enough and though I have now got my staff all onboard here (it was hopeless in *Lord Nelson*) and work is continuous, it is hard to keep pace with the various calls that are made. A fleet would be easy to run but when you have an Army on your hands, it is the devil. The General, Ian Hamilton, and his C.O.S. Braithwaite[45] are delightful people to work with, but lower down the scale there are some real 'blockers' − R.E., Head Medical Officer, and one or two more, these do not appear to have any idea of method, certainly not ours. However, we have kept them going in spite of themselves and if the Army could only push on and make a little more room for themselves, all would be well. At present machine guns and barbed wire always bring up our attack and the Turk counter attacks with fresh troops, which is hard on our tired soldiers. But these general frontal attacks which we make, do not appear to be a success and certainly not the value of the losses; though on the 4th June it appears the French let us *down* very badly and prevented our having a brilliant success. The French have a good general and very poor infantry, but excellent artillery and lots of ammunition, which our Army have not got!

As regards ourselves, I am naturally distressed beyond measure at the loss of the ships, but what was one to do. I could not put all the ships in harbour at Mudros and leave the Army to be shelled off the Peninsula! Our net defence is apparently no use against the German torpedo and think the only net defence that will meet the situation is a double net a few feet apart; bring the old or lighter net outside to explode the net cutting charge and trusting to the heavy net to stop the torpedo afterwards and propose to work on this idea as nets become available. At present here at Kephalo I put colliers alongside any ship of value if it is possible to do so and the ships only bombard for short intervals. Still when we get all these additional trawlers and nets the German submarines will have a very anxious time if they come to attack us off Helles.

As soon as the Monitors arrive I hope to start again inside the Dardanelles and give more support to the Army on that flank, at present the French are supposed to do so and assist the right flank of their army, but it is very hard to get this new French V.A. to do anything, he will do nothing as well as anyone. He suggested taking some of his ships to Egypt the other day; in fact has the submarine fever very badly! Nicol is a very different man from dear old Guépratte who is a gallant fellow and the most loyal friend! Nicol is a little man of the most unprepossessing appearance; does not look a gentleman and don't think his name would be in the 'Stud Book'! We get on very well with the French, but they want everything and do as little as possible (most of them). It was a great pity the French Admiralty did not leave Guépratte here in command, he feels the situation very keenly of having this other man put over his head! But I quite understand that you cannot do anything in the matter at the present time!

I have been most loyally served by all hands and everybody has done their best and it should be remembered we are largely manned by R.N.R. officers and men, who are not up to the same standard as one would expect in the Grand Fleet, still they have done their best and in some cases splendidly! The people who feel the strain most are a ship's company like *Majestic*'s made up of very old men, many of them grandfathers, their nerves do not stand the work and I sent most of them home in *Carmania*. Some Captains also feel it and want rest before going to sea again, though they can do good work on shore; for that reason I have sent Dent[46] and Hayes-Sadler[47] home! Others like Nicholson[48] who had his flag in *Majestic* don't seem to mind the experience in the least and was ready to have another turn at once!

As regards the general situation here, the Army does not appear likely to make any grand [?] advance while the Turk is able to pour fresh troops into the peninsula, on the other hand the Turk is not in a position to turn them out; but do not place too much reliance on reports of their shortages of ammunition, evidently a lot comes in through Roumania or Bulgaria, the latter also assisted the German submarine near Thaso if one can believe these agents. So if the Army cannot push forward on the peninsula what is to be done? The General talked to me about landing an Army at Enos, well there should be no great difficulty in actually landing there, as it is an excellent beach and the transports could be run on shore if there was danger of a submarine attack. But the maintenance and general support of an additional army with my present available small craft did not seem a possibility; unless it was only for a few days. So I told him that and telegraphed to that effect to Admiralty. Of course if Enos Gulf was dredged out it would be a different matter, but believe that one cannot rely on more than 3ft. 6 inch on the bar at present though as much as 18 ft. in a hole off the town. Any other place in the Gulf of Xeros has much the same drawbacks and on the whole not as good as Enos. The only other solution to my mind is an attack on Smyrna using Port Eiro, Mitylene as a base and landing the Army at one of the small harbours like Ali Aghi opposite. But this is a military question and from the very beginning I have not offered any opinion to the General in what seems to be for the Army to decide!

I understand if the Greeks join in the war their idea is to attack Smyrna using 120,000 men, which at the present time would be ample. Venizelos[49] gives one the impression of being sincere and if he is not murdered he is certainly going to rule Greece for some time to come. Bulgaria appears to be entirely 'out' for what she can get and German money is keeping the government neutral, a few millions would bring them in and it would be a cheap way of ending the deadlock here!

How far the Navy will be able to destroy the Chanak forts with our Army in its present position depends on these new monitors, if they can stand howitzer fire we can do a great deal, as the mines will not be the same danger to them as it was to the old Battleships. The Turks send down a few mines and we are always destroying them in Morto Bay, our nets are almost impossible to keep in place in the Dardanelles on account of the current. But hope to have a net protected area near Cape Helles when the nets arrive. Kephalo Bay is a difficult place to do anything with as the NE wind blows right in and seems to blow 9 days out of 10. However our bogus defence will probably assist us, as it is sure to be reported to the enemy and they will think it a formidable net defence! We will I hope soon have the squadron rearranged when the monitors arrive and give the Turk all he wants, in the meantime the submarines are doing invaluable work in the Marmora and we will see the business through somehow, though if the Bulgarians came in, it would be over in three weeks! The Russians I can't make out, do they intend to help? With all good wishes and kind regards to Lady Jackson. Believe me . . .

P.S. R. Keyes sends his best wishes, etc. How is golf these days, I have not played since the war started and you will beat me easily now!

10 *De Robeck to Limpus*

[Holograph]   *Triad,*
Secret   21 June [19]15

Many thanks for your letter and the information in regard to the feast of Bamayh [Bairam]. It might come in very useful as about then the Army should have received the three new divisions and be able to make another push somewhere or other. I have great hopes [in] these heavy anti-submarine nets which can be laid by the two paddle steamers *Prince Edward* and the other. My anxiety is of course the landing of troops in large bodies should an enemy submarine be about, even though one might run the transports on shore. What we are trying to do now is to get our small craft, tugs, lighters, steamboats, etc., into some sort of repair, they have been run off their legs and if this show is not over before the winter it will be very hard to keep an army provided on an open beach during SW winds. Also we require to make some sort of secure anchorage for store ships, etc., when anchored off Helles; [at] Anzac it is impossible to do so and must take the risk!

Should the Army land elsewhere then of course our commitments will be increased in accordance with the size of the force. We will require rafts similar to those used at home for boom defence at our defended ports for supporting heavy net defence and I should like to try using the old light net in front of the heavy net in order to fire the German explosive cutter! I would have a place like enclosed rough sketch for the battleship doing supporting ship at Cape Helles with net protection; also will put a heavy net protection at Rabbit Island and hope if net is available to put a heavy anti-submarine net at Tenedos just across the Strait at Gadaro Island and block the Strait entirely for enemy's submarines. – Then (*very secret*) if the Army land at Yukheri [Yukyeri] Bay where I want them to; directly they land, put a second anti-submarine net on southside from Galley Point to Suffren Shoals and so make a large anchorage where transports could lay and discharge in safety. Tell me what you think of this idea, it is what I am urging on Hamilton and tell him I will engage to put 25 to 30 thousand men on shore in first flight and another 30,000 second day if landing has been secured. Yukyeri Bay is the best winter anchorage about these parts nearer than Mudros. Enos is very exposed, of course everything would be done to make the enemy think we are going there or Bulair. I imagine Turks at most have not more than 40,000 on south side of Straits and not of the same class of those on the north side.

Of course one does not know when the army will be ready, or when the monitors are likely to reach me; they shall make all the difference as though sending battleships to bombard in Straits are not in great risk of submarine attack, they are so vulnerable to torpedo attack when hit that it is always fatal to them and therefore becomes a question is it any use having them risked. I do not think it is the least use hanging old type torpedo nets round any ship and if the nets being sent out are of that sort (weaker than G or H)! the nets can be better used as previously suggested.

Can you send me up some large baulks of timber, we have practically none up here and they would be invaluable for working at net defence, also for a slipway at Kephalo which I want to repair lighters. Don't forget the possibility of a small floating dock for Mudros!

Nothing much fresh here, French made a small advance yesterday. Turkish guns on the Asiatic side have been active and a nuisance by shelling our beaches at Helles. *Lord Nelson* will be the next battleship to send you after *Swiftsure*, she has been a long time without a refit and got a blow from a large projectile below the belt some time back.

Kind regards and excuse scrawl. Been disturbed every moment and hard to write . . .

11   *Limpus to de Robeck*

[Holograph]   H.M. Dockyard, Malta.
Private   29 June [19]15

My writing is so appalling that I made Stark my Sec[retar]y — whom I would trust with my life — type my long letter for you.

Ashmead-Bartlett[50] — whom I judged to be like another Winston — humoured me by showing me his ideas.[51] They are logical and plausible, but the *size of the operation*, the number of transports requiring a base while assembling and protection while landing and the uncertainty of the weather make his plan impracticable from a *sailor* point of view and in this business both sailors and soldiers must be satisfied together that the plan to be carried out is really sound and workable. Your scheme will I think stand the test of practicability from both a sailor's and soldier's point of view. And besides — though it will not immediately give us the whole peninsula — it will make our position comfortable and secure with the troops which are available.

I expect you know that I think we should never have fired one round at the entrance forts (about November 4, 1914) until we had a force ready to throw ashore under cover of the panic that a serious [?] and sustained bombardment would have caused.

However it is no use crying over the far distant past. The thing now is to see what is still really practicable, and I think that you have hit it. Hence my long letter with this one.

I think the force for your new landing should be assembled where it may be pretended that it is meant for:

an offensive across the Suez Canal
a landing at Alexandretta
a landing in great strength at Enos
a landing at Bulair

and one or more of these schemes should be darkly hinted at as a great [?] secret followed by a bit of coast reconnaissance.

7.30 p.m. I must shut up and run [?] over [?] to the office!!

[P.S.] Young Marine [?] who runs the Mudros boom defence guns and helios tells me that he visited Strati [?] to see why they could not get Helio communicated − rearranged matters a bit and improved it − but − found that on one occasion the man there [?] had seen a submarine lying up under the island for *two hours* and began his message to Mudros *'nothing to report'*.!! I don't know if they tell you these things − but I expect if they do that you have by now a reliable [?] W.O. or Marine sergeant living there with ten stout Marines and rifles at least − possibly a lancer bomb or two.

Beagle had nothing in his defect but about his boilers − but the Capt. tells me they are all wrong [?] and I am having the matter looked into. This last hot 6 weeks has been pretty stiff for me but I hope we are nearly through with it now.

The Bulgars are murderous [?] devils. I have no fear about the Roumanians. But for the Bulgar I do hope that our people will get Sari Bair [?] and Biyuk Anafarta before the winds begin.

I am so glad you will meet the French C.-in-C. I believe in talking with people and I think the old man will fall in love with you at first sight and that will be sound [?]. He is doing much better now in the way of submarine hunting, but I feel now will strain every nerve after meeting you. Of course I am writing after he has met you, but he acted so quickly to your wire that I could not get a letter in before he started. I am jolly glad to pass on all these monitors, lighters and steam and motor boats to you − but Lord they *do* want a heap of tinkering on the way. I feel that the hotter you make it for German submarines round the Peninsula, the more they will base themselves in places like Enos, Porto Lagos, Euboea and Kos and the more they will give you up to turn attention to the transport routes, Alexandria, Port Said and Malta. The Standard Oil Company of New York has now come to terms with the British Government − I hope you have received a copy of the agreement ratified? − and they are sending a white man to Athens as general manager − an American called Thomas [?] − who may be trusted to play the game and who replaces a rank pro-German.

Must shut up. Things go *well* even if slowly [?] everywhere. Not counting yours I have good reason to believe 33 German submarines are satisfactorily done for . . .[52]

N.B.   The Greeks at Strati are extremely friendly and willing to have our post there (so Captain Horne [?] RMLI says).

12   De Robeck to Rt Hon. Arthur J. Balfour[53]

[Copy]   H.M.S. *Triad,*
Secret   9 July 1915

The present position in the Dardanelles is much the same as when I wrote last. Our troops in the southern section have made an appreciable advance on both wings, inflicting very heavy loss on the Turks during the counter attacks. On the northern section at Anzac things remain very quiet beyond the usual shelling. The great annoyance to our troops is in the southern area and is due to the fire of the Asiatic guns; the bombardment at times is very heavy, though the loss to personnel is small. The serious wounding of General Gouraud[54] is an irreparable loss to the Army − a brilliant officer and a great leader of men. The effective dealing with these Asiatic guns is a problem which will certainly have to be faced in the near future; they can, I think, only be permanently and satisfactorily dealt with by a landing on the Asiatic side and the clearing of the southern shore of the Dardanelles. It would probably mean an opposed landing anywhere between Kum Kale and Yukyeri Bay, but the number of Turks on the southern shore is estimated at 10,000 only.

Enemy supplies seem to get through in sufficient quantities, judging by the amount of ammunition they expend and the reports of prisoners as to their feeding, but whether this can continue, in view of the activity of our submarines, is considered very doubtful.

We have again bombarded various places on the northern end of the peninsula which are reported to be depots of supplies such as Gallipoli, Examil, Erenkeui, etc., and our submarines continue to destroy a number of small steamers and sailing craft in the Marmora. At the present moment only one submarine − *E.7* − is in the Marmora, but I hope when all our large submarines are available to be able to keep three always cruising there.

Net defence has been laid at Kephalo. It is an anti-submarine net and was very quickly and well laid by the two specially fitted steamers *Prince Edward* and *Queen Victoria*. We are preparing a heavy submarine net for laying off Helles, but this will take some time, owing to special vessels being required to lay it. In the meantime an attempt is being made to place an indicator net below the surface between Seddul Bahr and Kum Kale.

Drifters are improving in their work and it is quite possible that they successfully dealt with one of the Austrian submarines on the 6th and 7th off Helles.[55] The supervision of the drifters and trawlers has now become a big organisation, but the work has been much improved by the placing of *Hussar* at the disposal of the Captain in charge of sweepers.

The destroyers continue to do good work but unfortunately the 'River'

(E) class are showing signs of wear, and the fact of our having to send 3 or 4 away at a time keeps the numbers available very short.

The battleships are all being refitted in turn at Malta and are now all efficient. They have not often been used lately – only when the object has appeared worth the expenditure of ammunition. This will enable us to have sufficient ammunition in the Fleet when our next serious effort commences in the Dardanelles.

None of the new monitors have yet joined but I note the advanced ones have arrived at Malta; they should prove invaluable if the ammunition supply can be assured. The small monitor *Humber* continues to be usefully employed in the Anzac section. She is rather lightly built and is showing signs of hogging, but it is hoped that this weakness will not increase.[56]

Other small craft, boarding steamers, auxiliary sweepers, etc., are doing useful patrol and ferry service work. My chief difficulty in regard to small craft and auxiliaries is the provision of officers and men to man them; the best solution for this is to utilise a portion of the R.N. Division, especially active service ratings and R.N.R. stokers.

Officers are hard to find and there is a considerable amount of sickness amongst them – not of a serious nature – but often requiring hospital treatment; it usually takes the form of a severe diarrhoea. As I quite realise the impossibility of sparing many officers R.N. from home I would point out that R.N.R. Officers can all be usefully employed by me.

As regards the Air Service – Colonel Sykes,[57] who is now out here, is forwarding certain recommendations, so I will not remark on this yet.

The health of the squadron continues to be good. I am issuing the report of a cholera committee to all commanding officers for information and guidance.

A small number of cases of typhoid are being sent from the peninsula. All men of the Fleet are being encouraged to be inoculated against the disease.

The position at Mudros has never been satisfactory. There is continual leakage of information and no doubt the island contains a large number of enemy agents, including the Greek Civil Governor who is, I think, not above suspicion. It is therefore a matter for consideration whether some arrangement could not be come to with the Greek Government whereby the military control of the island of Lemnos is placed entirely under our jurisdiction.

I attach some remarks on the present situation as regards – and proposals for dealing with – the Greek contraband trade . . .[58]

13 *Admiralty to de Robeck with note by General Hamilton*

[Typescript]   [21 July 1915]

Copy of telegram

From . . . . Admiralty
To . . . . Vice-Admiral, Mudros
Date . . . . 21st July 1915.   No. 714
Urgent

Personal. Mr Churchill now finds himself unable to leave England. Colonel Hankey[59] and Captain Staveley[60] will arrive at Brindisi 6.17 a.m. Saturday next, 24th July, and embark on board *Chatham*, who should be instructed accordingly.

II.

General Sir Ian Hamilton,
    G.C.B., D.S.O., etc.
    Referred for your information, please.
    Chatham will proceed to Mudros after embarking the two officers named.

Triad,   J. M. de Robeck,
21 July 1915   Vice-Admiral

[Holograph]   Imbros, 21 July [19]15
Confidential

My dear Admiral,

I do not know in the least whether Hankey is coming on your job or mine? If on *mine* I would not at all like him to be allowed to run loose about Mudros before I had got hold of him and set his feet firmly in the right path. Hankey is a most important man. Whether we think him doctrinaire, narrow and academic (as I do) or whether we believe him to have a real practical grip of naval and military matters, − there is no doubt at all he has the ear of the Cabinet, and especially of the P.M.

My idea would be to give him a shake down in the sand together with a few centipedes and flies. Then to send him in charge of a trusty Staff Officer to Anzacs and Helles to be shelled, and then he will be anxious to get back as quickly as he can without hearing too much naval and military irresponsible gossip.

yours sincerely,
Ian Hamilton

14 *Jackson to de Robeck*

[Holograph]   Admiralty, Whitehall.
                                                     27 July 1915

Your letters have been most useful and enabled us to grasp the situation and I am not going to bother you with a long reply. We are I hope doing all we can to help you. Wells[61] leaves today and we are sending out more officers − 500 (about) reserve men as soon as they can be collected.

You probably know Wells, he is better at a job in which he is the head than working under others and if you can find him one of that sort it will I think be worth it. He rather expected a special one before the situation was explained to him and in fact we had intended to send him in charge of civilian stevedores, but it fell through.

I hope the next big attack will be a success, as if not we are up against a very tough problem, as honestly I don't think any more troops can be spared and we are certainly squeezed dry as regards small vessels. The drain is really serious as the submarine hunting round our coasts requires an enormous flotilla. Thank goodness we are bagging a few each week, but say nothing about it. I hope Mitylene will be useful, it may at least relieve the congestion at Mudros if the non-attacking troops, etc., stay there. The Army are growling about piers and transport and, I regret, send their complaints indirectly instead of through you and as far as we can see they are based on wrong information and are mostly groundless.

It is about time Gamble left for home I think. I only expected he would be at most a week.

My very best wishes to you all . . .

15 *De Robeck to the Secretary of the Admiralty*

[Typescript]   H.M.S. *Triad*,
VERY SECRET   19 August 1915

With reference to your Memorandum marked 'Very Secret', M.0097, No. 53, I have the honour to forward herewith my remarks on the appreciation therein contained, together with some general remarks on the position of affairs in this war area.[62]

2. At the time the Admiralty appreciation was written, i.e. 24th June, the Army was concentrating on the attack and capture of Achi Baba ridge; this operation proving very slow and extremely expensive in men and material, the point of the main attack was changed on August 7th, to the Gaba Tepe area. In consequence, a certain number of the points mentioned in the appreciation have lost their immediate A   importance, − for instance, the landing of the Naval guns has of necessity been postponed until the Army are in a position to decide where they want to place them.

3. Before entering into details there are two points which should be borne in mind when dealing with the problem of forcing the Dardanelles.

The first point is that in order to destroy modern open forts at long range by high velocity guns mounted in ships, such an expenditure of ammunition is required as to render the operation impracticable − the only case of a fort being destroyed by long range fire is Fort

B No. I on the 25th February, when the *Queen Elizabeth* at 13,500 yards dismounted the two 9.4 inch guns it contained, but she was never able to repeat this performance. The total permanent damage she inflicted on the forts at the Narrows after many bombardments, was to dismount one gun of 9.4″ calibre.

C The second point is that for close support of infantry, the Naval gun, unless it is used on the flanks, no matter how it is mounted, is not a suitable weapon; for direction it is very accurate, but the flat trajectory and large 50% zone makes it too dangerous to use against trenches often only a few yards from our own front line.

D 4. There is no doubt that the landing of Naval guns would strengthen the Army. For the reason stated in paragraph 3, these guns could not be used in close support of the infantry, but only to engage and silence the enemy's artillery − but even for this purpose Naval guns are inferior weapons as compared to the Army heavy artillery, for, by reason of their flat trajectory, it frequently happens that enemy guns mounted on reverse slopes can not be hit, shells either falling short or missing over. The Army recognise this and do not attach great importance to the landing of guns for which there will only be a limited use.

E Given an adequate supply of ammunition for the Army heavy artillery, the Naval guns would not be required on shore.

For action against the Asiatic Batteries, the French have mounted some Naval guns, the range being too great for their Field Artillery; these are doing good work, but the contest between the enemy's guns firing at a large target, such as the beach at Helles, and the French naval guns firing at targets composed of one gun, is a most unequal one, and it has been found necessary to place long range monitors at Rabbit Island to rectify this inequality.

5. As regards the further operations with Achi Baba ridge in our hands and the consequent possession of observation stations and positions for the 4-inch Naval guns, I consider the attack should be continued principally by the Navy.

There are three main obstacles to pushing home the Naval attack on the Narrows. They are − firstly, the sweeping of a channel through the mine field; − secondly the protection of the sweeping flotilla; − thirdly, the silencing of the Forts at the Narrows. I write 'silencing' advisedly, the destruction is only possible at point blank range.

Though in theory these obstacles to the progress of the Fleet can be separated, in practice this is not so; and the three operations must go on simultaneously.

F In order to protect the sweeping flotilla it is necessary to dominate the guns placed to defend the mine fields; these guns can not all be dealt with by 4-inch guns on Achi Baba alone which position is within range of the Chanak forts − it will be necessary to cover the sweepers from inside the Straits, i.e. ships must enter the Dardanelles; again, to engage the defences of the mine fields, these ships must advance some distance into the Straits − this brings them under the fire of the Chanak Forts, and it is therefore necessary that these should be kept silent while the sweeping is in operation.

I trust that this view of the operations will be accepted, for I am convinced that it is the only practicable method by which the attack can be carried out.

The suggestion on page 4, paragraph 5, of the Admiralty appreciation − that Battleships should bombard for definite times and then withdraw − is not a sound one, as has been practically proved here on several occasions − from all intelligence the 9.4″ gun dismounted by the *Queen Elizabeth* on the 18th March, is the only material loss which any of the enemy's forts inside the Straits has suffered as the result of all bombardments up to and including that of 18th March.

The attack, when it takes place, must be continuous, and by threatening close action at any moment the Turks must be kept at their guns; only thus can we succeed. The attack at long range must be directed against the personnel rather than against the materiel − to achieve this, ships must threaten the materiel by closing the range, thereby forcing the enemy to man his guns, meanwhile the sweeping flotilla, working in short reliefs, would continue without any pause at the clearing of the channel through the mine field.

6. The discussion at this stage of the further action after the Narrows is in our hands, is, to my mind, unprofitable; everything depends on the attitude of the enemy, which must decide whether it would be politic to push on at once and strike while the demoralisation of the enemy lasts − or, as is suggested in the Admiralty appreciation, recommence the more deliberate method starting from Kilid Bahr Plateau instead of Achi Baba . . .

Minutes

[Holograph]

Par. 2. A From this it may be inferred that the *intention* to land naval guns exists, but is postponed.

Par. 3. B Although possibly only one 9.4″ gun was actually dismounted in the forts at the Narrows, no doubt a great deal of damage to materiel and personnel was inflicted.

C This was set forth in Admiralty appreciation.

Par. 4. D The first sentence give sufficient reason for guns being landed − even though they may be inferior to Army guns.

E   Why not if they can help? The French guns do good work
     apparently.

Par. 5. F   This par[agraph] seems to lay down that all that is required
     for the Fleet to attack the inside Forts is an observation
     station. If only we could gain the Sari Bair ridge such an
     observation station could be established at about the same
     distance from the forts as is Achi Baba and in a better relative
     position for spotting.

     The 4″ guns would not do very great damage at a range
     of 12,000 yards.

                         D. H. Gamble
                         31.8.15.

Concur.
     H. F. Oliver[63]
     31.8.15.

Seen.
     H. B. J. [Jackson]
     1 September 1915.

I think the observation at D must be a slip. It contradicts everything
else in the paper.

                         A. J. B. [Balfour]
                         2.9.15.

It is not quite consistent but when a dominating position is taken the
long range naval guns may be more appreciated than they seem to be at
present.

                         H. B. J.
                         3 September 1915.
                         A. J. B.
                         3/9

16   *Limpus to de Robeck*

[Holograph]   H.M. Dockyard, Malta.
                                         Sunday, 22 August 1915

A pity the soldier push between Anzac and Suvla seems to have hung
fire − as I gather that it did.

It means I am afraid that instead of a rather decisive advance ending
about August 12 it will be a case of slow progress occupying another 10
days during which time the Suvla Beach will be − uncomfortable.

I did see Stopford[64], but he did not say much about anything except
to say that he is satisfied they will get good water supply on shore there

and that he emphatically contradicted a rumour that came here that a 14-inch monitor had shelled our Australians (owing to the non-use by the latter of the distinguishing flag arranged). Indications now are that the Bulgars will NOT come in against us and that the Roumanians will come in for us – but date uncertain. I do sympathise with you in this delay – the weather will begin to fail us after September. So I hope Sir John Jackson[65] or some such force has been engaged to make you a shelter at Suvla – it would be sound even if costly and I hope and expect you will be through before it is needed.

Ormsby Johnson[66] didn't bring us much definite news about the positions held – but is I believe asking Bowlby[67] to mark them off on a map and send it along. I hope that Bowlby will.

25 August 1915 I've been trying to get this finished and sent but interruptions are many. What I principally want to say is that the French C.-in-C. has recently returned from a cruise to the eastward with 1 cruiser, 2 destroyers, etc., and I am extremely glad that he *has* been. I saw him on his return. He has a much clearer idea of what is needed to hunt away odd submarines, has rearranged and strengthened his patrols north and east of Crete considerably, and is making more use of Milo, Stampalia and Rhodes for his small craft. He has conferred with Peirse[68] and is glad he has met him. He also saw Maxwell[69] and the Sultan in Egypt and came back via the Sollum coast. He has conferred with Dartige.[70] He himself destroyed everything capable of floating at Alexandretta and has told Dartige to do the same for all places south of Samos on the ground that what is burnt or sunk cannot slip away to sea and have to be hunted for.

I asked him why he did not go and have a yarn with you. He said that he badly wanted to but didn't dare. He was afraid you might think he was shoving his nose into 'our job'. I told him that I was perfectly sure that a visit by him would *not* be so regarded and that I myself believed that you would be very glad to meet him and have a yarn and that you would both probably find cooperation at a distance easier after a personal talk. For example, in the matter of the border lands of your respective zones of small craft. He asked me to write to you and find out if you really would not object to his coming. Hence this. If you say you see no objection I shall tell him and he will probably come next time he makes a round trip. If you say better NOT, I simply shall not say anything more about it to the old man and if he raises the point I shall deny yet having had an answer – or say that it would be well to consult his own Admiralty – or some such evasive thing. So – in order to arm me send me a wire when you get this saying either 'no objection to a visit' or 'better not visit' and I shall know what it refers to.

A young staff surgeon has just come out for the *Europa* to deal with *Flies* in the Naval Division area and naval bases. His name is Atkinson.

He seems knowledgeable but not a pusher. Very quiet in fact. I will look out that all the stuff that comes here for him is urgent or quick, if he can deal – or make people deal effectively with the flies he will be a Godsend. He awaits stuff now and will leave here Saturday 28th.

I am kicking at the awful turn taken here by the submarines. I *know* you want them and supplies of guns, etc., from England have gone very awry [?]. I have at last pulled guns out of ships here to fit in them and will rearm the ships when the ones from England come. Anyway weather permitting I now see *E.12* sailing 26th and all four 'H' class before end of August.

Must shut up.

Why the deuce could not the 11th Div. push to Buyuk Anafarta while they are about it. I feel sure Anzac would have played up and done [?] their bit and stopped on [Hill] 971 if they had. However – dogged [?] will do it.

So long old chap . . .

17 *Jackson to de Robeck*

[Holograph]   Admiralty, Whitehall.
                                                     25 August 1915

The General's telegrams are not very encouraging at present and I fear the situation must give you a good deal of anxiety, but you seem to keep up your spirits and we know the Turks are getting very despondent, so personally I am not so depressed as some of the Cabinet appear to be.

We all of us want to help the Army as much as possible, but don't quite know the situation. We think artillery is the best weapon, as it is proving itself on the continent, and wonder if any heavy guns 6" and above have been landed to bombard the Turkish positions, and if the little monitors could assist. We quite understand ships cannot attack the enemy's first line trenches for fear of hitting our own people, but could not an almost universal slow fire be sent over the heads of our troops to the Turkish reserves, roads, etc. We have plenty of 6" Q.F. though not over well supplied with heavier shell yet.

Could you let me know what is being done in that way, a short written report with a tracing to apply to a squared map would be worth anything to us as the G.O.C. is not very communicative as regards detail. We will back you up in any risk you like to take, but our late First Lord suggests the monitors can rush the Straits and command the situation. I have had to sit on that proposal and say they'd never get through and if they did would not command anything except perhaps ridicule. I don't think they'll send out more troops as they are all wanted on Western Front.

Let me know if we can help you further only don't ask for Destroyers.

Hoping you keep fit and with best wishes from all here . . .

18   *Jackson to de Robeck*

[Holograph]   Admiralty, Whitehall.
                                                    8 September 1915

I much appreciate your long descriptive letter of August 25th which clears up all points and shows also what a lot you have had on your hands. This is likely to increase as you know but it is evidently not all clear sailing as there are restraining influences at work and the date may be put off too long for good weather conditions.[71] We, however, are doing all we can to hasten the decision, the departure and the attack. We are sending you 4 scouts which will relieve Destroyers for refit too and also some coastal T.B.D.s which may be useful locally for S.M. hunting. This is getting more difficult daily. They spread more and more and are getting more cute and daring and if possible more unscrupulous.

I won't bother you with a long letter but with best wishes remain . . .

19   *Balfour to de Robeck*

[Typescript]   Admiralty, Whitehall.
(Dictated)   10 September 1915
Private

My telegrams will have kept you abreast of the present situation so far as we know it.

I am sorry Joffre's[72] influence has sufficed to delay the sending out of the four French Divisions. The explanation I gave you in my telegram appears to be the correct one. He is quite determined to attempt an advance in Flanders, and is equally determined not to allow the four Divisions to go to the East until the attempt on the German lines has been made. I cannot discover that anybody (except the Generals concerned) is very sanguine of success. It is true that by all accounts the German forces on the West front are weaker than those of the Allies; but it is hard to believe that modern trenches and modern machine guns will not make up the difference.

I ought to add that the responsible Generals appear to think that the conditions in the West are now far more favourable than they have been in the past. Time will show.

Some information has reached me which suggests that we should be careful about Greek susceptibilities. They have on the whole behaved very well to the Allies; and I suppose if Germany wanted to pick a quarrel with them, their un-neutral acts would give ample excuse. But they have, I gather, been rather painfully impressed by the way in which we have interfered with their coastal traffic in the search for contraband. They greatly dislike our negotiations with Bulgaria; and the Russians are reported not to have treated them with any great consideration. We must do all we can to smooth their ruffled feathers.

Lord K.[73] seems quite confident that if the six new Divisions (two

English and four French) get out to the East in time, the Allies should make a good job of the Peninsula. We must however be prepared for all eventualities; and among these eventualities a defensive campaign extending through the winter is the one which requires the longest preparation and the most careful thought. I know you are giving all your mind to this subject; and I need not say that we will do our best to ease your task. Give us the longest notice you can of anything that you want.

It is very hard to get at any authentic information about the Turkish position. All the accounts that reach us seem to show that they are very uncomfortable, are losing heavily, and are sick of the war. If there is any truth in all this, I do not see how their position is to improve, unless the Germans break down to the south-east, or unless the Bulgarians throw themselves in against the Allies. It would seem that as winter approaches, the want of coal will make itself more and more seriously felt, while the access to Gallipoli by road becomes (as I am informed) extraordinarily difficult as soon as the rains begin. I think we may trust your glorious submarines to make the alternative line of communication by the Sea of Marmora precarious, if not impossible.

Talking of submarines however, the augmented strength of the German and Austrian submarine force in the Eastern Mediterranean is causing us great anxiety. I hope the additional anti-submarine force which we are sending out to you will be of material assistance; but we cannot, I fear [?] hope to avoid further disasters to our transports. We must admit that, *so far*, our good fortune in this respect has been extraordinary . . .

20 *Jackson to de Robeck*

[Holograph]   Admiralty, Whitehall.
                                                    12 September [1915]

If you think they deserve it and you have the opportunity, can you say a word in an official despatch relative to the work of the officers and men of the Transports, as I hear privately they are feeling rather hurt that no one has apparently ever mentioned them, and I believe they have frequently been under fire and some of them have done extremely well.

I hope they'll hurry up the troops as much as we are trying to hurry up transport for them, as time appears to me to [be] very precious both from political and weather considerations.

Very sorry we have lost the submarine. I hope *E.20* with her 6″ gun will not get brought up by the net and be able to do something.[74]

I've been a bit off colour and am just going to try and take a week's leave and shoot a few partridges for a change.

Best wishes to you from . . .

21   *De Robeck to Jackson*

[Carbon]   *Triad*,
                                                      16 September 1915

We have had a visit from the French Commander-in-Chief which I think will have excellent results, and he will no longer look on us with a certain amount of jealousy and suspicion. He could not have been more cordial and I feel that he will now make much greater efforts to hunt enemy submarines; also I hope that he will be more generous with his destroyers. It struck me that he was by no means friendly – or at any rate sympathetic – with the Italians, and that he rather sneered at them and wanted to know why they declared war against the Turks unless they intended to make war. I promised to assist him at Milo island, where he has a base for twelve oil-burning destroyers and keeps an oiler in the harbour. It is proposed to send him one mile of the deep heavy anti-submarine net that we could not use in the Dardanelles and to use indicator nets on a trot at the two ends – nearly two miles of these being required.

We seem to have a good many enemy submarines about in the Aegean and so far have not accounted for any of this new lot. The arrival of the Sixth Light Cruiser Squadron and Torpedo boats will be of great assistance. I propose they shall work on the transport route between Mudros and Doro Channel, together with two sloops and twelve trawlers, which will leave *Doris* and the armed boarding ships to continue the work of hunting up submarines at their bases and stopping contraband trade.

I am dealing with the questions arising out of the important movements of troops you inform me are about to take place. Wemyss and Contre-Amiral de Bon[75] are going into all details and I gather that the French will be quite satisfied with the assistance we shall be able to offer them. As, however, I am going to write officially on the whole of this question I will not worry you with it now beyond saying that I do not see any insurmountable difficulty.

The military situation on the peninsula remains the same – things being quiet – with the usual amount of intermittent shelling. Our people are entrenching themselves and preparing for the winter. The Turks are also busy strengthening and putting down wire in the Anafarta valley, so it looks as if we shall be up against the same proposition there as at Helles, and that the French landing elsewhere will be the true solution. We have now got about a month's reserve supply of stores ashore at Suvla and Anzac and rather more at Helles. The water question continues to improve, but I still have occasional scares and am consequently looking forward to the arrival of the water lighters.

The distilling plant at Mudros is up and working. The boilers of the plant for Imbros are now being landed, and I understand the military intend to erect one at Anzac.

As regards the working of supplies, matters are straightening themselves out rapidly, thanks largely to General Altham[76] – a capable person and one easy to work with.

Captain Fitzmaurice[77] is proving a success as P.N.T.O. and I hope the Admiralty will see their way to making him a Commodore, so as to enable him to carry more guns when surrounded by General Officers with whom he has to deal.

Certainly military methods are not always ours and one of my principal difficulties is to make military officers realise certain necessities, such as that running supply ships only partially loaded is not business and that the military method of working in watertight compartments is impossible. I think they will soon realise it. Another point is that they do not understand they must not keep big ships off the beaches as a target for enemy submarines, and I am continually impressing on them that we cannot afford to lose big ships and that they must use the small craft sent out for the purpose; but I have now no real cause of complaint in this respect and I think that as regards supplies we shall shortly be in a very strong position on the Peninsula.

Tenedos has now been taken over by the French and we are only retaining there a small party employed in repairing indicator nets; we have 40 Greeks at Tenedos employed repairing nets continuously and they are very capable at that class of work.

With regard to the Fleet, owing to sickness and casualties we are in want of some Captains and Commanders in connection with the beaches and transport work.

The health of the fleet is improving, there being less trouble from enteritis, due probably to the cooler weather.

I have a committee considering the winter clothing requirements of beach crews and men employed in boats at beaches.

The battleships are all efficient – I am sending them one by one to refit and rest their crews. *Cornwallis* returned yesterday from Malta. Refits of other ships are being arranged for – the Destroyers being the most difficult owing to nearly all the 'Beagle' class having Yarrow boilers, and I wish Malta was able to take more of them in hand at a time. Refit of Boarding steamers and auxiliary sweepers is being done in Egypt. The trawlers are being hauled up and having their bottoms coated on the slip at Syra, two at a time, and I have given them *Aquarius* to deal with their defects, which should mean that they will all have been repaired and refitted before Christmas.

Each class of monitor has her own particular trouble – 14″, the steering engines are too weak; 9.2″, the exhaust fumes in the funnel; 6″, weakness of decks under the guns; but they are mostly being successfully dealt with by *Reliance*, where Engineer Captain Humphreys is worth his weight in gold and never makes a difficulty.

We must not expect too much from these monitors, especially the 14″, which could not navigate the Dardanelles without tugs, so the question of forcing the Narrows with monitors is, I am afraid, for the present not a workable proposition.

22   Jackson to de Robeck

[Holograph]   Admiralty, Whitehall.
Private   27 September 1915

We will send you some tugs and small storeships as requested and try and find a small floating dock. We are also asking if you want more monitors (12″), but are not certain if we can spare them, as it depends how the present grand attack progresses. It has upset our Eastern strategy much to my regret and I hope we shan't fall between 2 stools. In any case it means a great delay in getting reinforcements to you and I expect when they arrive bad weather will have set in. It is not Admiralty doing in any way but political grand strategy beyond our control.

I shall be glad to know what you think of the situation shortly if you can send me a line. I've been away for 10 days leave. I felt I must have it not having been out of London for 2 years except on duty and I am much better for it. I hope you have sufficient staff and beach parties now, if not let me know.

North Sea work almost dead at present, all small craft being used for escort work and S.M. hunting and the place strewn with mines. I hope air service is all right and no friction among the personnel. We are trying to bring them into line now at home. Excuse haste . . .

23   Jackson to de Robeck

[Holograph]   Admiralty, Whitehall.
Personal   4 October 1915

Many thanks for your letters but don't answer this, as I expect your hands will be full for some time to come, though I fear not so much in overpowering the Turks as deflecting our forces. I think the Allied Govts. have made a mess over the Bulgarian-Greco-Serbian business. We can't manage another campaign properly, and it would have been better to stick to the one we have in hand, viz. 'Yours'. Perhaps it may be so but it depends on the success or failure on the Western front where we are doing well, but slowly, so decision as to what is really to be done may be deferred for some weeks. If we cannot advance there will be plenty of troops to spare, but if the French break through I doubt if there will be many over to send to you. We are sending you 2 more sloops which I hope you will find useful.

The airship sheds will be ordered at once, but I doubt if they will be much use before the spring. The 2 12″ Monitors will not be able to leave for another week or two. Hodges[78] leaves tomorrow for Salonika and I'll try to rake up some more officers for you, but they are scarce. Wire your requirements if the Salonika business seems likely to develop.

I've had 10 days leave and so has Jellicoe[79] and we are both much better for it. Evidently you keep fit and well in spite of the worries you must have.

Have just got a request that your force should convoy Greek transports. It is what I expected and I hope you'll deal with them firmly and make them do it themselves. We are referring it through F.O. and Athens to you to talk it over with Greek naval officers. However it won't be for long and then their small craft ought to help us . . .

24 De Robeck to Jackson

[Carbon]   *Triad*,
                                                          8 October 1915

The Bulgarian entry into the war seems practically an accomplished fact which will undoubtedly complicate matters for us and it appears to me that the situation in Athens is very doubtful. From what one can see the Greeks have no desire to fight and, were it not for Mr Venezelos, would desert Servia tomorrow.

Our troops on the peninsula are marking time and are secure in their positions; they would not easily be turned out unless an overwhelming force of artillery could be brought against them, though it does not seem that they are capable of making much headway against the Turks. The most serious thing with them is sickness, which is high, the average evacuation from the peninsula being now about 1000 per day, largely dysentery.

The reserve of stores is accumulating and I hope the water question will be relieved when the rains arrive.

The first of our motor water lighters are now reaching Mudros and they should be invaluable.

In regard to the fleet the enemy's submarines are extremely active and doing a great deal of damage in the south of Greece and Crete, which is all in the French patrol area.

The French Commander-in-Chief appears to realise the seriousness of the situation and is sending more destroyers to patrol this part of the transport route. Unfortunately French patrols spend a large percentage of their time in harbour and do not seem to understand what sustained effort means. In the last few days we have lost two fleet colliers and a water lighter, which is serious.

We are badly in need of more oilers – also oil fuel itself is very short. We have barely five days' consumption left and the French are asking us to lend them oil fuel. Unless some arrives it means laying up 'L' class destroyers, monitors, motor lighters and oil-burning torpedo boats.

To meet submarine menace *Clacton*, disguised, with submarine *H.2.* in company, is cruising to the south west of Anti Kithera. *Jonquil*, with 6 trawlers and 6 drifters, has also proceeded to join the French in that area. This is of course weakening my own force and the effectiveness of their patrol, but I judge it to be necessary.

E.12 and *H.1* are in the Marmora but their wireless has not been good, so I have not had much information nor learnt how *H.1* fared when passing through the net.

Otherwise there is not much of interest outside my weekly report to tell you.

The Air service seems to be settling down and I do not anticipate any internal trouble.

The destroyers are being sent to refit as arranged and the length of these refits will be a great benefit to the officers and men, who have had a most strenuous year.

Christian[80] has nearly recovered from his wound and Nicholson is having a rest at Malta which he stood badly in want of.

I hope you are feeling better yourself and it is a pity you cannot get a longer holiday. For myself, I am fairly well, and would be better if I could sleep regularly. Various worries are at times rather trying. We are all cheerful and ready for anything.

25   *Jackson to de Robeck*

[Holograph]   Admiralty, Whitehall.
Personal   9 October 1915

Sir Arthur Wilson[81] has taken a lot of trouble in working out the paper I send you and I feel I cannot but send it on semi-officially though whether it is practicable or not only a trial will prove. We are in a deplorable mess in the Balkans thanks to the political conduct of the war by France and ourselves. On October 7th the 'War Council of the Cabinet' came to the conclusion that they did not know what to do and that perhaps it might be worthwhile asking their professional Naval and Military advisers as to what they ought to do. This is the first time, *I believe*, since the outbreak of war that they have taken any advice except through the Heads of Departments.

Personally, I say go for Constantinople tooth and nail, without further procrastination or delay and I expect they will do so as our joint War Office and Admiralty report will practically rule out anything else.[82] If so I know you and Ian Hamilton (when he gets more troops) will do all you can. We can spare more battleships for Constantinople if you can open the way with those you have got, but delay is fatal as ammunition is sure to reach Turkey in 5 or 6 weeks from now, and then Gallipoli may become untenable. I'll send out motor launches which are now beginning to arrive from Canada in small numbers but can't get them to you yet. We are taking up more hospital ships and hope they'll clear the Mediterranean Hospitals ready for the future requirements.

I don't think it is worth wasting much ammunition on the Bulgarian

Coast and a good line of mines outside Dedeagatch will bother their submarines. I should lay them with fitted moorings and not use the automatic ones as they are not reliable and give us a lot of trouble. Could your seaplanes carry and drop really heavy bombs on the forts (500 lb) instead of Whitehead torpedoes, it seems worth a trial.

Excuse haste and best wishes . . .

26   *Jackson to de Robeck*

[Holograph]   Admiralty, Whitehall.
                                                           13 October 1915

I fear no final decision regarding military operations in Eastern Med. has yet been arrived at by the various Govts. who are mixed up in the matter. The First Lord's telegram to you (114 of 10/10/15) described the situation pretty accurately.

Since then, by order, we have given a joint naval and military opinion[83] on the matter which after pointing out the danger of a Serbian campaign ends as follows:

> The most useful way in which to employ troops that can be relieved in France by French troops (under certain conditions) would be in operations designed to secure the vital important interests of the British Empire in India, Mesopotamia and Egypt; and for that purpose (subject to conditions) the operation recommended is a renewal of the attack on the Gallipoli peninsula. For this a force of two corps and 2 Indian divisions (total 8 divisions) organised as an army under a selected commander should suffice. This force should move in the first instance from France to Egypt for necessary reorganisation and preparation.

We strongly recommended a renewal of the offensive on the western line in France.

I enclose a copy of my appreciation which was included in the paper and which apparently meets with approval by most and certainly by the naval people in the Admiralty.[84] I hope the Government will come to the same conclusion.

100 copies of Admiral Wilson's proposed scheme of using ships against shore positions are being forwarded. After reading it carefully, most of us are of the opinion that it will probably prove impracticable. There is nothing very new in the gunnery part, but the aircraft people will probably soon say that their scheme is useless; if so, don't waste any further valuable time. Unfortunately a telegram (116 of 11/10/15) was sent to you by error without my approval. (I had ordered the original to be much condensed intending to warn you only that something was on the way). Don't take it therefore as a literal order, but if you can do something it will greatly please Sir A. Wilson. The Recodolites [?] shall be sent by the first opportunity.

You seem to be doing fairly well – gaining ground surely if slowly.

I hope the weather will keep fine, or at least give you warning when it is going to change. Wire your requirements, and we'll do all we can to meet them.

I've just heard Greece and Roumania are being given 48 hours to state their intentions and that if they will both join us we'll send troops to Greece, if not, none are to go. We are going to send some 6″ guns to Serbia rather late in the day . . .

27   *De Robeck to Balfour*

[Carbon]   H.M.S. *Triad*,
20 October 1915

I send this letter by Commodore Keyes − my excellent chief of staff − who will give you all information about the naval situation in the Dardanelles. He will put before you a scheme for a plan of attack by the Fleet on the Turkish defences of the Dardanelles and I hope every consideration will be given to the proposals.[85]

My chief reason for sending my chief of staff is that I differ profoundly from him as to the chances of success of the scheme − as I do not think it would achieve the object we desire. I do not propose in this letter to criticize the plan beyond saying that if carried out it would, in my opinion, be a most costly and desperate effort whether successful or otherwise and further that it would lead to no definite result.

Please do not think that there is any ill will between us over this difference of opinion; on the contrary there is none whatever. I have always encouraged officers under me to state their views in the most candid manner possible and as Commodore Keyes is an officer of so much experience, I think that it is desirable he should personally lay his views before you.

I would just touch on one or two points. First of all no attack can be considered successful that does not admit of the passage of our colliers and other auxiliaries into the Marmora. For example, if we succeed in getting a few battleships in a fighting condition into the Marmora the Turks would be perfectly aware of the approximate time they can continue without replenishing and my view is that the bombardment of Constantinople or other methods of attack in the Marmora that would be carried out would not make the Turks lay down their arms. Secondly, the Turkish army on the peninsula is reported to have several months supplies with it and therefore the temporary stoppage would not force them to surrender or abandon the peninsula.

To my mind the only possible solution is the absolute destruction step by step of the forts and defences of the Dardanelles and this can only be done with the assistance of the army.

Again − if this attack, carried out on the lines proposed, fails the loss of personnel and ships must be great. One cannot expect that if ships are sunk in the minefield or near the forts at the Narrows many of the crews will be saved.

Also the effect on the morale of our army now on the peninsula and the encouragement a failure would give to the enemy has to be considered. The position of the army would, I fear, be critical and the problem of how to deal with such a situation would be hard to solve.

In any case, before undertaking such an effort, it would be necessary to build up a large reserve of ships out here – especially light craft, destroyers, etc. – otherwise owing to shortage of these craft it would leave the enemies' submarines a clear field to deal with our transports and supply ships.

In conclusion I may say that I have talked the matter over with several senior officers (including French) under me and they are of practically the same opinion as myself.

In addition Commodore Keyes takes with him notes for discussion on a number of other points connected with the squadron and our work here which I feel will be of interest to you . . .

28   *Limpus to de Robeck*

[Holograph]   Admiralty House, Vittoriosa.
                                                     Sunday, 24 October [19]15

I see that a spell for you is impossible for the moment. I wish it were otherwise. But I guess you are physically fit to stick it out as I am and more so – and now I already feel the relief of the cooler weather. But – do take a spell when you are able. I am expecting *Price of Wales, Queen*, and *Implacable* in turn here to follow *Weymouth* – or rather *Bacchante*, for the men I have for the *Weymouth* are due to return to England unless Admiralty comply with my request to keep them. If they do that I can take another, *Exmouth*, on the same terms – not fully man[ned?] – but to a bit. Will tell you the moment the Admiralty tell me.

The French are – and have been for some weeks – doing far more *escorting* of Transports. But I am pressing the French C.-in-C. (and giving the Admiralty full copies of what I say) to organise a regular *attack* on the submarines as well. It means more destroyers in the first place and perhaps more drifters too and they *must* come from the north as the submarines certainly have. I am so glad the Adm[iralt]y can at last gun many of the transports and tramps. It will certainly reduce casualties. Staveley and Godfrey[86] came back in *Exmouth*. We shall feel the loss of de Lapeyrère for a bit – but I think the new man should do. I *am* sorry you are losing dear old Guépratte.

Serbia is being hard pressed. But so also is *Germany*. They are even exporting small quantities of copper by sea to Panderma from Constantinople and then from Smyrna to Austria – in returning submarines – seems hardly worthwhile but it is a fact.

Well done *E.20* and *Turquoise* and well done Sir James Porter.[87] The feeling here is one of general relief that I. H. [Ian Hamilton] seems to be being replaced. Best of luck old chap. It's dogged as does it — and it *does* do it . . .

29   Jackson to de Robeck

[Holograph]   Admiralty, Whitehall.
Strictly Personal   7 November 1915

I just missed the last mail to you so tore up my letter as things here change daily thanks to the indecision of our rulers. They don't know how to save their face, so talk, talk, talk and let things slide. Lord K. will have reached you before this and will we think take up the Dardanelles for all he can and let the mess at Salonika settle itself. May I warn you that his brain power and knowledge of detail are not up to his will power and push, and that his statements should be taken with reserve. We all agree in this in spite of all he has done for the Army. He is more ignorant of the sea and its ways than most soldiers and only looks on it as a way to send [?] and fancies it is quite conquerable. However he has plenty of go and power and won't evacuate the peninsula unless it is seen to be absolutely necessary. If it is I don't envy you the job. We'll try to get some yachts, sloops and such like out to help to patrol the waters the French are not patrolling as they ought to do.

The Turks are short of mines, torpedoes, 6″, 4″ and 8.8 cm shell and the first consignment will be 8000 rounds of shell. Railway trucks and lighters are scarce in Bulgaria and I fancy that the stuff won't arrive as soon as expected nor in very large quantities. They are also to have sent some very large aeroplanes which will probably be put in a shed close to the railway near Adrianople. Please do not quote the above, it is from our most secret source of information but is correct. Use it best, don't say you heard it from England.

I hope you are better, if not take some leave if there is a lull. Keyes has not made much impression except perhaps on K. However, he has given up plenty of information.

I won't worry you with a long letter.

Don't let Salonika drain Mudros. The latter is of infinitely greater importance. Egypt is going to be a trouble and if you can help Peirse please do so . . .

30   De Robeck to Limpus

[Holograph]   *Triad*,
                                                        9 November 1915

Excuse a scrawl in great haste by *Wahine*. There never seems a moment when it is possible to write, there is so much going on and so many things to think of. We have Lord K. and staff, Generals from Egypt and

McMahon[88] H.C. [High Commissioner] all coming here for a conference, please goodness some useful result will be achieved. As soon as things are decided and if nothing exceptional is to take place, I propose to run home for a short rest as my health requires it and am run down. Cannot sleep at night, but think all I require is a little actual rest. In which case I would send *Triad* to Malta, if she could have some alterations made in her accomodations and sanitary arrangements just in order! *Doris* I had to send at once, as her condition seems so bad that her defects must be dealt with in order to make her seaworthy! *Euryalus* must wait, but she requires refit, as does *Talbot*. Am sorry we should keep you so busy, but please remember none of my ships are in their first youth! It is very bad case from what I hear about *Louis*.[89] She was allowed to drag on shore over ½ mile, however the C.M. will bring the facts out; what can one do with officers who do such things?

The present situation is curious to my mind, the first thing that must be done is to get a clear statement from the Greeks, in fact send a squadron to the Piraeus to demand it and insist on getting rid of the brothers Dousmanis[90] and others who are entirely in the Germans' pay, if we do not do it and take strong action we will have the Greeks coming in against us, they or rather their King and staff are perfectly capable of it.

The Admiralty, probably on the advice of Roger Keyes, are evidently anxious that we should again attack the Dardanelles with the Fleet. I am perfectly determined to do nothing of the sort, as it would probably lead to a colossal disaster and then Roumania and Greece would come in against us and we should lose our army on the peninsula and Salonika. Unless we can clear the mines away and destroy the torpedo tubes it is madness, fancy bringing these old battleships into the Narrows to be torpedoed. It is like sending an unfortunate horse into the bull ring blindfolded! We must keep our heads and keep pegging away, if the Servians can stick it until we have troops enough at Salonika to join with them, Bulgaria will be very sorry that they joined the Germans. The French are sending some splendid troops to Salonika, one had no idea the French had such fine men in the country, also Sarrail[91] impressed one and has the reputation of being a good General which is what the Allies want most! Hope you are better old friend, these are strenuous days and quite realise how heavy the strain is on you! God bless you . . .

P.S. So glad you are putting plenty of ginger into French C.-in-C. Keep at him.

31 *Limpus to de Robeck*

[Holograph]   H.M. Dockyard, Malta.
Personal   12 November [19]15

You are absolutely right. It wants an independent and strong man to tell the Admiralty so. I am horrified to hear that they even contemplated

such an operation. It is true that some armoured ships might get through
– and we have always known that. It is equally true that they could do
nothing real if they *did* get into the Marmara, unless collier transport
supply ships and other soft vessels got in too. We did bluff the Russians
in 1878 with Geoff. Hornby's[92] Fleet. But the Germans know their job
better; *and* the limitations of a fleet pitted against land defences and land
forces. We have already played into German hands by fighting the Turkish
Army; instead of blockading the Turkish coasts alone. Heaven forbid that
we are smitten by madness again and allow ourselves to exhibit a visible
disaster to our Fleet to the world – especially to the Arabs, Greeks, and
Roumanians. I believe that an attempt by the Fleet to rush the Dardanelles
would provide us with the biggest disaster of the whole war. Imagine my
thankfulness that – this time – we have a man who is strong enough
to say NO.

My dear old chap I am disturbed at your feeling run down. But take
a short spell directly you can and you'll get as fit as a fiddle and be back
again ready to help the soldiers through the winter. They will want you
and we all want you to see the show through.

It *will* be seen through – if only we are not tempted to make fools of
ourselves by running our heads against a brick wall. I am glad Lord K.
is to be with you. I think he has the gift of knowing a man whose word
is worth taking.

Personal

Of course there is another big suggestion in the air – that of evacuating
the peninsula. I do trust the soldiers will decide that they can hang on.
For that would be a costly business in men and stores and almost as bad
as a visible failure of the Fleet to force the passage. Once having started
– I believe it is dogged as does it.

At any rate things are going more favourably than I dared hope in Serbia
and I believe the most telling move would be an advance of the Italians
via Montenegro or Albania and an advance of the Japanese to help the
Russian south push forward. Meantime I am digging away side by side
with the new French C.-in-C. to block all further entry of German
submarines into the Mediterranean and to hunt and harry those now in.
I am glad to say that Dartige du Fournet shares my views in this matter,
and is asking for 40 more British-French destroyers to do it with. I think
Thursby got one submarine early this week and the French seem to have
probably got one down south east of Crete.[93] But we want to make Gib
Straits and Otranto Straits and Cattaro as hot for them as the Dardanelles
entrance now is. And also to hunt the life out of them on the transport
routes.

Malta could easily keep your lot going but for these infernal Yarrow
boilers – they make it a bit hard. But with the help of Gib and the

Home[?] yards we shall manage. *Doris* will be 3½ weeks from today.

Dartige sums up the Greeks by saying they want the fruits of victory without the fighting. Maybe he is right but I think they − or rather their King and his party in the Army, are dallying with the Germans − we need a clear success in Serbia or a clear indication of Japanese action to turn the scale in Greece − and perhaps also in Roumania. But a visible disaster to which the Germans could point − such as the sinking of several battleships and the absence of any favourable result in spite of it would almost certainly tilt the scales the wrong way and much prolong the war.

We must keep our heads and keep pegging away.

So long old chap, and God bless you . . .

32   De Robeck to Limpus

[Holograph]   *Triad,*
                                                        26 November 1915

I am on my way to England for a short holiday and hope to be back in three weeks, it was absolutely necessary as not being able to sleep pulls one down to such an extent that there is no reserve to draw after a time. With no worries for a few days one ought to pick up fast, insomnia is the devil and of late I have been getting a certain amount of neuralgia in the head. One has to realise that the summer was rather trying and all our insides got rather a bad time! I hate running away even for a day, but Rosie Wemyss is such a good fellow, he will not be induced into any foolish action by R. Keyes. The latter the most capable and best of C.O.S. but at present he is obsessed with the idea of forcing the Straits with the Fleet and is quite incapable of weighing the consequences in case of failure.

The military have made up their mind to leave the peninsula, it will take at least six weeks and lose at least 30 percent in men and material unless we have the most wonderful luck. It was a very grave decision for Lord K. to make and think he was much influenced by the written appreciation of Sir C. Monro.[94] Naturally I do not like it and asked that at least Helles should be kept as otherwise the dangers of submarines and T.B.D. attacks in the Aegean will be enormously increased. The execution of this must take some six weeks so I will be back to carry out the critical part, one does not like it, but as one put them on shore, it is necessary to show we can take them off! What is to happen then or at Salonika I don't know, but these great authorities can talk of nothing else except Egypt and the Moslem world about which I confess to know little or nothing, though considering the great trouble we have in arming our armies, also the Russians, we cannot see how the Moslem world is going to be a great danger! There is a feeling that we are being 'bluffed' off the Peninsula by the Germans and the question [is] have they the men or the ammunition to spare to make a sustained attack on our troops there? Helles people in any case think they could not be pushed off from their position and the Australians equally so. The Suvla people are the ones that are in doubt about themselves. In any case I hope to get to London in time to make them think a little.

In the meantime in regard to the enemy's submarines. There are two things that one must do and it is outside my area so perhaps you can do it or make better arrangements with the French C.-in-C.

(a) To mine all places used by the enemy's S.M. on the African or Asiatic coast. I feel sure that nothing frightens them more, it is a simple method and is a great economy in our small craft, which would always be overworked looking for them − to insure the efficiency of this system we must destroy all enemy's craft, boats, caiques, etc., so there can be no question of their removing the mines. I think it is a preventative; take Smyrna as an example, there has been no submarine there for ages, though possibly one was blown up off Long Island some three months ago. Surely if they were not afraid of the mines they would use the place.

(b) The establishment of proper squadrons on the transport routes, under commodores, both to east and west of Malta. It is impossible for me to control vessels south of Crete and our friend C.-in-C. East Indies appears to [be] such a curious person one never knows what is actually happening in Egypt!

As long as we hunt these submarines wherever they go and keep their heads below water during the day they will not do a great amount of harm to our shipping! But [to] do that we must have vessels and above all good communication, all our steamers to be armed and to have W/T, but under the most strict rules as regards its use!

What is your view of a real attack on Smyrna, if undertaken should it be by A[rmy] and N[avy] or could Navy round up the Turks alone. What would the effect be on the Turkish mind, apart from destruction of factories, docks, etc. It seems a good side show and ought to be done in case the Germans wished to make use of it later on! Give me your opinion as I suggested it to Lord K., but the Moslem world representatives don't like it!

Lambart[95] is required at Mudros on some staff work and Captain Potts,[96] *Imogene*, should be sent to dock after *Triad*, his ship being used by staff. Weather getting too bad for *Imogene* to run the King's Messenger from Athens to Mudros. Please do what you can for *Triad*, she is not comfortable at present for the Staff, especially now the winter is coming on. Trust the change will do me good, if one could only buy [?] a new head that would finish all the trouble. I must get the Admiralty to decide also on a definite line of action for the future and think we can do a good deal more if one has more precise instruction!

Hope this finds you well my dear old friend, what the Mediterranean would have done without you heaven only knows. My kind regards and Believe me . . .

P.S. There are two Midshipmen in *Triad*, one going to pass shortly, Bethune [?], and the other the son of the padre [?] at Constantinople Whitehouse[97] who perhaps you know. Please keep a friendly eye on them.

33 *Jackson to de Robeck*

[Holograph] Admiralty, Whitehall.
3 December [19]15

I'm very sorry you have a chill as it will spoil your holiday, but in some ways it may be good as we can't get you here for innumerable conferences to worry you. Don't make notes for us but get well and enjoy yourself ready to go out later and have another try which I feel certain will be the policy adopted. I hope we shall get a game before you sail. Propose your own date and we'll lunch at 1.15 and motor to Roehampton and finish by dark . . .

34 *Captain S. R. Drury-Lowe*[98] *to Captain Herbert Richmond*

[Holograph] H.M. Hospital Ship *Liberty*, No. 10.
5 December [19]15

. . . This is Lord Tredegar's yacht, a very fine one, fitted up and lent to Adm[iral]ty who gave it for use of Sir James Porter – Naval Medical D.G. here – in control of all Hospital Ships. Now the old man has suddenly received recall orders and is returning home with the yacht and will drop me at Malta. Naturally Sir J. is sick at sudden recall, especially as usual no warning given. But Military Medical fellows have been against it all the time as they consider it interfering with their own show, and apparently War Office have badgered and persuaded Admiralty to give in and return to same arrangement as before Sir James took it on in July last. Which proved a failure and was the very reason why Sir James was sent out here to take it on under his own single control. That is the ship part of it only. Military control of ships cannot be satisfactory for 2 reasons, 1st that there are 4 heads controlling – viz. the Q.M.G.s at Gibraltar, Malta, Alexandria and Mudros – instead of 1 head, and 2nd that a soldier simply does *not* understand the requirements of a ship, or that she ever requires docking, coaling, provisioning, cleaning of boilers, etc., etc. Nothing has been so clearly demonstrated out here in our combined work than their inability to understand the purely sea work of a ship or fleet and their movements and requirements. Unfortunately the confusion that must arise from 4 Q.M.G.s all issuing orders to 60 odd

Hospital Ships will undoubtedly fall on the shoulders of the unfortunate naval officers and of the sick and wounded themselves.

De Robeck has just gone home for a few weeks' rest. I know he's against it and so is the new C.-in-C. — Sir Charles Monro. We may well wonder how 'such things are!' I'm glad de Robeck is getting a rest. He's been wonderful under a continuous strain and I hope he'll be back before long. Of course he's had far too much work to do which should never have bothered him with an adequate staff. Both he and Roger Keyes. Their sole staff consists of a retired Commander (Lambart, *excellent* fellow but no training), a Commander G. never anything much of a flier, and 2 young Flag Lieuts. who work signals only + a Marine for Intelligence (V.G.). And since April the fleet has gradually grown and expanded in every single direction besides auxiliaries, trawlers, armed boarding steamers and what not, but never an addition to the staff. They ought to have a junior Flag Officer right away. Wemyss is now temporarily in command, but still carrying on his own particular show as well (SNO Mudros) which will give him far more than any man can possibly manage. It's the old naval way, praiseworthy but not organised war . . .

35   *Limpus to de Robeck*

[Typescript]   7 December 1915

How the days fly! I have not had a half hour in which to answer yours of the 26th November,[99] though I *wanted* to write and especially to consider and to answer some of your questions. But first, I am really happy that you have managed to obtain that sorely needed spell. Of course you will have spent much time at the Admiralty and War Office, but I do trust that you will have managed, or will manage, some time in the country, perhaps on shank's mare with a scatter gun.

Meanwhile we shall be doing with the *Triad* as much as possible in the time allowed. I keep her at 48 hours' notice so that when you wire there will be little time lost in getting her away, though proposed work may be half done, or even some of it unstarted. We hope to have it *all* done by the *24th December*.

I hope that the Military have *not* definitely decided that evacuation is necessary. But it is entirely and absolutely a military question and must be decided after giving full weight to the military considerations. But, as I say, I hope they will *not* evacuate.

First because the victorious shouts of the Germans and Turks will resound far and wide, especially will they reach that Mahommedan world which it is *our* interest to convince that we shall win. Also they will reach Roumania and Greece and far away Sweden, Holland and Denmark; and even the German party in America will take heart from their echo and the latter will redouble their efforts to make America press for peace — when peace would be disastrous for us and the Allies.

Secondly because the actual business of evacuation will be very difficult and very costly in lives, guns, and other material of war at any time. More especially so in the winter. How costly I cannot gauge; that again is a military question. But I have heard soldiers estimate it at 30% of the force evacuating.

Thirdly, as you say, the evacuation of Helles will make it much easier for submarines, T.B.D.s and T.B.s to get out of the Dardanelles, and to use freely the strong current to take floating mines out to sea.

I think that while the Germans are by no means at the last gasp, they *do* begin to see an end in sight unfavourable to them. I also think that their semi-final effort was the Serbian push and the acquisition of Bulgaria, Greece, and Roumania to their side. Even this would not ensure them final success but it would add to the time and difficulty of *our* success. This semi-final push has *not* succeeded so soon or so well as they hoped. In fact Roumania and Greece may even yet keep out. But I fear the effect of evacuation on them.

11 December – Such a nuisance being so busy. I *cannot* get my answer off to you and I do wish you to have it before you start back for the Mediterranean.

About the submarines. Dartige du Fournet is already keen on laying mines across their lairs, but I am rubbing it in, and the acquisition of the fine mine-layer *Angora* with 300 mines on board will help a lot.

Also, as you say every caique and boat that might be used for sweeping, etc., must be destroyed.

Your (b).

I rejoice to say that this very day I learn that the impossible task of escorting every vessel and so tying up all the available destroyers is being dropped as from 12th December and though I have not got the sequel in writing yet, it must follow that patrols and hunting squadrons will be established instead.

And I strongly endorse, and have done so in writing, the necessity of patrol squadrons under special Commodores or active young Admirals both east and west of Malta. And I would base a third in Egyptian waters to hunt between Port Said and Crete.

I think a British W/T station in south Crete is most desirable and a scout balloon at Malta to be established now for use when the windy weather passes.

All steamers should have a 12 pdr. gun. This is being done as fast as the Admiralty can lay hands on the guns.

As to a real attack on Smyrna. If SMYRNA HARBOUR is meant, it is Army and Navy; and a fairly big job for the Army, because the Turco-Germans in force would try and oust us at once. If what is aimed at is a further fairly good harbour for the winter such as ERITRA Bay between Chios and the mainland and/or GUL BAGTCHE Gulf, then it will be naval but with a land force sufficient to *take* the Peninsula of Kara Burnu and Chustan Island and to hold absolutely the neck of land between Sigajik Bay and Gul Bagtche Gulf, and of course to picket or hold all the Kara Burnu Peninsula and Chustan Island.

As to the desirability of the operation; either would deny the use of Smyrna Harbour to the Germans and from that point of view it *is* desirable. But it is essential first to learn if the Military can be sure of their part.

As to the larger operation, Smyrna and later on to Smyrna-Panderma railway; that involves meeting and defeating the Turco-German army and is a military question and a question of men and munitions and ships to carry them and supply them.

This would best be done with the help of a Russian landing on the south Black Sea coast, on that fine and suitable (I believe) stretch between the Bosphorus and Erekli (Cape Baba). But whether the Russians have sufficient sea command to do it I do not know. Nor do I hold out great hopes of *any* landing on that coast *in the winter*. Local men will know the latter.

Certainly the operation would *cut* the German, etc., move into Asia if done in time.

If that cannot be done then the German move south can be immensely hampered by a serious landing at Alexandretta and the seizure of the railway running west to Adana and south to Aleppo and beyond, thus spoiling their access from Constantinople and Haidar Pasha to any place south of Alexandretta.

If the Germans really mean to pass south as apparently they do, then it is certainly worth while seriously considering whether to stop them at Haidar Pasha (via Smyrna-Panderma and the coast of the Marmora; and with a Russian landing at the south west of the Black Sea and marching on Ismidt and Haidar Pasha) or, failing that, at Alexandretta. The effect on the Moslem world would be to convince them that the Germans are *not* invincible and *can* be stopped and that the Allies *are* going to win. But it is all far more than a naval question. It needs many men.

Triad shall be done by 24th December.

You do not want a new head. Your own is singularly clear and determined. You *did* need a rest for it and I trust that you will have it before starting back.

I will keep an eye on the two Midshipmen, or rather, to be honest, my wife will.

It's dogged as does it and dogged as will do it. I am much hurt and grieved that Porter and one man control has gone.[100]

I do trust that your health will let you see the thing through. I think it will . . .

[P.S.]   I find this cannot catch you in England so send it to Marseille to meet you.

Admiral Dartige du Fournet has just gone to Taranto to talk to Duke d'Abruzzi[101] and will be back 16 Dec.

A. H. L. 12/12/15.

18 December So this missed you at Marseille too!

36 *De Robeck to Limpus*

[Holograph]   *Lord Nelson*,
                                                        24 December 1915

A Merry Xmas and all good luck in 1916 and may it bring you and yours all success and great victory and peace to our Empire. They pulled off a great performance here and every credit is due to those who did it and Wemyss and Keyes especially. They certainly were very foolish and sent many telegrams that showed they had no true appreciation of their responsibilities, however all's well that ends well. R. W. [Wemyss] is off as C.-in-C. Egypt and I have [had] a heart to heart talk with R. Keyes and told him that he must in future be C.O.S. and not 'leader of the opposition'! I had not the heart to send him away. I am only just back from Kephalo, so excuse the short note. God bless you. All kind regards . . .

[P.S.] Do what you can for Burmester,[102] no better young Captain in the Navy, he is the very best class of officer.

37 *Captain Heathcoat S. Grant*[103] *to de Robeck*

[Holograph]   28 December 1915

We are all delighted to hear you are back and D.V. all the better for your short spell at home, though don't doubt you had worries enough when there. The evacuation was well done and was backed in my humble opinion by extrdy [?] good luck, the Turks apparently not being suspicious of the event. Before we left Suvla we had the Bay to the north of Suvla Pt. surveyed and handed it over to Sir Julian[104] who settled on its use [?] and the building of the Pier there forthwith and I guess [?] it came in useful. On the whole I was pleased [?] they did it as my brother's accounts of the front at Suvla, at the back of Chocolate Hill in the floods and cold weather afterwards were really ghastly, the dead Turks and our fellows' bodies being washed right over the parapets and the men being [?] drowned actually in the trenches, etc.

Re the attempt to have another naval debacle in the Straits, with in my opinion no object in view for the enormous cost to the Navy and the inevitable cheering effect on the Turk. I do not like to say too much, but expressed my own views very openly to Chief of Staff and asked him to notify the fact that personally I was absolutely opposed to it in every way and no doubt he has told you so . . .

38   *Jackson to de Robeck*

[Holograph]   Admiralty, Whitehall.
2 January 1916

My best congratulations on the very thoroughly earned K.C.B. and best wishes for the New Year.

I hope the weather will favour you in the distasteful task you are engaged in. The First Lord did his best, but if the soldiers say they won't supply troops, which is practically what they did say, we can't but accept the Govt. decision and protest as we have done. The First Lord *now* thinks Salonika may be a good move after all, especially as the Turks are beginning to think that all is not well to the north [war] d and we *know* the Germans are extremely perturbed about the political situation there.

I hope you'll soon be able to answer our telegrams to you about the future disposition of forces, R.N.D., air sheds, ships, etc. I am having rather a hot correspondence with C.-in-C. about robbing him of *Lowestoft* to relieve *Chatham* but I've told him it must be done and we'll get her out to you about end of the month. *Breslau* is being armed with 6" guns, perhaps only 2, but they have reached Constantinople. How can you tackle *Goeben* if she appears? She must be 18 months out of dock and damaged, and in the restricted areas amongst the islands battleships might manage to keep within range.

Our idea [is] to have good look-out stations on Imbros and Tenedos using Lemnos as a good base and garrisoning them all with R.N.D. which suits the W.O. too. Patrols of course would have to be out, but the fighting ships as a rule in harbour at short notice. Perhaps your ideas are different, if so let us know as soon as possible . . .

Notes

1   De Robeck to Keyes, 15 September 1914 in Paul G. Halpern (ed.), *The Keyes Papers*, Vol. I: *1914–1918*, N.R.S. Vol. 117 (1972), Document 10, pp. 22–3.

2   The letter is reproduced in Admiral of the Fleet Sir Roger Keyes, *The Naval Memoirs* (London: Thornton Butterworth, 1934), Vol. I, p. 220.

3   Admiral John H. Godfrey, *The Naval Memoirs of Admiral J. H. Godfrey* (7 volumes in 10, privately printed, 1964–6), Vol. II, p. 2. Good accounts of the naval aspects of the campaign are in: Keyes, *Naval Memoirs*, Vol. I; Arthur J. Marder, *From the Dreadnought to Scapa Flow: The Royal Navy in the Fisher Era*, Vol. II: *The War Years to the Eve of Jutland: 1914–1916* (London: OUP, 1965) chapters ix-xiii; Marder, 'The Dardanelles Revisited: Further Thoughts on the Naval Prelude', *From the Dardanelles to Oran: Studies of the Royal Navy in War and Peace, 1915–1940* (London: OUP, 1974); Captain Eric Wheler Bush, *Gallipoli* (London: Allen & Unwin, 1975); Admiral of the Fleet Lord Wester Wemyss, *The Navy in the Dardanelles Campaign* (London: Hodder & Stoughton, 1924); and the exhaustive Sir Julian S. Corbett, *Naval Operations*, Vols. II–III (London: Longman, 1922–3).

4   The telegram is reproduced in Keyes, *Naval Memoirs*, Vol. I, pp. 335–6. Keyes scornfully wrote in the margin of his copy: 'A reply was received to the effect that the hour had passed − the Army would do it!', Keyes MSS. 5/15, Churchill College, now in the British Library.

5 Martin S. Gilbert, *Winston S. Churchill*, Vol. III: *The Challenge of War, 1914–1916* (London: Heinemann, 1971) chapter xiii; Marder, *Dreadnought to Scapa Flow*, Vol. II, chapter xi.

6 Paul G. Halpern (ed.), *The Keyes Papers*, Vol. II: *1919–1938*, N.R.S. Vol. 121 (1980), Documents 40, 53, 64, 65.

7 ibid., Documents 114, 122, 267, 269.

8 Winston S. Churchill, *The World Crisis*, Vol. II (London: Butterworth, 1923), ch. xiii.

9 See also *The Keyes Papers*, Vol. I, Documents 98, 110.

10 *The Keyes Papers*, Vol. II, Document 137, pp. 160–1. Keyes also concluded that unless occupation of the Gallipoli Peninsula was part of the main plan for imposing their will on Turkey the use of troops for this purpose was not justified.

11 *The Keyes Papers*, Vol. I, Documents 135, 136.

12 ibid., Document 109.

13 ibid., Document 110.

14 *The Keyes Papers*, Vol. II, Document 195.

15 Christian to Keyes, 23 October 1915, *The Keyes Papers*, Vol. I, Document 111.

16 Mrs J. Proby to the editor, 8 September 1982.

17 Admiral Sir Arthur Henry Limpus (1863–1931). Naval adviser to the Turkish Government, 1912–14; Admiral Superintendent, Malta, September 1914–October 1916; President Shell Committee at the Admiralty, 1917.

18 Rt Hon. Sir Winston S. Churchill (1874–1965). First Lord of the Admiralty, October 1911–May 1915.

19 Vice-Admiral Sir Sackville Hamilton Carden (1857–1930). Admiral Superintendent, Malta, 1912–14; commanded allied naval forces in the Eastern Mediterranean, September 1914–March 1915. Carden was then in the naval hospital at Malta.

20 After their escape to the Dardanelles in August 1914, the German battle cruiser *Goeben* and light cruiser *Breslau* were sold to the Turkish Navy and renamed *Yawus Sultan Selim* and *Midilli*. Although they flew the Turkish ensign, the sale was fictitious and their German crews remained aboard. Throughout the war the Germans usually used their old names in official documents. The escape of the ships and subsequent court of inquiry and court martial is covered in depth in E.W.R. Lumby (ed.), *Policy and Operations in the Mediterranean, 1912–1914* N.R.S. Vol. 115 (1970).

21 The pre-dreadnoughts *Ocean* and *Irresistible* had been sunk in the attack on 18 March.

22 Gerald H. Fitzmaurice (1865–1939). Entered Foreign Office, 1888; Vice-Consul Smyrna, 1895; 2nd Dragoman, Constantinople, 1897–1905; Chief Dragoman, 1907; 1st Secretary, 1908; retired, 1921. Rear-Admiral Hall, Director of Naval Intelligence, employed Fitzmaurice after the war began, and in February and early March he had been one of those engaged in abortive negotiations aimed at Turkey's withdrawal from the war, the opening of the Dardanelles and the surrender of the *Goeben* in return for a large sum of money. For details see: Admiral Sir William James, *The Eyes of the Navy: A Biographical Study of Admiral Sir Reginald Hall* (London: Methuen, 1955), pp. 60–4; Captain G. R. G. Allen, 'A Ghost from Gallipoli,' *The Royal United Services Institution Journal*, Vol. CVIII, No. 631 (August 1963), pp. 137–8.

23 Document **3**.

24 Later Admiral of the Fleet Baron Wester Wemyss (Rosslyn Erskine Wemyss, 1864–1933). Created 1st Baron, 1919; Senior Naval Officer, Mudros, 1915; C.-in-C. East Indies and Egypt, 1916–17; Deputy First Sea Lord, September–December 1917; First Sea Lord, January 1918–November 1919.

25 Rear-Admiral [later Admiral Sir] Cecil F. Thursby (1861–1936). Commanded 2nd Squadron at the Dardanelles, 1915; after Italy's entry into the war detached to the Adriatic with 4 battleships and commanded British Adriatic Force, 1915–16; C.-in-C. Eastern Mediterranean, 1917; commanded Coast Guard and Reserves, 1918; C.-in-C. Plymouth, 1919–20; retired list, 1920.

26 On 10 May de Robeck's Chief of Staff Roger Keyes noted in a letter to his wife they had reports of one and probably two German submarines on their way. On the 14th de Robeck shifted his flag from the new super dreadnought *Queen Elizabeth* to the older *Lord Nelson*. See *The Keyes Papers*, Vol. I, Document 78, p. 135.

27 *Blenheim* was a depot ship for destroyers and *Ark Royal* a seaplane carrier.

28 *A.E.2* experienced difficulties with her torpedoes and had only one success. On 30
April she was sunk by a Turkish torpedo boat after a loss of control (possibly caused
by the difference in density between the salt and fresh water currents of the Marmara)
caused her to break surface.

29 The old battleship *Goliath* was torpedoed and sunk on the night of 12/13 May off
Morto Bay by the destroyer *Muavanet-i-Miliet* with a mixed German-Turkish crew
commanded by Kapitänleutnant Rudolph Firle.

30 Captain [later Admiral] Herbert A. S. Fyler (1864–1934). Commanded *Agamemnon*
at Dardanelles, 1915–16; Escort Admiral to Atlantic convoys, May, 1917.

31 Contre-Amiral [later Vice-Amiral] Emile-Paul-Aimable Guépratte (1856–1939).
Commanded Division de complement [old battleships] August 1914; French squadron
off Dardanelles, September 1914–May 1915; Vice-Amiral and Préfet Maritime, Bizerte,
October 1915; retired, 1917. Guépratte's gallant conduct during the Dardanelles
campaign made him a rather beloved figure in the Royal Navy. His superiors in France,
however, took a somewhat more reserved view of his judgement and efficiency.

32 Captain T. L. Shelford, commander of the *Goliath*, went down with his ship.

33 Vice-Amiral Ernest-Eugene Nicol (1858–1917). Commanded Escadre des Dardanelles,
April – September 1915; Préfet Maritime, Rochefort, 1916; retired, 1917.

34 Admiral of the Fleet John Arbuthnot Fisher (1841–1920). Created 1st Baron Fisher
of Kilverstone, 1909. C.-in-C. Mediterranean, 1899–1902; First Sea Lord, 1904–10;
October 1914–May 1915. Although it was Churchill who had brought back the now
elderly Fisher as First Sea Lord in October 1914, they fell out over the Dardanelles
and on 15 May Fisher resigned. The affair is examined in great detail in Martin Gilbert,
op. cit., Vol. III, ch. xiii.

35 Vice-Admiral [later Admiral Sir] Douglas Gamble (1856–1934). Naval adviser to the
Turkish Government, 1909–10; commanded 4th Battle Squadron, 1914; War Staff,
Admiralty, 1915–17; retired list, 1917.

36 Captain [later Admiral Sir] Herbert W. Richmond (1871–1946). Assistant Director
of Operations, 1913–15; liaison officer with Italian fleet, 1915; President Royal Naval
War College, Greenwich, 1920–3; C.-in-C. East Indies Squadron, 1924–5; Commandant
of the Imperial Defence College, 1927–8; retired list, 1931; Master of Downing College,
1936–46.

37 Vice-Amiral Augustin Boué de Lapeyrère (1852–1924). Minister of Marine, July
1909–March 1911; C.-in-C. Ière armée navale (Mediterranean), 1911–October 1915.
The Anglo-French Naval Convention of 6 August 1914 gave the French general direction
of operations in the Mediterranean but local operations in the Adriatic and Dardanelles
escaped their control, and barring the extremely unlikely eventuality of a sortie by
the Austrian fleet eluding the Italians, Lapeyrère's role as allied commander-in-chief
was nominal.

38 Special Service Ship No. 14 was the former transport *Merion* (11,650 tons) fitted with
dummy guns and superstructure to resemble the battle cruiser *Tiger*.

39 Commander William B. Forbes (1845–1928). Retired from Royal Navy, 1888; recalled
and appointed to Special Service Squadron, January 1915; appointed to armed drifters
of Dover Patrol, July 1915, but later forced to retire by ill health.

40 The battleships *Triumph* and *Majestic* were torpedoed on May 25th and 27th
respectively. Both were victims of *U.21* which had come from Germany via the Straits
of Gibraltar, refuelling at the Austrian naval base at Cattaro.

41 General Sir Ian Hamilton (1853–1947). Chief of Staff to Kitchener and commanded
mobile columns in western Transvaal, 1901–2; Quartermaster-General to the Forces,
1903–4; Adjutant-General to the Forces, 1909–10; C.-in-C. Mediterranean Expeditionary
Force, March–October 1915.

42 Enver Pasha (1881–1922). Ottoman Minister of War; one of the leaders of the 'Young
Turk' revolution in 1908 and the coup d'état of 1913. Enver Pasha was considered
one of the most energetic and effective of the Turkish leaders and, as former military
ataché in Berlin, was regarded as strongly pro-German.

43 Admiral [later Admiral of the Fleet] Sir Henry B. Jackson (1855–1929). Commanded
R.N. War College, 1911–13; Chief of the War Staff, Admiralty, 1912–14; First Sea
Lord, May 1915–December 1916; President R.N. College, Greenwich, 1916–19.

44 The Royal Naval Division, composed of Royal Marines and Naval Reservists, first served in the defence of Antwerp in October 1914 and subsequently at Gallipoli and on the Western Front.

45 Major-General [later General Sir] Walter P. Braithwaite (1865–1945). Director of Staff Duties, War Office, 1914–15; Chief of Staff, Mediterranean Expeditionary Force, March–October 1915; commanded 62nd Division, December 1915–August 1918; IX Corps, August 1918–September 1919; Adjutant-General to the Forces, 1927–31; retired, 1931; Bath King of Arms, 1933.

46 Captain [later Admiral] Douglas Lionel Dent (1869–1959). Commanded battleship *Irresistible* sunk during the attack on 18 March; Principal Naval Transport Officer in preparation of landing before returning home in early May; subsequently commanded blistered cruiser *Edgar* and a squadron of supporting monitors and destroyers off the Dardanelles, 1915–16; Chief of the Submarine Service, 1919–21; Director of Naval Equipment Department, Admiralty, 1922–4; retired list, 1926.

47 Captain [later Vice-Admiral] Arthur Hayes-Sadler (1863–1952). Commanded battleship *Ocean* sunk in the attack on 18 March; commanded Aegean Squadron, 1918; relieved of his command following the sortie of the *Goeben* 20 January, which resulted in the loss of the monitors *Raglan* and *M.28* (as well as the German light cruiser *Breslau*); retired list, 1919.

48 Rear-Admiral [later Admiral] Stuart Nicholson (1865–1936). Commanded covering squadron at the Dardanelles 1915–16; flew flag in *Majestic* when she was torpedoed 27 May; Vice-Admiral commanding East Coast of England, 1916–18; retired list, 1920.

49 Eleutherios Venizelos (1864–1936). President of Cretan National Assembly, 1897; led Cretan insurrectionary movement, 1904; Prime Minister of Greece, 1910–15; 1917–20; 1924; 1928–32; 1933.

50 Ellis Ashmead-Bartlett (1881–1931). Well-known war correspondent who was selected to represent the London press during the Dardanelles campaign. His observations made him extremely pessimistic and on his return to London in October he worked diligently for an evacuation before winter set in; represented London press at Joffre's H.Q. in France, 1916; MP(C),N. Hammersmith, 1924–6. Author of the highly critical *The Uncensored Dardanelles* (London: Hutchinson, 1928).

51 This presumably was a scheme for landing the Army at Bulair. There are some interesting comments on Ashmead-Bartlett's relations with authorities at the Dardanelles in Alan Moorehead, *Gallipoli* (New York: Harper, 1956), pp. 305–7. See also *The Keyes Papers*, Vol. I, Document 85, pp. 147–8.

52 This estimate is wildly optimistic. As of 29 June 1915 only 14 German (and no Austrian) submarines had been destroyed in all theatres. Only one German loss took place in the Mediterranean, the small *UB.3* which disappeared from unknown causes en route to Smyrna. Robert M. Grant, *U-Boat Intelligence, 1914–1918* (London: Putnam, 1969), pp. 182–3.

53 Rt Hon. Arthur James Balfour (1848–1930). Created Earl, 1922. Leader of the House of Commons and First Lord of the Treasury, 1891–2; 1895–1906; Leader of the Opposition, 1892–5; Prime Minister, 1902–5; First Lord of the Admiralty, May 1915–December 1916; Foreign Secretary, 1916–19.

54 General Henri Eugène Gouraud (1867–1946). Commanded 10th Infantry Division (wounded in Argonne), 1914–15; commanded French Expeditionary Corps at Dardanelles (wounded, losing right arm), May-June, 1915; Resident General in Morocco, 1916–17; commanded IVe Armée, 1917–19; Governor of Strasbourg, 1918–19; High Commissioner in Syria and Cilicia and C.-in-C. Armée du Levant, 1919–22; Military Governor of Paris, 1923–37.

55 No German or Austrian submarine was lost that day.

56 *Humber* (1520 tons [deep], 2 6″ and 2 120mm howitzers) had been one of three monitors under construction for the Brazilian Navy and taken over by the Admiralty at the beginning of the war. Details of the class are in Ian Buxton, *Big Gun Monitors* (World Ship Society: Trident, 1978), pp. 81–91.

57 Colonel [later Major-General Rt Hon. Sir] Frederick Sykes (1877–1954). Commanded R.F.C. Wing in France, 1914–15; commanded R.N.A.S., Eastern Mediterranean, 1915–16; Chief of Air Staff, 1918–19; MP(C) Harlam division of Sheffield, 1922–8; Governor of Bombay, 1928–33; MP(C) Central division, Nottingham, 1940–5.

58 Not reproduced.
59 Colonel Maurice P. A. Hankey (1877–1963). Created 1st Baron, 1939; entered Royal
    Marine Artillery, 1895; Assistant Secretary, Committee of Imperial Defence, 1908;
    Secretary, C.I.D., 1912–38; Secretary of War Cabinet, 1916–17; Imperial War Cabinet,
    1917–18; British Secretary to Paris Peace Conference, 1919; Secretary of the Cabinet,
    1919–38; Clerk of the Privy Council, 1923–38; Minister without portfolio in the War
    Cabinet, 1939–40; Chancellor of the Duchy of Lancaster, 1940–1; Paymaster-General,
    1941–2.
60 Captain [later Admiral] Cecil M. Staveley (1874–1934). Admiralty War Staff, 1914–15;
    Beachmaster Gallipoli Peninsula, 1915–16; Principal Beachmaster at both Anzac and
    Cape Helles during evacuation; senior officer of detached squadron, N. Aegean,
    1916–18; naval attaché, Constantinople during Armistice, 1918–20.
61 Possibly Captain Lionel de Lautour Wells, R.N. (1859–1929). Formerly Chief Officer
    Metropolitan Fire Brigade and originator of 1898 scheme for protection of London
    against fire.
62 The Memorandum by Admiral Oliver, Chief of Staff, took the position that the most
    effective use which could be made of naval guns to help the Army was to land a number
    of them. It was the result of an inquiry and suggestion by Lord Selborne, Minister
    of Agriculture and Fisheries and former First Lord of the Admiralty (1900–5), to the
    Dardanelles Committee. In forwarding the Memorandum, the Admiralty remarked
    that the appreciation of the position 'commends itself generally to Their Lordships,
    but must not be taken as conveying to you any specific directions for compliance'.
    Admiralty to de Robeck, 24 June 1915, P.R.O., ADM 137/1090, fols. 183–202.
63 Vice-Admiral [later Admiral of the Fleet] Sir Henry F. Oliver (1865–1965). Director
    of Intelligence, Admiralty War Staff, 1913–14; Chief of Admiralty War Staff, 1914–17;
    Deputy Chief of Naval Staff, 1917–18; commanded 1st Battle Cruiser Squadron, 1918;
    Second Sea Lord, 1920–4; C.-in-C. Atlantic Fleet, 1924–7.
64 Lieut.-General Hon. Sir Frederick William Stopford (1854–1929). Military
    Secretary to Sir Redvers Buller in South Africa, 1899–1900; G.O.C., London
    District, 1906–9; commanded IX Corps and in charge of Suvla operations;
    harshly criticised for failure to exploit the initial surprise and relieved of his command,
    15 August.
65 Sir John Jackson (1851–1919). Leading civil engineer and contractor responsible for
    major civil engineering work (including docks, harbours, railways) throughout the world;
    MP (U) Devonport, 1910–18.
66 Lieutenant Lionel S. Ormsby Johnson, Flag Lieutenant to Admirals Carden and de
    Robeck at the Dardanelles.
67 Lieutenant [later Captain] Hugh S. Bowlby (1888–1977) Flag Lieutenant to de Robeck
    during the war. Brother-in-law of Roger Keyes.
68 Vice-Admiral [later Admiral Sir] Richard H. Peirse (1860–1940). C.-in-C. East Indies
    Station, 1913–16; commanded allied naval forces defending Suez Canal, 1914–16; Naval
    member of Central Committee, Board of Invention and Research, 1916–18; retired
    list, 1919.
69 General Sir John Maxwell (1859–1929). Commanded forces in Egypt, 1908–12;
    September 1914–October 1915; C.-in-C. Ireland, April–November 1916; C.-in-C.
    Northern Command, 1916–19; retired, 1922.
70 Vice-Amiral Louis-René Dartige du Fournet (1856–1940). Senior Admiral of
    International Squadron at Constantinople, 1912–13; Préfet Maritime, Bizerte, 1913–15;
    commanded Escadre des Dardanelles, May–October 1915; succeeded Lapeyrère as C.-
    in-C. Ière armée navale (C.-in-C. Mediterranean), October 1915–December 1916;
    relieved of his command 11 December 1916 after the Minister of Marine blamed him
    for the fiasco caused when Greek forces fired on Allied landing parties at Athens,
    1 December.
71 This probably refers to the proposal to send 4 French divisions to the Dardanelles under
    General Sarrail before Bulgaria's entry into the war on the side of the Central powers
    diverted the force to Salonika. See Jan K. Tanenbaum, *General Maurice Sarrail,
    1856–1929: The French Army and Left-Wing Politics* (Chapel Hill, N.C.: University

of N.C. Press, 1974), pp. 62–5; and George H. Cassar, *The French and the Dardanelles* (London: Allen & Unwin, 1971), pp. 178 ff.

72 General Joseph Jacques Césaire Joffre (1852–1931). Chief of French General Staff, 1911; C.-in-C. of French armies in north and north-east, 1914; C.-in-C. French armies in the west, 1915–16; created Marshal of France, 1916.

73 Horatio Herbert Kitchener (1850–1916). Created Baron, 1898, Viscount, 1902; Earl (Kitchener of Khartoum), 1914. Sirdar of Egyptian Army,1890–9; commanded expedition for reconquest of the Sudan, 1896–9; C.-in-C. British armies in South Africa, 1900–2; C.-in-C. India, 1902–9; British Agent and Consul General, Egypt, 1911–14; Secretary of State for War, 1914–16; lost at sea en route to Russia when H.M.S. *Hampshire* was mined, 5 June 1916.

74 *E.7* was lost 4 September after fouling the Nagara net. *E.20* was torpedoed 6 November by *UB.14* in the Marmora after her rendezvous was betrayed to the Germans by papers left aboard the captured French submarine *Turquoise*. The events are described by Eric Bush, op. cit., pp. 217–18, 221–2.

75 Contre-Amiral [late Vice-Amiral] Ferdinand de Bon (1861–1923). Director of Naval Bases, Eastern Expeditionary Corps, 1915; Chef d'état major général, 1916, 1916–19; member of Interallied Naval Council with an important role in formulating naval clauses of Treaty of Versailles, 1918–19; C.-in-C., Ière armée navale, April 1919–July 1923; Chief Technical Advisor of French Delegation, Washington Naval Conference, 1921.

76 Lieut.-General Edward A. Altham (1856–1943). Inspector-General Communications, Dardanelles, July–November 1915; Egyptian Expeditionary Force, December 1915–November 1916; Quartermaster-General in India, 1917–19.

77 Captain [later Vice-Admiral Sir] Maurice Swynfen Fitzmaurice (1870–1927). Commanded *Triumph*, 1914–15; P.N.T.O. Dardanelles and Salonika, 1915–16; Chief of Staff, Eastern Mediterranean Squadron, 1916–17; S.N.O. coast of Palestine, 1918; commanded British Aegean Squadron, 1919; D.N.I. Admiralty, 1921–4; C.-in-C. Africa Station 1924–7.

78 Captain [later Admiral Sir] Michael Henry Hodges (1874–1951). Naval Attaché in Paris, 1914; Principal Naval Transport Officer, Salonika, 1915–16; Naval Secretary to First Lord, 1923–5; 2nd-in-Command, Mediterranean Fleet, 1925–7; Second Sea Lord, 1927–30; C.-in-C. Atlantic Fleet, 1930–1.

79 Admiral of the Fleet Sir John R. Jellicoe (1859–1935). Created Viscount Jellicoe of Scapa, 1918; 1st Earl, 1925. Second Sea Lord, 1912–14; C.-in-C. Grand Fleet, August 1914–November 1916; First Sea Lord, December 1916–December 1917; Governor-General and C.-in-C. of the Dominion of New Zealand, 1920–4.

80 Rear-Admiral [later Admiral] Arthur Henry Christian (1863–1926). Commanded 'Southern Force' consisting of Harwich submarine and destroyer flotillas and 7th Cruiser Squadron (Nore), 1914; Rear-Admiral in Eastern Mediterranean (commanded naval forces at Suvla Bay landing), 1915–17; retired list, 1919.

81 Admiral of the Fleet Sir Arthur Knyvet Wilson (1845–1921). 3rd Bt. Awarded V.C. for heroism at El Teb, 1884; C.-in-C. Home and Channel Fleets, 1903–07; First Sea Lord, 1910–11; loosely attached in unofficial and unpaid capacity to War Staff, 1914–16.

82 Admiral H.B. Jackson, First Sea Lord and Lieut.-General A.J. Murray, Chief of the Imperial General Staff, *An Appreciation of the existing situation in the Balkans and Dardanelles with remarks as to the relative importance of this situation in regard to the general conduct of the war,* 9 October 1915, Copy in P.R.O. ADM 137/1145.

83 ibid. The printed version contains minor variations.

84 Jackson concluded ('Note on the Situation in the Eastern Mediterranean by the First Sea Lord', 7 October 1915, ibid., Appendix I, p. 10):

Instead, therefore, of weakening our Dardanelles forces, they should be strengthened with the utmost rapidity possible, kept fully supplied with ammunition, stores, and drafts, and the attack pushed home with determination.

When the heights are occupied and artillery brought into position, the Fleet should push into the Straits to reduce the forts, even at the risk of serious losses, which, as far as older types of battleships are concerned, can be replaced without endangering the naval situation in home waters.

85 De Robeck sent a similar letter to Jackson. Reproduced in *The Keyes Papers*, Vol. I, Document 110. On the plan and variations see ibid., Documents 98, 100, 113.

86 Captain [later General Sir] William Wellington Godfrey (1880–1952). Captain R.M.L.I., 1907; War Staff Officer on Carden's and de Robeck's Staff, 1915–16; Colonel Commandant, Portsmouth Division, Royal Marines, 1933–5; Adjutant-General Royal Marines, 1936–9.

87 Surgeon Vice-Admiral Sir James Porter (1851–1935). Director-General Medical Department, Royal Navy, 1908–13. Porter came out to the Dardanelles in the hospital yacht *Liberty* as Principal Hospital Transport Officer to direct the movement of sick and wounded of all services by sea in the Mediterranean. The military objected to this complication of a rather muddled medical situation and in December Porter was recalled. Discussed in Robert Rhodes James, *Gallipoli* (New York: Macmillan, 1965), p. 249. See also Document 34.

88 Colonel Sir A. Henry McMahon (1862–1949). Foreign Secretary to the Government of India, 1911–14; First High Commissioner, Egypt, 1914–16; British Commissioner on Middle East International Commission (Peace Conference), 1919.

89 During a southwesterly gale early on the morning of 1 November the destroyer *Louis* dragged her anchor in Suvla Bay, grounded on a sandbank and subsequently became a total loss.

90 General Dousmanis was Chief of the Greek General Staff while his brother, Rear-Admiral Dousmanis, was Chief of the Greek Naval Staff. In conversations with the German naval attaché in Athens, both had indeed expressed pro-German sympathies. Freiherr von Grancy to Staatssekretär des Reichsmarineamts., 14 August 1915. Microfilm copy in U.S. National Archives, T-1022, Roll 485, PG 69104.

91 General Maurice Paul Emmanuel Sarrail (1856–1929). Director of Infantry, Ministry of War, 1907–11; commanded VI Army Corps and Third Army, 1914; relieved by Joffre, July 1915; thanks to connections with polticians of the Left, the pro-republican Sarrail was named to command of Armée d'Orient (destined for the Dardanelles but diverted to Salonika after Bulgaria entered the war), August 1915; C.-in-C. Allied Eastern Army, January 1916–December 1917; High Commissioner in Syria and Lebanon, 1924–6.

92 Admiral of the Fleet Sir Geoffrey Thomas Phipps Hornby (1825–95). Commanded Flying Squadron, 1869–71; Channel Squadron, 1871–4; C.-in-C. Mediterranean, 1877–80; led Fleet through Dardanelles to Constantinople during diplomatic crisis caused by Russo-Turkish war and Russian threat to Constantinople, 1878; President Royal Naval College, 1881–2; C.-in-C. Portsmouth, 1882–5; First President of The Navy League, 1895.

93 Once again these hopes were unfounded, no German or Austrian submarines had been sunk.

94 General Sir Charles C. Monro (1860–1929). Commanded 2nd Division, August–December 1914; I Corps, December 1914–July 1915; Third Army, July–October 1915; named to command Mediterranean Expeditionary Force (Gallipoli), October 1915; named C.-in-C. Eastern Mediterranean Forces (Gallipoli and Salonika) 23 November 1915–9 January 1916; commanded First Army, February–August 1916; C.-in-C. India, 1916–20; Governor and C.-in-C. Gibraltar, 1923–8.

95 Commander [later Captain] Hon. Lionel J. O. Lambart (1873–1940). Son of 9th Earl of Cavan; served in *Queen* and after she was mined served as Chief Staff Officer to S.N.O. off Anzac; joined de Robeck's staff before Suvla landings; retired list, 1918; returned to active service to command yacht *Grive* during Dunkirk evacuation and lost with his ship in German dive bomber attack on his fourth run, 1 June 1940.

96 Lieutenant Thomas M. Potts, R.N.R., captain of *Imogene*.

97 De Robeck's hand writing is not clear, but if it is the word 'padre' it probably refers to Rev. Francis Cowley Whitehouse, Chaplain to the Embassy at Constantinople before the war.

98 Captain [later Vice-Admiral] Sidney R. Drury-Lowe (1871–1945). Commanded cruiser *Chatham* in Mediterranean, 1915–16; battlecruiser *Princess Royal* in Grand Fleet, 1916–18; retired list, 1921. Drury-Lowe was laid up after having his left foot crushed between a picket boat and ladder during a gale at Salonika.

99   Document **32**.
100 See Document **32**.
101 Prince Luigi Amadeo di Savoia, Duke of the Abruzzi (1873–1933). 3rd son of Amadeo,
     Duke of Aosta. Noted explorer before the war; Inspector of Torpedo Craft, 1911;
     C.-in-C. Italian Fleet, 1915–17.
102 Captain [later Admiral Sir] Rudolf Miles Burmester (1875–1956). Commanded *Euryalus*
     at Dardanelles, 1915–16; Chief of Staff in Mediterranean, 1917–19; Chief of Staff
     Portsmouth Command, 1920–2; commanded *Warspite*, 1923; Director of Mobilization
     Dept., Admiralty, 1926–8; C.-in-C. Africa Station, 1928–31; retired list, 1933; recalled
     to active service, 1940; Flag Officer-in-charge, Cardiff, 1942–4.
103 Captain [later Admiral Sir] Heathcoat S. Grant (1864–1938). Naval Attaché in the
     United States, 1912–14; commanded battleship *Canopus*, 1914–16; Senior Naval Officer,
     Gibraltar, 1917–19; retired list, 1920.
104 Lieut.-General [later Field Marshal] Sir Julian Byng (1862–1935). Created baron, 1919;
     viscount, 1926. Commanded 3rd Cavalry Division, October 1914–May 1915; Cavalry
     Corps till August 1915; IX Corps (Suvla) till February 1916; XVII Corps till April
     1916; Canadian Corps, Third Army, 1917–19; Governor-General, Canada, 1921–6;
     Field Marshal, 1932.

List of Documents and Sources

1	De Robeck to Vice-Admiral Sir Arthur H. Limpus	26 March 1915	National Maritime Museum, Limpus MSS.
2	De Robeck to Limpus	11 April 1915	Limpus MSS.
3	Limpus to de Robeck	7 May 1915	Churchill College, De Robeck MSS. 4/36
4	De Robeck to Limpus	16 May 1915	Limpus MSS.
5	De Robeck to Limpus	22 May 1915	Limpus MSS.
6	Thursby to de Robeck	24 May 1915	De Robeck MSS. 4/35
7	De Robeck to Limpus	3 June 1915	Limpus MSS.
8	Admiral Sir Henry B. Jackson to de Robeck	9 June 1915	De Robeck MSS. 4/79
9	De Robeck to Jackson	15 June 1915	Naval Historical Library, Jackson MSS.
10	De Robeck to Limpus	21 June 1915	Limpus MSS.
11	Limpus to de Robeck	29 June 1915	De Robeck MSS. 4/36
12	De Robeck to Rt Hon. Arthur J. Balfour	9 July 1915	P.R.O. ADM 137/1144
13	Admiralty to de Robeck with note by General Hamilton	21 July 1915	De Robeck MSS. 4/40
14	Jackson to de Robeck	27 July 1915	De Robeck MSS. 4/31
15	De Robeck to the Secretary of the Admiralty	19 August 1915	P.R.O. ADM 137/1144
16	Limpus to de Robeck	22 August 1915	De Robeck MSS. 4/36

17	Jackson to de Robeck	25 August 1915	De Robeck MSS. 4/31
18	Jackson to de Robeck	8 September 1915	De Robeck MSS. 4/31
19	Balfour to de Robeck	10 September 1915	De Robeck MSS. 4/31
20	Jackson to de Robeck	12 September 1915	De Robeck MSS. 4/31
21	De Robeck to Jackson	16 September 1915	De Robeck MSS. 4/70
22	Jackson to de Robeck	27 September 1915	De Robeck MSS. 4/31
23	Jackson to de Robeck	4 October 1915	De Robeck MSS. 4/31
24	De Robeck to Jackson	8 October 1915	De Robeck MSS. 4/70
25	Jackson to de Robeck	9 October 1915	De Robeck MSS. 4/31
26	Jackson to de Robeck	13 October 1915	De Robeck MSS. 4/31
27	De Robeck to Balfour	20 October 1915	De Robeck MSS. 4/69
28	Limpus to de Robeck	24 October 1915	De Robeck MSS. 4/36
29	Jackson to de Robeck	7 November 1915	De Robeck MSS. 4/31
30	De Robeck to Limpus	9 November 1915	Limpus MSS.
31	Limpus to de Robeck	12 November 1915	De Robeck MSS. 4/36
32	De Robeck to Limpus	26 November 1915	Limpus MSS.
33	Jackson to de Robeck	3 December 1915	De Robeck MSS. 4/31
34	Captain S. R. Drury-Lowe to Captain Herbert Richmond	5 December 1915	National Maritime Museum, Richmond MSS. RIC 7/4
35	Limpus to de Robeck	7 December 1915	De Robeck MSS. 4/36
36	De Robeck to Limpus	24 December 1915	Limpus MSS.
37	Captain Heathcoat S. Grant to de Robeck	28 December 1915	De Robeck MSS. 4/38
38	Jackson to de Robeck	2 January 1916	De Robeck MSS. 4/31

13

Selections from the Memoirs and Correspondence of Captain James Bernard Foley, CBE, RAN (1896–1974)

Edited by

J. V. P. GOLDRICK

The Memoirs of Captain Foley

James Bernard Foley[1] was born in Ballarat of Irish parents on 24 June 1896. In 1914, at the suggestion of his headmaster, he took the examination for the Accountant Branch of the Royal Australian Navy, and was one of two successful candidates to be entered as Paymasters' Clerks, with seniority of 1 March 1915.

He received sketchy initial training at H.M.A.S. *Cerberus*[2] and after a few months was appointed to join H.M.A.S. *Australia*, then serving in the Grand Fleet as Flagship of the Second Battle Cruiser Squadron. After a long passage in the S.S. *Persic*, and a short leave in London, Foley was sent north to join the *Australia*. He has left this vivid account of his early years at sea.

I

Having arrived at Inverkeithing Station and discovered where the ship was, I plus sea chest eventually found myself at the gangway of my first ship. At the head of the gangway I found the Officer of the Watch, a Lieutenant named Hodgkinson[3] who was in his early 20s. He seemed a friendly sort of fellow, who having learned who I was and why I was there, sent me down to the

Gunroom and ordered my sea chest to be taken down to the Cabin Flat.

I was about as raw as a young carrot and completely out of my depth. I cannot recall much of the following two or three hours, but by about 10 p.m. my sea chest had been installed in a passage way outside the Gunroom, the servant allotted me had been produced, and had found me a hammock and a slinging billet in the Gunroom Flat. I never saw Hodgkinson again, he was apparently a sick man and was landed into a hospital next day, or soon afterwards, where he died almost at once.

I had never slept in a hammock and was glad to be able to try it and find my balance before the main leave body returned on board about 11 p.m., by which time I felt that I would not over-balance and fall out. There were over 20 Gunroom officers – Sub Lieutenants and Midshipmen. There were not enough slinging billets in the Gunroom Flat or the passage outside the Gunroom to accommodate all. The Sub of the Mess (i.e. the President and Senior Member) was Sub Lieutenant Creswell RN,[4] and he was the only Gunroom member who had a cabin. Some Mids, as did many Ratings, preferred to spread their hammocks on the steel deck. There was a space of perhaps 18–24 inches between hammocks.

I heard the chatter and clatter of the others as they arrived. John Loudon-Shand[5] had warned me before I left Australia that there would probably be 'fun and games' and that I should be prepared for some such. I had given the matter some thought before turning in and wondered what form the initiation proceedings would take, and was, to be honest about it, in some sort of trepidation. I knew that I was older in years than all or most of the Midshipmen, though not than all of the Sub Lieutenants or Acting Subs. As I had not seen any of them, I was not aware of their physical qualities.

As for myself, I was very fit, having had nothing else to do for the previous 8 weeks but play deck games and keep fit. I did not drink or smoke. I also knew that owing to war requirements the Admiralty had been pushing Cadets to sea as Midshipmen a year or more earlier than their normal time. I had therefore some vague idea that, while I may have to put up with something from the Subs, I would object to being kicked around by those younger and (I hoped) smaller than myself.

Nothing happened immediately, and I was dozing off to sleep when I felt my hammock shaken and a voice say, 'Why, the bugger's alive'. There was some discourse about cutting down my hammock, but another voice said something about it being too late and leaving me 'for next day'. So ended my first day.

Next morning I was one of the first up and about and took myself to the Bath Room – a space of probably four or five hundred square feet with two full-sized (long) baths, and in a corner a pile of hip-baths about three feet in diameter and eight to ten inches deep. A length of hosing was available to attach to the hot or cold taps to fill these hip baths. As one of the two long baths was unoccupied, I filled it and got in. While I was thus engaged, a couple of what seemed to be boys of 16 came in, got up and filled hip baths and sat in them and with large sponges squelched water over themselves.

One said he assumed I was the new boy from Australia, and that evidently I did not realise I was not entitled to use a long bath, which were only used by Senior members of the Gunroom – all Junior members should use hip-baths.

I made some appropriate reply, completed my bath, and got dressed, had some breakfast and, it being after 8 a.m., went in search of my immediate Head of Department, Fleet Paymaster R. F. Wardroper RN.[6] He turned out to be a small, very quiet, soft voiced man with a wispy beard, who I thought must have been the age of God.

During the day, I suppose that I must have seen the Commander, the Captain,[7] the other officers in my Department and finally, Sub Lieutenant Creswell, who took me into his cabin to talk to me. I told him I was completely raw and without any knowledge of Gunroom or Ship's procedures. I mentioned the incidents of the night before and the bathroom that morning and told him that I was not a rebel but that I had no intention of being pushed around by a bunch of small boys. Creswell told me that he had been staying at the home of the Australian Naval Liaison Officer, Captain Haworth-Booth[8] at the time I appeared in London – that Captain Haworth-Booth had been agreeably impressed with me and that he (Creswell) had decided that because of my age I was to be regarded as a Senior Midshipman for ordinary mess purposes.

This, of course, suited me and I was thus free of all 'initiation' problems. As I myself have not had to undergo such traditional inductions, my views are not very relevant, but I have no objections to reasonable inductions provided that they are carried out in good spirit and without bullying and the dangerous practices which sometimes creep in, or are stupid in other ways. Crossing-the-Line ceremonies, for example, can be quite harmless fun, and I have seen hundreds of soldiers, sailors and civilians put through them without any problems.

As an example of the stupid type; some time after I joined we got a new batch of 4 Mids, all of the Church of England. On the morning of the first Sunday after they joined, one of the senior Sub Lieutenants (also Anglican) asked them collectively whether they had attended the morning Communion Service. They all meekly replied, 'No, Sir'.[9] The Sub expressed to them his view that they should have done so, so as to make a good Gunroom showing there, and he directed that they appear in the Gunroom Flat at 10 p.m. that night when they would each be given six cuts of the cane, which punishment he duly administered.

The next Sunday, the Sub asked the four the same question and received the cheerful reply of 'Yes, Sir'. 'Oh,' replied the Sub, 'so you are showing up the rest of us. See you at 10 p.m. in the Gunroom Flat.'

Later in the day, I saw the Sub concerned and told him that I didn't like what he proposed to do and that he should not do it. I told him that, as a Roman Catholic, I did not wish to become involved in Church of England or any other religious questions, but that, in my view, it was obnoxious in any Christian faith to do what amounted to a mockery of the Eucharist, and that unless he undertook there and then not to punish the four for the reason he gave them, I would run him in. The Sub in question was really not a bad fellow − we were in fact good friends − and he did not carry out the threat.

One or two of the Subs and the Senior Mids thought that Creswell had been a bit weak in letting me straight into the Senior Midshipman group and rather resented it. One in fact told me so. He was an RAN officer of my own branch who said he had been put through the hoop a couple of years earlier and thought I should have been also, as he was just as old as I was when he joined the Gunroom. I subsequently learned that he had been very unpopular and had, as a result, been a fruitful case for bullying.

I had only two slight incidents. On one occasion a Senior Mid (he was due to be made an Acting Sub within a week) directed me to vacate (for him) one of the two or three armchair type of chairs in the Gunroom. I replied that he could have it if he liked to turn me out, but warned him that he might get hurt in the attempt. As I was probably two stone heavier than he was, he wisely went away muttering. On another occasion, I was sitting in the Mess with a few others nearby − one of whom was an Acting Sub (he was in fact the hammock shaker of my first night). I was reading and heard a voice a few feet away saying, 'Hey, you, pass me my cigarettes'. I took no notice, though I realised it was directed at me. He repeated the order a couple of times, finally by name, and when I told him to get his own cigarettes he said something about giving me half a dozen for impertinence, to which I replied that I would be delighted if he cared to try it. He was a much smaller person than I and that was the last I heard of it. He left the ship soon afterwards.

I have often wondered whether my brashness helped me at this time, or whether it was my comparative size. It wasn't that I was outsize − I was about 5' 10½" in socks, but I weighed something over 13 stone and was in good condition. I heard that a couple of years later when the first outfit from the RAN College joined the Gunrooms in the Grand Fleet they were inclined to, and mostly did, resist the cane. They had done the full College Course[10] and would have been substantially older (as I was) than their RN contemporaries.

I had left the UK for other parts long before our first lot arrived, but I did hear that they succeeded in 'cleaning up' one or two Gunrooms.

There was a constant movement of Gunroom officers because, as Mids became Acting Sub Lieutenants they were moved off to courses, other jobs (mainly destroyers and other small craft), etc. Within a short period of my joining our Sub (Creswell) departed to specialise in submarines, in one of which he was lost later in the war.

In a Gunroom group of 20 (3 Subs, 17 Mids, of whom 1 Sub and myself were RAN) which must have been taken in late 1915, I can still name each of them. Some are dead, none achieved any great Service success. Of the RN, three or four served on loan in the RAN in later years. Six or seven of them I saw occasionally after I left the ship in 1917. As far as I know, only one, H. T. T. Bayliss,[11] reached Captain's rank on the Active List. Some retired soon after the end of the 1914–18 War. One of these did some blackbirding and, I believe, a stretch in jail.

I must have settled in reasonably quickly and well, as I cannot recall any major 'growing pains'. *Australia* was the Flagship of the Second Battle Cruiser Squadron, which consisted of three battle cruisers of the same type, *Australia, New Zealand* and *Indefatigable* with Rear-Admiral William Pakenham in command.[12]

Almost all the Seaman officers were Royal Navy, loaned to the RAN. Two, at least, were Australian born, one of whom, J. G. Crace[13] was I think, the only one of all the Seaman branch, including the Gunroom, to achieve Flag Rank on the Active List. Two or three of the RN Midshipmen were also Australian born and had entered the RN as Colonial Cadets – a method of entry to Osborne and Dartmouth for two or three Australians every year.

In my own branch, the boss was dear little Digby Wardroper. He had married a very nice Tasmanian girl who was then living in Edinburgh with a small baby girl. They were extremely kind to me and I was a frequent guest for afternoon tea – almost every time I went to Edinburgh, in fact. Despite his smallness and gentleness, Wardroper was a really good and wily tennis player of the old type.

As I have mentioned, I thought he must be very old – in fact, he would have been only 40 or little more when I joined and I can well remember, whenever I had occasion to be in the Wardroom about noon, seeing him, usually with the Commander (N) and the Engineer Commander, in a corner of the Wardroom, drinking pink gins, and thinking what a pity it was to see them drinking themselves to death. That was in 1915. In 1965, or thereabouts, I met the then Secretary of the Kooyong Tennis Club who, on being told that I was ex-Navy, said, 'Oh, I wonder if you know an old Naval Officer – a wonderful old boy – well over 80, who plays tennis almost every day at Kooyong and is quite indefatigable'. His name was Wardroper.

The Number Two in the Branch was L. H. Mosse Robinson,[14] ex-Royal Navy, who had married an Australian girl just before the War and later transferred to the RAN. I believe that they had not a bean beyond his modest pay. She was then living outside South Queensferry. Since he had had to meet among other expenses the cost of her passage to England, he had to live extremely frugally – never smoked or drank.

The former Commander of *Australia* had been appointed away a month or so before I joined, so I missed the man with whom I subsequently spent about one third of my whole Naval Service – George Francis Hyde.[15]

Apart from my Departmental work, I found myself put into the cypher organisation. After a crash course in cyphering and coding, I was made a cypher officer, which was practically a full-time, three-watch job. Unlike my Seaman contemporaries, who were also in 3 or 4 watches when at sea, but less in harbour when they had the Naval Instructor's classes, I had to keep a regular cypher watch in addition to my branch duties. When at sea, there were of course normally only incoming messages and interceptions to decypher, but there were not many moments either at sea or in harbour when there was a let-up throughout the full watch, and many times when one had to stay on to help one's relief cope with the heavy traffic. Being the Flagship, we had to do the Flag Cyphers as well as the General Cyphers.

At sea, the cypher office was a small space off the main W/T Office, well down in the bowels of the ship, where I was working on the occasion in 1916 when *Australia* and *New Zealand* were in collision during a sweep into the Skagerrak. When the bump came, the crash threw my coding assistant, Leading Writer Louis Irving,[16] off his chair on to the deck. It was a lean few minutes. Almost immediately the bridge ordered all watertight doors closed, and we had no knowledge what happened. One of our cruiser escort had been torpedoed a little earlier, so we didn't know whether we had also been torpedoed or mined. As I was the only officer in the W/T and Cypher Offices, I had to forget my instinctive desire to get up to the upper deck, and to try to convey to six or eight ratings that there was nothing to worry about and that whatever it was should ensure us all a few weeks leave during repairs. Actually, I was mentally kicking myself for my stupidity in having left my Gieves' waistcoat in my sea chest. There was an official issue of a blow-up rubber tube life belt, but many people claimed that it was dangerous and liable to break the wearer's neck if he had to jump into the sea from any appreciable height. Most of the officers bought and used a Gieves' waistcoat made of heavy warm blue cloth, which had a rubber tube inside, with a blow-up nozzle in the top pocket, just long enough to reach the mouth. This was a good and efficient article and was fine for those officers in exposed positions as it was so warm. Anywhere down between decks at sea, however, when all hatches were closed and the fug became heavy, it wasn't so comfortable, and down in my action station cubby hole, where even in the coldest weather it was like an oven, one could not wear such a hot garment – this was the reason it had not been my practice to take it down with me.

After perhaps 10 or more minutes we found out by telephone what had happened and were greatly relieved. I had got Irving back on his chair, none the worse, although his language was rather warm.

No result of an inquiry (if any) into this collision was ever made public that I am aware of. There was the inevitable expert opinion in the Gunroom completely exonerating ourselves from any blame. The Battle Cruiser Fleet was at that time carrying out a sweep into the Skagerrak and, as there were known grave dangers from submarines in that area, the whole force was carrying out the approved zig-zag procedure when a pea soup fog came down. The Gunroom experts were somewhat divided in deciding where the responsibility for cancelling the zig-zag procedure lay once the ships entered a fog. Apparently one ship ceased and the other did not, with the result that *New Zealand* loomed up suddenly and did a 'bumps-a-daisy' about midships with *Australia* and then sheered off into the fog.

That the fog was really thick may be judged from the fact that 2 or 3 minutes after the waist-to-waist bump, the *New Zealand* appeared again directly in the path of *Australia*, which crashed bows onto her, with the result that *Australia* needed a completely new stem, and the replacement of much of her bow structure. *New Zealand* apparently suffered much less damage, which was repaired in time for her to participate in the Battle of Jutland. There was a considerable amount of sourness in the *Australia* at this bad luck, though hindsight indicates that *Australia* may well have been one of the unfortunate battle cruisers which were lost in the battle. No one seemed to have been censured for the event. The Captain of the *Australia*, S. H. Radcliffe, was not promoted to Active Flag Rank, but I had gathered that this was not unexpected anyhow.

We had hobbled back at very slow speed, first to Rosyth, then to Newcastle-on-Tyne where we went into the Floating Dock to be made more or less seaworthy before going south to Devonport for a full refit, which took over 4 weeks. It was regarded as lucky that we did get back, as our speed was down to 8–10 knots, and we could have been a sitting shot for the numerous German submarines which were known to be in the area. Evidently, the pea soup fog, which was the cause of our collison in the first place, was our salvation and permitted us to get back unseen.

After we got in, I had to decypher a long signal from the Admiralty, containing detailed orders and instructions for the ship to proceed for the docking and temporary repairs. I knew the routine, i.e. that when I took the decyphered version to the Captain, he would tell me to get the Commander (N) for him. I also knew that the Commander (N) had been having a party in both the Wardroom and Gunroom, an understandable reaction for the past 36–48 hours.

It was about midnight when I completed the decypher, and I went first to 'N's' cabin, where he was asleep, half undressed, in his armchair. I shook him awake, told him the general tenor of the signal, gave him about 20 minutes to pull himself together and then took the message to the Captain, who had of course turned in. The Admiral had to be told also, so I woke his Secretary. The Admiral, with Staff and retinue, had to transfer to *New Zealand*. Fortunately, we did not have to sail for a number of hours and I never heard any references to 'N's' state. He was a known hard drinker and a 'quick recoverer'.

After our refit was completed, we left Plymouth for Scapa via the West Coast of Ireland to rejoin the battle cruisers, and for the usual work-up, on the morning of 31 May, 1916.

I was on the upper deck as we passed out through the breakwater, and I remember one of our senior RN Lieutenant Commanders, Alan MacDonald,[17] making the remark to me that he was very glad indeed that we were on our way back to the job, as he had had an uneasy feeling that the long awaited clash between the Grand Fleet and the German High Seas Fleet would have occurred while we were out of action. Not many hours later that day, we were off the South West Coast of Ireland when we began to pick up the signals from the Battle of Jutland. *Australia*, plus destroyer escort, increased to full speed, but, by late that night and early next morning, it was clear that we *had* missed the scrap. I think the only personnel from *Australia* in that battle were Father Gibbons,[18] who being the Squadron Catholic Chaplain had shifted over to *New Zealand*, and a few wireless ratings who were attached to the Admiral Commanding the Second Battle Cruiser Squadron, who had also of course moved over to *New Zealand* when we left Rosyth.

The ship's company in *Australia* were a mixed bag. There were ratings, especially amongst the CPOs and POs, who had transferred from the RN to the RAN permanently, within, of course, the normal naval engagements (12 years first engagement, followed by two volunteer periods of 5 years, making 22 years man's time, i.e. to 40 years of age). There were also RN loan ratings, i.e. those who had signed loan engagements for 2 or 3 years (the normal loan periods), and RAN ratings, who had been trained in Australia. Many of these latter had been trained in H.M.A.S. *Tingira*, harbour training ship in Rose Bay, Sydney, and others such as Stokers, Cooks and Stewards had entered and trained at Williamstown Naval Depot, H.M.A.S. *Cerberus*. All these ratings were in receipt of RAN rates of pay and allowances, which were substantially higher than were those of RN personnel of similar rates and grades. An AB or Stoker received 5/- per diem, plus a daily uniform allowance.

General messing was in force and the standard of feeding was probably much better all round than in RN ships where General Messing had not then been introduced. The RN ship operated on a Standard Ration, i.e. an issue of x pounds of basic items, such as bread, butter, tea, sugar, etc., per person to a stipulated financial amount, and the balance as a daily allowance in cash. Each mess then made the most or best they could out of the rations in kind and the daily cash allowance.

The RAN had started out with General Messing in the larger ships — it was soon extended to the smaller ones — but the RN took a few years to adopt it so generally. The Able rate for Ratings in the RN at that time was 1/- or 1/2 per diem, though a married man's wife got a separation allowance, at that time I think about 7/6 or 10/- *a week*.

Fifteen years later, when the Invergordon mutiny occurred, there had not been a very great improvement in pay conditions, and it is little wonder that sailors claimed that the reductions in pay and separation allowances proposed by the UK Government would result in wives having to become 'street walkers' to keep their homes and children going. The Admiralty had the proposed reductions forced upon them, but I was told subsequently by the Paymaster Director-General — Admiralty[19] at the time that he, as the head of the 'S' Branch of the Navy, had no knowledge of the intended reductions, and he was quite certain had he been consulted by Their Lordships of the Admiralty on the general question, that he had available sufficient evidence and knowledge to have made so strong a case that the Government could have been persuaded not to proceed with the reductions ordered, or at least modified the reductions for married men. When he did get into the act, the reductions were cancelled or modified substantially on the case he presented. These were the days when the 'old brigade' had not yet learned to seek the best advice available, especially if the colour between the gold lace were not black.

As time went on, and replacements or additions of personnel became necessary, RN Ratings were drafted direct from RN sources to fill vacancies in complement. These Ratings got *RN* rates of pay, as did the 'Conshies' we got from time to time. I cannot recall exactly how this came about, but I recall one Rating who was a conscientious objector whose civil occupation was a church organist. He was excused work on board other than playing the small organ in the ship's chapel and the pianos (Wardroom and Gunroom) with the Ship's Band and other non-warlike jobs. He was paid his 1/2 per diem.

This variety of rates of pay was scarcely conducive to happiness, and I think it was not long before authority was obtained to pay all ratings serving on board at RAN rates. Our sailors were not over-popular ashore in the canteens, as they were comparative millionaires and, unhappily, some were rather inclined to make too much of this comparative affluence. RN personnel were entitled to a daily rum ration (or 2d per diem in lieu of the ration). The rum issue had never been approved for the RAN.

The normal harbour routine at that time for me, as well as all Mids, was physical jerks on the Quarter Deck at 6.30 a.m. (except Sundays and when on watch), not always pleasant in the cold winter months, with a coating of ice on the deck. These PT sessions were taken by Lieutenant Commander

Allen, the Snotties' Nurse.[20] Then a bath, breakfast at 8 a.m. and the office by 8.30. Divisions at 9 a.m., followed by all those at divisions doing a 10 to 15 minutes jog around the whole upper deck length of the ship, with Bandmaster Joshua Ventry[21] and the Band providing the necessary music, which always included 'Colonel Bogey'.

In RN ships, the Royal Marine Corps provided officers' servants, but as RAN ships did not carry Royal Marines, Steward Ratings were provided for Wardroom officers and volunteer Bandsmen (many of whom had been Royal Marine Bandsmen) provided the servants for Gunroom officers, for which the officer concerned had to pay his Bandsman servant (of which there was one to two or three Mids) 2/6 per week. There was never any lack of volunteers as the extra 5/- or 7/6 per week was welcome to most.

Any extras in the Gunroom, such as fruit, biscuits or cake at tea had to be paid for by the consumer. Each Thursday night was a guest night, which meant an extra course at dinner, usually a savoury of some kind. Gunroom officers could invite (and, of course, pay for) one guest, or two if there were enough room. Except at sea, we dressed for dinner – and wore stiff fronted shirts.

Guests were either friends from other ships or our own Wardroom officers. Junior Mids were permitted a wine bill of 10/- per month, Senior Mids 15/- a month and Sub Lieutenants either 25/- or 30/- a month. These amounts included guests' consumption as well as hosts'. Ten shillings didn't go very far even if one had even one 'expensive' guest. All alcoholic drink served was entered in the daily wine book, which by rules was to be seen and initialled by the Captain each week. Junior Mids were not supposed to drink spirits. Beer was more expensive than spirits. Gin – Coates Plymouth was the popular, in fact almost the only brand and cost 1d per tot. A year or two later it went up to 1½d a tot, and the moaning and groaning could be heard from Scapa Flow to Plymouth! Whisky was 2d per tot, Port and Marsala were 2d or 3d a glass. Cigarettes, cigars and tobacco were also duty-free. I was a non-drinker and a non-smoker, so was not greatly concerned. Wardroom officers, even Commanders, were permitted a Wine Account of five pounds per month, and this limit was still in existence in the 1950s. I do not know the position today. The same procedure of noting consumption in the daily wine book operated in the wardroom, and the Captain also saw and initialled the book each week.

Long 'General Leave' in all ships of the Grand Fleet was usually given only when a ship was refitting and I think that in the slightly over 2 years I was in the *Australia* I had only about 10 days leave, except for leave after our collision with *New Zealand*, when I had 14 days. The Irish leave party got an extra day, as travelling time, and I was usually placed in charge. For the rest of the time, there was only recreational leave of a few hours' duration. When the ship was at one hour's notice for steam (i.e. to be ready to leave harbour not more than one hour from the time sailing was ordered) noshore leave was granted. At 2½ hours notice for steam, officers were permitted leave, but were to remain within sight of the ship, so as to be able to see a 'recall' signal. Recreation parties (e.g. football teams) were also given permission to land under similiar instructions, and with an officer accompanying the team, either as a member or in charge. The normal notice for steam was 4 hours, when shore leave was granted in accordance with usual Service routine, in watches, etc. This permitted officers and ratings to go ashore and follow their own devices, but as all such leave expired at about 4 p.m. or 4.30 p.m. in the winter, and only another hour or so later in the summer, having commenced at about 1 p.m., after the Noon meal, there was little opportunity to go far afield.

Australia, with the other nine battle cruisers (fewer, of course, after Jutland), was moored inside the Firth of Forth Bridge and Hawes Pier, South Queensferry was the landing place, and it was a very busy and interesting sight in the evening, with anything up to 20 picquet boats jockeying for position, with occasionally an Admiral's barge pushing its lordly way through them.

The whole ship's company, both officers and men, were on board for the evening meal, and in my opinion it speaks volumes for all concerned that about 1,000 officers and men cooped up night after night for months on end, often under considerable strain, should have got through it all with such little bother. I wonder whether the mods of today, young or old, would acquit themselves so well. No TV, no radio to ease the monotony. Discipline, patience, good manners, restraint and much consideration for others were the keys. I never sighted a single instance of the trouble one might expect from 20 or more people who had to live in such a confined space or under such crowded conditions as the Gunroom Mess of probably 25 feet by 15 feet for months on end. Wardroom officers were better off, of course, as they could always escape to their own cabins, small though most of these were. Most had room for a bunk, a small desk, a chair and a small wardrobe or chest of drawers. Ratings, at least those below Petty Officer rate, were even worse off than Gunroom officers. Conditions on the Lower Deck are greatly improved these days.

Australia and the other battle cruisers of the day were coal burners, and another of the tasks which befell all (or nearly all) officers and men was 'coal ship'. It was essential, and part of the normal procedure, that ships should be kept complete with coal, so as to be fully ready for sea at short notice. The first thing therefore on return to harbour from any foray into the North Sea or exercises, etc., was to complete with coal. No sooner had the ships secured at their moorings, than a collier would come alongside, whatever the time of day or night, and all hands would get busy with the filthy and rather hard job of coaling, which involved hours and hours of shovelling coal into bags or baskets in the holds of the collier, or pushing barrows on deck to the coal shutes. The coal dust filled one's eyes, ears and hair, as well as the whole ship via its ventilators, all of which took almost another day to clean up. In the cold or even mild climate of Scotland, it was bad enough, but that was easy compared with a coal ship I experienced later in the war, when in the harbour of Dili, Timor, we in *Pysche* commenced coaling at 7 a.m. and finished at 9 p.m., all through the humid tropical day.

It was the common view, I could almost say 'boast', then and still that Australian Service personnel were not amenable to discipline. I do not agree with this view, which I believe probably had its origins in reasons advanced by Australian politicians, press and other extreme partisans in an endeavour to excuse the larrikanism (mainly alcoholic) of our troops when they burnt down the Wuzza in Egypt, practically wrecked Capetown, and in other places where their misbehaviour was nothing to be proud of.

On scores of occasions, I was in charge of football parties (30–40 Ratings) ashore and had absolutely no trouble, except on one occasion. These were Australian Rules Football parties, so were not cowed or disciplined 'Pommies'. And the one exception was an occasion when I had refused the party permission to make a call at the Wet Canteen at Rosyth after the game (only because the time factor would have prevented the party getting the boat ordered to pick us up). One stoker decided the call of the beer was worth it, and was thus left ashore. He got back aboard 4 hours later – suffered the usual penalty scale of losing 2 days pay and 2 days leave – and I got ticked off by the Commander. I was privately informed some time later that a number of members of the team thought he deserved a further penalty which they duly applied.

Generally speaking, this period of little more than 2 years in *Australia* was a very monotonous existence, with little excitement after the collision with *New Zealand*. Some events which remain in my memory from this time were:

(1)   A visit to *Australia* by H.M. King George V, when all officers were presented to him.

(2)   A visit from Mr W. M. Hughes, then Labor Prime Minister[22] who harangued the ship's company on the quarter deck. As we had just finished an 8 hour coaling ship after a return from a North Sea sweep, and the decks were still wet from washing down, it was not surprising that there were a few sarcastic sniffs from the sailors who were being told how much unionism was doing for our great country, and how greatly the RAN and AIF were loved by all.

(3)   The floral wreath on *New Zealand*'s mainmast on the day Prince George of Battenberg,[23] married the Grand Duchess Nadia Toby of Russia. He was then a Lieutenant in *New Zealand*. He was subsequently the Marquess of Milford Haven – the elder brother of Lord Louis Mountbatten. Prince George retired as a Commander after the war, to take on a job in industry. Unfortunately, he died a few years afterwards. From what I heard in later years, he was considered more brilliant than his younger brother Louis – which is saying a lot.

(4)   Hockey games against the ladies of Edinburgh – about the roughest hockey games I ever played in, not excluding games against Australian State Teams in later years. Sometimes, with a coating of snow on the field, it was difficult to see the white ball.

(5)   Walks to Kirkliston from South Queensferry to have tea.

(6)   Occasional visits to the ship by Admiral Beatty.[24]

(7)   The change over of command which took Admiral Beatty to command the Grand Fleet vice Jellicoe,[25] Admiral Pakenham to *Lion* vice Beatty, and Rear Admiral Leveson[26] to *Australia* vice Pakenham.

(8)   My first hearing of a Court Martial gun and, as far as I can recall, my first, even though distant, proximity to a Court Martial. It was held in *New Zealand*, although the accused did not belong to that ship. He was a Lieutenant Commander RN, a 'T' Specialist, and he was charged and found guilty of sodomy with a member of the ship's company, for which he was Dismissed the Service with Disgrace and sentenced to 2½ years imprisonment. Nobody whom I heard refer to the incident seemed to think that the penalty was harsh, in fact some spoke of it being fairly light.

Early in 1917, Captain Radcliffe sent for me to tell me he had had information from Navy Office that my co-entry Freyer[27] had been found medically unfit for service in the Tropics – he was in *Psyche*, then on the China Station – and that it was intended that Freyer and I should exchange appointments. He said that neither he nor Fleet Paymaster Wardroper wished me to leave the ship, but before doing anything about it, he wanted to know whether *I* wanted to go. I certainly did not, and told him so. He replied that he would write to Navy Office and ask for cancellation of the exchange.

Communications in those days were not as simple as they are today, of course, and his letter crossed with one from Navy Office. The latter said that a medical board had recommended Freyer's immediate removal from the Tropics and that he was even then en route to UK. Further, that there was an urgent requirement for me in *Psyche* and I was to depart at the earliest date and without awaiting the arrival of my relief. I subsequently learnt that Mosse-Robinson (by now a Staff Paymaster), who had returned to Australia in the latter half of 1916, had been appointed to *Psyche* as (S) officer and had fixed it at Navy Office for me to go as his Assistant. There was nothing more which could be done, so I packed up my old sea chest again, had a few days' leave which permitted a quick dash to Cork to say goodbye to my Grandmother, whom I then saw for the last time, and got my sailing orders from Australia House, where the Naval Adviser was by then installed.

II

Foley served in H.M.A.S. *Psyche* for most of the remainder of the war and, after promotion, held a variety of supply appointments before, in 1921, becoming Assistant Secretary to the Flag Officer Commanding the

Australian Fleet, Rear-Admiral J. S. Dumaresq,[28] in H.M.A.S. *Melbourne*.

In 1923 Foley came under the eye of Captain G. F. Hyde, RAN, Second Naval Member of the Australian Commonwealth Naval Board. Foley was appointed Hyde's Secretary, a crucial step in his career, because Hyde was already marked for promotion to flag rank and eventual service as First Naval Member. For most of the next fourteen years, Foley was to serve as Hyde's Secretary, following him around the world through a wide range of appointments.

To gain experience of RN methods, Foley was attached to the staff of Vice-Admiral Sir Frederick Field,[29] commanding the Special Service Squadron in H.M.S. *Hood* on the world tour of 1924. On arrival in England, Foley attended the Secretaries' Course, which he topped, before joining the staff of the C.-in-C. Portsmouth, Admiral Sir Sidney Fremantle.[30] Hyde, during this time, attended the Senior Officers' War Course and served in command of H.M.S. *Vindictive*.

In 1926, Hyde was appointed Commodore First Class Commanding the Australian Squadron,[31] with Foley as his Secretary. In 1928, Hyde was promoted Rear-Admiral and Foley, Lieutenant Commander. In the next year both returned to the United Kingdom where they undertook further courses before Hyde assumed command of the Third Battle Squadron with his flag in H.M.S. *Emperor of India*.

Hyde became First Naval Member in 1931, retaining Foley as his Secretary. Their association continued until Hyde's death, shortly before he was due for relief, in 1937. Foley, however, continued to serve as Secretary to the First Naval Member until 1944.

His experience proved to be of the greatest value to the next two officers to serve in the position, Admiral Sir Ragnar Colvin[32] and Admiral Sir Guy Royle.[33] Foley was the ideal Secretary for the British Admirals to have during their loan service. Though discreet and intensely loyal, he was not afraid to offer advice and criticism to his chiefs, and the monumental knowledge of the RAN and of the Australian Government as a whole which he possessed made him more than a match for politicians and the civil service.

Perhaps the greatest problem faced by the RAN during Hyde's term as First Naval Member was that there was simply not enough money. This lack of finance was to result not only in construction programmes being too small, but even more dangerously, attempts to reduce pay and remunerations for serving personnel.

A notable difference between Australia and the United Kingdom between the wars was the existence of a powerful Department of Defence in addition to the single Service administrations. This had significant ramifications for the RAN:

Admiral Hyde was constantly pressing the Government for more money for the Navy and pointed out, year after year, that Australia was 'botting' on the people of the United Kingdom, who were paying many times more per capita on defence, especially naval defence, than Australians. Very few people today have even the faintest idea of how the Service Boards of those times kept their Services going. In 1929/30 the Navy Estimates totalled £2,107,191, which by 1931/32 had been reduced to approximately £1,400,000. The Army received substantially less, and the Estimates for the Royal Australian Air Force in 1929/30 were £444,650 and, in 1930/31, only £395,895.

In 1929/30, the sea-going personnel allowed by Estimates was 4858. In 1930/31 this had been reduced to 3929. The actual number borne on 15 March 1931 was 3442.

It should be realised that one of the tricks of the day was to put forward estimates of expenditure, together with the personnel numbers (officer requirements given in actual ranks). These estimates would then go through the Defence Department and the Treasury machine, and eventually find their way into the Parliamentary Estimates, usually mutilated en route.

Parliament would then approve 'x' millions as the total Defence appropriation. The three Services would then be told to prune their requirements to come within the total allotted. Since each of the Services had put up their minimum requirements, naturally none of the Chiefs of Staff would be prepared voluntarily to cut down his own Service's estimates. This gave the Defence Department Secretary his opportunity to put it to the Minister that, as the three Chiefs of Staff (inevitably) could not agree to a division of the inadequate amount provided, *he* should deliver a 'Judgement of Solomon'.

This suited the politicians, as it saved them the responsibility, but it ended up in making first Shepherd[34] and later Shedden[35] feel that they were the real masters.

Furthermore, whatever amount had finally been approved by Parliament, it was the almost invariable practice, about three quarters of the way through the financial year, for a direction to be received that a stipulated amount of 'savings' had to be effected in the year's expenditure. There was no real desire or intention to do more than pretend to make provision for defence.

From the Naval point of view, matters were not improved by the peculiar constitution of the Naval Board:

The Finance Secretary of the Department of Defence was Colonel Thomas[36] who doubled up jobs by also being the Finance Member of the Naval Board. It was a delightful situation, where Colonel Thomas could agree to a proposal at the Naval Board table, walk back to his Defence Department office at the other end of the Blue Stone Building and reject the proposal. A more absurd situation could not be imagined, yet it continued to last for many years, despite all attempts by Hyde to get it rectified.

The assumption by the Defence Department of the financial initiative might well have resulted in a tragedy when, in late 1931, the Government was searching about for ways to reduce expenditure:

Shortly after Hyde became First Naval Member, the Government of the day decided to cut pay rates in the Services. On receiving the decision (arrived at without consultation with the Naval Members of the Board), Admiral Hyde stormed along to the Minister[37] and, in objecting most strongly to the proposed reduction, informed the Minister for the information of Cabinet that if the cuts were insisted upon, he and his Naval colleagues would refuse to accept any responsibility whatever for the outcome and would make the press aware of this if need be. He added that the Minister and the Government should by now realise that the Navy was the only fully disciplined force in the country in the event of domestic troubles, and that if the Government alienated the Navy they might well be cutting their own throats and the blood would be upon their own heads.

We had discussed the line of approach to the Minister on the subject and thought, correctly as it transpired, that fear was the best ingredient to instill into him. It may sound a little extreme to claim that the Navy was the only disciplined force, but it should be remembered that there had been a serious police strike in Victoria only a few years earlier, that there was a very small permanent Military Force, and only a handful of Air Force personnel, and a lot of general unrest because of the bad world economic conditions.

However, the arguments advanced, plus the implied threat of the resignation of the First Naval Member and the reversion to the Royal Navy of the FOCAS and other senior RN officers apparently did the trick with the Government.

Nevertheless, I had not been a great believer in threats to resign after having heard views on such threats from Admiral Field. During a private lunch at Beckenham, I had brought up a well publicised problem at the time relating to the number of cruisers the Admiralty claimed to be necessary. The First Sea Lord at the time was Lord Beatty, and his requirement, backed up by Lord Jellicoe in the House of Lords, was 70. The Government was not prepared to authorise any more than 50, which was substantially less.

I asked Admiral Field (who had been Deputy Chief of the Naval Staff during the affair) why did not Lord Beatty and the Board of Admiralty resign in protest. Admiral Field's answer was that resignation may be effective sometimes, but very rarely, and *never* when there are others ready to accept the alternative. He pointed out to me that, at the time there were quite a number of senior or very senior officers who would have loved to become First Sea Lord, and would have accepted such an appointment, which acceptance automatically implied agreement with the Government's proposals. Would it not, he asked, be better for the Service if the Board remained in office and exerted every effort to achieve their desired objective, or at least to do their utmost towards that end?

In 1932, a Disarmament Conference was held in Geneva. Mr S. M. Bruce[38] was Australia's representative and the Australian Services were to be represented by Mr Frederick Shedden, one of Shepherd's staff. The Chief of the General Staff,[39] on hearing of this, proposed to the First Naval Member that they should protest. Admiral Hyde's reply was that he did not intend to send an officer to participate in any reduction in the Navy, but that if the CGS wished to send someone, he would raise no objection.

He was actually speaking with his tongue in his cheek, because we had already been in close contact with the Admiralty and were well aware that our interests would be better looked after by them. From an Empire Navy point of view, they were most anxious that the RAN should be kept as large as possible.

The worst feature of the whole thing in the long run was that Shedden, who was a hard worker, very ambitious, and not very favourably disposed to the Armed Services, gained the important favour of S. M. Bruce. This alone was bad enough[40] but when subsequently Shedden was sent to do the Imperial Defence Course, he returned to the Department of Defence, in which he was to succeed Shepherd, and became regarded in political and other circles as the Alpha and Omega of all things relating to defence.

A succession of conferences followed:

In 1933, Admiral Hyde attended a Naval Conference in Singapore. I went with him, travelling by Orient Line to Colombo and by P & O from Colombo to Singapore via Penang. After the Conference, we returned to Australia in a Burns-Philp ship via Java. The Conference was between the C.-in-C. China Station, Admiral Sir Frederick Dreyer,[41] who was the senior Admiral and Chairman, the C.-in-C. East Indies Station, Vice-Admiral Sir Martin Dunbar-Nasmith,[42] Vice-Admiral Hyde, and the First Naval Member of the New Zealand Naval Board, Commodore Burges Watson RN.[43] The latter had joined us in Melbourne from Wellington.

Admiral Dreyer was a pompous product of the old school − a big man physically, with a high domed shaped head. I believe he was clever and had invented various gunnery gadgets. We soon found on arrival that the 'Report of the Conference' had for all practical purposes been drawn up by him before our arrival, and he thought all that was required were the signatures of the other three leading members on the final page. He got something of a shock when he found that Admiral Hyde, supported usually by Commodore Burges Watson, was not in agreement on many points, and wished them and many others on which they only partially agreed, to be discussed fully.

The basis of the Conference was co-operation in the area in the event of war with Japan − a problem upon which Australia had strong views.

Admiral Dreyer's Chief of Staff was Captain George Pirie Thompson RN,[44] who subsequently became Second Naval Member of the Commonwealth Naval Board. He told me after the Conference that he had disagreed with Admiral Dreyer on many points, not only in connection with the Conference, and that he was so fed up that he informed Their Lordships that he did not wish to be considered for promotion to Rear-Admiral on the Active List.

In 1935, the London Naval Treaty Conference took place. On this occasion, Admiral Hyde and I again went to London by Orient Line to Toulon, and thence through France to the United Kingdom. The Conference was an intensely interesting experience, and it had tremendous international implications, which are well publicised by historians of the era. To me, some of the highlights were the very clear documentary evidence of the rise of Hitler and the quite obvious belief in British naval circles that war with Germany was absolutely inevitable, the only question being, when?

We had wished to get an Admiralty paper prepared, following the Conference, which we would use to help us when the Naval Board would be putting forward to the Commonwealth Government recommendations on the structure of the future RAN in the light of the agreed world fleets and the impending Hitler menace. We knew from experience that any Naval Board recommendations not fully supported by Admiralty and the United Kingdom Government would be murdered by our Defence Department and Parliament. We had therefore produced a long paper in draft, and Admiral Hyde had given a copy to Vice-Admiral William James,[45] who was then in the Admiralty as Deputy Chief of the Naval Staff, asking him to have it examined and commented upon by the various Admiralty Staff Divisions. It took us a long time − many weeks −

to get these comments, and it delayed our departure, but Admiral Hyde felt it worthwhile our waiting, as agreement on the spot would save unending trouble later.

Apart from these conferences and financial economies, Hyde's administration was much preoccupied with the provision of new cruisers to strengthen the Australian Squadron and replace the remaining obsolete ships of the 'Town' class.[46] The problem had already arisen in the previous decade over the acquisition of two 'County' class cruisers.

In 1924, the battle cruiser *Australia* had been sunk off Sydney Heads in compliance with the Washington Disarmament Treaty. Two new 'County' class cruisers were to be built, but, as usual, political trouble arose in regard to the place of building. The parochial attitude was that they *must* be built in Australia. The Naval Board was able to show that, apart from such aspects as the capability of Australian shipyards to build such large warships (twice as big as anything previously built in Australia), the time it would take and the various political and minor involvements, the ships could be built in the United Kingdom in not more than 3 years from the date of placing the order, and there would be a financial saving of sufficient magnitude to permit the building at Cockatoo Island Dockyard in Sydney of a seaplane carrier.

The Labor Opposition and the unions were pacified by this – after all, the only factor with them was work for the unionists – and so H.M.A.S. *Albatross*, seaplane carrier, came into being. I do not remember how long it took to complete *Albatross*, but I have little doubt it would have been many years longer than it should have, in the true tradition of the Australian unionist. (During the 1939–45 War, the Labor Minister of the Navy, Mr Makin,[47] at the launching of a destroyer at Williamstown Naval Dockyard in Victoria, informed the dockyard mateys that the Government was so pleased with their work it had been decided to place an order for another destroyer with the Williamstown Yard, adding 'and this should ensure adequate employment in the Yard for years to come'. It did, too!)[48]

This attitude eventually prevailed in the early 1930s, and although the Naval Board managed to obtain Government approval in principle for a new cruiser to be built in Britain, Hyde was aware that this would not satisfy the requirements of the Australian Squadron.

Hyde sought to resolve the dilemma of a Government unwilling to spend large capital sums, and still more unwilling to spend them outside Australia by suggesting a scheme whereby new ships could be built in and by Britain, at considerably less cost than possible in Australia, and maintained by the RAN.

The British, thinking that they would be bearing an additional financial burden, were not enthusiastic. Hyde, however, prepared a lengthy argument for the Minister for Defence[49] to transmit to the Committee of Imperial Defence. The major point was:

. . . that the expenditure on the building of the ships could be balanced by the maintenance of additional ships by the Commonwealth, the British Government thus being relieved of the cost of the maintenance of the *additional* ships.

The financial situation in the United Kingdom and in Australia, at present and as it will be for some years to come, as far as can be foreseen, makes it imperative that money available for Empire Defence be expended to the best possible advantage and this proposal appears to offer the best solution. It is certain that 3 cruisers could be built in the United Kingdom at no greater cost than 2 in Australia, and there are insurmountable difficulties in the way of placing orders for ships in the United Kingdom as an Australian commitment. The loan or permanent transfer of ships by the British Government to Australia would not be open to the same objections.

The advantages to the Royal Australian Navy would be considerable, and would be obtained without additional cost to either Government.

The attached paper read:

The capital cost of a 'Leander' class cruiser built in the United Kingdom is approximately £2,000,000 excluding exchange (built in Australia approximately £3,000,000). The life of a cruiser is 20 years. The cost of maintenance in commission of a 'Leander' class cruiser would be approximately £200,000 per annum at Australian rates of pay.

Australia's existing allocation of the Empire's cruisers is four, the cost of replacement of which (as they become obsolete) by 'Leander' class cruisers would be approximately £8,000,000 (or £400,000 per annum for 20 years) at present rates. (If H.M.A. Ships *Australia* and *Canberra* were to be replced in due course by 10,000 ton cruisers the cost would be greater.)

The proposal means therefore that over a period of 20 years the Imperial Government would incur on Australia's behalf an average annual expenditure on construction of approximately £400,000. It can be anticipated that the Imperial Government would expect a quid pro quo and it is suggested that this should be given in the form of maintenance in commission by Australia of two additional cruisers at an annual cost of approximately £200,000 each. Australia would thus be responsible for the maintenance in commission or reserve of six cruisers plus any additional vessels such as *Albatross*, destroyers, sloops, etc. The two cruisers referred to would be maintained in commission in addition to the ships normally kept in commission by Australia.

The proposal appears to have distinct advantages in that an economy would ensue as ships would be obtained for an expenditure equal to United Kingdom building rates, which would be less than if the ships were built in Australia, or if built in the United Kingdom and paid for by Australia. The money made available for defence would be used to better advantage.

The greater number of ships in full commission would increase efficiency generally and would mean an increased personnel with enhanced prospects of advancement, etc., which would remove the present tendency to stagnation. It would also result in an ultimate increased reserve of personnel for war.

There are, however, certain aspects which would require to be very clearly defined and decided upon after careful investigation, e.g.

PERIOD OF AGREEMENT

If the proposal matured into an agreement, it would be essential that such an agreement be binding on both sides for a stated period, say 20 years, so that its continuity could not be broken through changes in Governments.

NUMBER OF SHIPS TO BE KEPT IN COMMISSION

An agreement would be necessary as to the number of vessels to be kept in commission. An agreement on the minimum annual expenditure on Naval defence (exclusive of the expenditure of the £400,000 per annum referred to above) for the period concerned would appear to meet the case.

CONTROL OF SHIPS IN TIME OF PEACE

No insurmountable difficulty in this respect should arise. It is the practice to keep H.M.A. Ships in a state of material efficiency on a par with the same class of ship in the Royal Navy. Any alterations, etc., found necessary by Admiralty are effected in RAN Ships and it is believed that the Admiralty would agree that RAN officers, men and ships are interchangeable at any moment with opposite numbers in the Royal Navy. There is no reason to suppose that the Imperial Government would ask for or desire any greater control than that desired over the 'gift'[50] destroyers. It would, however, be desired to make the position in this respect quite clear.

CONTROL OF SHIPS IN TIME OF WAR

This is a matter of Government policy. It can, however, be anticipated that the Imperial Government would require some definite undertaking in regard to the control, distribution, etc., of the ships in time of war. All cruisers and destroyers are part of the Empire by treaty and it is scarcely likely that the Imperial Government would agree that 12% of that quota (the building of which had been at its expense) would be so far removed from its control that it would not be assured of the availability of the ships in time of war or strained relations. The Naval Board would welcome a definite decision that H.M.A. Ships and RAN personnel under either the existing or the proposed conditions would be placed at the disposal of the Admiralty in time of war or strained relations.

If some such decision were not arrived at, difficulties might arise if the Imperial Government required the ships in an emergency and the Australian Government of the day raised objections to the ships being moved and/or the Australian personnel being employed.

STRATEGIC DISPOSITION OF SHIPS IN TIME OF PEACE

Under the arrangements visualised above, Australia would at certain periods have five cruisers in commission. From a strategical or training point of view (or both) it would probably be inconvenient to Admiralty if these were all kept on the Australian Station. This could be overcome by temporarily attaching one or two of the Australian cruisers to a Royal Navy Squadron, for example Mediterranean, East Indies or China (as desired by Admiralty) either in lieu of or in addition to the existing system of exchange of cruisers. Such an arrangement would be of immense value to the RAN generally, particularly in regard to the experience which would be gained by personnel.

TYPE OF SHIPS TO BE PROVIDED

The chief requirement in this respect is a homogeneous Squadron of reasonably modern ships. It is assumed that the ships provided would not necessarily all be new and it would be necessary to make some stipulation regarding the degree of obsolescence acceptable. Observing that one of the objections raised in the earlier days when the system of subsidy was in practice was that ships kept by the Admiralty on this Station were of an obsolete type.

STATUS OF THE ROYAL AUSTRALIAN NAVY

It would be desirable that it be made very clear that the principle of the RAN as a *Dominion Navy* was not being brought into question and that there was no intention of suggesting the re-introduction of a subsidy system but that the RAN would retain in all respects its existing status as a separate Service.

The proposal was not agreed to by Britain, for a number of reasons, but principally because at the time the latter could little more afford the capital expenditure involved than Australia. In addition, the Statute of Westminster, although not yet ratified by Australia, raised very considerable questions concerning the employment of RAN-manned ships for British purposes in peace or war, without the clear consent of the Australian Government.

Hyde, however, was eventually successful in achieving a limited expansion and modernisation programme. Four new sloops had been commissioned or were building by the time war broke out in 1939. In addition, two cruisers of the Modified 'Leander' class, *Hobart* (ex-*Apollo*) and *Perth* (ex-*Amphion*) had been purchased to join the *Sydney* (ex-*Phaeton*). The seaplane carrier *Albatross* had been given to the Royal Navy as part-payment for the ships, but the elderly cruiser *Adelaide* had been modernised and would prove a useful trade protection vessel. Finally, three 'Tribal' class destroyers and a large number of 'Bathurst' class minesweepers had been approved and were building in the country.

III

The war years had brought a massive increase in work with little consequent increase in the establishment of Navy Office in Melbourne. Ever since Hyde's death in 1937, Foley had wanted to move on to a new appointment. The demands of the war and the need to support the successive British First Naval Members kept him in Navy Office.

By 1944, however, Sir Guy Royle was happy enough with the situation to let Foley go to be Australian Naval Liaison Officer in London. Foley's relief was Paymaster Commander Patrick Perry, RAN[51] who was fresh from serving as Secretary to the outgoing FOCAS, Rear-Admiral V. A. C. Crutchley.[52]

Foley's translation to London was a natural step in his career, but his arrival in the city came at a particularly opportune time for the RAN. All Foley's recent career had been involved with policy making at the highest level. He had the friendship of many senior RN officers and the complete confidence of the First Naval Member in Australia. Tactful and discreet, he was the obvious emissary for negotiations between the RN and the RAN. As a Paymaster Captain, raised in the tradition of secretarial silence, he was more likely to be admitted to the councils of the naval great than a Captain of the Executive Branch. So high was Admiral Sir Ragnar Colvin's opinion of Foley that he resigned his appointment as Naval Adviser to the Australian High Commissioner for the reason that he thought Foley's presence made his own unnecessary.

The impending end of the European war and the drive against Japan highlighted the existence of the RAN and its need for reconstruction. In 1939, the RAN possessed six cruisers and five destroyers. In 1944, although there were hundreds of smaller units in service, there were only four cruisers (one a gift from the RN) and eleven destroyers, seven of which were Australian-manned RN-owned units. Three cruisers and four destroyers had been sunk.

Relations between the Australian and British Governments were not good, and a variety of Admiralty proposals for larger RN units to be manned by the RAN had foundered because the British had not wished to pass operational control to Australia. The Australian Government, remembering the debates over the AIF Divisions in the Middle East in 1941–2, was determined that the ships should be employed in theatres of Australian interest, something which the Admiralty could not guarantee.

Proposals were being developed in London and Melbourne from late 1943 on for the creation of an Australian Fleet Air Arm and the transfer of modern light cruisers. These discussions had to be carried out, if not in secrecy, then at least with great discretion, and the presence of an officer in London fully briefed on the Australian problems and with access to all the Admiralty Staff Divisions was essential. Foley was given such access and, believing his loyalty to lie with the RAN, he ignored most of the Australian Defence organisation in London and acted directly on the orders of the First Naval Member.

The first scheme, for the transfer of a carrier and cruisers on loan, was not a success. Although the Admiralty eventually agreed that the ships could become RAN units under Australian control, matters were removed from its hands by the intervention of Churchill,[53] who insisted that Australia should pay for the ships.

The Australian Naval Board was unable to persuade the Government to provide the necessary funds. This incident clearly demonstrated the political weaknesses of the RAN, and the suspicion with which the Labor Government, the Department of Defence, and the other Services regarded its strong links with the Royal Navy.

Successive British First Naval Members were always viewed as manipulating the RAN's plans to suit the best interests of the Royal Navy and Great Britain rather than Australia. In consequence, their opinions, as well as those of RAN officers in general, were discounted in any Anglo-Australian dispute.

The end of the Second World War and the appointment of Admiral Sir Louis Hamilton as First Naval Member brought some improvement in the situation.[54] The shrewd and diplomatic Hamilton enjoyed better relations with the Government, particularly with the new Labor Prime Minister, J. B. Chifley,[55] than his predecessors, and he was able in the end to obtain consent for a number of measures towards the post-war reconstruction of the RAN.

The programme devised by Hamilton was three-pronged. With only a trio of Australian-built destroyers, there was an urgent requirement for the retention of some of the destroyers on loan from the RN in order that a full flotilla could be made up. The Admiralty suggested that the four 'N' class destroyers remain in the RAN.[56] These had been Australian manned since their completion in 1941–2, and were well armed and in reasonable condition. Hamilton, however, asked for five 'Q' class, some of which were already in RAN hands.[57] Although armed only with single 4.7″, as opposed to the 'N''s twin mountings, they carried extra fuel tanks – highly desirable in Australian conditions.

Hamilton then proposed that six destroyers (two 1942 'Battle' and four 'Daring' class) be built in Australia. This suggestion was warmly received by a Government eager to ensure full post-war employment.[58]

Finally, Hamilton was convinced of the RAN's need to create a substantial Fleet Air Arm around at least two light fleet carriers. He knew that the Royal Navy had the spare hulls available, but the fiasco in 1945 over the *Ocean* convinced him that two conditions had to be met. The first, that Australian shipyards and unions should not be able to raise any objections was dealt with by the destroyer programme. The second was that Britain had to agree to part with the necessary ships at a cut price. It was this second condition that Foley set out to meet – with some success:

> Because of the time lag with mails – the letters between us were sent chiefly by Diplomatic Bag – much of our written correspondence was overtaken by signals, and I find a letter from me to the First Naval Member dated 17 February 1945, offering congratulations on his apparent success in getting the Government's provisional approval for Australia to accept an offer from the United Kingdom to lend us a modern light fleet carrier (*Ocean*) and two modern 'Tiger' class cruisers to be delivered some time between 1945 and 1947. Some work on this scheme had been

going on for some time − it had in fact commenced in a quiet unofficial way before I left Australia.

On 1 March 1945, in a letter received by me on 26 March, Admiral Royle said:

> Wasn't it a remarkable change for the Government to offer to man RN ships after having wasted a whole year trying to make up their minds. I feel that the factors which probably influenced them in this decision were the knowledge that their AIF Divisions were not being used, that there was a huge surplus of air crews in the country who were complaining of their inactivity and, finally, the excellent work done by the RAN in recent operations and the publicity given to this work, due to the casualties sustained by the *Australia*.[59]
>
> Your preliminary proposals, as cabled out, were of great assistance . . . It is most unfortunate that we cannot get a modern cruiser earlier than February 1946. I am afraid that anything less than 'Tiger' class cruisers would arouse suspicion, and so the only alternative left to us was to man a modern carrier as soon as we can get our crew to the United Kingdom . . . The main thing we wish to get settled is acceptance of the principle with as few strings attached as possible . . .

In this same letter he mentioned that he had heard Louis Hamilton's name as his successor as First Naval Member. Evidently my letter to the First Naval Member of 17 February had not reached him by March as it contained the following paragraph:

> In regard to yourself I saw the Naval Secretary − both the outgoing (Admiral Harcourt)[60] and the incoming one (Admiral Barry)[61] − yesterday. The First Sea Lord saw your probable successor when he was at Malta last week . . . and I gather that he is very keen on Admiral L. K. Hamilton taking on the job. The Naval Secretary is seeing Mr Bruce next Tuesday to put up the name.

My letter of 17 February also referred to the matter of the loan carrier and cruisers and mentioned that I had seen Admiral Sir Denis Boyd,[62] the Fifth Sea Lord, who had promised every assistance, and that I would also be seeing the Controller and the Director of Plans (Grantham),[63] which three, with the First Sea Lord, would have most to do with the matter.

In fact the negotiations broke down, ostensibly on financial grounds. In this connection I had learned and informed the First Naval Member privately on 12 March that I had not yet seen the 'Out' signal from the United Kingdom Government on the ship problem, but that I had seen the Admiralty's proposed one and gathered that the Treasury was interesting itself more than I liked to think of, and that Winston Churchill intended to discuss it with the Chancellor of the Exchequer.

I mentioned also that the whole problem had been dealt with on rather closer lines than usual and it was apparently not until I informed Mr Bruce of it that he began to ask Dominions Office for copies of the relevant messages.

Other items related to problems concerning the *Australia*'s refit, which included questions of carrying it out in South Africa, Canada or the United Kingdom. On the matter of the carrier, I mentioned that:

> . . . the carrier question is easy as far as a 'Colossus' type is concerned except that I could not light on a conveniently completing one fitted as a flagship

and I was relieved to get your reply that this was not essential . . . I couldn't get far with the proposition to take over a 1943 class.[64] There are only four to be built according to present intentions and they seem to be dropping so far back in their completion dates that the Admiralty view was that it was too distant. I tried to get it recorded, at any rate, that it was intended to make this replacement in due course.

On 24 March 1945, I wrote to Admiral Royle again:

I am sorry to say that the reply about the ships has not yet left. The situation, briefly, is that the Admiralty proposed reply (which offers a 'Colossus' type carrier this year, and two 'Tigers' when they are finished − but in view of the delay involved, suggests we might like to take over 2 modernised 6″ cruisers in the interim) went to the First Lord and from him to the Prime Minister, and I understood that Alexander[65] mentioned the question of finance and proposed a reply in principle, with the question of finance to be dealt with separately. I am told that the P.M. considered the financial aspect should be dealt with now, and directed the 1st Lord to discuss the matter with the Chancellor of the Exchequer. It is here that the matter has been for some days now . . . I have had an almost daily 'prod' at the Admiralty people about it, and the First Sea Lord's Secretary has 'touched up' the First Lord's people three times this week. Mr Bruce was to see the Chancellor this week on another subject and I asked him (Mr Bruce) to try to get the matter decided. He promised me he would speak to the Chancellor and to the First Lord.

On 29 March, I wrote to the First Naval Member to say that Mr Bruce rang me that day to say that he had done as I had asked and that he expected a very early and favourable reply.

On 22 March, Admiral Royle sent me a copy of a questionnaire he had received from Admiral Hamilton, together with his answers. He said that he had told Hamilton that I could elaborate on the answers he had given and that 'when I was tired of telling him things he can go to "Rags" Colvin for the remainder'.

Royle ended his letter to Hamilton by saying:

Captain Foley will be able to elaborate on the answers to many of the questions and give you a lot more useful information. You will probably be the last of the RN First Naval Members and Foley will explain to you the possible sequence of events, presuming that John Collins[66] comes to the surface again after his recent injuries. I notice that this Government has approved your appointment for 2 years, after which it is intended that your place should be taken by an RAN officer.

The matter of the ships was still awaiting decision on 1 May 1945, when Admiral Royle wrote to say that it was very sad that the decision should take so long and noted that a signal from me the previous day indicated that there might be some financial strings attached to the loan of the ships. He added that he quite understood the British Treasury's point of view, when the Australian Government had demanded that:

UK should pay all of the 21 million pounds expended on facilities for the British Pacific Fleet.

The amount the UK Government had requested was 9 millions for the modern light fleet carrier and the two 'Tiger' class 6″ cruisers – and as the latter were not yet complete they had agreed to the Admiralty proposal to lend two modernised 6″ cruisers until the 'Tigers' became available.

I have little doubt in my mind that the parochial attitude of the Australian Government over various matters had peeved Winston Churchill to the extent that he and his political colleagues had concluded that it would be unjust to the British taxpayer and the British people at large to keep on hand feeding a Government and a country which had not really suffered the anguish of war (except by the actual fighting services themselves and their immediate relatives). There had also been considerable acrimony between the Australian and the United Kingdom Governments on various strategic problems during the war.

Still full of optimism about the provision of the carrier, Admiral Royle said he had Armstrong[67] in mind to command her and thought he should get some experience in the United Kingdom before taking over command. He also included some cracks about the Deputy Prime Minister, Mr Forde's[68] 'brilliant' remarks about the arrival of the WRNS in Australia having put Britain on the map, and warning Great Britain not to slack up when the German War ended because there was still a battle going on in the Pacific.

The last letter on the subject of these ships from Admiral Royle was dated 23 May 1945. The United Kingdom Government's telegram regarding the transfer of the ships from the RN to the RAN had at last been sent. Admiral Royle enclosed a copy of the reply *he* suggested to the Minister of the Navy (Makin). Up to that date (23 May), the Cabinet had not yet discussed the matter, though he understood that Chifley, the Treasurer, had a talk with the Prime Minister on the subject and he had a talk with Mr Makin, who was not 'what you could call optimistic'. He went on to say:

> I have an uneasy feeling that if the Government could see an easy way out without loss of face, they would welcome it. They do not like telling the Caucus that they have spent 9 millions on ships built in another country. Like you, I have always been afraid that if we gave this Government the slightest chance of getting out of this naval commitment, they would snatch at it. The future of the RAN is in the balance again and may be decided next Monday. I hope for the best but fear the worst.

Admiral Royle's proposals to the Minister included arrangements to commission *Ocean* in August 1945 with personnel from *Australia*, which would then be in the United Kingdom undergoing refit and, subject to adequate recruiting being approved and commenced, to commission *Kenya* (6″ cruiser) in December 1945 while awaiting a 'Tiger'.

In the event, of course, the whole proposal for a loan carrier and the 'Tiger' class cruisers fell flat and the carrier proposals did not come up again until later in 1945. I wrote to Admiral Royle on 3 August 1945 bemoaning the decision about *Ocean*. Amongst other things, this decision meant that some occupation had to be found for the crew of *Australia*. My letter included the following:

> I was indeed glad you approved the proposal to man *Suffolk* with a nucleus crew. I was at my wits end to devise any valuable use for the men for such a brief period and no bright thoughts came from Admiralty Staff. Luckily one morning at the Admiralty Staff meeting some question of *Suffolk*'s next trooping trip arose and it struck me as just the thing – so I put it forward

and it was jumped at with great joy. Armstrong agreed readily when I discussed it with him subsequently.

Although we had lost out on Admiral Royle's proposals, Admiral Hamilton before he left for Australia told me he was determined to revive the matter of light fleet carriers, of which he was convinced the RAN needed at least two. He was insistent in his view, which he pressed hard upon the Government, that two carriers were the minimum requirements.

I wrote to Admiral Hamilton on 24 September 1945, referring to the matter of the 'N' and 'Q' class destroyers being turned over to the RAN:

> Admiralty are anxious to help in this matter but it seems they must go warily with the Treasury. Money is very tight here, and the Treasury view is that they just can't see why Australia, which they say is in a much stronger financial condition than UK at present, should expect 'something for nothing' all the time. I do not know the facts of the relative financial state, but the latter part of the argument sounds reasonable. However there was a keenness on the part of the *Admiralty* for the RAN to take over the 'N' class and 20 AMS[69] and it was thought any Treasury objection could be avoided by merely extending the present loan period . . . I have shown your reply to Plans and they are now scratching their heads about it because I believe the other 'Q's are probably to be sold (for hard cash) to one of the smaller foreign powers. This may make the proposition a bit 'tricky' vis-a-vis the Treasury.

I also referred in this letter to the fact that I had recently in unofficial discussions in Admiralty Plans Division raised the question whether in their post war proposals they had sufficiently in mind the intentions, or at least the aspirations, of the RAN. I had found that their general ideas were that we should probably have one light fleet carrier, three cruisers and four to six destroyers in commission, with possibly the same numbers in reserve. My letter stated:

> I understand from Admiral Royle that this corresponds more or less with the Naval Board's proposals, except that we were asking for 8″ cruisers.[70] If however you have it in mind that we should maintain in commission more ships than Plans anticipate as mentioned above, I suggest it would be desirable for you to make it known very definitely to them, because if Admiralty puts down on any paper which gets circulated in Australia a proposed RAN which is *less* than the Board's proposal to the Australian Government it would be a bit strange and in any case would completely finish any prospect the Naval Board might have of getting their own proposals approved . . . Admiralty intentions in general are to have a reserve of approximately 100% in ships, i.e. as many in reserve as in commission on the basis that the Admiralty were again caught without a sufficient reserve of war vessels on the outbreak of this war.

My letter to the First Naval Member of 1 October 1945 commenced:

> I hope Admiralty reply to ACNB's signal re 'N' class meets with your approval. The reply is substantially my own draft, which I had handed to the Director of Plans after receiving your signal of 19th, and it gives you a completely free hand to get whatever of the 'N' or 'Q' class you desire to retain. From earlier discussion with various Admiralty people, the oblique approach to the 'Q's was the most likely to get through without opposition.

Since then I have again been in discussion with Director of Plans and others in regard to the revival of the carrier, and after our success with the 'Q's it seems possible that a similar approach for a light fleet carrier *on loan* may now succeed.

It will be remembered that in the case of the *Ocean* we were purchasing (nominally, at any rate), not being given the ship on loan. The letter continued:

If the carrier question is revived now, and it appears that Dr Evatt[71] could help the case along, I will ask him to do so. At the moment he is full of joy as his efforts were successful in getting Australia the Japanese disarmament proposals. He is giving an informal luncheon to the Australian Cricket Team at Claridges on Monday and asked me if I would try to get the First Sea Lord to come to it. I'm glad to say that A. B. C.[72] is coming and I've asked D of P to brief him in case he gets an opportunity to talk to Dr Evatt on RAN matters.

At Dr Evatt's lunch, I found myself seated between Admiral Cunningham and C. B. Fry,[73] one of England's famous old cricketers. During luncheon, A. B. C. asked me whether I thought the RAN would be interested in taking over a number of partly built destroyers. He said there were quite a number, some 75% completed, which would be redundant now that the war in Japan was over. We could have them for the cost of completion, which would make it a very good financial proposition. I replied that I did not think that there was the slightest hope of the Australian Government taking over UK destroyers or other small craft, as we had the capability, as he knew, of building them in our own shipyards, and that no Australian Government would be prepared to spend money to buy such ships abroad, even on such a good financial basis.

I asked whether his offer extended to larger ships, e.g. aircraft carriers, and whether there were any such available on similar terms. I mentioned that I was aware of the Naval Board's desire to get one or two light fleet carriers and thought that such a proposition as he had suggested with destroyers might well come off if carriers were available. He replied that he would look into the matter.

In a postscript to my letter of 1 October, written after this lunch, I gave Admiral Hamilton the substance of Admiral Cunningham's conversation with me. It would seem therefore, that the subsequent acquisition of two light fleet carriers, *Sydney* (ex-*Terrible*) and *Melbourne* (ex-*Majestic*) for the price of one probably arose from this conversation.

Sydney commissioned into the RAN in 1948, and, after serving in Korea and as a fast troop transport during the Vietnam War, was finally paid off for disposal in 1973. *Melbourne* did not commission until 1955, having been equipped with a steam catapult, angled deck and mirror landing aid. She remained operational until 1982, when she paid off into material reserve. She was declared for disposal in 1983.

Foley was to remain as Australian Naval Liaison Officer in London until 1948, when he returned to Navy Office as Administrative Assistant to the Second Naval Member. In 1951, he was again appointed to London and remained there until 1955. In the early months of that year he became Australian Director-General Supply Branch, Chief Naval Judge Advocate and Director of Administrative Planning, in which positions he remained until 1957. Although Foley had reached the highest appointment in his Branch, there were at this stage no Rear-Admirals (S) on the establishment of the RAN and he retired as a Captain. James Bernard Foley lived in retirement in Melbourne until his death on 9 February 1974.

Notes

1   The unpublished memoirs written by Captain Foley in his retirement, three long excerpts from which are printed here, were based on his own correspondence and papers. These, together with the memoirs, have been preserved by his family. The letters quoted by Foley and those used by the present writer are all from this source.

2   H.M.A.S. *Cerberus* was at that time located at Williamstown Naval Depot in Melbourne. The present site of the establishment at Westernport was still under construction.

3   Hodgkinson, Lieutenant Samuel Charles Lindsey, RAN. Died 1915.

4   Creswell, Lieutenant Colin Fraser, RN. Killed 1917.

5   Loudon-Shand, Commander Alexander John, OBE, RAN. Commander 1926; commanded RAN College 1941–5.

6   Wardroper, Paymaster Captain Richard Francis, RN. Fleet Paymaster 1909; Paymaster Commander 1919; Paymaster Captain (Retired) 1924.

7   Radcliffe, Vice-Admiral Stephen Herbert, CMG (1874–1939). Commander 1904; Captain 1911; Rear-Admiral (Retired) 1922; Vice-Admiral (Retired) 1927; commanded H.M.A.S. *Australia* 1913–17, H.M. Ships *Drake, Achilles* and *Superb* 1917–19; North–East Coast of England 1920–2.

8   Haworth-Booth, Rear-Admiral Sir Francis Fitzgerald, KCMG (1864–1935). Captain 1905; Rear-Admiral (Retired) 1917; Naval Advisor to the High Commissioner for Australia in London 1911–20.

9   A slip of memory by Captain Foley. Sub Lieutenants were addressed by their surnames by Midshipmen.

10 The RAN College training had in fact been reduced by three months from the intended course of four years. Although the RAN Midshipmen refused to put up with bullying when they were Juniors in their Gunrooms, it was notable that they indulged in 'evolutions' in their turn. See Captain G. N. Brewer, 'The Melody Lingers On', *The Naval Review*, Vol. LXI, No. 4, October 1973.

11 Bayliss, Captain Horace Temple Taylor, DSO, RN. Commander 1934; Captain 1941.

12 Pakenham, Admiral Sir William Christopher, GCB, KCMG, KCVO (1861–1933). Commander 1896; Captain 1903; Rear-Admiral 1913; Vice-Admiral 1918; Admiral 1918; a Lord Commissioner of the Admiralty 1911–13; commanded Third Cruiser Squadron 1913–15; Second Battle Cruiser Squadron 1915–16; Battle Cruiser Fleet 1917–19; Admiral-President RN College; Greenwich 1919–20; Commander-in-Chief North America and West Indies Station 1920–2.

13 Crace, Admiral Sir John Gregory, KBE, CB (1887–1968). Commander 1920; Captain 1928; Rear-Admiral 1939; Vice-Admiral (Retired) 1942; Admiral (Retired) 1945; commanded H.M. Australian Squadron 1939–42, Admiral-Superintendent H.M. Dockyard, Chatham 1942–6.

14 Mosse Robinson, Paymaster Lieutenant Commander Leslie Herbert, RAN. Assistant Paymaster 1907; Paymaster 1911; RAN 1914; Staff Paymaster 1916; Paymaster Lieutenant Commander 1919.

15 Hyde, Admiral Sir (George) Francis, KCB, CVO, CBE (1877–1937). Commanded H.M. *TB No. 6* 1907–8, H.M.S. *Rother* 1908–9, H.M.A.S. *Warrego* 1912, H.M.S. *Adventure* 1915–17, H.M.A.S. *Suva* 1919, H.M.A.S. *Brisbane* 1919–21; Second Naval Member Australian Commonwealth Naval Board 1923–4; commanded H.M.S. *Vindictive* 1924–5; commanded H.M. Australian Squadron 1926–9; Third Battle Squadron 1930–1; First Naval Member A.C.N.B. 1931–7.

16 Irving, Commander (S) Louis Charles, MBE, RAN.
17 Macdonald, Lieutenant Commander Allan Robert Armitage, RN.
18 Gibbons, Reverend Father Patrick J.
19 Manisty, Paymaster Rear-Admiral Sir Henry Wilfred Eldon, KCB, CMG (1876–1960). Finance and Civil Member A.C.N.B. and Paymaster-in-Chief RAN 1911–14; Paymaster Director-General RN 1929–33.
20 Allen, Rear-Admiral Hamilton Colclough (1883–1964). Commander 1916; Captain 1924; Rear-Admiral (Retired) 1935; commanded RN College, Greenwich 1931–3; H.M.S. *Iron Duke* 1933–5; Reserve Fleet, Nore 1935; Commodore of Convoys 1939–41; Admiralty 1941–8.
21 Ventry, Commissioned Bandmaster Joshua, MBE, RAN.
22 Hughes, the Right Honourable William Morris, CH, KC (1864–1952). Australian Minister for External Affairs 1904; Attorney-General 1908–12, 1914–15; Prime Minister 1915–23; Minister for Repatriation and Health 1934–5; Minister for External Affairs 1935–9; Attorney-General and Minister for the Navy 1939–41.
23 Battenberg, Captain Prince George of, GCVO, RN (1892–1938), later Mountbatten and Second Marquess of Milford Haven. Commander 1926; Captain 1932; retired 1932.
24 Beatty, Admiral of the Fleet Earl, GCB, OM, GCVO, DSO, PC (1871–1936). Commander 1898; Captain 1900; Rear-Admiral 1910; Vice-Admiral 1915; Admiral 1919; Admiral of the Fleet 1919; Naval Secretary 1912; commanded First Battle Cruiser Squadron 1912–15; Battle Cruiser Fleet 1915–16; Grand Fleet 1916–19; First Sea Lord and Chief of Naval Staff 1919–27.
25 Jellicoe, Admiral of the Fleet Earl, GCB, OM, GCVO (1859–1935). Commander 1893; Captain 1897; Rear-Admiral 1907; Vice-Admiral 1911; Admiral 1914; Admiral of the Fleet 1919; Director of Naval Ordnance 1905–7; Rear-Admiral Atlantic Fleet 1907–8; Controller 1908–10; commanded Atlantic Fleet 1910–11; Second Division Home Fleet 1911–12; Second Sea Lord 1912–14; commanded Grand Fleet 1914–16; First Sea Lord 1916–17; Governor-General of New Zealand 1920–4.
26 Leveson, Admiral Sir Arthur, GCB (1868–1929). Director of the Operations Division, Admiralty 1914–15; commanded Second Division, Second Battle Squadron 1915–16; HM Australian Fleet and Second Battle Cruiser Squadron 1916–18; Second Battle Squadron 1919–20; Commander-in-Chief China Station 1922–4.
27 Freyer, Paymaster Commander Allan, MVO, RAN. Paymaster Commander 1934.
28 Dumaresq, Rear-Admiral John Saumarez, CB, CVO (1873–1922). Captain 1910; Rear-Admiral 1921; commanded H.M.S. *Shannon* 1913–17, H.M.A.S. *Sydney* 1918; Commodore and Rear-Admiral Commanding H.M. Australian Fleet 1919–21.
29 Field, Admiral of the Fleet Sir Frederick Laurence, GCB, KCMG (1871–1945). Captain 1907; Rear-Admiral 1919; Vice-Admiral 1924; Admiral 1928; Admiral of the Fleet 1930–3; Third Sea Lord and Controller 1920–3; commanded Battle Cruiser Squadron 1923; Special Service Squadron on World Cruise 1923–4; Deputy Chief of the Naval Staff 1925–8; Commander-in-Chief Mediterranean Fleet 1928–30; First Sea Lord and Chief of the Naval Staff 1930–3.
30 Fremantle, Admiral Sir Sidney Robert, GCB, MVO (1867–1958). Captain 1903; Rear-Admiral 1913; Vice-Admiral 1919; Admiral 1922; commanded Ninth Cruiser Squadron 1916; Second Cruiser Squadron 1917; Aegean Squadron 1917–18; Deputy Chief of the Naval Staff 1918–19; commanded First Battle Squadron 1919–21; Commander-in-Chief Portsmouth 1923–6.
31 The Australian Fleet was renamed the Australian Squadron in 1921, due to its reduction in size and the need to ensure the subordination of the Flag Officer Commanding to the Naval Board. The Squadron was renamed a Fleet in 1953.
32 Colvin, Admiral Sir Ragnar Musgrave, KBE, CB (1882–1954). Captain 1917; Rear-Admiral 1929; Vice-Admiral 1934; Admiral 1939; Chief of Staff Home Fleet 1930–2; commanded Second Battle Squadron 1932–3; Admiral-President RN College, Greenwich 1934–7; First Naval Member A.C.N.B. 1937–41; Naval Advisor to the High Commissioner for Australia in London 1942–4.
33 Royle, Admiral Sir Guy Charles Cecil, KCB, CMG (1885–1954). Captain 1923; Rear-Admiral 1935; Vice-Admiral 1939; Admiral 1942; commanded H.M.S. *Canterbury* 1927–9, H.M.S. *Excellent* 1930–2, H.M.S. *Glorious* 1933–4; Naval Secretary 1934–7; Aircraft Carriers 1937–9; Fifth Sea Lord and Chief of Naval Air Services 1939–41; First Naval Member A.C.N.B. 1941–5.

34 Shepherd, Malcolm L., CMG, ISO. Secretary, Australian Department of Defence 1925–37.
35 Shedden, Sir Frederick, KCMG, OBE (1893–1971). Lieutenant First AIF; attached British Cabinet Office and Committee of Imperial Defence 1932–3; Secretary Department of Defence 1937–56; Member, Australian Council of Defence 1945–6; Chairman, Australian Defence Committee 1948–56; Secretary, Australian War Cabinet 1939–40.
36 Thomas, Colonel John Thomas, OBE (1872–1961).
37 Francis, the Honourable Sir Josiah (1890–1964). Member, Australian House of Representatives 1922–55; Assistant Minister for Defence 1932–4; Minister for Repatriation 1933; Minister for the Army 1949–55; Minister for the Navy 1951, 1954–5; Minister and Consul-General for Australia in New York 1955–61.
38 Bruce of Melbourne, Sydney Melbourne, First Viscount, PC, CH, MC, FRS (1883–1967). Australian Treasurer 1921–3; Prime Minister 1923–9; Minister Without Portfolio 1932–3; Australian Minister in London 1932–3; Australian High Commissioner in London 1933–45.
39 Bruche, Major General Sir Julius Henry, KCB, CMG (1873–1961). Military Commandant Western Australia 1914–16; New South Wales 1920–1; GOC Field Troops, Queensland 1921–5; First Division, New South Wales 1926–7; Adjutant-General A.C.M.B. 1927–9; Australian Representative on Imperial General Staff 1929–31; Australian Chief of the General Staff 1929–31.
40 As High Commissioner in London, Bruce played a major part in determining defence policy and the advice passing between Australia and the United Kingdom.
41 Dreyer, Admiral Sir Frederick Charles, GBE, KCB (1878–1956). Commander 1907; Captain 1913; Rear-Admiral 1923; Vice-Admiral 1929; Admiral 1932; retired 1939; Assistant Chief of the Naval Staff 1924–7; commanded Battle Cruiser Squadron 1927–9; Deputy Chief of the Naval Staff 1930–3; Commander-in-Chief China 1933–6; Commodore of Convoys 1939–40; Inspector Merchant Navy Gunnery 1941–2; Chief of Naval Air Services 1942–3.
42 Dunbar-Nasmith, Admiral Sir Martin Eric, VC, KCB, KCMG. (1885–1965). Commander 1915; Captain 1916; Rear-Admiral 1928; Vice-Admiral 1932; Admiral 1936; retired 1942; Rear-Admiral Submarines 1929–31; Commander-in-Chief East Indies 1932–4; Second Sea Lord 1935–8; Commander-in-Chief Plymouth and Western Aproaches 1938–41; Flag Officer in Charge London 1942–6; Vice-Admiral of the United Kingdom and Lieutenant of the Admiralty 1945–62.
43 Burges Watson, Rear-Admiral Fischer, CBE, DSO* (1884–1960). Commanded H.M.S. *Nelson* 1930–1; First Naval Member N.Z.N.B. and Commodore Commanding New Zealand Division 1932–5; retired 1935; Commodore of Convoys 1939–42; Captain Landing Forces 1943–4; Flag Officer in Charge Harwich 1944–5.
44 Thompson, Rear-Admiral Sir George Pirie, CB, CBE (1887–1965). Captain 1927; Rear-Admiral (Retired) 1939; Second Naval Member A.C.N.B. 1937–9; Chief Press Censor, Ministry of Information 1940–5.
45 James, Admiral Sir William Milbourne, GCB (1881–1973). Commander 1913; Captain 1918; Rear-Admiral 1929; Vice-Admiral 1933; Admiral 1938; Chief of Staff Atlantic Fleet 1929–30; Mediterranean Fleet 1930; commanded Battle Cruiser Squadron 1930–2; Deputy Chief of Naval Staff 1935–8; Commander-in-Chief Portsmouth 1939–42; Chief of Naval Information 1942–4; MP (Unionist) North Portsmouth 1943–5.
46 H.M.A. Ships *Brisbane* (completed in 1916) and *Adelaide* (completed to a modified design in 1923).
47 Makin, the Honourable Norman John Oswald, AO (1889–1982). Member (Labor), Australian House of Representatives 1919–46, 1954–63; Speaker 1929–31; Minister for the Navy and Munitions 1941–5; Minister for Aircraft Production 1943–6; Australian Ambassador to the United States 1946–52; First President, United Nations Security Council.
48 Foley has a point, although there were other factors than union troubles in the protracted building time for the two 'Battle' class (completed in 1950–1) and four 'Daring' class (completed 1958–9) destroyers of the post-war programme. Only the minimum funds were made available for the construction of the ships, which proceeded at a snail's pace, particularly in the mid-1950s. Funds were so short that the RAN was eventually forced to have the fourth 'Daring', which was to have been named *Waterhen*, scrapped on the slip at Williamstown.

49   Pearce, Senator the Right Honourable Sir George, KCVO (1870–1952). Federal (Labor) Senator 1901–16; National Party Senator 1916–38; Minister for Defence 1908–9, 1910–13, 1914–21, 1931–4; Minister for Home and Territories 1921–6; Minister for External Affairs and Territories 1934–7; Vice-President of the Federal Executive Council 1926–9; Leader of the Opposition in the Senate 1929–31.

50   In 1919, the leader *Anzac* and five 'S' and 'T' class destroyers, among other units, were 'gifted' to Australia. In 1933, they were replaced by the 'Campbell' class leader, *Stuart*, and four 'V' and 'W' class destroyers, which were handed over on loan. These five ships later earned distinction in the Mediterranean as the 'Scrap iron Flotilla'. The older ships were finally disposed of in 1935–6, having seen little operational service.

51   Perry, Rear-Admiral (S) Patrick, CBE (1903–79). Barrister-at-Law; Secretary to FOCAS 1942–4; to First Naval Member 1944–8; RAN Liaison Officer London 1948–52, 1955–8; Director-General Naval Supply and Secretariat Branch 1952–5; Fourth Naval Member A.C.N.B. 1958–62.

52   Crutchley, Admiral Sir Victor Alexander Charles, VC, KCB, DSC (1893–   ). DSC Ostend 1918; VC and Croix De Guerre Ostend May 1918; commanded H.M.S. *Warspite* 1937–40; Commodore RN Barracks Devonport 1940–2; FOCAS 1942–4; Flag Officer Gibraltar 1945–7.

53   Churchill, the Right Honourable Sir Winston Leonard Spencer, KG, OM, CH (1874–1965). First Lord of the Admiralty 1939–40; Prime Minister, First Lord of the Treasury and Minister of Defence 1940–5; Leader of the Opposition 1945–51; Prime Minister and First Lord of the Treasury 1951–5.

54   Hamilton, Admiral Sir Louis Henry Keppel, KCB, DSO (1890–1957). Rear-Admiral (D) Home Fleet 1940–2; FOIC Malta 1943–5; First Naval Member A.C.N.B. and Chief of Naval Staff 1945–8.

55   Chifley, the Right Honourable Joseph Benedict (1885–1951). MHR (Labor) Macquarie, NSW 1928–31, 1940–9; Minister for Defence 1931–2; Treasurer 1941–9; Minister for Post-War Reconstruction 1942–5; Prime Minister 1945–9; Leader of the Opposition 1949–51.

56   H.M.A. Ships *Napier, Nizam, Norman* and *Nepal*. A fifth, *Nestor*, had been sunk in the Mediterranean in 1942. Two others were serving in the Royal Netherlands Navy and one with the Poles.

57   H.M.A. Ships *Queenborough* and *Quality*, H.M. Ships *Quickmatch, Quiberon* and *Quadrant*.

58   The 'Battle' class *Anzac* and *Tobruk*, were completed in 1950 and 1951. Only three of the 'Daring' class were eventually completed – *Voyager, Vendetta* and *Vampire*, in 1958–9. The fourth, *Waterhen*, was scrapped on the slip at Williamstown Naval Dockyard.

59   *Australia* had been struck by a Kamikaze on 21 October 1944 in Leyte Gulf, causing severe damage to her bridge and many casualties. In early 1945, off Lingayen, she was repeatedly struck by Kamikazes, five in all, and forced to withdraw from operations for extensive repairs.

60   Harcourt, Admiral Sir Cecil Halliday, GBE, KCB (1892–1959). Captain (D) Australian Destroyer Flotilla 1935–7; Deputy Director Operations Division 1938–9; Director Operations Division 1939–41; commanded H.M.S. *Duke of York* 1941–2; Tenth, Twelfth and Fifteenth Cruiser Squadrons 1942–4; Naval Secretary 1944–5; commanded Eleventh Aircraft Carrier Squadron 1945; C.-in-C. Hong Kong 1945–6; FO (Air) and 2-in-C. Mediterranean Fleet 1947–8; Second Sea Lord 1948–50; C.-in-C. The Nore 1950–2.

61   Barry, Admiral Sir Claud Barrington, KBE, CB, DSO (1891–1951). Flag Officer Submarines 1942–4; Naval Secretary 1945–6; Director of Dockyards 1946–51.

62   Boyd, Admiral Sir Denis William, KCB, CBE, DSC (1891–1965). Commanded H.M.S. *Illustrious* 1940–1; Rear-Admiral Aircraft Carriers 1941; Eastern Force 1942; Fifth Sea Lord and Chief of Naval Air Equipment 1943–5; Admiral (Air) 1945–6; C.-in-C. British Pacific Fleet and C.-in-C. Far East 1948–9.

63   Grantham, Admiral Sir Guy, GCB, CBE, DSO (1900–   ). Director of Plans Division 1945; COS Mediterranean Fleet 1946–8; Flag Officer Submarines 1948–50; 2-in-C. Mediterranean 1950–1; VCNS 1952–4; C.-in-C. Mediterranean 1954–7; C.-in-C. Portsmouth 1957–9; Governor and C.-in-C. Malta, 1959–62.

64 The 1943 class carriers, which were larger than the first light fleet carriers and had a sustained speed of 28 knots, as opposed to the 24¼ of the 'Colossus' and 'Majestic' classes, were eventually completed in 1953–4 (*Centaur, Albion* and *Bulwark*) and 1959 (*Hermes*, ex-*Elephant*). Three others, *Arrogant* (ex-*Hermes*), *Monmouth* and *Polyphemus*, had been cancelled earlier in 1945.

65 Alexander of Hillsborough, First Earl, PC (1885–1965). First Lord of the Admiralty 1929–31, 1940–6; Minister of Defence 1947–50; Chancellor of the Duchy of Lancaster 1950–1; Leader of the Labour Peers 1955–65; Viscount 1950; Earl 1963.

66 Collins, Vice-Admiral Sir John Augustine, KBE, CB (1900–   ). Commanded H.M.A.S. *Sydney* 1939–41; A/COS Singapore 1941–2; commanded Java Sea Force 1942; NOICWA 1942; commanded H.M.A.S. *Shropshire* 1943–44; commanded H.M. Australian Squadron 1944, 1945–7; wounded in action H.M.A.S. *Australia* 1944; Rear-Admiral 1947; IDC 1947; First Naval Member A.C.N.B. and C.N.S. 1947–55; High Commissioner to New Zealand 1956–62.

67 Armstrong, Captain John Malet, CBE, DSO, RAN (1900–). Commanded H.M.A.S. *Australia* 1945.

68 Forde, the Right Honourable Francis Michael (1890–1983). MHR (Labor) Capricornia, Queensland 1922–46; Minister for the Army 1941–6; Minister for Defence 1946; Deputy Prime Minister 1941–5; Prime Minister 6–12 July 1945; Australian High Commissioner to Canada 1946–53.

69 AMS – 'Bathurst' class Australian MineSweepers. Of a total of sixty built in Australia, twenty were to Admiralty order, but were manned by the RAN. Most were to remain in the RAN until their disposal in the late 1950s. Some, however, went to Turkey and one, ex-*Bendigo*, is still serving in the Chinese Navy.

70 Unless it was intended that the ageing *Australia* (completed in 1928) and *Shropshire* (1929) be retained in service indefinitely, the Naval board were indulging in wishful thinking. No British 8″ cruisers had been built since the *Exeter* of more than a decade before. In the event, *Shropshire* paid off into reserve soon after the war, although *Australia* was to soldier on until 1954.

71 Evatt, the Right Honourable Dr Herbert Vere, KC (1894–1965). Justice High Court of Australia 1930–40; MHR (Labor) Barton, NSW 1941–60; Attorney-General and Minister for External Affairs 1941–9; President UN Assembly 1948; Leader of the Opposition 1951–60; Chief Justice of NSW 1960–2.

72 Cunningham of Hyndhope, Admiral of the Fleet First Viscount (Andrew Browne), KT, GCB, OM, DSO (1883–1963). Rear-Admiral (D) Mediterranean Fleet 1934–6; Vice-Admiral Battle Cruiser Squadron and 2-in-C. Mediterranean 1937–8; DCNS 1938–9; C.-in-C. Mediterranean 1939–42, 1943; Head Admiralty Delegation to Washington 1942; First Sea Lord and CNS 1943–6.

73 Fry, Charles Burgess (1872–1956). World Long Jump Record Holder; Hon. Captain RNR; represented England at Cricket and Association Football.

INDEX

NAVY RECORDS SOCIETY
(FOUNDED 1893)

The Navy Records Society was established for the purpose of printing rare or unpublished works of naval interest. The Society is open to all who are interested in naval history and any person wishing to become a member should apply to the Hon. Secretary, c/o The Royal Naval College, Greenwich, London SE10 9NN. The annual subscription for individuals is £10, the payment of which entitles the member to receive one copy of each work issued by the Society in that year. For Libraries and Institutions the annual subscription is £12.

The prices to members and non-members respectively are given after each volume, and orders should be sent, enclosing no money, to the Hon. Treasurer, c/o Barclays Bank, 54 Lombard Street, London EC3P 3AH. Those volumes against which the letters 'A & U' are set after the price to non-members are available to them only through bookshops or, in case of difficulty, direct from George Allen & Unwin (Publishers) Ltd, PO Box 18, Park Lane, Hemel Hempstead, Herts HP2 4TE. Prices are correct at the time of going to press.

The Society has already issued:

a Contemporary Englishman. Edited by Admiral Sir Cyprian Bridge. (*Out of Print.*)

Vol. 16. *Logs of the Great Sea Fights*, 1794–1805 (Vol. I.). Edited by Vice-Admiral Sir T. Sturges Jackson. (*£12.00/£15.00.*)

Vol. 17. *Papers relating to the First Dutch War*, 1652–54 (Vol. II.). Edited by Dr S. R. Gardiner. (*Out of Print.*)

Vol. 18. *Logs of the Great Sea Fights* (Vol. II.). Edited by Vice-Admiral Sir T. Sturges Jackson. (*£12.00/£15.00.*)

Vol. 19. *Journals and Letters of Sir T. Byam Martin* (Vol. III.). Edited by Admiral Sir R. Vesey-Hamilton. (*See* 24). (*£6.50/£12.00.*)

Vol. 20. *The Naval Miscellany* (Vol. I.). Edited by Professor J. K. Laughton. (*Out of Print.*)

Vol. 21. *Papers relating to the Blockade of Brest*, 1803–5 (Vol. II). Edited by Mr John Leyland. (*Out of Print.*)

Vols. 22 and 23. *The Naval Tracts of Sir William Monson* (Vols. I and II.). Edited by Mr M. Oppenheim. (*Out of Print.*)

Vol. 24. *Journals and Letters of Sir T. Byam Martin* (Vol. I.). Edited by Admiral Sir R. Vesey Hamilton. (*£6.50/£12.00.*)

Vol. 25. *Nelson and the Neapolitan Jacobins*. Edited by Mr H. C. Gutteridge. (*Out of Print.*)

Vol. 26. *A Descriptive Catalogue of the Naval MSS. in the Pepysian Library* (Vol. I.). Edited by Mr J. R. Tanner. (*Out of Print.*)

Vol. 27. *A Descriptive Catalogue of the Naval MSS. in the Pepysian Library* (Vol. II.). Edited by Mr J. R. Tanner. (*£6.50/£12.00.*)

Vol. 28. *The Correspondence of Admiral John Markham*, 1801–7. Edited by Sir Clements R. Markham. (*Out of Print.*)

Vol. 29. *Fighting Instructions*, 1530–1816. Edited by Mr Julian S. Corbett. (*Out of Print.*)

Vol. 30. *Papers relating to the First Dutch War*, 1652–54 (Vol. III.). Edited by Dr S. R. Gardiner and Mr C. T. Atkinson. (*Out of Print.*)

Vol. 31. *The Recollections of Commander James Anthony Gardner*, 1775–1814. Edited by Admiral Sir R. Vesey Hamilton and Professor J. K. Laughton. (*Out of Print.*)

Vol. 32. *Letters and Papers of Charles, Lord Barham*, 1758–1813 (Vol. I.). Edited by Sir J. K. Laughton. (*Out of Print.*)

Vol. 33. *Naval Songs and Ballads*. Edited by Professor C. H. Firth. (*Out of Print.*)

Vol. 34. *Views of the Battles of the Third Dutch War*. Edited by Mr Julian S. Corbett. (*Out of Print.*)

Vol. 35. *Signals and Instructions*, 1776–94. Edited by Mr Julian S. Corbett. (*Out of Print.*)

Vol. 36. *A Descriptive Catalogue of the Naval MSS. in the Pepysian Library* (Vol. III.). Edited by Dr J. R. Tanner. (*Out of Print.*)

Vol. 37. *Papers relating to the First Dutch War*, 1652–1654 (Vol. IV.). Edited by Mr C. T. Atkinson. (*Out of Print.*)

Vol. 38. *Letters and Papers of Charles, Lord Barham*, 1758–1813 (Vol. II.). Edited by Sir J. K. Laughton. (*Out of Print.*)

Vol. 39. *Letters and Papers of Charles, Lord Barham*, 1758–1813 (Vol. III.). Edited by Sir J. K. Laughton. (*Out of Print.*)

Vol. 40. *The Naval Miscellany* (Vol. II.). Edited by Sir J. K. Laughton. (*Out of Print.*)

Vol. 41. *Papers relating to the First Dutch War*, 1652–54 (Vol. V.). Edited by Mr C. T. Atkinson. (*£6.50/£12.00.*)

Vol. 42. *Papers relating to the Loss of Minorca in* 1756. Edited by Capt. H. W. Richmond, R.N. (*£6.50/£12.00.*)

Vol. 43. *The Naval Tracts of Sir William Monson* (Vol. III.). Edited by Mr M. Oppenheim. (*£6.50/£12.00.*)

Vol. 44. *The Old Scots Navy*, 1689–1710. Edited by Mr James Grant. (*Out of Print.*)

Vol. 45. *The Naval Tracts of Sir William Monson* (Vol. IV.). Edited by Mr M. Oppenheim. (*£6.50/£12.00.*)

Vol. 46. *The Private Papers of George, second Earl Spencer* (Vol. I.). Edited by Mr Julian S. Corbett. (*£6.50/£12.00.*)

Vol. 47. *The Naval Tracts of Sir William Monson* (Vol. V.). Edited by Mr M. Oppenheim. (*£6.50/£12.00.*)

Vol. 48. *The Private Papers of George, second Earl Spencer* (Vol. II.). Edited by Mr Julian S. Corbett. (*Out of Print.*)

Vol. 49. *Documents relating to Law and Custom of the Sea* (Vol. I.). Edited by Mr R. G. Marsden. (*£6.50/£12.00.*)

Vol. 50. *Documents relating to Law and Custom of the Sea* (Vol. II.). Edited by Mr R. G. Marsden. (*£6.50/£12.00.*)

Vol. 51. *Autobiography of Phineas Pett.* Edited by Mr W. G. Perrin. (*£6.50/£12.00.*)

Vol. 52. *The Life of Admiral Sir John Leake* (Vol. I.). Edited by Mr G. A. R. Callender. (*£6.50/£12.00.*)

Vol. 53. *The Life of Admiral Sir John Leake* (Vol. II.). Edited by Mr G. A. R. Callender. (*£6.50/£12.00.*)

Vol. 54. *The Life and Works of Sir Henry Mainwaring* (Vol. I.). Edited by Mr G. E. Manwaring. (*£6.50/£12.00.*)

Vol. 55. *The Letters of Lord St. Vincent*, 1801–1804 (Vol. I.). Edited by Mr D. B. Smith. (*Out of Print.*)

Vol. 56. *The Life and Works of Sir Henry Mainwaring* (Vol. II.). Edited by Mr G. E. Manwaring and Mr W. G. Perrin. (*Out of Print.*)

Vol. 57. *A Descriptive Catalogue of the Naval MSS in the Pepysian Library* (Vol. IV.). Edited by Dr J. R. Tanner. (*Out of Print.*)

Vol. 58. *The Private Papers of George, second Earl Spencer* (Vol. III.). Edited by Rear-Admiral H. W. Richmond. (*Out of Print.*)

Vol. 59. *The Private Papers of George, second Earl Spencer* (Vol. IV.). Edited by Rear-Admiral H. W. Richmond. (*Out of Print.*)

Vol. 60. *Samuel Pepys's Naval Minutes.* Edited by Dr J. R. Tanner. (*Out of Print.*)

Vol. 61. *The Letters of Lord St. Vincent*, 1801–1804 (Vol. II.). Edited by Mr D. B. Smith. (*Out of Print.*)

Vol. 62. *Letters and Papers of Admiral Viscount Keith* (Vol. I.). Edited by Mr. W. G. Perrin. (*Out of Print.*)

Vol. 63. *The Naval Miscellany* (Vol. III.). Edited by Mr. W. G. Perrin. (*Out of Print.*)

Vol. 64. *The Journal of the First Earl of Sandwich.* Edited by Mr R. C. Anderson. (*Out of Print.*)

Vol. 65. *Boteler's Dialogues.* Edited by Mr W. G. Perrin. (*£6.50/£12.00.*)

Vol. 66. *Papers relating to the First Dutch War*, 1652–54 (Vol. VI.; with index). Edited by Mr C. T. Atkinson. (*£6.50/£12.00.*)

Vol. 67. *The Byng Papers* (Vol. I.). Edited by Mr W. C. B. Tunstall. (*£6.50/£12.00.*)

Vol. 68. *The Byng Papers* (Vol. II.). Edited by Mr W. C. B. Tunstall. (*£6.50/£12.00.*)

Vol. 69. *The Private Papers of John, Earl of Sandwich* (Vol. I.). Edited by Mr G. R. Barnes and Lieut-Commander J. H. Owen, R.N. (*£6.50/£12.00.*)

Corrigenda to *Papers relating to the First Dutch War*, 1652–54 (Vols. I. to VI.). Edited by Captain A. C. Dewar, R.C. (*Free.*)

Vol. 70. *The Byng Papers* (Vol. III.). Edited by Mr W. C. B. Tunstall. (*£6.50/£12.00.*)

Vol. 71. *The Private Papers of John, Earl of Sandwich* (Vol. II.). Edited by Mr G. R. Barnes and Lieut-Commander J. H. Owen, R.N. (*£6.50/£12.00.*)

Vol. 72. *Piracy in the Levant*, 1827–8. Edited by Lieut-Commander C. G. Pitcairn Jones, R.N. (*£6.50/£12.00.*)

Vol. 73. *The Tangier Papers of Samuel Pepys.* Edited by Mr Edwin Chappell. (*Out of Print.*)

Vol. 74. *The Tomlinson Papers.* Edited by Mr J. G. Bullocke (*£6.50/£12.00.*)

Vol. 75. *The Private Papers of John, Earl of Sandwich* (Vol. III.). Edited by Mr G. R. Barnes and Commander J. H. Owen, R.N. (*Out of Print.*)

Vol. 76. *The Letters of Robert Blake.* Edited by the Rev. J. R. Powell. (*£6.50/£12.00.*)

Vol. 77. *Letters and Papers of Admiral the Hon. Samuel Barrington* (Vol. I.). Edited by Mr D. Bonner-Smith (*£6.50/£12.00.*)

Vol. 78. *The Private Papers of John, Earl of Sandwich* (Vol. IV.). Edited by Mr G. R. Barnes and Commander J. H. Owen, R.N. (*Out of Print.*)

Vol. 79. *The Journals of Sir Thomas Allin*, 1660–1678 (Vol. I. 1660–66). Edited by Mr R. C. Anderson. (*£6.50/£12.00.*)

Vol. 80. *The Journals of Sir Thomas Allin*, 1660–1678 (Vol. II. 1667–78). Edited by Mr R. C. Anderson. (*£6.50/£12.00.*)

Vol. 81. *Letters and Papers of Admiral the Hon. Samuel Barrington* (Vol. II.). Edited by Mr D. Bonner-Smith. (*Out of Print.*)

Vol. 82. *Captain Boteler's Recollections* (1808 to 1830). Edited by Mr D. Bonner-Smith. (*Out of Print.*)

Vol. 83. *Russian War*, 1854. *Baltic and Black Sea: Official Correspondence.* Edited by Mr D. Bonner-Smith and Captain A. C. Dewar, R.N. (*Out of Print.*)

Vol. 84. *Russian War*, 1855. *Baltic: Official Correspondence.* Edited by Mr D. Bonner-Smith. (*Out of Print.*)

Vol. 85. *Russian War*, 1855. *Black Sea: Official Correspondence.* Edited by Captain A. C. Dewar, R.N. (*Out of Print.*)

Vol. 86. *Journals and Narratives of the Third Dutch War.* Edited by Mr R. C. Anderson. (*Out of Print.*)

Vol. 87. *The Naval Brigades in the Indian Mutiny*, 1857–58. Edited by Commander W. B. Rowbotham, R.N. (*Out of Print.*)

Vol. 88. *Patee Byng's Journal.* Edited by Mr J. L. Cranmer-Byng. (*Out of Print.*)

Vol. 89. *The Sergison Papers* (1688–1702). Edited by Commander R. D. Merriman, R.I.N. (*£6.50/£12.00.*)

Vol. 90. *The Keith Papers* (Vol. II.). Edited by Mr C. C. Lloyd. (*Out of Print.*)

Vol. 91. *Five Naval Journals*, 1789–1817. Edited by Rear-Admiral H. G. Thursfield. (*£6.50/£12.00.*)

Vol. 92. *The Naval Miscellany* (Vol. IV.). Edited by Mr C. C. Lloyd. (*Out of Print.*)

Vol. 93. *Sir William Dillon's Narrative of Professional Adventures (1790–1839)* (Vol. I. 1790–1802). Edited by Professor Michael A. Lewis. (*Out of Print.*)

Vol. 94. *The Walker Expedition to Quebec, 1711.* Edited by Professor Gerald S. Graham. (*Out of Print.*)

Vol. 95. *The Second China War*, 1856–60. Edited by Mr D. Bonner-Smith and Mr E. W. R. Lumby. (*Out of Print.*)

Vol. 96. *The Keith Papers*, 1803–1815 (Vol. III.). Edited by Professor C.C. Lloyd. (*£6.50/£12.00.*)

Vol. 97. *Sir William Dillon's Narrative of Professional Adventures (1790–1839)* (Vol. II. 1802–1839). Edited by Professor Michael A. Lewis. (*Out of Print.*)

Hungerford Pollen, 1901–1916. Edited by Dr Jon T. Sumida. (*£6.50/£20.00*—A & U.)

Vol. 125. *The Naval Miscellany* (Vol. V.). Edited by N. A. M. Rodger (£6.50/£30.00.)